Commercial Property Risk Management and Insurance

Volume I

Commercial Property Risk Management and Insurance

Volume I

WILLIAM H. RODDA, CPCU
President, Marine Insurance Handbook, Inc.

JAMES S. TRIESCHMANN, D.B.A., CPCU, CLU
Associate Professor and Acting Head
Department of Risk and Insurance
University of Georgia

BOB A. HEDGES, Ph.D., CPCU, CLU
Professor of Insurance and Risk
Temple University

First Edition • 1978

AMERICAN INSTITUTE FOR
PROPERTY AND LIABILITY UNDERWRITERS
Providence and Sugartown Roads, Malvern, Pennsylvania 19355

Third Printing • July 1980

Library of Congress Catalog Number 78-52690
International Standard Book Number 0-89463-004-0

Printed in the United States of America

This text was made possible
through a generous grant
provided by the
Thomas and Dorothy Leavey Foundation
through the Robert E. Early
Visiting Scholar Program
named in honor of
the late Robert E. Early,
former Executive Director
of the Farmer's Insurance Group.

Foreword

The American Institute for Property and Liability Underwriters and the Insurance Institute of America are companion, nonprofit, educational organizations supported by the property-liability insurance industry. Their purpose is to provide quality continuing education programs for insurance personnel.

The Insurance Institute of America offers programs leading to the Certificate in General Insurance, the Associate in Insurance Adjusting Diploma, the Associate in Management Studies Diploma, the Associate in Risk Management Diploma, and the Associate in Underwriting Diploma. The American Institute develops, maintains, and administers the educational program leading to the Chartered Property Casualty Underwriter (CPCU) professional designation.

Throughout the history of the CPCU program, an annual updating of parts of the course of study took place. But as changes in the insurance industry came about at an increasingly rapid pace, and as the world in which insurance operates grew increasingly complex, it became clear that a thorough, fundamental revision of the CPCU curriculum was necessary.

The American Institute began this curriculum revision project by organizing a committee of academicians, industry practitioners, and Institute staff members. This committee was charged with the responsibility of determining and stating those broad goals which should be the educational aims of the CPCU program in contemporary society. With these goals formulated, the curriculum committee began writing specific educational objectives which were designed to achieve the stated goals of the program. This was a time-consuming and difficult task. But this process made certain that the revised CPCU curriculum would be based on a sound and relevant foundation.

Once objectives were at least tentatively set, it was possible to outline a new, totally revised and reorganized curriculum. These outlines were widely circulated and the reactions of more than 1,800 educators and industry leaders were solicited, weighed, and analyzed.

These outlines were then revised and ultimately became the structure of the new, ten-course curriculum.

With the curriculum design in hand, it was necessary to search for study materials which would track with the revised program's objectives and follow its design. At this stage of curriculum development, the Institute reached the conclusion that it would be necessary for the Institute to prepare and publish study materials specifically tailored to the revised program. This conclusion was not reached hastily. After all, for the Institute to publish textbooks and study materials represents a significant broadening of its traditional role as an examining organization. But the unique educational needs of CPCU candidates, combined with the lack of current, suitable material available through commercial publishers for use in some areas of study, made it necessary for the Institute to broaden its scope to include publishing.

Throughout the development of the CPCU text series, it has been—and will continue to be—necessary to draw on the knowledge and skills of Institute staff members. These individuals will receive no royalties on texts sold and their writing responsibilities are seen as an integral part of their professional duties. We have proceeded in this way to avoid any possibility of conflicts of interests.

All Institute textbooks have been—and will continue to be—subjected to an extensive review process. Reviewers are drawn from both industry and academic ranks.

We invite and will welcome any and all criticisms of our publications. It is only with such comments that we can hope to provide high quality educational texts, materials, and programs.

Edwin S. Overman, Ph.D., CPCU
President

Preface

A Chartered Property Casualty Underwriter must have thorough knowledge of the protection provided by property and liability insurance. This text is designed to aid in the acquisition of that knowledge with respect to "commercial" property insurance—that is, property insurance used by businesses, institutions, and other organizations. The kinds of property insurance included are fire and allied lines, marine (ocean and inland), crime insurance (burglary, robbery, fidelity, etc.), boiler and machinery, and a few miscellaneous types. For convenience and with some logic, a few types of property insurance—automobile and aircraft physical damage covers and surety bonding—are dealt with in the text for CPCU 4, *Commercial Liability Risk Management and Insurance*. On the other hand, the liability protection provided in fire and allied lines forms, in marine insurance contracts, and nuclear energy liability insurance, are treated in this text.

The usefulness and significance of any insurance coverage depend on its relationship to the loss exposures of some potential insureds, *and* to other means that might be used for dealing with that exposure. That is, the usefulness and significance of any insurance coverage depend on its value as a risk management device for some organizations. Therefore, this text begins with an overall analysis of organizations' exposures to property loss. Then, as each general class of insurance coverage is taken up, the discussion includes consideration of (1) the nature of the loss exposures to which that coverage relates, and (2) the risk management techniques other than insurance that can be useful in helping to deal with those exposures. Understanding of these two related subjects is essential to efficiency and professionalism in the application of insurance to risk management problems.

The great variety of property insurance covers—their range of subject matter, their differences from territory to territory, from company to company, and from time to time—makes complete treatment in a single text impossible. The insurance professional must add, on his or her own, the additional information needed with respect to a particular cover in a given place at a given time. Hence the professional must always have reliable, detailed, up-to-date sources of information on policies and forms available. To use such sources, one must know what to look for and where to look; and must know the meaning of what is found. A thorough knowledge of both the common features and the principal special characteristics of most property covers will help the student to know what to look for, and to know the meaning of what is found.

The usual starting point in deliberate, planned acquisition of such knowledge is to obtain nearly complete *acquaintance* with, and *understanding* of, the regular content of a wide range of the property insurance forms in general use at a particular time. *Understanding* is obtained through learning (1) the exposures, losses, and hazards to which the coverages relate; (2) the history and principles from which the coverages and provisions have come; and (3) the relationships among the many classes of coverages and forms.

The student should keep these points in mind when studying this text. It is necessary to remain aware that the specific details of coverage presented here are illustrations of practice as expressed in forms in general use when the material was written (1976-77). They are thus illustrations of particular applications of general characteristics. And they can be used as benchmarks against which to compare other forms.

No review exercises or discussion questions appear in this text. These are included in a companion study aid—the CPCU 3 Course Guide. The Course Guide contains educational objectives, outlines of the study material, review terms and concepts, review questions, and discussion questions.

The extensive range of subject matter in this text required the authors to seek an equally wide range of assistance from others. Many insurance technicians have contributed information and comment. Their assistance was particularly important in providing information about company practices and special forms. Such information was especially necessary in the marine and surplus lines, where there are few rules, but was needed with other subjects, too. With respect to variations by company, and also by territory, we have attempted to present representative current practices.

Several contributing authors prepared manuscripts upon which some chapters, or parts of chapters, of this book were based. These are separately acknowledged following this preface. Obtaining the assistance of the many persons involved, and helping to coordinate their efforts, was a heroic contribution of several members of the staff of the American Institute for Property and Liability Underwriters.

Special thanks also go to E. J. Leverett, of the University of Georgia, and to R. G. Covin, of the Southeastern Region of the

Insurance Services Office, for extensive assistance with material for the fire and allied lines chapters.

We would particularly like to express our gratitude to Dennis A. Stimeling, CPCU, Product Manager, Insurance Company of North America, for his extensive review of the entire manuscript.

We would also like to specially thank the following persons who reviewed major sections of this text and provided us with valuable comments: Frederick J. Dugle, CPCU, CLU, Director of Education, Kemper Insurance Companies; William K. Ghee, Ph.D., CPCU, CLU, Professor of Finance and Insurance, Virginia Polytechnic Institute; John R. Lewis, Ph.D., CPCU, CLU, Professor Risk Management, Insurance and Real Estate, College of Business, The Florida State University; Thomas S. Marshall, CPCU, CLU, Marshall General Agency, Inc.; Robert H. McDowell, CPCU, Insurance Service of Charleston; Joseph R. Pierpont, Insurance Manager, Richardson-Merrell, Inc.; Frances M. Pommer, CPCU, University Extension Division, Rutgers University; August Ralston, Ph.D., Associate Professor and Chair, Department of Finance and Insurance, Bowling Green State University; John P. Stanford, CPCU, CLU, Vice President, Safeco Insurance Company; John L. Stewart, Vice President, Fireman's Fund American Insurance Companies; Seeman Waranch, CPCU, President, Insurance Agency of Norfolk, Inc.; Bernard L. Webb, CPCU, FCAS, Professor of Actuarial Science and Insurance, Georgia State University; Numan A. Williams, Ph.D., Associate Professor of Finance and Insurance, College of Business, Ball State University; Glenn L. Wood, Ph.D., CPCU, CLU, Professor of Finance and Insurance, California State College at Bakersfield.

In addition, we would like to thank the following individuals who reviewed chapters in their areas of specialty: Patrick F. Genovese, CSP, Loss Control Property Manager, CNA/Insurance; Ralph E. King, CPCU, Professor, Canton Agricultural and Technical College; John E. Linck, Resident Secretary, Insurance Company of North America; Milton M. Nachbar, P.E., Assistant Vice President, Director of Loss Control, CNA/Insurance; June Ann Roberts, CPCU, Marketing Research Manager, Meridian Mutual Insurance Company; Homer O. White, Jr., CPCU, Assistant Secretary, Insurance Company of North America; James D. Youd, CPCU, President, Attleboro Mutual Fire Insurance Company.

We would also like to thank the following for their extensive reviews of material in their areas of specialty: Charles R. Bardes, Vice President—Liability Underwriting, Leo P. Mariani, Ph.D., Vice President—Liability Underwriting, and Richard S. Pye, Vice President—

Property Underwriting, American Nuclear Insurers; and the Hartford Steam Boiler Inspection and Insurance Company.

Finally, authorship requires support and cooperation from the author's family. Donna, Martha, and Catherine Trieschmann are hereby added to the fraternity of "those who know how." They are entitled to wear the invisible badge of the fraternity, with its motto, *sine qua non;* the Hedges and Rodda families have earned another oak leaf cluster.

William H. Rodda
James S. Trieschmann
Bob A. Hedges

Contributing Authors

The American Institute for Property and Liability Underwriters and the authors acknowledge, with deep appreciation, the work of the following contributing authors whose manuscripts in their areas of expertise helped make this text possible:

Wallace L. Clapp, Jr., CPCU
Editorial Director
The Rough Notes Company, Inc.

A. Hawthorne Criddle, CPCU
Managing Partner
Warren, McVeigh & Griffin of Delaware Valley

David Warren, CPCU
President
Warren, McVeigh and Griffin

Table of Contents

CHAPTER 1

Commercial Property Exposures

INTRODUCTION

This is a text in commercial property risk management and insurance. Because insurance is the primary method used to treat commercial property loss exposures, the emphasis of this text is on insurance. But insurance cannot be studied in isolation. Insurance exists as a system for handling loss exposures. To study insurance, it is necessary to study exposures to loss and all the techniques which can be used to handle those exposures.

Chapter 1 will begin with a brief review of the risk management process discussed in CPCU 1. Following this, the topic of commercial property exposures is introduced by analyzing types of property, types of perils, and types of losses. Although the discussion at this point may seem somewhat elementary, its purpose is to develop an awareness of the vast variety of property loss exposures that will be considered in this course.

It is necessary to begin with an overview of the important characteristics of various types of property. Each type of property is subject to loss from a variety of perils. The discussion of perils approaches this subject in two ways, since perils can be grouped according to a generic classification system (a system which entirely disregards insurance), or can be grouped by considering their insurability. When property is damaged by a peril, various types of losses may result. Either direct or indirect losses may be insured, regardless of whether owned or nonowned property is damaged.

In identifying commercial property loss exposures—the first step in the risk management process—it is desirable to use an organized approach in accumulating the information. The latter part of this chapter will introduce several structured systems for identifying loss exposures. The insurance survey method, discussed in some detail, is particularly useful to insurance personnel in identifying loss exposures so that they can provide insurance which gives appropriate coverage. This method is of less value for identifying exposures for which risk management techniques other than insurance should be considered.

The insurance survey method will receive considerable attention in this chapter. Because of the insurance orientation of most CPCU candidates, it is an approach that will frequently be encountered in practice. Other methods or systems of exposure identification, particularly flow chart analysis and financial statement analysis, will all be discussed but in less detail.

The discussion in this chapter will not present any magical formula for identifying all insurable and noninsurable property exposures which face producers, underwriters, or risk managers. Even with the burgeoning use of computers, and the use of various systems to be explored, exposure identification requires experience, imagination, insight, and education.

REVIEW OF THE RISK MANAGEMENT PROCESS

The risk management process is discussed extensively in CPCU 1. Because this process will be used in this text in analyzing commercial property loss exposures and methods of treating those exposures, it is worthy of review. The risk management process is summarized in the following outline:

1. Identifying and analyzing loss exposures
    a. Identifying things of value exposed to loss
    b. Measuring potential loss frequency and severity
2. Selecting the technique or techniques to be used to handle each exposure
    a. Avoidance
    b. Control
    c. Noninsurance transfers
    d. Insurance
    e. Retention
3. Implementing the techniques chosen
4. Monitoring the decisions made and implementing changes when appropriate

This chapter deals with step (1a) in the risk management process—identifying things of value exposed to loss.

The first major section of this chapter deals with various ways in which commercial property loss exposures can be classified. The remainder of the chapter deals with various systems that may be used to analyze a business operation in order to identify possible exposures to loss.

Step (1b) of the risk management process, measuring potential loss frequency and severity, will be the subject of Chapter 2. The following chapters deal more specifically with particular types of commercial property loss exposures and the insurance and noninsurance methods used for their treatment.

TYPES OF COMMERCIAL PROPERTY LOSS EXPOSURES

The first step in the risk management process involves identification of things of value exposed to loss. This section will discuss various types of commercial property, the perils which may cause property losses, and the types of losses involved.

Types of Property

There is no single widely accepted system for classifying commercial property. Property can be divided into the categories of real property and personal property, but these broad categories are too broad to be of much use for the present discussion. It will be of more value to discuss narrower categories of property types, with most of the property in each category having similar loss exposures. A good classification system is one that meets the needs of its user. The classification system used here is merely illustrative of the type that might be adapted for use by a commercial firm attempting to identify types of property exposed to loss.

A brief analysis of each of the property types should make clear the usefulness of this kind of classification. The property types used for this discussion are unimproved land; buildings and structures; money and securities; accounts receivable; inventory; equipment, fixtures, and supplies; machinery; data processing equipment and media; valuable papers, books, and documents; mobile property; and intangible assets.

Unimproved Land Real estate, excluding all permanent property improvements, is known as "unimproved land." Often it is desirable to classify unimproved land separately for two reasons. First, values may be difficult to determine. Second, perils which can damage unimproved land are unique, or at least unusual.

Consider some of the reasons values may be difficult to recognize. Unimproved land may contain (1) water (lake, river, creek, springs, or underground water table); (2) mineral resources (coal, iron, oil, copper, bauxite, potash, sand, stone); (3) natural attractions of commercial value (caves, therapeutic springs or pools, historic sites, artifacts); (4) growing plants (timber, fruit trees, grazing pasture); or (5) resident wild animals.

Some perils which might affect unimproved land are rather obvious. Growing crops or timber are subject to brush or forest fires and plant diseases. And agricultural crops (such as vegetables and grains) may be damaged by rain, hail, snow, drought, and other weather conditions. The soil itself may be lost by erosion (caused by water or wind) and landslide. Even unimproved land that is not in use for any purpose has a value. Yet, if it is unattended and unsupervised for long periods, others may obtain rights to the property through easements or "squatter's rights."

Many of the potential losses to unimproved land are seldom covered by insurance. Yet loss to unimproved land may present significant exposures.

Buildings and Structures Buildings—including equipment used for the service of the buildings—and unattached structures usually must be subdivided into various categories. The loss exposure of buildings and structures depends primarily upon the type of construction, occupancy, and location of the property. Loss potential may be influenced significantly by loss control measures. A sprinklered building, for example, is much less likely to suffer a major fire loss than an identical but unsprinklered building.

The major characteristics of buildings and structures are:

1. They often represent substantial values.
2. The exposures are almost always insurable, at least against a large number of perils causing physical property losses.
3. Income is frequently lost until the damaged property is repaired or replaced.

Money and Securities The term "money and securities" includes many types of monetary assets. It may include cash, bank accounts, certificates of deposit, securities, notes, drafts, and evidences of debt.

The magnitude of this exposure varies widely by business and is not always related to the size of the business. Some small firms have relatively large monetary assets. Supermarkets, for example, usually have large sums of cash and checks. A large manufacturer, on the other hand, may have a small exposure for monetary assets.

The money and securities exposure fluctuates considerably in some companies. Firms that have seasonal patterns often have wide variations in monetary assets during the year.

Monetary assets are subject to many perils, but one of the most important is theft. Monetary assets may be stolen by employees or outsiders, by simple schemes or very elaborate, sophisticated plans.

Accounts Receivable The tangible property (paper or other media on which accounts receivable are recorded) is subject to physical damage, destruction, or removal from possession. However, the value of the media usually is insignificant when related to the property right that they represent. If accounts receivable records are damaged or destroyed, a company may be unable to reproduce the records or may reproduce them from underlying data at a large cost. In either event the exposure can be significant.

Another outstanding characteristic of this exposure is that loss potential may be virtually eliminated by reasonable loss control methods. If duplicate records are kept in a remote location, simultaneous loss of both sets of records is practically impossible.

Inventory For a wholesaler or retailer, inventory represents goods ready for sale. For a manufacturer, inventory is usually further divided into raw material, stock in process, and finished goods.

There are several characteristics of this exposure. One is that inventory is subject to a wide range of perils. This is due, in part, to the fact that inventory may be at a fixed location but is often subject to the perils of transportation. Many of the perils are insurable, but one important cause of financial loss, obsolescence, is not.

Inventory values may fluctuate widely and valuation is sometimes difficult. Goods in process, for example, are often difficult to value because value is being added at each stage in the production process.

In some cases, raw material is obtained from sources that may be difficult or impossible to replace. In these circumstances a company can suffer a loss when a supplier has a loss and is unable to deliver its goods.

Equipment, Fixtures, and Supplies Most personal (as opposed to real) property, other than inventory, machinery, and EDP (electronic data processing) equipment, can be conveniently classified as equipment, fixtures, and supplies. Examples include office furniture, file drawers, typewriters, photocopy equipment, showcases, counters, office supplies (such as stationery and printed forms), cleaning supplies, and packaging materials.

The basic rationale of this classification is that it provides, in effect, a miscellaneous category of personal property that would be difficult and impractical to otherwise classify. As such, one outstanding characteristic of this classification is that usually it consists of many separate pieces of property, each with a relatively low value. Also, replacement equipment, fixtures, and supplies are usually readily available, so an extensive interruption of the business resulting from loss of these items is unlikely. Another characteristic of property in this category is that it often is difficult to establish total values. Valuation is difficult for two reasons: (1) with numerous items of low value, it is impractical to devote much attention to precise valuation of each item; and (2) this property frequently shifts from one location to another, making it difficult to keep an accurate inventory.

The above characteristics provide, at best, only a general description of property in this category. Since this is a miscellaneous class of property, there is a real danger that some property will not conform to the general pattern. This exceptional property can cause risk management problems. Suppose, for example, that a risk manager decides that equipment, fixtures, and supplies are low value items that could be replaced easily. A manufacturer, however, may have a significant investment in packaging materials, fuel, chemicals, or cutting oils. And, even if the values are not large, and most such property is readily replaceable, it is possible that some property may not be easily replaced, and a loss could shut down the firm's operations. It is important, therefore, to analyze the property in this general category to determine if it includes any property of special importance. It is easier for special property in this category to escape detection because the category consists of miscellaneous property.

Machinery Machinery could logically be included in the previous category—equipment, fixtures, and supplies. Machinery, however, often has particular importance to a firm.

Machinery is characterized by large values. Often the values are subject to rapid depreciation—true physical depreciation, as opposed to accounting depreciation.

In many cases, losses caused by breakdown of machinery cause additional losses, independent of any other peril. Loss to power, heating, cooling, and lighting machinery, for example, may interrupt a company's operations. Since replacement or repair of damaged machinery often requires specialized parts or technical expertise, repair or replacement may require a long time. As a result, the lost income during the business interruption can be substantial.

Machinery is subject to some unique perils. Mechanical breakdown, for example, may result from improper use or maintenance, electrical malfunctions, inherent defects, metal fatigue, rust, and overheating. Many of these perils are uninsurable and must be handled by some risk management technique other than insurance.

Data Processing Equipment and Media Many companies have electronic data processing (EDP) equipment with substantial values. This property classification includes not only the computer but also computer programs, tape libraries, and equipment such as keypunches, tape punches, verifiers, and printers. Many computer facilities also require a special environmental control system. This may involve a raised floor and separate temperature and humidity controls. Magnetic tape loses its characters at high temperatures and a card reader cannot function if the humidity is high.

In addition to the unusual perils that may cause physical damage to the computer facilities and loss of income if the business is interrupted, EDP systems make other losses possible. Computer fraud by employees and outsiders has increased dramatically in recent years. Usually the criminals intend to steal money, but some ingenious schemes are designed to perpetrate the theft of other property. In some cases an employee or outsider is interested in sabotaging the EDP equipment. Sometimes the crime is to obtain confidential information. Industrial espionage probably has been stimulated by computers because corporate information is now more centralized than it previously was. Thus, a long list of criminal activities may be associated with computers.

Computers are frequently owned by the user, but many are leased. Normally, the leasing company retains responsibility for maintenance and accidental losses to the computer and its equipment, but this is not always true. Consequently, the lease agreement must be reviewed carefully to identify loss exposures.

Valuable Papers, Books, and Documents Most business firms of any size generate a huge volume of accounting, financial, and statistical records. In addition, many companies have valuable books, drawings, films, maps, abstracts, deeds, photographs, and other documents. Physicians maintain medical histories on their patients, and photographers, architects, engineers, and others maintain files of their previous work in order to work more efficiently.

These pieces of property create special loss exposures because they are small, light, easily destroyed or lost, and can be quite valuable. If valuable papers can be reproduced promptly, with little cost, the exposure may not be significant. Often, however, reproduction of valuable papers is time consuming or impossible, and a company may lose income or incur additional expenses because of the loss.

Mobile Property Automobiles, aircraft, boats and ships, heavy mobile equipment used by contractors, and other mobile machinery represent a separate class of property.

Mobile property is exposed to special hazards that arise from transportation. Collision is a major cause of loss but movable property can be damaged or destroyed from a large number of other perils.

Often extremely large values are concentrated in single items of mobile property. Airplanes, ships, and earth-moving equipment may be valued in the millions.

Intangible Assets Some assets, although valuable, have no physical substance. These include such items as copyrights, patents, trademarks, trade names, leases and leasehold interests, licenses, and trade secrets.

The outstanding characteristic of these assets is that they generally are difficult to recognize and value. If a firm consistently earns a larger profit than seems warranted on the basis of the company's physical assets, the implication is that a portion of the profits is being generated by intangible assets. But it is difficult enough to determine the rate of profits that should be earned on physical assets. Furthermore, the identification of the specific intangible asset that is responsible for the increased profits is difficult. The larger profits may be a result of a key employee's efforts, trade secrets, or even competitive advantages.

Although some intangible asset exposures are insurable, others are not—at least at a reasonable rate. Other risk management techniques, therefore, are especially important for these exposures.

Perils Affecting Property

A sound property risk management program requires a strong ability to identify perils affecting the various types of property. The potential frequency and severity of losses cannot be analyzed properly unless perils are recognized. More important, an unrecognized peril might produce a loss for which no risk management technique has been planned. If a large unanticipated loss occurs, the unintentional retention of the exposure can be catastrophic, or even fatal, to a firm.

Despite the importance of peril recognition, it is impossible to identify all potential causes of loss. There simply is no method available capable of the task. There is, in addition, a huge number of ever-changing perils.

Some peril classification systems give the illusion that practically all perils have been identified. Indeed, some listings of perils are quite lengthy and detailed, and it is difficult to imagine any perils that have been omitted. This, however, would be a false conclusion. Classification systems always omit some perils, and their inherent limitations must be kept in mind.

Perils may be classified by many different systems. Two systems—the generic classification system and classification by degree of insurability—will be discussed here.

Generic Classification System Under a generic classification system, perils may be divided into three categories: (1) natural forces, (2) man-made forces, and (3) acts of men and governments. From these broad classes, lists of specific perils can be constructed. Such lists are illustrated in Figure 1-1.

As complete as these lists appear to be, they must omit a huge number of perils. The list can be expanded by imagination and research, but it is sometimes helpful to consider other classification systems.

Classification by Degree of Insurability Perils can be classified according to their insurability, an approach somewhat more useful to the student of insurance. Within this system, perils can be divided into (1) insurable perils; (2) difficult-to-insure perils, or perils insurable only by the government; and (3) uninsurable perils.

It must be recognized that insurance does not cover all losses caused by every insurable peril. Therefore, the definitions and limitations of the insurable perils will be discussed to further specify what kinds of loss caused by the perils can be insured and what kinds of loss can only be handled by noninsurance techniques.

Classification by degree of insurability also recognizes that certain identified *perils* are uninsurable, and require treatment by a noninsurance technique. For example, losses caused by the inability of retail consumers to pay their debts might be recognized as an uninsurable peril.

Insurability is subject to change as loss exposures, underwriting, regulation, and market availability change. Although such changes affect the categories into which the various perils are placed, they do not affect the value of this approach in classifying loss exposures.

Since the discussion in this section deals with insurable perils, the information is presented according to standard insurance policies: fire, extended coverage, and optional additional perils. The discussion will be kept brief since later chapters are more specific with respect to these perils.

Standard Fire Policy Perils. In the fire policy three basic perils are insured: fire, lightning, and removal.

FIRE. Fire is often defined as rapid oxidation with a flame or glow. For insurance purposes, "fire" means a hostile fire, a fire outside its intended container. This definition means that a fire is not a fire, for insurance purposes, if it is in a fireplace or on a stove. Associated with and included in the fire peril is smoke damage caused by the fire, and water damage occurring from extinguishing the fire. In addition, any other damage to the property done by a fire department in fighting the fire is covered by fire insurance. If a fireman has to break out windows and knock down doors to fight the fire, these losses are considered to have resulted from fire.

LIGHTNING. The second peril covered in the fire policy is lightning. This peril can be defined as a natural discharge of electricity, usually

Figure 1-1

Generic Peril Classification System

I. Natural Forces		
Sun	Water	Rust
Rain	Flood	Mold
Fog	Tides	Corrosion
Snow	Tidal wave	Rot
Ice	Perils of the air (icing, clear air turbulence)	Fungi
Hail		Vermin
Lightning	Perils of the sea (icebergs, waves, sandbars, reefs)	Weeds
Static electricity		Uncontrollable vegetation
Wind (tornado, hurricane, typhoon, tempest)		Landslide/mudslide
	Fire of natural origin	Erosion
Temperature extremes	Volcanic eruption	Cave-in
Humidity extremes	Earthquake	Subsidence
Drought	Mildew	Smoke
	Evaporation	Meteors

II. Man-Made Forces		
Fire	Discoloration	Obsolescence
Pollution (smoke, smog, water, noise)	Contamination	Dust
	Electrical overload	Discrimination
Excessive odor	Changes of temperature	Sonic boom
Toppling of high piled objects	Shrinkage	Chemical leakage
	Water hammer	Vibration
Building collapse		
Radioactive contamination		

III. Acts of Men and Governments	
Strikes	Theft, forgery, fraud
Loss of trained personnel	Terrorism
Human carelessness, error, mistake, omission, malpractice, incompetence, or incomplete knowledge	Kidnapping
	Extortion
	Libel, slander, malicious prosecution, infringement of personal or property rights
Arson	
Vandalism, malicious mischief	
Riots, civil commotions	Expropriation, confiscation
Sabotage	False arrest
War, rebellion, insurrection	Currency fluctuations
	Depreciation

from a cloud. It is often hard to establish where lightning damage ceases and fire damage begins.

REMOVAL. The last peril covered in the fire policy is loss resulting from the removal of insured property from a building damaged or threatened by an insured peril. Coverage is afforded on a virtual "all-risks" basis until the property is permanently placed in another location. This coverage is one of the few examples of real "all-risks" coverages available since there are few, if any, exclusions. (Because the act of removal increases the chance of loss, some people consider removal a hazard rather than a peril.)

Extended Coverage Perils. Under the extended coverage endorsement, the basic fire policy is extended to insure against additional perils. These perils are windstorm, hail, explosion, riot, riot attending a strike, civil commotion, aircraft, vehicles, and smoke.

WINDSTORM AND HAIL. The windstorm peril includes damage caused by a wind of unusual strength that has produced general damage in an area at a particular time. It is not just any damage caused by wind. Wind erosion is not covered. Hurricanes, tornadoes, and cyclones are all considered windstorms.

The hail peril is included with the windstorm peril in the extended coverage endorsement. The hail peril involves actual direct physical damage to property caused by hailstones. Damage caused by freezing rain, snow, sleet, and ice is not covered. Typically, hail will cause automobile roofs to be dented, and it damages roofing and siding.

EXPLOSION. Explosion is a sudden and forceful expansion of air or other gas. For insurance purposes, it includes "the explosion of accumulated gases or unconsumed fuel within the firebox (or combustion chamber) of any fired vessel or within the flues of passages which conduct the gases of combustion therefrom."[1] This expression is fairly broad, and the extended coverage endorsement uses seven exclusions to limit it.

SMOKE. Another peril in the extended coverage form is that of smoke. The smoke peril here includes only loss which results from a sudden and accidental release of smoke from a vented heating or cooking unit. If the unit is not vented, no coverage is provided. (As mentioned before, smoke damage from a hostile fire is covered by the fire policy.)

AIRCRAFT AND VEHICLE DAMAGE. Aircraft damage and vehicle damage are usually treated simultaneously in the extended coverage form. Coverage for these perils is for direct physical contact between insured property and the vehicle or aircraft. Damage done by owned vehicles is sometimes excluded, but not damage done by owned aircraft.

RIOT PERILS. The last perils covered in the form are the riot perils: riot, riot attending a strike, and civil commotion. Riot as used in this form has been considered to be "an assembly of individuals who commit a lawful or unlawful act in a violent or tumultuous manner to the terror or disturbance of others."[2] Civil commotion can be considered an uprising of citizens. The two perils are quite similar, and it is difficult to distinguish between the two. The third part of riot coverage, riot attending a strike, covers direct physical damage done by striking employees who are occupying the insured's property during a sit-down strike. Under the riot attending a strike peril, loss or damage from pillage and looting is covered if such loss occurs during and at the place of the riot. The same is true with respect to riot and civil commotion.

Vandalism and Malicious Mischief (V&MM). The vandalism and malicious mischief peril (which is not one of the extended coverage perils) includes damage that might be caused by racketeers, cranks, spiteful employees, and other persons who maliciously damage property.[3] Typically, the forms which provide V&MM coverage define the perils to mean willful and malicious damage to or destruction of the insured property. Little distinction, if any, is made between vandalism and malicious mischief.

Optional Perils. The next group of perils that deserve attention are those which can be insured against through the optional perils endorsement. These perils include the following: falling objects; weight of snow, ice, or sleet; collapse; water damage; and glass breakage.

FALLING OBJECTS. The falling object peril includes property damage to the exterior of the building caused by any item falling on it. If the exterior is damaged, any interior damage caused by the falling object is also covered. For instance, when a tree falls on a building and damages the structure and the contents therein, the damage to both the exterior and the contents is covered. If a person drops a load of bricks on a warehouse floor and chips the floor, no coverage exists because no damage occurred to the exterior of the building.

WEIGHT OF SNOW, ICE, OR SLEET. The weight of snow, ice, or sleet peril involves situations where the roof or some other part of a building is damaged by the accumulation of snow, ice, or sleet. For instance, if a snowstorm deposits two feet of snow on a roof, the roof may not collapse, but the rafters may bend or crack. Structural damage has resulted and needs to be repaired, or more serious losses may result.

COLLAPSE. Coverage against the collapse peril provides protection when a structure actually caves in. Strict court interpretations have stated that the structure must actually fall into a heap of rubble. More liberal courts have said that even a partial collapse is collapse for insurance purposes.[4] However, recent exclusions that pertain to earth movement and subsurface water have been added to insurance forms and seem to have made the strict definition the majority view.

WATER DAMAGE. The water damage peril is intended to include particular types of damage caused by water. The present exposition pertains to limited water damage. Flood will be analyzed in the next section on difficult-to-insure perils. Limited water coverage concerns damage resulting from the accidental discharge or leakage of water or steam from within a plumbing, heating, or air conditioning system or domestic appliance. Such damage is covered only when the discharge or leakage is the direct result of the breaking or cracking of any pipes, fittings, parts, or fixtures forming a part of such system or appliance. Damage resulting from sprinkler leakage is specifically excluded. Since they are not mentioned in the definition of water damage, destruction resulting from flood, tidal wave, or other natural sources of water damage are not covered.

GLASS BREAKAGE. The last peril of the optional perils endorsement that needs attention is that of glass breakage. Technically, one might say that glass breakage is a type of loss rather than a peril or cause of loss. Nevertheless, glass breakage is usually treated as a peril. This coverage is limited to breakage of glass that is a part of a building, but not neon signs. Besides limitations as to the type of glass broken, this peril has very low limits—such as $250. The actual peril covered is any action that damages glass as defined in the form. It is an "all-risks" contract in nature but specific to one type of property—glass.

Other Insurable Perils. Besides these commonly insured perils, there are several other types of insurable perils that should be reviewed: sprinkler leakage, crime perils, boiler explosion, and perils of transportation.

SPRINKLER LEAKAGE. The peril of sprinkler leakage includes loss caused by the accidental discharge of a sprinkler system. If the system is accidentally activated and discharge damages or destroys an insured's property, the loss is covered. If a fire starts the discharge and the discharge damages the property, the damage is considered a loss caused by the fire.

CRIME PERILS. The crime perils involve the felonious taking of another person's property. With respect to insurance, there are three types of crime perils: burglary, robbery, and theft. *Burglary* is the felonious taking of property from a premises where force was used to enter and signs of forceful entry are visible. *Robbery* is the use of violence or threat of violence to take property from a person. *Theft* is the most general peril of the three and is the unlawful taking of another person's property. The theft peril would include burglary and robbery.

Boiler Explosion. The discussion of extended coverage stated that the definition of explosion did not include damage resulting from an exploding boiler or from mechanical breakdown. To insure against this peril, boiler and machinery insurance is needed. This peril protects against losses arising out of the utilization of pressure, mechanical, and electrical equipment. Protection can be provided for damage to the equipment itself as well as damage to other property.

Perils of Transportation. While property is being transported in an automobile, truck, ship, or aircraft, loss can occur from a variety of causes peculiar to property in transit. Planes, trains, and cars are damaged due to collision or upset; ships sink due to the "perils of the seas." All those losses result directly from transportation.

The preceding material is not exhaustive. The purpose of the discussion has been to illustrate types of insurable perils. Similarly, the next section concerns types of perils that are difficult to insure when any exposure exists.

Difficult-to-Insure Perils. What is difficult to insure depends on insurance market conditions. Two perils often difficult to insure are earth movement and flood. The term earth movement includes earthquake, landslide, mudflow, earth sinking, earth rising, or shifting. This wording is typical of the earth movement exclusion in most property insurance contracts. This peril is difficult to insure where the threat is great because of its catastrophic nature. If a strong earthquake were to occur in downtown Los Angeles or St. Louis, the losses could be in the billions. In earthquake-prone areas like California, rates are high and some companies are not anxious to provide insurance. However, in southern Florida, coverage should be readily available since that area has an earthquake rating of zero on a scale of zero to three. California's rating is three, as it is in St. Louis, Missouri and Charleston, South Carolina.[5]

The insurance definition of the flood peril includes more than just flooding from streams. It includes overflow of inland or tidal waters, unusual and rapid runoff of surface waters from any source and mudslides which are caused or precipitated by accumulations of water on or under the ground. It does not include seepage or backup of water or hydrostatic pressure.

Noninsurable Perils. Noninsurable perils are numerous. Some of these are war; rebellion; insurrection; intentional losses; fading; rust; dry rot; pollution; and settling of pavements, foundations, and walls. In addition, most losses resulting from political, production, and marketing activities are not insurable.

The perils of war, rebellion, and insurrection are typically considered the war perils and as a group or singly are not insurable. While special forms may be used to insure aircraft and oceangoing vessels against losses caused by war, this coverage is issued primarily by the United States government. The war exposure is privately uninsurable because of its catastrophic nature. If a hydrogen bomb were exploded over the Chicago Loop, the devastation would be enormous. Losses would be in the billions of dollars. If private insurance companies were providing coverage, they and their reinsurers would be bankrupt (assuming the reinsurer is not the United States government). While the losses could be spread throughout the general population, the losses that could happen at one time would be too great to absorb.

Intentional loss is not insurable for the obvious reason that if it were, people would deliberately destroy much of their property in order to be able to collect from the insurance company. Any time a business could not sell an old building or its inventory became obsolete, it could burn the inventory or building and collect from the insurance company.

Fading, rust, dry rot, pollution, settling of pavements, foundations, and walls can be called the natural wear and tear perils. These causes of loss are part of the natural order of things. If iron is exposed to air and moisture, it will rust. If a painting is directly exposed to the rays of the sun, it will eventually fade. A greenish coating forms on copper when it is placed in the open air. After prolonged use, most items will simply wear out. These perils do not cause accidental losses. The losses are certain to happen, and insuring them would prove of no benefit—uncertainty would not be reduced.

Production, marketing, and political activities which cause losses are what might be called business perils. While losses may result from them, gains may also be made. These perils are generally considered "speculative risks" rather than "pure risks," and are not suitable for insurance coverage. For instance, if a firm overproduces, it cannot buy insurance to cover the losses involved. If it could, there would be little incentive to control the level of production. Likewise, if a company enters a new market and fails, it cannot purchase insurance to cover the losses. If it could, the company could recklessly enter all types of new markets without fear of financial loss. The chance of production and marketing loss is largely in the hands of the insured. The moral hazard and adverse selection would be just too great to insure.

Classification of perils by degree of insurability is summarized in Figure 1-2. Although this list is much shorter than the generic list in Figure 1-1, it should be noted that the definitions of these insurable perils are rather broad.

Figure 1-2
Classification by Degree of Insurability

Insurable Perils	Difficult-to-Insure Perils
Standard fire policy perils	Earth movement
fire	Flood
lightning	**Noninsurable Perils**
removal	War perils
Extended coverage perils	Intentional losses
windstorm and hail	Wear and tear perils
explosion	fading
smoke	rust
aircraft and vehicle damage	dry rot
riot perils	settling of pavements, foundations, and walls
Vandalism and malicious mischief	Business perils
Optional perils	production
falling objects	marketing
weight of snow, ice, or sleet	political
collapse	
water damage	
glass breakage	
Other insurable perils	
sprinkler leakage	
crime	
burglary	
robbery	
theft	
boiler explosion	
transportation	

Types of Property Losses

Previous sections have discussed types of property that may be lost or damaged, and perils which might cause loss or damage. This section will discuss the types of loss that may be involved when property is destroyed or damaged by a peril.

Losses can be divided into several useful categories. Various authors have used a variety of classification systems. For our purposes, the most useful classifications are direct losses and indirect losses, and losses to owned and nonowned property.

Direct Losses A direct property loss occurs when a peril causes actual physical destruction, damage, or taking of property. A direct loss causes an immediate diminution in the value of the affected property.

Direct losses to tangible property are easy to visualize, although the exposures are not always easy to identify. Direct losses to intangible property, however, are also possible. The theft of trade secrets or valuable corporate information, for example, are direct losses of intangible property.

Indirect Losses Indirect losses result from direct losses. Indirect property losses can be further subdivided according to a variety of classification systems. For example, one approach recognizes two types of indirect losses—*net income losses,* which result from a reduction in the *net* income of the insured caused by either a reduction in gross revenue or an increase in expenses; and *consequential losses* (such as spoilage of meat in a freezer that was without power because of a direct damage loss).[6]

The following sections briefly describe many types of indirect loss, which are discussed in greater detail in later chapters of this text.

Business Interruption. When property used for producing goods for sale is destroyed or rendered unusable, sales may be impaired and business lost. A direct loss that causes a business slowdown or shutdown, therefore, may cause a company to lose (1) net income that would have been earned, (2) additional expenses required to minimize the reduction in income, and (3) expenses that necessarily continue when the property is damaged or destroyed. (Even if the property is completely destroyed, there may be continuing expenses, such as taxes on the land, noncancelable contracts for heat, light, and power, interest on debt, and salaries for executives.) These losses are known collectively as business interruption losses, and they are perhaps the most important of all indirect losses.

Contingent Business Interruption. Many firms are highly dependent on the activities of other organizations. The most common type of contingent business interruption loss arises when a company has a single major supplier. For example, if a manufacturer is dependent upon a supplier for a particular unique component, it may be impossible to avert a shutdown if the supplier's property is damaged. In these cases, a direct loss to a company causes a business interruption loss to another company.

The same type of loss can result when a consumer or wholesaler suffers a direct loss, and causes an indirect loss to the seller or manufacturer who no longer has a customer. The loss to the seller can be substantial if the customer represents all, or a large portion, of the seller's business.

Contingent business interruption losses can even result when a nearby firm suffers a loss. A number of small stores, for example, may be located near a large store. If the large store is shut down, business at the smaller stores may stop or decrease, even though they are not physically harmed.

Rental Income. Owned property that is leased or rented to others produces income. If the property is damaged or destroyed, the lessee or tenant may be excused from rent or lease obligations. The owner of the property, then, would suffer a loss of rental income. In effect, this is a business interruption loss for those who rent or lease property.

Rental Value. If property is occupied and used by the owner, there will be no loss of rental income, but the loss of use represents a loss of rental value (potential rental income). Suppose, for example, that a company owns a five-story building. Four stories are rented to others and one story is used by the owner. If the building is totally destroyed, the company may lose not only rental income, but also the rental or use value of the one story it occupies. Without the direct loss, the company could have rented the story to others. The loss, therefore, is a genuine loss because the company loses the use of a valuable asset.

Tuition Fees. Educational institutions have unusual business interruption loss exposures. Tuition fees usually are paid at the beginning of the school year or semester. If a major loss of facilities occurred shortly before or after the beginning of school, it is possible for tuition for the entire year to be lost even if the building could be repaired or reconstructed within a short time.

Profits and Commissions. Direct damage to a given building may have little impact on some operations. Consider the case of a manufacturer who stored finished products in a warehouse. If the warehouse and its contents were totally destroyed, the factory would continue to produce as usual. In the usual sense, there would be no business interruption. This is not, however, to say that there would be no indirect loss. In addition to the direct loss of all raw materials and labor that had gone into the finished product stored in the warehouse, there would be the loss of profits because these destroyed products could not be sold. In addition to loss of profits for the manufacturer, sales people paid on a commission basis would suffer loss of their commissions.

Accounts Receivable and Other Records. If a business loses its records of accounts receivable (or other transactions) it may not be able to collect the amounts due the company from debtors. Under the worst circumstances, the company would not be able to reconstruct its records and many customers would not pay their bills. At best, extra expenses will be involved in reconstructing the accounts and collections would be delayed.

Costs involved in the loss of accounts receivable may also include interest charges to borrow money to substitute for delayed payments, extra collection expenses incurred to collect accounts, and expenses to reestablish the records.

Extra Expenses to Operate. Business interruption losses may often be reduced by incurring extra costs. These costs are really part of the business interruption loss. Some companies, however, can altogether avoid a slowdown or interruption of the business by incurring additional costs. Many such companies are strongly inclined to continue operations at all costs.

Leasehold Interest. If a company occupies or uses property as a lessee and the lease is subject to cancellation if a direct loss renders the property untenantable, the company could have a loss of leasehold interest. Consider this example. A company obtains a twenty-year lease on a building in 1980 at a cost of $5,000 per month. In 1990, with ten years remaining on the lease, equivalent property might lease for $12,000 per month. If so, and the company lost the lease, it would lose the present value of $7,000 per month for the remaining ten years of the lease.

Improvements and Betterments. In many cases a tenant will install improvements in rented or leased property. If these improvements are permanently attached they become part of the realty and become the property of the building owner. Nevertheless, they are installed because they have value to the tenant. If destroyed and not replaced by the building owner, the tenant will lose the use of these improvements and betterments for the remaining period of the tenancy. Of course, the tenant might replace the improvements and betterments. The loss then would be the value of the replaced property.

Demolition and Increased Cost of Construction. The building codes of many jurisdictions may have a significant influence upon a loss. Some codes state that if a building is more than 50 percent destroyed, the entire structure must be demolished and rebuilt according to the prevailing building code. This may involve three major types of losses. First, the demolition cost. Second, the loss of the *undamaged* property that must be demolished. This cost is in addition to the direct loss because it pertains to the undamaged property. Third, the existing building code is likely to require higher quality and more expensive construction. In most cases, electrical codes call for more modern wiring, plumbing may be different, and the structure itself might need improvement. For example, a fire resistive structure might be required in place of a building of frame construction.

Consequential Losses. In a sense, all indirect losses are consequential. The term, however, often is used to describe changes in conditions of property following a direct loss. The identification of potential consequential losses can be difficult. So is estimation of loss severity. The variety and variables that can be involved are suggested by a few examples: thawing of frozen food following failure of a freezer, shutdown of a data processing machine following failure of an air conditioning system, or solidification of electrically heated molten metal when electrical power fails.

Pairs or Sets Losses. Some property items derive a large part of their value from the fact that they are used together. When one part of the set is lost or destroyed, the value of the undamaged property may be substantially reduced. For example, consider a clothing manufacturer that produces men's suits. If a fire or other peril destroys the trousers, the coats may be worth only a fraction of their value when included as part of a suit. Some property, in fact, such as costume jewelry earrings, may not have any value if one-half the set is lost or destroyed.

Owned Versus Nonowned Property Companies may suffer losses, direct or indirect, to both owned and nonowned property. Losses caused by damage to owned property are fairly obvious. Less obvious are the situations that can produce direct losses to nonowned property, such as those involving bailees, leased property, property on consignment, or employees' property.

Bailee Operations. Dry cleaners, laundries, warehouses, repair firms, and others have property of customers (or others) on their premises for which they are usually legally responsible.

Leased Property. Companies often lease computers, automobiles, and other machinery. The terms of the lease agreement usually determine who is responsible for losses.

This also applies to leased real property. Some leases require that the tenant pay for repairs and reconstruction following damage to the premises.

Property on Consignment. Distributors and retailers sometimes have property on their premises to be sold, although ownership rests with another company. Responsibility for losses should be spelled out in a contract between the parties, but this is not always the case.

Employees' Property. Employees often keep property, such as clothing and tools, on the employer's premises. Some union contracts even make the employer directly responsible for loss of employees' tools, imposing a loss exposure where none might otherwise exist.

In some cases, the legal responsibility for nonowned property is difficult to determine. To compound the problem, sometimes a company feels a moral responsibility for losses to nonowned property even though there is no legal obligation to bear the loss. To make things still more complex, indirect losses may result from the direct losses discussed above.

SYSTEMS FOR IDENTIFYING COMMERCIAL PROPERTY LOSS EXPOSURES

Identification of property loss exposures is no simple task. Fortunately, several systematic approaches to exposure identification are possible, and will be discussed in the remainder of this chapter.

The systems which will be discussed include the insurance survey method, flow chart analysis, and financial statement analysis. Other analysis systems are mentioned briefly. A risk manager may have to use several of the systems discussed in this chapter in order to identify, as completely as possible, exposures subject to loss.

The discussion which follows inevitably makes reference to some exposures and types of insurance discussed in greater detail later in this text. Emphasis in this chapter is not on the specific methods used to treat loss exposures, but on methods for identifying those exposures.

The Insurance Survey Method of Loss Exposure Identification

The most commonly employed system of loss exposure identification is the insurance survey questionnaire. Forms for this purpose are supplied by many insurance companies in conjunction with survey procedures they have developed as an aid to their producers. Insurance survey forms are also available from a few publishing houses that specialize in insurance publications, and some survey practitioners have developed their own.

All such questionnaires have undergone substantial revision as the business of insurance has changed, and they have been significantly affected by the increased use of the multi-peril policies or package forms. Some current survey forms include multi-peril policy applications.

Understandably, insurance survey forms like the one discussed here are totally insurance oriented. They are designed to reveal the insurable loss exposures of the prospect or client, in terms of available insurance coverage, and to provide the information necessary to underwrite and rate each policy. They do not attempt to develop loss exposure information on exposures for which insurance is not currently available.

Some insurance companies have several questionnaires, each especially designed to meet the particular requirements of certain classes of business. A retail store questionnaire does not develop the information required to survey a bank. Neither does a manufacturing questionnaire meet the needs of a long-haul truck operation. As more special purpose multi-line package policies are developed, the special questionnaire will become increasingly important as a tool for surveying different classes of business.

The insurance survey is one effective way of identifying exposures that can be treated with insurance. When combined with the knowledge, skill, and experience of an insurance professional, the insurance survey can develop the information needed to design a combination of insurance coverages that meets the needs of the firm surveyed. Insurance surveys are most useful for the small-to-medium sized firm that commonly uses insurance as its primary risk management technique. However, the approach can be adapted for use on firms of almost any size, including the larger firm used as an example in the following pages. To illustrate both the format and use of the insurance survey, a combination survey form and application for a multi-peril policy is presented. The responses given to the survey questions are illustrative and represent a hypothetical case.

To develop the information shown in an insurance survey like the one illustrated, it is typically necessary for the surveyor to tour the premises of the firm, at least in part, and to interview personnel at the firm who are capable of providing the necessary information. Throughout the information-gathering process, the surveyor assimilates the information received and combines it with his or her knowledge of insurance coverages.

General Information The first page of the survey (Figure 1-3) identifies the business entity, its organizational form, its locations, a subsidiary company, the nature of the business, the individuals to be contacted for physical inspections, the premium payment plan desired, and the various forms of insurance quotations required. To illustrate the use of this form, only those sections of the survey questionnaire relating to direct property loss exposures will be completed and commented upon. (Identification and evaluation of indirect loss exposures will be discussed in detail in Chapter 5.)

It is of critical importance to identify all the entities that are to be insured. This particular case reveals the ownership of a subsidiary engaged in a different but related business. The reasons for this separate corporation could be many. One is an effort to limit liability to subsidiary corporation assets in connection with a hazardous operation.

Three types of interests in the property locations can be indicated in the survey—those of owner and occupant, those of tenant, and those of a tenant who has made improvements and betterments to real property owned by another.

Four classifications of property are revealed—buildings, machinery and equipment, inventory, and office furniture and equipment.

This general information required by the questionnaire is very sketchy and should be supplemented by any other sources of information available to the person completing or using the survey.

For example, an underwriter might order a Dun & Bradstreet report to obtain more information about the business, history, operations, and finances. It would also reveal the names of the officers and directors, with some biographical data, a history of past business operations, financial statement as given, credit standing and, in some cases, loss history, particularly fire losses. If the organization is publicly-owned, a stockholders' annual report and, upon request, a public corporation's Securities and Exchange Commission Form 10-K can be obtained, both of which provide a great deal of information about the company. Catalogs or product brochures will describe products and services in considerable detail and add to a better understanding of the business activities being conducted.

Part I—Property Property—Part I (see Figure 1-4), both owned and occupied by the organization, is described as a fire-resistive building, ten years old, sprinklered, and used as a chemical plant and office. There is no other occupancy, and one of the items of property exposed to loss is inventory.

The note is made that inventory fluctuates because this is a seasonal business. Production is at its peak in late winter in preparation for the high product demand which will occur in the spring. The finished stock is warehoused at location #3 and it, too, fluctuates, reaching a peak of $3 million prior to spring distribution.

Because location #1 is fire-resistive and sprinklered, the surveyor realized that it is eligible for the highly protected risk fire form which includes extended coverage, vandalism and malicious mischief, and sprinkler leakage. In this case, the surveyor decided it would also be desirable to consider coverage on a blanket building and contents basis, but the problem of fluctuating inventory will have to be dealt with. (Discussion of these insurance considerations may appear to be placing the cart before the horse. But completion of such an insurance survey must be done with full knowledge and understanding of the insurance implications, so that additional information can be obtained where necessary.)

Location #2 is simply a sales office located near the area of the organization's largest sales distribution. It would be eligible for an office contents special form.

Location #3 is a sprinklered warehouse, also located near the point of greatest product distribution. Polywog, Inc. has a ten-year lease from 1975. At that time, it installed the sprinkler system with a secondary

Figure 1-3
Commercial Account Survey and Application

COMMERCIAL ACCOUNT
SURVEY AND APPLICATION

General Information

Name of Applicant POLYWOG, INC.

P.O. Address 000 (No) Main Street (Street) Anytown (City) USA (State) 00000 (Zip Code)

Producer (Name) (Address)

The Applicant is

☒ Corporation ☐ Partnership ☐ Individual ☐ Other ( )

COMPLETE ADDRESS OF EACH LOCATION TO BE INSURED		APPLICANT'S INTEREST		
Location No.		Owner & Occupant	Gen. Lessee	Tenant
1 Plant & Office	000 Main St., Anytown, USA	☒	☐	☐
2 Sales Office	000 High St., Another Town, USA	☐	☐	☒
3 Field Warehouse	001 " " " " "	☐	☐	☒
4 Plant & Office	1340 North St., Boomville, USA	☐	☐	☒

(Use separate sheet if more than four locations)

Name, Address and Relationship of All Affiliated and Subsidiary Companies to be Insured
100% owned—APPLICATORS, INC., 1340 North St., Boomville, USA

General Description of Business and Operations

(1) POLYWOG, INC.—Herbicide Manufacturer and Distributor

(2) APPLICATORS, INC.—Designers & Builders of Spraying Equipment (2) Contract Spray Applicators

Person Engineer Should Contact — Phone Number

Main Plant and Office—John Doe — 111-222-3333

APPLICATORS, INC.—Richard Roe — 111-322-2333

Premium To Be Payable ☐ 3-Year Prepaid ☐ Annual Installments

Premium Budget Plan to be used? ☐ Yes ☐ No

If Answer Is "Yes," Indicate Payment Option To be Used.
☐ 5 Months ☐ 10 Months ☐ 20 Months ☐ 22 Months

Proposed Effective Date: January 1st

Date Quotation Desired: December 1st

Quotation Desired For The Following Insurance
(Check Appropriate Block)

COMPREHENSIVE POLICY

- ☒—Part I —Property
- ☐—Part II —Business Income
- ☒—Part III —Inland Marine
- ☐—Part IV —Automobile Physical Damage
- ☐—Part V —Comprehensive Automobile Liability
- ☐—Part VI —Comprehensive General Liability
- ☒—Part VII—Crime

ADDITIONAL COVERAGES

- ☐—Workmen's Compensation
- ☐—Comprehensive Catastrophe Liability
- ☒ Plate Glass
- ☐
- ☐

The signing of this Application does not bind the Applicant nor any Company to complete the insurance, but it is agreed that the information contained herein shall be the basis of the contract should a policy be issued. The information contained herein has been prepared from our records and is true and correct to the best of my knowledge and belief. Please recognize the producing agent whose name appears herein as my agent for the handling and negotiating of the policy herein applied for with the company herein named to whom this application is submitted.

By ______________________
Owner, Partner, or Officer

Title ______________________ Date __________

Signed ______________________
Producer

Figure 1-4
Part I—Property

Part 1—PROPERTY

Standard Perils: Fire, lightning, windstorm and hail, explosion, riot, riot attending a civil commotion, aircraft and vehicles, sonic shock waves, smoke, vandalism and malicious mischief, sprinkler leakage, elevator collision, accident to an object (steam boiler, fire pressure vessel or electric steam generator).

Loc. No.	Coverage	Amount of Insurance	Co-ins %	ACV	RC	Prot. Class	Const.	BLDG. AGE	NO. OF FLOORS	Spklrd.	OCCUPANCY
1	Building	3,700,000	90		x	5—C	F.R.	10	1	Yes	Chemical
	Machinery	800,000	90	x		"	"	"	"	"	Plant &
	Inventory	900,000 *	90	x		"	"	"	"	"	Office

BUILDING IS ☒ SINGLE OR ☐ MULTI-OCCUPANCY FLOOR(S) OCCUPIED BY APPLICANT Entire

	Coverage	Amount of Insurance	Co-ins %	ACV	RC	Prot. Class	Const.	BLDG. AGE	NO. OF FLOORS	Spklrd.	OCCUPANCY
	Office Equip.	65,000	90	x			F.R.	"	"	"	

Loc. No.	Coverage	Amount of Insurance	Co-ins %	ACV	RC	Prot. Class	Const.	BLDG. AGE	NO. OF FLOORS	Spklrd.	OCCUPANCY
2	Office Equip.	15,000	80	x		7	Ord.	15	2	No	Sales Office

BUILDING IS ☐ SINGLE OR ☒ MULTI-OCCUPANCY FLOOR(S) OCCUPIED BY APPLICANT Part of first

Loc. No.	Coverage	Amount of Insurance	Co-ins %	ACV	RC	Prot. Class	Const.	BLDG. AGE	NO. OF FLOORS	Spklrd.	OCCUPANCY
3	Inventory	1,500,000 *	90	Sales Price		7	Ord.	7	1	Yes	Warehouse
	Office Contents	5,000									
	Improvements	100,000									

BUILDING IS ☒ SINGLE OR ☐ MULTI-OCCUPANCY FLOOR(S) OCCUPIED BY APPLICANT Entire

Loc. No.	Coverage	Amount of Insurance	Co-ins %	ACV	RC	Prot Class	Const.	BLDG. AGE	NO. OF FLOORS	Spklrd.	OCCUPANCY
4	Office Contents	15,000				6	Ord.	5	1	No	Mfg. Spray Equipment
	M & E	100,000	90	x							Equip. Storage
	Inv.	300,000									Office

BUILDING IS ☒ SINGLE OR ☐ MULTI-OCCUPANCY FLOOR(S) OCCUPIED BY APPLICANT Entire

(Use separate sheet for additional locations)

Optional Coverages Desired (check)	☒ *Highly Protected or Superior Form (if eligible) (Location 1) ☐ Special Extended Coverage (Bldgs.) ☐ Glass (attach schedule) ☐ Inflation Guard (Bldgs.) ☒ Agreed Amount Clause (Bldgs.) (Location 1)
Deductible:	☐ As provided in basic coverage form $250 ☐ $1000 ☐ $3000 ☒ $5000 Franchise Disappearing at $25,000 Flat Deductible ☐ $500 to $75,000 $ ______ Other ______
Form(s) To Be Used (Check Block)	☐ Specific Building ☐ Specific Contents ☒ Blanket Building and Contents (Loc.1) ☐ Scheduled Building and Contents ☐ *Public and Institutional—Blanket ☐ *Public and Institutional—Scheduled ☐ *Commercial Property—Non-Reporting ☐ *Commercial Property—Reporting ☐ *Multiple Location—Form 1 Reporting ☐ *Multiple Location—"A" Reporting ☒ Office Contents Special Form (Loc. 2) ☐ *Multiple Location—Bldg. and Equip. *Submit appropriate completed application for rating.
☒ Mortgage ☐ Loss Payee ☐ Contract of Sale ☐ Additional Insured Under Property Only	Loc. 1 Name Third Savings and Loan Association Bldg. ___ Address 111 Main Street, Anytown, USA Loc. ___ Name ______ Bldg. ___ Address ______ Loc. ___ Name ______ Bldg. ___ Address ______ Loc. ___ Name ______ Bldg. ___ Address ______

Comments *Location 1—Inventory is maximum during 6 month Peak Production
Period—drops to low of $150,000 other 6 months.
Location 3—Inventory is 50% of maximum of $3,000,000 which will be reached in
March-then decline to $50,000 by June when it will start to rebuild.

Continued on next page

Part 1—PROPERTY (Continued)

BOILERS, PRESSURE VESSELS AND MACHINERY OBJECTS

	Kind of Object	Part I—PROPERTY DAMAGE (Check block if to be insured)	Part II—BUSINESS INCOME (Check block if to be insured)
Mandatory	Steam Boilers, Fired Pressure Vessels, and Electric Steam Generators	☒	☐
Optional	Unfired Vessels	☒	☐
	Refrigerating Vessels	☐	☐
	Compressors or Pumps—Rotary	☒	☐
	Compressors or Pumps—Reciprocating	☐	☐
	Fans or Blowers	☐	☐
	Gears	☐	☐
	Steam Turbine Units	☐	☐
	Electric Motors	☒	☐
	Electric Generators	☐	☐
	Transformers	☒	☐
	Switchboards—Cables—M.E.A.	☒	☐
	Describe any other kind		

Important In order to accurately rate your **boiler & machinery** coverages, please submit **a current** schedule of objects indicating direct, **indirect** and consequential limits desired.

Number of Working Days per year 250

Optional Coverages

Is Repair and Replacement to apply? ☒ Yes ☐ No

Is Blanket Group Plan Desired? ☒ Yes ☐ No

water supply at a cost of $100,000. Because of the fluctuating inventory, a reporting form should be considered.

Location #4 is used for the manufacture of spray equipment for applying the parent company's products. In an interview, it was learned that some of this equipment is sold to others and some is retained and used in the application of herbicide on a contract basis. The inventory consists of new and used equipment for both sale to others and use in the business of applying herbicides.

The surveyor, at this point, is asked to report decisions with respect to insurance forms to be utilized in the program and is also required to select a deductible. Naturally, such decisions are not properly made until analysis of relevant exposures has been completed, by use of this form or some other means. In the example, a $5,000 deductible was selected.

Finally, the mortgage interest in the owned real property is identified. This particular survey questionnaire does not ask how the values were selected for coverage amounts on the various properties. Values are critical and their source should be questioned. For the owned building, the key valuation is replacement cost. Using this as a base, actual cash value can also be ascertained. The best source of such data is a current appraisal or a current builder's estimate. Very often, in practice, neither of these will be available and alternate methods must be employed, such as an insurance company appraisal based on square foot costs for the type of construction and area. No matter which method is used, it is essential that some basis of evaluation be established.

With respect to machinery and equipment, the best source of valuation is the current replacement cost of the machinery and equipment involved. Again, a professional appraisal is the best source, but a secondary source may be the manufacturers' current day prices. Other chapters in this text will deal more extensively with the subject of valuation.

Boiler, Machinery, and Electrical Apparatus The manufacturing process utilizes a variety of machinery and equipment. Such equipment is covered under a fire and extended coverage insurance contract for those perils, but it is also subject to loss by perils which are either specifically excluded or which are not within the scope of coverage provided. Steam explosions are an example of the former, and mechanical breakdown an example of the latter. (See Figure 1-4.) The surveyor should identify the classes of equipment and the inherent perils to which it is subject. Inspection by the underwriter's boiler inspector should be made, listing and describing each item and its rating factors. Because this class of insurance is a specialty, most surveyors need the assistance of those especially qualified in the field.

Objects may be individually listed and insured or they may be insured under "blanket group" descriptions which include all objects within a given class. The latter is considered better practice because of its automatic features applicable to changes and additions.

In considering the amount of loss exposure, attention should be given to the loss characteristics of each class of objects. Any object subject to explosion not only can destroy itself but can also cause substantial damage to other property, including the building. On the other hand, the burnout of an electric motor is unlikely to extensively damage other property unless fire ensues and then fire insurance would apply.

Plate Glass Insurance on plate glass covers breakage from any cause except fire, which is covered by the fire insurance contract. A manufacturing company usually has a minor loss exposure (like the exposure identified by the survey questionnaire—see Figure 1-5). A mercantile business with large and expensive show windows or a modern glass-walled building has greater loss exposures, especially with respect to perils that can cause loss to multiple plates.

Part III—Inland Marine An index to various inland marine insurance policies serves as a guide to the sections to be completed. (See Figure 1-6.)

From the facts previously presented, certain things may be deduced. The two organizations are engaged in the sale of products and/or services and have not been identified as "cash only" businesses. Therefore, they must have accounts receivable, supported by accounts receivable records. On the survey questionnaire, the accounts receivable data section is completed.

Their herbicide formulas, spray equipment designs, and research activities are undoubtedly recorded. They must have books of account, a deed to the real property, and may have research records. These constitute valuable papers, and the valuable papers section is completed.

There are no neon or other signs, and this section is not completed.

It is obvious that the plants receive raw materials and supplies from outside sources and ship their own products. They may require a transportation floater, so this section is completed.

It has been stated that Applicators, Inc. does work for others under contract, using its own equipment. This shows an exposure of mobile equipment, so the contractors equipment section is completed as shown.

An oil portrait was observed by the surveyor in the company president's office, and further inquiry developed the information listed under "Miscellaneous Schedule Property."

There is no indication from the stated facts that there is a loss exposure of the kind insured by bailees, installation, installment sales, or

Figure 1-5
Plate Glass

PLATE GLASS

Loc. No.	Location of Premises
1	000 Main Steet, Anytown, USA

IS GLASS NOW FREE FROM IMPERFECTIONS?	IS GLASS SET IN WOOD OR METAL FRAMES?	ARE FRAMES & SETTINGS IN GOOD CONDITION?	HAS INSURED SUSTAINED ANY LOSSES DURING PAST THREE YEARS? IF SO, STATE CAUSE
Yes	Metal	Yes	1 Partition Plate-Struck by object.

The glass, lettering and ornamentation insured hereby are described and located as stated below. Unless specifically described as such hereunder, this policy does not cover lettering or ornamentation, or clamped, glued, bent, wired, leaded, or cathedral glass, or mirrors, or show case glass, or any glass not set in frames, sashes, or bars, or any glass other than fully-glazed plain plate glass. (State whether plates are interior or exterior glass is six feet or more within the outer building line.)

LOC. NO.	NUMBER OF PLATES	LENGTH IN INCHES	WIDTH IN INCHES	DESCRIPTION OF GLASS, LETTERING AND ORNAMENTATION	SPECIFIC LIMIT (If Any)
1	18	5'	3'6''	Office Partition Glass—3'6'' above floor level	
1	5	3'	2'	Private Office Doors	

Figure 1-6
Part III—Inland Marine

PART III — INLAND MARINE

Check coverages to be included and complete appropriate section of this application.	Check coverages to be included and complete appropriate special company application indicated.	
☒ Accounts Receivable	☐ Motor Truck Cargo	☐ Parcel Post (Open Form)
☒ Valuable Papers and Records	☐ Installation Floater	☒ Patterns and Dies
☐ Neon Signs	☐ Bailees Customers Floater	☐ Processing Floater
☒ Transportation Floater	☒ Fine Arts Floater	☐ Salesmen's Floater
☒ Contractors Equipment Floater	☐ Installment Sales Floater	☐ Camera Dealers Form
☐ Scheduled Property	☐ Other ______	
	☐ Other ______	

ACCOUNTS RECEIVABLE ☐ Reporting Form ☐ Non-Reporting Form (limit must not exceed $100,000 on non-reporting)

Loc. No.	Location of Premises	Limits of Insurance
1	000 Main Street, Anytown, USA	$1,750,000
		$
		$

	• RECEPTACLE DESCRIPTION				( )CHECK COVERAGE APPLICABLE
	Kind	Name of Maker	"Class" or Label	Name of Issuer of Label	
Loc. 1	F. P. Cabinet	Mosler	A	Und. Lab.	☒ Accts. Rec. ☒ Val. Pap.
Loc. 4	File Cabinet	Steelcase	A	" "	☐ Accts. Rec. ☒ Val. Pap.
					☐ Accts. Rec. ☐ Val. Pap.

VALUABLE PAPERS AND RECORDS

Loc. No.	Location of Premises	
Loc. 1	000 Main St., Anytown, USA	
Loc. 4	1340 North St., Boomville, USA—F.P. File Cabinet	
	Coverages	Limits of Insurance
	Valuable Papers and Records(Chemical Research Notes-Equipment Drawings)	$ 25,000 - Loc. 1
	(a) Specified Articles	$ 10,000 - Loc. 4
		$
		$

A. The published 90 % coinsurance fire contents rate is $ .24 (Loc. 1) 80% $.75-Loc. 4

B. Give Details of Previous Losses None

C. During the last three years the estimated percentage of uncollectible accounts receivable to total of accounts receivable is:
19 76 1%   19 75 1%   19 74 1%

D. On what floor is vault or safe located? 1st   Number of floors in building? 1

E. Can the papers to be insured be duplicated or reproduced? Yes x No ____

F. If records or accounts receivable are kept in a vault, is vault built on a solid foundation from the ground up? ____

G. Does applicant understand he must furnish the company with a written statement of the total amount of the accounts receivable 20 days after the end of each month? yes

H. How often does the applicant have a certified public accountant audit his records? Annually

I. Does the applicant keep duplicant records? some   a. In same building some b. Elsewhere some

J. List Accounts Receivable for 12 months immediately preceding date of this application:

Month		Amount Outstanding Accounts	
1. January	7. July	1. 450,000.	7. 516,250.
2. February	8. August	2. 525,000.	8. 473,750.
3. March	9. September	3. 787,500.	9. 431,250.
4. April	10. October	4. 1,672,500.	10. 489,500.
5. May	11. November	5. 1,475,000.	11. 474,500.
6. June	12. December	6. 823,750.	12. 628,500.

Continued on next page

SIGNS

Type ☐ Neon
☐ Mechanical NONE
☐ Electric

How is sign mounted and where located? ______ It is ☐ Inside ☐ Outside

If outside, how high is sign above street level? ______ If roadside sign, how far from road? ______

Coverage desired: Full coverage with ☐ Std 5% Deductible or ☐ Other $ ______

Give details of previous losses ______

Description of lettering and size of sign. (Use space below for sketch.)

ANNUAL TRANSPORTATION FLOATER

Type of Property Shipped: Chemicals-Packaging Material

Limits of Liability: $ 100,000 Any One Location; $ 100,000 Any One Disaster

Carrier's Release from Liability: $ Yes Freight; $ No Express; $ Yes Truckmen

Coverage Desired (Please Check)
☐ Named Perils
☐ All Risks

Deductible Desired
☐ $50 ☐ $100 ☐ $500
☐ Other ______

Method of Shipment	Estimated Annual Shipments To Be Insured: Incoming	Outgoing	Inter Location	Maximum Value Any One Shipment
Railroad	$3,000,000	$ None	$ None	$25,000
Railroad Express	$ None	$ None	$ None	$
Public Truckmen	$2,000,000	$ None	$ None	$15,000
Trucks Owned Leased or Hired By Insured	$ None	$11,000,000	$9,000,000	$50,000
Other (Describe) Supplier	$250,000	$	$	$
Truck Totals	$5,250,000	$11,000,000	$9,000,000	$

Give Details of Previous Losses: 1975-Railroad Derailment-Tank Car $20,000—Recovery from carrier $10,000

CONTRACTORS EQUIPMENT — ☐All-risk ☐Named Peril If Deductible desired, please show amount $ ______

Yr. Built	Trade Name or Mfg.	Description, Capacity or Body Type	Serial or Motor No.	Radius of Operation	Value
1970	Crane Co.	Yard Crane-5 Ton	0123	Yard	15,000
1975	APPLICATOR, INC.	2—500 Gallon	567 & 568	50 miles	@3,500
1976	APPLICATOR, INC.	3—1,000 Gallon	1026-7-8	" "	@6,500

Where is Insured Property Kept When Not in Use? St. 1340 North Street City Boomville State USA

Loss Payee or Mortgagee on Item ______ is: Name

Is a Certificate of Insurance Required? ☐Yes ☒No Address

Give Details of Previous Losses 1975 - 500 Gallon - Sprayer mired in quicksand - cost of recovery and cleanup - $1,250

MISCELLANEOUS SCHEDULE PROPERTY WITH $______ DEDUCTIBLE. ☐Named Perils ☒All Risks

DESCRIPTION OF ITEM, ABOVE (attach list if necessary)—Show name of manufacturer and serial number if possible.	Actual Cash Value
Portrait of founder of POLYWOG, INC. by famous artist—appraised 1970	$1,500

salesman's samples floaters. At this point, there is also no indication of the need for processing or patterns and dies floaters, which will be discussed later.

Part VII—Crime The most frequently purchased crime coverages are listed first and the surveyor has selected those applicable to Polywog, Inc. (See Figure 1-7.)

The section which follows is designed to provide a basis for estimating the employee dishonesty loss potential at each location. The remainder of the questions on the first page of the crime section are related to procedures and practices which affect loss prevention, detection, and control.

The crime section contains loss history, prior coverage, and a census of employees by positions. There are also questions on burglary or theft of merchandise. In the case under study, the merchandise is not considered attractive to thieves. The surveyor has learned that the chemical products have a specialized and limited use, and the value is small in relation to bulk. There are probably no "fences" through whom the product could be sold. The spraying equipment has similar characteristics. There *is* a property loss exposure, but one with a low frequency and severity.

Questions are then asked about money, securities and checks. Cash is usually a minor loss exposure to a manufacturer—purchases and sales are usually check transactions. Securities, if owned, are usually in a safe deposit box. Incoming checks can be handled by a procedure that minimizes loss exposures. The questions asked are clues to some of these techniques.

The depositors forgery section relates to specifics of forgery coverage requested on a previous page. A small fringe benefit is available by including the personal accounts of officers or partners. In Polywog's case, coverage on officers or partners was not desired. There are no valuable metals involved in the account under study.

Flow Chart Analysis

One of the most useful methods of exposure identification is the detailed analysis of a flow chart of a firm's business operations. A flow chart is a diagram of the firm's operations showing, in the case of a manufacturer, the flow from suppliers' raw materials to purchasers of the finished product.

For many firms, a flow chart will be quite complex. It may be necessary to use numerous flow charts (perhaps one for each product line) in the exposure identification process for a large conglomerate organization. However, the basic procedures are the same for firms of any size.

It is often desirable to draw two flow charts. The first covers the flow of goods from the supplier to ultimate consumers. Such a chart, illustrated in Figure 1-8, can be used to identify those points in the production and distribution chain where a loss could create considerable problems because of the interrelationship of various operations. This flow chart indicates that the warehouse is a potential trouble spot—information that might not be revealed with use of a questionnaire.

Another chart, or series of charts, could depict the movement of goods within a plant. Such a chart might help identify critical processes in which a minor direct damage loss could cause substantial business interruption losses, because all goods flow through one machine or one point in the manufacturing process. A chart depicting movement of goods within a plant is illustrated in Figure 1-9. In this chart, it will be observed that minor damage to process AB might make it necessary to shut down the entire plant.

The number, variety, and format of flow charts that can be drawn depends on the exposures present, the amount of information available and the creativity of the person making the flow chart(s). Figure 1-10 depicts a flow chart showing the water utility operation of a large city. Although the format is different from those of manufacturing operations, the concept is the same.

Applying the Flow Chart Technique Different information is required for flow chart construction than is provided by the survey questionnaire. This supplementary information is risk management data—it reveals the factual situations which create or significantly affect loss exposures. Specific information may show it is possible to eliminate or reduce some of the exposures by changing current practices.

Polywog, Inc. will again be used to illustrate how a flow chart may be applied to loss exposure analysis. In this case, assume the preceding survey questionnaire had already been completed and the flow chart is being used as a supplement. (In other cases, it may be desirable first to construct a flow chart.) The flow chart in Figure 1-11 forms a basis for the following exposure identification and analysis.

Because Polywog's manufacturing process begins with the acquisition of raw materials or final product components, the first section of the survey form that needs expanded information is the "Annual Transportation Floater." Since the owner of goods has the primary loss exposure, it is important to establish when title passes from seller to buyer. This makes it essential to know the terms under which the purchase and sale are made. The various possibilities are that (1) title can pass to the buyer

Figure 1-7
Part VII—Crime

Part VII—CRIME

AMOUNT OF INSURANCE DESIRED — COMPREHENSIVE 3D POLICY

Insuring Agreement I	Employee Dishonesty Coverage	Commercial Blanket Blanket Position	Form A Form B	$ 50,000 $	
Insuring Agreement II	Loss Inside the Premises Coverage	Money & Securities Securities Only		$ 1,000 $	BLANKET CRIME POLICY
Insuring Agreement III	Loss Outside the Premises Coverage	Money & Securities Securities Only		$ 1,000 $	$ . . . .
Insuring Agreement IV	Money Orders and Counterfeit Paper Currency Coverage			$	
Insuring Agreement V	Depositors Forgery Coverage			$ 25,000	
	Additional Optional Insuring Agreements				

EMPLOYEE DISHONESTY Office Locations (Show largest amount of Money and Merchandise on hand at each location)

Loc. No.	Address	Main Office/Branch	Money	Merchandise
1		Main	1,000.	200,000
2		Sales	100.	None
3		Warehouse	100.	500,000
4		Branch	100.	75,000

AUDITS AND PROTECTIVE CONTROLS

(a) How often will there be an audit by an outside C.P.A.? Annually Name of firm Doe & Roe

(b) Is unqualified opinion rendered by C.P.A.? ☒ Yes ☐ No

(c) Is verification or spot check made of Accounts Receivable Ledger? ☒ Yes ☐ No How Often? Monthly
By Whom? Treasurer

(d) Will there be an audit by an officer or employee who is a C.P.A? ☐ Yes ☒ No How Often? ______

(e) Are audit reports given directly to Owner, or Partners, or Board of Directors? ☒ Yes ☐ No

(f) Do Branch Locations bank locally? ☐ Yes ☒ No
If so are duplicate copies of monthly bank statements and deposit slips sent directly to head office by bank? ☐ Yes ☐ No

(g) Is a complete inventory made with physical check of stock and equipment? ☒ Yes ☐ No How Often? ______
By Whom? ______

(h) Is a perpetual inventory kept? ☒ Yes ☐ No

(i) Is monthly bank statement reconciled by one not making deposits or withdrawals? ☒ Yes ☐ No

(j) Will employer agree to furnish completed applications (FK 310) on all new or not previously bonded employees of his organization? ☒ Yes ☐ No

(k) Will employer enforce vacations of all officers and employees? ☐ Yes ☒ No as to officers

(l) Will employer agree to furnish Loss Prevention Questionnaire? ☒ Yes ☐ No

AUTHORITY OF EMPLOYEES List names of employees authorized to do any of these activities:

Sign Checks	Issue-Cancel Warehouse Receipts	Handle Bank Deposits	Approve Payroll
Any two of Pres.-VP—Treas.-Bookkeeper	NONE	Bookkeeper	Treasurer

DISTRIBUTION OF MERCHANDISE AND SERVICES

Employer's merchandise or services are sold by: Full Time Employees ☒
Agents or Others ☐

Cash and charge sales have been approximately Cash 1 %
Charge 99 %

DUTIES OF OUTSIDE EMPLOYEES

Carry Merchandise Yes ☐ No ☒
Collections Are Cash 1 % Checks 99 %
Handle Refunds Yes ☐ No ☒
Deposit Collections Yes ☐ No ☒
Value of Merchandise $______
Average Daily Collections $______ Per Person
Handle Trade-ins Yes ☐ No ☒
Deduct Commissions Yes ☐ No ☒

How often is merchandise inventories?
Daily ☐ Weekly ☐ Other: Annually
How often are collections turned in? No collections
Daily ☐ Weekly ☐ Other:
Are salesmen subject to written agreement?
Yes ☐ (Attach Copy? No ☒
Average Earnings
Salary $ 12,000 Commission $______
Bonus $4-6,000

Continued on next page

Part VII—CRIME—(Continued)

LOSSES DURING PAST 6 YEARS BY EMPLOYEE DISHONESTY, FORGERY, BURGLARY, ROBBERY, THEFT, DISAPPEARANCE, DESTRUCTION. CHECK IF NONE ☐

Description of Loss	Date	Amount	Describe Corrective Measures Taken (If Employee Dishonesty, Furnish Complete Details)
NONE			

Has any employee dishonesty, forgery, burglary, robbery, theft, disappearance or destruction insurance carried by the applicant been declined or canceled within the last five years by any insurer) If answered affirmatively, please explain.

PRIOR FIDELITY COVERAGE TO BE SUPERCEDED—CHECK IF NONE ☐

Form of Bond or Policy	Effective Date	Amount	Name of Insurer
Blanket Crime	1-1-70	$50,000	XYZ Insurance Co.

PERSONNEL INFORMATION

COMPLETE THIS LIST OF POSITION DESIGNATIONS WHICH APPLY TO THE PERSONNEL OF THE EMPLOYER. SINCE PREMIUM IS BASED ON THE UNDERWRITER'S ANALYSIS OF THE PERSONNEL LIST, ITS ACCURACY AND COMPLETENESS ARE MOST IMPORTANT.

OFFICIALS	NUMBER	MANAGEMENT	NUMBER	SALES	NUMBER
Chairman	1	Managers		Sales Manager	2
President	1	Assistant Managers		Assistant Sales Manager	0
Vice President	3	Branch Managers		Branch Sales Manager	0
Treasurer & Asst. Secty.	1	Department Managers		Salesmen (Outside Who Collect)	0
Assistant Treasurer	—	Superintendents		Salesmen (Outside—No Collect)	5

Secretary & Asst. Treas.	1	Factory Superintendents	2	Salesmen (Inside)	0
Assistant Secretary	—	Purchasing Agents	2	Demonstrators	0
Comptroller	—	Supervisors		Canvassers	0
Assistant Comptroller	—	Buyers		Collectors	0
				Drivers (Collections)	0
				Drivers Helpers	4
				Chauffeurs (Collections)	0
				Chauffeurs (No Collections)	4
ACCOUNTING		STOCK			
Accountants	0	Shipping Clerks	2	Messengers (Inside) & outside	1
Auditors	0	Receiving Clerks	2	Messengers (Outside)	—
Assistant Auditors	0	Helpers—Shipping Dept.	1	All Inside Clerical	11
Cashiers	0	Helpers—Receiving Dept.	1		
Bookkeepers	2	Checkers		All Other Positions	
Paymasters	0	Stock Clerk	1	Research Chemist	1
Payroll Clerks	0	Supply Clerk		Hourly employees	150
Cash Handling Clerks	0	Custodians			
Timekeepers-Foremen	2	Watchmen			
Adjusters	0				

Does the employer contemplate any expansion of its business during the coming year which is likely to result in a substantial increase in the number of employees? Yes ☐ No ☒

Is the number of employees likely to be increased substantially during the premium year because of seasonal activity or any other circumstances peculiar to the employer's business? Yes ☐ No ☒

Continued on next page

Part VII—CRIME—(Continued)

OPEN STOCK

Is open stock burglary insurance desired? ☐ Yes ☒ No

Is open stock theft insurance desired? ☐ Yes ☒ No

What types of merchandise or material are to be insured? ____________

Is there a predominance of one type? ☐ Yes ☐ No

Is any merchandise kept off premises? ☐ Yes ☐ No

If all locations to be covered, please state amount $____________

Does applicant maintain on premises a burglar alarm? ☐ Yes ☒ No

Is burglar alarm system certified? ☐ Yes ☐ No

Does applicant employ private watchmen who are on duty when the premises are closed? ☐ Yes ☒ No.

Is surrounding area enclosed by fence? ☒ Yes ☐ No

Is there barbed wire on top? ☐ Yes ☒ No

Gates locked at night? ☒ Yes ☐ No

If premises is entirely surrounded by a fence how high is the fence and what is its construction and condition?

8' Cyclone Fence—good

Please list below the locations to be covered under the insurance and state the kind and amount desired at each

Loc. No.	Location	Kind of Merchandise	Amount of Burglary Insurance	Amount of Theft Insurance
			$	$
			$	$
			$	$
			$	$

MONEY AND SECURITIES

Loc. No.	On Premises Location	Exposure		Type of Safe	Daytime Guards	Watch-men	How Often Make Rounds	(a) Register on watchman clock (b) Signal outside central sta.
		Cash & Sec. Except Checks	Check					
1	Chemical Plant	$ 1,000	$ 50,000	A	No	No	—	—
4	Equip. Plant	$ 1,000	$ 10,000	B	No	No	—	—
		$	$					
		$	$					

Are Checks Kept Separate from Cash? ☒ Yes ☐ No

Are Adequate Records Maintained So That Duplicate Checks Can Be Obtained for Replacement? ☒ Yes ☐ No

Are Checks Stamped "For Deposit Only" as They are Received? ☒ Yes ☐ No

Loc. No	Off Premises Location	Exposure		Messengers			Guards	Public or Private Conveyance
		Cash & Sec. Except Checks	Checks	Bank	Salesmen	Drivers		
1	Chem. Plant	$ 1,000	$ 50,000	1	0	0	0	Private
4	Equip. Plant	$ 100	$ None	1	0	0	0	Private
		$	$					
		$	$					

DEPOSITORS FORGERY

If depositors forgery coverage is desired for personal accounts of officers or partners of the applicant, complete the following:

Name	Position	Amt. of coverage
Not Wanted		$
		$
		$
		$

Is Employee Dishonesty to Be Eliminated from Forgery Coverage? ☐ Yes ☐ No

Is Credit Card Forgery Coverage Desired? ☐ Yes ☐ No

Number of Card Holders ________

VALUABLE METALS NONE

Please indicate those metals kept on Premises whose average value exceeds $500.

☐ Chromium ☐ Copper ☐ Gold ☐ Iridium ☐ Mercury ☐ Nickel ☐ Osmium ☐ Palladium ☐ Platinum ☐ Radium ☐ Rhodium ☐ Ruthenium ☐ Silver ☐ Tin ☐ Tungsten

BURGLAR ALARM SYSTEM NONE

Loc. No.	Location	(A) Signal Outside Central Station (B) Gong on Outside of Premises	Are Keys to Premises in Possession of Alarm Company?	Is Alarm Connected to Safe?	Class	Installation	Certificate Number	Expiration Date

Figure 1-8
External Flow*

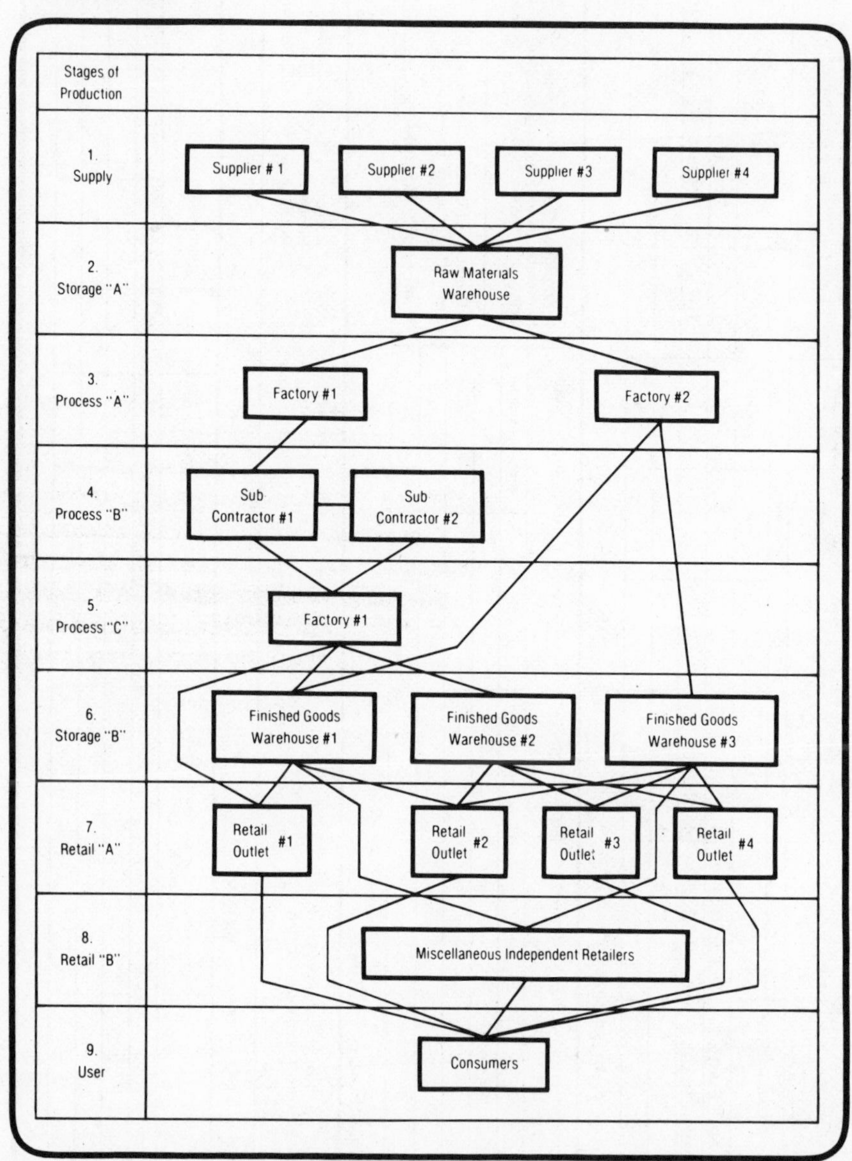

*Reprinted with permission from Matthew Lenz, Jr., *Risk Management Manual* (Santa Monica: The Merritt Company, 1976), p. 17.

Figure 1-9
Internal Flow*

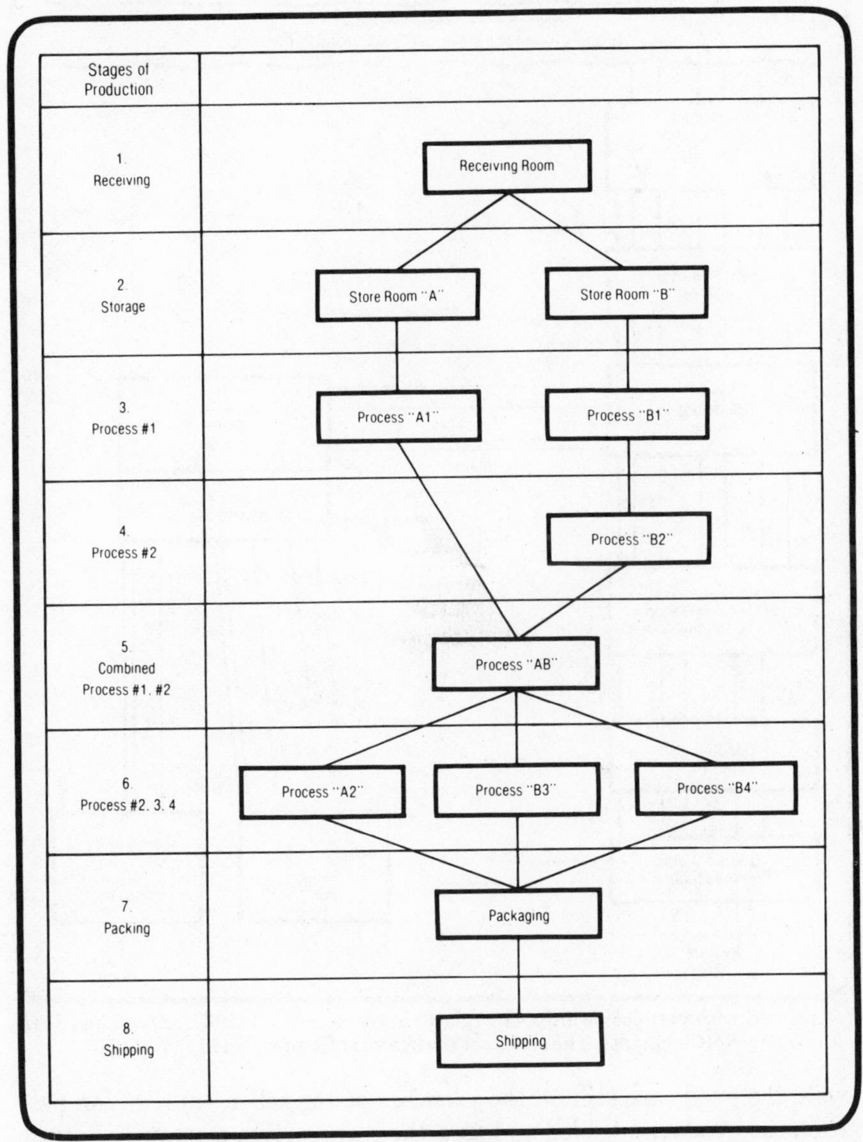

*Reprinted with permission from Matthew Lenz, Jr., *Risk Management Manual* (Santa Monica: The Merritt Company, 1976), p. 18.

Figure 1-10

Water Utility Flow Chart of a Large City*

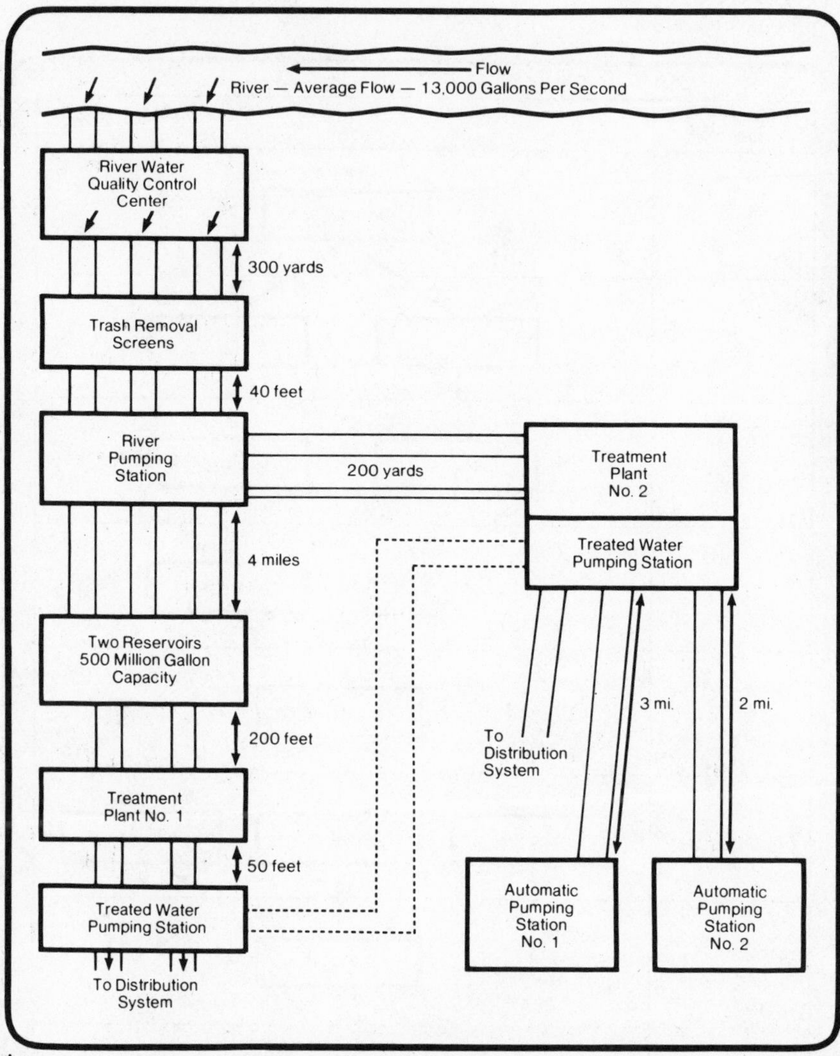

*Reprinted with permission from Georgia Chapter Society of CPCU, *Municipal Risk Management* (Cincinnati: The National Underwriter Company, 1971), p. 6.

while the goods are still on the premises of the seller, (2) title can pass when the goods are loaded on board the transporting conveyance at the seller's loading dock (F.O.B. seller's premises), (3) title can pass when the goods are delivered to the buyer's premises, and (4) title can pass when the goods are delivered to the premises of another at the direction of the buyer. If title passes on the seller's premises, the buyer has a loss exposure at that location. If title passes F.O.B. the seller's premises, the buyer's loss exposure begins when the loading is completed. The flow chart helps identify the need to determine when title passes, and further research may be necessary to determine the actual loss exposure.

In addition to the terms of purchase, information should be obtained on the nature of the raw materials or components. Are the items generally available from a number of sources or are they specialty items available from only one source? If the latter, this single source of supply of critical items could represent a "bottleneck" in the production process. If the items are available from other sources but would cost significantly more, then special attention should be given to the valuation placed upon the loss exposure.

If transportation from seller to buyer is by common carrier—rail, truck, or vessel—the tariff governing the valuation, in event of loss, should be ascertained. This controls the amount for which the carrier would be liable for loss or damage during transit. Shippers frequently employ "Released Bills of Lading" to obtain lower freight rates and this represents a trade-off for a lower amount of loss liability of the carrier. Finally, the carrier is not liable for any and every loss event during transportation—for example, there is no liability for "acts of God," "acts of the public enemy," and under certain conditions if the consignees fail to pick up goods within the tariff time limits.

If the F.O.B. purchaser uses an owned truck to pick up the merchandise at the seller's location, the purchaser's loss exposure begins when loading is completed. If the goods have been bought on a "delivered basis," the buyer's loss exposure begins when the transporting conveyance has been unloaded at the delivery point.

In some situations, purchasers will place an order for more material than they can receive and handle, except over an extended time period. In the case under study, further inquiry revealed that this applies to the special chemicals and to the printed packaging materials because there is a significant price advantage in quantity buying. The seller has agreed to warehouse the material and to ship it on order. Usually, title passes to the buyer upon the completion of the goods and a buyers' loss exposure is created on the premises of the supplier.

In the case of the packaging materials, it was learned that a unique situation exists because the terms of sale are on a "delivered basis" (i.e., no charge to the buyer, and the seller's truck is going to be used for the transit after title has passed to the buyer). The purchase order should clearly fix the responsibility for loss during transit.

The "Annual Transportation Floater" section of the survey limited its questions to "Type of Property Shipped," "Method of Shipment," "Estimated Annual Shipments to be Insured—Incoming," "Limits of Liability for Any One Location and Any One Disaster," and "Carriers

Figure 1-11

Polywog, Inc.—Flow Chart

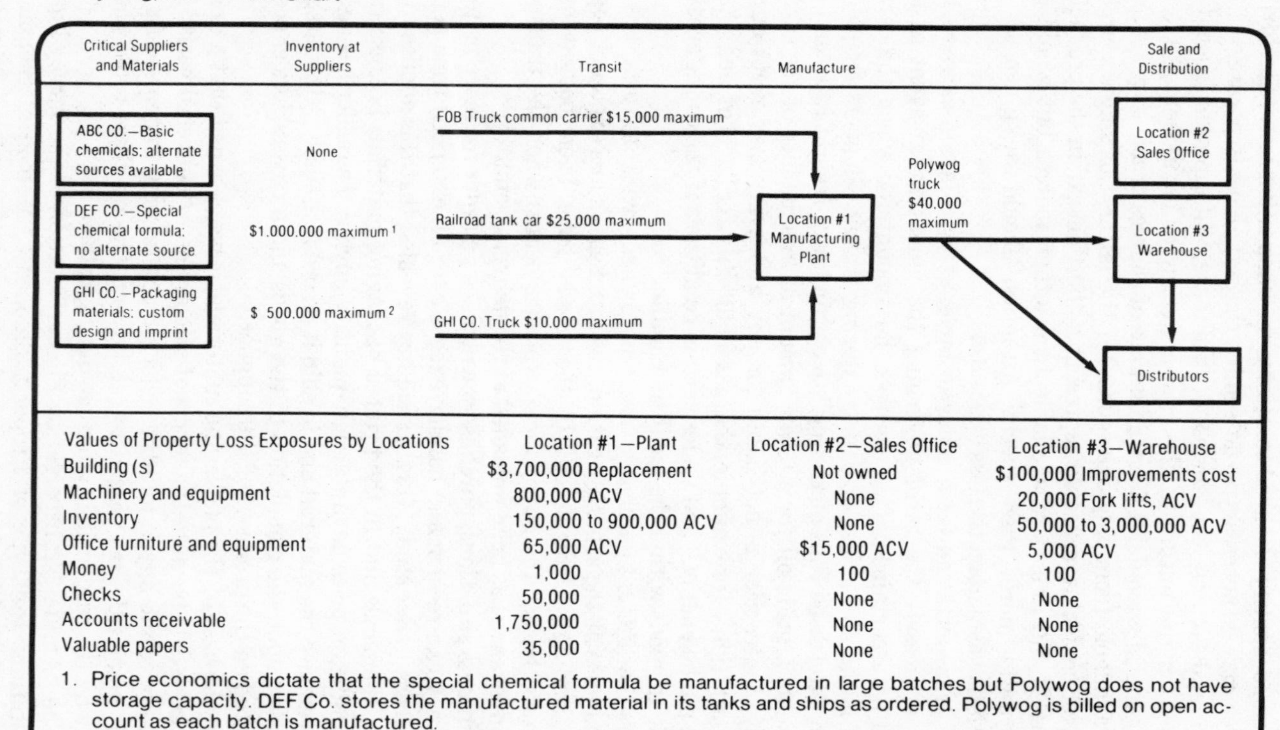

Values of Property Loss Exposures by Locations	Location #1—Plant	Location #2—Sales Office	Location #3—Warehouse
Building (s)	$3,700,000 Replacement	Not owned	$100,000 Improvements cost
Machinery and equipment	800,000 ACV	None	20,000 Fork lifts, ACV
Inventory	150,000 to 900,000 ACV	None	50,000 to 3,000,000 ACV
Office furniture and equipment	65,000 ACV	$15,000 ACV	5,000 ACV
Money	1,000	100	100
Checks	50,000	None	None
Accounts receivable	1,750,000	None	None
Valuable papers	35,000	None	None

1. Price economics dictate that the special chemical formula be manufactured in large batches but Polywog does not have storage capacity. DEF Co. stores the manufactured material in its tanks and ships as ordered. Polywog is billed on open account as each batch is manufactured.
2. For the same pricing reason Polywog orders its packaging material, which is specially designed and imprinted. GHI Co. stores the material and delivers by its own truck as ordered. Polywog is billed when manufacturing is complete.

Release from Liability." If this is all the information obtained, the surveyor could write an insurance policy but the ability to analyze the loss exposures would be limited and the surveyor would be unable to construct a meaningful flow chart.

Applicators, Inc., illustrated in Figure 1-12, purchases forgings and castings from JKL Co., who keeps patterns and molds owned by Applicators. A pattern and die floater may be needed to insure these items.

The next step is to assume the safe and undamaged arrival of the raw materials and product components at the manufacturing location, represented by blocks on the flow chart diagram. To the extent that space permits, these blocks should contain loss exposure data, i.e., building construction; blanket group descriptions of boiler, machinery, and electrical objects eligible for that class of insurance; the production activities conducted; values of the building, machinery, and equipment; inventories—peak, average, and low—with separate values for any stored in the open; accounts receivable; and valuable papers and money. With respect to automotive and contractors equipment, there are two possible approaches. One is to list all such equipment on a physical damage schedule which includes the street address of the garage location and the other is to prepare a schedule for each location. Either method provides the data to determine the aggregate value exposed to loss at a single location. Some such equipment may be garaged within the building or in the open.

Some raw materials may be received at the buyer's plant where part of the manufacturing process is performed and the partially manufactured goods are sent out to another to perform some special function. For example, after the metal body of the spray equipment has been formed, it might be sent out for heat treatment or annealing and then returned to be assembled into the completed machine. If this situation existed, additional property loss exposures would be created by the transit in both directions and while at the location of the processors.

The end result of the manufacturing process is a finished product and the flow chart information reverts back to the "Annual Transportation Floater" section, to follow the distribution of the final product from the manufacturing location to the point at which title passes to another and the property loss exposures cease for the case under study. The production of herbicides in a seasonal business and from fall until early spring, the product is manufactured, transported, and accumulated in a distribution warehouse. Sales are wholesale only on open account to various distributors on a "delivered basis." Title passes to the distributors when delivered by the maufacturer's trucks. Intercompany sales are also made to Applicators, Inc. to be used in their contract spraying operations.

The outgoing shipments of herbicides, intermediate warehousing, and shipments to distributors are all loss exposures of Polywog, Inc.—since their trucks are used for transportation to the warehouse and to their distributors.

Similarly, Applicators, Inc. sells only to dealers on open account on a delivered basis and retains the loss exposures until delivery is completed.

If, for example, Polywog or Applicators made consumer financing available to customers through their dealers, they would have a continuing loss exposure until full payment had been received. The exact nature of the exposure would depend upon the nature of the financing arrangements and applicable provisions of the Uniform Commercial Code, the Federal Consumer Protection Act, and state laws.

In the delivery process, the vehicles of Polywog and Applicators are exposed to physical damage loss.

In summary, the flow chart (Figure 1-12) depicts property loss exposures graphically from origin (acquisition of title) through transit and the production and distribution processes until the exposures cease through passage of title to another and, in some cases, until final payment.

For accounts of substantial size and complexity, a master flow chart may be supported by underlying charts that provide greater detail.

The Financial Statement Method

Early in the development of risk management, it was recognized that the insurance survey method of identifying loss exposures had a number of inadequacies. These inadequacies are attributable to the origin and authorship of surveys by the insurance industry, primarily to improve the techniques of insurance sales and service. Surveys deal primarily with exposures that are commercially insurable. Insurance surveys were not designed to encourage objective consideration of alternative methods of treating exposures nor to develop information on commercially uninsurable exposures, no matter how serious the exposure to loss may be. Because risk management involves more than insurance, it is necessary that the identification of loss exposures be on a broader basis than the insurance survey.

Risk management encompasses the entire field of exposure to accidental loss and requires that each exposure be identified, analyzed, and evaluated. This includes taking appropriate action to eliminate and reduce hazards to a practical minimum and, finally, deciding to insure or not insure in accordance with the best interests of the firm exposed to loss over a reasonable time interval.

The initial effort to create a better system for loss exposure identification consisted of expanding the insurance survey into risk

Figure 1-12

Applicators, Inc. (Subsidiary of Polywog, Inc.)—Flow Chart

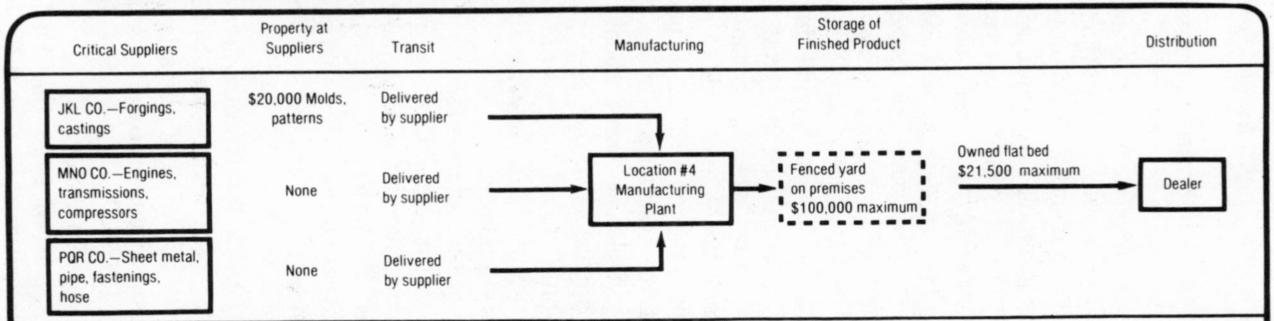

Critical Suppliers	Property at Suppliers	Transit	Manufacturing	Storage of Finished Product	Distribution
JKL CO.—Forgings, castings	$20,000 Molds, patterns	Delivered by supplier	→ Location #4 Manufacturing Plant		
MNO CO.—Engines, transmissions, compressors	None	Delivered by supplier	→ Location #4 Manufacturing Plant →	Fenced yard on premises $100,000 maximum → Owned flat bed $21,500 maximum →	Dealer
PQR CO.—Sheet metal, pipe, fastenings, hose	None	Delivered by supplier	→ Location #4 Manufacturing Plant		

Contract Operations

Contractors' Equipment	Value	Stored When Not in Use	Transported	Operated by	Remains Overnight at Work Site
500 gal. sprayer	3,500	Fenced yard on premises	Owned flat bed	Applicator employee	0 to 7 days
500 " "	3,500				
1,000 " "	6,500				
1,000 " "	6,500				
1,000 " "	6,500				

Values of Property Loss Exposures at Location #4

Building	Not owned
Machinery and equipment	$100,000
Inventory	300,000
Office furniture and equipment	15,000
Money	100
Checks	None[1]
Accounts receivable	None[2]
Valuable papers	10,000[3]

1. Customers pay bills to parent company office.
2. Accounts receivable are handled by parent company.
3. Working production drawings including detail. Original design drawings in parent company office, but not detail.

management areas. The problem with this effort was that it was still heavily dominated by insurance practices and did not deal adequately with the internal procedures of firms which might be changed to eliminate or reduce loss exposures.

Since the function of risk management is to protect an organization's capital, assets, and income against loss, or to provide financing in the event that losses do occur, the conclusion was reached by some that risk management is a function of financial management. A method was needed that was sufficiently comprehensive to identify all exposures to accidental loss, whether or not currently insurable. Workable criteria were also required to establish all sources of possible loss causes, analyzing the degree of probability of their occurrence, and evaluating the potential financial consequences. Techniques were needed for the absolute avoidance of some exposures, for reducing the degree of probability of occurrence of some losses, and for mitigating the financial consequences of losses which occurred. The data source should be one readily available in substantially standardized form for any medium or large organization. The logic of the system should be understandable and acceptable to directors, executives, stockholders, accountants, bankers, and investors. The developed facts should be capable of clear, concise presentation in terms that conform to reports on other corporate matters, as distinct from the jargon of the insurance business. The principles upon which such a system should be based should be scientifically supportable and universally applicable, so that they can be employed for any type of organization, located anywhere, with assurance that all significant loss possibilities will be disclosed, analyzed, evaluated, and dealt with in a comprehensive manner.

In 1958 it was suggested that such a system could be based upon the utilization of corporate financial and accounting records as the initial data source.[7] These records are the common denominator of all business organizations, reflecting everything that is owned, all its current activities and, in many cases, what it hopes to do in the immediate future. For this purpose, the surveyor must go beyond the condensed type of annual report usually issued to stockholders. Behind this brief annual report are much more detailed reports for internal use. For example, there are considerable underlying data with respect to asset accounts, income accounts that break down the result of operations by profit centers or by classes of business, administrative or selling expenses, loan agreements, and litigation. From all of these accounts, a substantial index of probable loss exposure can be deduced.

It is necessary that the hypothesis derived from the financial statement method be supported by several subsystems. The flow chart analysis previously mentioned may be used to supplement financial statement analysis. Financial statement analysis leads naturally to the employment of the flow chart because each of the items is analyzed for loss exposures in the same order as it appears in the financial statement.

Cash "Cash" is ordinarily the first item in every balance sheet. It is necessary to learn how cash comes into the possession of the organization, whether it is in the form of money or checks, what happens to it between the time of its receipt and the time it is banked, the safeguards that are employed, and the amounts that are involved—with particular reference to the maximum amounts which can occur in a seasonal business or one which has built up over weekends and holidays. The money loss exposure will vary widely among different classes of business. Retail stores and supermarkets handle a great deal of cash, but the large manufacturer handles only modest amounts. The next cash item to be explored is checks received. A number of questions may be asked. How are they received? Do they go to the office of the organization or is there a post office box number through which they go directly to the bank? What is the deposit practice? What is the ability to reconstruct checks that come to the organization and are then sent out to the bank? Is there a duplicate deposit slip or record from which a lost or stolen group of checks could be replaced? With respect to both cash and checks, it is important to investigate the control procedures exercised with respect to the verification of cash and checks received and credits to customers' accounts.

For Polywog, Inc. it is learned that there is only a small amount of petty cash exposed to loss and the primary exposure is that of checks. Checks are received by mail and an adding machine tape made immediately. The daily cash journal is then prepared on an accounting machine and the customers' accounts ledger is posted. The adding machine tape, the cash journal, and customers' ledger posting are balanced and the checks deposited that day.

Accounts Receivable The next asset item is usually "accounts receivable." Very few organizations do business on an entirely cash basis. With respect to those who do a credit business, it is important to establish whether or not it is their own charge account and what the system is with respect to credit approval or verification. In some businesses, it is also important to find out whether they use any credit cards, either local or national, in their operation. This is more likely to occur in a retail operation than in a manufacturing operation, but volume of credit card purchasing is large and apparently increasing. Accounts receivable entry procedures should be traced from the source document to the ledger posting. The posting of payments and credits to the account should also be checked for procedure and control.

The safeguarding of accounts receivable records should be verified, as should the ability to duplicate them in the event of loss or destruction.

The range of protection which will be found will vary from unlabeled filing cabinets to safes bearing two- or four-hour Underwriters Laboratory labels. Another method is to have the accounts receivable ledger cards in rolling trays, which are removed from a protective vault during the day when being used. This temporarily unprotected exposure should not be overlooked. Accounts receivable, when not in use, should be kept in a vault or otherwise adequately protected under lock and key, and persons authorized to unlock or remove accounts receivable should be identified. Vandalism by disgruntled employees has caused a number of accounts receivable losses. From these data, a flow chart of accounts receivable has been prepared for Polywog, Inc. (See Figure 1-13.)

Inventory The third item appearing on the financial statement is usually "inventory." Inventories can consist of merchandise purchased ready for sale or of raw material or components that are used to manufacture the final product of the organization. Applying the axiom, "Exposure to loss follows title," the task is to ascertain the terms of purchase to determine when title passes to the organization.

If purchases are on a "delivered basis," title passes upon receipt by the buyer at his premises, and the transit loss exposure falls on the seller. If, on the other hand, the purchase is "F.O.B. Seller's Shipping Dock," title passes when the goods are loaded on board the transporting conveyance and the transit exposure is the buyer's. The transporting conveyance could be a common carrier, either railroad, truck, or vessel. If so, the goods move under a bill of lading which describes the extent of liability of the common carrier for loss of the goods during transit. This makes it necessary to examine the bills of lading which are representative of the incoming shipments to determine whether or not the carrier's limit of liability is adequate. Some shippers, in order to reduce freight rates, will take what is known as a "release bill of lading," which may limit the liability of the carrier to considerably less than the value of the goods being transported. Under these conditions, the purchaser has a loss exposure equivalent to the excess valuation.

It is also important to remember that the carrier's liability is not absolute. For example, they have no liability for so-called "acts of God" or "acts of the public enemy." Shipments by rail are delivered to a freight terminal, rather than to the consignee. The railroad will have only a warehouseman's liability if the goods are not picked up by the consignee within the stated number of hours.

Another mode of transport used by some is called contract carriers. Contract carriers are usually used on an annual contract or an individual contract basis. The terms and conditions of the agreement between the purchaser and the contract carrier, with respect to liability, should be carefully examined. Some organizations buying a variety of products

Figure 1-13

Polywog, Inc. and Applicators, Inc.—Accounts Receivable Loss Exposure Analysis

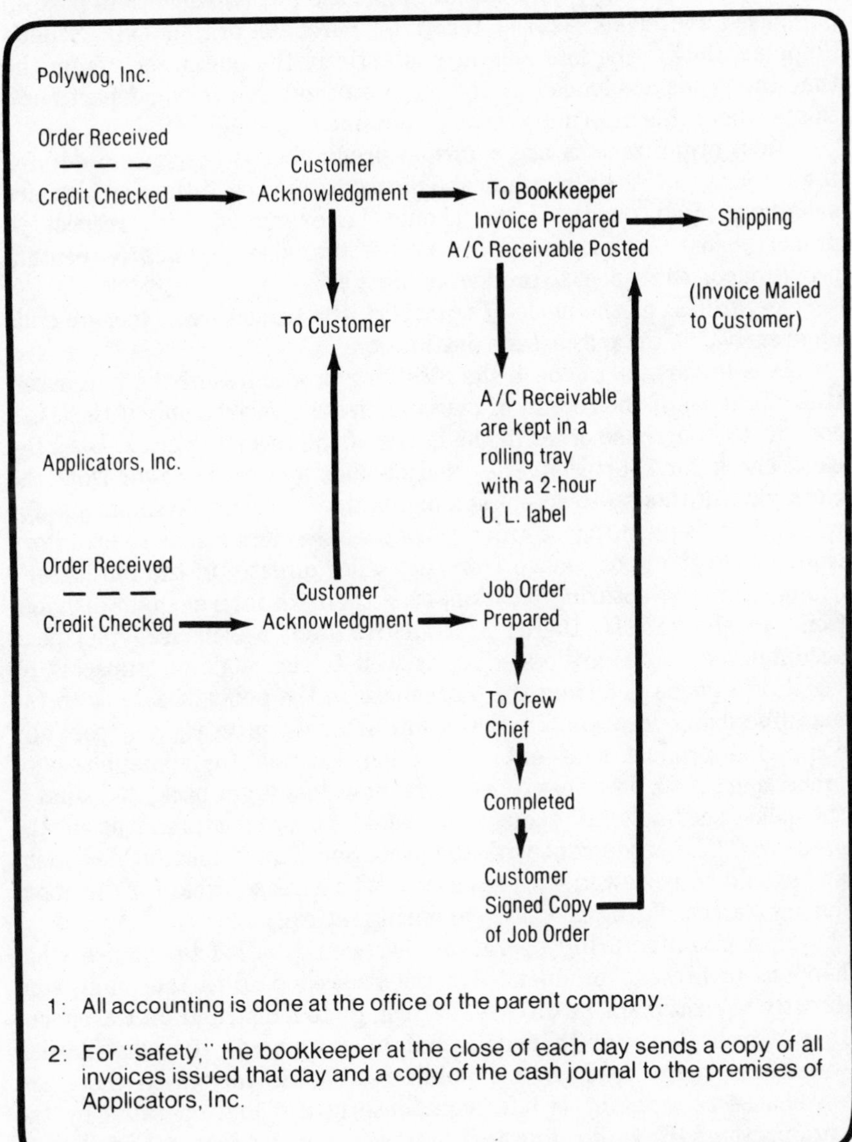

1: All accounting is done at the office of the parent company.

2: For "safety," the bookkeeper at the close of each day sends a copy of all invoices issued that day and a copy of the cash journal to the premises of Applicators, Inc.

might find it advisable to use a so-called freight consolidator. Under this system, goods are accumulated in the terminal of the consolidator until a full load is reached and then shipped. It is important to establish the values that might accumulate at such a location, as well as the values per shipment. Finally, a purchaser might use owned vehicles to pick up purchased materials. If the terms of purchase are "F.O.B. Seller's Shipping Dock," the loss exposure is entirely the purchaser's from the time the goods are loaded. If the organization has a traffic department, this is where this information can be obtained.

Most organizations use a formal prenumbered purchase order for the majority of their purchases. The terms and conditions, which are usually printed on the back, should be examined with respect to property loss exposures. (Purchase orders also frequently contain provisions with respect to product liability.)

Regardless of the mode of transport, the transit loss exposure ends upon arrival at the purchaser's destination.

It is important to check the receiving procedures of the purchaser. One might ask if the receipt of merchandise is approved only if there is a copy of the purchase order in the hands of the receiving clerk. Does the clerk check for short deliveries and obvious loss or damage? Does the clerk have authority to accept shipments that are short or shipments for which there is no purchase order? How does the clerk report to inventory control? Do the goods move from the seller directly to the purchaser's selling or manufacturing location, or is there an intermediate distribution warehouse? If there is a distribution warehouse, the peak accumulated values are essential, as well as the mode of transport by which the goods get from the warehouse to the point of sale or to the manufacturing location. In the manufacturing process, is a partially completed product sent out to another location for some phase of processing? If so, how does it get there, how does it get back, and what is the peak accumulated value that would be on the premises of the processor? The agreement with the processor is an important document and should be reviewed with respect to who is responsible for the goods during transit, during process, and during return.

In a manufacturing operation, one would be led to inquire what happens to finished products. Are they warehoused at the plant, sent directly to customers, or do they, in turn, go to a distribution warehouse from which they are then delivered to customers? If a distribution warehouse is involved, is it a public warehouse for which there are warehouse receipts, or is it a warehouse owned and operated by the organization? How do finished products get from the distribution warehouse to the customer? Is the sale on a delivered basis or an F.O.B. seller's warehouse? Mode and terms of transport in all instances are important to identification of inventory loss exposures.

The property loss protection in all phases of the inventory movement from the original seller to the final disposition of it to the final customer, are critical. Are trucks involved equipped with alarm systems? Are warehouses staffed with security people during the day? Are there sprinklers? Are there automatic alarms? Are there guards at night? Are receiving and shipping procedures under adequate control? Are inventory shortages within the "normal range" for the type of business involved? Even though sales may be F.O.B. the seller's plant or warehouse, are there circumstances which still make it necessary for business reasons for the organization to assume responsibility for shipments that are lost in transit to a valued customer?

For either insurance or risk management purposes, it is necessary to obtain values in all stages of the inventory flow from the maximum single shipment in one vehicle or one freight car to the maximum accumulation at manufacturing, warehousing, and processing locations. This can be done with the aid of a flow chart like the one illustrated in Figure 1-11.

Assets The foregoing items usually constitute what the accountants call "current assets," but some organizations will also own "marketable securities" which are likewise classified as "current assets." These are usually represented by bonds or stock certificates and are most often in a safe deposit box or custodian account at a bank. Sometimes, they may be held by a stockbroker or investment banker. The related loss exposures include:

1. Having purchased stolen, lost, counterfeited or altered securities. This loss exposure can be eliminated or mitigated by purchasing only from reputable stockbrokers, investment bankers, or banks who are guarantors of good title.
2. Theft, damage, destruction, or disappearance of the securities. These loss exposures can be treated by safekeeping procedures previously referred to, including the requirement of two signatures to enter a safe deposit box or to authorize the purchase or sale of securities. Special care is required with respect to bonds identified as "bearer" or "Coupon," which are not registered as to the owner. The risk management treatment is to change them to registered bonds or, where this is impossible, a custodian account. Alternatively, they should be fully insured because of the problem related to replacement.

Under noncurrent assets, an item may appear entitled "Investment in Affiliates" for corporations which have subsidiaries or affiliated companies. Figures in the financial statement may or may not truly represent the value of the affiliate to the parent organization. The financial statements of any such affiliates should be reviewed on exactly the same basis as the parent. In some instances, different financial interests may appear, for example, joint owners or minority stockholders. The details of each of these in their relationships to the parent should be explored and recorded.

The next item in the financial statement will usually be headed "Fixed Assets." Fixed assets consist of land, building, machinery and equipment, and other property items owned by the organization which are not converted to cash during a company's normal business cycle.

As previously pointed out, land may, in special instances, be subject to loss exposures that need investigation. Is land merely a site for a business building, such as a retail store or manufacturing plant, or is it "unimproved" land containing valuable resources which are subject to loss? In either case, one of the loss exposures is impairment of title. Quite frequently, title is secured by title insurance but in many jurisdictions of the United States it is simply secured by a lawyer's search of past transactions related to the property. All facets of a potential loss exposure should be explored.

The next items are usually buildings and equipment. In the search for building loss exposures, an additional subsystem must be employed to supplement the financial statement method. This subsystem involves physical inspection and an estimation of replacement valuation. Physical inspection should cover the basic perils, the hazards of occupancy, the inherent perils of machinery and equipment involved, and loss prevention systems and procedures. In valuation, obsolescence must be considered if the structure is old and outmoded. Buildings also may be subject to building code restrictions which would require a more expensive type of construction and partial demolition of the building in the event of partial loss. Machinery and equipment may also be obsolete in view of the development of more advanced machines for the process. Another factor is location. In the event of a total or a nearly total destruction, would rebuilding be on the same site? Many businesses have found it advantageous to move from their existing location to other regions of the country. This may be simply a move from a metropolitan district to a nearby suburb or a move from one state to another.

Most organizations own automotive vehicles, and some own aircraft, watercraft, or mobile equipment. The capital asset accounts will contain a schedule of such equipment, original cost, and annual depreciation. Depreciated values will usually be less than the current actual cash values. With respect to automotive equipment, it will not be necessary to establish values if they are to be insured on an actual cash value basis, but for risk management purposes, individual current values should be established. It is of critical importance that the concentrated values subject to a single loss be ascertained. Fleet insurance policies contain a one-location or catastrophe limit and, of course, a company which retains its vehicle loss exposure is vitally concerned. In one recent instance, forty loaded trailers were backed up against a terminal building and an explosion and fire of unknown origin completely destroyed all of them, together with twelve private passenger cars, the terminal, and its contents. This single loss involved two classes of property in a single event—building and contents, and vehicles. Building and contents would normally be considered subject to a single loss, but forty loaded trailers would not.

With respect to the vehicle collision peril, the most probable occurrence involves a single vehicle, but collisions between two vehicles of the same owner occur with sufficient frequency to justify consideration. Most often they occur when two vehicles on the same run are "tailgating" and the lead vehicle has an accident.

Aircraft ownership varies from a single company plane to a fleet of ten or more. The capital asset account usually reflects depreciated value—not replacement or current cash value. If several are housed in a single hangar, the concentrated values are important. Midair or taxi collisions of two aircraft of the same owner are much less likely than collisions of two tractor trailer rigs.

Owned watercraft would also be shown as capital asset items. Values range from modest to very significant, and are dealt with as marine loss exposures. The most reliable values for insurance purposes are those established by qualified marine surveyors. For risk management purposes, the values used may be the depreciated book values or utility values to the organization. With respect to those who carry cargoes owned by the organization, those values must be included in the loss exposure evaluation.

Mobile equipment is necessary for some organizations. Contractors require bulldozers, trenchers, cranes, road-building and earth-moving machines. Strip miners also require draglines. These items also appear in capital asset accounts on an original cost and depreciated basis. Many have long useful lives beyond the depreciation period and valuation is an important function of property loss exposure evaluation.

Another item occasionally found in financial statements is valuation on patents and royalties. This may frequently be carried at a one dollar nominal value but, in fact, the ownership of the patent, copyright, or process may be considerably more valuable. Many organizations have developed formulas or processes that they can license to others on a royalty basis. If such is done, and the royalty contract with others is such that the organization benefits on the basis of the material produced and sold by the licensee, then a property loss exposure is created with respect to the licensee's business or manufacturing premises. In the majority of cases, the assets which have been reviewed here will be common to most business enterprises. Of course, there is always the possibility that some unique or unusual property will be owned that requires special analysis based on the facts.

All of the foregoing property loss exposures are derived from the basic principle that the one who owns the property is the first to suffer loss of such property. However, this principle can be abrogated or limited by contract.

By contract—lease or construction, for example—the owner organization may have effected a noninsurance transfer of all or part of its property loss exposure to the contractor. Conversely, by a premises lease, it may have assumed the property loss exposure of another owner.

Therefore, a further subsystem of the financial statement method must be introduced (i.e., the analysis of contracts and agreements relating to property loss exposures). Such loss exposure assumption may be considered either a direct property loss exposure or a contractual liability exposure.

Types of contracts which may affect the property loss exposures of an organization are as follows: (1) leases of real or personal property, including data processing equipment; (2) construction; (3) mortgages; (4) agreements of sale or purchase of real property; (5) railroad sidetrack agreements; (6) contracts for the transportation of goods; (7) repair and servicing contracts; (8) equipment purchase agreements (special machinery, aircraft, etc.); (9) processing agreements; (10) warehouse receipts; (11) custodial agreements with respect to securities; (12) contracts for services (janitorial, office temporaries, security, "in-plant" maintenance, etc.); or (13) purchase or sales order forms.

This brief illustration of the financial statement method of identifying loss exposures has been confined to direct property loss exposures which can be identified by an analysis of the assets side of the balance sheet. An analysis of the liabilities shown in the balance sheet may identify further exposures. Analysis of financial statements other than the balance sheet may further aid in recognizing loss exposures.

Some of the data collected by financial statement analysis also reveals liability exposures. The study of contracts and agreements is as essential to liability loss exposure identification as to property. Additional subsystems have to be employed in the search for liability exposures.

Other Methods and Subsystems

Exposure Meter Frederick J. Flynn, CPCU, devised a system many years ago which he called the "exposure meter." Like the financial statement method, this system involved the identification of assets or property of the organization. On a large spread sheet, these items were listed in the left column and headings of loss exposures ran across the page from left to right so that the existence could be checked and brief notes inserted with respect to protective measures being employed. The exposure meter is considered to be one of the first attempts to approach loss exposures from the viewpoint of the organization to be served rather than from that of insurance sales. Hence, it was one of the earliest methods compatible with the risk management concept. It is still useful for the small to medium size organization and the financial statement method differs from it only in depth of inquiry and emphasis upon operational or procedural changes which can eliminate or reduce loss exposures.

Coverages Applicable Another completely insurance-oriented system can be identified as coverages applicable. This method makes use of a publication by the Rough Notes Company, entitled *Coverage Applicable,* which lists kinds of available insurance by classes of business or commercial activities. The insurance surveyor is spared the task of examining every form of insurance in order to determine which are applicable to the account under study. It might also direct attention to kinds of insurance that would not otherwise have been recognized as applicable.

Loss History Approach Another method being used by some consultants may be called the loss history approach. The assumption is that if the organization under study can produce a history of its losses over the past five years, the loss exposures will be revealed. The obvious defect of this method is that it will not reflect loss exposures of a catastrophe level with a very low probable frequency of occurrence—the "100-year flood," the longer interval earthquake, the concealed dishonesty loss, the "long tail" product liability claim, and so on.

Organizational Chart Analysis Exposure identification through organizational chart analysis is similar to flow chart analysis. The difference is that an organizational chart is used instead of a flow chart. Organizational charts tend to be less detailed than flow charts, showing only the personnel relationships of the firm rather than detailed product flows. Consequently, the analysis tends to be less detailed, and the likelihood of overlooking exposures is greater if organizational chart analysis is used as the sole means of exposure identification. This method may be useful, however, in conjunction with other techniques. The value of organizational chart analysis depends to a large extent on the operation involved and the managerial structure.

Physical Inspection Any exposure identification procedure should be accompanied by a physical inspection of the firm's premises and operations. However, it is very doubtful that a physical inspection alone is sufficient. An inspection is a prerequisite to the preparation of a flow chart and is almost as necessary with other exposure identification methods.

A physical inspection should not be a simple tour of the firm's facilities. It should follow a carefully planned procedure designed to reveal potential sources of fortuitous losses.

Published Information A wide variety of published information is useful in the exposure identification process. Such published information may deal with (1) the operations of the firm, (2) exposures common to certain kinds of businesses, or (3) loss exposures arising from certain processes or products.

Information about the firm is more likely to be published if the firm's stocks or bonds are publicly traded. Investment advisory services, such as Moody's or Standard and Poor's, publish extensive data concerning the finances, products, markets, and other pertinent characteristics of such firms. Careful scrutiny of such publications may reveal loss exposures which might otherwise be overlooked.

Published information concerning the loss exposures connected with specific processes or products is especially helpful in the exposure identification process. The potential sources of such information are too numerous to list here in detail. Some particularly helpful sources are the National Safety Council and the National Fire Protection Association. Two agencies of the federal government, the Occupational Safety and Health Administration and the Consumer Product Safety Commission also publish material in this category.

Various types of exposure identification surveys or checklists are also published by firms selling protective equipment. These checklists are useful in exposure identification, but risk managers must realize that their objective is usually similar to that of many insurance surveys. Protective equipment manufacturers wish to sell protective equipment and overreliance on their surveys may lead the manager to inappropriately use noninsurance techniques for treating loss exposures.

Comparison and Evaluation of Techniques

The use of any of the techniques alone is likely to result in a failure to identify some exposures to loss. This is especially true of the questionnaire approach, because the questions must be general enough to apply to many firms.

As an example, executives of one large greeting card manufacturer indicated, when interviewed for an insurance survey, that the firm did not have any valuable papers the destruction of which would cause a financial loss to the firm. However, a flow chart analysis of the manufacturing process revealed a storage area containing several thousand items of original artwork that had been used in the company's high-priced lines of greeting cards. Additional questioning revealed that the company earned about a half-million dollars each year by licensing similar firms in foreign countries to use the artwork from the collection. In addition, the firm frequently used the material in its own lower-priced lines. Since the artwork was not shown as an asset on the firm's balance sheet, it is doubtful that this loss exposure would have been identified by any method other than flow chart analysis.

In general, the questionnaire method and financial statement analysis are likely to be satisfactory in identifying exposures to direct property loss. However, some care must be exercised even in regard to those exposures. Some assets may not appear on financial statements, either because they have been fully depreciated or because management does not think of them as assets. The greeting card artwork mentioned in the preceding paragraph is an excellent example of the latter.

The questionnaire method also is likely to be satisfactory in identifying the exposures that are common to a large number of firms, such as loss of earnings, goods in transit, and the more common liability exposures. It is much less satisfactory in identifying unusual exposures to which a particular firm may be subject. The list of such unusual exposures is virtually endless, but examples are (1) the inability to obtain merchandise or raw materials from a key supplier; (2) the increased probability of loss of profits or prolonged loss of profits because of the failure of a key machine or key process; (3) the loss to goods in process and possibly processing machinery if processing is stopped because of power failure or other reasons; and (4) the expense to reproduce research results if records, test animals, or other research materials are destroyed. Such unusual exposures are much more likely to be found through flow chart analysis.

The best approach to loss exposure identification is a combination of several methods. One effective combination relies on flow chart analysis and financial statement analysis for the initial identification effort. A comprehensive questionnaire is then used as a final checklist to be sure that none of the common exposures have been overlooked in searching for the unusual ones. Of course, a physical inspection of the firm's facilities and operations must be included, since it is virtually impossible to prepare and analyze a flow chart without an inspection. Other combinations of methods are possible, of course, and each analyst will develop techniques which are compatible with his or her abilities and methods of operation.

Chapter Notes

1. Extended Coverage Endorsement—Form FAL-1 (Ed. 6-75).
2. FC&S Bulletins, *The National Underwriter*, January 1975, Misc. Fire Sc-5.
3. Ibid., MSC Fire Rcd-1.
4. Ibid., Dwellings Col-1.
5. S. T. Algermissen, "Seismic Risk Studies in the United States," Fourth World Conference on Earthquake Engineering, 1969, p. 26.
6. J. J. Launie, J. Finley Lee, and Norman A. Baglini, *Principles of Property and Liability Underwriting* (Malvern, PA: Insurance Institute of America, 1976), p. 109.
7. A. Hawthorne Criddle, CPCU, "How Can the Part Time Insurance Manager Know His Risks?"—address to the Delaware Valley Chapter of RIMS (formerly ASIM), delivered on October 8, 1958.

CHAPTER 2

Commercial Property Risk Management

INTRODUCTION

The preceding chapter discussed the identification of loss exposures. This chapter is concerned with measuring potential loss frequency and severity, and selecting the technique or techniques to be used to handle each exposure. Among the techniques that can be used are avoidance, control, noninsurance transfers, insurance, and retention. These techniques were introduced in CPCU 1 and are specifically applied here to commercial property exposures.

MEASUREMENT OF LOSS EXPOSURES

After loss exposures have been identified, the next step in the risk management process is the analysis or measurement of those loss exposures. That is, the risk manager must formulate a realistic estimate of the potential economic effect on the firm of the possible losses arising from the exposure. The potential economic effect of losses depends upon (1) the potential frequency of loss, (2) the potential severity of loss, and (3) the financial ability of the firm to absorb such losses. These three measures of loss exposure will be discussed, but first it is desirable to examine the goals behind loss exposure measurement.

Goals of Loss Exposure Measurement

In theory, the risk manager should attempt to predict the impact on an organization of the sum of all losses each year. As a practical matter,

Figure 2-1

Range of Predicted Losses

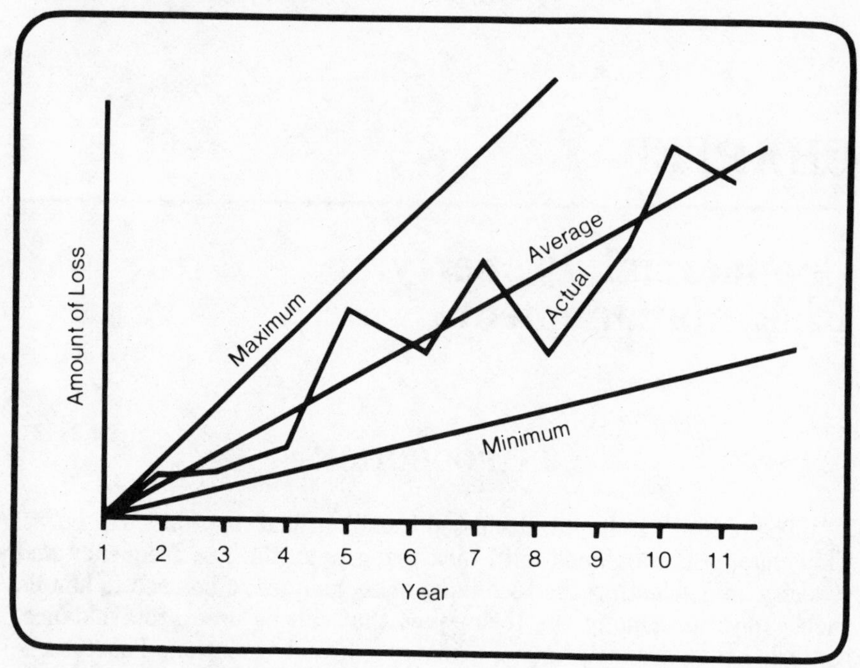

the forecast will be limited to those types of losses which lend themselves to forecasting because of the availability of loss data from one source or another, but will recognize all the other rarely occurring losses and lump them all together. The risk manager will then attempt to meet financial management goals by identifying those predictable losses which exceed the company's tolerable loss level and transfer that exposure.

Loss Prediction The degree to which losses are predictable plays a large role in determining what insurance or noninsurance techniques will be used. Suppose, for example, that losses can be predicted within a narrow range as shown in Figure 2-1.

This might be a typical pattern for the transportation claims of a large shipper with ten years in business and a steadily increasing volume. If this is the case, there is little uncertainty and the losses can be handled readily by budgeting. No insurance or other transfer mechanism is needed.

On the other hand, a more usual situation is illustrated in Figure 2-2. This might represent fire losses. A few losses usually occur each year. In year four, however, there were no losses while in year eight, there

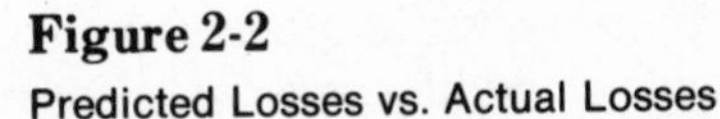

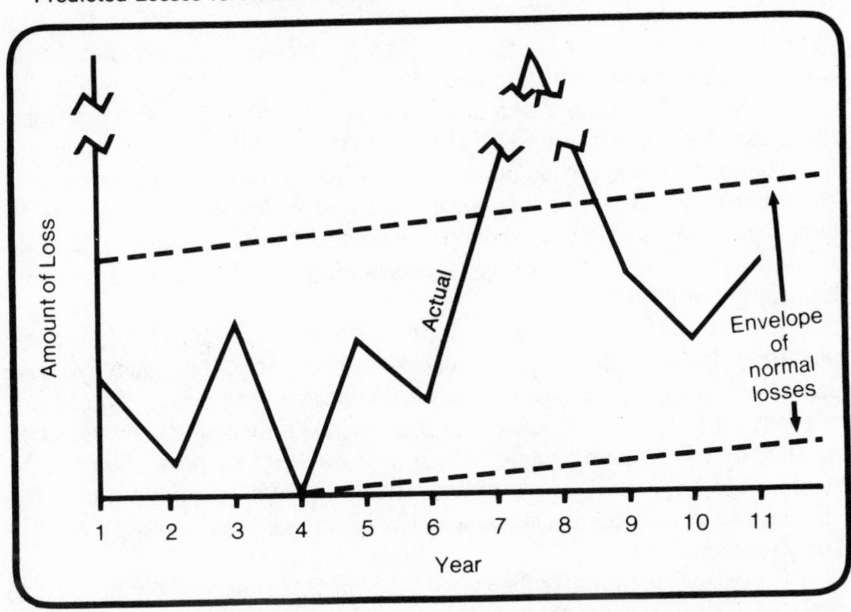

was at least one major fire. These losses are predictable to a certain extent at lower levels, but possibilities exist for substantial losses which cannot be budgeted.

Financial Management Goals Loss exposures are measured so as to treat the exposures with a technique that fits the company's financial management goals. Financial management of all organizations is concerned with the goals of minimization and cost stabilization.

Cost Minimization. Minimizing costs is an obvious goal, but there sometimes exists a conflict between immediate and long-range cost savings. Management sometimes is willing to cut costs in a period of temporary adversity, realizing that they are taking a chance of incurring greater cost, and knowingly gamble by retaining their exposures because of financial exigencies. This can occur, for example, when a company purchases low limits of liability insurance, hoping that a large loss will not occur while the lower limits are in effect. Companies also will go without automatic sprinklers or other fire protection devices which will lower long-range costs in the hope that fire will not strike or that the additional insurance costs will not be great.

Cost Stabilization. The goal of cost stabilization is less obvious and less subject to quantification. Every organization experiences fluctuations in revenues, costs, and earnings from year to year. Some concerns are willing to accept rather large fluctuations while others are more concerned about maintaining stability and are willing to pay a price for it. To the latter, the ability to forecast losses is important, so that the financial manager will be able to take whatever steps are needed to achieve the degree of stability desired.

Companies aiming for a high degree of stability may emphasize insurance to a greater extent than retention, realizing that they are increasing their costs by so doing. Organizations looking for greater cost reductions may be willing to accept a greater degree of variability in cost from year to year in order to minimize the long-range cost. Cost minimization and cost stability or consistency can be evaluated best by knowledge of future losses.

It is not possible to calculate loss patterns for each individual peril, not only because some perils occur infrequently, but also because conditions which give rise to the perils change frequently. The list of perils is almost limitless. Larger organizations may develop statistics on an aggregate of many perils which will enable loss projections to be made. It is important to know not only the probable amounts but also the degree of possible variation and the confidence that can be placed in the variations.

Statistical techniques discussed later in this chapter may be used to develop loss patterns, though the precision of all such calculations is limited. Whether or not complex statistical methods are employed, it is always desirable for the forecast of future losses to be as accurate as possible, and to have knowledge of the approximate degree of accuracy of the predictions.

Throughout this discussion, it is necessary to remember that measurement of loss exposures is, in effect, an attempt to predict the future. Predictions are useful for planning purposes, but do not guarantee what will happen. In fact, if the future could be predicted with absolute certainty, there would no longer be a chance of loss, but a certainty of loss, and insurance and risk management would be rendered obsolete.

Probable Loss Frequency

As a general rule, loss frequency is more predictable than loss severity. In fact, loss frequency can be predicted with reasonable accuracy for some exposures for large firms or organizations. For example, an organization with a thousand motor vehicles probably would be able to predict the number of accidents involving physical damage with reasonable accuracy. A firm that makes dozens of shipments each day probably can predict with reasonable accuracy the number of transit losses it will sustain in a given year. Some firms may even be able to make satisfactory projections of the number of fire losses to be expected. An example would be a fast food chain with, say, two thousand stores throughout the country.

However, most kinds of property insurance losses occur infrequently and most firms do not have a sufficiently large number of exposure units to permit accurate prediction of loss frequency. In spite of the relatively low accuracy of property loss forecasts, some estimate must be made. An estimate with a substantial margin for error is better than no estimate at all, as long as the risk manager recognizes its limitations. The paragraphs that follow will discuss some considerations and problems involved in the estimation of future loss frequency.

Sources of Data Any projection into the future, if it is to be more than a wild guess, must have some factual basis. In most cases, the basis for the projection of future loss frequency is past loss frequency—the past loss frequency of the firm under consideration, of some group of firms, or of a geographic area. Loss experience data must be modified, of course, to reflect changes in the exposure that have taken place since the experience was developed or that are expected in the future. For example, a firm that makes frequent waterborne shipments to foreign ports may have experienced one pilferage claim for each ten shipments over the past three years. If the firm does not contemplate any change in its method of shipping or packaging, it might use this figure to project future pilferage loss frequency. However, if it has recently started shipping all goods in large, sealed containers, it may be desirable to adjust the estimate of future loss frequency downward. On the other hand, if the firm will continue its former methods but will increase its shipments to a port where pilferage losses are frequent, the estimate may be adjusted upward to reflect the increased exposure.

Environmental and economic factors beyond the direct control of the firm also may affect future loss frequency. For example, automobile accidents usually decrease during a period of economic recession, as they decreased substantially during the gasoline shortage of the early seventies. The shift of many industries from natural gas to coal furnaces is likely to have some effect on the frequency of fire and explosion losses. The risk manager must reflect such influences in estimates of future loss frequency to the extent possible by modifying the data used.

Past Experience of the Firm The most useful data for estimating future loss frequency is the past experience of the firm concerned, if the firm has a sufficient number of exposure units for the figures to have meaning. It is important, however, to evaluate the reliability of experience data before they are used. Some of the factors that may affect the reliability of data are discussed below.

Reporting. The first step in assembling loss data is to keep a record of all losses in some organized system. In the case of workers' compensation, there is usually little problem because all such losses should be reported on forms as required by law. Public liability suits are easily monitored because lawsuits are important events calling for considerable attention. This may not be true for some property damage liability claims. Frequently an organization will have a deductible on insurance for property damage liability only and be less inclined to keep accurate records on settlements. However, the deductible does not eliminate the importance of good record keeping.

Property losses present the most difficult problem in regard to reporting, particularly in a large organization. Many small fire, wind, theft, and other property losses are not reported because they appear trivial or because the entity suffering the loss sees no advantage in having them reported.

A second important problem in reporting property losses is obtaining a figure that accurately represents the amount lost. Direct loss is easier to measure than indirect loss, but the direct damage will not reflect a number of intangibles such as disruption of work flow, losses or gains in accounting or tax treatments, benefits from replacing old property with new, and many unrecorded expenses such as executive time taken for planning and expediting repairs, long-distance telephone calls, and so on.

The indirect loss costs are sometimes ignored and almost always inaccurately stated. To the extent that losses have been covered by insurance, a reasonably accurate representation of past losses may be made. For uninsured portions, an informed estimate is the only practical means of producing figures. For both extra expense and business interruption, these loss cost estimates, even if they are made, may be off by 50 percent or more.

Recording. Once the loss is reported, it must be recorded in a written log or a computer memory. Even when this is done, those familiar with computer loss reports know that inaccuracies frequently occur for no apparent reason. Written logs, of course, depend upon the conscientiousness and accuracy of the person recording them. Sometimes reports are maintained for a client by an insurance producer or company, in which case the amounts recorded would usually be only the incurred or paid insured losses, omitting deductible portions or uninsured losses.

Changes of Organization. All organizations are subject to change, some to a great degree—they may manufacture different products, change officers, or merge with other companies. Nearly all such changes affect loss exposures to some extent, so the losses incurred during one year may represent a different environment from that of future years.

Changes of Protection. The Occupational Safety and Health Act, influence of insurance inspectors, and improvements of protection through the years continually alter property exposures. For the most part, these changes are for the better, but there may be regressions, such as when a hazardous new operation is not accompanied by concurrent safety improvements. But whatever the situation, changes do occur and will affect losses.

Environmental Changes. Changes occur in the economic and social environment in which organizations operate. Inflation is the most apparent change and fast inflation can be measured, with at least a moderate degree of accuracy. All dollar figures for losses in different years should be adjusted by an inflation factor if they are to be compared on a common basis. Another environmental change is the increasing restrictiveness of building codes and other laws which may require rebuilding damaged facilities to a higher degree of safety and pollution control.

Volume. The extent of past experience is a major determinant of the reliability of data. There must be a sufficient number of exposure units for the data to be statistically credible. The number of exposure units required for statistical credibility varies with the relative frequency of loss. The method of determining the required units is beyond the scope of this discussion. In general, the larger the number of units, the more credible the data. All these limitations on the projection of loss frequency are not to say that experience is unusable but simply to point out the need for careful analysis and recognition of the need to estimate the degree of credibility for different types of loss reports.

Experience of Other Firms In some cases, the experience of organizations in similar fields may be a good indicator of probable loss frequency. In fact, insurance rates are normally based on the loss experience of many firms with reasonably homogeneous loss exposures. However, it may be difficult or impossible for some kinds of firms to use this technique. First, the loss histories of other firms are pertinent only for organizations with reasonably homogeneous operations, such as gasoline stations, schools, apartment houses, and so forth. Second, companies large enough to have credible information of their own are not always willing to share it. Even smaller firms may be reluctant to furnish such information to a competitor. However, trade associations frequently compile data on an aggregate basis in such a way that it can be useful to all members without disclosing proprietary data of any single member.

A small company, without credible statistical data of its own might use available information regarding similar companies as a basis for its own calculations. A large company, on the other hand, might first of all find that it is not sufficiently like other companies for their data to be useful and, second, data of its own might be statistically credible. Thus, the usefulness of another company's experience diminishes as the size of the company wanting to use the experience increases.

As an example, consider a small retailer owning four stores in four different cities. The retailer has no basis for estimating probable losses from the experience of the four stores. However, the retailer might be able to determine the experience of a retail chain with a thousand similar stores scattered throughout the country. These statistics may be useful to the small retailer for such things as estimating the value of automatic sprinkler systems in reducing loss severity. Nevertheless, it would be fallacious to assume that one year's losses for a four-store chain would be four one-thousandths of those of a large chain.

Insurance Statistics Loss data collected by insurance organizations represent the most comprehensive accumulation of loss information available. Many insurance companies subscribe to the services of the Insurance Services Office or the American Association of Insurance Services, rate-making organizations that promulgate rates nationwide. As insurers collect data on the losses they pay, information is forwarded to these organizations which then promulgate insurance rates based on the loss data. These rates develop a premium which is intended to enable the insurer to pay losses and expenses while making a profit.

For fire insurance, loss statistics are broken down by classes for those types (dwellings, etc.) that can be class rated. Loss statistics are also considered for adjusting specific rates on larger buildings that are individually rated, giving rating credits for better-than-average features and debits for those below average. Unfortunately, the statistics are not sufficiently refined to be any more than a rough indicator of future losses, for a large group of exposure units. It is never possible to predict with much accuracy the losses at a single location. Though the aggregate statistics used in rate making may be accurate, they represent an average of thousands of different properties. Any single fire insurance rate is not a predictor of whether a loss will occur.

Both the Insurance Services Office and the American Association of Insurance Services collect loss statistics for inland marine insurance. However, the data seldom are in sufficient detail to be of much assistance to risk managers. Perhaps the most useful application of such statistics would be the establishment of trends in loss experience. The same limitations would apply to crime insurance statistics collected by the Insurance Services Office and fidelity and surety statistics collected by the Surety Association of America.

Other Sources Trade organizations represent a good source of data for many types of industries. The Machinery and Allied Products Institute, for example, collects data on the loss experience of some classes of industrial firms. The National Fire Protection Association also is a useful source of information on fire losses. Their publications discuss such subjects as the fire hazards of various industrial processes, the effectiveness of sprinkler systems in extinguishing fires, fire resistance of building materials, explosion hazards of industrial materials and processes and many others. Underwriters Laboratories and the Factory Mutual Research Corporation also provide information on fire hazards and fire resistance of materials.

The uniform crime reports compiled by the Federal Bureau of Investigation may be useful in estimating crime losses. They are especially useful in the establishment of loss frequency trends and the comparison of crime trends by geographic area.

The U.S. Army Corps of Engineers is a source of information on flood frequency and magnitude. Though they cannot estimate the dollar loss potential, they can give some indication of the height to which flood waters may rise and the frequency with which floods may reach a certain level. For example, they can project that a certain height of flood waters might be expected every 100 years, on the average.

Earthquake insurance statistics are kept by the Insurance Services Office, but are of value only in a general way because of the low frequency of damaging earthquakes and the small percentage of earthquake damage which is covered by insurance. More extensive information on earthquake activity can be obtained from governmental sources.

Windstorm and hail statistics are well documented by the U.S. Weather Service and provide a highly useful background for building design or risk analysis. Catastrophe data collected by the Insurance Services Office also may be useful in estimating the probability of damage by tornado or hurricane.

Potential Loss Severity

The sources of information for estimating the size of loss are the same as those cited above for loss frequency. However, the estimation of severity may be even less precise.

The severity of a particular loss, particularly a fire loss, depends on many variables that are unpredictable to a very large degree. For example, a fire that starts at night, when the premises are not open for business, is likely to cause more damage than one that starts in the daytime, when it is likely to be detected and extinguished more promptly. The difference between a minor fire and a total loss may hinge on some action such as an employee's erroneously turning off a sprinkler system valve.

For this reason, the risk manager must consider not only the most probable size of loss but also the potential range of losses. There is little comfort in knowing that the most probable amount of loss is $25,000 if a $1 million loss actually occurs.

Amount Subject The first important consideration in estimating loss from fire or other perils to buildings and contents is the amount subject, sometimes called the maximum possible loss. The amount subject is the total values exposed to loss at any one location or from any one event. For the peril of fire, this would usually be the amount contained in any one fire division. It is the amount subject that should be considered by the risk manager when choosing among retention, avoidance, or insurance, and in establishing insurance limits if insurance is elected.

The foregoing discussion was couched in terms of fire loss, but fire is not always the most serious peril, in terms of severity, to which buildings and contents are exposed. If a building is fire resistive and well divided by approved fire walls, fire damage may be relatively minor, even in the worst possible situation. However, the fire resistive construction and fire walls may offer little protection against damage by earthquake, landslide, subsidence, or explosion.

The amount subject must be considered with regard to other property also, not just for buildings and contents. For example, what is the amount subject to physical damage loss for a fleet of motor vehicles? Is it the value of the most expensive unit? Are several vehicles stored in the same building at night? What are the chances of flood or tornado damage at the company's parking area?

At first glance, the amount to which goods in transit are subject in a single loss would seem to be the value of the largest shipment. However, one must also consider the possibility that several shipments might be in the carrier's terminal at one time.

Probable Maximum Loss The largest loss *likely* to occur may involve less value than the amount subject. The probable fire loss will be limited by the fire protection present, such as automatic sprinklers, public fire departments, and so forth. This loss figure might be termed probable maximum loss.

The diagram in Figure 2-3 may be used to illustrate the concepts described above. The premises consist of two buildings: Building A and Building B. Building A is subdivided into three areas by two standard fire walls. The values of buildings and contents in Area 1 of Building A are $1 million, $2 million in Area 2, and $3 million in Area 3.

Figure 2-3
Probable Maximum Loss

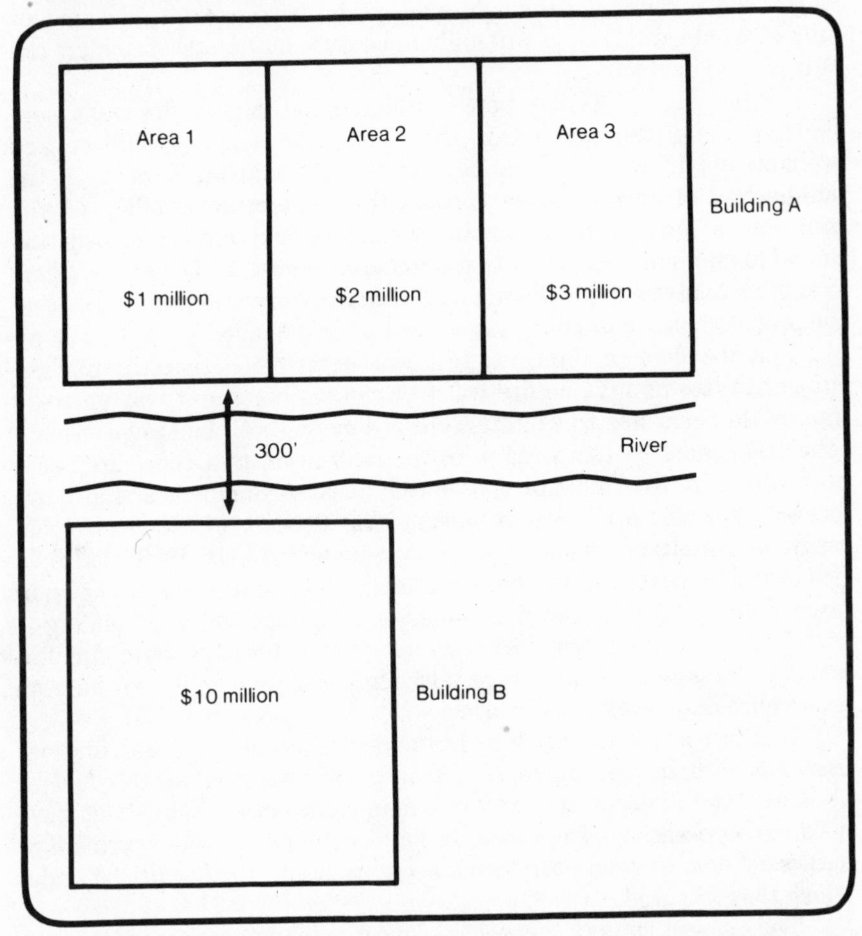

Another building, Building B, is separated from Building A by 300 feet, including a river 200 feet wide, and contains total values of $10 million. In determining the amount subject and probable maximum loss, it must be determined whether the fire walls and the separation distance between buildings will be recognized as effective fire separation. This sometimes calls for an engineering evaluation of the premises, considering the combustibility of the materials and the effectiveness of the separations. Assuming the engineers reported that all separations are standard and effective, then the amount subject would be $10 million and the probable maximum loss would be $10 million (the value of Building B). Building A and Building B would not be deemed subject to a single fire loss. If, however, all buildings are sprinklered with an adequate sprinkler system, then the probable maximum loss might be judged some fraction of the values exposed, say 40 percent. The amount subject would still stay at $10 million, because automatic sprinklers can be rendered ineffective.

If Building A by itself were considered and the two fire walls were deemed completely standard, then both the amount subject and probable maximum loss might be considered $3 million. However, if the building is of fire resistive construction and combustibility of the contents is low, or if automatic sprinklers had been installed, the probable maximum loss might be considered some fraction of $3 million. A similar analysis might be made of a multi-story building, estimating the probable maximum number of floors to be damaged.

For the firm in Figure 2-3, it was determined that the amount subject to loss in any one fire was $10 million, because it was virtually impossible for a fire to simultaneously damage both buildings. Such a conclusion must be tempered with the realization that there are perils other than fire that must be considered. Because Buildings A and B are located alongside a river, it is possible that flooding of the river would result in simultaneous damage to both buildings. The likelihood of a flood at this location must be considered. Even less likely, though not impossible, is the possibility of windstorm damage to both Building A and Building B. It is not inconceivable that a tornado could simultaneously damage both buildings, although the probability of such an occurrence may be extremely low.

It is important to note that in the discussion above, the definitions used and figures reached represent only one approach which could be used by some underwriters and risk managers—other individuals have different approaches. Therefore, in any discussion of these terms it is necessary first to define the terms being used and the conditions under which they are used.

The amount subject concept is of most value to a risk manager who can use the concept to establish the severity of exposures that must be treated. The probable maximum loss concept is of more use in underwriting, since underwriters benefit from the averaging effect of a large number of exposure units.

Normal Loss Projected losses may be considered in two categories. First is the loss which occurs with a reasonable degree of predictability so that plans may be made to establish expense allowances from year to year to cover the total amount. Common examples are automobile collision in a large fleet or workers' compensation in a large organization.

Since these losses occur in a reasonably predictable manner, they sometimes are referred to as the *burning layer*. The use of the term "burning layer" does not indicate that this technique is applicable only to the fire peril. The concept is equally applicable to all perils, whether property or liability. A second category consists of large losses which do not appear with predictable regularity and which may not ever occur. This category may be termed the *catastrophe layer*.

For estimating purposes, it might be considered that losses of a magnitude which can be expected at least once every five years constitute the burning layer, while larger losses would constitute the catastrophe layer. The importance of the distinction is that burning layer losses may be funded from current revenues as a cost of doing business, while catastrophe layer losses normally would require advance funding through reserves, insurance, or some other formalized funding device.

Total Loss Concept The discussion up to this point has dealt with relatively simple events in which a single peril caused only one kind of loss. Unfortunately, actual events are seldom that simple. The risk manager must prepare for more complex events involving more than one type of property or peril, or more than one kind of loss.

Single Peril. The discussion of amount subject in terms of damage to building and contents was a convenient way to introduce an important concept. However, it is very important to realize that a loss to building and contents may be, and frequently is, accompanied by other losses caused by the same peril. To name a few possibilities, there may be (1) a loss of production or earnings as a result of the damage to building and contents, (2) a loss from inability to collect accounts receivable because of destruction of records, (3) workers' compensation losses, and (4) liability claims for damage to the property of others or injuries to other persons. A firm that decided to retain the building and contents fire loss without consideration of other potential losses from the same fire might find that its total retention is far greater than it is willing to bear.

It is not sufficient for risk managers to define one amount subject for physical damage and a separate amount subject for business interruption. These and other types of losses may be involved in a single incident. The distinction between direct damage and indirect damage is useful for identifying loss exposures, and is used in insurance contracts, but must not be carried too far. When a loss occurs, the entity suffers all of it, and that total effect is what must be managed. Therefore, the important figure to consider in estimating a loss potential is the maximum dollar loss which could occur, considering all its aspects. This will be useful in establishing retention levels to be certain that the tolerable loss level is not exceeded.

To illustrate this point, consider a manufacturer of electronic parts who leases a large building in a desirable industrial park. The lease says that in the event of total destruction of the building the lease may be canceled. A fire occurs which totally destroys the building and contents. This is the only manufacturing plant of the company, and it has sales commitments to a number of customers. These sales are exceedingly important in maintaining a continuity of business.

The manufacturer's losses are as follows:

1. Direct loss of manufacturing equipment and stock amounts to $5 million.
2. Lost profits and continuing expenses for the year amount to $1 million.
3. Because of the critical need to maintain deliveries to customers, some operations are delegated to other firms so that deliveries can be made. This reduces the business interruption loss somewhat, but for many product lines the expenses are increased over and above the amount by which profits are saved. The amount of this extra expense is $800,000.
4. The manufacturer was about at the midpoint of a very favorable building lease. Upon rebuilding the structure, the building owner now wants to double the rent. The difference between the present value of the remaining payments under the old lease and the payments for the same time period under the new lease comes to $200,000.

Under these conditions, the amount lost is $7 million. One could also say that the normal loss expectancy was $7 million, though with values of this magnitude the building probably would have been sprinklered or otherwise protected so as to reduce the normal loss expectancy.

Combination of Perils. When calculating maximum loss potential, attention must be given to the fact that some major losses can involve substantial values in several different peril and line categories. An earthquake may be followed by a fire. Flooding may be accompanied by a fire. Hurricane and flooding may come together, as may hurricane and fire. In regard to other than property losses, a major explosion could involve workers' compensation, bodily injury liability, property damage liability, as well as direct and indirect losses to property.

The combination of physical damage perils will not normally exceed the amount subject established for fire loss, except possibly where there is a considerable amount of noncombustible or fire-resistive construction not subject to fire loss and there is a simultaneous earthquake and fire. The chief reason for considering a combination of perils in assessing a company's loss potential is to be certain that excessive loss exposures are

Table 2-1
Annual Losses

Size of Loss	Number of Losses	Total Amount of Loss
$0 to $1,000	159	$76,200
$1,000 to $5,000	32	61,412
$5,000 to $10,000	5	41,216
$10,000 to $25,000	2	26,500
Over $25,000	0	0

not retained. It is also possible for loss to involve property in several different classifications (see Chapter 1).

Consider the case of a chemical plant where an employee is driving a truck. The truck goes out of control and strikes a processing unit which explodes, doing a great deal of damage to the plant and releasing toxic chemicals which spread for a considerable distance beyond the plant, damaging property and injuring people. A number of employees of the chemical plant are also injured. This single incident could involve automobile physical damage, direct property damage, business interruption, extra expense, workers' compensation, and public liability, both bodily injury and property damage. If the chemical company has a high retention in all these lines, they could combine to the point where the retention has exceeded the company's loss-handling capacity.

Stratification of Loss Levels Loss data may be most easily analyzed if separated into various strata. They may be prepared, for example, as in Table 2-1.

If tables like this one are prepared covering a five- to ten-year period, then a fairly clear picture may be obtained of how many losses of a particular size may be expected.

In the example above, no losses over $25,000 occurred in the year represented by that table. If this were the case for at least five years, it would be reasonable to assume that losses over $25,000 would not normally occur and would therefore be considered in the catastrophe category. Likewise, if such tables were duplicated for at least five years—that is, some numbers appeared in all categories below $25,000—then it might safely be stated that losses up to $25,000 might be anticipated unless considerable improvements in protection or processes were made.

If a loss in the $10,000 to $25,000 category occurred only once in five years, there would be a question whether this was an unusual event or one which might be expected. In this case, data for more years would be necessary. If such losses occurred twice in ten years, then it might be considered as falling in the burning layer.

A table of stratified losses like Table 2-1 can be very useful in the selection of deductibles or retentions under excess insurance policies. The deductible amount usually should be slightly above the largest loss that may occur frequently. From Table 2-1, a deductible of $20,000 or $25,000 would be indicated. Of course, the difference in premium levels for insurance with various deductible levels also must be considered, as well as the firm's ability to absorb the indicated deductible one or more times during the year.

Frequency and Severity by Peril

Loss frequency and severity vary rather widely according to the peril or perils involved. This section discusses the patterns of frequency and severity associated with some of the more common property perils. Although it is not possible to discuss all perils here, those that are discussed account for a large proportion of property losses.

Fire Among perils with large potential for property damage, fire has the greatest frequency for most types of operations. The chief difficulty in estimating probable fire loss frequency and potential severity is obtaining accurate information. Many small fires occur which are extinguished without causing damage and may, therefore, never be reported. Even those which cause moderate damage may not be reported if deductibles are in effect. It is natural for most persons to avoid filling out a report form unless forced to do so by a management directive with effective penalties for failure to comply. Since few managers consider fire loss reporting to be that important, the data base may be deficient in regard to past loss frequency.

Simple stratification of loss levels, as described above, is an easy, effective technique for obtaining a clear picture of the frequency of losses of various sizes. Very large concerns may have sufficient data to call for more sophisticated statistical analysis whereby the data are fitted to a probability distribution curve so the curve itself may be used to predict losses at various levels. Care must be taken, however, to apply appropriate trend factors to losses of different years. One trend which can be fairly well quantified is that of inflation. Other trends may not be so easy to quantify, such as changes in operating procedures and increase in protection facilities. Here, however, a good guess is usually better than no guess at all.

Fire loss severity potential is best determined by estimates of trained fire protection engineers or underwriters. Severity varies greatly as a result of differences in protection, construction, and occupancy, and care must be used in severity estimates.

Explosion Explosion is quite a different peril from fire and is subdivided by the insurance industry into two types: steam explosion, and all others. Steam explosion refers to rupture of vessels which normally contain steam (steam boilers, steam pipes, steam condensers, and so on). The distinction is made because separate insurance policies are usually employed for boiler insurance and because loss statistics are separately maintained.

The extended coverage endorsement to fire insurance policies covers most explosions other than steam explosions, including combustion explosions and explosions of pressure vessels. Different types of explosions have considerably different characteristics, and low frequency leaves them little subject to statistical analysis, although there are exceptions. Certain processes have large numbers of explosion-prone devices where the experience might be considered credible—for example, an explosives manufacturing operation. In most cases, however, explosions arise from unpredictable causes, and loss frequency is difficult or impossible to quantify.

Potential severity on the other hand is relatively easy to determine, though still not with a high degree of accuracy. The severity of a steam explosion is roughly proportional to the total volume of water which may be turned to steam and released by sudden failure of the containing vessel. Higher pressure also means a larger potential explosion. Such explosions can be extremely violent, causing damage within a wide radius. Parts of the containing vessel can also be hurled hundreds of feet by the force of the explosion. The maximum magnitude of the explosion can be determined by analysis of the value of property surrounding the object, making an informed judgment of the extent of damage possible and relating that to the value of the property. Pressure vessels such as air tanks present much less of a severity problem than either steam or combustion explosions but can damage property within a radius of the object which is proportional to the size and operating pressure of the object.

Explosions not involving pressure vessels are different. Combustion explosions can occur almost anywhere. Leaking gas can accumulate in a building and then be ignited, causing widespread explosion damage. A truck containing explosives may explode near a building. Combustion explosions are therefore difficult to analyze for severity, but it is common practice to assume the same loss potential as for fire, though in most cases the loss is considerably less.

In estimating the potential severity of explosion losses, careful consideration must be given to construction characteristics of the building and to explosion control equipment provided. Buildings for which there is a relatively high probability of explosion, such as spice manufacturing or grain grinding operations or others handling combustible dusts, are usually designed with roofs or wall panels which can be blown off easily by explosion without damage to the basic structural components of the building. Explosion suppression equipment is very effective against combustion explosion, though not against explosion of steam vessels or other pressure vessels.

Windstorm The frequency and maximum velocity of windstorms in particular areas can be obtained from the U.S. Weather Service, but it is not easy to determine the potential loss severity resulting from such winds. Most buildings and structures are designed to withstand the most serious winds reasonably foreseeable in the area, but experience has proven that weaknesses are often present, and damage can be considerable. Roofs, particularly those which are older and in need of repair, are often particularly susceptible to loss, as are tall structures and movable property. Loss potentials vary with the type of property and can be estimated by (1) outlining the maximum geographical area in which a single windstorm can be expected to be damaging, (2) considering that mobile equipment and other properties not firmly anchored would be a total loss, and (3) considering that permanent structures anchored to the ground are less likely to be a total loss, depending upon the type of construction and maintenance.

Areas subject to hurricanes are treated differently from those subject to tornadoes. Hurricanes often have winds of one hundred miles per hour or more and may be dozens of miles in extent. Tornadoes are less extensive in area but sometimes more violent in intensity; thus, properties which consist of many items widely dispersed may be 100 percent subject to a hurricane but only 10 percent subject to tornado damage. Property which will withstand hurricane winds may also be seriously damaged by a tornado. The U.S. Weather Service has compiled extensive data on the frequency of both hurricanes and tornadoes in various geographical areas, including data on wind velocities.

Earthquake Earthquake frequency is so slight, even in the most seismically active parts of the world, that statistics are not reliable indicators of future loss potentials. Few structures will be subject to more than one damaging earthquake in any century and no one can say with certainty when, or even within what reasonably precise time span, it might be expected. In parts of California, estimates are that major earthquakes occur every sixty to one hundred years, but the accuracy of this prediction is questionable since it is based only on a few hundred years' data.

The matter of severity can more easily be estimated but precision is not great. There are many variables: type of ground soil (whether rock or loose-fill), proximity to faults, type of construction, height and configuration, quality of earthquake resistant design, proximity to other buildings, and other factors.

The possible loss magnitude of an earthquake can best be expressed in terms of probabilities because every structure has the possibility of total loss from earthquake. However, for well-designed buildings the probability of total loss may be exceedingly small. Though the probability of major damage to most structures cannot accurately be assessed in most cases, it is usually significant enough to warrant consideration by the risk manager. The best that can be done is for the risk manager to consider all applicable variables and make a mental determination of the maximum loss which seems in the realm of reasonable probability.

Some firms use computer simulation models to assess the potential damage to a particular building by an earthquake of a given intensity. While these models offer considerable promise for the prediction of loss severity, their use is expensive and can be justified only for high-value properties and probably only at the design stage, when corrective measures can be taken. The cost might be justified if the results of the simulation can be used to convince an underwriter to accept coverage on the property.

Flood Frequency of floods along major rivers and streams can be estimated reasonably accurately from data developed by the U.S. Army Corps of Engineers. The frequency of flood waters reaching certain levels can be estimated fairly closely, though there is always the possibility of an unusual event (such as a dam breaking) upsetting the estimates. Frequency of loss can therefore be determined fairly closely, but to this must be added another element of uncertainty to increase this frequency figure somewhat.

The next element to determine, after frequency, is the level to which flood waters will rise. This can be calculated fairly accurately from data given by the Corps of Engineers. Even flood levels resulting from dam breakage can be calculated and such data are usually available from flood maps obtainable from various governmental sources.

Once the frequency and flood height have been determined, the next step is to question the susceptibility of the concerned property to flood water damage. Some industrial buildings, if they do not contain a great deal of precision equipment, can come through a flood with little damage, whereas some paper, electrical equipment, and other property will be seriously damaged by soaking or even corrosion and mildew from excessive humidities developed in flooded buildings. Loss magnitudes will therefore depend greatly on the type of property which would be involved.

There is one other aspect of flood to consider. Flood losses are not always confined to riverside areas and flood plains. Sometimes the runoff from unusually heavy rains can be ponded by new structures, construction operations, or temporary barriers of one sort or another. Water can then back up to cause flooding. Potential frequency and severity of this type of flooding is virtually impossible to determine, but the possibility should be recognized. Some intuitive assessment may be necessary; for example, the possibility of such losses would cause the risk manager to recommend against putting an important computer facility in the basement. Even though the flood frequency may be low, the potential severity would be high enough to rule against such a location.

Other Insurable Perils Depending on the property, many other perils call for frequency and severity analysis. Theft is perhaps the major consideration for much personal property. Frequency might be established from historical records and from knowledge of the environment, type of merchandise, and methods of storage. The Uniform Crime Reports compiled by the Federal Bureau of Investigation also may be useful in this regard. The magnitude will depend generally on the amount of goods concentrated in one area, the marketability of the goods, and the relationships among value, weight, and volume.

One type of theft which is much more difficult to evaluate is employee dishonesty. Some trusted employees, particularly in computer departments, can embezzle huge sums of money over a period of time. In 1971, a moderate size fruit packing firm in rural California found that a trusted computer programmer had embezzled over $1 million over a six-year period before auditors discovered it. The loss frequency of such crimes may be low but the magnitude is potentially very high, generally related to the financial magnitude of the firm. In large firms, considerable sums can be taken before auditors become aware of the problem, but in all firms the potential is considerably greater than most people realize.[1]

Building collapse is another peril with low frequency but high magnitude which can best be assessed by an engineering study of the structure. As a practical matter, engineering studies seldom predict that a building will fall down, so the risk manager must simply remember that it can happen.

Water damage from broken pipes or tanks rather than from flood is another significant peril which has a low frequency and moderate magnitude and which can best be judged by consideration of the premises, their layout, and the susceptibility of building and contents to water damage. Say, for example, that there is a five-story industrial building with wood floors and an automatic sprinkler system fed by a large wood water tank on the roof. Each of the five floors contains garment manufacturing operations or printing shops, all of which have high susceptibility to water damage. The wood floors would probably not be watertight, so a rupture of this water tank would cause a large loss and the loss probability may not be low, especially if it is an older tank. In this regard, the risk manager may want to distinguish between a water tank used to supply an automatic sprinkler system, and one which supplies water for domestic or industrial use. Loss from the former would be insured under a sprinkler leakage insurance policy, while loss from the latter would be insured under a water damage policy or an "all-risks" property policy. Consequently, the frequency estimates may need to be kept separate for analysis of insurance needs.

Hail damage is a peril which is strongly influenced by geography and type of property. Major hailstorms occur only in certain parts of the country. Hailstones the size of golf balls and larger are sometimes encountered which can damage many types of property. Growing crops are particularly susceptible, but wood and aluminum siding and glass also may be severely damaged. Frequency can readily be predicted from weather bureau records and severity will be a function of the property involved.

Uninsurable Perils The risk manager is concerned with all perils, whether insurable or uninsurable. It makes no difference to the company financial statement whether the loss occurred from an uninsured insurable peril such as fire, or from an uninsurable peril such as pollution. The dollar result is the same. Identification of the frequency and severity of all perils is therefore useful.

Each firm will have somewhat different exposures to uninsurable perils and each calculation will be dependent on the peculiar circumstances of the concern. No general procedures have been developed for calculating frequency and severity of miscellaneous perils. Each organization should work out its own technique. The main thing to remember is that these perils exist and that they should be treated, or at least recognized. Often a firm will be suddenly hit with a major loss and have no provision made for funding the loss. This causes some disruption in finances and rescheduling of projects as the money is moved to the proper account. In most cases the loss is absorbable by the company without undue dislocation because the loss retention capability of most firms is greater than generally realized. A good example is the case of

Table 2-2

Loss History

	Number of Losses	Total Loss	Average Loss	
Year 1	9	$ 35,762	$3,918	
Year 2	7	19,292	2,756	
Year 3	72	63,283	879	} $1,100 average
Year 4	83	129,519	1,560	
Year 5	99	108,511	1,096	

Seattle First National Bank which lost over $22 million through failure of a correspondent bank in Herstatt, Germany. This of course is a serious loss (subsequently, some of the money was recovered), but the interesting point to note is that even a loss of this magnitude did not seriously affect the commercial banking operations of the company and certainly did not come close to bringing it to bankruptcy, even though the loss to the bank was not insured. On the other hand, smaller losses have caused other banks to collapse.

Loss Analysis

When the data have been determined, stratified where desirable, and frequency and severity estimated, the most important process may be started: analysis of the data to determine what they may mean. The first step is to examine the data to try to understand their sources, the conditions under which they were gathered, and all the changes that may have occurred from the time they were recorded to the present. These have been enumerated elsewhere in this chapter.

Some conditions will continue into the future, while some factors need only be applied to the old statistics to bring them up to current values. Many of the changes cannot be expressed accurately in numbers, but the closest possible approximation should be made in order to convert old figures to current figures. Then, future trends should be estimated.

Updating Loss History The example used here illustrates how a loss history can be updated to improve its use as an indicator of future loss trends. The firm in this example had a five-year loss history as shown in Table 2-2.

Reporting procedures were lax in Years 1 and 2. A new report form

Table 2-3

Loss History for Years 1 and 2

	Number of Losses	Total Losses	Average Loss
Year 1	9 x 10 = 90	$99,000	$1,100
Year 2	7 x 10 = 70	77,000	1,100

issued to the field brought out more complete and accurate figures. This is indicated by the low number of losses reported in Years 1 and 2 and by the relatively large average loss. Apparently, smaller losses were occurring but not reported.

The risk manager estimates (using Years 3 through 5 as a guide) that average losses should have been about $1,100 and number of losses about ten times the number actually reported. Then the loss history for the first two years should have been as shown in Table 2-3.

Inflation has occurred, according to the Consumer Price Index, at the following rates:

Year 1—6 percent from January 1 to December 31
Year 2—8 percent
Year 3—11 percent
Year 4—9 percent
Year 5—7 percent

To adjust loss values to equivalent figures at the end of Year 5, they should be factored as shown in Table 2-4. Though 6 percent is the figure for Year 1, the occurrence of losses must be assumed to operate uniformly throughout the year. Thus, the average effect on all losses to year end will be one-half of 6 percent, or 3 percent. A similar rationale applies to Year 5. While the Consumer Price Index was deemed appropriate for this particular firm, some other index might be more appropriate in other circumstances. Examples include the wholesale price index, index of industrial commodity prices, construction cost indexes, and others.

At the end of Year 1, management sold one manufacturing facility which was estimated to be responsible for 15 percent of all losses. Thus, the amounts for Year 1 should be multiplied by a factor of 0.85.

The more realistic loss history is shown in Table 2-5. This is a very rough estimate, based on the risk manager's knowledge of the reporting system in use in Years 1 and 2, and the average losses in Years 3, 4, and 5. In practice, no further modification might be made on such rough

Table 2-4

Adjustment of Loss Values

Year 1	\$ 99,000 x 1.03 x 1.08 x 1.11 x 1.09 x 1.07	=	\$142,570
Year 2	77,000 x 1.04 x 1.11 x 1.09 x 1.07	=	103,671
Year 3	63,283 x 1.055 x 1.09 x 1.07	=	77,866
Year 4	129,519 x 1.045 x 1.07	=	144,822
Year 5	108,511 x 1.035	=	112,309

Table 2-5

Loss History Reconstituted as of End of Year 5

	Number of Losses	Total Losses	Average Loss
Year 1	77	\$121,185	\$1,574
Year 2	70	103,671	1,481
Year 3	72	77,866	1,081
Year 4	83	144,822	1,745
Year 5	99	112,309	1,134

estimates. For the sake of discussion, however, we will assume that these rough estimates indicate actual loss experience.

Allocating Losses In a large organization, liability losses and workers' compensation losses are often related to an exposure base such as annual sales or payroll. This allows loss projections to be made or charges assessed to operating units. For example, a manufacturer may have the experience described in Table 2-6.

These figures develop the data shown in Table 2-7.

We now know that for the company as a whole, losses are experienced at the rate of \$254 per million dollars of sales, and may be projected on that basis if future sales can be estimated. It is also apparent that Division 1, with 7.5 percent of sales, suffers 14.3 percent of losses (\$486 per million dollars of sales compared to \$235), more than double the rate of the larger Division 2. This information may be used to direct loss prevention efforts or to charge costs of insurance or retained losses to the two divisions.

Property losses may be treated this way but are usually more closely related to values. They may be further refined into losses per unit value in a certain kind of process. For example, a conglomerate would keep losses per \$100 of building value for what is a predominantly office

Table 2-6

Loss Experience Related to Annual Sales

	Division 1		Division 2		Total	
	Sales	Losses	Sales	Losses	Sales	Losses
Year 1	$13,000,000	$ 5,612	$163,000,000	$ 32,111	$176,000,000	$ 37,723
Year 2	13,000,000	6,019	158,000,000	38,712	171,000,000	44,731
Year 3	14,000,000	7,875	175,000,000	46,118	189,000,000	53,993
Total	$40,000,000	$19,506	$496,000,000	$116,941	$536,000,000	$136,447
Percent of Total	7.5	14.3	92.5	85.7		

Table 2-7

Dollar Losses Per Million Dollars of Sales

	Division 1	Division 2	Total
Year 1	$432	$197	$214
Year 2	463	245	262
Year 3	563	264	285
	$486	$235	$254

occupancy separate from loss figures for a manufacturing facility. An example is shown in Table 2-8.

Note that for simplicity these figures were not trended, as they should be, for inflation and other factors. Results show that the Sales Division might anticipate future losses of $34 per million dollars of property values while the Manufacturing Division can project $142.

Larger organizations also may make use of statistical analysis where the loss data are fitted to curves representing different loss distributions. If losses fit a particular distribution curve, it is possible to show the probability of losses of a certain size occurring. The value of this approach may be in discriminating among loss prevention opportunities. Thus, a loss which has a probability of one in 10,000 may call for special protection devices before a loss which has a probability of one in one million. In some cases, it may be useful in determining whether or not insurance should be purchased. Examples would be earthquake or

Table 2-8

Losses Related to Property Values

	Sales Division		Manufacturing Division	
	Values	Losses	Values	Losses
Year 1	$1,500,000	$212	$ 385,000,000	$ 38,512
Year 2	1,600,000	42	398,000,000	87,608
Year 3	1,600,000	0	430,000,000	25,012
Year 4	1,700,000	36	512,000,000	118,606
Year 5	1,900,000	0	590,000,000	59,718
Totals	$8,300,000	$290	$2,315,000,000	$329,456
Average	$1,700,000	$ 58	$ 463,000,000	$ 65,891
Losses per $1 million of sales		$ 34		$ 142

flood insurance or higher limits for fidelity bonding. If data are not numerous enough to fit to a curve, a particular distribution may be assumed.

All such projections should be tempered by the knowledge that even if the probability of a specific loss is remote, if it *can* happen, it *may happen tomorrow.* The fact that the probability was low would be little consolation if no protection or insurance had been employed.

ABILITY TO ABSORB LOSS

Simply stated, an uninsured loss reduces a firm's net worth. A risk manager, therefore, needs to determine how much of a reduction in net worth the firm can absorb.

A firm's ability to absorb loss is a very important consideration in the design of a risk management program. It is a major deciding factor, along with cost, in the choice between retention and insurance. If insurance is selected, the ability to absorb loss is a major factor in the selection of deductible amounts. Unfortunately, a firm's ability to absorb losses is not a quantity which can be calculated precisely. However, it is possible to single out certain factors which may need to be considered.

The factors to be considered in the determination of the ability to bear loss, and the weight to be assigned to each factor, vary somewhat with the nature of the firm and its ownership. In most cases, the factors to be considered include (1) liquidity, (2) income stability, (3) net worth, and (4) management attitude toward uncertainty. The factors are not necessarily of equal importance, and their relative importance will vary from one firm to another.

Liquidity

The liquidity of a firm, in the sense used here, is measured by the relationship between its actual liquid assets and the minimum amount of liquid assets needed to maintain operations at substantially the existing level. In other words, the measure of liquidity is the amount of liquid assets which the firm can lose without being forced to curtail operations to an unacceptable level. Liquid assets are cash and other assets which can be converted to cash in a short time, such as marketable securities and, for some firms, inventory.

No general rules can be given for determining the minimum liquidity needed to maintain operations. Consequently, no general rules can be given for determining excess liquidity or the ability to absorb loss. The chief financial officer of the firm is the best judge in this case. Some indicators of excess liquidity can be given, however.

Occasionally, a firm will hold investment securities as a means of realizing some earnings from funds not currently needed in the firm's normal business operations, so the existence of a substantial investment portfolio may be an indication of sufficient liquidity to absorb substantial losses. However, it is also possible that the invested funds have been accumulated for a planned expansion or modernization program. Substantial bank balances, especially in savings accounts or certificates of deposit, also may indicate excess liquidity. On the other hand, rapid growth in notes payable or accounts payable may indicate a shortage of liquidity.

Income Stability

Profit is the principal incentive for the formation of most business firms and, other things being equal, the owners of most firms prefer predictable profits rather than fluctuating profits. Stability in profits (preferably around an increasing trend line) is important to firms whose stocks or other securities are publicly traded, because there is some evidence that investors prefer such stability. They will bid more for a stable $100 of earnings per share than for a series of varying earnings that average $100 per share. And the price of a corporation's stock is a major determinant of management's job security. Stable profits also may be a very important consideration in a closely held firm, especially if major stockholders are dependent on dividends from the company's stock for their livelihood. Lending institutions also look at the stability of profits in their consideration of a loan application. Management must consider all of these elements in determining what part of profit they can afford to expose to fortuitous loss.

Earnings per share of common stock are frequently used in determining a corporation's ability to retain loss, since it is the measure which most directly affects dividends and stock prices. It is calculated by dividing the total net profit by the number of shares outstanding. Management may sometimes prefer to use cash flow per share, which is calculated by dividing the number of shares outstanding into the sum of net profit and depreciation charges deducted for tax purposes. The latter measure might be more meaningful for a firm engaged in a manufacturing industry, such as a steel mill, which involves a large investment in machinery and equipment. Other relevant measures include rate of profit on owner's investment (net worth) and on total investments (assets) in the business. For any or all of these there often are minimum acceptable values.

In nonprofit operations, including governmental units, there is usually a maximum amount of acceptable fluctuation in relationship of revenues to expenses (which is, after all, what "net earnings" means in a business). And nonprofit organizations are every bit as interested in protecting cash flow as businesses are.

The exact percentage of earnings which a firm may be willing to expose will depend on many factors. However, as an illustration, a conglomerate firm with earnings of $2.35 per share decided that it could not expose more than five cents per share to fortuitous loss. The market price of its stock was a major consideration in this decision because management was concerned about the company's ability to acquire other firms through exchanges of stocks. Another firm, for which stock prices were a less pressing consideration, was willing to expose ten cents (out of per-share earnings of $1.73) to fortuitous loss. The latter firm was closely held and all of the stockholders were independently wealthy. The firm also held over $2 million in negotiable securities and was unlikely to need significant amounts of credit in the foreseeable future.

Preservation of Net Worth

As noted earlier, property losses usually result in a reduction in the value of one or more assets on the firm's balance sheet. Since liabilities normally are not reduced by a loss, the firm's net worth (the excess of total assets over total liabilities) is reduced. Net worth is an important factor in a firm's ability to obtain credit. Consequently, management will be concerned about possible reduction of net worth to the extent that the reduction impairs the firm's ability to obtain credit needed to finance its operations. The ratio of net worth to total assets and the ratio of net worth to liabilities frequently are used as a measure of financial strength and credit security. The acceptable ratios vary from one industry to another, but the chief finance officer of a firm probably would be familiar with industry standards.

Management Attitude

The preceding paragraphs have dealt with quantifiable factors in a firm's ability to absorb losses. However, the attitude of management toward uncertainty is at least as important.

Some people are gamblers by nature. They have a high tolerance for uncertainty, and may even enjoy pitting their luck against the laws of probability. Other people find uncertainty very unpleasant. While this psychological difference in people is difficult to measure, it is real, and it must be considered in any risk management program.

Multiple Losses

The discussion up to this point has avoided the mention of time, but a risk management program must be built within a time frame, usually one fiscal year. A year's *normal* losses can often be projected with some accuracy, and losses within this "burning layer" can be treated like other business expenses. It is much more difficult to plan for catastrophe losses, particularly when it is necessary to consider the possibility of multiple losses within a given year. Because the time frame must be considered, the amount of catastrophe loss that a firm can afford to retain usually refers to the aggregate amount for one year, and not to the amount of a single loss. On the other hand, the risk manager may have to think in terms of a single loss. For example, excess or deductible insurance coverage may be available only on a per-claim or per-accident basis. The amount to be retained in a single accident would then be calculated by dividing the permissible annual retention by the estimated probable maximum number of occurrences.

For example, assume that a firm has decided that it can afford to retain catastrophe losses in one year equal to ten cents per share of its common stock. It has two million shares outstanding, so its total permissible retention is $200,000. Four catastrophe losses per year is believed to be the *maximum* number that is likely to occur, so the risk manager can consider any deductible up to $50,000 per occurrence.

SELECTING RISK MANAGEMENT TECHNIQUES

After future losses have been estimated and the firm's ability to absorb losses has been determined, the risk manager is in a position to select among the various alternatives available in the formulation of a risk management program. This choice should be based on cost-benefit analysis; that is, the benefits to be derived from each method should be weighed carefully against the cost of that method. The method selected should be the one for which the benefit is greatest in relation to the cost.

The discussion in this section on selecting risk management techniques is general, and serves only as an introduction to the subject. The majority of the chapters to come will deal with the specific treatment of commercial property loss exposures, including both insurance and noninsurance techniques.

Avoidance

The ideal method for dealing with any loss exposure is to eliminate it, though in most cases this is not practical. Careful consideration of alternatives, however, may often lead to a more desirable, less hazardous operation.

Loss exposures can be completely eliminated in some cases, such as contracting out a hazardous operation or discontinuing a hazardous process. For example, there may be a painting activity in a metal manufacturing plant which might constitute the only serious fire hazard in the plant. If the painting is given to an outside painting contractor, then this hazard can be completely eliminated, although the potential for fire loss from other hazards remains.

In some cases, a large manufacturer may decide that due to excessive hazards, the production of one item is not economically feasible. One manufacturer of many products found that so many products liability claims were developing from ladders that he discontinued that product line. Another manufacturer discontinued one of its chemical products because of the explosion hazard inherent in the manufacturing process.

Loss Control

Loss control as it relates to property loss exposures will be discussed in greater detail in later chapters of this text. In general, loss control measures may be used to supplement either insurance or noninsurance transfers or retention programs. A primary consideration when loss control measures are employed is the cost-effectiveness of the measures. However, this is not the only consideration.

For example, in designing a new building, the question frequently arises as to whether or not it should be provided with automatic sprinklers for fire protection. In other words, is the cost of insurance for a sprinklered building plus the cost of sprinklers less than the cost of insurance without sprinklers? Where values are high, the total costs with sprinklers are usually less; in smaller buildings, the total cost without sprinklers is less. The borderline decisions are determined by a careful analysis of all pertinent factors including insurance costs, cost of retained losses, initial cost of sprinkler installation, maintenance costs, and taxes. Similar decisions are often necessary in buildings with a high theft potential to determine whether or not elaborate security measures are cost-effective. Notwithstanding the cost-effectiveness of loss control activities, it is often necessary to consider factors less tangible than cost, such as worker safety or the loss of market that might follow a loss. Loss control measures may be of value, even if not cost-effective, if they reduce potential for such intangible losses.

Noninsurance Transfer

When two parties are involved with a single building or other property, it is common practice for them to decide that one or the other is to be responsible for fortuitous losses and to so state in the contract or lease agreement. For example, a building owner may lease a building to a tenant and in the lease agreement require the tenant to be responsible for all loss. On the other hand, the owner may retain the exposure to loss if total costs will be lower.

When a contractor works at a large construction site, the construction contract may state that the owner will be responsible for all losses of property, which could include the property being installed by the contractor. On the other hand, the contract may make the contractor responsible for such damage.

Intercompany Agreements Intercompany agreements are special cases of transfer of losses by noninsurance contract. Following a fire or other crippling casualty, the principal concern of many organizations is how to supply their customers. In some industries, it may be possible for work to be farmed out to competitors or other contractors.

Some large oil refineries have an agreement among themselves that if one is put out of commission by a catastrophe, the others will expand their output to supply the customers of the inoperable refinery. With this sort of agreement, the refineries need not purchase business interruption insurance because there would be no business interruption; however, there would be considerable extra expense.

In some major cities, laundry and dry cleaning companies have agreements among themselves that if one is unable to operate because of a casualty, the others will do the work and let the disabled company use their own name and labels. Some milk product distributors have had the same arrangement, which is possible wherever the products are sufficiently similar so that the customer would not be aware of a difference. This is the case far more often than many distributors would like the public to believe.

Intercompany agreements also may be used to protect against exposures for which insurance generally is not available. For example, there are several intercompany agreements providing for indemnity against losses from strikes.

This technique of intercompany agreements provides a method of risk sharing reminiscent of early colonial times when if a family's barn burned, all the neighbors helped to rebuild. It entails no preloss cost and is perhaps the most effective way of treating a business interruption loss, provided the capacity for fulfilling orders is available and everyone cooperates. If it is not completely reliable, it can be supplemented by insurance or other techniques.

Insurance

In recent years, insurance has been the principal technique for handling loss exposures; but as modern technology has multiplied both the number and magnitude of loss exposures, alternate risk management techniques have been developed. These techniques often supplement the insurance protection or substitute for only a part of it. In some cases there is no risk management alternative other than insurance, because insurance is mandatory. In other cases, insurance is voluntarily selected as the risk management technique of preference.

Mandatory Insurance In a few cases, the options available to the risk manager may be limited. The only option available may be the transfer of the exposure through insurance, and the principal duty of the risk manager will be the selection of the most suitable coverage and the insurer best able to provide the needed coverage and service at the most attractive price.

Required by Law. Property insurance seldom is required by law, though liability and workers' compensation insurance frequently are required. Federal law requires flood insurance for any real property located in a flood zone and financed by a federally insured or federally regulated lending institution. Federal regulations also require some interstate common carriers to carry cargo insurance.

Required by Contract. It is quite common for mortgages and other contracts to require that certain property be insured. Leases sometimes require the tenant to carry fire insurance, plate glass insurance, or other coverages on the leased property. Automobile leases and leases of other personal property may contain similar provisions. The risk manager should review all leases, of either real or personal property, to be sure that such contractual obligations are fulfilled.

Bond indenture agreements frequently include requirements that certain of the firm's assets be insured. This contractual obligation often is overlooked.

If a firm wants to retain losses, it may be able to satisfy its contractual insurance requirements by arranging for an insurer to file a certificate of insurance with the other party. The insurer would, of course, require an indemnity agreement in which the firm would agree to reimburse the insurer for any losses paid under the certificate. Some consideration for the certificate also would be required, since the insurer is exposed to the possibility that the firm would be unable to fulfill the indemnity agreement. The consideration might be a specific charge for the certificate, the placement of other coverages with the insurer, or both.

Voluntary Insurance Insurance is often the most practical technique for transferring large loss exposures. It is important that the risk manager analyze all loss potentials carefully to be certain that the selected insurance contract covers everything which poses a serious loss exposure. This ideally means an "all-risks" rather than a named-perils contract. On the other hand, it is often desirable to use noninsurance techniques wherever the loss potential does not exceed the tolerable loss limit.

In almost all cases, even where most losses are retained, insurance will be necessary in excess of the tolerable loss limit. Insurance is increasingly purchased over a retention which may vary from the $100 deductible of dwelling policies to a $10 million retention of a large petroleum company.

Insurance organizations through the years have developed loss prevention, claims administration, boiler inspection, and other services which are important and often vital adjuncts of the insurance contract, and may influence the decision to purchase insurance.

Loss Retention

Once the tolerable loss level has been determined, losses to that level should generally be retained and exposures transferred for losses which exceed this level. This is the starting point but, of course, there are many other considerations.

First of all, the cost of insurance in excess of the tolerable loss level as compared to insurance to a lower level must be considered. Premium savings between the two levels are frequently perceived as being inadequate to justify high retention levels, so insurance to a lower level is carried. Sometimes this is true, but more often than not the premium saving is realistic and only appears low because of the low statistical incidence of losses in the range between deductible options. When considering a rate credit between a $10,000 loss retention and a $50,000 loss retention, the premium saved may appear small in relation to the additional exposure retained. However, the frequency of losses between $10,000 and $50,000 must be assessed in order to make an accurate judgment in this regard, as well as management attitude.

Important as they are, premium savings are not the only consideration. Any organization which develops substantial insurance premiums will find its insurance costs strongly affected by the actual losses paid by the insurer. When a firm goes many years with few losses, rate credits will often be granted. Conversely, if a number of adverse loss years are experienced, rating surcharges may be applied. For these reasons, a decision on loss retention based only on credits perceived initially is not realistic.

Many organizations are apprehensive about moving from fully insured positions to higher loss retention levels, but a good part of the apprehension is due to ignorance of loss exposures and the customs of past insurance buying practices. If a manager considers all the many loss exposures which are faced by the firm every day without insurance—changes of buyer preference, competitive activities, changes in interest rates, and an almost infinite number of other events, the insurable section of the exposure spectrum can be put in its proper perspective.

Captive Insurance Companies In many respects, a captive insurance company is nothing more than a formalized method of retaining losses, but there are unusual characteristics of the captive which make it desirable in many cases. A captive insurance company is an insurance company formed for the purpose of insuring the loss exposures of the firm which establishes it. The captive insurer may be domiciled in a location which has favorable insurance regulation and income tax laws—for instance, Bermuda. A captive insurance company may also be established by a group of companies, usually in the same line of business, to underwrite the exposures of all participants. An organization must have large insurance premiums before establishment of a captive insurance company offers significant advantages. At least several hundred thousand dollars in premiums are necessary. There have been a number of reasons for forming captives, chief of which are:

1. The belief that a captive insurance company could buy its reinsurance on favorable terms in the reinsurance market, which is sometimes more flexible and responsive than the primary insurance market.
2. The hope that the premium paid to a captive company would be treated as any other insurance premium, which would allow it to be tax deductible. Statutory insurance reserves could then be maintained in the captive company free of income tax and available for investment. The taxes are then not assessed until money is brought back to the parent in the United States. However, the Internal Revenue Service has currently disallowed the tax advantage of captives, although this question is still before the courts and could be resolved against the IRS.[2] Thus this advantage may not persist.
3. Some companies find that an insurance premium is a more acceptable way to charge costs to separate operating cost centers than a "self-insurance" charge.

The captive insurance company concept has become so popular that Colorado passed a special law providing for the administration of captive insurance companies in that state. The law exempts the captive from a number of requirements that must be faced by conventional insurers, such as participation in assigned risk pools.

Whatever the reasons, the use of captive insurance companies has become increasingly common in larger organizations. In times of shortage of capital for insurance companies in general, this provides a source of insurance which might not otherwise be available. Many captive insurance companies have expanded into underwriting the exposures of others, and some have become full-fledged insurance companies.

A CASE STUDY—FEETON DESK CORPORATION

A case study of a hypothetical business firm will illustrate some of the considerations involved in the selection of risk management techniques. The example has been kept relatively simple in order to keep

Table 2-9
Shipments

Mode of Transportation	Incoming		Outgoing	
	Number	Total Value	Number	Total Value
Railroad	81	$ 972,000	107	$ 4,280,000
Owned trucks	189	3,778,000	179	3,581,000
Contract carrier	634	9,297,000	987	19,740,000
Totals	904	$14,047,000	1,273	$27,601,000

the illustration within manageable proportions. This analysis is concerned only with property risk management.

Feeton Desk Corporation

The Feeton Desk Corporation is a manufacturer of steel desks, filing cabinets, shelving, and other office equipment. It also upholsters office chairs with steel frames. Some of these chairs have cast aluminum bases and casters. Desk tops may be of plastic with simulated wood grain or actual wood. The furniture is manufactured in the company's plant in a suburban industrial park near a major midwestern city. However, plastic desk tops and the base castings for chairs are purchased from other manufacturers who make them to Feeton's specifications. Feeton now has one supplier for each of these items. Other parts, materials, and supplies purchased by Feeton are standard items and can be purchased readily from several sources.

There is a railroad siding on one side of Feeton's plant and a truck loading dock on the opposite side. Both modes of transportation are used for both incoming and outgoing shipments, and Feeton is responsible for loss on all shipments. The company's nine owned tractor-trailer units are used for some shipments, but most truck shipments are hauled by an unrelated contract carrier. Last year, which was a reasonably typical year, shipments were as shown in Table 2-9.

The largest single shipment by railroad was $63,000, and the largest single shipment by truck was $41,000. Transportation losses last year, which were typical of the last several years (except that the loss over $25,000 is very unusual), are as shown in Table 2-10.

The values of incoming shipments are shown at cost and outgoing shipments at selling price in both of the above tables.

Table 2-10
Transportation Losses

Size of Loss	Number of Losses	Total Amount of Losses
$0 to $1,000	203	$ 65,163
$1,001 to $2,000	41	60,639
$2,001 to $3,000	12	30,432
$3,001 to $4,000	5	17,435
$4,001 to $5,000	2	8,973
$5,001 to $10,000	2	15,032
$10,001 to $25,000	1	13,729
Over $25,000	1	33,462
Totals	267	$244,865

Most of Feeton's products are sold on open account to retailers or distributors. One large mail order and retail store chain buys approximately 25 percent of production each year. Feeton also has been testing a lease plan, under which it leases equipment to medium- and large-sized offices. The company currently has 107 leased installations throughout the U.S. and Canada, totaling $5,228,000 in actual cash value. The installations range from $25,000 to $60,000 each. The lessee is relieved of any liability for accidental damage to the leased equipment except in the case of gross negligence on the part of the lessee. The terms of the leases vary, but generally are for the expected useful life of the equipment. There have been no significant instances of loss or damage to leased equipment.

Feeton's building is of masonry construction with a concrete slab floor and a steel roof deck on unprotected steel bar joists. The receiving department (including the office) and the shipping department are cut off from the manufacturing area by approved fire walls and fire doors. The wall between the office and the receiving department is gypsum board on wood studs, and the boiler room is cut off by masonry walls. The replacement cost of the building is $2.8 million and the actual cash value is $2.4 million. Figure 2-4 shows the layout of the building. There are several production lines running through the various departments, but only the departments are shown in Figure 2-4. The figure is not to scale.

There are no walls between the various departments within the manufacturing area. It is one large open area. The broken lines in the figure merely indicate the relative sizes of the departments.

The woodworking department makes and finishes wood tops for

Figure 2-4

Factory Layout of Feeton Desk Corporation

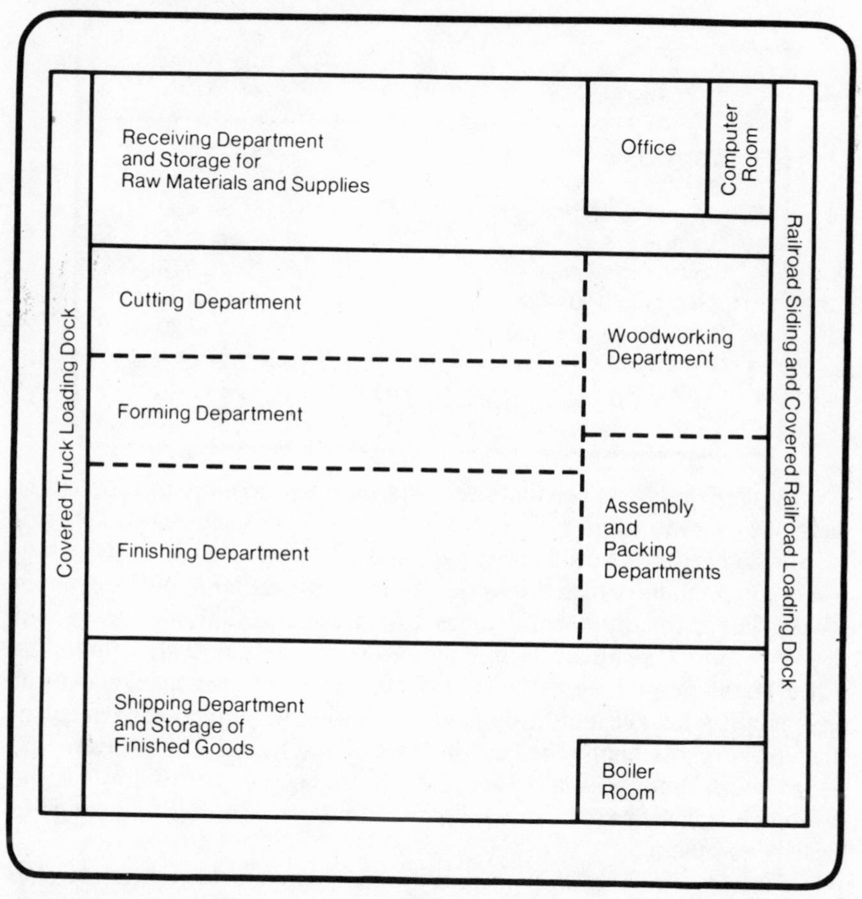

desks, and includes the machinery and equipment usual to such work, such as saws, planers, sanders, and so forth. The first stop along the production line for the steel parts of furniture is the cutting department, where sheets of steel and steel tubing are cut to length and size. Several kinds of cutting devices are used, including saws, abrasive blades, and torches, depending on the kind of material to be cut.

The next step in production is the forming department, where the cut steel sheets and tubing are formed into desk and chair legs, drawer parts, and so forth. The forming is done by punch presses, sheet metal brakes, and similar equipment. Any necessary welding also is done in this department.

From the forming department, the parts move to the finishing department, where various finishes are applied. Parts to be painted are first dipped in vats of solvent to remove oil, grease, and other contaminants and then dipped in vats of paint. Metal plating, galvanizing and anodizing also are done in this department.

After finishing, the various parts are taken to the assembly and packing area. They are assembled into finished products and packed in cardboard containers for shipping. The assembly department installs upholstery on chairs and plastic or wooden tops on desks along with the other assembly work. The assembled furniture is then packed and moved into the shipping and storage area to await shipment.

All factory machinery and equipment is standard, stock equipment which can be replaced quickly. The present facilities, both building and equipment, are believed to be adequate for the next few years. However, it might be necessary for Feeton to move to a larger building in three or four years. Steam for heating and for use in the manufacturing process is furnished by an oil-fired boiler in the boiler room of the plant. A compressor in the boiler room provides compressed air. The warehouse and manufacturing areas are cooled by fans, but the office is air conditioned by a central unit. A separate air conditioning unit cools the computer room.

All of Feeton's accounting, including accounts receivable and accounts payable, is computerized. The computer also is used for inventory control, ordering of materials, maintenance of payroll records, issuance of payroll checks, and similar chores. The computer equipment is leased from the manufacturer, and Feeton is responsible for any damage to it.

Feeton's current balance sheet is shown in Table 2-11. Liabilities have not changed significantly over the last three years. The only substantial changes in assets have been an increase of $50,000 in investment securities and the normal increases in accounts receivable and inventories as a result of the company's growth.

Table 2-12 shows Feeton's profit and loss statement for the latest year. It also is reasonably typical of the past few years except that sales and profits have been increasing steadily at about 5 percent each year.

Feeton is a closely held corporation. All the stockholders are heirs of the company founder, who was the sole stockholder until his death. Most of the owners depend on dividends from Feeton stock for their livelihood. The company pays out in dividends over half of its net profit after taxes. The remainder is retained to support the company's growth.

Insurance Quotations

The company's broker has obtained the quotations shown below for various kinds of property insurance. In each case, the policy limits

Table 2-11
Balance Sheet for Feeton Desk Corporation

Assets		
Current Assets		
Cash	$ 276,593	
Investment securities	387,438	
Accounts receivable	2,100,079	
Inventory	1,735,333	
Office equipment leased to others	5,228,000	
		$ 9,727,443
Fixed Assets (after depreciation)		
Building	$1,927,000	
Machinery and equipment	3,431,217	
Automotive equipment	270,874	
		$ 5,629,091
Total Assets		$15,356,534

Liabilities		
Current Liabilities		
Accounts payable	$1,770,583	
Notes payable	75,269	
		$ 1,845,852
Long-Term Liabilities		
Mortgage on building		$ 1,327,864
Total Liabilities		$ 3,173,716
Net Worth		
Paid-in Capital	$2,900,000	
Paid-in Surplus	1,300,000	
Retained Earnings	7,982,818	
		$12,182,818
Total Liabilities and Net Worth		$15,356,534

Table 2-12
Profit and Loss Statement for Feeton Desk Corporation

Gross Sales	$27,601,583		
Less returns and allowances	9,327		
		$27,592,256	
Revenue from Leased Equipment		1,280,205	
			$28,872,461
Expenses			
Cost of materials and supplies		$14,833,279	
Salaries and wages			
Officers and key employees		1,163,421	
Ordinary payroll		6,249,127	
Heat, light, and power		487,016	
Depreciation		567,329	
Sales and general administration expense (including insurance)		2,992,257	
			$27,042,477
Net Profit Before Income Taxes			1,829,984
Income Taxes			805,193
Net Profit After Taxes			$ 1,024,791

quoted are adequate for full coverage on the valuation basis indicated, so policy limits are not indicated. Where "none" is indicated as a deductible, the standard policy deductible is implied.

The following premiums were quoted for "all-risks" transportation coverage for shipments by rail, owned trucks and nonowned trucks:

Deductible Amount	*Annual Premium*
None	$408,000
$ 5,000 per occurrence	99,600
25,000 per occurrence	10,000
300,000 annual aggregate	10,000

However, the insurance company's loss control representative has suggested that Feeton adopt a new packaging method which would be expected to reduce losses by 50 percent. The new method would require an initial capital outlay of $10,000 and an increase of $8,000 per year in the cost of packaging materials and labor. Most of the loss reduction would be in the smaller losses. The new method would not be as effective against the larger losses, which usually result from severe collisions, truck fires, and similar occurrences.

The insurer has agreed that it will reduce its quoted premiums if the new packaging method is adopted. The revised premiums are:

Deductible Amount	*Annual Premium*
None	$210,000
$ 5,000 per occurrence	79,000
25,000 per occurrence	9,000
300,000 annual aggregate	2,000

The following quotations were given for "all-risks" coverage on office equipment leased to others, with the coverage to apply anywhere within the United States and Canada:

Deductible Amount	*Annual Premium*
None	$7,840
$ 5,000 per occurrence	6,300
10,000 per occurrence	5,800
25,000 per occurrence	4,200
100,000 annual aggregate	2,000

The premiums for "all-risks" actual cash value coverage on the building would be:

Deductible Amount	*Annual Premium*
None	$42,000
$ 5,000 per occurrence	41,000
10,000 per occurrence	40,500
25,000 per occurrence	39,000

If automatic sprinklers are installed throughout the plant, the premiums, including sprinkler leakage, would be:

Deductible Amount	*Annual Premium*
None	$18,000
$ 5,000 per occurrence	17,000
10,000 per occurrence	16,800
25,000 per occurrence	16,600

The initial cost of installing sprinklers would be $180,000, and the annual cost of maintenance, alarm system, and inspection would be $10,000. The estimated remaining useful life of the plant is twenty years, and the sprinkler system would last for the life of the plant.

The cost of "all-risks" contents coverage, with and without sprinklers, is:

	Annual Premium	
Deductible Amount	*Unsprinklered*	*Sprinklered*
None	$97,000	$46,000
$ 5,000 per occurrence	95,200	45,000
10,000 per occurrence	94,000	44,200
25,000 per occurrence	92,500	43,000

It should be noted that the annual premium for coverage with sprinklers includes sprinkler leakage coverage.

Replacement cost coverage would be 17 percent more for the building and 25 percent more for contents in each case mentioned above. The contents premiums do not include coverage for the leased computer system or for Feeton's data processing media, such as punched cards, paper tape, and magnetic tape.

Feeton has asked the computer manufacturer about revising the lease agreement to relieve Feeton of any liability for damage to the equipment. The manufacturer has agreed to relieve Feeton of liability for all accidental damage except that caused intentionally or through gross negligence of Feeton or its employees. However, the annual rental for the equipment would increase by $3,000 if the amendment is made. The cost to Feeton of "all-risks" coverage on the computer system is:

Deductible Amount	*Annual Premium*
None	$4,500
$ 5,000 per occurrence	3,700
10,000 per occurrence	3,200
25,000 per occurrence	2,300

The insurer has suggested that Feeton install (1) an automatic Halon extinguishing system in the computer room, and (2) a computer-checked identification card system to be sure that only authorized persons can enter the computer room. (Halon is a nontoxic gas that extinguishes fires by breaking the chain reaction in the combustion process without depleting the oxygen supply.) The initial cost of these measures would be $30,000 and the annual upkeep would be $500. If the loss prevention measures are adopted, the premiums for the computer system would be:

Deductible Amount	*Annual Premium*
None	$2,500
$ 5,000 per occurrence	1,800
10,000 per occurrence	1,000
25,000 per occurrence	800

"All-risks" coverage on data processing media, with and without the loss prevention measures recommended above, would be:

Deductible Amount	*Annual Premium* *Without*	*With*
None	$4,300	$2,200
$ 5,000 per occurrence	3,600	1,400
10,000 per occurrence	3,000	900
25,000 per occurrence	2,100	650

In addition, the insurer has recommended that duplicate master magnetic tapes be run each day and stored at a separate location. This would facilitate reconstruction of data and software following a loss. This measure would cost an estimated $2,000 per year, and the insurer would allow a 50 percent rate credit for it.

"All-risks" business interruption coverage, including ordinary payroll coverage, is available at the following premiums (either with or without the sprinkler system previously mentioned):

Deductible Amount	*Annual Premium* *Unsprinklered*	*Sprinklered*
None	$48,384	$23,500
$ 5,000 per occurrence	47,129	22,100
10,000 per occurrence	46,315	21,200
25,000 per occurrence	44,000	20,000

Boiler and machinery coverage has been quoted separately for (1) steam boilers, pipes, and equipment; and (2) air conditioners, air compressors, and other pressure vessels. The premiums are:

Deductible Amount	*Annual Premium* *Steam Equipment*	*Other*
None	$12,500	$1,250
$ 5,000 per occurrence	12,000	1,000
10,000 per occurrence	11,600	900
25,000 per occurrence	10,800	700

The premiums listed above for boiler and machinery include adequate business interruption and extra expense coverage for incidents arising from accidents covered under the policy. The laws of the city in which Feeton is located require that steam boilers and associated equipment be inspected at least twice each year by a licensed inspector. The insurance company's inspectors, whose services are included in the quoted premiums, are licensed to make these inspections. The cost of the inspections, if purchased separately from an independent engineer, would be $2,000 per year.

Table 2-13
Feeton's Insurance Program

Coverage	Renewal Premium
Transportation	$408,000
Leased equipment	7,840
Building (ACV)	42,000
Contents (ACV)	97,000
Computer	4,500
Data processing media	4,300
Business interruption	48,384
Boiler and machinery—all objects	13,750
Total	$625,774

Feeton's current insurance program includes the coverages shown in Table 2-13. Each of the exposures is insured with no deductible. Also shown below are the premiums quoted to renew coverage on the present basis.

Because Feeton's insurance costs have reached such a high figure, the board of directors wonder whether they have relied too heavily on insurance for treatment of their property loss exposures. Feeton has hired a risk manager to analyze the current insurance program, together with the alternatives cited above, and to make appropriate recommendations.

The risk manager was given the following policy statement:

"Feeton Desk's risk management objective is to minimize Feeton's cost of coping with loss exposures while providing protection needed to enable the company to meet its financial objectives. We recognize that reduced cost may in some cases lead to increased chance of loss. Feeton should not be exposed to any single foreseeable uninsured loss greater than $50,000. We also recognize that unforeseeable losses may occur. In no case should Feeton incur losses in any one year exceeding $100,000, which might have been avoided with the purchase of insurance."

In view of this policy statement, the risk manager was requested to make an interim report, suggesting methods of treating each of the exposures for which insurance has been quoted. After the interim report has been approved, and any necessary additional studies have been completed, Feeton will implement a revised risk management program.

The highlights of the interim report follow.

Table 2-14

Cost of Transportation Insurance with Different Deductibles

Cost of full insurance (no deductible)		$408,000
Normal losses under $5,000 per loss	$182,642	
Normal losses over $5,000 x $5,000 deductible (3 x 5,000)	15,000	
Insurance premium with $5,000 deductible	99,600	
Expected total loss and premium costs with $5,000 deductible		$297,242
Normal losses under $25,000 per loss	$211,403	
Insurance premium with $25,000 deductible	10,000	
Expected total loss and premium costs with $25,000 deductible		$221,403
Normal losses under $300,000 aggregate†	$211,403	
Insurance premium with $300,000 aggregate deductible	10,000	
Expected total loss and premium costs with $300,000 aggregate deductible		$221,403

†The $33,462 loss last year was unusual.

Proposed Risk Management Program

Transportation Exposures

Analysis of Loss Frequency and Severity. Loss frequency has been fairly constant, with approximately one loss for every eight shipments. As to severity, most losses fall below $25,000. However, since shipments are valued as high as $63,000, the amount subject to a single loss is $63,000. If several shipments may be exposed to a single loss, the amount subject could be even higher. Since this exceeds Feeton's $50,000 tolerable loss level, the entire exposure cannot be retained.

Analysis of Insurance Alternatives. Based on Feeton's risk management objective, a $25,000 deductible seems reasonable. However, before selecting the $25,000 deductible, it is necessary to compare the cost of insurance with lower deductibles, based on the information in Table 2-14.

The $25,000 deductible still appears attractive. However, before making a final decision, Feeton must analyze the cost of handling its own claims adjustment.

Use of the $300,000 aggregate deductible is not favored for the following reasons: (1) such a choice would tolerate single retained losses in excess of $50,000, in violation of Feeton's risk management objective; and (2) given the above expected premium and loss costs, a single loss exceeding $25,000 appears more probable than aggregate losses exceeding $300,000. The former could occur with a single shock loss. The latter would require substantial increases in loss frequency and/or average loss severity.

Analysis of Noninsurance Alternatives. The cost per year of $8,000 for the proposed packing system would be offset by only a $1,000 reduction in insurance costs (assuming use of a $25,000 deductible). In addition, there would be the $10,000 initial cost to change packing systems. This is not a cost-effective alternative.

Other noninsurance methods for treating this exposure might further reduce the chance of loss, such as making other parties responsible for all shipments, using common carriers instead of the nine owned tractor-trailer units, or revising the contract with contract carriers so they are fully responsible for all losses. These alternatives should be explored.

Leased Office Equipment

Analysis of Loss Frequency and Severity. With over $5 million in leased office equipment, the loss exposure is substantial. The amount subject to a single loss is $60,000 (the maximum values at any one location). Because 107 different locations are involved, the possibility of a loss at one or more locations each year seems fairly high at a glance, despite the insignificant losses to date. A total loss at any location would involve from $25,000 to $60,000.

Analysis of Insurance Alternatives. Because the 107 remote locations are not under Feeton's direct control, it is impossible for Feeton to utilize loss control techniques to reduce loss frequency and severity. To determine an acceptable retention limit, it would be necessary to have some estimate of expected loss frequency and severity. Past experience cannot serve here as a basis for such calculations because the leasing operation is relatively new. Adjustment of retained losses could be difficult, since many of the locations with leased equipment are at locations remote from Feeton's base of operations.

Because past experience is limited, it seems advisable to recommend full insurance coverage. This will provide the added advantage of claim service from the insurer's claim adjusters at the remote locations.

Loss experience with leased equipment should be monitored closely, so that this recommendation can be re-evaluated as the data accumulate. It would also be desirable to obtain loss cost data from whatever outside sources might be available, including the experience of others engaged in the office equipment leasing business, and loss statistics from insurance rating bureaus and others accumulating loss data. Such data could supplement Feeton's developing experience and serve as an aid in future risk management decisions.

It might be noted that the $7,840 annual premium to provide full, "all-risks" coverage on $5,228,000 of leased office equipment amounts to only $.15 per hundred dollars of insurance, which seems to be a very reasonable rate. However, for a firm of this size, insurance costs alone should not be a major criterion in a decision to insure or retain loss exposures. If claims are made, there is a possibility of premium increases. Also, different insurers may quote different premiums or deductible credits at various times.

Analysis of Noninsurance Alternatives. It might be possible to transfer this loss exposure by changing the lease agreement to make lessees responsible for all loss. It may, however, be impossible to give lessees adequate consideration to induce them to accept the loss exposure, and may also run counter to practice in this industry. It may also be that, based on the premiums above, Feeton can obtain insurance at a lower rate than would be available to individual lessees.

Building, Contents, and Business Interruption These exposures need to be considered together because any single loss might affect all three exposures.

Analysis of Loss Frequency and Severity. Despite the fire wall which may limit the probable maximum loss from fire, the entire building is subject to a loss from other perils such as an explosion caused by solvents or paint. The potential severity should be considered as the replacement cost value, since that would be the amount spent by Feeton to replace damaged property. In view of the hazardous operations being performed, there is a fairly high probability of loss frequency. Because contents can be replaced quickly, any business interruption would not likely extend beyond the time required to replace or repair the building. Despite bottlenecks in the manufacturing process, it appears they could work around an interrupted operation for a few days, if necessary.

Analysis of Insurance Alternatives. It appears that loss frequency would probably be higher for contents than for the building, and higher for the building than for business interruption. In view of the above, and in view of the $50,000 tolerable loss level, it appears a $25,000 deductible on business interruption and a $10,000 deductible on building and contents would be feasible choices (total deductible, $45,000). Replacement cost coverage is recommended.

The premium differentials for these deductible levels appear to be rather small. (The credits granted for deductibles are substantially less

Table 2-15
Building, Contents, and Business Interruption Premiums

	Unsprinklered	Sprinklered
Building ($10,000 deductible, RC coverage)	$ 47,385	$19,656
Contents ($10,000 deductible, RC coverage)	117,500	51,714
Business Interruption ($25,000 deductible)	44,000	20,000
Total	$208,885	$91,370

than those suggested by the ISO table of credits for deductible coverage.)[3] This should be discussed with the insurer, in an attempt to gain greater premium credits for the deductible levels recommended.

Analysis of Noninsurance Alternatives. At the deductible levels chosen, for replacement cost coverage, sprinklered versus nonsprinklered premiums are as shown in Table 2-15. It is obvious that, at these premium levels, the cost of the sprinkler system would be less than two year's premium savings, and should definitely be purchased. Even if the building is sold in three or four years, the value of the sprinkler system will not be lost because it will increase the value of the building. (More refined analysis, beyond the scope of this case study, would also consider the effect of income taxes. Automatic sprinkler systems are a capital investment which may be deducted only by depreciation charges over a period of twenty to twenty-five years. Savings from reduced insurance expense is an increase of profits which is taxed at the full rate.) It should be recognized that a sprinkler system will reduce probable fire loss severity, but not frequency. Likewise, a sprinkler system will be relatively ineffective against windstorm or explosion damage.

The loss exposure may be further reduced if it is practical to subcontract some of the more hazardous operations to other parties, or to locate them in separate buildings, or to enter into agreements with other suppliers to provide services during a business interruption.

In addition to premium cost, Feeton should consider the business losses following any substantial interruption of operations. If the outlet selling 25 percent of Feeton's output should choose another supplier, or if a substantial number of other outlets should change suppliers, the indirect losses could be substantial. The sprinkler system and other loss control measures will reduce the chances of such an indirect loss.

Computer Equipment and Media

Analysis of Loss Frequency and Severity. Loss frequency does not appear to be a problem with this computer equipment and media, because no previous losses were cited. Loss severity, however, could be catastrophic. The computer system is Feeton's nerve center, and even a small direct loss to the computer or computer media could result in a substantial indirect loss. It is highly desirable to prevent losses. Therefore, it is recommended that noninsurance treatment of this exposure be given primary consideration, with insurance as a backup.

Analysis of Noninsurance Alternatives. An insurer has suggested Feeton install a Halon extinguishing system in the computer room, as well as a computer-checked identification card system. Much of the equipment associated with these recommendations would be permanently installed in Feeton's building. Since Feeton is likely to move in three or four years, the initial cost of this system can be averaged only over (conservatively) three years. The initial cost of this recommendation ($30,000) would then be approximately $10,000 per year plus $500 for upkeep, or $10,500 per year. These safety measures would reduce the highest quoted premiums (no deductible) on both computer and media by only $4,100 per year. The loss control measures proposed are not cost-effective. Such measures might be recommended despite their cost, in view of the importance of loss prevention. However, other alternatives are better.

The recommended duplicate record system will effectively prevent any chance of loss to data and software, at a cost of $2,000 per year. In addition, it might be possible to make a reciprocal agreement with the owner of a nearby compatible computer, to use their system following a loss. The only consideration for such an agreement might be an agreement to provide computer services for the other party if their computer is damaged.

If duplicate records are kept, and a duplicate computer system is made available, Feeton is not exposed to extensive loss unless records at both locations are destroyed in a single loss, or the backup computer is unavailable when needed.

The above discussion has treated the indirect loss exposures arising out of lost media, or lost computer time, but has not addressed loss arising out of direct damage to the computer. The most reasonable approach to this exposure seems to be to transfer it to the computer manufacturer for $3,000 per year. This would be less than the cost of insurance with a $10,000 deductible. (Choice of this alternative also recognizes the possibility of a loss involving building, contents, business interruptions, and the computer.) A $10,000 deductible (in addition to the deductible on other coverages) would exceed the tolerable loss limit in a multiple loss of this nature—full insurance coverage would cost even more. With such a noninsurance transfer, Feeton would retain the exposure to loss arising out of intentional damage or gross negligence, but these can be handled with an effective loss control program.

The likelihood of damage to the computer can be reduced if it is separated from hazards. A separate fire resistive building would be preferable. However, the computer seems to be well located within the present structure.

Analysis of Insurance Alternatives. Most exposures to computers and computer media have been treated with the above-suggested noninsurance techniques. There remains, however, a remote exposure to catastrophic loss if the duplicate tapes and master tapes are both destroyed in a single occurrence. This low frequency/high severity event could be insured for a premium of $1,050 (considering a 50 percent rate credit and a $25,000 deductible). Such catastrophe coverage is recommended. Loss of a single day's records, not yet duplicated, can be retained. There is no alternative to retaining the slight chance that the duplicate computer would be unavailable if needed, unless, perhaps, an alternate substitute computer can be arranged for.

Boiler and Machinery

Analysis of Loss Frequency and Severity. The potential loss severity is greater for steam boiler explosion than for loss arising out of other pressure vessels and machinery. Air conditioner breakdown could cause damage to the computer system, but this has been previously considered.

Analysis of Insurance Alternatives. A steam explosion could result in catastrophic loss not covered by other insurance. Retention of this exposure would cost $2,000 per year for inspection service (which also reduces potential loss frequency). Therefore, the effective cost of insurance is $2,000 less than the premiums indicated. Because a boiler loss might be a low frequency/high severity exposure, retention is not deemed advisable. The premium differentials between different deductible amounts appear realistic, and coverage on the boiler with a $25,000 deductible is indicated.

Analysis of Noninsurance Alternatives. Because of the low severity loss potential of "other" pressure vessels, it is recommended that this exposure be retained. The hiring of a specialist to inspect this equipment and thus reduce potential loss frequency should be investigated, and the cost of this inspection service should be compared with the cost of insurance including inspection service.

Summary of the Proposal

If all of the above suggestions are accepted, the direct cost of

Table 2-16

Comparison of Proposed Risk Management Program with Present Insurance Program

		Proposed Cost	Present Insurance Cost
Transportation			
Normal losses under $25,000 per loss	$211,403		
Insurance with $25,000 deductible	10,000		
		$221,403	$408,000
Leased Office Equipment			
Full coverage, no deductible		$ 7,840	$ 7,840
Building, Contents, Business Interruption			
Building insurance ($10,000 deductible, replacement cost coverage)	$ 19,656		
Contents insurance ($10,000 deductible, replacement cost coverage)	51,714		
Business interruption ($25,000 deductible)	20,000		
⅓ initial cost of sprinkler system (remaining half to be expensed over the next two years)	60,000		
Annual upkeep on sprinkler system	10,000		
		$161,370	$187,384 (ACV)
Computer Equipment and Media			
Duplicate record system	$ 2,000		
Transfer of exposure to computer manufacturer (no deductible)	3,000		
Insurance on media ($25,000 deductible)	1,050		
		$ 6,050	$ 8,800
Boiler and Machinery			
Insurance on steam equipment only ($25,000 deductible)		10,800	13,750
		$407,463	$625,774
Difference Between Present Program Cost and Proposed Program Cost			$218,311

insurance and noninsurance treatments of the exposures discussed will be as shown in Table 2-16.

The following points should be emphasized regarding the above presentation. First, under the proposed program building and contents are insured to replacement cost; the old program insured these items to actual cash value. Second, out of the apparent $218,311 in savings retained losses and loss adjustment expenses for retained losses must be paid. Last, the sprinkler system has been conservatively valued, for the sake of a concise presentation, with the installation expense written off in only three years. With a useful life of twenty years, it has an actual annual depreciation much lower than the figure indicated. Even if Feeton sells the building, the value of the sprinkler will increase the value of the building.

Analysis of Loss Control Program as Proposed The above program does not *entirely* preclude the possibility of a single catastrophe loss in excess of $50,000, nor does it *guarantee* that retained catastrophe losses will not exceed $100,000 in any one year. However, considering the $218,311 savings over the cost of the present program, and the low probability of loss frequency and severity exceeding the tolerable loss limit, the above proposal seems acceptable. However, lower retention limits could be selected, if the board sees fit, in the interest of greater security.

If the above proposal is acceptable, it will be necessary to explore the other questions raised (i.e., loss adjustment expenses, availability of alternate computer facilities, and so on) before arriving at a final proposal.

Conclusion

The Feeton Desk case study presents an excellent example of how insurance and noninsurance techniques can be combined to form a sound risk management program. The program described here is certainly not the only way the exposures could be analyzed and treated. It merely illustrates one way in which the data can be analyzed and solutions found.

Chapter Notes

1. *How Much Honesty Insurance?* (Surety Association of America). This booklet may be helpful in estimating the potential magnitude of employee dishonesty losses. This is discussed in greater detail in Chapter 12.
2. Rev. Rul. 77-316 August 29, 1977. [Reported in *Risk Management*, October, 1977, p. 7.]
3. See Table 3-3 in Chapter 3 of this text.

CHAPTER 3

Fire and Allied Lines: Common Forms

INTRODUCTION

Insurance is the most widely used risk management technique for transferring the exposures of loss to property due to fire and other perils. Lengthy insurance contracts have been written in an attempt to define precisely what losses are or are not covered and to spell out specifically the responsibilities of both parties.

In the early days of fire insurance, coverage was written almost entirely by individual underwriters who concentrated on insureds with whom they were personally acquainted. The brief policies they wrote merely included a description of the property, the term, and the premium. However, as insurance operations became more widespread, additional controls were needed. Many promissory and restrictive provisions were incorporated into the policies to protect the insurer against unnecessary exposures to loss and the payment of unjust claims. Policies now contain full descriptions of the property insured, provisions to prevent concealment of facts prior to the issuance of the policy, and wrongful conduct in the maintenance and care of the property after the owner had purchased insurance.

Insurance policies became voluminous and there was very little uniformity among different policies. Each company used its own policies. The character of policy forms in the late 1800s was described in a court decision:

> Forms of applications and policies (like those used in this case) of a most complicated and elaborate structure, were prepared, and filled with covenants, exceptions, stipulations, provisos, rates, regulations, and conditions, rendering the policy void in a great number of contingencies. These provisions were of such bulk and character that

> they would not be understood by men in general, even if subjected to a careful and laborious study; by men in general, they were sure not to be studied at all. The study of them was rendered particularly unattractive by a profuse intermixture of discourses on subjects in which a premium payer would have no interest. This compound, if read by him, would, unless he were an extraordinary man, be an inexplicable riddle, a mere flood of darkness and confusion. Some of the most material stipulations were concealed in a mass of rubbish, on the back side of the policy and the following page, where few would expect to find anything more than a dull appendix, and where scarcely any one would think of looking for information so important as that the company claimed a special exemption from the operation of the general law of the land relating to the only business in which the company professed to be engaged. As if it were feared that, notwithstanding these discouraging circumstances, some extremely eccentric person might attempt to examine and understand the meaning of the involved and intricate net in which he was to be entangled, it was printed in such small type, and in lines so long and so crowded, that the perusal of it was made physically difficult, painful, and injurious.[1]

Fortunately, this situation has improved. Insurance policies today, while still classed as "least-read best sellers," are much more understandable and uniform than those of the nineteenth century. In fact, a fire insurance policy issued by one company reads much the same—often exactly the same—as a policy issued by another company, although some nonstandard forms are still in use for specialized situations. This uniformity provides great benefits to insurance buyers, sellers, and regulators; and, no less important for purposes of this course, to the student of insurance.

This chapter and the following chapter will explore the insurance coverages available under fire and allied lines forms. There is no generally accepted definition of "allied lines." However, the term is commonly applied to coverages closely associated and usually sold with fire insurance.

This chapter introduces fire and allied lines insurance with a study of the general nature of fire and allied lines insurance and the structure of fire and allied lines insurance contracts. After a brief review of standard fire policy forms, there is an extensive discussion of the general property form, chosen because it is an example of the most common approach to insuring most types of commercial property. Emphasis in this chapter is on the types of property covered and policy conditions affecting coverage. Perils will be discussed in more detail in Chapter 4.

The last major section of this chapter deals with a variety of methods for handling amounts of insurance including deductibles, reporting forms, blanket insurance, replacement cost insurance, builders' risk forms, and other variations on the standard approach.

NATURE OF FIRE AND ALLIED LINES INSURANCE

Fire and allied lines insurance can be categorized in two ways: first, according to property covered ("property" includes certain types of assets at certain locations); second, according to perils insured against.

Property and Locations Covered

Historically, fire and allied lines coverages have dealt with buildings and their contents. The location of each covered structure was specified in the contract. Personal property was covered while within the specified structure or within a given distance from it.

Such strict limitations are no longer the case. In current policies there is usually some limited off-premises coverage—for example, coverage on such items as storm windows away from the described location for cleaning or repair.

However, since coverage essentially applies at a specific location, fire and allied lines insurance is not used to insure items in transit. Businesses that ship materials and/or goods or deliver or receive goods would use a marine insurance policy to protect that property. If coverage is required to cover property off premises wherever it is situated, marine coverage is generally more appropriate.

Such items as watercraft, bridges, tunnels, vehicles used on public highways, and aircraft are not insured under fire and allied lines contracts. These types of property are covered under ocean or inland marine policies, automobile policies, or aviation contracts, examined in other chapters of CPCU 3 and 4.

Money, securities, and valuable papers and records are generally not covered by fire and allied lines policies or are covered on a very limited basis. Such property is better covered under crime or inland marine forms discussed later in this text.

Fire and allied lines insurance is the type of insurance most commonly used to insure buildings and their contents. Coverage may be provided under single-line policies or under a package policy such as the SMP. Package forms will be discussed more specifically in Chapters 14 and 15 of this text.

Perils Covered

Because fire and allied lines insurance has centered on buildings, the perils covered traditionally have been those that may cause damage to real property (buildings), such as fire, lightning, windstorm, hail, explosion, and riot. Conspicuous by their absence from this list are such perils as burglary, robbery, collision, and jettison that would primarily affect personal property.

Traditionally, fire and allied lines insurance has been written on a named perils basis. Many policies are still issued for fire and extended coverage. However, in recent times there has been an expansion to make available a broad list of named perils or even "all-risks" protection on buildings and contents. ("All-risks" coverage protects against all direct physical losses except those excluded in the policy.)

In summary, fire and allied lines insurance *generally* applies to buildings at a fixed location and property inside those buildings. Insurance has traditionally been written on a named perils basis, but broader coverage including "all-risks" coverage is now frequently available on a fire and allied lines form.

Standardization

Apart from the material in the declarations, most fire and allied lines insurance policies are composed entirely of standardized wording. Even the information typed in the declarations tends to consist of certain standard phrases. All forms published by the Insurance Services Office are standardized, including the general property form (discussed later in this chapter), the gross earnings business interruption form (discussed in Chapter 5), and others.

In the material that follows, the basic nature of standardized policies, forms, and endorsements in fire and allied lines insurance policies is analyzed.

STRUCTURE OF FIRE AND ALLIED LINES INSURANCE CONTRACTS

The structure of insurance contracts in general was extensively discussed in CPCU 1, Chapter 11. As noted there, the content of an insurance policy can be broken down into five categories—declarations, insuring agreement(s), exclusions, conditions, and miscellaneous provisions. Many policies are assembled by expanding some foundation document through the addition of one or more other documents, called "forms." Such an approach is usually taken in fire and allied lines insurance.

The standard fire policy (discussed in detail in CPCU 1, Chapter 15) is the foundation document for most fire and allied lines insurance policies. The New York standard fire policy is the one most commonly in use although slight variations exist in some territories.

The declarations of the standard fire policy individualize the policy by describing the person(s) insured, the mailing address, the property insured—location, construction, type of roof, occupancy—limits of coverage, the inception and termination dates, added interests (e.g., mortgagee), and the policy number. The declarations also show the premium applicable for each of the types of perils covered (e.g., fire, extended coverage, vandalism and malicious mischief, and so forth).

The standard fire policy is not a complete insurance contract by itself, but requires the addition of one or more forms to make it complete. The declarations contain the words: "Subject to form No(s). Attached Hereto." When the policy is issued, the person preparing the policy enters in the space following these words the numbers and edition dates of each form attached to the standard fire policy. The addition of one or more forms makes it a complete contract of insurance. (The edition date is the publication date of the form in use. Forms are frequently modified, and different edition dates of the same form number may contain some variances in coverage.)

A variety of forms may be attached to the standard fire policy, singly or in combination. The purpose of the form or forms is to provide a complete description of the subject matter(s) of insurance—the property, income and expense, or liability loss(es) covered, and the perils insured against.

Various forms may be used singly or in combination to provide the combination of coverages required by a given firm. Each of these forms contains a number of clauses which, together, form a contract of insurance.

Forms Describing Insured Subject Matter

Figure 3-1 depicts the three major classes of subject matter forms or endorsements that can be attached to the standard fire policy. The three classes are forms that describe the property covered, forms that describe the income and expense losses covered, and forms providing for liability coverage. It should be noted that these are not completely independent categories. A single form may provide coverage for more than one class of subject matter. Nonetheless, it is true that there are generally separate forms for covering direct property losses (e.g., buildings and contents), for covering income and expense losses (e.g., business interruption, rent, extra expense), and for liability (e.g., sprinkler leakage liability, fire liability).

Figure 3-1
Subject Matter of Fire and Allied Lines Insurance

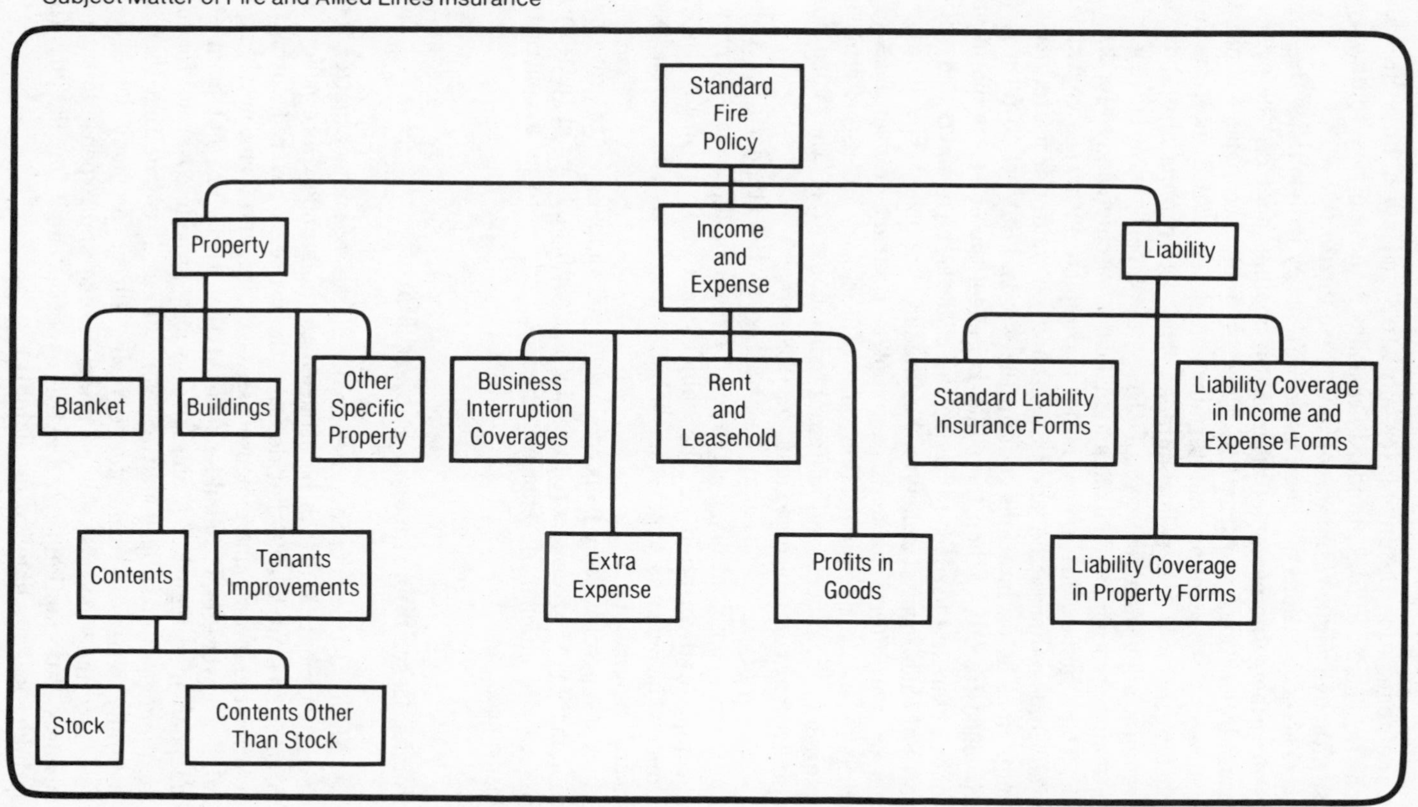

Property Damage Forms The various types of property identified in property coverage forms are shown on the left side of Figure 3-1. Coverage may be blanket, providing coverage on several types of property within a single insuring agreement. Or, coverage may be specific with a separate amount of insurance applying to each type of property—coverage applicable to one type cannot be used for losses to other kinds of property. Buildings may be one specific category. Covered personal property may then be blanketed together as "contents," or "personal property of the insured," or further subdivided. The common subdivisions are "stock" (e.g., goods held for sale and raw materials and stock in process, plus certain other property as defined in the forms), and "other contents" (e.g., machinery, furnishings, equipment, materials, supplies, and other personal property as defined in the forms). Another standard property category is "tenant's interest in improvements and betterments." Although this is a *use* interest and therefore an income or expense exposure, it is treated as a property exposure. Additional property subdivisions also appear in some standard forms and, of course, are possible with the use of endorsements.

Income and Expense Forms The general categories of income and expense forms are depicted in the center of Figure 3-1. This category includes "business interruption" forms that are used to cover loss of income due to physical damage from an insured peril to a concern's facilities (or the facilities of others, depending on the form used). "Extra expense" forms are used to cover costs that increase because an insured peril has damaged property. "Rent and leasehold" forms deal with losses that occur because of loss of use of real property. The "profits in goods" entry refers to those forms and clauses that cover the seller's markup in finished goods. When finished goods are destroyed, the manufacturer loses that potential profit.

Liability Forms The various types of liability forms are shown on the right-hand side of Figure 3-1. Although most liability insurance protection is provided by regular liability insurance, some liability for damage to property—such as fire liability insurance—can be provided in fire and allied lines forms.

Forms Identifying Perils Covered

All the types of forms described in Figure 3-1 provide coverage contingent on damage by an insured peril. Unless such a peril causes the loss, there is no coverage. The way in which forms describing perils covered can be arranged is given in Figure 3-2. The content of such forms is discussed in detail in Chapter 4 of this text, but the perils added

Figure 3-2
Perils Forms

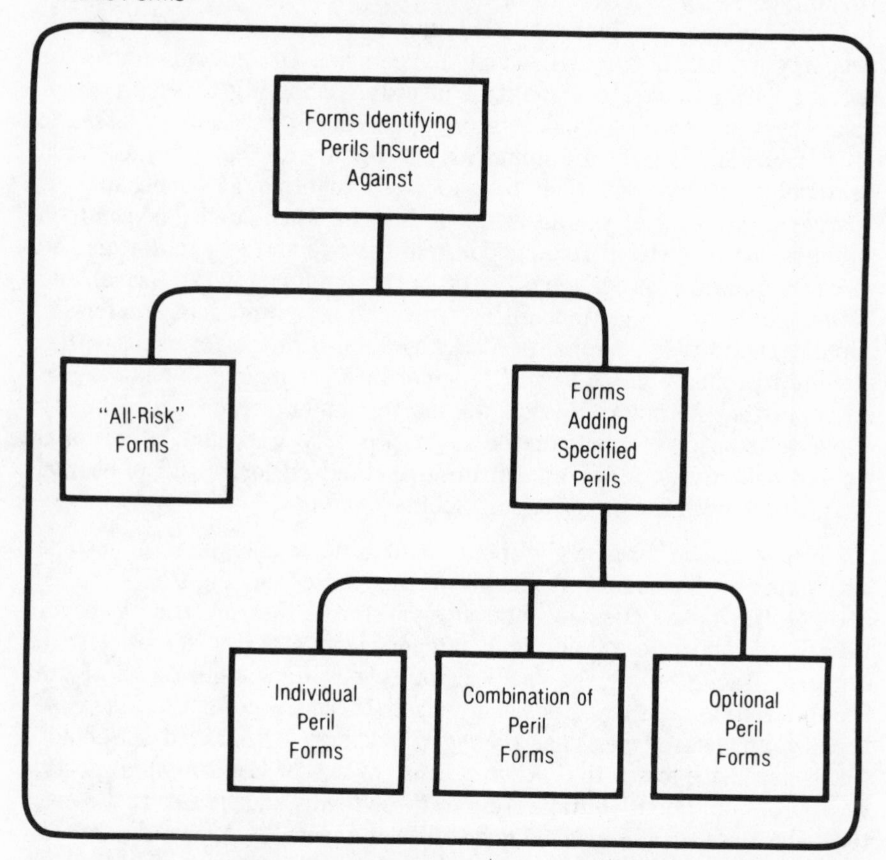

can range from just one specified peril to "all-risks" protection. In between, the insured can add a package of a combination of perils like the extended coverage endorsement or a selection from a standard set, as with the optional perils endorsement.

Subject Matter and Perils Forms Combined

Figure 3-3 shows how the previous figures relate to each other. On the left side of Figure 3-3 are the types of insured subjects: property, income and expense, and liability. All of these forms specify *what property* must be damaged in order for the insurance contract to cover the loss. To these documents are added forms that describe the perils insured against. Together with the declarations and the standard fire policy, they tell what property is insured, which perils are insured

Figure 3-3
Relationship Between Subject Matter and Perils Forms

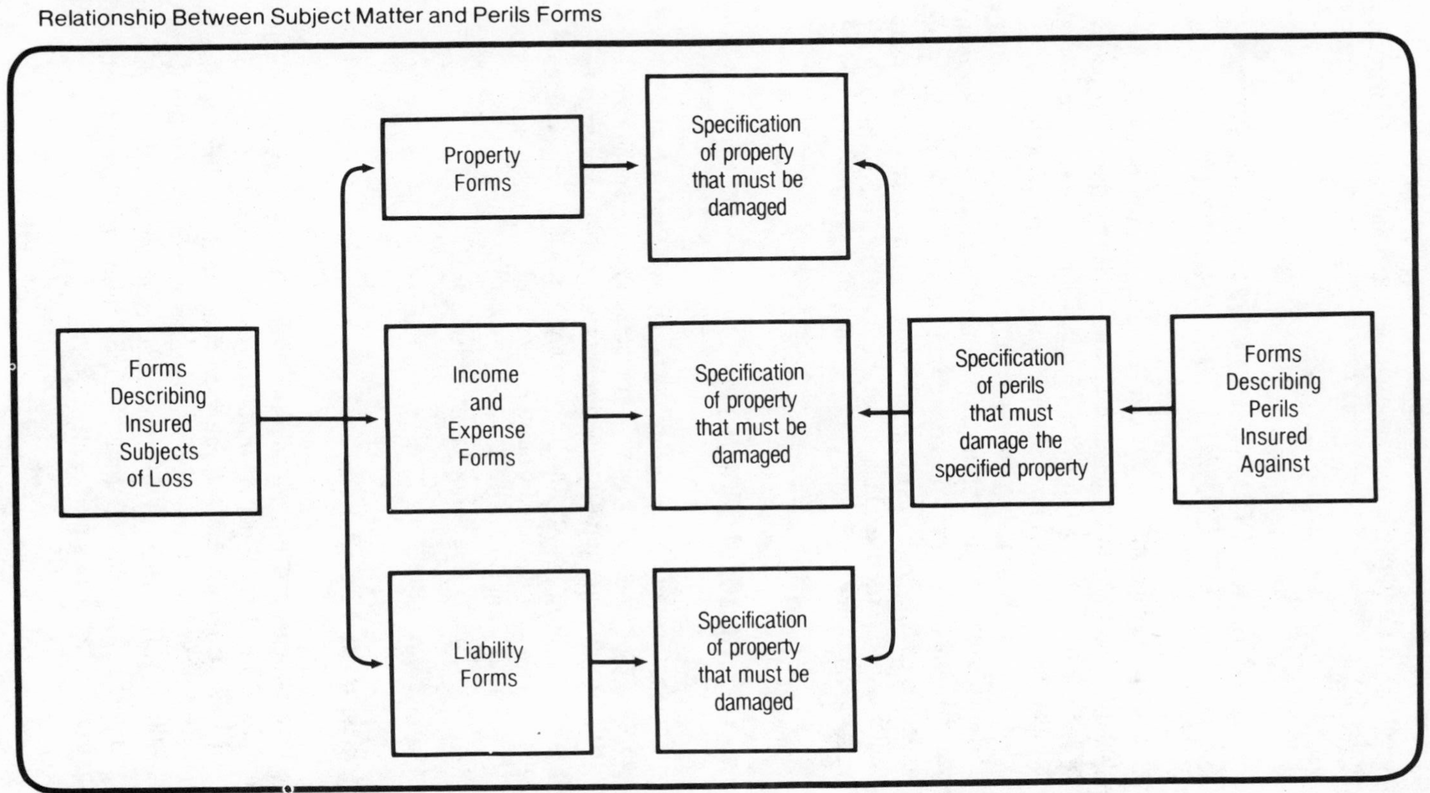

against, and under what circumstances. One form which describes the subject matter and perils may be used, or a combination of forms may be required.

STANDARD FIRE AND ALLIED LINES FORMS FOR COMMERCIAL PROPERTY

The discussion in this portion of the chapter deals briefly with foundation documents such as the New York standard fire policy, the Texas standard policy, and other standard fire policies. There is also a brief discussion of allied lines policies other than fire policies.

All discussion of policy forms is subject to territorial and company variations. Forms change from time to time and, at any given moment, more than one edition of the same form may be in use. In applying the discussions of this text to any specific case, it is necessary to consult the specific form(s) in use. This must be kept in mind throughout the discussion on forms.

New York Standard Fire Policy

The most common fire policy in the United States is the New York standard fire policy. The New York standard fire policy contains an insuring agreement, an assignment clause, and 165 numbered lines that describe the coverage of the fire policy, subject to provisions in the forms attached to it. Since Chapter 15 of CPCU 1 discusses this policy, no further explanation will be given here. However, there are some minor variations to this policy in several states.

Variations in Fire Policies

Fire policies are not all identical, as illustrated by the following examples. The Oregon policy omits the countersignature provision; the North Dakota policy has a three-year time limit for suits rather than twelve months; the Maine version requires ten day's written notice of cancellation rather than five days; Kansas requires that return premium be tendered with cancellation. Policies used in Massachusetts and Minnesota differ more significantly.

Texas Fire Policy

The policy used in Texas differs enough to deserve a more detailed review. Unlike the New York policy, it does not always require the addition of forms to make it complete. The extended coverage perils are listed in the policy itself, and when the proper premium is paid and so indicated on the policy for these additional perils, coverage is in force. Also, the Texas policy defines the terms "building" and "contents," so no separate form is required to define these subject matters of insurance.

Actually, through the declaration page one can delete coverage provided in the standard contract. If an amount of insurance is not placed next to a type of property listed in the declarations page, no protection is afforded even though the conditions for that coverage are included in the policy language. For example, if the declarations page does not indicate that coverage is provided on improvements and betterments, all the information concerning them inside the policy is irrelevant to that particular contract.

The Texas policy is a valued policy. In the event of total loss to the insured structure, the insurer must pay the insured the face value of the policy. (Some other states have similar requirements by law, but they do not appear in the contract.) Another difference is a two-year statute of limitations on claims.

From this short discussion of the Texas policy, it is apparent that its structure is quite different from the New York standard fire policy, but the differences in coverage are less substantial. However, any generalization in this course based on the New York standard fire policy must be checked against the Texas form whenever Texas coverage is contemplated.

Standard Allied Lines Forms

Aside from different types of standard fire policies, there are some similar policies for other perils. Included among these policies are rain and crop damage policies, and earthquake policies.

There are at least three other coverages that can be issued without underlying fire insurance. Sprinkler leakage, windstorm and hail, and the optional perils endorsements may be issued and placed with a fire policy without purchase of insurance against the peril of fire. In this situation, the fire policy is used as an instrument to provide the declarations page and the certain contract provisions, but the space indicating the amount of fire insurance is left blank. No fire coverage then attaches. The optional perils form makes the situation explicit by stating: "Insurance under this endorsement attaches only to those items specially described in the form attached to this policy for which a specific amount is shown and insurance under this endorsement is provided against only those perils listed below for which option(s) a specific premium charge is indicated." The endorsement further states that all conditions of the fire policy apply except as otherwise provided in the endorsement.

TYPICAL PROPERTY FORMS AS ILLUSTRATED BY THE GENERAL PROPERTY FORM FGP-1

The general property form illustrates the approaches most commonly taken to provide fire and allied lines coverage. Discussion in this text will be based on the June, 1975 edition of the general property form (FGP-1) published by the Insurance Services Office. The material in this section will be most easily understood if the reader keeps a copy of the policy at hand.

The discussion will first deal with the categories of property covered by the policy—owned real property, owned personal property, and nonowned property. Following this, the discussion deals with locations at which property is covered, rights of insureds, special provisions relating to perils, provisions dealing with conditions or hazards, clauses defining the amount of covered loss, and other clauses. Perils will be discussed in detail in Chapter 4. Likewise, this analysis of the general property form does not deal extensively with valuation of insured property. Methods of handling amounts of insurance are discussed in the last major section of the chapter, where the approach of the general property form is compared with other approaches to value.

This section of the chapter analyzes the specifics of coverage in typical fire and allied lines property damage forms. The general property form is widely used and has replaced such forms as the building and contents, lumberyard, whiskey, wool, apartment building, automobile garage, school, and coal mining plant forms. Because of its wide use and generality, this form is particularly useful for illustrating the common content of fire and allied lines property forms. It is not the only way to handle the situation, but it is a common way.

Of course, the general property form varies slightly from territory to territory, so the discussion will occasionally involve more than just one version of the form. This approach provides a better understanding of possible ways to provide coverage.

Coinsurance Clause

The general property form (FGP-1), like most property forms, has a coinsurance clause. Although discussed in detail in CPCU 1, the clause will briefly be reviewed here because it is so fundamental to the coverages discussed shortly.

The coinsurance clause reads:

> This company shall not be liable for a greater proportion of any loss to the property covered than the amount of insurance under this policy for such property bears to the amount produced by multiplying the actual cash value of such property at the time of the loss by the coinsurance percentage applicable (specified on the first page of this policy, or by endorsement).

Eighty, ninety, or one hundred percent coinsurance is commonly used. In exchange for a reduced rate, the insured agrees to carry insurance to the specified percentage of the actual cash value of the building. If the specified amount of insurance is not carried, the loss is adjusted according to the formula:

$$\frac{\text{Amount of insurance carried}}{\text{Amount of insurance required}} \times \text{Loss} = \begin{array}{c}\text{Amount paid by insurance} \\ \text{(never more than policy} \\ \text{limits or amount of loss)}\end{array}$$

The "amount of insurance required" in the above formula can be determined by multiplying the actual cash value of the insured property (at the time of the loss) by the coinsurance percentage. The effect of this clause is to penalize an insured who does not insure to the specified percentage of value, the penalty being proportional to the amount of underinsurance. Even if insurance meets the requirements of an 80 or 90 percent coinsurance clause, the amount paid following a loss will never exceed policy limits. It might be misleading to say that a firm with all the insurance required by the coinsurance clause is insured in full. The insurance might still not be sufficient to pay for a *total* loss.

Categorization of Property

As discussed in Chapter 1 of this text, the two basic categories of property are (1) real property, and (2) personal property. Real property is generally identified as land, buildings, and other improvements attached to the land. Personal property is commonly more mobile and not so attached to land or buildings.

Three categories of property covered—owned real property, owned personal property, and nonowned property—will be discussed in the following section.

Three similar categories of property are described on form FGP-1—building(s), personal property of the insured, and personal property of others. The policy notes that "insurance applies only to item(s) specifically described in this policy for which an amount of insurance is shown. . . ." Therefore, coverage in any of these categories applies only if an amount of insurance for that category is indicated in the declarations. The owner of a building rented to others might purchase coverage only for the building. A tenant might cover only personal property of the insured, or might also desire coverage on the personal property of others. An owner-occupant might purchase coverage in all three categories.

Owned Real Property

The description in the declarations includes the building's principal construction characteristics and the nature of its occupancy. If these are materially wrong, the coverage *may* be voidable, since coverage applies only to items specifically described.

Building(s) FGP-1 defines "building(s)" as follows:

> Building(s) or structure(s) shall include attached additions and extensions; fixtures, machinery and equipment constituting a permanent part of and pertaining to the service of the building; yard fixtures; personal property of the named Insured used for the maintenance or service of the described building(s), including fire extinguishing apparatus, outdoor furniture, floor coverings and appliances for refrigerating, ventilating, cooking, dishwashing and laundering (but not including other personal property in apartments or rooms furnished by the named Insured as landlord); all while at the described locations.

Besides the building and attachments, the building coverage provisions include some additional property. Stationary building service equipment and its detachable parts are included in the definition of building. So this definition would include fixed motion picture projection machines in movie theaters, refrigeration equipment in cold storage and ice houses, and fixed seats and permanently installed pipe organs in auditoriums. These last items reflect incorporation of parts of the old school and church forms into the general property form. The influence of the old apartment building form can be seen in the inclusion of some of the furnishings of an apartment under the building coverage. These include floor coverings and refrigerating, ventilating, cooking, dishwashing, and laundering equipment owned by the landlord.

The building(s) coverage section also provides protection for personal property used to service the building. Property representative of this category includes window washing, floor cleaning, and lawn mowing equipment. Coverage for such service equipment applies while that property is located on the described premises. In older forms this protection was limited to 1 percent of the building coverage: if the buildings were insured for $500,000, then $5,000 of it could be applied (by the insured) to building service equipment. In newer forms this limitation is eliminated, and yard fixtures (flagpoles, for example) are also added to the building coverage. Some property is excluded unless the items are specifically listed in the declarations. Included in this category are outdoor signs, whether or not they are attached to a building. Likewise, outdoor swimming pools; fences, piers, wharves, and docks; beach or diving platforms or appurtenances; retaining walls not constituting a part of buildings; and walks, roadways, and other paved surfaces are similarly excluded.

Excavations, Foundations, Pilings When the coverage purchased contains a coinsurance agreement, underground property and the cost of excavations are excluded from coverage:

> THIS POLICY DOES NOT COVER THE FOLLOWING PROPERTY WHEN SECTION IV—COINSURANCE CLAUSE APPLIES, UNLESS ADDED BY ENDORSEMENT:
>
> 1. Cost of excavations, grading or filling;
>
> 2. Foundations of buildings, machinery, boilers or engines which foundations are below the undersurface of the lowest basement floor, or where there is no basement, below the surface of the ground;
>
> 3. Pilings, piers, pipes, flues and drains which are underground;
>
> 4. Pilings which are below the low water mark.

The excluded property is seldom damaged by fire. Even when a building is a total loss, the excavation (the hole for the basement), underground pipes, and so forth are seldom damaged. If these items were covered, the insured would have to include their value in determining the amount of insurance to be carried to meet coinsurance requirements. Thus, the insured would be required to purchase insurance against an exposure with a very low probability of loss. To prevent this, the above property is excluded from coverage and is not included in determining values to meet coinsurance requirements. It should be noted, however, that while the probability of loss to this property is extremely low, such property is not totally immune from damages, as from an explosion. Coverage can be added by endorsement.

To determine just how significant the removal of this property from coverage is, one can investigate building cost data. In the *Stevens Valuation Quarterly*, information is given on the costs of underground foundations and excavations. The figures in Table 3-1 reflect some of that data. Examination of Table 3-1 shows that as much as 11.1 percent

Table 3-1

Percentage Cost of Construction of a Building Due to Excavations and Below Surface Foundations*

	High	Low
Excavations	5.0%	1.0%
Foundations		
Below Ground	6.1	2.4
Total	11.1%	3.4%

*Reprinted with permission from *Marshall Valuation Service* (Los Angeles: Marshall and Swift Publication Co., 1976), Fire Insurance Exclusion Section.

of the cost of a building can be due to the cost of excavation and subbasement foundations. This figure represents a substantial portion of the cost of a structure, and the insured needs to realize this item is not covered. If the building were totally destroyed and new excavation work and new foundations had to be completed, the insured would have to provide the extra funds. Since this provision may be removed by endorsement, one needs to determine if the exposure is serious. When the exclusion is removed, the amount of insurance purchased should reflect the increased coverage.

Architects' Fees One of the hidden costs of a building is the cost of architectural plans. Under some older property forms, architects' fees were excluded. This exclusion is not present in form FGP-1, so architects' fees are covered. When the building value is determined on the basis of an appraisal, some appraisals include architects' fees as a separate item. Their cost should be considered in determining the value of the building to be insured.

Trees, Shrubs, and Plants Trees, shrubs, and plants fall into the general definition of real property, but are not included in the definition of building(s). Such items receive differing treatment in various property forms in use.

In form FGP-1 growing crops and lawns are specifically excluded. Outdoor trees, shrubs, and plants are also specifically excluded from the broad coverage of the policy, but limited coverage is provided as an extension of coverage. (Trees, shrubs, and plants held for sale or sold but not delivered are covered in full.)

The effect of this treatment is that outdoor trees are *not* covered for damage by windstorm or hail, vehicle damage, smoke, or vandalism. Such damage would normally result in high frequency, low severity losses best handled by noninsurance techniques. Where loss occurs due to a covered peril, coverage is limited to a nominal amount.

In addition to the preceding limitations, another condition applies to the coverage: for the protection to be valid, there must be an 80 percent or higher coinsurance clause. Furthermore, this extension of coverage to trees, shrubs, and plants does not add anything to the total amount of insurance. If the limits are used up by the damage to other property, the extension adds nothing. Thus, for the extra coverage to be useful, there must be adequate insurance relative to exposed value.

Insureds needing more extensive coverage on landscaping can purchase a separate amount of insurance specifically applying to such property.

Owned Personal Property

Coverage for owned personal property can be included in a variety of ways. No one method can be considered the most common. Two frequently used methods will be discussed.

In the older of the two methods, a building's contents are separated into two categories: stock, and contents other than stock. A newer practice is to combine both categories as contents or as personal property of the insured. The latter approach is taken in FGP-1. The form describes personal property of the insured as follows:

> Personal property of the Insured means only business personal property, owned by the named Insured usual to the occupancy of the named Insured, including bullion, manuscripts, furniture, fixtures, equipment and supplies, not otherwise covered under this policy. . . .

Such a broad definition is best examined in the light of what it does *not* cover, as provided elsewhere in the policy. Some types of personal property are accorded special treatment in common standard forms. Coverage is either restricted or eliminated for such items.

Money and securities are excluded by the standard fire policy to which the form is attached. A separate exclusion is not necessary in the general property forms.

Motor vehicles, aircraft, and watercraft are subject to exclusions in most forms. Where significant off-premises exposures exist, coverage should be purchased elsewhere. The exclusions, however, are not usually so broad as to exclude all coverage for these classes of personal property.

In form FGP-1, aircraft are excluded. "Watercraft, including motors, equipment and accessories (except rowboats and canoes while out of water and on the described premises)" are also excluded, unless such watercraft is held for sale or sold but not delivered, and is not afloat. Personal property while waterborne also is excluded.

The "held for sale . . ." exclusion to the exclusion, like that for trees, shrubs, and plants, provides full coverage for a boat manufacturing or selling operation, where the loss exposure is similar to that of other contents. Coverage, however, is excluded in other circumstances.

"Vehicles designed for use on public thoroughfares" are also excluded, although coverage may be added by describing such vehicles on the policy declarations, or by endorsing coverage to the policy. There is no exception for this class of property when it is held for sale.

Animals and pets are specifically excluded in the general property form. As with trees and boats, the exclusion applies only to animals not held for sale.

Valuable papers and records coverage was quite limited under the building and contents form and the old general property form. Books of account, abstracts, drawings, card index systems, and other records (except electronic data processing records) were insured, but only for the cost of blank materials and the cost incurred to transcribe such record. Electronic data processing records were covered only for the cost of blank cards, tapes, and discs. Thus, the cost of redeveloping the information and the loss suffered because the information could not be redeveloped were not covered.

The new form FGP-1 provides similar treatment. However, an extension of coverage adds a small amount of true valuable papers insurance: 5 percent of the personal property limit, but not to exceed $500, may be used to cover the cost of research and other expenses to restore damaged records. However, this protection applies only for the named perils covered under the fire and allied lines form. The amount of coverage provided here will only meet incidental needs; it is not intended to cover valuable papers losses of any real significance. If a serious loss exposure exists, regular "all-risks" valuable papers coverage or a form specifically for electronic data processing should be purchased. These forms are discussed in later chapters of this text.

Nonowned Property

The insured may have an insurable interest in property of others (1) because of right or privilege to use the property, (2) because of a lien or other claim for payment, (3) because of possible liability for damage to the property, and (4) because damage to the property may mean loss of goodwill. More than one of these interests may be present in a particular piece of property. For example, with respect to a piece of borrowed equipment, damage to the equipment may cause suspension of operations until a replacement is obtained (class 1); the borrower will generally have a legal obligation to reimburse the owner for many types of damage (class 3); and, in event of other types of damage, the borrower may feel that continued good relations with the owner require that damage should be paid for even in the absence of an enforceable legal obligation (class 4). Another example is a machine shop that has customers' equipment in for repair. Again, there will generally be some situations in which there is legal liability for damage to the equipment, and a potential loss of goodwill in other damage. In addition, the machine shop is unlikely to be able to collect for labor and materials already expended in repairing the equipment if it is lost or damaged before delivery back to the customer, a class 2 type of exposure.

Two types of nonowned property are covered in form FGP-1—tenant's improvements and betterments (which are real property) and personal property of others.

Tenant's Interest in Improvements and Betterments Special coverage provisions are used to protect a tenant's interest in improvements which have been added by the tenant to the landlord's building. In form FGP-1, this coverage is included whenever coverage on personal property of the insured is provided. The description of property covered under personal property of the insured reads:

> This coverage shall also include Tenant's Improvements and Betterments when not otherwise specifically covered. Tenant's Improvements and Betterments means the named Insured's use interest in fixtures, alterations, installations or additions comprising a part of the buildings occupied but not owned by the named Insured and made or acquired at the expense of the named Insured exclusive of rent paid by the named Insured, but which are not legally subject to removal by the named Insured.

This description does not include repairs or maintenance, such as painting the inside or the outside of the premises. An improvement or betterment generally changes the building and enhances its value. Modifications such as a new store front, decorations, partitions, acoustical insulation, elevators, floor coverings, and air conditioning systems are illustrations of improvements and betterments.

Often a question arises as to whether an item is a trade fixture or an improvement. Trade fixtures, characterized by the right (or obligation) of the tenant to remove them when the premises are vacated (or before), may include counters, machinery, and appliances. Whether an item is a trade fixture cannot always be told by looking at it, not even by examining the apparent firmness of its attachment to the structure. Many cases are determined by trade customs. Thus, walk-in freezers and refrigerators and the stage machinery in a theater, although completely built in and necessarily firmly attached to the structure, are, by custom, trade fixtures and not building improvements.

When a tenant buys improvements and betterments coverage, what is covered thereunder is subject to general legal interpretation as to which installations constitute improvements to the landlord's building and which remain the tenant's trade fixtures.

A landlord's interest in any improvements is included, of course, under the landlord's coverage on the building. The amount of building insurance carried by the landlord, therefore, should reflect the value tenants have added to the structure.

Since landlord and tenant have simultaneous but separate insurable interests in the same property, each may buy insurance. Such coexistent insurance on separate interests is enforceable; the landlord can collect for the loss of owned property, and the tenant can collect on the basis of loss of use of the property. Paying for such separate insurance contracts on the same property can be inefficient. Other solutions are available.

One technique is for the owner and tenant to be named as insureds in a single policy. Underwriters generally do not favor this arrangement because it negates the possibility of subrogation against either of the parties when that party's negligence causes the loss. The landlord's insurer, for example, may collect from the tenant when the latter has legal responsibility for the insured loss and is *not* someone to whom the landlord's insurer has promised protection.

Owners and tenants do not always favor the arrangement either. One reason is that the collectibility of the insurance can then be jeopardized by acts of either party. The contracts provide for suspension of coverage upon an increase of hazard "within the knowledge or control of the insured." And contracts are voidable in event of fraud by an insured. When owner and tenant are jointly insured, acts of one may affect the coverage of the other; this does not usually happen with separate contracts.

Another approach is for the lease to oblige one party to make repairs in the event of damage. Then the other party is protected to the extent the obligor can fulfill his or her obligation. A common arrangement is to provide assurance of financing by requiring the obligor to carry adequate insurance on the property. Then one premium pays for protection for both parties. Of course, there is still the problem that the coverage may be abrogated by acts or omissions by the insured party.

The most common arrangement is for the landlord to carry insurance on the building and the tenant to insure the improvements. This is why some standard forms, like form FGP-1, provide automatic coverage on a tenant's interest in improvements when the tenant buys coverage on contents. For coverage beyond any automatic protection and for coverage in the many other forms with no automatic extension, a standard improvements and betterments coverage form can be used.

The major feature of this coverage deals with how the amount of insured loss is measured. There are three measures, depending on events after the loss. These measures are outlined in Section VIII of FGP-1 dealing with valuation. When the owner replaces the improvements without charge to the tenant, the tenant's insurance pays nothing. The tenant has had no loss. When the tenant pays for restoration, the improvements and betterments coverage pays the actual cash value of the improvements just as though the tenant owned the improvements. When the improvements are not replaced, payment is based on unamortized cost. For example, suppose improvements costing $50,000 were installed June 1, 1972. On June 1, 1977, the improvements are destroyed and not replaced. At the time of the loss, the tenant's lease ran to June 1, 1987. The tenant's right to use the improvements thus had a known life of fifteen years (1972 to 1987) at the time of installation. Over this period, the tenant had the opportunity to recover the $50,000 cost. However, at the time of the loss, five of the fifteen years, or one-third of this known life had been used up. Therefore, the insurer pays two-thirds of the original $50,000 or $33,333 to cover the lost portion of the total time the tenant had in which to recover the original investment. Note the following points about this third method:

1. The dollar figure used as the basis is *original* cost, including necessary cost to prepare the premises before the improvements could be installed. Neither actual cash value nor replacement cost is relevant.
2. The only lease whose expiration date is considered is the one in effect at time of loss. Previous leases (including the one in force when the improvements were installed, if different from the one at time of loss) are irrelevant.
3. The relevant lease need not be in writing. But if it is oral, the insured may have trouble providing satisfactory proof as to its expiration date.

Personal Property in Insured's Custody. The insured's interest in property of others because of resources expended in repairing or otherwise servicing it, is specifically covered in many standard forms. This interest is also covered under coverage B—Personal Property of the Insured, which includes "the named Insured's interest in personal property owned by others to the extent of the value of labor, materials and charges furnished, performed or incurred by the named Insured...." Different forms treat this exposure differently.

The amount of insurance automatically provided for personal property of others is strictly limited. A limit equal to 2 percent of the amount of insurance on owned personal property, but not to exceed $2,000, is common. This is the approach taken in form FGP-1 under the first extension of coverage.

There is no coverage at all unless the relevant coverage on owned property is subject to 80 percent or higher coinsurance. However, the covered property of others is not included in computing coinsurance requirements, and the amount provided for property of others is in addition to the amount of coverage purchased on owned property.

Insureds who need more than the automatic amount of coverage on property of others may purchase coverage C—Personal Property of Others. The coverage must be indicated in the declarations and an amount of insurance and premium must be shown.

Locations at Which Property Is Covered

As noted, fire and allied lines insurance applies almost exclusively to fixed or specified locations. Standard policies contain explicit specifications of the locations covered. Forms, however, often do extend small amounts of coverage elsewhere.

Building(s) There are only a few exceptions to the requirement that a building, to be insured, must be individually specified in the policy. In some specialized standard forms (or in a manuscript endorsement), all the buildings at a set of premises may be covered without individual identification.

In form FGP-1, newly acquired buildings at different locations, as well as newly constructed buildings at the designated location, are insured under an extension of coverage. The newly acquired buildings must be in the territorial limits of the policy and occupancy must be for either the same purposes as stated in the declarations or for a warehouse. Coverage is limited to 10 percent of the indicated building coverage up to a maximum of $25,000 and terminates after thirty days. This thirty-day period should give the insured enough time to purchase specific insurance on the new location. After that time has elapsed, there is no more protection for it unless the policy limit has been increased to include the values and the declarations have been modified to include the new building.

In many standard forms, including the general property form, insured attachments to buildings (such as awnings and storm windows) are covered even while removed from the building: they are covered while stored in any building on the designated premises; they also are covered at premises not owned or occupied by the insured when there to be cleaned or repaired. The off-premises coverage applies only when the building insurance has a coinsurance requirement of 80 percent or more and is limited in amount. In form FGP-1, coverage is limited to 2 percent of the amount of insurance on the building and personal property of the insured, or $5,000, whichever is the smaller.

Personal Property In form FGP-1, personal property is insured while in a described building, while in the open (or within a vehicle) within 100 feet of the described premises. Elsewhere, personal property *other than* stock or merchandise is covered by the same extension of coverage previously described for building attachments: the policy must have an 80 percent or higher coinsurance clause; the property must have been moved for cleaning, repair, reconstruction, or restoration; and it must be at premises not owned or controlled by the named insured. Property is not covered while in transit.

Property belonging to persons other than the insured is covered only while in the custody of the named insured and only while on premises described in the policy.

Off-premises protection uniformly includes the provisions that (1) the coverage is excess over other applicable coverage, and (2) the extension shall "not directly or indirectly benefit any carrier or other bailee."

As was the case with location coverage for buildings, form FGP-1 provides coverage for personal property at newly acquired locations similar to that for buildings at such locations; again, this automatic coverage is for up to thirty days, and the property must be within the territorial limits of the policy. Excluded from coverage is property located at fairs and exhibitions. The policy does not provide automatic additional coverage for newly acquired property at the premises described in the policy. The off-premises coverage is limited to 10 percent of the personal property limit up to a maximum coverage of $10,000.

The basic way of specifying several locations in a single policy is to list each in the declarations, with a specific amount of insurance applying to each covered type of property at each location. In short, the coverage is the same as though a separate policy had been issued for each item.

For an insured with a large number of locations, this method is cumbersome and lacks flexibility. For such situations there are multiple location forms, discussed later.

Rights of Insureds

In fire and allied lines insurance there are two basic classes of insureds. One class consists of those who may enforce coverage for claims on their own initiative and in their own names. The other basic class consists of persons whose interests are protected only if the named insured chooses to apply the protection.

Insureds Who Can File Claims Two types of insureds may directly enforce claims for coverage under fire and allied lines insurance: named insureds (including their legal representatives) and named mortgagees for real property. Much of the detail regarding the rights of these types of insureds appears in CPCU 1. A few additional points appear here.

Named Insureds. Named insureds and their legal representatives may enforce the contract subject, of course, to their having fulfilled all policy conditions. The important point to be noted here is that when a policy condition has been violated by any one of the named insureds in a particular policy, that violation gives the insurer a defense against claims by any named insured in the same policy.

Named Mortgagees. Coverage of named mortgagees is not voided by acts of named insureds, subject to the following requirements:

1. If the named insured fails to pay the premium, the named mortgagee, when requested to make the payment, must then make it if the protection is to be continued. The named mortgagee is not required to pay the premium, but the policy can be canceled for nonpayment if the premium is not paid. Payment on request is a condition of coverage; it is not an obligation of the mortgagee.
2. A standard requirement is that "the mortgagee (or trustee) shall notify [the insurer] of any change of ownership or occupancy or increase of hazard which shall come to the knowledge of said mortgagee (or trustee) and, unless permitted by this policy, it shall be noted thereon. . . ."
3. In circumstances when the mortgagee has protection under the policy but the named insured does not, the insurer is subrogated to the mortgagee's rights under the mortgage. The rights are specified both in standard policies and in property insurance forms and are examined in detail in CPCU 1.
4. The mortgagee's right to file proof of loss (the key to enforcing payment) arises only when the insured fails to do so. The clause relating to the mortgagee's right to file proof of loss is found in the standard fire policy, not in form FGP-1. The two forms must be read together.

A special right of named mortgagees, as specified in FGP-1 and most standard forms that cover loss from damage to real property, is that mortgagees are entitled to ten days notice before cancellation by the insurer, compared to the usual five days notice required for named insureds.

Other Persons Insured Within the group of persons whose interests are protected only if the named insured chooses to enforce the protection there are two subclasses. As noted before, the property of some persons is protected solely at the option of the named insured. This is commonly the case under policy provisions that extend coverage to ownership interests in property not owned by the named insured. The named insured may collect for owned property without putting in a claim for nonowned property, or nonowned property in the insured's care also may be included. The owners of the property in the insured's care have no choice in the matter.

The second category of persons whose interests are protected only if the insured chooses to enforce a claim are those named as *loss payees* in a loss payable endorsement. Here the insurer agrees to pay the named insured and the named loss payee(s) "as their interest may appear." If the insured enforces a claim against the insurer, the loss payee is entitled to be named on the claim check. But if the insured chooses not to pursue the claim, the loss payee has no independent right to do so. And, of course, the loss payee cannot collect if the named insured cannot, if the named insured has violated policy conditions, for example.

A loss payable clause usually is attached to the policy at the request of a creditor who has a claim other than a real estate mortgage against specific property covered by the insurance. Chattel mortgages, conditional sales, and installment sales are common examples of such claims. However, whereas real estate mortgagees regularly require that they be named in insurance policies covering the property, other creditors seldom ask to be named in fire insurance policies. The difference in the enforceability of the protection afforded loss payees by fire and allied lines insurance is part of the reason for this difference in practice.

Most extensions of coverage to nonowned property do not apply when the named insured's interest in that property is otherwise specifically insured.

Most of the content of the general form with respect to insurance on the property of persons other than the named insured has already been described in the discussion regarding protection of the named insured's interest in nonowned personal property. As already noted, the named insured's goodwill interest is protected by applying some insurance to the ownership interest of others when the named insured wants this done.

In addition to the provisions previously detailed, form FGP-1 has another extension that allows a small amount of the personal property coverage to be applied to the personal effects of owners and employees of the insured organization. The limits are nominal: $100 per person, $500 aggregate per loss (not to exceed 5 percent of the amount of personal property coverage). Another important restriction is that this extension does not apply at all if the loss is covered by any other insurance.

Clauses that provide coverage for property away from the specified premises or for personal property of others regularly contain the provision that the protection shall not apply to bailees or carriers other than the named insured.

Special Provisions Relating to Perils

Fire and allied lines perils are discussed in the next chapter. However, included with property damage forms, such as form FGP-1, are a few clauses interpretive of certain terms in the basic fire policy.

Clauses Interpreting "Fire" Situations arise in which there is question as to what constitutes a fire with respect to fire insurance. Reference here is to situations other than the basic ones discussed in CPCU 1, involving the distinction between hostile and friendly fires. Such basic distinctions are not spelled out in the contracts; but have been read in by judicial decision. The interpretations to be discussed here are those that are written into the contracts in standardized forms.

Electrical Apparatus Clause. When electrical equipment or appliances suffer electrical damage, the common phrase is that they have "burned out." This phrase suggests loss by fire. Such damage, however, was not intended to be covered in fire insurance. To make this clear, standard forms, including FGP-1, regularly contain the electrical apparatus clause. It states that the insurer "shall not be liable for any loss resulting from any electrical injury or disturbance to electrical appliances, devices, fixtures, or wiring caused by electrical currents artificially generated unless fire ensues, and then this company shall be liable only for its proportion of loss caused by such ensuing fire." The term ensuing fire has been interpreted to mean a self-sustaining fire which continues after the electrical currents artificially generated have been interrupted. Damage to vacuum tubes, transistors, electronic equipment, or electrical machinery from a surge of artificially generated current is excluded. Damage from a "brown out" would also be excluded. Also excluded is damage from electrical arcing and flashovers between parts of wiring, appliances, or equipment, or between such items and grounded objects. Electrical damage caused by lightning, which is naturally generated current, is covered of course, since lightning is a covered peril.

Nuclear Energy. Most property and liability insurance policies all contain nuclear energy exclusions. FGP-1 contains the provision:

> The word 'fire' in this policy or endorsements attached hereto is not intended to and does not embrace nuclear reaction or nuclear radiation or radioactive contamination, all whether controlled or uncontrolled, and loss by nuclear reaction or nuclear radiation or radioactive contamination is not intended to be and is not insured against by this policy or said endorsements, whether such loss be direct or indirect, proximate or remote, or be in whole or in part caused by, contributed to, or aggravated by 'fire' or any other perils insured against by this policy or said endorsements....

However, as previously mentioned, damage by a fire caused by nuclear reaction, radiation, or radioactive contamination is covered in FGP-1 and most similar policies. Consequently, if a nuclear reactor should go out of control and cause a fire, the fire damage would be covered under most forms, although the damage caused by the nuclear reaction apart from the ensuing fire would not be covered. If a fire causes the release of radioactive particles, contamination damage from them is not covered.

Special forms of coverage are available to cover nuclear energy and radioactive contamination hazards. They are discussed in the next chapter.

Clauses Dealing with Consequential Losses Standard fire policies cover only direct loss. Unless coverage is amended by some form attached to the standard fire policy, indirect losses, such as consequential losses and net income losses are not covered. (Indirect losses are those caused by some direct damage and take place over a period of time.) Several clauses in the general property form (FGP-1) clarify this intent to exclude indirect loss.

Power Failure. The power failure clause provides that there will be no coverage for loss caused or resulting from interruption of power or other utility service unless (1) the failure results from physical damage to equipment situated on premises where the covered property is located, and (2) such damage is caused by a peril insured against.

If a fire on the premises of a large restaurant damages electrical lines or refrigeration equipment so that refrigerated food spoils, the owner will receive payment under fire insurance coverage for the damaged food. However, if fire elsewhere (such as at a utility's power station) causes the loss of refrigeration and consequent spoilage, there is no coverage.

Any special provisions contained in clauses insuring against the perils of riot or vandalism which apply to indirect losses supersede this general provision. It is common for riot and vandalism coverage provisions to exclude entirely loss caused by changes in temperature or humidity.

Ordinance or Laws. In many cities and some other jurisdictions there are laws regulating the types of building construction in some areas. Buildings already standing when such regulations are adopted are allowed to continue in use, but it is customary to provide that when a building that does not meet requirements is severely damaged, it may not be rebuilt except in conformity to requirements. Suppose such a building suffers damage equal to 75 percent of its value. Repair would not be permitted. The remainder of the old structure must be demolished and a new, conforming structure erected. Thus there is a consequential loss of the remaining 25 percent of the old building's value, plus the expense of demolishing the 25 percent left standing and removing its debris.

The policy contains a provision stating that the insurer will not be responsible "for loss occasioned directly or indirectly by enforcement of any local or state ordinance or law regulating the use, construction, repair, or demolition of property, unless such liability is otherwise specifically assumed by endorsement hereon."

Of course, this wording also excludes any increased cost for reconstruction or repair for features which are necessitated by construction regulations but which were not in the old building. Such features might include additional fire exits, for example, or installation of a roof, more resistive to fire. Standard endorsements to cover some of these consequential loss exposures are discussed in Chapter 4.

Provisions Dealing with Conditions or Hazards

The following analysis concerns those provisions in form FGP-1 that involve clauses which either require the insured to perform certain tasks to receive insurance payment or give the insured permission to conduct given activities without prejudice to the coverage. In either case, they serve the purpose of informing the insured as to what the insurer considers acceptable behavior with respect to the protection offered by its insurance contract.

Protective Safeguards Clause The purpose of this provision is to reinforce the "increase in hazard" provision in the standard fire policy and inform the insured of the consequences if certain conditions are altered. If protective safeguards described in an endorsement to the policy are not maintained, the insured faces suspension of coverage at each location where a variance takes place. If four locations are listed on the policy and only one location is in violation, then the other three still have full coverage. Insurance coverage at the location with the violation is suspended until the situation is corrected.

Permits and Use The next series of conditions of form FGP-1 deal with waivers and permits. These clauses either permit the insured to perform certain acts or waive standard fire policy provision restricting the insured's actions.

Additions, Alterations, and Repairs. This clause, like the preceding clause, protects the insured from possible adverse effects of the increase in hazard clause in the fire contract. Making repairs or alterations to a building introduces different hazards. Some are important, including any welding or roofing activity, repairing of electrical systems, and possibly spray painting.

Under the alterations and repairs provision, the insured is given permission to make additions, alterations, or repairs to the building. If the policy covers the building, it is extended automatically to cover the additions, alterations, or repairs, including materials and supplies on the premises for use in the additions, alterations, or repairs. If the policy covers contents, it also covers the contents in such additions. This automatic coverage will not respond if it duplicates any other insurance on the alterations, additions, or repairs.

While this clause authorizes alterations and repairs, it does not relieve the insured of any responsibilities discussed under the protective safeguards clause. Notice is still required of changes in detection and protection equipment. In the case of a structure protected by an automatic sprinkler system, if the change is a reconstruction or an enlargement, not only must notice be given but the policy may have to be modified with a special endorsement and an additional premium charge. The analysis of sprinkler leakage insurance in Chapter 4 will explain this process in detail. Finally, the alterations and repair clause does not relieve the insured of any obligations under the coinsurance clause.

Vacancy and Unoccupancy. The standard fire policy suspends coverage when a building is vacant or unoccupied for more than sixty consecutive days. This restriction is modified in form FGP-1—unoccupancy that is usual or incidental to the occupancy is permitted, but vacancy is limited to sixty days. This permission is highly important to a business such as a school, which is customarily unoccupied during the summer months. If vacancy beyond sixty days is contemplated, additional coverage must be obtained. Once again, the insurer wants to know of any increased hazard involved with insurance on a vacant building.

Subrogation. In standard fire policies, the insurance company can require the insured to assign to the insurer any right of recovery against third parties. This procedure is called subrogation and often occurs when the insured's property is damaged by a known negligent third party. The insured collects under the fire and allied lines policy, and the insurer subrogates against negligent third parties. Fire policies provide that the insured is not to do anything to prejudice the insurer's right of recovery.

However, the subrogation clause in form FGP-1 allows the insured to nullify the insurer's subrogation rights when such forfeiture is done in writing before the loss occurs. In many lease agreements and some other contracts, one party or the other gives up rights of recovery. Because of this provision in the property insurance contract, the right of the insured to collect on his or her insurance is not jeopardized by such a waiver.

Control of Property. In this clause the insurer restricts its right to deny recovery because of the breach of a condition. The provision states that, "This insurance shall not be prejudiced by any act or neglect of any person (other than the named insured) when such act or neglect is not within the control of the named Insured." This waiver is only fair, since it is not equitable to hold the insured responsible for events beyond the insured's control. This provision is especially important to a building owner who leases a building to others. The tenant or tenants have actual physical control over most of the building and it would be unfair to hold the owner responsible for their actions. A tenant could disconnect the sprinkler system in the morning and a fire could occur in the afternoon. Obviously, this type of situation is beyond the control of the owner. Also, when a tenant rents an entire building, the owner does not have as much contact with the premises. The owner is exercising little or no control and has little opportunity to inspect the premises.

Divisible Contract Clause. This provision treats the insured more favorably than does the standard fire policy with respect to any breaches of warranty. The provision states that breach of warranty or policy condition in one building does not affect the insured's rights of recovery in other buildings. Of course, if there is only one building insured under the contract, this clause has no effect and coverage is voided or suspended while the violation exists.

The provision is equitable since each building is separately rated. The premium is supposedly adequate, and there should be no reason for the insurer to deny coverage. No increase in hazard has occurred at buildings for which no warranty or policy condition has been breached. Furthermore, it gives the same treatment to multiple locations insured in a single policy as if they were insured in separate policies. Thus, the efficiency of a single rather than multiple contracts is not affected.

Clauses Defining Amount of Covered Loss

There are two basic types of limitation on the amount of covered loss. One type has to do with valuation—how covered loss is defined and measured (e.g., by decrease in actual cash value of property or by cost to repair or replace). The other type consists of special limitations in the policy that may prevent payment of the full amount of loss as determined by the first type of limit. Thus, a policy may provide that the amount of covered loss is determined by the reduction in the actual cash value of the insured property. But when loss so measured is, say, $80,000, and the amount of property insurance carried is only $70,000, the provision that the insurer will pay no more than the policy amount prevents full payment of the $80,000 loss. Standard property insurance forms contain provisions dealing with each type of limitation.

Debris Removal The cost of removing debris is an expense that often accompanies property damage. In some cases, this cost is substantial. The value of the real property that contains debris is diminished, of course, by the presence of that debris. It is arguable that the presence of debris increases the "actual cash value" loss suffered, at least by the real property. The extent of this effect is commonly measured by the cost of removing the debris. However, these arguments do not apply equally well to coverage on contents for a tenant, who may be the one who has to pay for removal of debris. Furthermore, adding the cost of debris removal to the direct damage loss may make a sum greater than the actual cash value of the property before the damage. But a contract that covers only "actual cash value" will not pay any amount in excess of pre-loss actual cash value.

The debris removal clause avoids the debate by specifically including cost of removal of debris as a subject of coverage and providing for its payment in addition to the loss in actual cash value. However, this provision is seldom of value to insureds who suffer serious damage, because they seldom buy enough insurance to cover debris removal cost in addition to direct loss from major physical damage.

An important limitation in the debris removal coverage is that the debris must be from covered property damaged by a peril insured against. Thus, the landlord's policy does not cover removal of a tenant's debris, and vice versa. One frequent effect of this limitation is that the cost of removing debris of trees or of neighbors' property left on the insured's premises by a windstorm is not covered.

The debris removal coverage does not affect action of any

coinsurance clause. The amount of insurance required to meet coinsurance requirements is still based on the value of the insured property, without regard to expense of debris removal. And the part of the loss that will be paid, including the portion of loss that is for debris removal expense, is still determined by the ratio of insurance carried to insurance required. For example, suppose the insured property has an actual cash value of $250,000. Let the direct damage loss be $52,000 and the debris removal cost be $4,000, and suppose further that there exist an 80 percent coinsurance clause and $125,000 of insurance. The ratio of insurance carried to insurance required is 125/200. Thus, 125/200 times the covered loss ($52,000 plus $4,000), or the amount of $35,000, will be paid.

The debris removal clause does not overcome the restrictions in the ordinance or law clause. That is, when undamaged property has to be removed because of construction ordinances, that cost is not covered.

Maintenance of Policy Limits A standard provision, called the loss clause, states that any loss suffered under the policy shall not reduce the amount of insurance available for subsequent losses. This clause has an interesting history. Years ago, a loss under a fire or allied lines policy reduced the coverage by a sum equal to the loss payment. The original amount of coverage was restored only upon payment of an additional premium. This possible extra expense could be insured against by means of an unearned premium endorsement, which cost a small amount. Then provisions were inserted in standard forms that provided that losses less than a specified amount did not reduce the policy face; gradually the specified amount was increased. This type of provision has been replaced by the present terms, under which payment of loss does not reduce the policy amount. This provision does not appear in all kinds of property insurance contracts, so that in some kinds of property insurance, payment of loss still reduces the amount of insurance available for subsequent losses.

Special Amount Limits Policies and forms contain a variety of clauses restricting claims payment to something less than the loss or the amount of insurance. Some of these, such as the pro-rata provision in standard fire policies and coinsurance clauses in forms, are discussed at length in CPCU 1. Many of the others have been mentioned earlier in this chapter in connection with discussions about coverage on property away from the specified premises and on property not owned by the insured. These and other special limits are such an important factor in selection of fire and allied lines insurance forms, with so many choices and so much interaction among the choices, that a major section later in the present chapter is devoted entirely to them.

Other Clauses

There remain three types of provisions to consider that do not fit into any of the categories that have been discussed. These three are the liberalization clause, the waiver of inventory clause, and the clauses concerning premium payment.

Liberalization Clause If the insurer adopts any changes in the form attached to the policy, and these changes include some:

> . . . by which this form of insurance could be extended or broadened without increased premium charge by endorsement or substitution of form, then such extended or broadened insurance shall inure to the benefit of the named Insured hereunder as though such endorsement or substitution of form had been made.

Without this clause, insureds would request their policies be reissued every time a favorable form change was introduced. Barring this, insureds might have less coverage under an old policy form than they could obtain for the same price under a newer form. This provision benefits both insured and insurer. The insured gets the improved coverage without the insurer's having to actually amend the written contract.

Waiver of Inventory In standard fire policies, the insured is required to furnish a complete inventory of the destroyed, damaged, and undamaged property, showing in detail quantities, costs, actual cash value, and amount of loss claimed. This can be a time-consuming and expensive obligation. The waiver of inventory clause, a part of the coinsurance clause, offers some relief. For relatively small claims, the requirement to provide an inventory on the *undamaged* goods is waived.

It should be noted that there are two conditions on the waiver. First, the loss must be less than $10,000 (or other specified amount); and second, it must *also* be less than 5 (or other stated) percent of the insured amount. With the figures given, on a $5,000 loss of property insured for $75,000, there would be no waiver since the 5 percent requirement has not been met. Likewise, a $15,000 loss on property insured for $500,000 would not have the inventory provision waived. Both conditions must exist if the waiver is to be granted.

The clause does not modify any of the contract's requirements concerning coinsurance. One reason for the inventory requirement is to determine compliance with coinsurance requirements. With coinsurance, the insurer needs to determine the actual cash value of all the insured property on hand at the time of the loss. For small losses, the insurer allows this determination to be made for undamaged goods by methods other than actual inventory. The cost of an inventory of undamaged goods might be disproportionately high for a small loss. To make the point clear, the clause specifically states, "Nothing herein shall be construed to waive the application of [the coinsurance] clause."

This concludes the present analysis of the general property form, FGP-1. Not every clause of the policy has yet been discussed. The significant clauses that remain will be discussed in the following section or in other chapters. As previously mentioned, the perils covered in this and other forms will be discussed in Chapter 4.

DIFFERENT METHODS OF HANDLING AMOUNTS OF INSURANCE

Thus far this chapter has discussed the most common approach to commercial fire and allied lines insurance. Where appropriate, a few variations of the common approach have been mentioned. The remaining sections of this chapter will deal with various other ways in which amounts of insurance can be handled. The methods to be discussed can be implemented by endorsement to the general property form or may be used on different forms covering commercial property.

One can arrange the amount of insurance on property in several ways. One of the reasons for special handling of the amount of insurance is the presence of fluctuating value in the property covered. Another one is multiplicity of locations. Both topics will be addressed in this analysis. The discussion is divided into two major sections: coverage under (1) basic property forms, and (2) alternatives to basic forms. The coverage in form FGP-1 provides a classic example of the basic approach.

The Basic Approach

The basic approach is rather inflexible and is designed for smaller concerns with stable property values at one or two locations. This review investigates the basic approach along six different lines in regard to policy limits: (1) stated amounts, (2) specific property, (3) special limits, (4) deductibles, (5) insurance to value, and (6) "other insurance." Then the amount of loss is analyzed along two further divisions: (1) actual cash value, and (2) insured's interest. Many of the ideas discussed here were introduced in CPCU 1 and consequently should be familiar. Much of the present discussion is intended only as a review.

Fixed Amounts In the basic general property form, the amount of coverage is stated on the declarations page. Coverage is for the stated number of dollars for the duration of the policy. When the insured needs to change the amount, an endorsement can be added to either increase or decrease the amount of insurance. This method is sufficient for those who have fairly stable amounts of insured property. Examples of such situations include a building to which no major alterations or additions are made and the contents of an office, which are likely to be fairly constant. Situations that are not compatible with this approach include a building under construction and the inventory of a seasonal business such as a toy store.

Specific Coverage Protection under the basic property forms is specific to a particular type of property at a given location. For example, $20,000 protection for personal property only, located at 1980 Washington Avenue. No coverage is provided for property at 1984 Washington Avenue. And when the damaged property is a building, no coverage applies even if the loss occurs at 1980 Washington Avenue.

If an organization has several locations, property may be transferred on a regular basis from one location to another. Under the basic approach, one must constantly keep changing policy amounts to keep coverage in order. The sheer paperwork is not the only problem. When an insured reduces coverage at one location, the insurer will return some of the premium, so accounting time and expenses are also involved. Thus, the basic approach is fairly rigid, and flexibility can be gained only at some expense.

However, when a firm's insurance needs are met by the basic arrangement, there is no need to use a more complicated technique. That is why the general forms exist. More sophisticated forms often cause confusion, and sometimes result in only partial recovery on a loss where a less complex approach would have given complete recovery. This possibility will be seen in a later analysis of reporting forms.

Special Limits As has been noted in the earlier explanation of the general property form, special limits apply to certain types of property. For example, off-premises coverage of not more than 2 percent of the amount of insurance on property other than stock, up to $5,000 of coverage, is provided for items being cleaned, repaired, or restored. Personal property of others that is similar to that of the insured is covered for the amount of 2 percent of the insurance on a given item, up to a maximum of $2,000. Such property of others must be located on the insured's premises as described in the policy. Another special limit often applies to personal property used to service the described building. This item is considered a portion of the building for insurance purposes and up to 1 percent of the amount of insurance on the building may be applied to it. Form FGP-1 expands the special limits area. Table 3-2 contains a summary of these extensions.

It should be noted that these special limits are not designed to meet

Table 3-2

Special Limits in the New General Property Form

Item	Coverage
1. Valuable Papers	5 percent of personal property coverage up to $500.
2. Trees, Shrubs, and Plants	5 percent of building and contents amount up to $1,000. Maximum of $250 per tree, shrub, or plant.
3. Newly Acquired Property	Coverage for 30 days. Building—10 percent of building coverage up to $25,000. Personal Property—10 percent of personal property limit up to $10,000. Personal property cannot be located at described premises.
4. Personal Effects of Insured's Officers, Partners, or Employees While on Described Premises	5 percent of personal property limit up to $500. Maximum of $100 per person.
5. Personal Property of Others	2 percent of personal property limit, but not more than $2,000.
6. Off-Premises Coverage for Insured's Business Personal Property	2 percent of the sum of the building limit and the personal property limit, but not more than $5,000.

the needs of anyone with a serious exposure in any of these areas, only the needs of insureds in general. This condition reflects the overall goal of general property forms: to meet the insurance requirements of a large number of different types of insureds with few, if any, special exposures.

Deductibles A wide variety of deductibles may be used with basic property forms. Normally, a $100 deductible is used with the general property form, and this deductible is preprinted in form FGP-1. When a building and its contents are both insured, the deductible applies only once to each building and its contents. When only contents are insured, the deductible applies separately to the contents of each building. The deductible applies separately to personal property in the open. Also, the deductible applies per event. Because of these applications, an insured can retain more than $100 in a single loss by the action of a $100 deductible. Deductible amounts larger than $100 are available in most cases by endorsement to the policy.

Deductibles can be increased to as much as $75,000, and sometimes even higher. Rate credits are given on the basis of the relationship between the size of the deductible and the insurable value of the property. Table 3-3 illustrates the deductible credits in use in one state. Credits in other states may vary. In the example state, the minimum credit shown in Table 3-3 is 2 percent. This credit is for a $250 deductible on an insurable value greater than $25,000. A maximum credit of 39 percent can apply when a $75,000 deductible is taken on property with an insurable value less than $750,000. Each category with a $5,000 or higher deductible has a range of rate credits that can apply, and underwriters may use their discretion as to the actual percentage given.

Table 3-3 provides some interesting insights which reinforce some of the concepts discussed in Chapter 2 in connection with frequency and severity of loss exposures. As might be expected, higher rate credits are granted when higher deductible limits are chosen. Less obvious is the fact that deductible credits for a given deductible are higher when the insurable value is lower. The reason for this is best illustrated by an example. Examine the figures for a $3,000 deductible on fire. With an insurable value of $30,000, an insured with a $3,000 deductible would be retaining 10 percent of the loss exposure, and a 14 percent rate credit would be granted. For a $300,000 building, only 1 percent of the exposure would be retained, and a lower credit of 5 percent would be granted. The lower credits for higher values reflect the increased likelihood of a loss exceeding the deductible when higher values are involved.

Note also that for deductibles up to $3,000, the rate credits are substantially higher for perils other than fire. This reflects the fact that other perils generally cause smaller losses than the peril of fire.

When deductibles over $5,000 are involved, a range of credits are used permitting the insurer to exercise judgment in choosing what credit to grant. The insurer would evaluate loss probability due to differing perils, and physical features reflecting probable maximum loss, such as public protection, sprinklers, building construction, relative combustibility and damageability of occupancy, and exposures.

Table 3-3 is only an illustration; rate credits given for deductibles vary by rating territory and other factors. All the deductibles given in Table 3-3 are on a per item basis, just like the $100 mandatory deductible discussed earlier. Therefore, the same cumulative effect can occur but with a larger dollar result. To control this possibility, an aggregate deductible can also be used to limit the total loss retained.

Table 3-3

Table of Credits for Deductible Coverage*

Insurable Value (As defined in Rules)	(Percentage Relationship of Deductible to Insurable Value)	Deductible Rate Credits: Fire	Deductible Rate Credits: ECE & Other Allied Perils (including V&MM)
	$250. Deductible		
More than $25,000.	(Less than 1%)	2%	5%
12,251 to 25,000.	(1% but under 2%)	3%	5%
8,334 to 12,250.	(2% but under 3%)	4%	10%
8,333 or Less	(3% or More)	7%	10%
	$500. Deductible		
More than $50,000.	(Less than 1%)	3%	22%
25,001 to 50,000.	(1% but under 2%)	4%	32%
16,667 to 25,000.	(2% but under 3%)	5%	37%
16,666 or Less	(3% or More)	10%	43%
	$1,000. Deductible		
More than $100,000.	(Less than 1%)	4%	23%
50,001 to 100,000.	(1% but under 2%)	5%	33%
25,001 to 50,000.	(2% but under 4%)	7%	38%
25,000 or Less	(4% or More)	12%	47%
	$3,000. Deductible		
More than $300,000.	(Less than 1%)	5%	25%
150,001 to 300,000.	(1% but under 2%)	6%	34%
75,001 to 150,000.	(2% but under 4%)	8%	39%
37,501 to 75,000.	(4% but under 8%)	10%	46%
37,500 or Less	(8% or More)	14%	51%

Insurable Value (As defined in Rules)	(Percentage Relationship of Deductible to Insurable Value)	Deductible Rate Credits: Fire, ECE & Other Allied Perils (including V&MM) Min.		Max.
	$5,000. Deductible			
More than $500,000.	(Less than 1%)	6%	to	22%
250,001 to 500,000.	(1% but under 2%)	7%		23%
100,001 to 250,000.	(2% but under 5%)	10%		24%
50,001 to 100,000.	(5% but under 10%)	14%		25%
50,000 or Less	(10% or More)	20%		26%
	$10,000. Deductible			
More than $1,000,000.	(Less than 1%)	8%	to	24%
500,001 to 1,000,000.	(1% but under 2%)	10%		25%
250,001 to 500,000.	(2% but under 4%)	12%		26%
100,001 to 250,000.	(4% but under 10%)	17%		27%
100,000 or Less	(10% or More)	21%		28%
	$25,000. Deductible			
More than $1,250,000.	(Less than 2%)	13%	to	30%
833,334 to 1,250,000.	(2% but under 3%)	14%		31%
500,001 to 833,333.	(3% but under 5%)	17%		32%
250,001 to 500,000.	(5% but under 10%)	20%		33%
250,000 or Less	(10% or More)	25%		34%
	$50,000. Deductible			
More than $1,666,666.	(Less than 3%)	17%	to	34%
1,250,001 to 1,666,666	(3% but under 4%)	18%		35%
714,286 to 1,250,000	(4% but under 7%)	20%		36%
500,000 to 714,285	(7% but under 10%)	25%		37%
500,000 or Less	(10% or More)	27%		38%
	$75,000. Deductible			
More than $1,875,000	(Less than 4%)	20%	to	36%
1,071,429 to 1,875,000	(4% but under 7%)	22%		37%
750,001 to 1,071,428	(7% but under 10%)	26%		38%
750,000 or Less	(10% or More)	28%		39%

*Reprinted with permission from *Pennsylvania—Delaware Rule Book* (New York: Insurance Services Office, May 1975 Revision), p. 1-25c, d.

Aggregate Deductibles. With an aggregate deductible, the insured's total loss retention for the year or for each occurrence, depending on the type of aggregate purchased, is limited to a specified amount by the aggregate deductible feature.

Under an annual aggregate deductible, individual losses are divided into three categories: those less than 10 percent of the per event deductible, those from 10 percent to 100 percent of the per event deductible, and those exceeding the per event deductible. When a loss is less than 10 percent of the per event deductible, the insured retains the entire loss. Losses ranging from 10 percent to 100 percent of the per event deductible are also borne by the insured, but their amounts are noted and accumulated. With losses in excess of the per event deductible, the insured bears the loss up to the deductible, and this amount is also noted and accumulated. When, within a policy year, the accumulated amounts reach the aggregate deductible figure, the insurer pays the remainder of all losses for the rest of the policy year. With the next policy year, the full deductible amounts are reinstated until used up again. An example of what might happen in one policy year is presented in Table 3-4, using a $10,000 deductible per event and a $30,000 aggregate deductible.

After loss *G*, the insured would not absorb any more losses during the year. With *G*, the aggregate loss retention limit is reached, so even if a subsequent loss is below the per event limit (such as loss *H*), the insurer pays it. Consequently, in this example, rather than retaining $67,000 of loss as would happen with just a $10,000 per event deductible, the insured retains $31,300.

The aggregate deductible has obvious advantages over a per event deductible as an aid to an organization's financial planning. It allows for more accuracy in anticipating such important items as cash flow and profits. However, from the insurer's viewpoint, the use of the aggregate deductible can lead to a larger payout to the insured. Given this possibility, when an aggregate deductible is chosen, the rate credit for the per event deductible is reduced. Table 3-5 shows a schedule of such rate reductions. The table is interpreted in the following manner: if two to five buildings are covered with a total insurable value of $1.5 million with a $25,000 per event deductible and an aggregate deductible of $75,000, then 85 percent of the per event rate credit shown in Table 3-3 will be allowed. Thus, the insured could receive a rate credit of between 11.05 percent (13% × 0.85) to 25.5 percent (30% × 0.85).

Disappearing Deductibles. Disappearing deductibles are available in some states. An illustration of the operation of these deductibles is given in Table 3-6. Deductibles under this option range from $500 to $5,000, and they disappear at varying loss levels. On a loss of $3,000 with

Table 3-4

How Aggregate Deductibles Operate[1]

Loss	Amount	Losses Above Per Event Deductible	Losses Retained	Losses Paid By Insurer	Loss Considered Part of Aggregate Deductible[2]
A	$ 800[2]	$ 0	$ 800		$ 0
B	10,000	0	10,000	$ 0	10,000
C	500[2]	0	500	0	0
D	1,000	0	1,000	0	1,000
E	25,000	15,000	10,000	15,000	10,000
F	5,000	0	5,000	0	5,000
G	15,000	5,000	4,000	11,000	4,000
H	4,000	0	0	4,000	0
I	15,000	0	0	15,000	0
J	700[3]	0	0	700	0
	$77,000	$20,000	$31,300	$45,700	$30,000

1. Per event deductible, $10,000; aggregate, $30,000.
2. Loss less than 10 percent of per event deductible.
3. After the aggregate deductible has been reached, the insurer pays all "whole losses" disregarding any deductibles.

a $1,000 disappearing deductible, an insured would make the following recovery. The $1,000 deductible would be subtracted from the $3,000 loss ($3,000 - $1,000 = $2,000). The difference, $2,000, is multiplied by the loss recovery factor ($2,000 × 1.11), and the insured receives $2,220. For a $10,000 loss, the same formula would be applied. The $1,000 deductible is subtracted from the $10,000 loss ($10,000 - $1,000 = $9,000). The difference, $9,000, is multiplied by the loss recovery factor (1.11), and the insured receives $9,999 ($9,000 × 1.11 = $9,999). All losses over $10,000 are paid in full. Of course, rate credits with a disappearing deductible are less than those given for flat deductibles.

Use of Deductibles. It is not just the percentage reduction in the premium that matters; the actual number of dollars saved is important. While a $10,000 per event deductible could save 20 percent on the premium, if the premium is only $2,000, the amount of dollar saving ($400) may not be important, especially when compared to the cost of one or more sizable losses during the contract year. One loss in excess of $10,000 equals twenty-five years of premium saving. The insured may

Table 3-5
Maximum Factors*

Number of Buildings or Structures Rated for Fire Insurance	Amount of Annual Loss Aggregate				
	2 Times Deductible	3 Times Deductible	4 Times Deductible	5 to 9 Times Deductible	10 or More Times Deductible
1	0.90	0.92	0.95	0.95	0.95
2 to 5	0.80	0.85	0.90	0.95	0.95
6 to 25	0.70	0.75	0.80	0.85	0.90
26 to 50	0.60	0.65	0.70	0.75	0.85
51 and over	0.50	0.55	0.60	0.70	0.80

*Reprinted with permission from *Pennsylvania—Delaware Rule Book* (New York: Insurance Services Office, May 1975), p. 1-25e.

Table 3-6
Disappearing Deductibles*

Disappearing Deductible	Loss Recovery Factor	Deductible Disappearing At
$ 500	1.11	$ 5,000
1,000	1.11	10,000
3,000	1.25	15,000
5,000	1.25	25,000

*Reprinted with permission from *Georgia Rule Book* (New York: Insurance Services Office, August 1974), p. 68c.

consider twenty-five years too long a wait to recover the money and, besides, there may be one or more additional losses in those years. This helps explain the low popularity of deductibles with many insureds. However, if the premium before rate reduction is $8,000, a 20 percent saving is $1,600. Then it would take only six years and three months of saving to equal the cost of one $10,000 loss borne by the insured. Of course, the larger premium would represent either more value insured, or a higher insurance rate, or both. More value insured would mean a smaller discount rate for the $10,000 deductible. A higher insurance rate would probably indicate a greater chance of suffering a loss. Therefore, the comparison given cannot be applied directly to a given case, but the concept involved is important and practical. That concept has been summarized as, "Don't risk a lot for a little"; e.g., do not take a chance of losing $10,000 to save $400. But risking $10,000 for $1,600 or some larger amount may be worthwhile.

Measure of Covered Loss The normal approach is to value property at its actual cash value. That is, standard forms measure loss by diminution of the actual cash value of the insured property or the cost to repair or replace it, whichever is less. One exception is debris removal coverage, as already discussed. Alternative measures of covered loss will be discussed later in this chapter.

Other Insurance The standard fire policies contain the basic provision for determining what share of a loss a particular policy should pay when more than one policy applies. As discussed in CPCU 1, the allocation provided for is in proportion to the amounts of insurance applying to the property in each policy. What the property damage forms add is that this rule applies to each extension in the policy, whether all the policies have similar extensions or not: coverage of debris removal, property off the described premises, and personal property of others. Therefore, if some of the policies do not have such extensions, the insured bears the portion of the loss which those policies would have paid if they had included the extensions.

Another regular provision states that off-premises coverage is excess over all other insurance covering the property, collectible or not. This is in accord with accepted insurance practice with respect to which coverages are primarily liable for loss to property away from specified locations. A similar provision, sometimes found, is that general insurance on nonowned property does not apply at all when the insured's interest is more specifically insured. The above provisions can be found in form FGP-1, previously discussed.

Alternatives to Basic Approach

The preceding discussion examined the coverage provided by basic property forms for persons with few unusual problems or special situations. However, not all organizations fit that category—many firms need insurance programs suited to their exposures. The following paragraphs discuss some alternative ways to cover property. The problem of varying values is explored, as well as that of property at several locations. In addition, recovery on a basis other than actual cash value at time of loss is explored. Also examined are property forms that do not use coinsurance clauses. These are among the tools presently available for improving the fit between property exposures and coverage.

Reporting Forms Fluctuating inventory values are a problem for many businesses. The volume of sales is seldom even throughout the year, and inventory values commonly change according to seasonal demand. Also, projections of future requirements can go astray and cause unplanned accumulations or depletions of inventory. Whatever the cause, an insured wants insurance to adjust to the circumstances and give efficient and economical protection.

As shown earlier, the basic approach of a single fixed amount of insurance is unsatisfactory for such situations. To cover temporarily large accumulations, the insured has to have high policy limits. Then when inventory values are reduced, the organization must either pay for unneeded insurance if high policy limits are maintained, or pay short-term rates if the policy limit is reduced. Either alternative is expensive. Reporting forms avoid this dilemma. When a reporting form is used, the insured makes periodic reports (monthly or quarterly) to the insurer which state the values exposed to loss. The earned premium is based on the values reported. The following analysis will focus on the specifics of reporting forms and their major distinguishing characteristics.

The major features that distinguish reporting forms from nonreporting forms are (1) provisional amount of insurance, (2) limit of liability, (3) treatment of specific insurance, (4) reporting requirement, and (5) penalties. The discussion below is addressed to these distinguishing characteristics.

Provisional Amount of Insurance. Reporting forms do not provide a fixed amount of insurance on property. A maximum limit of liability is established for each location covered by the policy. The insurer will never pay more than this amount in the policy at the time of loss. Once the limit of liability is determined, the insured usually must make a premium deposit of 75 percent of the premium which would be required to purchase nonreporting insurance for the same limit. However, for highly seasonal risks, the provisional premium may be lower. The actual premium earned by the insurer depends on the average values insured during the policy term. At the end of the contract period an additional premium may be due or a refund may be owed to the insured. Refunds are on a pro-rata basis. Short rate factors apply only when the insured cancels the entire policy. As long as the insured complies with the policy conditions, coverages increase and decrease automatically, even when the goods on hand at the time of loss are greater than those on hand at the time of the latest report, but always subject to the stated limit of liability.

The location of the property must be stated in the report. If several locations are to be insured, each location must be listed and a limit of liability at each location given. The insured can choose to include automatic coverage for later acquired locations. As long as the limit of liability for such locations is less than $10,000, no additional provisional premium is required. For coverage greater than $10,000, the insured must pay a larger deposit premium.

Limit of Liability. As stated above, each location has a maximum limit of liability; the insurer's obligation is limited by this maximum.

The insured is required to report all property on hand as of the report date. If $250,000 worth of goods are on hand and the limit of liability is $150,000, the insured must still report $250,000 and pay a premium on that amount. However, protection is limited to $150,000.[2] In such a case, the insured should increase the limits or purchase specific insurance to cover the additional $100,000 of value.

Specific Insurance. The reporting form defines specific insurance as "insurance other than contributing insurance." Contributing insurance is defined as "insurance written subject to the same terms, conditions and provisions as those contained in this policy." Consequently, if coverage is not on a reporting form, it is specific insurance.

Coverage under reporting forms is excess over specific insurance. If the specific insurance contract has a coinsurance clause, the reporting form coverage is not counted when determining whether the coinsurance requirement has been met. Suppose insured goods are worth $250,000. An 80 percent coinsurance clause would require $200,000 worth of coverage under the specific insurance contract. If the specific insurance amount is $100,000, then the specific insurance coverage would pay only 50 percent of any loss up to $200,000. The reporting form would pay the amount of loss in excess of the specific insurance payment. Thus, on a $100,000 loss, the specific insurance would pay $50,000 and the reporting form $50,000. On a $224,000 loss, the specific insurance would pay $100,000 (0.5 × 224,000 = 112,000, which is greater than policy limits, so the policy pays its limit of $100,000). The reporting form would pay $124,000, assuming its limit is adequate. When the specific insurance has no coinsurance clause, the specific coverage pays to its policy limit. The insured always receives his or her loss in full as long as the combined limits (specific plus reporting) are adequate.

Since the reporting form coverage is excess, the premium for the form is based only on the excess of covered value over the amount of specific insurance at each location. Thus, with specific insurance of $100,000 at a location and value of $250,000 in covered property, the reporting form rate is applied against the $150,000 difference. The insured and insurer must be alert to any change in specific coverage. In particular, when any specific coverage expires, the change must be noted in the next report.

Reporting. The monthly report usually must include (1) all locations covered, (2) total value of covered property at each location, and (3) the amount of specific insurance on the property at each location. Usually reports are made as of the end of each month, but the insured may choose any reporting date during the month. Each report is due within thirty days of the date to which it applies. Otherwise, the insured is subject to the penalty for late reporting.

Penalties. There are two types of reporting behavior that can cause less than full recovery on a loss. One is late reporting, the other is inaccurate reporting.

LATE REPORTING. When a report has not been filed within thirty days of the valuation date, it is late. As a consequence, the amount last reported becomes a limit on the amount payable on any claim. Thus, if a policy had a stated maximum of $250,000, a report was overdue, and the last report previously received was for $150,000, the maximum amount payable would become $150,000. Should a loss occur for $200,000, the policy would only pay $150,000. When the last value reported is at a low point of the inventory cycle, this can be a severe penalty.

When the first report is late, there is no previous report to use, and the maximum amount payable becomes 75 percent of the provisional amount of insurance, that is, 75 percent of the original limit of liability. Therefore, if the provisional amount were $250,000, the maximum amount payable would be reduced to $187,500. On a $200,000 loss, the insurer would pay $187,500 and the insured would retain the remaining $12,500.

Note that the nature of the penalty for late reporting means that there is no penalty for small losses. In the examples given, if the loss in each case came to $50,000, it would be paid in full.

Late reports are a fairly common problem with reporting forms. Therefore, despite the forms' apparent advantages, they should never be used unless a firm's books and procedures indicate a good probability that reports will be produced promptly and accurately.

INACCURATE REPORTS. The reporting form has no coinsurance clause, but it has a full reporting clause that amounts to a 100 percent coinsurance clause. It is commonly called the "honesty clause." This clause stipulates that claims will be paid according to the ratio of the last reported values to the actual values on hand as of the date of the report. Thus, if an insured, through error or deceit, reported values of $50,000 but actually had $100,000 on hand at the time, the insurer would pay no more than one-half of any loss.

When more than one location is involved, each location must be reported accurately. Even if the total for all locations is correct, there can be a penalty, since the honesty clause applies separately per location rather than on a blanket basis.

Inadequate Limits. Reporting forms require insurance to 100 percent of value but allow use of specific insurance in meeting this requirement. However, sometimes an insured is not able to obtain adequate limits. Under the standard reporting provisions, all values would nonetheless have to be reported and a premium paid on them. Premium must be paid according to values on hand, even when those values exceed the limit of insurance. In such situations, an insured would be paying for insurance which could never be used. To remove this inequity, a deficiency of insurance endorsement can be attached to the policy. This endorsement eliminates the insured's obligation to pay for coverage above the limit of liability. However, it does have one disadvantage; the insured must meet what amounts to a 100 percent coinsurance clause. Consequently, the insured is subject to a coinsurance penalty on any loss. If the insured cannot insure close to 100 percent, the deficiency of insurance endorsement may not be desirable, since the penalties under it may be greater than the premiums paid under the standard form. Regardless of how an insured handles the situation, a satisfactory solution is not really available using a reporting form in such circumstances.

Peak Season Endorsement Some firms have inventories which fluctuate according to predictable cycles. A toy store, for example, may predictably have double its usual inventory in the months preceding Christmas. For such accounts, the peak season endorsement can provide some of the advantages of the reporting form without the problems associated with reporting requirements. The peak season endorsement provides for an increased amount of insurance for a specified time each year, which is indicated by specific dates shown on the endorsement. Usually this endorsement is attached when the policy is issued (although it may be added mid-term), and a pro-rata increased premium is charged for the period when values are increased.

Blanket Coverage A blanket policy has been defined as "one which (a) covers for one amount two or more separate subjects of insurance, or (b) which covers for one amount at more than one location or separately rated area, or (c) a combination of (a) and (b)."[3] The usual example of two separate subjects of insurance is a building and its contents.

This approach is a particularly effective method of insuring property that is moved from one building to another if the total value involved does not fluctuate widely. A warehouse which supplies several retail outlets is an often used example of such a situation. In other cases, a firm may have stock located in several different buildings, and may have an inventory system which gives total values but does not break out values in each location. Some manufacturing operations move property from one building to another in the normal course of manufacture so that total values are relatively constant, but the value in any one building may vary substantially from week to week.

In general, the greater the number of locations and the higher the ratio of total value to value at any one location, the greater the virtue of blanket insurance. From the viewpoint of the insured, the point is that in such situations there is less and less value in knowing exactly how much value is in any particular place. Therefore, the regular bookkeeping procedures are less likely to reflect the value at each place, and it becomes onerous to report the insurable value at each location. From the insurer's point of view, the greater number of locations and the dispersion of values make it less important to know exactly the amount of exposure at each location because of the greater credibility of the insured's overall average experience.

Coinsurance Requirement. While the blanket approach has the advantage of not requiring precise knowledge as to where property values are located, it has some disadvantages also. With specific insurance, a 90 percent coinsurance clause earns a 5 percent reduction from the 80 percent coinsurance rate. A 100 percent clause earns a further 5 percent reduction (10 percent total). For blanket insurance, a 90 percent coinsurance clause uses the same rate as the regular 80 percent clause (no reduction) while a 100 percent clause earns only a 5 percent reduction. These higher rates are justified because an insured with blanket coverage does not have to buy insurance equal to 100 percent of total values to have 100 percent coverage at each separate location unless, of course, it is subject to a 100 percent coinsurance clause.

To illustrate the point of the preceding paragraph, consider the following example. A landlord owned two buildings on opposite ends of town, each valued at $50,000. Both were covered by blanket insurance with a 90 percent coinsurance clause. The policy limit was $90,000. If one building were totally destroyed, the coinsurance clause would be applied as follows:

$$\frac{\text{Amount of insurance carried (\$90,000)}}{\text{Amount of insurance required (\$90,000)}} \times \text{Loss (\$50,000)} = \$50,000$$

Of course, the loss payment would never exceed the policy limits of $90,000, but this is a moot point unless both buildings were involved in a single loss. In short, the loss would be covered in full. With specific insurance the landlord would have had to purchase two separate $50,000 policies ($100,000 total insurance) to provide the same loss adjustment. Because of this loophole, the pro-rata distribution clause is often used.

Pro-Rata Distribution Clause. Some blanket forms contain a pro-rata distribution clause. When x percent of the total covered property value is at location A, then x percent of the total amount of blanket insurance applies to location A, and so on. This produces a kind of divided coverage (insurance applicable to one location cannot be applied toward the loss at another location), but with flexible amounts; the amount of insurance at each location changes automatically as its percentage of total value changes. With $50,000 at A, $25,000 at B, and $5,000 at C, all covered by $72,000 of insurance: 50/80 times $72,000 or $45,000 of insurance applies to A; 25/80 times $72,000 or $22,500 at B; and $4,500 at C. If $5,000 of value is moved from B to C, $4,500 of insurance is automatically shifted from B to C. (Note that the ratio of insurance to total value, 72/80 or 90 percent, applies constantly to the value at each location.) Blanket insurance rates are affected by the presence or absence of a pro-rata distribution clause, and also by the level of coinsurance requirement with or without a pro-rata distribution clause. Combinations available may differ in various states and insurance companies.

Note that a pro-rata distribution clause does not affect coverage for partial losses up to the location limit. It requires that total insurance equal total value before any location is fully insured. Because the pro-rata distribution clause, in effect, makes blanket insurance specific at the time of loss, it is very seldom used. Normal blanket forms allow an insured to recover in full for a total loss at one location by carrying 90 percent insurance to value; with the pro-rata distribution clause the insured must carry a limit equal to 100 percent of values in order to fully recover for a total loss at one location. The small premium savings generated by the pro-rata distribution clause does not compensate for this penalty.

Rating. A potential disadvantage of blanket coverage arises when more than one rate applies to property covered by the form. The rating bureau may provide that the highest rate on the various types of property be used on all contents at all locations. However, this provision may be eliminated by the use of the average rate endorsement where allowed. This modification is discussed in the section on multiple location forms.

In the absence of an average rate, if a $1.50 rate applies to one item and a $.50 rate to another, the $1.50 rate would have to be used on both items. If the item with the $.50 rate is a substantial proportion of the total property, the insured would pay three times the normal premium for that item to obtain blanket coverage.

Multiple Location Plans As the name indicates, these plans are used in connection with insurance on property located at two or more sites. The locations can be in one or more states. Multiple location plans are characterized by use of average rates and by volume discounts for accounts with more than $1,000 in premium. The discounts were once automatic; in some cases, they are no longer given. The plans may be used with reporting or nonreporting and with blanket or specific coverage forms.

Eligibility. Since these are multiple location rating plans, two or more locations must be insured. The insured must have at least $50,000 of property at the secondary location or an amount greater than 10 percent of the value at primary location, whichever is greater. This latter requirement is quite minimal and would allow many insureds to qualify except for the fact that a $500 minimum annual premium also is required. Consequently, only larger firms tend to use these plans. These rules may vary in different states.

Many types of organizations (federal, state, and county governments; some cooperatives; mercantile and manufacturing businesses and distilleries; and hospitals, educational, and religious institutions) are eligible for multiple location forms.

All types of property may be insured. Formerly, coverage was limited to merchandise and stock, but present forms can be used to insure the following: (1) building and fixtures, (2) furniture and fixtures, (3) machinery and equipment, (4) improvements and betterments, or (5) stock. Typically, the first four items are written on nonreporting forms, and stock is written on a reporting form.

While most types of property may be written, some are not eligible. The rules vary by territory, so one must check in each particular territory before any conclusions can be drawn. For illustrative purposes only, the following list of property is ineligible in some territories: (1) dwelling property; (2) farm property; (3) railroad property; (4) property insured under public and institutional property form, industrial property form, highly protected risk plans, or petroleum property forms; and (5) farm produce insured in the farmer's name.

Available Options. Throughout this analysis the term *plans* has been employed because there are different multiple location forms.[4] These forms include:

1. ML-1—reporting form for general properties
2. ML-2—special reporting form for distilled spirits
3. ML-3—special reporting form for grain at grain elevators
4. ML-5—nonreporting form for general properties other than stock[5]

The most commonly used multiple location form is ML-1, and it operates in a manner very similar to the reporting form described earlier. However, because of the complexity of the average rate calculation, insureds are not encouraged and often not allowed to increase policy limits during the policy term.[6] Therefore, adequate limits must be established at the policy's inception. Also, the initial premium is based on 100 percent, rather than 75 percent of the policy limits. If the deposit premium exceeds the earned premium, excess is returned. In cases where an insured exposure exceeds the limits of liability an individual can buy specific insurance to cover the exposure since the ML-1 limits are difficult to raise.

Since ML-2 and ML-3 are special situation forms and not frequently used, they will not be discussed in detail here. The ML-5 is a nonreporting form used to insure nonstock exposures. Buildings and equipment are often insured under this form, which uses an average rate and has a coinsurance clause that applies to the aggregate of values insured but not to specific locations. The coinsurance percentage required is 90 or 100 percent. It is really the blanket approach to the multiple location situation. In this form, volume discounts and experience credits are mandatory. This is one of the few fire and allied lines forms that is experience rated.

Perils Insured Against. Not all perils may be insured against under a multiple location form, and no indirect losses may be insured under such forms. Examples of ineligible perils include collapse, earthquake, flood, and water damage. While these perils cannot be individually added to multiple location forms, some of them may be insured against in the same policy through the use of an "all-risks" form or an optional perils form. None of the forms available includes earthquake or flood coverage.

Changing Values Because of Inflation Actual change in property on hand is not the only cause of change in the value of insured property, of course. Inflation has been an important cause of underinsurance. In most territories there are standard forms designed to help with this problem. These forms are called automatic increase in insurance or "inflation guard" endorsements. The usual procedure is to provide for a quarterly increase in the amount of insurance at a predetermined percentage selected by the insured. Common choices are 1, 1.5, and 2 percent; sometimes higher percentages are also available.

Originally these endorsements applied only to buildings and their attachments. This has been extended in some cases to apply to contents also. Naturally, the insured has to pay an additional premium for this additional coverage.

Reporting forms, of course, reflect changes in values caused by inflation as well as by physical changes in inventory. But buildings and fixed assets are not subject to reporting forms, and most insureds do not have reporting forms on stock.

Fixed percentage increases in value do not exactly match rates of inflation, of course. Nor do they help much when applied to insurance that is inadequate in the first place. But they do ameliorate the problem imposed by inflationary times. (In order to solve the problems caused by predetermined fixed percentages, some insurers have developed non-standard endorsements which increase policy limits in accordance with some type of building cost index. Such a system provides much better protection against underinsurance caused by inflation.)

Replacement of Property

So far, the insured's recovery for property damage has been discussed in terms of actual cash value at the time of the loss. This measure of recovery has implicitly meant that depreciation would be deducted in loss adjustment. However, the insured is not limited to this approach. Coverage may often be purchased on a replacement cost basis. As noted earlier, replacement cost is sometimes increased by laws that require repairs to be made according to higher standards than the property damaged or destroyed. This section addresses itself to these two topics: (1) replacement cost insurance and (2) operation of building codes.

Replacement Cost Insurance According to basic insurance principles, an insured who sustained a property loss would be reimbursed for the actual cash value of the damaged property. Traditionally, it was held that any indemnification over and above the actual cash value of the loss would violate the principle of indemnity in that it would leave the insured in a better position after a loss. If the insurer paid for a new building, the insured's value in the new building was greater than the value in the building which had been destroyed and thus, the insured would profit from a loss.

On the other hand, an insured who suffers a loss needs to replace the damaged real or personal property. The out-of-pocket expenses following property damage (disregarding insurance) are the actual expenses to repair or replace the damaged property. Thus, insureds with actual cash value insurance face the chance of having to pay the difference between their insurance recovery and the actual cost of repair or replacement following a loss. With actual cash value insurance it is necessary for risk managers to recognize this potential expense and determine how it will be treated should a loss occur.

Insurers have historically been reluctant to write replacement cost coverage because the potential for betterment following a loss increases the chance of moral hazard. More recent thinking, however, recognizes that the potential out-of-pocket expense to repair or replace damaged property is a valid loss exposure which can be treated with the use of insurance. As a result, replacement cost coverage has come into frequent use.

If an insured expects to repair or replace damaged or destroyed property, then replacement cost insurance may be desirable. With this coverage an insured collects on the basis of the replacement cost at the time of loss. There is no reduction for loss of value through depreciation. On brand new buildings replacement cost is little different from actual cash value. On older buildings depreciation is a very important factor. However, insurers may be reluctant to issue replacement cost coverage on very old buildings, especially if the market value of the structure is significantly below its replacement cost. The potential for moral hazard is too great in such circumstances.

Eligible Property. Various categories of property are eligible for replacement cost coverage. This section will discuss the eligibility standards commonly applied to standard forms, but it should be noted that many other insurers will provide replacement cost coverage on other property as well. Common practice provides that one may insure buildings and permanent machinery, fixtures, and equipment in the insured building. This category coincides with the building coverage in the general property form without the extensions to personal property. A second eligible category is improvements and betterments. A third category of coverable property is machinery, furniture, fixtures, and equipment. Whether other contents are eligible depends upon the type of insured.

General contents can be insured on a replacement cost basis if owned by and contained in buildings owned and principally occupied by governmental units, hospitals, educational, and religious institutions. The exception to this rule is that the occupancy must pertain to the primary functions of these organizations. A drugstore operated by a governmental unit or an apartment house managed by a religious institution would not qualify. Other than for these organizations, replacement cost coverage is not offered for contents except machinery, furniture, fixtures, and equipment. The principal components of such other contents are stock, materials, and supplies, of course, and these classes of property usually are subject to little or no deduction for depreciation when determining actual cash value. Therefore, replacement cost coverage is usually not needed.

Some special types of property are usually excluded from coverage in the replacement cost endorsement. Among them are (1) property not covered by the actual cash value form, (2) art objects and items with historical value, and (3) research costs to reconstruct valuable papers and records.

Replacement cost coverage is usually added at no additional charge, or at a nominal charge such as $1. However, when the replacement cost clause is included, the coinsurance clause is applied to the replacement cost, rather than the actual cash value, of property covered. Therefore, the insured must carry higher limits of insurance to avoid a coinsurance penalty, and this increases the premium in line with the increased coverage.

Even if the insured takes settlement on an actual cash value basis, as permitted by the policy, the coinsurance provision is still based on the ratio of amount of insurance to the required percentage of replacement cost.

Loss Settlement. To recover replacement cost, the insured must actually repair or replace the damaged property. Usually payment is not made until this is done. An insured who wishes to collect something quickly can make a claim on the basis of loss in actual cash value. Within the time stated in the contract (usually 180 days), notice must be given of intent to claim replacement cost. When replacement has taken place, the insured can collect the appropriate additional amount.

If the insured does not replace or rebuild the property, payment is made on the basis of the actual cash value loss. Supposing the insured does replace or rebuild, the limit on claim payment is the smallest of (1) the amount of the policy applicable to the loss, (2) the replacement cost of the property on the same premises and intended for the same occupancy and use, or (3) the amount actually and necessarily expended in repairing or replacing the property.

The first condition restricts coverage to the policy limits. If the policy is for $100,000 and the loss $105,000, the policy will pay only $100,000. Of course, any failure to meet coinsurance requirements reduces the amount of the policy applicable to the loss.

The second condition limits recovery to the cost of replacing or repairing at the same location for the same occupancy, and using the same design. This clause is subject to varying interpretations. It does not require the insured to rebuild according to the specified conditions (same premises, same occupancy, and use). It merely says that the insured will not be paid more than the cost to reconstruct with those conditions. It seems to follow that if the insured replaces with a more expensive building at the same or a different location, the policy will pay only the amount it would have cost to replace the original building at the original location. However, this liberal interpretation is not accepted by all insurers because of the history of the coverage, plus fear of creating considerable moral hazard. Some hold that the replacement must be for exactly the same occupancy and use. The presence of the third limitation quoted seems to conflict with this view, especially since the wording, "for the same occupancy and use," formerly appeared in this third condition but is no longer included.

The third condition states that the actual expenditure on repair and replacement limits recovery. The policy may be for $200,000, with the cost to replace for the original occupancy and use at the original location $190,000; but if the insured builds at a different location for $150,000, the policy will only pay $150,000, the smallest amount of the three limits. As noted, this third limit says nothing about either the same premises or the same occupancy and use. Suppose the insured's new building is more extensive and expensive than the old one, costing, say, $220,000. The lowest limit is then the $200,000 amount of insurance. But the question previously mentioned arises: is replacement with a significantly different structure covered by replacement cost? It is difficult to see anything in the three limitations which says it is not. The matter seems to hinge on the extent to which a different structure can be said to be a replacement for the old one, especially when on different premises. The matter can only be resolved definitely by further court decisions or changes of wording in the form.

Time of Replacement. Replacement cost coverage requires that the replacement be accomplished with "due diligence and dispatch" or "within a reasonable time," depending on the territory. The insured may choose to disregard the replacement cost endorsement (although the coinsurance clause is still applied to the replacement cost) and make a claim under other policy provisions. This might happen, for example, if the insured should choose not to repair or replace the damaged property, in which case the loss would be adjusted on an actual cash value basis. When this is done, the insured can claim the additional replacement cost coverage by notifying the insurer of this intent within a certain time period, frequently 180 days.

When coverage is written, replacement cost coverage is usually added by endorsement, although some forms covering commercial property such as the business owners policy discussed later in this text automatically include replacement cost coverage in the basic form.

Operation of Building Codes The replacement cost endorsement does not provide payment for changes in design or materials if they make the replacement cost more than it would have been with unchanged design and materials. As noted earlier, building codes may require changes, sometimes extensive and expensive ones.

Increased Cost of Construction Cover. An increased cost of construction endorsement may be added to replacement cost coverage. This endorsement has its own specific amount of separate insurance available only for the one use: to cover the difference between cost of reconstruction of a building just like the old one and cost of reconstruction in accordance with current building codes. The endorsement has an 80 percent coinsurance clause separately applicable to its special subject matter.

Besides coinsurance, the endorsement includes the following restrictions.

SAME PREMISES. Unlike the replacement cost endorsement to which it must be attached, the increased cost of construction endorsement usually demands the property be replaced or repaired on the *same premises.* The "due diligence and dispatch" provision also has a fixed limit of two years from the date of building loss. The insurer may extend the time period by written consent. In addition, the repaired building must be of like height, floor area, style, and occupancy as the original building.

DEMOLITION. As noted earlier, loss from the operation of building laws is excluded by the ordinance or law clause of form FGP-1 and other property forms. Building laws might require demolition of undamaged portions of a severely damaged structure (typically, a structure damaged to the extent of 50 percent of its value) followed by reconstruction of a building that meets current requirements. This loss (loss of the value of the undamaged property that must be destroyed, plus cost of demolition) is specifically excluded in the increased cost of construction endorsement.

Coverage for Demolition Loss. Two endorsements apply to demolition loss: demolition coverage and coverage for contingent liability from operation of building laws. Demolition coverage applies to demolition expense; operations of building laws coverage applies to the loss of value of the demolished property.

DEMOLITION ENDORSEMENT. The demolition endorsement increases the insured's coverage by a sum that can only be used to demolish an undamaged portion of an insured building and to clear the site. The loss necessitating the demolition must be from an insured peril, and a governmental ordinance must require the demolition. If one policy on a property has this endorsement, all policies should have it because it contains a pro rata clause which otherwise would limit recovery.

OPERATION OF BUILDING LAWS FORM. The operation of building laws form provides actual cash value insurance on the portion of the property not directly damaged by a peril insured against, but lost because of the operation of building laws that require demolition of the remainder of a severely damaged structure.

Note that this form does not require an increase in the amount of insurance. The limit of liability is still the total actual cash value of the property, just as with the regular fire insurance. If that total value is adequately covered in the regular fire insurance, no increase is needed for this endorsement. However, where there is exposure to property loss from operation of the building laws, the question as to what percent of actual cash value should be insured by the basic policy needs careful examination. With such exposure, insuring to 80 percent or even 90 percent of insurable value may not be enough.

To add this endorsement to an insurance policy, property insurance rates are increased 15 to 25 percent, depending on the type of construction. Fire resistive buildings require a 15 percent increase and all others require a 25 percent increase.

The Complete Package. All together the several covers applicable to loss involving operation of building laws operate in the following manner. Regular property damage forms apply to the loss in actual cash value of the property actually damaged by insured perils, including the cost of removing debris from the direct damage. Contingent liability from operation of building laws cover pays the insured for the actual cash value loss of property that must be demolished. Replacement cost cover raises these payments from the actual cash value loss to the replacement cost of the old structure. Demolition insurance adds the cost of actually demolishing the undamaged portion of the structure. Increased cost of construction cover raises the replacement cost protection from replacement cost of the old building to the cost of putting up a building (same premises, size, and use) that meets the minimum requirements of the *current* building code.

It should be apparent from this discussion that the operation of building codes can create substantial loss exposures. Identification of the exposures requires awareness of building codes affecting property. If the exposures are not identified, insurance or noninsurance techniques for handling the exposure cannot be planned, and the exposure is unconsciously retained.

Alternatives to Coinsurance

Most fire and allied lines insurance policies includes a coinsurance clause. However, there are some situations in which coinsurance provisions are not standard. For example, in the old public and institutional property forms and the new businessowners forms, there is no coinsurance clause as such.

In some forms an agreed amount takes the place of the coinsurance clause. A yearly valuation is made of the property, and a figure equal to at least 90 percent of the value is inserted into the policy. If the insured maintains this amount of insurance in force, all claims are paid in full up to the policy limits. If not, losses are adjusted by multiplying the loss times the ratio of the insurance carried to the agreed amount.

Unlike the coinsurance clause where the required amount of insurance is determined at the time of loss, in forms using agreed amount coverage, the required amount of insurance (the agreed amount) is determined at the inception of the policy. Under this approach there is no uncertainty in meeting insurance-to-value requirements.

The businessowners policy goes one step further in not requiring a coinsurance clause or an agreed amount provision. The producer is warned in the manual for that program that one should insure to value, and the rates assume insurance of at least 80 percent to value, but the policy has no provision to penalize the insured for violation of this requirement.

Builders' Risk Forms

Structures under construction have special loss exposures to consider. They present the problem of changing values. A building's value varies from zero at the time construction begins to the full completed value when construction ceases. In addition, the hazards presented are different than for finished buildings. Normally, security is poor, fire detection or prevention devices may not be operational, there are many open spaces through which a fire can spread, combustible materials are scattered throughout the work place, and construction materials are unprotected from the elements. In addition, there may be several subcontractors working on the project, with varying degrees of care for loss control. These factors add up to a situation where both the insured and the insurer need a special form of insurance to meet their respective needs.

Property Covered The actual coverage under a builders' risk form may be separated into two different parts with each section having its own limits. The categories are (1) the building or structure, and (2) construction machinery and equipment.

Building or Structure. The building or structure section covers the structure, its roof, foundation, additions, attachments, fixtures, machinery, and equipment. Notice that foundations are insured; they are not excluded as they are under the general property form. Also insured under the building or structure coverage are temporary structures, materials, and supplies of all kinds, owned by the named insured to be used in construction of the building while on the insured premises or within 100 feet of it. The preceding coverage is fairly standard from one part of the country to the other. However, the treatment of property of others and of contractors' equipment varies.

Property of Others. Some forms state that coverage is only on a legal liability basis for property of others. Other forms make this coverage a separate item under the building coverage. In these forms, at the option of the insured, an additional amount of insurance up to 2 percent of the insurance on the building can be used to cover property of others in the care, custody, or control of the insured. However, a maximum of $2,000 of protection is placed on this additional insurance. In other forms coverage is provided automatically for these items without proof of legal liability, and the protection provided is considered part of the builders' machinery, tools, equipment, and supplies coverage.

Builders' Machinery and Equipment. Property in this category is insured one of two ways. Some forms include this item in the definition of the structure or building under the temporary structures, materials, and supplies coverage. Machinery and equipment is added to the list in those forms. In other forms, called "two-item" forms, builders' machinery and equipment is a separate amount of insurance with its own limits. Coverage in the two-item form is for machinery and equipment owned by the named insured only while on the premises or within 100 feet of it.

Conditions With respect to contractual conditions, the builders' risk form has many clauses that were contained in the general property form—the debris removal, liberalization, nuclear energy, subrogation, mortgagee, power failure, electrical apparatus, and operation of building laws clauses. However, as one would expect, there are conditions that differ.

Amount of Insurance Clause. This provision explains the provisional amount of insurance figure and sets the insurance-to-value requirements of the form. It states that the insurance amount is only provisional, and the actual amount of insurance on the structure is the proportion of the provisional amount to the value of the structure at date of completion, but in no case will the policy pay more than the provisional amount or the loss. This clause has the same effect as a 100 percent coinsurance clause except the finished value of the structure is the required amount of insurance rather than the value of the structure at the time of loss.

Occupancy Clause. This provision restricts the occupancy of the structure. It says that the structure cannot be occupied without obtaining the consent of the insurer and paying any additional premium needed. The only exceptions to this restriction are for the testing of machinery and for dwellings. Machinery may be set up and operated for testing purposes. A dwelling for four families or less may be occupied for a period not to exceed ninety days. After that time period, coverage under the builders' risk form ceases unless notice is given, and an additional premium paid if needed.

Different Types of Builders' Risk Forms Thus far the discussion has been general, dealing with material that it is common to all builders' risk forms. Now the major different types of builders' risk forms will be examined. These forms include the completed value form and the reporting form.

Completed Value Form. This section will explain how the coverage operates and will examine the different types of completed value forms. Under the completed value form, insurance at the beginning of the policy is written for the full value of the finished building. Obviously, at the initial point of construction the insurance limit is higher than any potential loss. The *average* value of the building during the policy term is approximately one-half of the completed value of the structure. Therefore, the rate used for the builders' risk form is 50 to 55 percent of the full annual rate. The insured is encouraged to insure to value since the amount of insurance clause requires 100 percent insurance to value. If the insured determines after construction begins that the provisional limit is too low, it can be raised.

In most territories, builders' risk policies may not be written for a period of less than one year. This does not penalize the owner of a building which is completed in less than a year, because when a policy is canceled because of completion of the structure, the return premium is computed on the pro-rata basis.

In builders' risk forms the interests of various parties may be protected. The owner, contractor, subcontractor or some combination of the three may be insured.

CONTRACTORS' AUTOMATIC FORM. This form was developed for large contractors. It gives automatic protection for thirty days for insureds engaged in construction at several different sites. The insured must arrange specific insurance on each site, through the issuance of a new policy, after the thirty-day period elapses.

Another version of this form allows coverage to attach permanently without a separate policy for each location. However, the policy must be endorsed to show the location of each new construction. Also, this form may be written without a time limit. In a sense, it is an open policy with respect to time. To accomplish this, the word "open" is inserted in the space provided to show the policy's expiration date. However, each of the endorsements to the policy is written for a time period not exceeding one year. This means the policy is not entirely "open," for it is the endorsement that actually covers the various new construction sites.

CONTRACTORS' INTEREST COMPLETED VALUE FORM. This form covers a contractor's interest in improvements, repairs, additions, or alterations to buildings that have previously been completed. Through the use of this form contractors can insure their interest in any building upon which they are performing major alterations. The provisional amount of insurance must equal the value of the contract for the remodeling. As with other builders' risk forms, when the job is completed and the policy canceled, the insured receives a pro-rata refund.

Builders' Risk Reporting Form. Under this approach, the reporting form technique is applied to the builders' risk problem. Values are constantly increasing in a building under construction, so a reporting form is used to place increasing increments of coverage in force. The provisional amount of insurance in the builders' risk form becomes the limit of liability of the reporting form. Since reporting forms have an honesty clause, there is what amounts to a 100 percent coinsurance clause, as in the completed value form. The occupancy clause and the provisional amount of insurance clause are basically the same as for the completed value form. Thus, the only significant differences between the two forms are the reporting and the rating.

Since each report includes only values that exist at the time of the report, the rate charged is the normal annual rate for the time period for which protection is provided. The rate is not reduced as it is in the completed value forms. However, the same effect occurs because the full rate is charged for reduced periods of time.

Perils Insured Against Under Builders' Risk Forms Builders' risk policies can be used to insure against the fire and extended coverage perils, vandalism and malicious mischief, and other named perils, such as falling objects, weight of ice and snow, collapse, limited water damage, and limited glass damage. However, the special extended coverage form is popular and can be used to provide "all-risks" coverage on many different types of buildings. The coverage of the special extended coverage form will be examined in Chapter 4.

Chapter Notes

1. DeLancy v. Rockingham Farmers Mutual Insurance Co. (1873) 52 N.H. 581, 587. Quoted in *Property Insurance* by S. S. Huebner. (New York: Appleton-Century-Crofts, Inc., 1938.)
2. Hiram Walker, Inc. v. Insurance Companies, 1937, U.S. District Court for Northern Illinois, not appealed so not reported. See F.C.&S. Bulletins, Misc. Fire Gd-3.
3. *Georgia Rule Book,* Insurance Services Office of Georgia, p. 10.
4. Some recognize five forms. However, the fifth, Reporting Form A, can be written at a single location. When more than one location is covered, specific rather than average rates are used.
5. There is currently no ML-4. At one time a multiple location form no. 4 provided floater coverage, but this coverage is currently written under inland marine forms.
6. Also, this action "prevents the insured from 'underestimating' needs at a high rate location and then increasing the limit at that location once the average rate has been established." F.C.&S. Bulletins, Misc. Fire Gc-5 and 6.

CHAPTER 4

Forms for Special Property, Perils, and Liability

INTRODUCTION

This chapter has three general areas of concentration. The first is a continuation of the previous chapter's discussion of fire and allied lines forms for insurance against property damage. The forms discussed here are those specifically designed for particular types of occupancies, such as farms, public and institutional properties, and highly protected properties. Second, this chapter discusses forms that add to or change the perils insured against. As noted in the preceding chapter, there are fire and allied forms that provide protection against liability claims or income or expense loss. Liability coverage in fire and allied lines forms is discussed in the final section of this chapter. Income and expense forms are discussed at length in Chapter 5.

SPECIALTY FIRE AND ALLIED LINES FORMS

General property forms, such as form FGP-1 discussed in Chapter 3, are usable on a great variety of business operations. They have been designed to provide insurance coverage applicable to a broad range of business activities and to cover many types of buildings and personal property. Yet, the basic general property forms are not usable for all types of commercial property exposures.

Because of their unique operations, unusual problems, or low-loss probabilities, certain organizations require property forms especially designed to meet their needs. The first part of this chapter addresses itself to some of these specialty forms. Included in this analysis are forms for farm operations, public and institutional properties, highly protected risks (HPR), and several miscellaneous occupancies.

Farm Operations

Farms may be insured under single-line fire insurance policies or under multiple-line policies like the farmowners-ranchowners forms discussed in Chapter 15. The single-line policies are subject to significant regional variations, whereas there is much greater uniformity in the farmowners-ranchowners program. For this reason, a detailed discussion of farm coverage is deferred to Chapter 15.

Exposures of Farm Operations Today there are 9.3 million people engaged in producing the farm products for 203 million other Americans.[1] Farming has become increasingly sophisticated since the time of the industrial revolution. Farmers have become production planners, scientists, and business experts. Significant values are exposed to loss, with land selling in the midwest for $2,000 or more an acre and combines and tractors costing thousands of dollars. A farm supporting a father and son and their families may have a total value of over $1 million.[2] Corporate farms, usually managed by an employee of a farm management corporation, become even more complex and involve larger values.

A variety of types of property are exposed to loss, including dwellings, barns, granaries, sheds, contents of buildings, livestock, poultry, hay, grain, milk, and farm machinery. Many of these properties have characteristics that require insurance treatment different from that which can be provided by a general property form.

Many farm buildings are of frame construction and contain contents such as hay and straw that burn readily. Yet public fire protection is often severely limited. As a result, loss severity may be high.

Farm Property Forms Because there are many regional differences in farm insurance forms, this text will not provide a detailed analysis of any one form. However, a brief overview of one of the more common farm property forms (Form No. 64) will illustrate the ways in which coverage has been adapted to meet the needs of the farmer.

Form 64 contains thirteen different coverages, each of which is activated when a specific amount for that coverage is shown in the policy declarations. A separate description of coverage applies to each of the following:

A. Dwelling Coverage
B. Barns, Buildings and Structures Coverage

C. Portable Building Coverage
D. Private Power and Light Pole Coverage
E. Outdoor Radio and Television Equipment Coverage
F. Household and Personal Effects Coverage
G. Grain Coverage
H. Hay Coverage (in buildings)
I. Hay Coverage (in the open)
J. Machinery, Vehicle and Equipment Coverage
K. Specifically Insured Machinery Coverage
L. Poultry Coverage
M. Livestock Coverage
N. Fire Department Service Charges Coverage
O. Fence Coverage

These descriptions of coverage are quite different from those in the general property form and contain provisions that adapt coverage to the specific exposures of each type of property. For example, grain in stacks and swaths or piles in the open are covered only against loss by fire. Fence coverage covers "fences, corrals, pens, chutes and feed racks on the described premises but not field and pasture fences." The specifically insured machinery coverage provides automatic coverage (for the same amount) on replacement equipment.

An examination of the perils insured against also reveals some striking differences from the general property forms. In addition to coverage for fire and the extended coverage perils, specific provisions apply to electrocution of livestock, theft of livestock and specifically described machinery, and overturn of specifically described machinery.

The "general exclusions" further illustrate the way in which the farm property form is adapted for a specific purpose. In addition to the familiar exclusions such as the water exclusion, the war risk exclusion, and the nuclear clause, there is a firing of tobacco clause and a brooder exclusion. The former clause excludes coverage for fire loss caused by the use of an open fire to cure or dry tobacco. The latter excludes coverage for fire caused by a brooder, heating stove, or portable heating device used for poultry. (It is possible to obtain coverage for both these exposures.)

Special farm forms are available in some areas, including such forms as the turkey farm form, the chicken-broiler flock farm form, and various forms relating to cotton growing and processing. A detailed discussion of these forms would be beyond the scope of this course. However, their existence serves to illustrate the way in which specialized farm insurance has been made available where specialized needs exist.

Public and Institutional Properties

As of this writing, the public and institutional property forms have been withdrawn from use in almost all states. Nevertheless, the public and institutional property program will be briefly discussed here, because it represents an interesting evolution in the use of special forms for special types of property.

Because public and institutional properties (hospitals, schools, churches, governmental properties, and so on) traditionally had favorable loss experience, and for competitive reasons, special forms had been developed for them. Also, since people seldom stand to gain financially from arson or other intentional loss to public or institutional property, the moral hazard was generally considered to be slight; consequently, broad coverage was built into the program. For instance, the public and institutional property form was one of the first to give replacement cost protection on personal property, to allow replacement at a different location, and to use an agreed amount clause in place of the coinsurance clause. Unfortunately, in the late 1960s persons who sought to gain from the publicity or pressure generated by acts of vandalism, riot, or terrorism, saw public and institutional properties as vulnerable and sensitive targets. Loss ratios on these properties went up. The special form remained broad, but became more expensive and was not always readily available.

With the withdrawal of the public and institutional property forms, the general property form is now used on such properties as hospitals, churches, schools, and municipal and governmental buildings. However, one special feature of the old public and institutional program remains available for properties of this type—agreed amount coverage on both buildings and personal property is available by use of the agreed amount endorsement. (For noninstitutional properties, the agreed amount endorsement is usually not available to cover personal property.)

Highly Protected Risks

"Highly protected risks" (HPRs) are properties that have a low loss exposure because of sophisticated use of protective devices. Naturally, highly protected risks also have low rates per $100 of insurance and broad coverage. Typically HPR rates range from $.04 to $.15 per $100 of coverage while standard rates for similar but less protected occupancies can be many times greater.

To qualify for insurance on an HPR basis, a firm must meet certain underwriting standards. These requirements usually include the following items: [3]

1. automatic sprinklers, plus special protective systems over special hazards;
2. sprinkler supervision by a central station or, as a substitute for the central station, watchmen with clock rounds;
3. adequate water supplies;
4. large amount of property to be insured;
5. loss conscious management;
6. main buildings of slow-burning or fire-resistive construction; and
7. properly installed electrical equipment, good housekeeping, and periodic inspection of protective devices.

Many large, sprinklered manufacturing plants in fire-resistive buildings with special hazards properly protected qualify as highly protected risks.

Markets HPR policies are predominantly sold by six different organizations: Factory Mutuals, Industrial Risk Insurers (successor to Factory Insurance Association), Kemper Group, Improved Risk Mutuals, Commerce and Industry, and Liberty Mutual. Each of these groups has a staff of trained fire protection engineers with the ability to perform local inspections and to test protective equipment. Since just two groups—Industrial Risk Insurers (IRI) and the Factory Mutuals (FM)—dominate this market, the following material concentrates on their policies.

Industrial Risk Insurers' Contract Because the Industrial Risk Insurers' version is considered the standard HPR policy, it will be analyzed first.

While one can insure liability, business interruption, and boiler and machinery exposures under the IRI contract, the present discussion is limited to direct loss to property excluding boiler coverage.

Coverage of Property and Locations. The insuring agreement reads, "This policy covers . . . property of the Insured designated below . . . ." The designation is in the declarations (or on added schedules). Designations tend to be broad, primarily by specification of locations (i.e., "property at ______."). Within the policy, separate provisions apply to real property and to personal property.

With respect to real property, the terms specifically include buildings and other structures and include those under construction as well as those completed. Extensions, additions, and attached building equipment are also covered, as are machinery and equipment for building service. Materials and supplies for construction, alteration, and repair are covered while on the premises, or in the open, or on vehicles on land within 500 feet of the premises.

Since the phrase "real property" includes land, and underwriters and insureds are seldom interested in land coverage, there is a specific exclusion for land. But all other real property is covered unless there is special provision (e.g., in the declarations) to the contrary.

The coverage for personal property is also broad. All personal property of the insured is covered as well as property of others in the insured's care, custody, and control. Personal property of employees is insured except for their motor vehicles, and bullion and manuscripts are also protected. These items of property are insured while on the described premises or within 500 feet of the described premises while on open land or in vehicles. Besides the preceding coverage, the insured's interest in and liability for railroad rolling stock and contents thereof while on or within 500 feet of the premises is insured. As in the general property form, there is coverage for property away from the premises while being repaired or serviced. Also there is coverage if removed to avoid damage by flood, in addition to the usual coverage of property removed to avoid damage by perils insured against. Automatic off-premises protection is limited to $50,000 and sixty days.

The IRI policy also covers debris removal (but provides no demolition or building ordinance protection), improvements and betterments if the insured is the tenant, and newly acquired property if located in the United States and valued at either $100,000 or 1 percent of the amount of insurance.

Few types of personal property are excluded. There is no insurance for owned motor vehicles, although there is some protection for others' vehicles while on the described premises. (Such vehicles are covered when being loaded or unloaded and repaired or adjusted. Of course, they are only protected against loss caused by the insured perils.) Although not excluded, coverage on records, drawings, and manuscripts is limited to copying costs. The information contained on or in electronic data processing media is not insured.

Perils Insured Against. Basically the IRI contract is a named perils contract. However, it can be endorsed with a special coverage endorsement which converts the protection to an "all-risks" basis for both real and personal property.

In the basic policy the following perils are insured against: fire, lightning, wind and hail, leakage from fire protective equipment, explosion, smoke, sonic shock wave ($5,000 deductible), riot, civil commotion, vandalism, molten material, civil or military authority, vehicles, and aircraft. Nearly all of these perils are discussed in CPCU 1.

However, there are a few notable differences in the perils covered by the IRI form.

"Leakage from a fire protective system" is similar to but a little broader than sprinkler leakage. The coverage in the IRI form includes discharge from water hydrants located on the premises while sprinkler leakage does not. The molten material peril insures against loss caused by heat from molten material which has been accidentally discharged. No coverage exists for damage to the discharged material, cost of removing the material, or repairing the fault which allowed the discharge.

Even though the contract is a named perils policy, it does specifically exclude certain losses. Among those excluded are flood and increased loss due to enforcement of building ordinances. There are the usual types of provisions with respect to artificially generated currents and loss from change of temperature and humidity. Boiler and machinery coverage (discussed in a later chapter) is also available.

Coinsurance and Deductibles. The basic IRI contract has no coinsurance clause. In its place an agreed amount provision is employed. As long as the insured purchases as much insurance as is required by this clause, there is no insurance-to-value penalty. When repair or replacement cost coverage is written, the endorsement does contain a 90 percent coinsurance clause.

The basic policy requires a minimum deductible of $500 but larger ones may be chosen. With the special coverage endorsement, the deductible is a minimum of $25,000 or one-half of 1 percent of the values insured, whichever is less.

Factory Mutuals' Contract The Factory Mutual (FM) policy is very similar to the IRI policy except that a few more perils are insured against in the basic FM policy. These perils include collapse, radioactive contamination, liquid damage, and volcanic eruption. These perils are discussed in the following paragraphs.

Collapse. The collapse peril has a $25,000 deductible in the Factory Mutual policy and pays because of collapse of buildings, structures, or a material part thereof. Collapse caused by or resulting from flood, earthquake, landslide, subsidence, or any other earth movement is excluded. In addition, the policy specifically states that settling, cracking, shrinking, bulging, or expansion of pavements, foundation, walls, floors, ceilings, or roof is not considered collapse. Property in transit or underground is specifically excluded and a blank is left in which to describe other property that the insurer might wish to exclude.

One of the problems associated with the collapse peril involves the definition of the term "collapse." Insurers prefer the strict interpretation: ". . . to break down completely; to fall or shrink together abruptly and completely; to cave in, fall in or give way; to undergo ruin or destruction by or as if by falling down." Using this interpretation courts held the following not to be collapse:

> A concrete "mat" [apparently a large concrete slab built over filled ground] upon which a house rested, dropped suddenly and caused a "twisting" of the foundation. The building remained intact, in that none of the floors, walls, or roof fell. However, cracks and holes appeared in the walls, doors were jammed, plaster fell from the ceiling, and the building itself broke away from the party wall of the adjoining building.[4]

Along this line some courts have ruled that there must be a falling or a loss of shape, or reduction to flattened form or rubble. The preceding definition represents a rather conservative judicial opinion and there are numerous cases where courts have accepted claims as collapse when only a partial collapse occurred. Both insurers and insureds should be fully aware of the distinctions relative to the definition of "collapse."

Radioactive Contamination and Volcanic Eruption. Radioactive contamination will be discussed in greater detail in the section on perils later in this chapter. A $5,000 deductible applies to radioactive contamination coverage in the Factory Mutual form.

The volcanic eruption coverage specifically excludes earthquake, subsidence, or other earth movement. Earthquake coverage, if desired, should be purchased elsewhere.

Liquid Damage. The liquid damage peril is similar to the water damage policy except protection is not limited to damage by water. Coverage exists for loss caused by accidental discharge, leakage, backup, or overflow of liquids from within piping, plumbing systems, or tanks other than fire protection systems. These systems are insured under the policy by the sprinkler leakage provision. The insurance covers damage caused by these liquids but no payment is made for replacement or removal of the discharged liquid. Like the collapse peril, there is a $25,000 deductible on this coverage.

Other Characteristics. Typically the FM policy is written on a blanket basis and contains an agreed amount clause based on 80 percent insurance to value for actual cash value coverage and 90 percent insurance to value for replacement cost coverage. The standard deductible is $500; higher deductibles are often used. Boiler and machinery insurance can be, and often is, written as part of the contract in a separate section.

Miscellaneous Specialty Forms

Other property forms are necessary to properly insure occupancies in which the property is so unusual that the general property form would not be adequate. This inadequacy may result from the hazards involved or problems in standard descriptions of the property insured. For instance, automobile filling stations need a form that gives coverage for underground tanks and piping and the general property form does not include these items. Therefore, a special form is required to meet the needs of this group of customers. Selected examples illustrate the treatment of some special problems. Discussion here is not exhaustive but illustrates the way in which special forms are adapted to meet special needs.

Cotton Gin Eight different categories of property are covered in the cotton gin form. These include the gin house, cotton ginning equipment, grist mill, boiler room, steam engines, gas, oil, or gasoline engines, the cotton house, and the seed house. By breaking down the property into all these different categories, the insured can choose which are to be insured and for how much. Likewise, the insurer can restrict its loss exposure on any one item if it so chooses.

This form contains most of the standard clauses found in property contracts: coinsurance, work and materials, debris removal, and so on. However, it does have three special conditions that uniquely adapt the form to the insurable exposures:

1. Special permission is required to store cotton or hay in the gin house.
2. Notice must be given the insurance company if the gin is to be idle during the normal ginning season.
3. The insured must use due diligence to prohibit smoking in the ginning section.

No cotton or cotton products are insured under this form, as these are insured under a cotton and cotton products form. From this discussion, one can see how an entire group of special standard forms has been developed to meet the needs of a specific industry—cotton growing and processing. The same is true of tobacco farming and poultry raising.

Lumber Forms There are at least two speciality forms in this area: one for retail lumberyards and one for manufacturing and other operations that have lumberyards on their premises. These forms were designed originally to insure all the different types of equipment and structures present on the premises of a lumberyard. In many areas, form FGP-1 is now used in place of a specialty form.

Retail Lumberyard. This form insures the buildings and merchandise found in a retail lumberyard. There is also coverage on a legal liability basis for property of others in the insured's control. In addition to this coverage, office furniture and supplies, machinery, tools, and equipment are protected. Even vehicles other than automobiles and gasoline trucks are insured. This provision is quite desirable since a lumberyard will often have mobile equipment on the premises that is used to move the lumber and other wood products.

Manufacturing and Other Lumberyard Operations. Protection under this form is restricted to lumber products. No coverage is provided for buildings, equipment, and other materials. Often there are clear space requirements around dry kilns, woodworking shops, and manufacturing areas.

Automobile Filling Stations Under this form all real and personal property above and below ground (not specifically excluded) is insured. Included in this definition of property insured are underground tanks, contents of tanks, piping and connections, pumps, hoists, and lifts. On a legal liability basis, property of others is also insured.

Since all real and personal property is brought under coverage by the basic coverage clause, one expects several exclusions. There are seven clauses that exclude different types of property. Excluded by these clauses are automobile storage garages, tire repair shops (other than patching), foundations, architects' fees, accounts, currency, securities, and motor vehicles. This last item represents a rather significant exclusion since many service stations own motor vehicles and almost all have motor vehicles of others in their care, custody, or control. When protection is desired for these exposures, automobile insurance forms are needed. (Automobile insurance is examined in CPCU 4.)

Careful reading of the exclusions section shows that coverage is provided only for buildings designed for filling station use or for certain joint occupancies. Most important is the provision that if a portion of the building is used as a restaurant or lunchroom, then the entire building and its contents are excluded.

Petroleum Property Form This form is designed for oil refineries, gasoline plants, pump stations, and oil terminals. As with the automobile filling station form, all real and personal property on the described premises is insured, as is property located on vehicles or railway cars in the open and within 100 feet of the premises.

Again, since the basic coverage is quite broad, exclusions play an important role. Normally excluded are cost of excavations and fillings, foundations, architects' fees, aircraft, watercraft, and motor vehicles.

Railway rolling stock and contents are insured only while on the premises for consignment to or while being loaded by the insured. If the railroad is just switching cars and some railroad cars are damaged, there is no coverage unless the railway stock was consigned to the insured or shipped out by the insured. Other exclusions include land values, earthen or concrete flow, or storage pits, reservoirs, and their contents. This last exclusion is unique to the petroleum form.

Due to the nature of the occupancy, a special settlement clause is inserted in the form. This clause values crude petroleum at market price plus transportation cost and any premium charges, subject to a maximum of replacement value of like quality crude at the site of and at the time of the loss. Other petroleum products are to be settled at replacement value.

An unusual clause in the petroleum form is the foam clause. The reference is to material used to extinguish petroleum fires. Protection is provided for loss of foam stored on the premises at the time of the fire and expended or destroyed in fighting a fire on the insured or adjacent premises. Chemicals brought in after the fire has started to try to extinguish it are not insured.

PERILS COVERAGE IN FIRE AND ALLIED LINES POLICIES AND FORMS

Whatever the subject matter of a fire and allied lines policy—property loss, income or expense loss, or liability—the contract contains provisions with respect to the perils that must damage specified property before the coverage applies. (Rain insurance is the only general exception to this statement in fire and allied lines forms. In it the peril is specified but property damage is never required. Rain insurance, discussed in Chapter 13, pays for loss of income when an outdoor event, such as a fair or a sports event, is canceled or interrupted on account of rain, hail, snow, or sleet.) In CPCU 1, the perils in the New York standard fire policy and the extended coverage endorsement are discussed at length. The content of these is therefore only reviewed here. Other policies and perils forms are considered at length.

Because forms and rules vary from one territory to another, and because there are sometimes fine points of difference between similar forms, the following discussion is general and subject to variation in specific forms or rating territories. It would be best to consult the specific form or rules involved in resolving specific points of coverage, availability, or applicability of coverage.

Review of Fire Policy Perils

In the fire policy, three basic "perils" are named: fire, lightning, and removal. The fire peril includes only hostile fires, that is, a flame or glow must exist and the fire must be outside its intended receptacle. Lightning is an electrical charge generated by nature as opposed to artificially generated electrical currents.

The removal "peril" provides coverage for "removal" of property from premises endangered by a peril insured against. Removal is actually a hazard rather than a peril. Removal of property from a threatened building increases the chances of loss to that property, and the policy provides coverage for removed property damaged by any peril during the actual removal process.

Review of Extended Coverage Perils

The emphasis here is on the definition of each of the perils. Conditions of the extended coverage form and property excluded are discussed only briefly.

The extended coverage endorsement extends the number of perils covered by the standard fire policy. These same perils are insured in other forms and/or policies and often have definitions different from those used in the extended coverage form. The definitions given in this section pertain only to the extended coverage form.

The extended coverage perils consist of windstorm and hail, explosion, riot, riot attending a strike, civil commotion, aircraft, vehicles, and smoke. A useful acronym for remembering their names is W. C. SHAVER (W = windstorm; C = civil commotion; S = smoke; H = hail; A = aircraft; V = vehicle; E = explosion; R = riot, riot attending a strike.)

Other acronyms used to remember the extended coverage perils are REV. SHAW and WHARVES. Whichever mnemonic device is used, it is important not only to know the names of these perils, but precisely what loss causes are included within their definitions.

Windstorm and Hail Except for policies covering growing crops, the perils of windstorm and hail go together. The terms "windstorm" and "hail" are not defined in insurance contracts. Coverage is partially delineated by describing what is not insured. The form provides no protection for losses occurring from (1) frost, cold, or ice (other than hail); and (2) snow or sleet whether driven by wind or not. If an object driven by the wind causes external damage to the insured structure, then subsequent damage caused by rain, snow, or any other object would be covered. Damage caused by rain blown through an open window is not covered. However, if the wind breaks the window and wind-blown rain enters the structure, coverage exists. This exclusion stands up better in theory than in practice. As Emmett J. Vaughan states, "It does not take a member of the bar to figure out how to cope with this exclusion. In many such losses the insurance company ends up paying for the water damage and the broken window."[5]

Damage due to flood, surface water, waves, tidal water or tidal wave, overflow of streams or other bodies of water, or spray from any of the foregoing, whether driven by wind or not, is not covered. This exclusion eliminates from coverage much of the water damage that occurs during a hurricane.

Riot, Riot Attending a Strike, and Civil Commotion The extended coverage form treats these three perils together and, again, does not define them. Riot has statutory definitions, but unfortunately each state does not use the same definition. A common definition is:

> Whenever three or more persons, having assembled for any purpose, disturb the public peace by using force or violence to any other person or to property or threaten or attempt to commit such disturbance or to do an unlawful act by the use of force or violence, accompanied with the power of immediate execution of such threat or attempt, they are guilty of riot.[6]

Some states say two persons can commit an act of riot while other states require up to five persons.

Civil commotion has been described as an uprising of citizens.[7] "Civil commotion" and "riot" are quite similar and the two terms combined should include most uprisings. The coverage for riot during a strike was developed during the labor strife of the 1930s to provide protection for damage occurring during a labor strike. The violent actions of the strikers at the Washington Post in 1975 is a more recent example of this peril: in cases like this, where strikers became very violent and damaged many of the newspaper's presses, loss can be quite severe.

The large number of civil disturbances over civil rights and the Vietnam conflict during the 1960s and early 1970s increased the seriousness of the riot exposure. Because of losses and the further possibility of catastrophic losses from the riot exposure, insurers restricted the availability of extended coverage to certain parts of urban areas. Therefore, the Fair Access to Insurance Requirements (FAIR) Plan was started, under which the federal government reinsured certain loss exposures, and private insurers made coverage available to the previously restricted areas.

Interestingly enough, while the federal government and insurers worked together to solve the problem, local government retreated. Before the riots of the 1960s and 1970s, many local governments were considered liable for riot damage, and some state legislatures had stripped the local governments of their sovereign immunity with respect to riots. When the large losses of the sixties started, many of these statutes were repealed and/or were held invalid by the courts.[8]

Smoke The extended coverage form does define the smoke peril as "sudden and accidental damage from smoke, other than from agricultural smudging or industrial operations."

Aircraft and Vehicles These two perils are treated together in the extended coverage form. Vehicles are described as "vehicles running on land or tracks but not aircraft." With vehicles, there usually must be direct physical contact between the vehicle and the damaged property or the building containing the property. With aircraft, the contact may be with something that fell from the aircraft. Examples of losses not covered because of the direct physical contact provision include: a vehicle collides with a pole owned by the telephone company and the pole hits the insured property; a chain is attached to a loading dock and to the vehicle, and the vehicle drives away causing damage to the dock; and the weight of a vehicle breaks a water pipe which causes extensive water damage to the insured premises. This direct physical contact requirement also eliminates sonic boom claims.

Regardless of whether direct physical contact occurs, all damage done by vehicles owned or operated by the insured is excluded. However, damage done by an aircraft owned or operated by the insured is covered.

Explosion The form does not actually define explosion, but it does contain some inclusions and exclusions. The form states, explosion shall include "direct loss resulting from the explosion of accumulated gases or unconsumed fuels within the firebox (or combustion chamber) of any fired vessel or within the flues or passages which conduct the gases of combustion therefrom." Explosion also includes combustion of gunpowder, dynamite, gasoline, and natural gas. Damage caused by a contractor's blasting is also covered. Loss due to malicious explosion as well as explosion of a container of compressed air is insured.

Some exclusions to the peril of explosion eliminate coverage best purchased on a boiler and machinery policy or serve better to define the peril. Excluded is, "explosion of steam boilers, steam pipes, steam turbines or steam engines if owned by, leased by or operated under the control of the insured." If the landlord owns and operates the steam boiler, the tenants' extended coverage includes damage to their property from that (or a neighbor's) steam boiler.

Also excluded as explosions are: shock waves caused by aircraft, electric arcing, and water hammer; rupture or bursting of rotating or moving parts of machinery caused by centrifugal force; rupture or bursting of water pipes or pressure relief devices; and rupture or bursting due to expansion or swelling of the contents of any building or structure caused by or resulting from water. This last exclusion means that when moisture in a grain storage silo or elevator causes a sudden expansion and collapse of the structure, there is no coverage under the explosion peril.

Perils Forms Added Only to Extended Coverage

The following discussion is limited to forms that are used only in connection with extended coverage.

Vandalism and Malicious Mischief The preceding section stated that a riot usually consists of three or more persons behaving in an unlawful manner and disturbing the peace. Situations in which only one or two persons are involved or when any number act quietly are not included under riot coverage. The vandalism and malicious mischief (V&MM) form fills this gap in coverage. Typically the V&MM form covers damage done by racketeers, spiteful employees, cranks, and mischievous persons of all ages.

Definition of Vandalism and Malicious Mischief. These synonymous terms are defined in the form as, "only the willful and malicious damage to or destruction of the property covered." The words "vandalism" and "malicious mischief" were undefined or only loosely defined in the earlier form. As a result, courts tended to rule that intent or malice were not necessary ingredients for a loss to be covered. With this new definition, intent and malice must be proven if a loss is to be covered.

Vacancy and Unoccupancy Provision. A vacant building is without furniture or occupants; an unoccupied building is without occupants. If a building is vacant or unoccupied beyond thirty consecutive days, V&MM coverage is suspended. There is a similar provision in the New York standard fire policy, analyzed in CPCU 1. Note that the V&MM provision is more restrictive than the standard fire policy and allows only thirty days, compared to the fire policy's sixty days. Also, provisions in forms attached to the fire policy granting permission for more extended vacancy or unoccupancy do *not* affect the V&MM limitation *unless* they *specifically* say so. It should be obvious that the probability of V&MM is greatly increased when a building is vacant or unoccupied.

EXCEPTIONS TO OCCUPANCY PROVISION. There are three exceptions to the V&MM occupancy requirement. The first two are for private dwellings and designated seasonal occupancies, such as schools or canning factories. Only unoccupancy is allowed; vacancy (beyond thirty consecutive days) is not.

The third exception is the broadest one. It states, "a building in the process of construction shall not be deemed vacant or unoccupied." However, the question does arise about the status of a building that is vacant because an insured peril has damaged the property and repairs are being completed. Technically the building is vacant, but the insurer knows the building is vacant and why it is vacant. It would not seem reasonable to force the insured to occupy the damaged building to keep the insurance effective. Consequently, most but not all courts have ruled that a building under reconstruction should be considered under construction.

MODIFICATION OF VACANCY AND OCCUPANCY PROVISION. This provision may be altered by the use of the vandalism and malicious mischief vacancy or unoccupancy endorsement. This form is needed to extend the number of days the building can be vacant or unoccupied. The form requires an additional premium and the extension period cannot go beyond the expiration date of the vacancy privilege in the fire policy to which the vandalism and malicious mischief form is attached. Since the standard fire policy vacancy provision is sixty days, this extension cannot be more than thirty days unless the fire policy's vacancy provision is modified.

Exclusions. The V&MM form exclusions which pertain: (1) to damage to glass; (2) to loss caused by theft, burglary or larceny; (3) to explosion of steam boilers; (4) to loss due to radioactive materials; and (5) to consequential losses.

GLASS. The glass exclusion states that loss "to glass (other than glass building blocks) constituting part of a building, structure, or an outside sign," is not covered. This provision eliminates windows, glass doors, and skylights from coverage.

CRIME. Loss by pilferage, theft, burglary, or larceny is not insured. However, willful damage to the building done by burglars is covered. Covered damage could result from persons ransacking the premises searching for money or from unsuccessful thieves who wreck the premises out of frustration.

EXPLOSION OF STEAM BOILERS. This exclusion is basically the same steam boiler exclusion found in the extended coverage endorsement. If vandalism or malicious mischief caused the boiler to explode, there would be no coverage. If a person wrecked the steam boiler or a steam engine without the occurrence of an explosion, coverage could exist.

Radioactive Materials. The specific name of this exclusion is the nuclear exclusion. It is a broad exclusion, eliminating coverage for any loss that might arise from nuclear reaction, radiation, or radioactive contamination. The radioactive contamination endorsement can be used partially to fill the gap created by this exclusion, but that endorsement only pertains to contamination from materials stored on the premises.

Consequential Losses. This clause states that the company shall not be liable for loss from depreciation, delay, deterioration, or loss of market; nor for any loss resulting from a change in temperature or humidity. This provision is designed to eliminate coverage for indirect losses; it is essentially the same as the one used in riot coverage.

To cover the spoilage loss exposure, the insured would need to purchase the riot and vandalism power failure loss assumption endorsement. This form will be discussed in connection with indirect losses in Chapter 5.

Clauses Limiting Recovery. There are two major clauses that limit recovery on an insured event. One is a deductible clause and the other is the apportionment clause found in the extended coverage endorsement, or other form to which the V&MM form is attached. These two clauses can force the insured to recover less than the full value of the loss.

Deductible Clause. This clause is usually either a flat deductible or a percentage of the amount of insurance carried by the insured. A typical flat deductible is $100. The percentage deductible is normally 2 percent of the amount of insurance carried, but not less than $250 nor more than $2,500. The $2,500 figure serves as an upper bound on the deductible. Property insured for $1 million would have a $2,500 deductible and not $20,000 (2 percent of $1 million). The percentage deductible, where used, applies to each building and contents loss.

Apportionment Clause. When attached to the extended coverage endorsement, the vandalism and malicious mischief form is considered to have the EC apportionment provision—if V&MM coverage is not carried on all policies covering certain property, the policy responds by paying its portion of the loss just as though all policies provided coverage. Were it not for this apportionment provision, some policyholders with more than one policy on a given location might carry V&MM coverage on only one policy, recognizing the relatively low probable loss severity of a V&MM loss. If this were permitted, premiums would not be adequate to cover the loss exposures. Insurance to value is encouraged by this provision, and a penalty is exacted for underinsurance.

Sonic Boom A sonic shock wave endorsement can be attached to policies containing an extended coverage endorsement. This endorsement modifies the extended coverage endorsement to include losses caused by sonic shock waves generated by aircraft. However, there is a $500 mandatory deductible that applies separately to each structure insured and to the contents of each. As a result, a person owning three buildings and their contents which were damaged might retain $3,000 in losses. The form also contains the standard nuclear exclusion.

Since a rather sizable deductible exists and the loss frequency is limited, the rate is fairly low. The 80 percent coinsurance rate in most areas is $.01 per $100 or $1.00 for $10,000 worth of protection. A higher no-coinsurance rate is also available. For insureds with relatively large values to insure but subject to small sonic boom losses, the no-coinsurance choice might be attractive even though the rate is higher.

These two forms—V&MM and sonic boom—are the only two endorsements used exclusively with extended coverage. All the remaining perils and forms reviewed in this section can be used with or without the extended coverage endorsement.

Optional Perils The optional perils form is an alternative for those who do not want to purchase the indivisible package of perils insured against in the extended coverage endorsement. It also allows an insurer to exercise some selectivity. For example, the underwriter may be willing to provide coverage for all the extended coverage perils except windstorm and hail. Thus, the optional perils form could be substituted for the extended coverage form when the chance of windstorm loss is too great to be insurable. Such might be the circumstances in beach areas and other places where windstorms frequently occur.[9]

The possible combinations of perils available under this endorsement are as follows:

1. explosion;
2. explosion with riot and civil commotion;
3. explosion, riot, civil commotion, vandalism and malicious mischief; or
4. aircraft and vehicle damage (can be combined with 1, 2, or 3 above).

The provisions of these optional perils are the same as in the extended coverage endorsement. However, the optional perils form is not often used today and may not even be available in some rating territories.

Damage by Water

Much property is exposed to the possibility of damage by water. The possible specific causes range from a sink overflow caused by a dripping faucet to a flood covering hundreds of square miles. Insurance practice does not treat all water loss exposures in one contract and coverage varies among policies. Thus, to obtain the most complete coverage available, it is necessary to combine several different contracts. In this section these various policies and forms will be examined. The forms to be discussed are as follows:

1. sprinkler leakage
2. water damage
    - limited
    - broad
3. flood
    - governmental
    - private

Sprinkler Leakage Insurance Automatic sprinkler systems are one of the most effective fire fighting tools ever developed. One example of a sprinkler system is shown in Figure 4-1.

An automatic sprinkler system usually consists of pipes placed along the ceiling of a building. These pipes are equipped at intervals (commonly ten- or fifteen-foot intervals) with sprinkler heads containing valves which are generally held in position by fusible links. Depending on the type, when the air around a sprinkler head reaches a given temperature, the valve in a sprinkler head opens and the water is sprinkled on the area below, thus extinguishing any fire. The heat that activates the system can originate from any source since the fusible link in a sprinkler head cannot distinguish between fire heat and heat from other sources.

Sprinkler systems may be "wet pipe" or "dry pipe." The wet pipe system contains water (or sometimes an antifreeze solution) in the pipes, and these pipes are connected to a water supply so that an immediate and constant supply of water is released upon the fire. In a dry pipe system shown in the refrigerated area in Figure 4-1, there is air instead of water in the pipes around the heads. The air is compressed to keep the water further down the line (behind the valve) under pressure. Quickly (although not instantly) after the opening of a sprinkler head, water rushes to it.

Wet systems have a faster response time than dry pipe systems.[10] However, dry systems are desirable where temperatures are such that the water would freeze.

Some automatic extinguishing systems use extinguishing agents other than water, such as carbon dioxide, halon, or a dry chemical extinguishing agent.

Although sprinkler systems are very beneficial in extinguishing fires, they introduce a new exposure—accidental discharge from the

Figure 4-1
Automatic Sprinkler System*

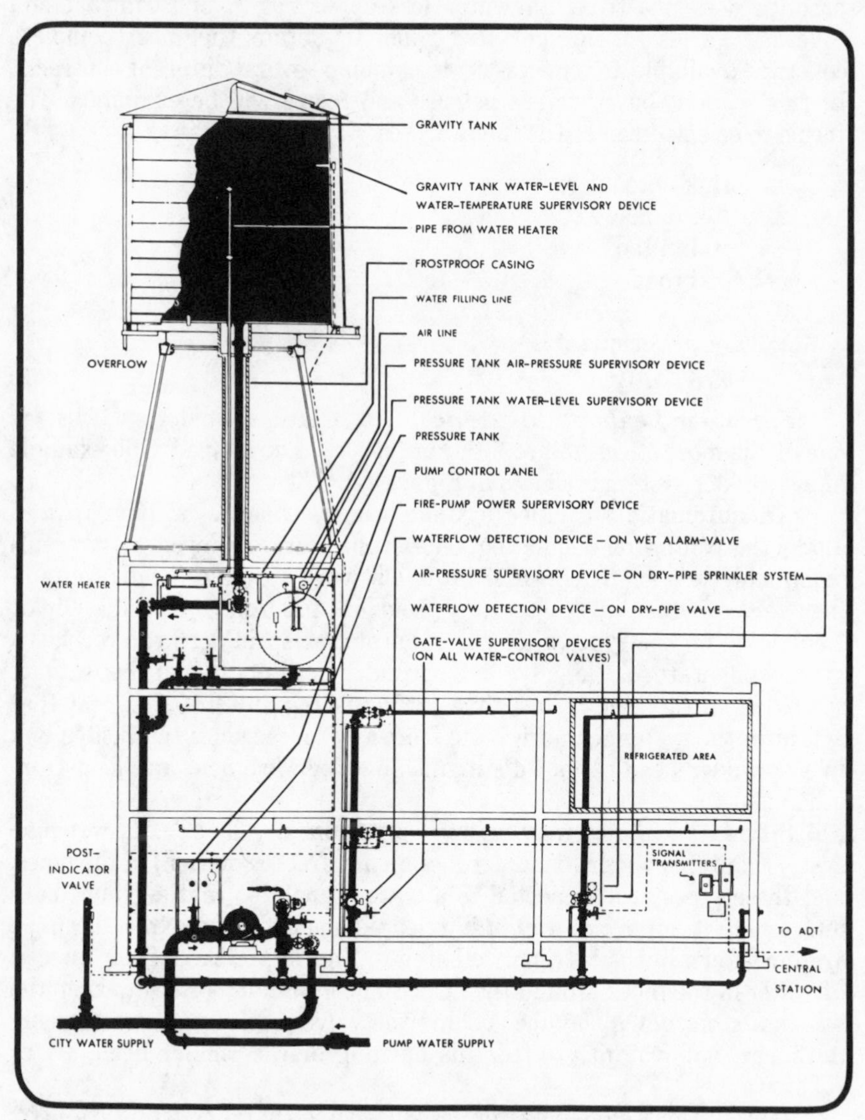

*Reprinted with permission of ADT Security Systems.

system that can damage property. The sprinkler system will activate at a given degree of temperature or rate of change in temperature, regardless of the heat source. Discharge can be caused by a welder's torch, overheating of unit heaters, or sunlight through a skylight in an attic room. A combination of high heat and a low temperature fuse can cause accidental discharge. Other events that can cause leakage include freezing of pipes in unheated areas, mechanical injury to sprinklers or pipes (e.g., from the operation of lift trucks), settlement of water storage tanks, and disintegration of fusing material on old sprinklers.[11] A large water storage tank is frequently installed to assure adequate water—quantity and pressure—to a system. Collapse of such a tank can cause much damage.

Automatic sprinkler systems solve more problems than they create. Automatic sprinkler systems have greatly reduced loss severity for firms so equipped. The possibility of an undetected discharge from a sprinkler system can be reduced by a simple local gong, driven by water pressure, that sounds when water flows through a system. More sophisticated systems, like that pictured in Figure 4-1, sound an alarm at a central station of an alarm company, such as Wells Fargo or ADT, whenever water flows. The primary purpose of these alarms is to alert plant personnel and fire departments to a fire, but they serve equally well for a false alarm. Sprinkler systems solve more problems than they cause, but nevertheless introduce another potential loss cause. Because of the potential damage from any of the components of an automatic sprinkler system, sprinkler leakage insurance was created.

There are variations in the sprinkler leakage forms used in different territories. The discussion which follows examines the sprinkler leakage endorsement used in some southeastern states (southeastern fire and allied form 781-8, 6-71 edition).

Definition of Sprinkler Leakage. The endorsement defines the term "sprinkler leakage" to mean "(a) leakage or discharge of water or other substances from within any 'Automatic Sprinkler System' or (b) direct loss caused by collapse or fall of tank(s) forming a part of such a system." The term "other substance" could include the accidental discharge from a system that contained CO_2 gas, Halon gas, or even an antifreeze solution in a wet pipe system. The phrase "from within any Automatic Sprinkler System" requires the discharge to come from the inside of the system. Condensation that occurs on the outside of the pipes and causes damage to property is not covered. The endorsement defines the term "automatic sprinkler system" to mean:

> . . . sprinklers, discharge nozzles, and ducts, pipes, valves, fittings, tanks (including component parts and supports thereof), pumps and private fire protection mains, all connected with and constituting a part of an automatic fire protective system; and non-automatic fire protective systems, hydrants, standpipes or outlets supplied from an automatic fire protective system.

Note that leakage from such a nonautomatic system is covered as long as it is supplied by an automatic system.

The second section of the automatic sprinkler system definition includes damage done by water storage tanks. Such tanks often stand on the roof of a building. If they collapse, a tremendous amount of water is released. Also, the weight of the tank itself adds to the damage. A 9,000 gallon steel pressure tank weighs 16,700 pounds and the water in it weighs 50,000 pounds.[12] When such a tank falls, considerable damage commonly results.

Because the form does not address the question of where the sprinkler system must be located, leakage from within any system is covered. Situations that could lead to loss in a nonsprinklered building include the collapse of or leakage from a storage tank on a nearby building or a tank on that building used to serve another building.

Property Insured. Property is insurable under seven categories: buildings, contents, stock only, furniture and fixtures, machinery, property of employees, and improvements and betterments. The broadest combination of property coverage is obtained by choosing the options for building and contents. However, if one does not desire to cover all contents, coverage can be limited to a combination of stock only, furniture and fixtures, and machinery. Insuring of only one of these three groups of items is also perfectly acceptable. If an insured believed that only the stock was likely to be damaged by sprinkler leakage, then the "stock only" option could be selected. The following discussion summarizes what is covered in these property categories.

BUILDING. As usual, "building" includes additions and extensions attached to it and permanent fixtures, machinery, and equipment forming a part of the building and pertaining to the service of the building. The sprinkler system is also insured and is covered against damage caused by freezing.

The building coverage section excludes the cost of excavations, grading, and foundations below the lowest basement floor. These items are not included in any coinsurance requirements and if coverage is desired, a special endorsement must be written to include them.

CONTENTS, STOCK, FURNITURE AND FIXTURES, AND MACHINERY. These four items are discussed together since the insured must decide which combination of them to select. When the "contents" option is chosen, then the other three options are not needed. If the "contents" option is not taken, then some combination of the remaining three should be considered.

The "contents" option simply states that contents owned by the insured and contained in the building located at the premises designated in the policy are insured unless specifically excluded. This section includes all exclusions of the basic fire policy to which the endorsement is attached, as well as the exclusions in the sprinkler leakage endorsement. In the "contents" option, personal property used to service and maintain the building is covered (i.e., not excluded). The other options that could provide coverage for these pieces of property specifically exclude them.

If it is not desirable to cover all contents, one or more of the other three options may be selected.[13] The "stock only" option insures owned merchandise, materials, and supplies usual and incidental to the occupancy. The "furniture and fixture" and "machinery" options also provide coverage on property as indicated by their names.

PROPERTY OF EMPLOYEES OR MEMBERS OF THE FIRM. This option provides coverage for sprinkler leakage damage to personal property of employees and members of the firm while such property is located in the building.

IMPROVEMENTS AND BETTERMENTS. This protection is only written when the insured is not the owner of the building. When feasible, this item should be insured by the owner of the structure, because the coverage costs 50 percent more when sold to the lessee. It would seem costs could be reduced if the owner insured the property and the lessee and lessor had a separate written contract concerning insurance proceeds pertaining to damage to improvements and betterments.

If coverage is purchased under this option, recovery is measured by the same three methods as discussed for improvements and betterments in the previous chapter:

1. When the owner pays for the repairs and makes no charge to the insured, the endorsement pays nothing.
2. When the insured makes the repairs, payment is based on actual cash value of property repaired or replaced.
3. When no repairs or replacements are made, claims are settled using the original cost of the improvements and betterments as the basis of recovery.

Extension of Coverage. Besides the preceding options, coverage is extended for two special situations: insured's interest in property of others, and property in the insured's care, custody, or control.

INSURED'S INTEREST IN PROPERTY OF OTHERS. This extension insures the value of labor and materials that the insured has in such property. The property must be similar to the personal property insured under the endorsement. If the insured buys only protection for machinery, then only machinery is covered by this extension.

PERSONAL PROPERTY IN THE INSURED'S CARE, CUSTODY, OR CONTROL. For this extension to apply, the insured must have at least a 25 percent coinsurance clause in the endorsement. Again, property must be similar to property insured under the form. Coverage is limited to an *additional* amount of insurance equal to 2 percent of the amount of insurance applicable to each category of personal property up to a maximum of $2,000. If the insured carries $10,000 coverage on stock and $5,000 coverage on furniture and fixtures, then coverage for this extension is $200 on stock and $100 on furniture and fixtures.

The usual conditions apply to this provision:

1. The insurer has the right to settle directly all claims with third parties.
2. The coinsurance clause does not apply to the extension.
3. There is an apportionment clause that reduces recovery if some of the insured's policies do not have this extension.

Restrictions on Property Coverage. Protection is restricted in amount on two special types of property. Books of account, abstracts, and drawings are insured for only the cost of blank material and the cost to transcribe or copy such records. Recovery for damaged film, tape, disc, drum, cell, and other magnetic recording or storage media is restricted to the cost of unexposed or blank materials.

Clauses Limiting Recovery. There are several clauses in the endorsement that apply to almost all items and limit recovery. These clauses include the coinsurance clause, the additional perils and property excluded clauses, the apportionment clause, and the conditions suspending or restricting coverage clause.

COINSURANCE REQUIREMENTS. Sprinkler leakage insurance may be written with or without a coinsurance clause. If written without such a clause, the minimum amount of coverage written is $25,000. Unlike some coverages, there is a wide range of coinsurance choices, as shown in Table 4-1. This wide range is used because, in many cases, loss severity can be expected to be as low as 10 percent or 25 percent of the values exposed, and it might be unrealistic to require insurance to a higher percentage of value.

The rate credits reported in Table 4-1 are interpreted in the following examples. If the no-coinsurance rate is $.50 per hundred, the 10 percent coinsurance rate is $.20 per hundred, and the 25 percent rate is $.10 per hundred. After the 25 percent choice, the rate credits are not nearly as significant, and insureds seldom choose a higher coinsurance clause.

One can select different coinsurance clauses for different categories of property. The insured could have a 10 percent clause on the building and a 25 percent clause on contents or some other personal property category.

ADDITIONAL PERILS NOT INSURED. The form excludes losses resulting from sprinkler leakage or collapse of a water tank caused by a number of perils. These perils include fire, lightning, windstorm, earthquake, blasting, explosion, rupture of steam boilers or flywheels,

Table 4-1

Coinsurance Choices and Credits for Sprinkler Leakage*

Coinsurance Clause	Rate Credit
10% clause	60%
25% clause	80%
50% clause	85%
80% clause	90%
100% clause	91%

*Reprinted with permission from *Georgia Rule Book* (New York: Insurance Services Office, May 1963), p. 1261.

riot, civil commotion, water (except from within sprinkler system), war, insurrection, and order of civil authority. Many of the losses caused by these perils are covered by standard policies and endorsements such as the fire policy and the extended coverage endorsement.

In addition to these excluded perils there is a clause containing the standard nuclear exclusion. The form also has another exclusion concerning personal property in which both the insured and parties other than the insured have an insurable interest. There is no coverage when the insured's interest in such property is otherwise covered by insurance.

APPORTIONMENT CLAUSE. The sprinkler leakage endorsement contains the same type of apportionment clause found in the extended coverage and V&MM endorsements.

Clauses Suspending Coverage. There are three clauses that suspend coverage in certain instances—the alarm or watchman service clause, the vacancy and unoccupancy clause, and the alterations clause.

ALARM OR WATCHMAN SERVICE CLAUSE. A major factor in the amount of damage done by accidental discharge from a sprinkler system (excluding fall of a tank) is how much time elapses before a sprinkler head is plugged or the master valve on the system is turned off. Therefore, rate discounts are given when there is a sprinkler alarm system or watchman service that will note the running of water in the system and sound an alarm. Given such a discount, the insured must use due diligence to maintain the service. If the service is impaired or suspended, the insured is supposed to give immediate notice to the insurer or the proper rating board. If such notice is not given, sprinkler leakage coverage is suspended while the service is inactive.

THE VACANCY AND UNOCCUPANCY CLAUSE. This clause states that when a building is vacant or unoccupied, coverage is suspended. As the clause does not mention any specific number of days, coverage is immediately suspended when a building becomes unoccupied. Permission may be obtained from the insurer for vacancy or unoccupancy and there is no specific charge for this permission.

ALTERATIONS AND REPAIR CLAUSE. Another situation that suspends coverage is when repairs, alterations, or extensions are made to walls, floors, roof supports, or to the automatic sprinkler system. Fifteen days after such operations begin, coverage is suspended. To remove this suspension, the alterations and repairs clause form is available. This endorsement allows for repairs as long as they are completed within a specified number of days. This endorsement costs 50 percent of the sprinkler leakage rate on a pro-rata basis. Thus, if the endorsement is in effect sixty days, the additional charge is one-twelfth the annual sprinkler leakage rate ($\frac{1}{2} \times \frac{1}{6} = \frac{1}{12}$).

Other Contract Provisions. Five more provisions deserve mention. These are the following: divisible contract, subrogation, debris removal, waiver of inventory, and time element coverage clauses. The first three are identical with provisions of the same name in the general property form (see Chapter 3). The waiver of inventory clause differs only in the detail as to how small the loss must be for inventory of undamaged property to be waived.

The time element clause declares that the sprinkler leakage form may be combined with time element coverages. It also specifies which conditions in the sprinkler leakage endorsement supersede the provisions of the time element contract. These conditions are as follows: definitions of "sprinkler leakage" and "automatic sprinkler system"; specification of additional perils not included; conditions suspending or restricting insurance; apportionment clause, alarm or watchman service clause, and nuclear exclusion.

Water Damage Water damage done by fire fighters extinguishing a fire is considered part of the fire loss and is covered by the fire policy. Accidental discharge from a sprinkler system is insured under a sprinkler leakage form. However, there are other exposures to damage caused by water, and the water damage policy addresses itself to some of these loss exposures.

Physically the insurance contract is in two parts—the policy and the form. The policy describes the perils insured against, and the form explains the property covered. There are two versions of the water damage policy—the broad form and the limited form. The latter covers accidental discharge of water and steam from within plumbing systems, industrial and domestic appliances, refrigeration equipment, and so on.

There is no coverage for damage done by anything other than water and steam. The broad form adds coverage for the accidental admission of rain or snow directly to the interior of the structure through defective doors, windows, skylights, transoms, or ventilators as well as loss caused by collapse or fall of a tank (or a component part) which forms a part of the plumbing system.

This coverage is written by only a few companies because of a lack of demand for the product. "All-risks" insurance includes water damage coverage and is frequently used when water damage protection is needed.

Exclusions. As with most insurance policies, the water damage coverage is not accurately defined until the exclusions are noted, and the exclusions in this policy are numerous.[14]

DAMAGE TO TANK. While the policy covers property of the insured damaged by water, it does not protect the tank, appliance, or portion of the building causing the loss. Neither will it pay for the replenishing of any contents that are discharged from the heating, cooling, or plumbing system.

FLOOD. No coverage is provided for loss due to flood, surface water, tidal wave, overflow of streams, water which backs up through sewers and drains, or water below the surface which flows, seeps, or leaks through to cause damage to the structure or its contents. The water damage policy is not a substitute for flood insurance.

LOSS DUE TO FUMES AND SPOILAGE. Loss caused by gases, fumes, or vapors (other than steam) is excluded. Also, loss due to the failure of refrigeration or air-conditioning equipment to maintain proper temperatures is not insured. Consequential damage insurance is needed to cover this exposure.

DAMAGE BY OTHER PERILS. Loss due to any of the common perils insured against under other contracts is excluded. These include but are not limited to fire, lightning, extended coverage perils, V&MM, sprinkler leakage, war, nuclear explosions, and theft. Since these perils (except war) can be insured by other contracts, they are specifically excluded from the water damage policy.

DAMAGE CAUSED BY INSURED'S FAILURE TO ACT. Once a loss occurs, the insured must take reasonable action to minimize the loss. After a water damage loss, if further loss results from failure of the insured to use reasonable care to protect the property, such additional loss is excluded. However, the original loss is insured. This clause is common in property contracts.

BUILDING UNDER CONSTRUCTION. No coverage exists for a building under construction unless entirely enclosed. The structure must have a permanent roof and all outside doors and windows must be permanently in place. The policy covers rain damage coming through open or defective doors, windows, and skylights, and if these pieces of equipment are not even in place, the probability of loss is almost 100 percent.

Endorsements. The water damage policy may be amended to provide broader coverage. The amendments providing the greater protection eliminate exclusions in the contract and consequently, if the following endorsements are not included, the exclusions remain in force.

VACANCY OR UNOCCUPANCY. Coverage by the policy is immediately suspended if vacancy or unoccupancy occurs. However, for no additional charge the policy may be amended (if an underwriter is willing) so that this exclusion is voided.

UNDERGROUND WATER SUPPLY AND FIRE HYDRANTS. The policy states that loss due to breakage or leakage from an underground water supply and fire hydrants is excluded. However, for an extra premium of 20 percent, this coverage can be given. When this protection is given, seepage through building walls is covered if the source of the water is from an underground water supply, main, or fire hydrant. However, seepage from other sources is still excluded. No endorsement is needed since the policy says coverage exists if the additional premium is paid and indicated in the declarations. If the policy shows no such notation, then this type of loss is excluded.

LEAKAGE OF CHEMICAL REFRIGERANT. The basic policy covers only damage done by water or steam. But with the payment of an additional premium of 20 percent, accidental discharge or leakage of a chemical refrigerant from any refrigeration or air-conditioning system is insured. Like the coverage for fire hydrants, no additional endorsement is attached. The coverage applies when the additional premium is noted on the basic policy. If the additional premium is not paid, accidental discharge of chemical refrigerants is excluded.

Other Provisions. Besides the preceding provisions, the water damage policy has numerous other clauses. The conditions found in the New York standard fire contract are replicated except those as to "uninsurable and excepted property," "perils not included," "conditions suspending coverage," and "other perils." In addition, the water damage policy has waiver of inventory and nonreduction of loss clauses. There is also a watchman service clause if a rate credit is given for an approved guard service. There is an alterations and repairs clause, but if the repairs or alterations are to take longer than fifteen days, the policy must be endorsed with a separate alterations and repairs endorsement or coverage is suspended. Thus, in many respects the water damage policy is like the fire policy.

Table 4-2

Rate Credits for Different Coinsurance Clauses in Water Damage Policies*

Coinsurance Clause	Rate Credit	Coinsurance Clause	Rate Credit
1.0%	5.0%	15.0%	71.0%
2.5%	15.0%	20.0%	76.5%
5.0%	35.0%	25.0%	80.0%
7.5%	50.0%	50.0%	86.0%
10.0%	60.0%	80.0%	90.0%

*Reprinted with permission from *Werbel's General Insurance Guide* (Greenlawn, NY: Werbel Publishing Co., September 1975), p. 878.

The Water Damage Form. The actual description of the property insured is given by the water damage form that is attached to the water damage policy. This arrangement is much like that of the general property form, which is attached to the standard fire policy. The categorization of property in the water damage form is like that used in sprinkler leakage: (1) building, (2) stock, (3) contents, except stock, (4) contents, (5) improvements and betterments, (6) property of employees, (7) furniture and fixtures, and (8) machinery. Certain types of excluded property (bullion and manuscripts) may be added to the contents section by endorsement and payment of an additional premium. Coverage is often limited on models, drawings, dies, or patterns to 10 percent of the policy's limits, although this coverage can be increased.

Protection under the form is limited to property located at and inside the described building. There is no coverage of property outside the building. But the source of the water damage does not have to be inside; water seeping through a ceiling from another business would be insured.

Coinsurance. Water damage contracts usually contain coinsurance clauses, and often a minimum coinsurance percentage is required. For instance, for property values of less than $50,000, a 25 percent or higher coinsurance clause must be used.[15] Rate credits given for the various coinsurance percentages are shown in Table 4-2.

Deductibles. As with other types of insurance, deductibles are available under the water damage form. Various rate credits are given for the use of deductibles and the size of the rate credit varies between buildings and contents.

Flood Damage In the United States losses from flood accompany hurricanes in the South and East, spring rains and the tail ends of hurricanes in the Midwest, and spring rains and melting snows in the West. Flood losses can have catastrophic effects. However, standard property contracts do not give relief, for almost all property contracts that apply to specified locations exclude flood. To cover this exposure, a special policy is needed.

Because of the nature of flood exposure, private insurers have been reluctant to provide insurance for this peril for real property and for personal property at fixed locations. Yet earthquake insurance is offered in earthquake zones, and windstorm insurance is written in the hurricane belt. Why not flood insurance along rivers and waterfronts? Floods are much more frequent than earthquakes. Whereas earthquake insurance premiums must cover a catastrophic loss once every 20 to 100 years (in the United States), flood insurance premiums would have to do so every 1 to 4 years. Hence, flood insurance would be tremendously more expensive than earthquake insurance for insureds with known exposures. Compared to windstorm there are far fewer locations with serious flood exposure. The hurricane belt is not the only area of severe wind damage. Almost all the states have tornadoes, and all have thunderstorms. There are hardly any places that are immune to windstorm as "high ground" is immune to flood. Hence, the premiums to cover windstorm losses can be spread over almost all buyers of property insurance, while the many occupiers of locations away from rivers and shores do not want to pay for flood insurance if there is no chance of flood loss.

Although many businesses do face an exposure to flood loss and need a method of treating this exposure, the peril of flood is not considered commercially insurable for several reasons. First, a flood loss at one location is not independent of losses at other locations. Catastrophic losses on a number of insured locations owned by various firms due to a single flood might be more than an insurer could tolerate. Flood losses are also fairly predictable, and the premium that would have to be charged on properties in flood-prone areas would be much greater than prospective insureds would be willing to pay. If the premiums were high, the only firms purchasing flood insurance would be those with a very high probability of loss. This adverse selection would make it impossible to develop adequate insurance rates. In short, it is difficult, if not impossible, to write insurance against predictable, frequent, severe losses. While many experts believe the problem could be overcome by including coverage against a combination of catastrophic perils (notably windstorm, earthquake, flood, and soil collapse) in an indivisible package like extended coverage (or in an "all-risks" form), the majority of insurers still have not been convinced. One troublesome factor has been that different studies have reached different conclusions about the predictability of flood frequency and severity.

Since the private market has not been able to meet the needs of the public at a price consumers were willing to pay, the federal government has created a flood insurance program. The National Flood Insurance Act was passed in 1968 and the National Flood Insurance Program was started in 1969. This program is a joint venture between the federal government and private insurance companies. As originally established, the government was represented by the Federal Insurance Administration (FIA) and the private sector by the National Flood Insurers Association (NFIA). This association has about 100 stock and mutual insurance company members. The FIA pays 90 percent of claims and operating costs. In 1977 some disputes developed between the FIA and the NFIA, and it is possible as of this writing that someone other than the NFIA will be servicing the flood program beginning in 1978.

The FIA sets policy (subject to the statutory restrictions) and the coverage is distributed through the private marketplace. Local agents currently market the product through selected insurers. These insurance companies have been designated NFIA Service Offices by the FIA and handle all flood policy applications in a given state. There is one service center for each state, and therefore only one company per state that performs this function.

In order for a firm to qualify for flood insurance, the community in which the firm is situated must perform certain tasks. As a sign of a community's desire to participate in the flood program, it must show legal authority to regulate land use; furnish flood plain maps of the community and a short history of local floods; provide a current report on the community's flood problems; and demonstrate that it will restrict land use in so-called "special" flood hazard areas (areas in which the probability of flood in a year is 1 percent or more).[16] When these steps have been taken, an area qualifies for the flood program. The reason for these requirements is that Congress felt that without them, people would build structures closer to flood areas, knowing that if a flood occurred the flood insurance would pay for the losses.

The initial program was not very popular with the public. Despite the subsidized rates, many thought the premiums too high. Two spectacular events in 1972 made this clear. Rapid City, South Dakota, and later many communities in eastern Pennsylvania and New York suffered catastrophic floods. Rapid City and many of the eastern communities were areas in which federal flood insurance was available, but very few policies were in force. To improve this situation, rates were later substantially reduced, and the free alternative, Federal Disaster Relief, was restricted—an owner of property in a "special" flood area cannot receive any flood disaster benefits until losses are above the limits of flood insurance available. If such limits were $100,000, then an uninsured firm would have to retain the first $100,000 and receive flood disaster benefits for losses above $100,000. Besides this requirement, certain financial institutions have been directed by their regulatory agencies to require flood insurance on structures in flood-prone areas if such coverage is available. Property with a mortgage from any institution regulated by the Federal Reserve System, the Federal Home Loan Board Bank, the Federal Deposit Insurance Corporation, or the National Credit Union Administration must meet this requirement. As a consequence, by law, almost all mortgaged structures built in flood-prone areas have to be insured for loss due to flood. These incentives to purchase flood insurance have helped the program to expand, and over 1 million policies had been issued by 1977.

Federal Flood Insurance. Since the actual contract is divided into two component parts, the following material is also in two sections. The first part pertains to the policy, which describes the peril insured against; the second part pertains to the property form, which describes the property insured.

THE FLOOD INSURANCE POLICY. The flood policy states it will pay for direct loss caused by flood at the premises described in the application and declarations forms attached to the policy. It will also pay on a pro-rata basis for thirty days at each proper place to which any of the property shall necessarily be removed for preservation from the peril of "flood," but not elsewhere. Unlike the standard fire policy, this flood policy has no coverage for damage caused by removal. Other coverage for property off premises might apply in such circumstances.

Definition of Flood. In the original policy, the term "flood" was defined as:

> . . . a general and temporary condition of partial or complete inundation of normally dry land areas from (1) the overflow of inland or tidal waters, (2) the unusual and rapid accumulation or runoff of surface waters from any source, or (3) mudslides which are caused or precipated by accumulations of water on or under the ground.

In 1973 this definition was expanded to include "collapse or subsidence of land along the shore of a lake or other body of water as a result of erosion or undermining caused by waves or currents of water exceeding the cyclical levels which result in flooding involving the overflow of inland or tidal waters."[17] This provision is primarily designed to give relief to those along the Great Lakes where serious erosion may accompany a storm, but the clause applies to all insureds regardless of location. However, it is not intended to provide coverage for ordinary erosion. In a 1973 case in Hawaii, a claim for ordinary erosion was denied.[18] For erosion to be covered a storm, unusually high water, or an unanticipated force of nature (flash flood or tidal surge) must happen.

Perils Excluded. The policy has seven exclusions pertaining to perils, of which five are fairly common:

1. war;
2. insured's neglect to use reasonable means to protect property from loss after an insured peril occurs;
3. loss resulting from power, heating, or cooling failure unless the power, heating, or cooling equipment is on the insured premises and damaged by flood;
4. nuclear energy; and
5. loss caused by the enforcement of local or state ordinances affecting the repair, construction or demolition of buildings or structures.

The remaining two exclusions are specific to flood insurance. One states there is no coverage for loss "by fire, windstorm, explosion, erosion, earthquake, landslide or any other earth movement except such mudslides as are covered under the peril of flood, or by theft." This exclusion eliminates perils that can be insured in other covers and makes a distinction between mudslides and landslides. To help clarify this distinction, the Federal Insurance Administration has defined mudslide to mean "a flow of liquid mud down a hillside, usually as a result of a dual condition of a loss of brush cover and subsequent heavy rains."[19] Of course, the mudslide is supposed to be sudden and unexpected by the insured.

The last exclusion to be examined in this analysis is actually the first in the policy and it is also the longest and most detailed. This exclusion has three basic parts. Loss due to the following events is excluded:

1. rain, snow, sleet, hail, or water spray;
2. freezing, thawing or by the pressure or weight of ice or water, except where the property covered has been simultaneously damaged by flood; and
3. water, moisture, or mudslide damage of any kind resulting primarily from conditions, causes, or occurrences which are solely related to the described premises, or are within the control of the insured (including but not limited to design, structural, or mechanical defects, failures, stoppages or breakages of water or sewer lines, drains, pumps, fixtures or equipment, seepage or back-up of water or hydrostatic pressure), or any condition which causes flooding which is substantially confined to the described premises or properties immediately adjacent thereto.

Part 3 of this provision was used by the U.S. District Court in Hawaii for denying liability for erosion.

Property Excluded. The policy contains three categories of property excluded:

1. accounts, bills, currency, deeds, evidence of debt, money, securities, bullion, manuscripts, or other valuable papers or records, numismatic or philatelic property;
2. fences; and
3. outdoor swimming pools, bulkheads, wharves, piers, bridges, docks or other open structures located on or partially over water or property thereon.

The property in the first exclusion can be insured under several different types of policies: valuable papers, accounts receivable, and money and securities forms. The latter two are more difficult to cover but may be covered against flood in a difference in conditions contract.

Other Clauses. Besides the various exclusions already discussed and the definition of flood, the policy contains many provisions common to fire and allied lines insurance generally. Included among these provisions are those relating to other insurance, cancellation, alterations and repair, property of others, liberalization, mortgage clause, loss clause, appraisal, and requirements in case of loss.

For the most part these clauses contain the standard wording. However, an interesting part of the cancellation clause deserves further exploration. The cancellation clause states that the insurer can only cancel for nonpayment of premium and must give twenty days' notice. The refund provision is also in this clause. If an insured cancels coverage and still has an ownership interest in the property, there is no refund. The premium is considered completely earned. If this condition were not the case, there would be a lot of cancellations after flood season. However, if the insured sells the property and cancels, a short-rate refund is given.

THE GENERAL PROPERTY FORM FOR FLOOD. In this form three subjects are covered: building, contents, and debris removal. The amount of insurance that one can buy is limited by program guidelines. Any money spent on debris removal must come from the stated limits; debris removal coverage is not an additional amount of insurance.

Buildings. The form defines "building" as including the structure insured, additions and extensions attached thereto; permanent fixtures, machinery, and equipment forming a part of and pertaining to the service of the building. This wording is basically the same as that found in general property forms for fire insurance. Besides this protection, materials and supplies used to alter or repair the structure are covered if they are in an enclosed structure on the premises. If these items are in the open, they are not insured. As part of the coverage for residence buildings there is a 10 percent extension of coverage for appurtenant structures on the premises. This extension is not an additional amount of insurance and does not apply to such structures if they are rented to persons other than the tenant of the described building or are used for commercial purposes.

Contents. Coverage for this property is separated into two categories—household goods, and other than household goods. Because this text concerns commercial property, only the "other than household goods" category will be analyzed. This coverage includes merchandise and stock held for sale, materials, stock supplies, furniture, fixtures, machinery, and equipment owned by the insured. The form provides no coverage for personal property of others. If the insured is a tenant there is coverage for improvements and betterments on a standard basis. Certain types of property are subject to limited coverage:

1. a $500 aggregate limit on fine arts, and
2. a $500 aggregate limit on jewelry and furs.

If more insurance is desired for these assets, specific insurance should be purchased from a private insurer under an inland marine form (discussed in Chapters 9 and 10).

Debris Removal. The form provides coverage for debris removal. There is a significant difference here from fire insurance coverage. Expenses incurred for removal of debris of *or on* the building or contents is covered. Thus, debris (such as mud) that is "on" the building or contents does *not* have to be debris *of* covered property. However, debris elsewhere on the described premises must be from covered property or removal cost is not insured.

Property Excluded by the Form. Besides the property excluded by the basic policy, there are additional property exclusions in the form. The following types of property are not insured:

1. land values, lawns, trees, shrubs, plants, growing crops, livestock, underground structures, equipment outside the foundation walls of the building, and personal property in the open;
2. portions of walks, driveways, and other paved surfaces outside the described building; and
3. contents covered by specific insurance except on an excess basis.

Analysis of these exclusions shows there is little coverage for anything outside the described building and appurtenant structures. Trees, shrubs, outside air conditioning equipment, and mowers left outside are all excluded.

Deductibles. The flood insurance form contains a mandatory deductible of 2 percent of the values insured or $200, whichever is

Table 4-3

Rates and Limits for Flood Insurance on Nonresidential Properties

Type of Property	Maximum Limits	Rates Per $100
Building	$100,000	$.40
Contents	$100,000	$.75

greater. This deductible applies separately to building and contents. Therefore, if both building and contents are damaged, one will have to retain at least $400 in losses.

RATES. In the National Flood Insurance Program there are two types of rates: *chargeable* and *actuarial*. The chargeable rates are subsidized by the federal government. The actuarial rates are those one would pay based on the real potential loss exposure of the location and are considerably higher than chargeable rates. Private insurers would have to charge actuarial rates if they were marketing the product without federal subsidy. One authority has stated that chargeable rates are generally only 5 percent of actuarial rates for any given location.[20] One can see that the federal subsidy is quite significant. Chargeable rates and their limits are shown in Table 4-3.

Another important aspect of the rate situation is that there is no coinsurance clause in the contract. While the authorities encourage insurance to value as much as possible, the contract has no provision to enforce this.

Flood Insurance from the Private Sector. As a general rule, flood insurance applicable at fixed locations is not sold by private insurance companies except in difference of conditions (DIC) contracts. Inland marine policies frequently include flood coverage, but this applies principally to property in transit or mobile property. DIC coverage is discussed later in this chapter, inland marine insurance in Chapters 9 and 10. Automobile insurance generally includes flood coverage on automobiles and will be discussed in CPCU 4.

Special Extended Coverage

Although the combination of fire, extended coverage, sonic boom, sprinkler leakage, vandalism and malicious mischief, and water damage coverages gives broad protection, expanded coverage is available in the form of the special extended coverage endorsement (SECE). This form is added to fire polices and extends coverage to all direct physical loss that may occur except for the perils and property excluded. It is an example of what is traditionally referred to as "all-risks" protection.

The SECE can be used to insure completed buildings and improvements and betterments, and is available for time element coverages (e.g., business interruption and extra expense covers). Personal property (contents) is not eligible for this protection, nor is every type of building eligible. Ineligible structures include farm property, aerial structures (e.g., smokestacks), aircraft hangars, amusement parks, camps, cattle and stock pens, greenhouses, lumberyards, mining properties, public utilities' property, and storage tanks. Buildings under construction are written under a different form—the builders' risk special extended coverage endorsement. "All-risks" coverage for completed buildings will be discussed first, followed by a discussion of the coverage for builders' risks.

Completed Buildings The SECE, like other "all-risks" policies, covers all risks of direct physical loss not otherwise excluded. As with other "all-risks" forms, coverage is best determined by an examination of the exclusions and conditions which limit coverage.

There are two types of exclusions in the form—one for perils generally, and the other for perils with respect to particular kinds of property.

General Exclusions. The insuring agreement of an "all-risks" contract covers all losses, including those which insurers feel are uninsurable. Among these are losses caused by wear and tear or exposure. Other uninsurable losses occur with high frequency or because of the insured's neglect in maintaining the property.

The SECE exclusions read as follows:

> . . . wear and tear, deterioration, rust or corrosion, mold, wet or dry rot; inherent or latent defect; smog; smoke, vapor or gas from agricultural or industrial operations; mechanical breakdown, including rupture or bursting caused by centrifugal force; settling, cracking, shrinkage, bulging or expansion of pavements, foundations, walls, floors, roofs or ceilings; animals, birds, vermin, termites, or other insects; unless loss by a peril not excluded in this policy ensues, and then this company shall be liable for only such ensuing loss.

These exclusions originated with marine insurance (especially inland marine), because that was the branch of insurance in which "all-risks" property insurance first appeared. Therefore, a more lengthy discussion of these familiar exclusions appears in Chapter 9 on inland marine coverage.

There are also some exclusions in the SECE which pertain specifically to theft. Excluded are theft by employees and any theft of property other than building equipment or part of a building. (Theft of an installed furnace or a chandelier would be covered.) Also, inventory shortage alone does not constitute a covered loss.

As might be expected, earthquake, flood, war, and nuclear energy losses are also excluded, as well as loss from operation of building laws. There is a provision that any damage directly attributable to alteration or repair work is not covered. However, if such work leads to loss through action of another peril, and the other peril is not specifically excluded, the loss is covered. Thus, if a welder damages the building through improper welding, such damage is not covered. But if improper use of a welding torch also produces a fire, the fire damage is covered.

Exclusions for Particular Property. Special extended coverage, like extended coverage, has some perils exclusions that apply only to particular kinds of property. For example, some provisions exclude coverage to hot water boilers, steam boilers and pipes, and electrical appliances for losses that could generally be covered under a boiler and machinery policy.

Glass coverage is limited to loss due to fire, lightning, the extended coverage perils, and discharge from fire protective or building service equipment. No coverage exists for glass damage due to vandalism. To obtain this protection, a firm should purchase plate glass insurance.

Fences, pavements, swimming pools, retaining walls, bulkheads, piers, wharves or docks, "when covered under this policy," are not insured for loss due to freezing or thawing, impact of watercraft, or pressure or weight of ice or water. When the SECE is used as an endorsement to the general property form, there would be no coverage unless these items are named in the declarations. In other cases, however, the form to which the SECE is attached may automatically include such items, and the phrase "when covered under this policy" makes it clear that these losses are still excluded by the SECE. Outdoor equipment of the type listed is highly susceptible to loss from freezing, thawing, or weight of ice or water, unless proper safeguards are taken. Loss exposures of this nature are best handled by noninsurance techniques.

Unless covered by specific endorsement, metal smokestacks, signs, outside fabric awnings, and radio and television antennae are not insured for loss due to ice, snow, sleet, wind, or hail. However, they are covered against all other insured perils, such as fire and damage by aircraft. Likewise, lawns, trees, or plants, when covered by the policy, have limited protection. Fire, lightning, aircraft, explosion, and riot are the only perils insured against. Noticeably missing in this last list are the perils of wind, hail, and V&MM.

Rain, snow, sand, or dust damage to the interior of a building is covered if it is the result of exterior damage from fire, lightning, an EC peril (excluding smoke) or V&MM.

Conditions. Special vacancy and unoccupancy conditions apply to some perils. Loss by vandalism or theft is not covered when the building has been vacant or unoccupied more than thirty consecutive days. However, there is also a provision like that previously noted as applying to damage incurred in the process of alterations or perils. If a vandal or thief creates a loss due to another peril (e.g., explosion), and that peril is not specifically excluded, the resulting loss is covered.

In the event of any vacancy or unoccupancy, the insured is expected to exercise due diligence to maintain heat or to shut off and drain pipes and equipment that might freeze. If this is not done, damage to such items from freezing is not covered. Note that damage to *other* property from this event *is* covered.

There is a provision that prevents seasonal property from being automatically classed as "unoccupied" during off seasons.

Other Provisions. The SECE does not increase the amount of coverage. Change of occupancy, vacancy, or unoccupancy does not affect coverage except for V&MM, theft, and loss to plumbing, heating, or air conditioning systems, and appliances.

"Riot" coverage includes direct loss by striking employees and by pillage and looting occurring during and at the immediate place of the riot. This definition matters only with respect to property not insured on an "all-risks" basis, only against a list of specified perils that includes riot (e.g., glass, lawn, shrubs, the interior of a building damaged by rain or snow, and a building under construction).

Provisions Applicable to Time Element Coverages. The term "direct loss" is defined as loss to the described property resulting from a peril insured against. If the business is interrupted by a strike, and any persons interfere with the rebuilding, repair, or replacement of damaged property or with resuming or continuing business, this is not covered.

Rates and Coinsurance. This endorsement requires an 80 percent coinsurance clause as a minimum, though higher percentages may be used. The rate paid is in addition to the fire and extended coverage premium and ranges from 0.01 to 0.069. Some illustrative rates are shown in Table 4-4. Sprinklered buildings have a higher rate because the sprinkler leakage peril exists in such structures and is covered. However, such structures should have lower fire rates, so an overall premium savings is still possible. The sprinkler leakage protection provided by the SECE has a low rate. Standard rates for such coverage with an 80 percent coinsurance clause run from 0.03 to 0.045, but in the SECE the addition to the rate is never more than 0.009. However,

Table 4-4

Illustrative Rates for Special Extended Coverage Endorsement*

Amount of Coverage	Fire-Resistive		All Other Construction	
	Nonsprinklered	Sprinklered	Nonsprinklered	Sprinklered
First $100,000	0.04	0.046	0.06	0.069
Next $100,000	0.02	0.023	0.04	0.046
Over $200,000	0.01	0.012	0.03	0.035

*Reprinted with permission from *Pennsylvania-Delaware Rule Book* (New York: Insurance Services Office, May 1975), p. 3-09x.

Table 4-5

All Other Perils Loading for $500,000 of Insurance on a Nonsprinklered Fire-Resistive Building

First $100,000 of coverage at 0.04/$100	$40.00
Next $100,000 of coverage at 0.02/$100	20.00
Next $300,000 of coverage at 0.01/$100	30.00
"All other perils" loading for $500,000	$90.00

separate sprinkler leakage coverage may be had with coinsurance percentages far below 80 percent. The premium for the SECE is added to the otherwise applicable fire and EC premiums to provide a premium for "all-risks" coverage.

The rate for the SECE is lower for values over $100,000. This is in marked contrast to fire and extended coverage rates, which remain constant regardless of the values involved. These rate reductions reflect the low probability of losses involving over $100,000 of property that would be covered by an "all-risks" policy but not by a named perils policy. The "all other perils" loading, as it is termed for a nonsprinklered fire-resistive building, would be calculated as shown in Table 4-5, using Table 4-4.

Buildings Under Construction Eligible occupancies under the builders' risk special extended coverage endorsement are similar to those for completed buildings. However, the list of ineligible occupancies is not as long and does not include aircraft hangars, camps, cattle and stock pens, greenhouses, lumberyards, and storage tanks. These properties can be insured under the builders' risk SECE, as can dwellings and farm structures under construction. The only types of buildings not eligible under this form but eligible under the completed structure form are petrochemical firms, piers, wharves, and a structure, when completed, that will be rated under the Nuclear Insurance Rating Bureau. In total, the builders' risk SECE can be used with more kinds of occupancies than the SECE for completed structures. Of course, a building under construction does not generally face the occupancy hazards involved with a building that has been completed and occupied.

Exclusions. Basically the same exclusions apply to the builders' risk SECE as to the SECE for completed buildings. One special limitation covers construction machinery, tools, and equipment on a named perils basis. The named perils are fire and lightning, the extended coverage perils except smoke, V&MM, and discharge from fire protective and building service equipment. Loss resulting from error, omission, or deficiency in design, specifications, workmanship, or materials is also covered only when one of this list of perils *except* V&MM is involved in causing a loss.

While the preceding items restrict coverage, the builders' risk SECE omits some of the exclusions found in the SECE for completed buildings. Since, by definition, a building under construction is unoccupied, a thirty-day vacancy or occupancy limitation on V&MM and theft coverage does not appear. And metal smokestacks, fabric awnings, signs, radio and television antennae are all covered by the builders' risk SECE.

Rates and Coinsurance. The builders' risk SECE follows builders' risk rules. Whether a completed value form or reporting form, the effect of a 100 percent coinsurance requirement is achieved.

Earthquake

One of the most catastrophic perils known to humanity is earthquake. Recent quakes in China and Italy caused tragic losses. In 1975 a quake in Hawaii caused $4.1 million damage, and the 1971 earthquake in San Fernando, California, resulted in losses over $550 million. The 1964 Alaskan quake produced losses of $500 million.[21] Such statistics point to a need for earthquake insurance for property, yet almost all types of property insurance policies exclude this peril.

The geographic areas most likely to have earthquakes are somewhat limited, resulting in a poor spread of exposure. Predictions regarding potential earthquake frequency and severity have been poor. Losses, when they occur, often affect many insureds in the affected area. It might seem appropriate for insurers to build catastrophe reserves against the contingency of a severe earthquake, but catastrophe reserves are discouraged by U.S. tax law. In view of all these facts, some find it surprising that earthquake insurance is, in fact, available from private insurers.

Earthquake insurance can be purchased:

1. as an endorsement to the fire policy (involving the extension of a fire form to cover earthquake); or
2. as an earthquake form used as an attachment to the standard fire policy when earthquake property damage insurance is to be provided, but not coverage for fire and other perils.

Until recently there were separate manuals and forms for the Pacific coast states and the rest of the country. However, in December 1976, the Insurance Services Office (ISO) published a revised commercial earthquake insurance program, along with a new manual which provides construction classifications and rating for all states. There are some specific variations for individual states or for the states designated as "western states" but, in general, the same earthquake coverage is now available countrywide.

The Earthquake Extension Endorsement This approach is the most widely utilized technique to obtain coverage. The endorsement extends the fire policy to cover earthquake. It does not add an additional amount of insurance. The term "earthquake" is never really defined in the forms. There is a statement, "if more than one Earthquake shock shall occur within any period of seventy-two hours during the term of this endorsement, such Earthquake shocks shall be deemed to be a single Earthquake." This explanation means most aftershocks will be considered part of the original event. Besides this explanation, the form further states that any loss caused directly or indirectly by fire, explosion, or flood of any nature, or tidal wave, all whether caused by an earthquake or not, is excluded. Consequently, loss from flood caused by an earthquake is not insured under an earthquake endorsement.

Foundations and Excavations. As mentioned in Chapter 3, foundations and excavations usually are excluded from coverage in the general property form when a coinsurance clause is used. This exclusion is logical, because such items are unlikely to be damaged due to fire or the other perils covered under that form. If foundations and excavations were covered, the insured would have to purchase insurance on the value of these items to meet coinsurance requirements but would be unlikely to sustain a loss to these items.

Foundations and excavations are susceptible to damage by earthquake. Therefore, the earthquake extension endorsement specifically states:

> When this Earthquake Extension Endorsement covers building(s), it shall cover direct loss by earthquake to foundations, excavations and all other portions of the building.

At first glance it would appear that this neatly resolves the problem of adequate coverage on foundations and excavations for the peril which is most likely to cause a loss. Unfortunately, it introduces another problem of maintaining insurance to value to meet coinsurance requirements. The present Commercial Earthquake Insurance Manual published by ISO specifies that the earthquake extension endorsement must use the same amount of insurance, and the same coinsurance clause, as used for fire insurance. Thus, an insured with a general property form and the earthquake extension endorsement, who is adequately insured for fire, may be inadequately insured to meet the coinsurance requirements for earthquake. There are several ways to work around this problem, but none of the current solutions are entirely adequate. For example, foundations and excavations coverage can be added to the fire coverage or deleted from the earthquake coverage.

As this text goes to press, ISO has assigned a committee to resolve this inconsistency in treating foundations and excavations. Interestingly, this inconsistency has not been caused by the use of new forms, but has always existed in earthquake insurance. Although it has not yet created any serious loss problems, it is a problem that should be resolved.

Coinsurance and Deductibles. For commercial buildings the fire coinsurance clause applies, subject to a minimum of 80 percent. Also, rather large deductibles are applied. A 2 percent deductible is mandatory in other than western states. In western states, mandatory deductibles range from 5 percent to 10 percent. The deductibles may be increased to as high as 40 percent. Even with the earthquake extension endorsement, retained losses may be high—a 10 percent deductible on a $20 million building equals $2 million.

Because of the size of the deductible, there is a market for a "first loss" or "primary" coverage. This covers the deductible amount. It often is purchased from a company other than the one providing the basic earthquake coverage. However, even first loss cover contains a ½ percent or $1,000 deductible, whichever is larger. The $2 million deductible on the $20 million building is reduced to $100,000.

Apportionment Clause. The earthquake endorsement must be put on all fire policies insuring the structure. If this is not done, all losses are prorated on the basis of the amount of earthquake coverage divided by the amount of fire coverage. This apportionment clause in the earthquake endorsement has the same effect as the one in the extended coverage endorsement.

The Earthquake Form This form is used to insure against only the peril of earthquake and is attached to the standard fire policy. The way in which the earthquake form modifies the standard fire policy is rather unusual. The earthquake form simply specifies that the word "fire" in the standard fire policy shall be interpreted to mean "earthquake."

> This policy covers direct loss by Earthquake only, and for the purpose of this policy the word "Earthquake" shall be substituted for the word "Fire" wherever appearing in this policy other than in this Earthquake Form.

The earthquake form also contains additional provisions relating specifically to earthquake coverage.

Coverage provided by the earthquake form and earthquake extension endorsement are very similar. However, the rate for the earthquake form is 25 percent higher than the rate used for the endorsement.

Nuclear Energy

Since humanity has developed various peaceful uses for the atom, the possibility of loss due to accidental exposure to nuclear material has greatly expanded. The general property form, as well as other property forms, contains a nuclear energy exclusion. Therefore, coverage must be specially purchased to cover this exposure. The two standard coverages in this area are the contamination assumption endorsement and nuclear energy property policy. The former insures against radioactive contamination of insured's premises, the latter protects property of those engaged directly in the nuclear field. Examples of such operations include an electric utility's nuclear power plant and a laboratory that uses a large quantity of radioactive substances in its operations.

Radioactive Contamination Protection Radioactive contamination protection is included in the nuclear energy property policy discussed in Chapter 13. For organizations whose exposures are not intense enough to require that policy, coverage is obtained by including a radioactive contamination assumption endorsement to their fire insurance contract.

Exposures are found among hospitals, medical clinics, educational and research institutions, and even welding shops. (This last occupancy could have an exposure because of X-ray welding that is performed on the premises.) Overall, the number of insureds who might require this protection is much greater than those needing the nuclear energy property policy.

The radioactive contamination assumption endorsement comes in two versions—the broad form and the limited form. They differ only in definition of the peril insured against.

Broad Form. Under the broad form (also called form B), protection is provided for sudden and accidental radioactive contamination that occurs on the premises from radioactive material stored on the premises. If contamination comes from off-premises sources, there is no coverage. Under this form, radioactive contamination becomes another peril insured against.

The form states there is no coverage "if either a nuclear reactor capable of sustaining nuclear fission in a self-supporting chain reaction or any new or used nuclear fuel which is intended for or which has been used in such a nuclear reactor is on the insured's premises." If such conditions as these exist, a nuclear energy property insurance policy is necessary.

The form contains an apportionment clause similar to the one found in extended coverage endorsements. Consequently, if one fire policy is endorsed for contamination, all fire policies should be so endorsed.

Limited Form. As its name indicates, the limited form (also called form A) provides restricted coverage for the radioactive contamination peril. Only contamination that results from a peril insured against in the rest of the policy in which the endorsement is inserted is covered. Thus, if the policy contains windstorm coverage, and tornado damage allows radioactive material to escape from its container so that contamination occurs, the limited form would pay. However, if a flood caused the contamination, it would not.

Rating. Radioactive contamination insurance is rated on an individual basis, since a large number of homogeneous exposures do not exist and tight underwriting control is desirable.

Difference in Conditions Insurance (DIC)

Previous discussions in this text have concentrated on *standard* forms used to insure property. Discussions in this section of the chapter, entitled "Perils Coverage in Fire and Allied Lines Policies and Forms," have listed the fire policy perils, the extended coverage perils, perils that can be added to extended coverage, the special extended coverage endorsement, and special forms that can provide coverage not included by the special extended coverage endorsement—flood, earthquake, and radioactive contamination. This discussion of perils coverage would not be complete without a discussion of difference in conditions insurance

Figure 4-2
DIC Coverage

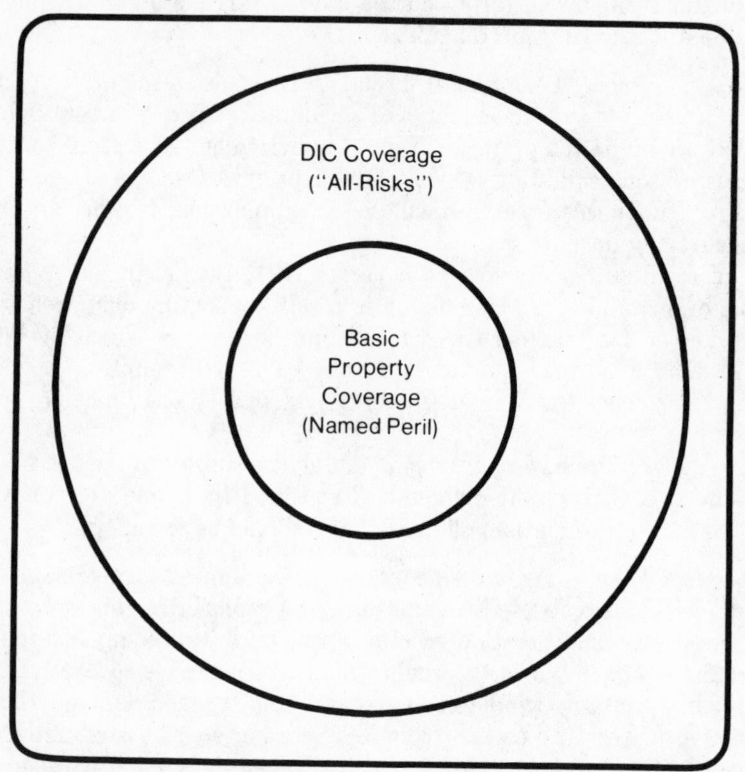

(DIC), a *nonstandard* form often used to "fill in the cracks" in other property policies.

The purpose of DIC is to cover the insured's property for all of the perils that are not covered by the basic property insurance policies (i.e., fire and extended coverage). It does not provide higher limits of coverage for these basic perils as the umbrella policy does. DIC insurance is primary or basic insurance coverage surrounding fire and extended coverage. It can be visualized eaily as a doughnut, as shown in Figure 4-2. DIC attempts to reduce the insured's chance of having an uninsured loss by providing "all-risks" coverage on the property.[22]

Unlike other "all-risks" contracts, including property forms with the SECE, the DIC is written as a separate policy to complement coverage provided on other forms. The DIC excludes perils, such as fire and EC which are covered on other forms. Because coverage can be custom-tailored to meet a given firm's needs and because coverage is, in many ways, less restrictive than the forms previously discussed, the DIC can be a useful tool in reducing the chance of an uninsured loss.

In addition to the types of property insured under fire and allied lines forms, DIC policies may be used to insure property in transit and overseas property. In fact, DIC coverage is often purchased to fill voids in policies purchased overseas. Many foreign countries require companies to purchase insurance locally and sometimes the local coverage is inadequate. The purchase of a separate DIC is one partial solution to the problem. The foreign country receives its premium dollars for the basic coverage, and the property that is being imported or exported typically is excluded.

Another feature of the DIC policy that is different from general property forms is that no exclusion generally exists with respect to foundations and excavations.

The term "difference in conditions" apparently originated in ocean marine insurance. There are occasions in maritime commerce where the coverage under a merchants open cargo policy is different from the coverage under a policy that is secured in connection with the sales contract. The merchant may buy a third policy to fill in the differences in conditions between these two policies, or in connection with other policies where the conditions are not identical. However, a DIC policy that is purchased in the United States to cover property on land has become essentially a catastrophe policy covering perils that are excluded from the coverage under basic property loss insurance.

DIC insurance is not standardized for two reasons. First, the insurance market for this coverage is limited. Insurance companies develop their own forms according to the kinds of businesses which they normally insure and according to their underwriting standards. Secondly, the DIC insurance contract generally is written to cover special exposures and circumstances. Underwriters develop the coverage to fit specific situations which may be quite different from any other exposures that are normally faced by policyholders. Policies issued by one insurer for different insureds may vary substantially.

Property Usually Covered The property that is covered by a DIC policy usually is the same property that is covered by the insured's other policies. This would include buildings, fixtures, and business personal property. It should be kept in mind that this policy is intended to cover loss from unusual or catastrophic exposures that are not covered by basic insurance policies. Therefore, the property that is covered would be the same as that covered by the basic insurance policies, but the losses covered would be different.

DIC policies exclude certain types of property which may be subject to special kinds of loss, or which might result in a higher frequency of loss than is contemplated by the usual difference in conditions policy. Excluded in many policies are special types of properties such as accounts, records, bills or deeds, money and securities or other evidences of debt, transportation tickets, stamps, jewelry, watches, furs, gems, or fine arts. These exclusions may not appear in policies where the property generally to be covered would include fine arts, or for jewelry stores where jewelry is the stock-in-trade, or fur stores where furs are the stock-in-trade. The exclusions which apply to such types of property in a given policy would depend upon the insured's business and exposures.

Property normally is excluded from coverage if it is of such a kind that full insurance to value could be provided by other policies. This would include such property as motor vehicles, watercraft, aircraft, livestock, or property that is covered under ocean marine policies. Property also would be excluded under most policies after the property has left the custody of the insured in connection with an installment sale. Property is also excluded if it is of a type normally covered by marine policies such as neon signs, valuable papers and records, and property in transit between locations.

Perils Usually Covered The coverage of a DIC policy tends to be of an "all-risks" nature. This is most likely to be the case where the basic insurance covers specified perils. It is, however, possible to obtain a specified perils DIC policy where the insured has an unusual or catastrophic exposure to loss by a named peril where there does not appear to be a need for the broad coverage of an "all-risks" form.

A very important exclusion in the DIC policy excludes perils that normally would be covered under basic insurance. Not covered by the typical DIC are damages from such perils as fire, the extended coverage perils, riot and civil commotion, vandalism and malicious mischief, and sprinkler leakage. It is important that these perils exclusions be carefully coordinated with the coverage of the basic insurance. The exclusions should be worded identically with the coverage provisions of the basic insurance.

It is also customary to exclude damage from steam boiler explosion and other steam explosion and also machinery damage. Here again it is important that the exclusion be coordinated with boiler and machinery coverage which the insured may have.

Infidelity losses generally are excluded. It is anticipated that the insured who has an infidelity exposure will buy coverage for that under a fidelity bond or under one of the package insurance coverages.

Certain other perils which are considered as too catastrophic to be the subject of private insurance are excluded. This includes damage from war and from the nuclear perils. However, a DIC policy might be written to cover certain nuclear exposures if such coverage is important to the insured and if the underwriter is agreeable to accepting the conditions.

There are also certain wear and tear type exclusions similar to those which are found in inland marine policies. These may be spelled out in some detail with the intent of excluding losses that may occasion a frequency of claims or that may be anticipated in the normal course of the insured's business.

There are certain perils that may be covered or excluded, depending upon the intent of both parties to the contract. The DIC often provides coverage for building collapse, earthquake and earth movement, and flood and water damage. One of the prime reasons for securing a DIC policy may be to obtain coverage for one or more of these perils.

Flood and water damage coverage ordinarily is not available to business policyholders in the private insurance market. There may be cases where the possibility of flood losses is slight but there is a possibility of a severe loss under unusual conditions. An insurer may be willing to provide a catastrophe coverage against loss from flood through a DIC. Usually there would be a substantial deductible applying to such coverage, perhaps even amounting to $200,000 or more. The object of flood coverage under such a DIC policy is to protect against the unlikely occurrence of a severe flood loss.

Somewhat the same thinking affects coverage against earthquake and earth movement. Insurers are wary of writing earthquake insurance even with a high deductible where the property is located in a high frequency earthquake zone. However, an insured whose business is located outside of a high frequency earthquake zone may feel that some protection is needed against the slight possibility of a severe earthquake loss. Here again a substantial deductible would be a usual part of such coverage.

The peril of building collapse, almost always covered by a DIC, deserves special comment. This is a peril that affects not only older buildings but also some of the newer buildings where current construction techniques appear to contribute to the possibility of a collapse.

Underwriters seem to be reluctant to provide complete coverage against a catastrophe loss. There is always the high deductible in order to eliminate any frequency of claims. In addition, an underwriter may intend to cover only a portion of a catastrophe loss from such perils as earthquake, flood, or building collapse. This portion that is covered by the difference in conditions policy may even be as low as 50 percent of the insured's loss above the deductible. Recovery by the insured may be on a pro-rata basis, or there may be an upper limit beyond which the coverage would not apply. These special conditions are all subject to discussion between the insured and the insurer depending upon the coverage desired by the insured and the insurer's willingness to provide coverage against the possibility of catastrophe loss.

There are occasions where the principal reason for choosing a difference in conditions policy is the exposure to major burglary and theft losses. It may be impossible for the insured, for example, to secure a mercantile open stock burglary coverage at the filed rate and through normal channels. The exposure may be such that the insured needs coverage against a severe burglary or theft loss. A DIC policy may be written specifically to provide such coverage, or coverage may be provided under an "all-risks" policy that includes the needed burglary or theft coverage. A deductible normally would apply in order to eliminate a frequency of losses. Here again the maximum limit of liability may be less than the total exposure. This is reasonable in many cases because even a severe burglary or theft loss is not likely to involve the insured's entire stock of merchandise. The coverage may amount to some percentage of the total value of stock, perhaps as high as 50 percent of the total value. This type of DIC policy may be particularly attractive to retail merchants whose exposure to loss is such that theft insurance is not available through normal channels.

Other Conditions of Coverage Territorial limits may be very broad in a DIC policy. Normal procedure is to cover within the United States and Canada, although worldwide coverage is written in some cases. The principal exposure normally is at the insured's business location, but there may be a need for broad territorial limits where the insured is shipping merchandise in high value lots throughout the United States or to foreign countries.

Special provisions may apply for determining the value of property, especially where it is business personal property. Coverage on improvements and betterments may be at replacement cost if the property is actually replaced. If the property is not replaced, then depreciation would apply to the valuation of such property. Real property such as buildings might be valued at actual cash value, or at replacement cost.

Merchandise and stock of materials normally would be valued at replacement cost, or perhaps at invoice cost in cases where the property is in transit. Any other property that is subject to coverage might be valued at actual cash value or might be subject to valuation provisions in the policy, depending upon the probable exposure to loss and the nature of the property.

A variety of valuation clauses are available, and it is best to purchase a DIC with a valuation clause that reads the same way as the clause in the firm's standard or basic property policies, if at all possible.[23]

Time element coverages such as business interruption can be written under a DIC policy where the exposure to such loss justifies the coverage.

The subject of "other insurance" is usually subject to specific provisions. The DIC policy is not intended to be excess coverage. The usual intent is to cover most losses that are not covered by other policies. Despite the fact that the exclusions in the DIC policy should be carefully coordinated with the coverages of other policies applying to the property, there may be cases where there is duplicate coverage. Therefore, the other insurance clause usually provides that the difference in conditions policy will be excess over any other insurance that should apply to a particular loss.

DIC policies do not generally have a coinsurance clause. The amount of coverage, limits of liability, and other features relating to value of the property covered are all carefully considered and discussed between the insured and the insurer. The agreed amount of coverage in many cases is only a portion of the total values exposed, perhaps 50 percent of these values. DIC policies are judgment rated, and the underwriter determines the premium on the basis of exposure to loss so that there is really no need for a coinsurance provision.

Typical Difference in Condition Losses Sometimes it is difficult for an insured to visualize the unusual occurrences that may cause severe loss. A brief review of some actual losses that have been paid under this type of policy will help to illustrate the possibilities.

1. An accident in a food processing plant in which molasses was an important ingredient resulted in spilling molasses into a complicated machine. It cost the company $38,000 to clean out the molasses and repair the machine.
2. Collections of dust on roofs have caused several building collapses. The dust from certain industrial operations is almost like concrete and solidifies layer upon layer when wet by rain or high humidity. In two such cases the dust had accumulated to thicknesses of eighteen inches and thirty-six inches, respectively, with subsequent collapse of the structure under the weight of the solidified dust.
3. The breaking of a thirty-six inch city water main flooded the basement and portions of the first floor in an industrial plant with damage running into the hundreds of thousands of dollars.
4. A clothing manufacturer had sent out a $50,000 shipment of clothing in an owned truck. The truck was hit by a train at a railroad crossing. This was a case where a broad and blanket type of coverage for all personal property, including property in transit, had been written under a difference in conditions policy.
5. A manufacturer had extensive shelving for the storage of metal components used in the manufacturing process. The shelving apparently had weakened through years of use (or perhaps newer parts were heavier than the old ones), and the shelving

collapsed. It cost more than $20,000 to repair the damage and to restore the parts to usable condition.

Water damage losses from faulty or broken plumbing occasionally cause losses. Such losses from interior water damage may be covered by some of the package insurance policies, but sometimes insurers are unwilling to accept this exposure at the filed rates which apply to package policies. This interior water damage exposure may be included in the coverage in the difference in conditions policy. Several such losses have been paid under difference in conditions policies.

There may be a question of where the coverage for the loss applies in the case of a collapse of a water tank that supplies water for sprinkler systems and also for domestic purposes. Collapse may result from structural weakness, from windstorm, or from some other occurrence such as earthquake. The examples of actual losses, plus the obvious possibility of confusion in the case of such a loss as the collapse of a water tank, illustrate the necessity for careful drafting of the DIC policy in relation to other insurance. Where possible, the DIC policy and the basic insurance coverages should be placed in the same insurance company or the same group of companies. An important advantage of the DIC policy is that when written as an "all-risks" type of coverage, it eliminates any need for the insured to pick specific exposures to loss. The miscellaneous exposures sometimes do cause catastrophic loss, and the DIC policy is ideally suited to this type of loss exposure to the insured.

Advantages and Disadvantages of DIC Combined with the basic coverage, the DIC gives comprehensive protection to the insured. Its advantages include these points:[24]

1. Both known and unknown perils may be insured against.
2. Coverages in a DIC are less costly than when purchased separately. Examples include flood, earthquake, and certain forms of crime.
3. One does not have to insure to value. The DIC contract does not have a coinsurance clause.
4. Elimination of multiple coverage. When a DIC policy is purchased, one does not need to maintain open stock burglary, installation floaters, inland marine cargo, inland waterway or intercoastal marine, or express shipments policies. Also, there is no need for separate earthquake and water damage (including flood) cover.

Disadvantages include:

1. limited and varying market, and

2. difficulty in interpretation of contract and negotiation with insurer (policy wording must be written very carefully in order for insured to obtain desired coverage).

FIRE AND ALLIED LINES INSURANCE FOR LIABILITY EXPOSURES

Most of the fire and allied lines forms discussed thus far protect a property owner against loss arising out of damage to his or her owned property. Fire and allied lines forms are also used in some cases to protect against loss arising out of legal liability for damage to property of others.

Legal liability insurance is usually considered liability insurance rather than property insurance. Yet there are situations where the loss exposures more closely resemble those typically covered by fire insurance than those typically covered by liability insurance. For example, a tenant may be legally liable for damage to a rented building if fire or water damage is caused by the tenant's negligence, and insurance may be selected to cover this chance of loss. In such a case, the property exposed to loss could be covered under a fire and allied lines policy, and the perils causing loss may be the same. Because of these similarities, several forms of liability insurance have developed which are written as fire and allied lines.

Coverage for liability exposures differs from coverage for damage to owned property in that the insured is not the owner of the covered property. Because of this, the insured is not exposed to direct loss arising out of *any* damage (such as fire damage) to the property in question. The insured is only exposed to loss if the damage is caused by a negligent act of the insured. An actual example of such negligence involved an auto mechanic who allowed gasoline from a leaking automobile gas tank to build up a puddle on the floor in a rented repair garage. Eventually the gasoline vapors were ignited by the flame in a hot water heater and a sizable fire resulted. In this case and most similar cases, the building owner had property insurance that paid for the loss, but the building owner's insurer subrogated against the automobile repair shop and was able to recover damages from the repair shop because the loss was caused by their negligence.

Following is a discussion of some liability coverages provided in fire and allied lines forms.

Legal Liability Coverage

There are three fire and allied lines forms that are specifically designed as liability insurance: (1) the fire liability form, (2) the sprinkler leakage liability form, and (3) water damage liability insurance.

Fire Liability Insurance The fire liability form applies to legal liability for loss to property caused by fire or other peril specified in the contracts. This coverage is sometimes written on a fire and allied lines form and sometimes written as an endorsement to the comprehensive general liability form.

Subject Matter. In the fire liability form, the insurance company agrees to pay on the insured's behalf, "all sums which the Insured shall become legally obligated to pay as damages because of injury to or destruction of such property, including the loss of use thereof, caused by accident and arising out of fire." Note the reference, "of such property." The form contains a space in which to identify the nature and the location of the property covered. This follows the fire insurance tradition of covering only at specified locations. Note also that claims for loss of use are covered, providing there has been injury or damage to the described property. Consequently, if the injured third party loses income because of a fire negligently caused by the insured, the fire liability form will respond.

Besides paying for damages up to the policy limits, the contract provides certain supplementary benefits similar to those in other liability insurance policies. The insurer promises to:

1. Defend any suit against the insured. The insurer can negotiate and make settlement without the insured's consent.
2. Pay premiums on bonds of release attachments. The insurer is not required to supply bond itself.
3. Pay all expenses incurred by the insurer and interest on judgment until the insurer pays the judgment.
4. Reimburse the insured for all reasonable expenses incurred at the insurer's request.

Insureds. In the form, the word "insured" includes any partner, executive officer, director, or stockholder while acting within the scope of his or her duties. However, ordinary employees are not considered insureds. If a negligent employee starts a fire, the employer is covered but the employee is not.

Perils. Inherent explosion, smoke damage, or extended coverage and vandalism and malicious mischief forms may be added to increase the perils insured against. Most extended coverage and vandalism and malicious mischief losses involve either acts of God or acts of others, so many question the need for legal liability coverage for these perils. Although the chance of loss is remote, it does exist, and the premium charge reflects the low probability of an insured loss. Of course, explosion and smoke legal liability losses are clearly valid items to provide for.

Exclusions. The fire liability form excludes (1) "nuclear" losses and (2) liability assumed under any contract or agreement. The contractual exclusion is important to most insureds because of lease agreements commonly in use. When a person assumes responsibility for loss to the property under the terms of the lease agreement, contractual liability is created. This type of contractual liability is excluded under the fire liability form. When a tenant has contractually assumed liability for fire losses to the building, the purchase of fire liability insurance does not cover to the extent the tenant has become liable for losses for which tort law would not have imposed liability.[25] Methods of treating liability assumed under contract will be discussed in CPCU 4.

Rates. Fire liability insurance is much less costly than direct property insurance. The rate for real property is 25 percent of the 80 percent coinsurance rate which would apply to direct property insurance. For personal property the fire liability rate is 50 percent of the 80 percent coinsurance rate for contents. The fire liability rate is lower because it only pays for fires negligently started by the insured. When extended coverage and V&MM are added, the relative charges are the same.

There is no coinsurance clause in the fire liability form. However, risk managers should carefully examine the degree of exposure to loss in establishing insurance limits. The maximum damages that could be sustained under this form would include loss of all property of others (described on the form) in the care, custody, and control of the insured as well as any indirect damages that might be sustained in a single loss. For a tenant occupying an entire building, the entire building might be in the tenant's care, custody, and control. A tenant occupying a portion of a multiple-occupancy building would only need to consider the value of that portion of the building in establishing insurance limits. Damage to other portions of the building, if caused by the insured's negligence, would be covered by property damage liability insurance, discussed in CPCU 4.

Noninsurance Techniques for Treating the Fire Liability Exposure As mentioned, the exposure to loss arising out of fire liability can be insured (under a fire or allied lines form or a liability form) or it can be retained. The exposure can also be transferred through the lease agreement if the building owner releases the lessee from liability for any fire damage to the building. As long as any such agreement is initiated before loss occurs, the building owner's insurer cannot subrogate against the tenant (or any other legally liable party) according to the terms of most policies. Such a release of liability agreement would normally have no effect on the building owner's insurance rate and might seem to be the best solution to this problem. Building owners should realize, however, that any such release eliminates their chance of recovery from a negligent tenant and may prevent full recovery if the building is not covered for its full insurable value.

Sprinkler Leakage Liability and Water Damage Legal Liability Since they were revised in 1966, general liability forms provide coverage for water damage to property of others not in the insured's care, custody, and control. Before this 1966 revision, sprinkler leakage liability and water damage legal liability insurance was used with much greater frequency than at present.

Sprinkler Leakage Liability. Like fire liability insurance, sprinkler leakage liability insurance can be used to provide the insured with limited coverage for damage to property of others in the insured's care, custody, and control. As expected, the form covers damage to others' property caused by accidental discharge from an automatic sprinkler system. Protection is limited to property of others for which the insured is legally liable.

The sprinkler leakage form can be amended to give coverage for property of others under the insured's control by deleting the words "except property in the portion of a building occupied by the insured" from the basic form. This increases the premium by 25 percent.

The exclusions section eliminates contractual liability, loss resulting from alterations and repair, and coverage while the building is vacant or unoccupied. Also excluded is loss due to fire, lightning, windstorm, earthquake, blasting, explosion, bursting of steam boilers, riot, civil commotion, water from other than a sprinkler system, war, and order of a civil authority.

Water Damage Liability Insurance. Water damage liability insurance protection is more restrictive than that in the other liability forms. Personal property in the insured's custody is *not* insured—only property of others outside the portion of the building occupied by the insured and damage to the building itself are covered under this form. As with the other property liability forms, contractual liability is excluded.

Fire and Allied Lines Property Insurance Used to Insure Property of Others

The preceding property forms only provide coverage for the insured if legal liability existed and an insured peril caused a loss. The following analysis describes situations where direct property insurance that pays without regard to liability is desirable to insure the property of others. The two areas of discussion involve leased real property and personal property held by the insured.

Leased Real Property Often when a tenant leases property, the lease requires the tenant to be responsible for accidental loss to the property. General liability (including contractual liability) insurance does not apply because of its "care, custody, or control" exclusion. Since the fire legal liability type policies exclude contractual liability, these forms are not useful. Consequently, the tenant must look to alternative means to insure the property. One approach is to have the tenant purchase direct property insurance on the building, since an insurable interest exists by contract. Since direct coverage pays without regard to fault and has no contractual liability exclusions, tenants can thus protect their interests. Of course, if a loss is caused by an uninsured peril, the tenant has a problem. Therefore, broad coverage is desirable in such situations.

Personal Property Held by the Insured Various types of business persons such as warehousemen, repair shop operators, cleaners, and tailors have personal property of others in their care, custody, or control. The liability property policies previously described can be used by them, but these covers pay only if the insured is legally liable. Good business practice may require the business person to cover the loss whether fault exists or not. A business may feel a moral obligation to pay for such losses, but these policies do not cover the peril of "moral obligations."

One way to provide the needed protection is to purchase direct property insurance on the customer's goods. Fire and allied lines coverage for this exposure can be attached through the use of the personal property of others in the care, custody, or control of the named insured endorsement, or the personal property of others coverage in forms like the general property form (FGP-1) can be purchased. In either case, a separate amount of insurance is set. The forms require the covered type of property to be specified and coverage applies only on the named insured's premises. The insured needs to make sure that the coinsurance requirement is met. Common alternative forms that cover in rather similar fashion are the bailee's customer's policies, described in Chapter 10 of this text.

Chapter Notes

1. "A Guide to Consumer Markets," 1975-76, The Conference Board, New York.
2. G. William Glendenning and Robert B. Holtom, *Personal Lines Underwriting* (Malvern: Insurance Institute of America, 1977), pp. 319-320.
3. "Highly Protected Risks," *Practical Risk Management*, B-5, July 1975.
4. Kattelman v. National Union Fire Insurance Co., 202 Atl. (2nd) 66, cited in National Underwriter Co., *Fire, Casualty and Surety Bulletins (FC&S)*, Dwelling Col-2.
5. Emmett J. Vaughan and C. H. Elliot, *Fundamentals of Risk and Insurance* (Santa Barbara: Wiley-Hamilton, 1972), p. 375.
6. Philip Gordis, *Property and Casualty Insurance*, 23rd ed. (Indianapolis: The Rough Notes Co., June 1974), p. 75.
7. *FC&S*, Misc. Fire, Sc-5.
8. S. S. Huebner, J. Kenneth Black, and Robert S. Cline, *Property and Liability Insurance* (New York: Appleton-Century-Crofts, 1968), p. 132.
9. N. O. Lincoln and G. W. Tisdale, *Insurance Inspection and Underwriting*, 8th ed. (Philadelphia: Chilton Co., Inc., 1965), p. 1061.
10. Ibid., p. 1066.
11. Ibid., p. 1073.
12. When blanket coverage is written for contents, a 10 percent coinsurance clause must be written into the contract. In addition, the highest specific rate applies except that, when supported by a satisfactory statement of values signed by the insured and subject to verification, an average blanket rate may be employed.
13. Bernard G. Werbel, editor, *Werbel's General Insurance Guide* (New York: Insurance Educational Publications, 1972), pp. 875-877.
14. Philip Gordis, p. 141.
15. Robert Riegel, Jerome S. Miller, and C. Arthur Williams, Jr., *Insurance Principles and Practices: Property and Liability*, 6th ed. (Englewood Cliffs, NJ: Prentice-Hall, 1976), p. 602.
16. Rough Notes Company, Inc., *Policy, Form and Manual Analyses*, Property Manual, p. 181.3.
17. Mason et al., Plaintiffs v. National Flood Insurers Association et al., Defendants: United States District Court for the District of Hawaii, No. 71-3350, July 13, 1973.
18. *FC&S*, Misc. Fire, Fl 6-7.
19. Riegel, Miller, and Williams, p. 604.
20. Insurance Information Institute, *Insurance Facts 1976*, p. 442.
21. *FC&S*, Misc., Fire, Nep-3.
22. Robert A. Hershbarger and Ronald K. Miller, "Difference in Conditions: The Coverage and the Market," *The CPCU Annals*, Vol. 29, No. 1, March 1976, p. 51.
23. Ibid., p. 54.

24. Ibid., p. 56.
25. Safeway Moving and Storage Co. v. Aetna Insurance Co., 1971, *C.C.H. (Fire and Casualty)* 810. See also *FC&S*, Multiple Line, Fk-4.

CHAPTER 5

Income and Expense Exposures and Insurance

INTRODUCTION

The preceding two chapters of this text have emphasized insurance used to treat direct damage losses to property. This chapter considers the treatment of net income losses that develop as a consequence of direct damage losses.

A firm's net income is its revenue less its expenses. When property is destroyed, a firm may suffer a loss in net income because its revenues decrease, because its expenses increase, or both. For example, if a firm's building is destroyed by fire, it may be out of business until the building can be rebuilt and suffer decreased revenues. Or, the firm may choose to operate from a temporary location and incur increased expenses.

This chapter will first examine the various types of net income losses. Following that introduction, loss exposures that can cause decreased revenues will be discussed in detail. Various types of business interruption insurance used to treat these exposures will also be discussed. Exposures that increase expenses following a direct loss will be analyzed along with extra expense insurance. Other types of insurance against net income losses are also discussed—combined business interruption and extra expense insurance, rent or rental value insurance, leasehold interest insurance, and tuition fees insurance.

INCOME AND EXPENSE LOSSES

Indirect losses may result as a consequence of direct damage to property. Fire is a major cause of indirect losses, but many also result from explosion, windstorm, and other perils. Perils that generally are uninsurable, such as strikes and war, also may cause indirect losses.

Indirect losses may even result when *nonowned* property is damaged. And indirect losses may result whether the damaged property is located on or off premises. A company that manufactures redwood furniture, for example, may suffer a loss of income if a forest fire destroys the redwood trees owned by the company's supplier.

Indirect losses arising out of direct damage by any peril to any property at any location may be categorized as (1) loss of profits, (2) loss due to continuing fixed expenses, (3) loss due to extraordinary costs, and (4) loss due to expenses to continue operations.

Loss of Net Profits

When a firm is partially or totally shut down following a direct loss, the company may lose (not receive) net profits that would otherwise have been earned during the period of the reduced or suspended operations.

This type of loss is only indirectly related to sales, gross earnings, or expenses. Specifically, the loss in net profits is the decrease in net income after taxes. A company that is not operating profitably does not have this exposure. For many companies, however, the exposure is critical. Many companies cannot survive very long without net profits.

Loss Due to Continuing Fixed Payments

Even when a business is shut down, certain expenses are likely to continue. These expenses are normal, recurring expenses that were incurred before the direct loss and continue (at least in part) even if the business is totally stopped.

After a direct loss there may be no earnings to pay for continuing expenses. The effect of a shutdown, therefore, is to convert some items from expenses to losses.

Continuing fixed expenses typically include salaries for officers and other key employees, mortgage payments, installment payments on other debts, insurance premiums, and expenses for heat, light, and power. These expenses are fixed in the sense that they continue even when business operations are interrupted—they are not necessarily fixed in the sense that they remain at the same level. Some continuing expenses may be reduced after a direct loss.

A business does not suffer a loss for payments that can be suspended when the company is shut down. The cost of raw materials, for example, may not be incurred while a plant is being rebuilt. Some payroll expense also may be avoided.

Even a business not generating net profits may face a loss due to continuing fixed payments following a shutdown.

Loss Due to Extraordinary Costs

A business shut down by a direct loss often incurs extra expenses. These losses are unlike continuing fixed expenses because they were not normal, recurring expenses before the direct loss.

The cost of cleaning the premises of debris and separating salvageable property from destroyed property is an extraordinary cost.[1]

Another type of loss that represents an extraordinary expense is the cost to demolish the remaining portion of a building to make the new building conform to the modern building code. This cost can be involuntary because many jurisdictions require a new building to meet the latest standards when a certain portion of the old building has been destroyed.

When a direct loss occurs, valuable papers, accounts receivable records, or patients' records may be destroyed. In addition to the cost of reconstructing these records, important losses may result from the loss of use of the records. Such indirect losses are likely to include increased bad debts and additional collection expenses.

Even when a business is shut down it may be desirable to rent substitute office space, machinery, equipment, or fixtures. Storage space for undamaged property may also be needed. Advertising costs, in anticipation of the resumption of business, may increase. If large numbers of employees are terminated during the interruption, the company may incur substantial expenses in hiring and training new employees. All these costs are genuine indirect losses. Many other examples could be cited.

Loss Due to Expenses to Continue Operations

Certain types of businesses cannot afford to shut down for any substantial period. Companies such as newspapers, laundries, dairies, and oil dealers are apt to lose their customers to competitors if they remain closed for even a short time. Public utilities, who have no competitors because of their monopoly, find it essential to provide continuous service to their customers who have no alternative source of service. These types of companies may incur substantial expenses, in addition to their normal expenses, in order to avoid a shutdown. The other losses mentioned above may be incurred when a business is interrupted; expenses to continue operations are incurred when an interruption cannot be tolerated.

Expenses to continue operations may include numerous types of cash outlay. A newspaper, for example, may continue to publish by using the "downtime" of presses owned by other companies. The costs of this approach might be much higher than costs under normal circumstances.

ANALYZING THE EXPOSURE

Before risk management techniques for income and expense loss exposures can be selected and applied, the exposures must be analyzed. The discussion which follows will analyze various aspects of these exposures—including loss frequency and severity, measuring the business interruption exposure, and distinguishing between continuing and noncontinuing expenses.

Frequency and Severity of Losses

It is difficult to estimate the probable frequency and severity of indirect losses. Businessowners and managers probably underestimate the frequency of these losses because there is a tendency to believe they are "less important" than direct losses.

Loss frequency would be much easier to predict if direct and indirect losses always occurred simultaneously. It is possible, however, to have an indirect loss even when there has been no direct loss—at any location. A strike, for example, may prevent the use of some property even though the property has not suffered a direct loss. Indirect losses may also arise when access to the premises is cut off because of property improvements or quarantine of an area.

The severity of indirect losses is also difficult to predict. One reason is that there is no consistent relationship between the values exposed to direct losses and the values exposed to indirect losses. Company A owns substantial assets but produces small profits and has few fixed expenses. The direct loss exposure is substantial, but the indirect loss exposure may be small. Compare this situation to Company B. Company B has few assets but it is highly profitable and has high fixed costs. Company B might have a larger indirect loss exposure than Company A, even with fewer assets exposed to direct loss.

Another reason why loss severity is difficult to predict is because some severe direct losses may cause few or no indirect losses. On the other hand, a minor direct loss sometimes can produce indirect losses that are severe.

Severe indirect losses often are associated with companies that have (1) production processes requiring a long time; (2) property requiring long periods for repair or replacement; or (3) bottlenecks in purchasing, production, or selling.

Time-Consuming Production Processes Consider a manufacturer whose production process requires a long time. Production time is not lost when finished goods are damaged or destroyed. However, there is an indirect loss (of time) when goods in process sustain a direct loss. The severity of the loss depends on the amount of time required to bring the goods to the same stage of production they had reached prior to the direct damage. The longer the production process takes, the greater the exposure.

Time to Replace Damaged Property The time required for repairing or replacing damaged property varies greatly among companies. Some companies can move into new quarters, with new equipment, almost immediately after a direct loss.

Some machinery or equipment may require a long time to repair or replace. This is especially true for companies that use highly specialized machinery or equipment. Replacement or repair time is also a problem in many cases when a company is dependent upon foreign companies for parts or repairs. Another factor to consider is the length of the production period of the equipment manufacturer. Consider a public utility that must replace a giant turbine. This machine may require months to manufacture and deliver.

In many cases, the time required to resume operations will depend on the time needed to repair or rebuild a damaged building. The most reliable method of estimating the rebuilding time for a damaged building is to obtain an estimate from a reputable contractor. If this is impractical, tables showing average rebuilding time may be useful. Table 5-1 is an example of such a table.

Table 5-1 is particularly helpful because it allows a person to recognize the effects on loss severity of grade of construction, type of construction, type of occupancy, number of floors, congested conditions, and weather. Of course the figures in the table can be adjusted to reflect judgments based on other factors.

Bottlenecks Bottlenecks refer to stages in business operations where problems can easily cause the process to slow down or stop. Production bottlenecks are easiest to imagine, but bottlenecks can also exist in purchasing and selling.

Some companies manufacture a product that must be developed in a long series of steps that must be performed in sequence. Automobiles,

Table 5-1
Average Rebuilding Time*

Grade of Construction	Average				Good			
Type of Construction[1]	A	B	C	D	A	B	C	D
Type of Occupancy								
Apartment, 1 story	125	105	90	72	156	131	100	90
Each additional story	15	13	12	10	19	16	15	13
Garages, public, 1 story	63	59	56	48	79	74	70	60
Each additional story	15	14	13	11	19	17	16	14
Hotels, clubs, 1 story	138	110	83	69	180	143	109	90
Each additional story	18	15	12	10	23	20	16	13
Industrial, 1 story[2]	69	66	63	52	86	82	79	65
Each additional story	13	12	11	9	16	15	14	11
Lofts, 1 story[3]	120	100	75	40	150	125	94	50
Each additional story	13	12	10	8	16	15	13	10
Offices, 1 story	130	117	88	79	175	158	119	107
Each additional story	17	16	13	11	23	22	18	15
Schools, 1 story	180	164	155	125	243	222	209	169
Each additional story	36	33	31	28	49	45	42	38
Stores, 1 story	124	104	79	42	155	129	99	52
Each additional story	14	13	11	9	17	16	14	11
Theaters	150	136	110	72	207	182	151	97
Warehouses, 1 story	92	81	66	39	110	97	79	47
Each additional story	13	12	10	8	16	14	12	10

1. A is reinforced concrete floors, roof and masonry walls on steel frame; B is reinforced concrete frame, floors, roof, and masonry walls; C is masonry walls with wood floors and roof (if no basement, grade floor may be concrete); and D is frame, stucco, iron-clad, or all steel.
2. Unfinished interior with very few partitions.
3. Plain interior finish and moderate amount of partitions to enclose space for light manufacturing occupancies.

*Reprinted with permission from E.C. Bardwell, *New Profits—Business Interruption Insurance* (Indianapolis: The Rough Notes Co., 1973), pp. 11-12.

Each figure represents an estimate of the number of working days that it takes to erect a certain building and covers the total period from commencement of the plans and specifications to the day when the structure is ready for occupancy. It is assumed that building will be carried on during one shift per day only and that the work would be neither abnormally expedited nor delayed. The construction time is shown for a one-story building, followed by a figure for each additional story above one. Full basements are considered an additional story.

This table presupposes ideal building weather; that is, no time lost due to enforced lay-offs. Increases of 15 percent are suggested in climates where a nominal amount of inclement weather may be expected, and increases up to 35 percent are suggested where uncertain weather is usually the rule or where rigorous winters occur.

The construction time estimates are based upon the location being in a nominally congested district. In highly congested districts of large cities it is necessary to build barricades and a roof over sidewalks, haul materials and refuse through crowded streets, and otherwise operate under adverse conditions. Under such conditions of location, the construction time estimates should be increased about 15 percent. In uncongested localities, the estimates may be reduced 10 percent.

Table 5-2

Business Interruption Exposures of Company X

Gross Earnings		$10,000
Continuing expenses	$4,000	
Noncontinuing expenses	$5,000	
Less: Total Expenses		$ 9,000
Net Profit		$ 1,000

If Company X has gross earnings of $10,000 and total expenses of $9,000, net profits will be $1,000. If expenses amounting to $4,000 would continue if the business is shut down, and $5,000 of expenses would be discontinued, what is the amount exposed to business interruption loss? One method of determining this loss is to add the net profits ($1,000) and the continuing expenses ($4,000) to arrive at an exposure of $5,000. A second method is to take the gross earnings ($10,000) and subtract the noncontinuing expenses ($5,000) to arrive at the exposure of $5,000.

for example, are assembled in the sequence dictated by the assembly line. Other companies manufacture a product which can be developed in steps that have no necessary sequence. These companies are less prone to production bottlenecks.

Bottlenecks are special problems in evaluating the business interruption exposure for two reasons. First, bottlenecks are often difficult to identify. (Flow charts can identify bottlenecks.) A second problem is that minor direct losses to bottlenecks may cause the entire business operation to shut down. As an example, some large plants are not permitted to operate without adequate pollution control devices.

Measuring the Business Interruption Exposure

The preceding discussion focused on general characteristics that influence indirect loss exposures. This section will proceed to measure more specifically the exposure to loss following an interruption of business.

The relationship between gross earnings, continuing expenses, noncontinuing expenses, and net profits is shown in Table 5-2. The most important losses incurred when a business is shut down are loss of net profits and loss due to continuing expenses. Loss exposures may be calculated in two ways: (1) net profits + continuing expenses, or (2) gross earnings – noncontinuing expenses, as illustrated in Table 5-2.

Since business interruption losses result from a passage of time, the time element must also be recognized in measuring the exposure. The

Table 5-3

Company A Income and Expenses, 1977

Sales		$2,540,863
Less: Discounts	$127,043	
Returns	143,068	
Bad debts	362,109	632,220
Net Sales		$1,908,643
Plus: Other income		109,534
Total Revenue		$2,018,177
Less: Cost of goods sold	$885,400	
Supplies	107,075	
Services purchased from others	100,001	1,092,476
Gross Earnings		$ 925,701
Less: All other expenses		684,320
Net Profit		$ 241,381

key concepts in measuring the time element are (1) the maximum period the business could be shut down, (2) the seasonal fluctuations in earnings and expenses (if any), (3) the trend in earnings and expenses, and (4) the distinction between expenses that would be continued and those that would not.

Assume that the exposure for Company A is being evaluated in February 1978. The first step, then, would be to analyze the company's profit and loss statement for 1977 as shown in Table 5-3.

The figures shown in Table 5-3 are annual figures, but it is unlikely that the business would be shut down for exactly one year. Therefore, an estimate of the longest period the firm could be out of operation is necessary. Generally this implies a severe direct loss requiring the construction of a new building. An estimate of the time this might involve can be obtained from a contractor or from tables such as Table 5-1. For our purposes, assume that Company A could construct a new building in five months. In addition, the company estimates that another month would be needed to install fixtures, reorient new employees, and prepare for reopening. The maximum length of the possible shutdown for Company A, therefore, is estimated at six months.

Which six months of the year would the company be shut down? It is impossible to predict when an interruption will occur, but the question is important if the company has a seasonal earnings pattern. If a seasonal pattern exists, the typical fluctuation in earnings must be identified either through the use of figures that show typical seasonal patterns for various types of businesses, such as shown in Figure 5-1, or by studying the past seasonal pattern of the company. Figure 5-1 shows

Figure 5-1

Ratios† of Monthly Sales to Annual Sales of Fourteen Classes of Retail Business*

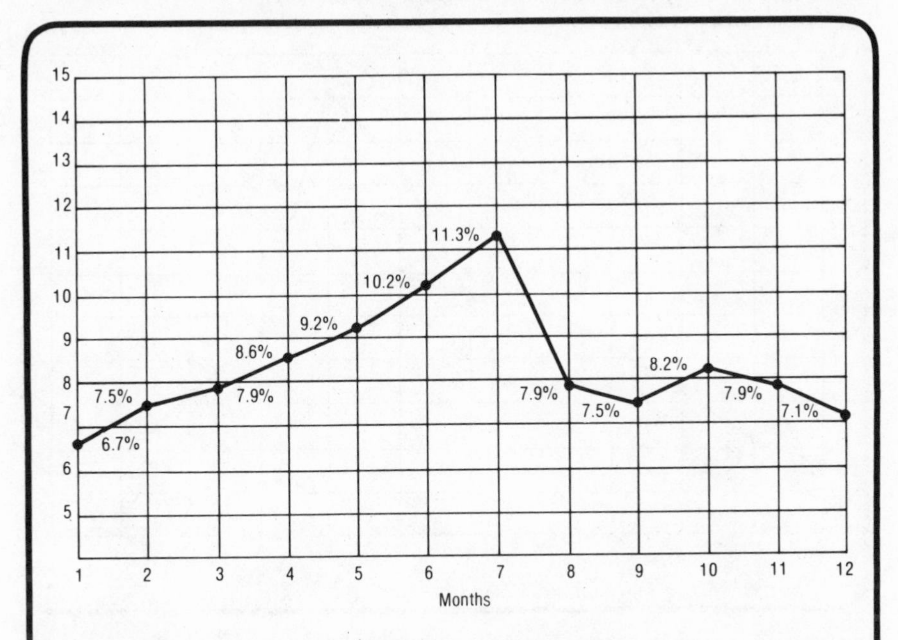

†These ratios are composites of fluctuation ratios of the following classes of business: (1) department stores, including mail order; (2) draperies and lamps; (3) drugs; (4) floor coverings; (5) furniture and appliances; (6) general merchandise, including dry goods; (7) lumber and building materials; (8) liquor stores; (9) home furnishings; (10) shoe stores; (11) variety stores; (12) women's ready-to-wear; (13) grocery stores; and (14) men's and boys' wear, clothing and furnishings.

*Reprinted with permission from E.C. Bardwell, *New Profits—Business Interruption Insurance* (Indianapolis: The Rough Notes Co., 1973), p. 14.

ratios of monthly sales in relation to annual sales for fourteen classes of retail businesses. Notice that 30 percent of the monthly sales occur in the peak three months of business activity for the composite of the retail stores in the figure.

Certain kinds of businesses, such as jewelry manufacturers, retail jewelers, and furriers transact as much as 45 percent of their annual business during their peak three months, and 60 to 80 percent of their annual business during the six consecutive months of highest business activity. Even more seasonal businesses, such as vegetable and fruit packers, canneries, and resorts might gain their entire annual income in a three-month period.

For purposes of measuring the business interruption exposure, the

Figure 5-2
Ratios of Monthly Sales to Annual Sales for Company A

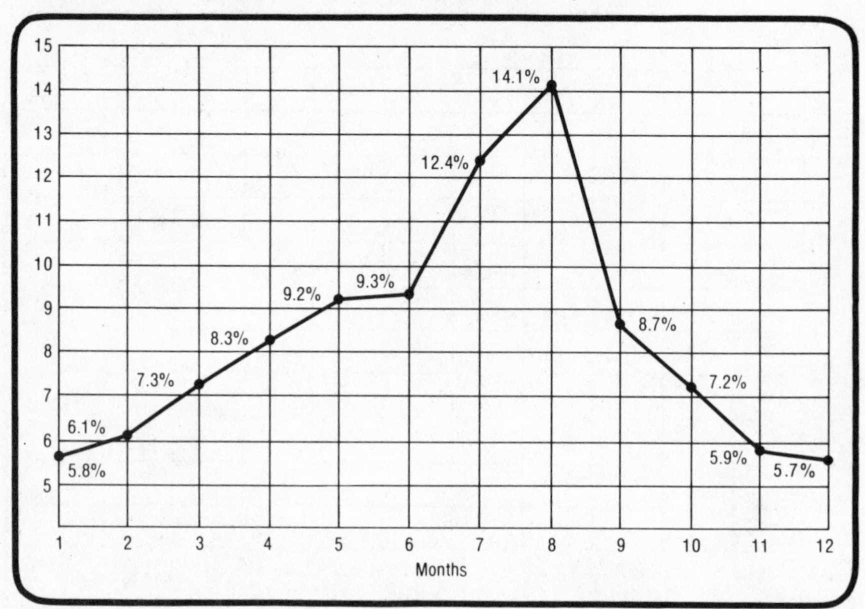

only safe assumption is that the maximum period of shutdown occurs during the months of greatest earnings. In Company A's case, we have estimated the maximum shutdown period to be six months. The net profits and continuing expenses during the highest consecutive six months of activity should be used.

Suppose Company A's seasonal pattern is as shown in Figure 5-2. The numbers of each month represent the percentage of annual earnings. For example, February produced 6 percent of Company A's annual earnings. For Company A, the highest six consecutive months of activity are April through September. In these six months (50 percent of one year) the company typically produces 62 percent of its total volume.

If Company A were shut down from April through September, how much expense would continue during the period? The only way this question can be answered accurately is to analyze each of the important expenses. The question must be asked: Would it be continued, or what portion of the expense would continue? This process will be described shortly, but for purposes of extending our example of Company A, assume that a detailed analysis shows that $205,296 of expense would continue during the shutdown.

From the preceding analysis we can conclude that Company A's business interruption exposure for 1977 was 62 percent of net profits

Table 5-4

Company A's Sales for 1973-1977

Year	Net Sales	Percentage Increase
1973	$1,520,468	—
1974	1,610,482	5.9
1975	1,706,500	5.9
1976	1,813,210	6.3
1977	1,908,643	5.3

($241,381), or $149,656. The total exposure, therefore, was $354,952, or $149,656 plus the continuing expenses of $205,296. This is expressed in the past tense because we are measuring the exposure in February 1978. We have used the figures from the most recent complete year, but our real interest is in projecting the figures into the future. This is necessary because the exposure only exists in the future.

Projections of earnings and expenses into the future can never be perfectly accurate and reliable. However, a simple approach usually provides a good estimate of the exposure. Expenses usually maintain a close relationship to income. Therefore, the trend in earnings should provide a reasonable estimate of the business interruption exposure in the future.

To make the point clear, suppose the net sales of Company A have been as shown in Table 5-4.

The average percentage increase in net sales over this five-year period is 5.85 percent. Furthermore, the deviations from this average have not been large. If, therefore, we assume that net sales will increase at the same approximate rate in the near future (and the other important relationships remain about the same), we can estimate the business interruption exposure in the future.

The exposure was calculated as $354,952 for 1977. At an increase of 5.85 percent, the business interruption exposure will be $375,717 in 1978 (354,952 × 1.0585), and $397,696 in 1979 (375,717 × 1.0585).

This method of projecting the business interruption exposure is simple. However, it yields a reasonably accurate estimate of the exposure. In some cases, more accurate methods of projecting income and expenses may be desirable. In sizable companies the accounting or finance department will already have projections of income and expenses. If available, these projected figures should be used.

Distinguishing Between Continuing and Noncontinuing Expenses

In the case of Company A, a figure was provided to represent continuing expenses. In practice, the determination of continuing expenses is a difficult problem, though very important in measuring the exposure. Although extreme precision is impossible when dealing with future expenses, it is possible to reach a reasonable estimate by considering the following types of expenses: payroll expense; expense for services performed by others; lease or rental expense; interest expense; taxes; advertising expense; royalties, franchise, and license fees; postage, telephone, and telegraph expense; collection expense; professional fees; travel expense, insurance expense; heat, light, and power expense; depreciation; maintenance expense; delivery expense; and shipping and packing expense.

Payroll Expense To what extent will a company continue to incur wage and salary expense during a business interruption? The answer depends upon the maximum duration of the shutdown, the number of employees who have special value to the company, conditions in the labor market, and other considerations.

If the maximum period of the shutdown is very long, it is unlikely that a company would continue the payroll expense for all employees. At the other extreme, few companies would dismiss all employees even in a prolonged interruption. At a minimum some employees usually are necessary (or desirable) in order to assure a smooth transition back to business.

One approach is to consider each job classification. In many companies income will be paid to the owners and officers regardless of the duration of an interruption. Salaries may or may not be continued for department managers, supervisors, or foremen. In some cases highly skilled employees who would be difficult to replace will continue to receive an income. Employees who have no special skills and would be easy to replace usually are not retained, unless the maximum period of an interruption is brief.

Expense for Services Performed by Others Many companies "farm out" functions or services to other companies. Part of the manufacturing process, for example, may be performed by other organizations. And many retailers, such as hardware, appliance, or jewelry stores have alteration, installation, or repair work performed by outsiders. Restaurants and bars often hire musical groups and other entertainers. These services, performed by others, may be under contract, that is, guaranteed. If so, a company may be obligated to make payments to the other companies even during a business interruption. More often, services performed by outside companies will not be continued and payments will not be required.

Lease or Rental Expense Whether or not the lease or rental expense for buildings and equipment would continue during a business shutdown depends upon the terms of the rental or lease agreement. Suspension of business normally does not free a lessee from rental payments for automobiles and trucks on a long-term basis. Rent on branch offices, warehouses, and storage facilities also normally continues during a business interruption at the main location.

Interest Expense Interest payments generally are a continuing expense. In the event of the total destruction of a building, the mortgage debt probably will be retired from property insurance proceeds. However, new loans are likely to be used to construct a new building, so interest expense will continue.

Interest on other loans, or mortgages on property away from the undamaged premises, is unaffected by a business suspension.

Taxes A conservative assumption is that property taxes will be a continuing expense. Depending on the situation, major losses may reduce taxable real property values. Partial losses, however, may cause a business interruption even when there is only a small reduction in taxable property values.

The same reasoning applies to personal property or excise taxes based on inventory or sales. These taxes may continue at the same level (or at virtually the same level) even though business is suspended.

Employer contributions for social security and unemployment compensation would not continue for employees who would not be working during the interruption.

Advertising Expense The advertising policies of companies differ greatly. Some spend large amounts for advertising; others spend little or nothing. Some advertising is intended to stimulate sales in the short run; other advertising is intended to enhance the image of the company and no short-run benefits are expected. Some advertising is designed as consumer education.

To determine whether advertising expense would be continued during a business suspension, the company's advertising policy must be considered. If advertising has been contracted for in advance and cannot be canceled, it would be a continuing expense. In many cases advertising would not be necessary except perhaps shortly before the business reopens. Some companies, however, will prefer to maintain their advertising even during a long shutdown.

Table 5-5

Accounts Receivable Aging Schedule

Age	Percent of Total
30 days and less	50
31–60 days	30
61–90 days	15
Over 90 days	5

Royalties, Franchise, and License Fees If based on sales or production, payment of royalties, franchise fees, and license fees would cease upon suspension of operations. These expenses may continue, however, if they are a flat fee or must meet a guaranteed minimum level.

Postage, Telephone, and Telegraph Expense Communication expenses would probably continue in full during a short period of suspension. In fact, these expenses might be increased because of the necessity to use long-distance telephone or telegraph service more extensively. In the event of a prolonged period of suspension, these expenses probably would be discontinued immediately, but they probably would be resumed sometime before the business reopens. As a general rule, communication expenses can be regarded as continuing for one or two months.

Collection Expense The cost associated with the collection of accounts receivable would continue, at least for the normal collection period. The company's aging schedule for its accounts receivable shows the percentage of accounts receivable not past due and the percent past due. Table 5-5 is a simple illustration of an accounts receivable aging schedule.

If a company normally has the experience indicated above, 95 percent of the accounts will be collected within ninety days. With this experience it might be reasonable to assume that collection expenses would continue for three months, possibly at a lower rate each month. When the maximum period of a shutdown is estimated at three months, the above figures suggest that collection expenses should be regarded as a continuing expense.

Professional Fees Fees for accounting and legal services normally are continuing expenses if paid on a retainer basis. However, additional legal and accounting services may be necessary as a result of the loss. If not on a retainer, it may be reasonable to assume one or two month's expenditure as a continuing expense.

Travel Expense Most companies would have no travel expenses if the business were shut down. Other companies, however, would incur increased and continuing travel expenses. The purposes of the travel should be ascertained as a guide to estimating travel costs.

Insurance Expense Insurance expense should be considered in relation to the type of insurance carried. Workers' compensation insurance premiums would continue only to the extent that they applied to persons continuing to be paid during the suspension.

In the event of the total destruction of stock, equipment, and buildings, insurance premiums on these items would cease. However, if only partially damaged, the insurance expense would continue and destroyed property would be replaced with new property that must be insured. The reasonable assumption, therefore, is that these premiums would continue.

For liability insurance, premiums based on gross receipts would probably be held to a minimum, since there would be no business activity during a shutdown. If the premium is based on a flat amount per location or on floor area, the premium would continue.

Automobile premiums would continue unless the autos were destroyed or coverage was suspended because they were not in use during a shutdown. Transportation insurance premiums would not continue during a shutdown.

Life, pension, and employee benefit insurance would continue to the extent that employees are retained. Business life insurance premiums would continue.

Heat, Light, and Power Expense The cost of heat, light, and power would probably be continued minimally during short periods of shutdown. During longer periods the expense would be discontinued until shortly before reopening. However, sometimes a minimum charge has to be paid to the utility companies.

Depreciation Depreciation continues on undamaged property but cannot continue on property that is totally destroyed. Since there is no way to know how much will be damaged, the conservative assumption would be to treat all depreciation expense as continuing.

Maintenance Expense In most instances maintenance costs would not continue in the event of a business shutdown. However, if the property consists of more than one building or fire division, the property not affected by the loss would probably require at least a minimum amount of maintenance.

Delivery Expense The determination of whether delivery expense would continue depends upon the method of making deliveries. With total suspension of business, deliveries would cease. In some cases delivery expense might continue because of minimum charges to be paid under an existing delivery contract.

Shipping and Packing Expenses Generally shipping costs would not continue during a period of interruption. However, if finished goods of a manufacturer were not damaged in a fire or other loss, the cost of shipping would continue for a short period and be absorbed in the selling price. Packaging includes containers of individual units of production, such as cans, bottles, boxes and cartons, and protective packaging materials. These items are really part of the product, so should be considered raw stock. Shipping containers and crates are generally considered shipping expenses rather than raw stock. Neither packaging nor shipping costs would continue during a business interruption.

General Observations of the Business Interruption Exposure

Several observations regarding the business interruption exposure can now be made. First, since the exposure consists of net profits *and* continuing expenses, it is clear that an exposure may exist even for companies that are not earning a profit. Even a nonprofit company or a company that is operating at a loss is normally generating earnings to cover all, or a portion of, the company's continuing expenses. In many cases continuing expenses are larger than the company's profits.

Second, continuing expenses may be less if a total loss occurs than if the loss is partial. As we have seen, many of the expense items will be discontinued if the property is totally destroyed. The business interruption exposure may not be at all proportional to the direct loss exposure. As a general rule, then, the conservative approach is to assume that a small direct loss can suspend operations. Extreme care should be exercised before deciding that any expense would be discontinued.

BUSINESS INTERRUPTION INSURANCE

Business interruption insurance contracts have gone through a long evolution. Earlier forms were often known as Use and Occupancy insurance, or simply U and O. Many people still refer to business interruption insurance by these names.

Today there are only four business interruption forms in general use in fire and allied lines. They are:

1. gross earnings form 3
2. gross earnings form 4
3. earnings form
4. combined business interruption and extra expense form

The following discussion is primarily concerned with the first two forms—the others will be described later in this chapter. In general, the business interruption forms insure against loss from interruption of business resulting from direct damage to real or personal property caused by a peril insured against.

Form 3 is intended for mercantile and nonmanufacturing companies. Form 4 is designed for manufacturing and mining organizations. The basic difference between these two forms is the way they define gross earnings.

In the mercantile form, gross earnings are defined as "the sum of: (a) Total net sales and (b) Other earnings derived from operations of the business, less the cost of: (c) Merchandise sold, including packaging material therefor, (d) Materials and supplies consumed directly in supplying the service(s) sold by the Insured, and (e) Service(s) purchased from outsiders (not employees of the Insured) for resale which do not continue under contract."

The manufacturing form defines gross earnings as "the sum of: (a) Total net sales value of production, (b) Total net sales of merchandise, and (c) Other earnings derived from operation of the business, less the cost of: (d) Raw stock from which such production is derived, (e) Supplies consisting of materials consumed directly in the conversion of such raw stock into finished stock or in supplying the service(s) sold by the Insured, (f) Merchandise sold, including packaging materials therefor, and (g) Service(s) purchased from outsiders (not employees of the Insured) for resale which do not continue under contract."

The differences stem from the fact that mercantile and manufacturing companies are back in business at different times. A merchant can resume operations when the building is repaired, the fixtures replaced, and the stock replenished. A manufacturer, however, recovers from a loss only after the plant is repaired, machinery replaced, and the work in process brought to the same stage of production it had reached before the loss. Stated differently, a mercantile business is protected against interruption of the *selling* process, while a manufacturer is protected against suspension of the *manufacturing* process.

Table 5-6

Business Interruption Data for Company A

	1977	1978†
(1) Gross earnings (annual)	$925,701	$979,855
(2) Net profit (annual)	241,381	255,502
(3) Expenses continuing during six-month interruption	205,296	217,306
(4) Maximum net profit during six-month interruption (2) x 0.62	149,656	158,411
(5) Maximum potential business interruption exposure (3) + (4)	354,952	375,717

† 1978 figures are 1977 figures increased 5.85 percent.

Determining the Amount of Insurance to Purchase

After the proper form has been selected (depending on the type of business) the amount of business interruption insurance to purchase must be decided. A detailed analysis of the business interruption exposure, like that described for Company A, will provide figures that can be used in determining the amount of insurance to purchase. Unfortunately, such detailed analyses are done infrequently, and the amount of insurance chosen is somewhat arbitrary. Nevertheless, the proper approach is first to measure the exposure and then to determine the amount of insurance needed.

The preceding discussion of Company A developed the information shown in Table 5-6. It would seem that a firm wishing to be fully protected against the business interruption exposure should simply buy the amount of insurance that matches the maximum potential exposure. Thus, if Company A were purchasing business interruption insurance in February 1978, it would seem appropriate to purchase business interruption insurance covering $375,717, the probable maximum exposure during the February 1978—February 1979 policy year. (The 1979 figures would not be used because the maximum exposure is during the months from April to September.) Such thinking is essentially correct, but there are two additional factors to consider: (1) the effect of the coinsurance requirement (contribution clause), and (2) coverage of ordinary payroll.

Contribution Clause or Coinsurance Clause In order to encourage insurance to value, business interruption gross earnings forms contain a contribution clause or coinsurance clause which operates the same as the coinsurance clause in direct damage insurance policies.

The policies used in some territories use the term "contribution clause," whereas others use the term "coinsurance clause." The term "coinsurance clause" will be used here, but the reader should be aware of the regional differences in terminology. In most territories, the insured may choose 50, 60, 70, or 80 percent coinsurance (90 and 100 percent coinsurance are available in some areas).

The important point regarding the coinsurance percentage is that it does not apply to the maximum loss exposure. As indicated earlier, the exposure consists of maximum net profits plus continuing expenses (or gross earnings less noncontinuing expenses) for the maximum anticipated period of interruption. The coinsurance percentage in the gross earnings form applies to the gross earnings that probably would have occurred during the twelve-month period following the beginning of the shutdown. For example, if a loss had occurred on January 1, 1978, Company A would have needed $489,928 with a 50 percent coinsurance clause (50 percent of $979,855) to meet coinsurance requirements. If Company A had used the data in Table 5-6 and bought $375,717 of coverage, they would be able to collect only 76.7 percent of a loss ($375,717/[50% × $979,855] = 76.7%).

The coinsurance clause may require an insured to purchase more business interruption insurance than seems necessary for a maximum loss. It might seem more logical if the coinsurance percentage applied to gross earnings less noncontinuing expenses. Those who drafted the contract language, however, recognized that estimates of noncontinuing expenses are difficult to make before a loss occurs, and such a requirement might make it difficult to comply with the contribution clause. Furthermore, the disadvantage of buying more insurance than may be needed is supposed to be offset by lower insurance rates.

Another aspect of the coinsurance clause which should be considered is that it applies to the gross earnings, not in the past or present, but in the future. Specifically, it applies to the gross earnings the company probably would have achieved in the twelve-month period starting at the beginning of the loss. This approach arises because the insurance is intended to "do for the insured what the business would have done" if there had been no loss.

Since business interruption insurance provides protection for future net profits and continuing expenses, the values (as we have seen) must be projected into the future. Because the projections are only estimates, the usual practice is to project figures for one year. Then, during the term of the policy the amount of insurance should be reviewed frequently, usually not less than every six months but more often if there are major changes in earnings or expenses. Some business interruption authorities believe that values should be projected at least two years. This is because a loss might occur near the expiration of the first year of coverage and extend into the second year.

Coverage of "Ordinary" Payroll A second major consideration in determining the amount of business interruption coverage to purchase is to determine how "ordinary" payroll will be handled. Ordinary payroll is defined as "the entire payroll expense for all employees of the insured, except officers, executives, department managers, employees under contract and other important employees." Its special importance arises because payroll expense is a major cost in most companies and because a company may need some latitude in how it will be handled with insurance.

Ordinary payroll may be handled in one of three ways. One approach, which is found in the unendorsed gross earnings forms, is to cover all ordinary payroll expense. This provides coverage since payroll cost is treated as a continuing expense, but it also increases the amount of insurance necessary to meet the coinsurance requirement. Coverage of ordinary payroll may be suitable for some insureds, especially if the maximum duration of a shutdown is brief or if all employees would be difficult to replace and would not be laid off during a shutdown.

A second approach is to use an endorsement that excludes all ordinary payroll. If ordinary payroll is excluded, coinsurance of at least 80 percent is mandatory. However, the amount of insurance required will be decreased because ordinary payroll will be deducted from gross earnings before application of the coinsurance percentage.

To illustrate, assume that the annual expected gross earnings are $300,000 and the ordinary payroll amounts to $100,000. The required amount of insurance under a policy totally excluding the ordinary payroll would be as shown in Table 5-7.

The required amount of insurance with an 80 percent coinsurance clause, if ordinary payroll is included, would be $240,000 (80 percent of $300,000). (Of course lesser amounts of insurance could be purchased if a 50, 60, or 70 percent coinsurance clause is used, but the rate would be higher for each dollar of coverage.)

The third approach is to cover, by endorsement, ordinary payroll for a limited period of time. Coverage may be provided for 90, 120, 150, or 180 days. This endorsement also requires coinsurance of at least 80 percent.

The operation of this endorsement can be illustrated by extending the previous example. Using the same figures as above, how much insurance is required if the insured wishes to cover ordinary payroll for

Table 5-7
Calculation of Required Amount of Insurance

Gross earnings	$300,000
Less ordinary payroll	100,000
	$200,000
Required Amount (80% of $200,000)	$160,000

Table 5-8
Required Amount of Payroll Insurance for Ninety Days

Gross earnings	$300,000
Less ordinary payroll	100,000
	$200,000
Plus coverage for 90 days (¼ of $100,000)	25,000
	$225,000
Required Amount (80% of $225,000)	$180,000

ninety days? If the ordinary payroll is projected at $100,000 for the year and the payroll expense does not fluctuate, the amount of insurance required would be as shown in Table 5-8.

When the ordinary payroll expense has a seasonal pattern, it would be wise to determine the highest amount of ordinary payroll anticipated for any consecutive ninety-day period. If, for example, the ordinary payroll is expected to be $100,000 for the year, but will be $40,000 in one ninety-day period, the above figures should be modified. The amount of insurance required then would be $192,000 (i.e., 80 percent of $240,000).

As with full payroll coverage, when ordinary payroll is covered for a limited time, the insured will be indemnified only for necessary payroll expenses, and only if such expenses are actually incurred. The coverage is not a "valued form" merely because it is provided for a limited period. Also, note that this coverage is not segregated from the coverage for other expenses. If an insured chooses a coverage limit based on ordinary payroll coverage for a limited period but does not incur all the estimated payroll expense during a shutdown, the coverage may be used to offset other expenses that are higher than anticipated.

The choice among the three approaches to ordinary payroll depends upon the insured's situation. However, ordinary payroll should be excluded entirely only after considering the following: (1) the labor market might be tight in the insured's locale at the time of a loss and there may be some difficulty in hiring employees—it may be easier to retain existing labor; (2) often there is a higher expense than anticipated in training new employees—existing employees are already trained; and (3) disputes in loss adjustments may develop over which employees should be classified in the ordinary payroll category.

Important Policy Provisions

Perils Insured Against The perils insured against are not described or listed in the gross earnings form itself; instead, the perils covered for business interruption are named on the policy and in endorsements to which the business interruption form is attached. Thus, business interruption insurance can be written for the same perils or combinations of perils as direct damage policies. When the basic policy is endorsed to include additional perils, such as burglary, weight of ice and snow, building collapse, and sprinkler leakage, loss from the same perils would be covered by the gross earnings form.

Although business interruption insurance may be written in conjunction with direct loss property insurance, the items must be separate. That is, it does not provide blanket coverage for direct and indirect losses. Direct loss insurance cannot be used to provide business interruption protection, and business interruption proceeds cannot reimburse the insured for direct losses.

Business interruption insurance cannot be written to cover such perils as flood, landslide or subsidence, except in some difference in conditions (DIC) contracts. Some perils are particularly important as causes of business shutdowns but are uninsurable under any standard insurance contract. Strikes, for example, cause many business suspensions. These perils must be managed by risk management techniques other than insurance.

The Insuring Agreement The gross earnings form protects against loss resulting directly from the necessary interruption of business caused by damage to or destruction of real or personal property by the insured perils.

An interruption may be total or partial but it must be necessary, that is, beyond the insured's control. Furthermore, the interruption must be caused by the perils insured against, occurring on the premises occupied by the insured. If a fire occurs to a neighboring property and causes the insured to lose business, there is no protection afforded in the insuring agreement. Shutdowns caused by uninsured perils obviously are not covered.

When an interruption occurs, the insurer is liable only for the *actual loss sustained,* not exceeding the reduction in gross earnings, less charges and expenses that do not necessarily continue. In effect, actual loss sustained is similar to actual cash value, and the purpose is to make the contract one of indemnity. This requires a determination of the amount the insured would have earned if there had been no loss. In cases of partial suspension, the *reduced* earnings must be compared to what the insured would have earned if a loss had not occurred. Business interruption losses, therefore, are not always easy to measure, but in most cases loss adjustments are handled without undue difficulty.

In determining the actual loss sustained the time element is measured by the length of time required, with the exercise of due diligence and dispatch, to rebuild, repair, or replace the damaged or destroyed property. The due diligence and dispatch requirement is important. The insured cannot delay the repair or rebuilding process, and he or she must see that all work is reasonably expedited. There can be a large difference between the actual time required for repairing or replacing the damaged property and the time required by due diligence and dispatch. In fact, the policy does not require that the damaged property ever be repaired or replaced. If the property is not repaired or replaced, the form would still provide reimbursement for the time it *would have* taken to repair or replace the property. This can be very important to a tenant of a building who has no control over the decision to repair or replace the rented premises.[2]

Notice that a landlord might delay the reopening by not exercising due diligence and dispatch, but the insured would not be reimbursed for the additional loss caused by delay.

The time element is not terminated when a damaged or destroyed building is repaired or rebuilt. Time is permitted for the insured to refurnish supplies and restock merchandise. For a manufacturer, time is allowed to bring the production process to the same place where it was before the loss.

The time element also is not terminated by the expiration of the policy. If a fire, for example, damages the property one week before the policy expiration date and causes a three-month suspension, the entire loss would be covered, whether or not a renewal premium was paid. (It might be desirable to carry business interruption insurance during the period of interruption in case another direct damage loss during the reconstruction causes a further period of interruption.)

Fortifying the due diligence and dispatch concept, the insuring agreement states that due consideration shall be given to the continuation of normal charges and expenses to the extent necessary to resume operations with the same quality of service which existed before the loss.

Resumption of Operations The gross earnings form states, "... if the insured could reduce the loss resulting from the interruption of business, (a) by complete or partial resumption of operation of the property herein described, whether damaged or not, or (b) by making use of merchandise or other property at the location(s) described herein or elsewhere, such reduction shall be taken into account in arriving at the amount of loss hereunder."

This clause requires the insured to take steps that will reduce the loss. If the insured can reduce the loss by using temporary rented quarters, for example, he or she is required to do so. When the insured could reduce the loss by taking reasonable steps but does not, the insurance company will not pay for the portion of the loss that could have been avoided.

Expenses to Reduce Loss The contract provision permitting the insured to use extraordinary means and expenses to reduce the loss is closely coupled with the insured's duty to get back into business as soon as possible. The cost of these measures—if they effectively reduce the loss—will be met by the insurer.

The policy reads:

> This policy also covers such expenses as are necessarily incurred for the purpose of reducing loss under this policy (except expense incurred to extinguish a fire), but in no event shall the aggregate of such expenses exceed the amount by which the loss otherwise payable under this policy is reduced.

Thus, if the insured spends $15,000 over and above normal expenses to expedite recovery of operations and this expenditure reduces the loss by $15,000, the insured will be reimbursed for the expense. If the expenditure reduced the loss only by $12,000, the insured would collect all but $3,000 of the extra cost.

The business interruption loss can be reduced by expediting the restoration of damaged properties with overtime work or by adding extra personnel. Extra expenses incurred in operating at a temporary location would also be eligible for reimbursement under this clause.

Expense to reduce the loss can have a dramatic effect on the actual loss sustained. In one case, a manufacturer operating two plants suffered a loss at one of the plants. In cooperation with its insurer, the firm doubled its capacity at the surviving plant to reduce losses during the period of restoration. The workers from the damaged plant operated as a second shift at the surviving plant, which now produced double its normal output. After the damaged plant was back in operation, it was determined that these measures had resulted in an operation more efficient than the original operation at two separate plants and that the expenses to reduce the loss had so reduced the loss that no business interruption loss was sustained.

Interruption by Civil Authority It is not uncommon for a fire or other peril to cause an interruption at a number of adjacent businesses. For example, police and firemen may deny access to an entire city block when a serious fire occurs. An insured's business, in such a situation, may be interrupted even though the fire occurred away from the insured's premises. This type of loss will be covered for a maximum of two consecutive weeks according to the "interruption by civil authority" clause.

To be eligible for this coverage, access to the insured's business must be denied by the order of governmental authorities. The denial of access must be caused by damage or destruction of property from an insured peril. A riot, for example, if it is an insured peril, could lead to reimbursement. The mere threat of a riot or a curfew imposed because of a possible riot would not be an insured peril. Furthermore, the insured peril must damage or destroy property that is adjacent to the insured's property. The word "adjacent" is interpreted to mean nearby; it does not necessarily mean adjoining. However, losses occurring at some distance, that is, not nearby, would not be covered.

EDP Media Limitation If a business is interrupted by an insured peril that damages or destroys electronic data processing programming records, media, or equipment and no other property has been damaged, coverage is limited to a period of thirty days. This limitation does not necessarily apply if other property has been damaged along with the EDP equipment. In this case, the time element is the time required to repair or replace the other property, if longer than thirty days.

In most territories the EDP limitation, for an additional premium, may be extended to 90 or 180 days or eliminated entirely.

Exclusions In addition to the exclusions previously mentioned, the gross earnings form contains several special exclusions.

Losses caused by the enforcement of a state or local ordinance or law pertaining to the construction, repair, or demolition of buildings are excluded. This exclusion corresponds to a similar exclusion in most fire, multi-peril, and other direct damage policies. It intends to exclude any increase in the length of time required to repair or rebuild a building to meet the modern building code. This exclusion may be eliminated for an additional premium.

An insurer is not liable for a loss resulting from interference at the described premises by strikers or other persons with rebuilding, repairing, or replacing the property or with the resumption or continuation of business. Although this contingency usually is beyond the insured's control, no increase in time caused by a strike or labor troubles on premises is covered. However, if there is a strike at other locations, such as at a supplier's location, increased time of interruption due to this off-premises strike would be covered. This would affect the time required to return to operations with due diligence and dispatch.

The third special exclusion excludes losses caused by the suspension, lapse, or cancellation of a lease, license, contract, or order. However, if these losses result directly from the interruption of the insured's business, they are covered. Consider, for example, a company that has an order to manufacture parts for a new airplane. If the order is canceled and a shutdown results, there would be no coverage. If, on the other hand, a fire causes a shutdown and the order is lost as a result, the earnings that the order might have generated during the period of interruption would be considered in determining the insured's actual loss sustained.

Important Endorsements

The most important endorsement, in many respects, is the endorsement that might be used to exclude or provide limited coverage for ordinary payroll. This endorsement has already been described because it is important in determining the amount of insurance to purchase. There are several other endorsements, however, that are often used with the gross earnings form, such as the endorsement extending the period of indemnity; the power, heat, and refrigeration deduction; the agreed amount endorsement; and the premium adjustment endorsement.

Endorsement Extending the Period of Indemnity One of the long-standing criticisms of business interruption insurance is that an insured may carry an adequate amount of insurance and still be unable to collect for the full loss. Without an endorsement the contract provides protection only for the time needed to repair or replace the damaged property. In many cases, however, this time will run out before the insured's business has returned to normal. The insured's personal property may be restored, but business activity may still be depressed. For example, a bowling alley might be entirely restored and ready for business following a shutdown but might have few customers because all leagues for the season have already formed at other bowling alleys.

The extended period of indemnity endorsement extends the time period for which the insured will be reimbursed by continuing the coverage beyond the time allowed in the basic contract.

Coverage under this endorsement begins on the date when repair or replacement of the property is completed or on the date when the insurer's liability under the basic form ceases, whichever is later. Normally the insurer's liability ceases when the property is repaired or replaced. In this case, coverage would be continuous with the extended period until the business is back to normal. Even with the endorsement there can be a gap in coverage, and this is the reason for the alternate starting dates of the coverage in the endorsement. Suppose a fire occurs and the insured's business is shut down. With due diligence and dispatch it would require three months to repair the property. If the insured takes four months for repairs because due diligence and dispatch are not applied, the basic form would provide coverage for three months and the extended indemnity endorsement would not begin until the start of the fifth month.

It should be noted that the endorsement does not guarantee that the insured will achieve the same level of activity that existed prior to the loss. The coverage terminates when the business is returned to the condition that would have existed if no loss had occurred. This is a difficult level to determine and, in fact, some businesses will never reach such a level. For these reasons, the endorsement adds a further limitation: ". . . but in no event for more than ____ consecutive calendar days from said later commencement date."

Insurance under the endorsement may be extended in multiples of 30 days, up to 360 days.

Any firm whose business is not likely to reach normal levels as soon as the property is restored faces a loss exposure that is not covered by the usual business interruption loss exposure. This extended loss exposure can be insured with the endorsement extending the period of indemnity.

Another good reason why such an endorsement should be used is that coverage is afforded for (1) an increase of loss occasioned by a local or state ordinance or law regulating construction and repair of the building, and (2) increases in losses caused by the suspension, lapse, or cancellation of a contract or order. As mentioned earlier, these are excluded in the basic contract.

When the endorsement is used, higher limits usually should be purchased for the policy. The longer period of indemnity usually will require a larger amount of insurance.

Power, Heat, and Refrigeration Deduction The cost of power, heat, and refrigeration used in manufacturing operations may be deducted from gross earnings by adding the following language to the coinsurance clause:

> Less the same percentage of the cost of only such power, heat and refrigeration, in excess of any minimum guaranty [sic] continuing under contract, as would have been consumed in the conversion of raw stock into finished stock or in supplying the service(s) sold by the insured, during that 12 month period.

The use of this endorsement allows a manufacturer to deduct nonguaranteed heat, power, and refrigeration from gross earnings and, therefore, requires less insurance to be carried. Coinsurance of at least 80 percent is required if this endorsement is used, and rates are higher than for comparable coverage without the power, heat, and refrigeration deduction. The endorsement is available only on Form 4 (manufacturing and mining companies).

Agreed Amount Endorsement Many business interruption insurance problems are associated with the coinsurance clause. If the danger of a coinsurance penalty is to be avoided, the insured must purchase an amount of insurance based on future gross earnings. But in many businesses gross earnings are difficult to forecast accurately.

The problem can be approached by frequent monitoring of changes in earning potential and costs and adjustments in the amount of insurance. This is not practical in most companies because they do not want to take the time and expense of developing frequent estimates. Another approach is to simply purchase more insurance than is needed, but this can be a costly way of avoiding coinsurance penalties.

The insurance industry has developed several methods of dealing with coinsurance problems. One of these approaches is the agreed amount endorsement.

In effect, the agreed amount endorsement substitutes a dollar amount for a coinsurance percentage. If the insured maintains the amount of insurance stipulated, all losses will be covered in full up to that amount. There will be no penalty even if gross earnings have increased above the agreed amount at the time of a loss. To illustrate, assume that the insured estimates gross earnings of $1 million. Applying 80 percent coinsurance, the rating organization agrees that $800,000 of insurance is sufficient and this amount is purchased and inserted in the endorsement. If, at the time of a $500,000 loss, the insured expects gross earnings of $1.2 million, the full $500,000 will be paid. There will be no coinsurance penalty even though the insured carried less than 80 percent insurance to value. Notice, however, that there would not be enough insurance if the loss amounted to more than $800,000.

The agreed amount in this endorsement is based on a business interruption statement of values that the insured files with the insurance rating organization. The agreed amount of insurance selected is normally a percentage (such as 80 or 100 percent) of the amount expressed in the statement of values. If the statement of values understated the figures, the insured might be required to purchase less coverage than if accurate figures were given. Therefore, the endorsement contains a full amount (honesty) clause similar to those in reporting form property policies. The clause limits the insurance company's liability to the proportion that the reported values bear to the actual values for the past period shown. Suppose, for example, that an insured had $1 million in gross earnings for the fiscal year just ended but shows only $700,000 of gross earnings for the same period. With this knowledge the insurer would pay no more than 70 percent of any loss.

If the insured reports accurately and maintains the agreed amount, there can be no coinsurance penalties. Therefore, strict rules must be met when this endorsement is used. In some states manufacturers are not eligible. Businesses that have been in operation less than twelve consecutive months are not eligible because they have not developed the necessary financial information. In some states only sprinklered or fire-resistive buildings are eligible.

The endorsement may not be added to the policy until application is made to the rating bureau or Insurance Services Office which has jurisdiction. The application that must be used is reproduced in Figure 5-3. Notice that values for the past year are shown in column 1 of the form, and projections for the coming year are shown in column 2. The agreed amount of insurance is derived by multiplying the gross earnings estimated in column 2 by a coinsurance percentage (50, 60, 70, 80, 90, 100). The resulting dollar amount of insurance is inserted in the endorsement. When approved, the endorsement is valid for one year.

The endorsement may be attached either on the inception date or after the policy inception. Usually within ninety days after the end of the next fiscal year the insured must file another application based on the previous fiscal year and projections of gross earnings. If the endorsement is not renewed, the endorsement no longer applies and the coinsurance clause again takes effect.

An agreed amount endorsement may be used with either of the ordinary payroll endorsements, but in such a case the agreed amount must be at least the equivalent of 80 percent coinsurance.

Premium Adjustment Endorsement Another method of minimizing coinsurance problems is the premium adjustment endorsement. This endorsement converts the policy to a reporting form that is similar in some respects to reporting forms used with direct damage contracts. It is available for use with both the manufacturing and mercantile forms.

The application of the premium adjustment endorsement is best explained by an example. (For the sake of simplicity, the values have

Figure 5-3
Application for Rate for Agreed Amount Endorsement

APPLICATION FOR RATE FOR AGREED AMOUNT ENDORSEMENT

(For Use with Gross Earnings Business Interruption Form Nos. 3 and 4)

To ....
INSERT NAME OF RATING BUREAU

Name of Insured ....

Location of Risk ....

ALL ENTRIES TO BE ON ANNUAL BASIS	COLUMN 1 Actual Values for Year Ended 19	COLUMN 2 Estimated Values for Year Ending 19
A. Total annual net sales value of production from Manufacturing Operations; and total annual net sales from Merchandising or Non-Manufacturing Operations, (Gross sales less discounts, returns, bad accounts and pre-paid freight, if included in sales)	$	$ ....
B. Add other earnings (if any) derived from operations of the business:		
1. Cash Discounts Received	....	....
2. Commissions or Rents from Leased Departments	....	....
3.	....	....

C. Total ("A" plus "B")		$		$ ....
D. Deduct only cost of:				
1. Raw stock from which such production is derived	$		$	
2. Supplies consisting of materials consumed directly in the conversion of such raw stock into finished stock or in supplying the service(s) sold by the Insured	....		....	
3. Merchandise sold, including packaging materials therefor	....		....	
4. Service(s) purchased from outsiders (not employees of the Insured) for resale which do not continue under contract	....		....	
5. Total Deductions		$		$ ....
E. GROSS EARNINGS ("C" Minus "D")		$		$ ....
IF INSURANCE IS TO BE WRITTEN WITH ORDINARY PAYROLL EXCLUSION ENDORSEMENT, Deduct From "E" Above:				
F. All Ordinary Payroll Expense		$		$ ....
G. Business Interruption Basis for Contribution ("E" Minus "F")		$		$ ....
IF INSURANCE IS TO BE WRITTEN WITH ORDINARY PAYROLL-LIMITED COVERAGE ENDORSEMENT, Complete the Following:				
H. Select the largest Ordinary Payroll Expense for 90* .... consecutive calendar days		$		$ ....
I. Business Interruption Basis for Contribution ("G" plus "H")		$		$ ....

Continued on next page

CONTRIBUTION PERCENTAGE
. . . . (50, 60, 70, 80, 90 OR 100) . . . . %

Amount of Insurance: Apply to Item "E", "G" or "I", Column 2, the percentage factor to be used in the Contribution Clause in the policy to develop the Agreed Amount which shall be shown in the Agreed Amount Endorsement . . . . AGREED AMOUNT $ . . . .

We hereby apply for rate for the Agreed Amount Endorsement on the above basis and certify that the above statement of Actual Values as shown in Column 1 is true and correct.

Insured's Signature . . . .

Official Title . . . .

Date . . . .

This statement must be signed by the Insured if an individual, by a partner if a partnership, or by an officer if a corporation. A true copy of entries in Items A to I inclusive must be shown in the Agreed Amount Endorsement attached to the policy.

*NOTE: 120, 150 or 180 days may be selected as provided in the rules.

been kept small. Most firms using this endorsement would have much higher values.) The following facts pertain to Company B:

- Actual gross earnings for 1977 were $100,000.
- They selected the premium adjustment endorsement and 50 percent coinsurance clause.
- They purchased a provisional amount of insurance of $150,000.
- They paid a provisional premium of $225.

If, at the end of the 1978 policy period, Company B reports actual gross earnings of $120,000, the insurer will refund the unearned premium. (If the earned premium was $180, Company B would receive a $45 refund.)

Company B cannot suffer a coinsurance penalty as long as actual 1978 gross earnings are less than $300,000. But to illustrate a possible coinsurance problem, assume that 1978 gross earnings increase to $350,000. The company would collect no more than 85.7 percent of a loss, calculated as follows:

$$\frac{\$150{,}000}{(0.50 \times \$350{,}000)} = 85.7\%$$

If a premium adjustment endorsement is used, the provisional amount of insurance should be set at a figure that is comfortably above the maximum expected gross earnings. There is a cost to the insured, however, if the provisional amount is much too large. The provisional premium is based on the provisional amount of insurance. The insured will recover any unnecessary premium at the end of the policy period, but the company has tied up funds that could have been used for other purposes.

With the premium adjustment endorsement there are four important limitations on the insurance company's liability. Three of these are common—the company's share if there is other insurance, the coinsurance requirements, and the "honesty" clause (losses will not be paid in a greater proportion than reported earnings bear to actual earnings).

The fourth limitation is a source of much misunderstanding because it is often confused with the conventional coinsurance clause. The insurer's liability for loss shall not exceed the stated coinsurance clause percentage of gross earnings that would be earned during the twelve months following a loss. To illustrate this, assume Company B had an $80,000 loss in 1978 and that it was determined that Company B's gross earnings in 1978 would have been $120,000, had no loss occurred. The policy limitation mentioned would limit the insurer's liability to 50 percent of $120,000 or $60,000. Company B would retain $20,000 of the loss. If Company B could have foreseen that a loss might result in loss of more than 50 percent of their annual gross earnings, they should have purchased insurance with a higher coinsurance clause, such as 80 percent.

A report of gross earnings values is submitted at the inception of the policy and at each anniversary thereafter. The reports cover values derived from operations of the previous fiscal year. When the policy expires or the anniversary date arrives, another report is required. Reports must be submitted within a period of 120 days after the close of the insured's last fiscal year or within 120 days after expiration or cancellation of the contract.

The report of values for the premium adjustment endorsement is similar to the application for the agreed amount endorsement, except projected earnings are not required. Both endorsements cannot be used on the same policy.

Earnings Forms

Despite the confusing similarity in names, the gross earnings forms discussed previously must be distinguished from the earnings forms. Although gross earnings forms are the only business interruption insurance contracts available to some businesses, they involve some problems. They are relatively complex and sometimes difficult to understand. The operation of the coinsurance clause causes problems because the percentage applies to the full gross earnings that probably would have been earned in the twelve-month period following a loss, a figure difficult to predict in many cases. Another problem is that some businessowners and managers are reluctant to divulge to the insurer confidential figures or business secrets.

In an effort to respond to the problems inherent in the gross earnings forms the earnings forms have been developed.

Earnings forms insure the business interruption exposure, and many provisions are the same or at least similar to the other forms. The distinguishing features of the earnings forms result from the fact that these forms are simplified for use by small companies.

Earnings forms do not contain a coinsurance provision. If probable earnings have been underestimated, the amount of insurance may be inadequate, but there can be no coinsurance penalty. Insurance to value is encouraged by a limit that applies to each month of a business interruption. The insurer will pay no more than a given percentage of the policy limits for any month of interruption.

Usually an insured has a choice of the monthly limitation percentage—33⅓, 25, or 16⅔ percent. If the insured estimates that the maximum duration of an interruption is four months, the 25 percent limit would be the appropriate choice. Up to 25 percent of the policy limit could be collected for each of four months of interruption. A three-month maximum shutdown indicates a limit of 33⅓ percent, and 16⅔ corresponds to six months.

After estimating the maximum duration of a shutdown (and the appropriate percentage limitation) the highest net profit and continuing expense for *any single month* should be determined. This is necessary because no one can forecast when a loss will occur. The amount of insurance to purchase is simply the maximum number of months multiplied by the highest monthly exposure.

To illustrate, assume that a company has a seasonal business and estimates that February is its best month. In February net profits and continuing expense would be, say, $8,000. The maximum duration of a shutdown is estimated at four months. Therefore, the 25 percent monthly limit is selected. The amount of insurance indicated, therefore, is 4 × $8,000 or $32,000.

Now, assume that the business is shut down for two weeks and a loss of $5,000 is sustained. The loss would be paid in full because the 25 percent ($8,000) limit is not allocated evenly over the month. In other words, the $8,000 monthly limit is not further subdivided into $4,000 for two weeks. The full $8,000 is available for any loss lasting less than one month.

Suppose the loss is $6,000 in the first month and $9,000 in the second month. The insurer will pay the full $6,000 for the first month, but only $8,000 of the second month's loss. The total reimbursement would be $14,000. If the full amount of insurance is not used in a month, the "unused" insurance is not carried forward to future months. The limit is not cumulative. It applies to each month separately.

The earnings form does not require an insured to purchase an amount of insurance equal to his or her full earnings. Nor does it require that a certain percentage of earnings must be insured. The amount an insured should carry depends upon the maximum amount that can be lost and how long an interruption could persist.

Sometimes the monthly limits create the impression that the coverage is a valued form. It is not. The form covers the actual loss sustained, the same as the gross earnings form.

As indicated, the earnings form contains many of the provisions included in the other forms including the resumption of operations clause, expenses to reduce loss clause, interruption by civil authority, special exclusions clause, and electronic media limitation clause.

The rates for the earnings form are substantially higher than the rates for the gross earnings form. Although the amount of insurance that can be purchased is not limited specifically, the higher rates make the earnings form inappropriate for large companies. Even with higher rates, the premium difference may be small for companies that need only a small amount of insurance. In many territories, manufacturing companies are ineligible for the earnings form.

INSURANCE FOR OTHER INCOME AND EXPENSE LOSS EXPOSURES

The business interruption forms previously discussed are not available to all types of businesses. Furthermore, some types of exposures are not covered in the preceding forms, even for normal manufacturing and mercantile companies. For these reasons, other forms or policies are available, such as contingent business interruption commissions of selling agents, loss of personal income coverage, and multiple location business interruption coverage.

Contingent Business Interruption Insurance

The usual business interruption forms insure against net profits and continuing expense when the business is interrupted by an insured peril causing damage or destruction of property at the insured's premises. These forms, therefore, provide no coverage when the insured's business is interrupted by damage or destruction of property off the insured's premises.

The exposures can be explained by examining the relationships of two firms illustrated in Figure 5-4. Contributing Manufacturing Company manufactures goods sold to Recipient Sales Corporation. If Contributing is Recipient's major supplier, a severe fire at Contributing's plant would cause Recipient's operations to be interrupted, even though there was no fire damage at Recipient's location. Conversely, if Recipient is a major purchaser of Contributing's products, a windstorm at Recipient's sales outlet might result in an interruption of Contributing's business, even though Contributing's plants were untouched by the tornado. These exposures, known as *contingent business interruption exposures*, arise when one company's business may be interrupted if another company is shut down.

There are three types of contingent business interruption exposures. One is when a company is dependent upon one or a few manufacturers or suppliers. The manufacturer or supplier would be known as a *contributing* property or company. A second type arises when only one or a few companies purchase all or most of the insured's products or services. In this case, the buyers are called *recipient* companies or properties. A third type of contingent business interrup-

Figure 5-4
Contingent Business Interruption Illustrated

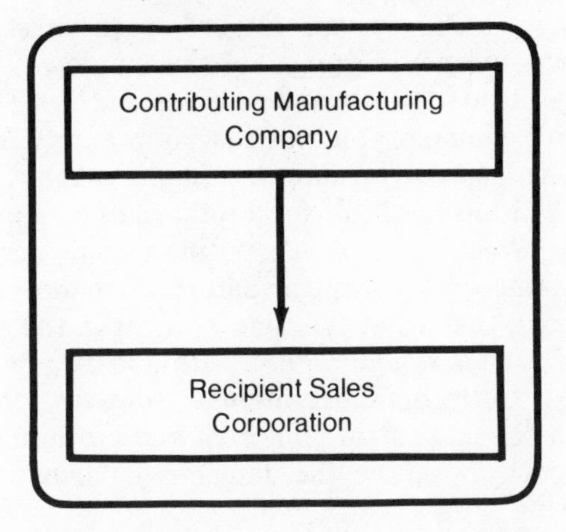

tion may exist if a company derives all or most of its business from a neighboring company known as *leader* companies. For example, small stores in many shopping centers depend on the traffic drawn to the shopping center by a large chain store. If the chain store is damaged, nearby small stores will suffer an interruption in business even though their shops sustain no damage.

It should be apparent that most businesses do not have a significant contingent business interruption exposure. Most companies have alternative sources of supply and a large number of customers. The loss of one buyer or supplier, therefore, usually would not cause a major loss. However, the contingent business interruption exposure may be important for certain companies.

Protection against contingent business interruption losses is provided under two forms: (1) the contributing properties form (the supplier shutdown situation), and (2) the recipient properties form (the buyer shutdown situation). The exposure arising from the shutdown of neighboring leader properties may be insured by the contributing property form if it is modified.

Insuring Agreement The policy may be written separately from the business interruption form covering perils at the insured's location. It covers only losses resulting from the interruption of the insured's business caused by damage or destruction of property at the specified location(s) of contributing (or recipient) properties not operated by the insured.

Note that the contributing (recipient) property must not be used or operated by the insured. If operated by the insured, the policy would be eligible for blanket business interruption rather than contingent business interruption coverage.

For coverage to apply, an insured peril must occur at the contributing (or recipient) property, but the shutdown (total or partial) must affect the insured's business. An insured peril might destroy finished goods, for example, at a contributing property. This could cause a shutdown of the insured's business but might not shut down the other company at all. It is also possible for a total shutdown at a contributing property not to affect a recipient's business. This could happen, for example, if the insured has a large inventory when the loss occurs.

It would seem, then, that the time element in the coverage should be the length of time it would require, with due diligence and dispatch, for the insured to resume operations. However, the form limits compensation to the amount of time required (with due diligence and dispatch) to repair or replace the damaged contributing or recipient property.

Normally an insured peril must occur at the named contributing (or recipient) properties. The policy can be extended to unnamed locations, not operated by the insured, within the continental U.S. This coverage, however, is limited to an amount not exceeding one-half of 1 percent of the amount of the policy for any one month of interruption of the insured's business. It would require a $200,000 policy, for example, to provide benefits of $1,000 per month.

Amount of Insurance to Purchase If the insured's business is dependent upon one contributing property, the amount of contingent business interruption insurance is determined in much the same way as the amount of (direct) business interruption would be figured. The insured may select a coinsurance percentage as low as 50 percent, and if either ordinary payroll endorsement is used, coinsurance of at least 80 percent is required.

In some cases a company will not be completely dependent upon one other company. Suppose a company has gross earnings of $500,000 and receives 70 percent of its supplies from a company and 30 percent from another company. If only the largest supplier is named in the form, the coinsurance requirement will be based on 70 percent of $500,000, or $350,000. This situation may not be uncommon because the insured may reason that it needs protection against shutdowns caused by perils at its major supplier, but protection may not be needed for other suppliers.

Resumption of Operations For exposures to loss resulting out of direct loss or damage at the insured's premises, the insured can control exposures, to some extent, by the use of noninsurance techniques. Loss prevention measures can reduce the probability of loss, and expediting of repairs is somewhat within the insured's control. When contingent business interruption exposures are involved, the insured has little control over the probability of loss and the time necessary to recover.

Contingent business interruption forms have a unique provision that is designed to minimize losses. These forms require the insured to "use his influence to induce" the contributing (recipient) property to resume operations and delivery (acceptance) of materials to (from) the insured. The insured is supposed to encourage the other company to use other machinery, equipment, supplies, or locations if this will expedite matters. The insured, however, is not obligated to contribute financially to the other company unless such an expenditure is authorized by the insurer.

The insured is also obligated to reduce his or her loss by (1) partial resumption of business, (2) using other sources of materials (or outlet for the product), and (3) in the contributing property form, using stock wherever located.

Commissions of Selling Agents

Some companies have a contingent business interruption exposure but are ineligible for the usual forms. These are intermediaries, such as selling agents, factors, or brokers, who do not receive title as goods are sold.

In many cases a selling agent represents only one or two manufacturers. Although the selling agent does not take title to the goods, the agent receives a commission for selling the product. This income can be lost if the manufacturer is shut down or if finished goods are destroyed. In fact, this type of exposure for a selling agent probably is more important than the contingent business interruption exposure for a typical manufacturer. Most manufacturers are not dependent upon one or two suppliers or customers. Many selling agents, on the other hand, will suffer a severe financial loss if their manufacturer(s) cannot deliver the product.

This exposure can be insured by a standard form called the commissions of selling agents form. It is very similar to other contingent business interruption contracts.

The coverage is limited to the reduction in gross selling commissions (rather than gross earnings) less noncontinuing expenses. The form provides a schedule for the name and description of each of the manufacturing properties supplying products that are sold by the insured. An amount of insurance for each manufacturing property is required.

If two or more manufacturing properties are listed, the amount of insurance at each location is important because the coinsurance clause applies to each separately (unless a blanket policy is used). In the event of a loss, the coinsurance percentage will be applied to the commissions that probably would have been earned from the next twelve months.

Loss of Personal Income Coverage

Sole proprietors, as well as partnerships and corporations, may be faced with important business interruption exposures. Individuals who are not businessowners also may suffer severe financial losses if business is interrupted.

As a practical matter, most employees would suffer only minor losses if the business that provides their incomes were shut down. The loss to the employee may not be significant if the employer continues the employee's income (or a portion of it), or if the employee can obtain employment from another company within a short time. Consider the situation, however, for those whose income would be discontinued and for whom it would be difficult to find other employment. These people have a contingent business interruption exposure. Usually these are store managers, department managers, and sales agents whose income is based largely on commissions and bonuses.

This exposure may be insured under a loss of income form. (The selling agents commission form is appropriate for business firms, not individuals.) The form covers the insured's loss of income when a designated business is interrupted by an insured peril. The loss is limited to the time required to rebuild or repair the damaged property. Income is defined in the policy as the total salary, commissions, and other earnings that would have accrued to the insured from the operation of the named business, less any income guaranteed to the insured by the business. The coverage includes an 80 percent coinsurance clause.

Multiple Location Business Interruption Coverage

In many companies, usually manufacturers, business operations are conducted at more than one location. If the operations are interdependent it is impractical to separately insure the various activities in each building or location. A multiple location form, therefore, should be used to provide blanket coverage for all locations.

A mercantile company often has more than one location. The business functions are usually independent of each other. If they are interdependent, a multiple location form should be used. If they are independent, a multiple location form may or may not be desirable.

A major requirement for blanket business interruption insurance is that all premises must be owned, managed, or controlled by the insured. Coverage, of course, is limited to loss resulting from damage to the insured's property.

For example, assume that Company Z is a manufacturer of mobile homes and owns Plants 1, 2, and 3. Plant 4 is owned and operated by another company, but it uses material supplied by Company Z. All four plants should be covered by Company Z's blanket business interruption policy. If, however, Company Z did not own the materials used to manufacture the mobile homes in Plant 4 but only contracted for the materials, Plant 4 could not be included in the blanket coverage. In fact, the operations at Plant 4 could not be insured except under a contingent business interruption form by Company Z.

Garages, offices, and warehouses used in connection with the insured's plant or store are not considered additional locations. This is true even if they are not located at the insured's main plant or location.

When the functions at two or more locations are independent, either specific or blanket coverage may be purchased and several factors should be considered. In some cases the premium cost will be lower with blanket coverage.

A possible disadvantage of blanket coverage is that the minimum coinsurance percentage is increased. In most territories, at least 70 percent coinsurance is required with blanket coverage, and at least 90 percent is required if either of the ordinary payroll endorsements are selected.

Another disadvantage of blanket coverage arises with loss adjustments. With a blanket policy, the insured must exhibit all of the books and accounting records (even those not involved in the loss) in order to determine whether the coinsurance requirement had been met. If each location were specifically covered, only the books of the damaged or destroyed location would have to be checked.

VALUED BUSINESS INTERRUPTION CONTRACTS

Most business interruption insurance is written under one of the gross earnings forms or the simpler earnings form. These forms provide reimbursement to the insured on an actual loss sustained basis.

Business interruption insurance is also available from some companies on a valued form. Although these contracts are less popular than the indemnity contracts, the proponents of valued business interruption policies are enthusiastic about their merits.

The valued approach is simple. In some plans the insured is paid a specified amount for each day the business is interrupted, up to a limited number of days. These policies are appropriately called per diem forms. In other plans, the amount of reimbursement may be on a weekly or monthly basis.

Valued policies contain no coinsurance provision. Obviously, therefore, it is impossible to have a coinsurance penalty. This does not mean, however, that the insured will necessarily be fully reimbursed for a loss. The amount of insurance may be inadequate either in the daily, weekly, or monthly amount and in terms of the maximum period benefits will be paid.

A business need not be totally shut down to receive valued business interruption benefits. Partial interruptions are also covered according to the percentage the business is reduced. Suppose, for example, that a company is entitled to receive $50,000 each week it is totally inoperative. If the company is able to operate at 40 percent of capacity, the insured will receive $30,000 each week. For a manufacturer the percentage of activity is determined by the percentage reduction in production or output. For mercantile companies, partial suspensions are measured by various methods. The reduction in gross sales probably is most common.

Valued forms have several advantages. One is their simplicity. With no coinsurance and a daily, weekly, or monthly benefit, the coverage is easy to understand.

Loss adjustments are much simpler and probably more prompt with the valued forms. It is not necessary to project the amount of gross earnings less continuing expenses for the twelve-month period following the loss. With a valued form only two things need to be ascertained: (1) the number of days of the interruption, and (2) the percentage of the shutdown.

Another advantage of valued forms is the federal income tax treatment of the insurance proceeds. With an actual loss sustained policy the amounts received from the insurer are taxable as ordinary income. This is reasonable because policy proceeds are received in lieu of profits which are taxable. With a valued form, however, the proceeds are taxable as capital gain rather than as income to the insured.[3]

The critics of the valued policy approach point out several possible disadvantages. First, the simplicity of the valued form may be mostly an illusion. If the insured does not estimate the amount exposed to loss or is not required to estimate full gross earnings following a loss, the amount of insurance purchased may not be determined accurately. If the amount purchased is not much more than a sheer guess, the amount is likely to be inadequate. On the other hand, if the amount of insurance is excessive, the insurer may feel a serious moral hazard is involved.

The speed of recovery may not be a genuine advantage of the valued forms. Recovery under a valued policy may be prompt, but even with the other policies, most companies will advance payments, at least for serious losses.

Another problem with the valued forms, according to the critics, is that their cost tends to be higher than the cost of the other forms. This may or may not be true. From an individual insured's point of view, the appropriate comparison should be made between two specific contracts.

EXTRA EXPENSE INSURANCE

Most businesses would cease to operate for a time following a direct loss to business property which would disrupt business activities. For such businesses, one of the various types of business interruption insurance discussed in the preceding pages may be an appropriate means of treating the loss exposure.

Other businesses—some service businesses, for instance—cannot, under any circumstances, sustain an *interruption* of business activities. Such firms must remain in operation "at all costs." To remain in operation when the building or equipment normally used has been damaged or destroyed, a firm will incur substantial extra expenses. These extra expenses are the subject of extra expense insurance. Where business interruption insurance indemnifies the insured for loss of income *during the interruption*, extra expense insurance reimburses the insured for extra expenses that must be incurred *to avoid an interruption.*

An important ingredient to the success of any program providing recovery after a loss utilizing the extra expense insurance approach is the availability of suitable temporary premises for immediate occupancy by the insured business. Another consideration is the availability of plants of other similar businesses willing to assist in accommodating the insured temporarily during the emergency. Extra expense insurance would provide the funds with which to pay the extra expenses of moving into and renting temporary premises and reimbursing others for the use of their facilities.

If there is a possibility that other organizations and businesses or suitable temporary premises are not available, then the insured might have no choice but to fully or partially suspend its operations. Extra expense insurance might not be the proper type of insurance to purchase, and business interruption insurance—either the gross earnings or the earnings form—should be considered.

Certain types of businesses would have an easier job of finding emergency facilities than others. For instance, a large laundry or dry cleaner might have difficulty in locating another plant with sufficient capacity and available machine time to handle the insured's volume as well as its own. However, a smaller independent dry-cleaning shop that frequently farms out much of its work to large plants would not have much difficulty in making temporary arrangements.

Small local newspapers that publish on a biweekly or weekly basis frequently can make arrangements with other nearby newspaper publishers for mutual assistance in the event of an emergency. Large newspapers that do job printing for others and are practically operating on a full-time basis might require business interruption insurance in preference to extra expense insurance, or might need a combination of both forms (discussed later).

Offices and banks are among nonmanufacturing businesses for which extra expense insurance is feasible. Insurance agents, architects, accountants, attorneys, consulting engineers, and real estate brokers have to continue operations with a minimum of lost time in the event of damage by a fire or other peril. Temporary premises would have to be rented and additional expense incurred to equip the temporary office. Physicians, dentists, opticians, and veterinarians would be in the same situation, and they would also need to replace specialized equipment in a hurry. If such equipment would be rendered inoperable by an insured peril, such an exposure might indicate the need for business interruption insurance rather than extra expense.

Insuring Provisions

The extra expense insurance form covers the necessary extra expense incurred by the insured in order to continue as nearly as practicable the normal operation of the insured's business following damage to or destruction of real or personal property caused by the peril(s) insured against during the term of the policy. The insurer is liable for this necessary extra expense incurred only for the length of time known as the "period of restoration." The period of restoration begins with the date of the damage and continues until the damaged parts of the property are rebuilt, repaired, or replaced with the exercise of due diligence and dispatch. Expiration of the policy does not limit the period of restoration.

By now it should be obvious that most fire and allied lines policies include provisions to encourage insurance to value. Insurance to value is difficult to determine when extra expense is involved, because there is no objective measure of extra expenses that might be incurred. Furthermore, it is very difficult to estimate the extra expenses that might be incurred until a loss actually occurs. The extra expenses to be incurred are subject to the availability of temporary premises, substitute equipment, and so forth at any given time. This uncertainty, however, does not alleviate the need for the insurance contract to encourage insurance to value.

The form provides for stipulated limits of liability expressed as a percentage of recovery of loss for necessary extra expense incurred during the time needed to repair or replace damaged property. The basic form is written with the following limits of liability:

1. 40 percent of the amount of the policy when the period of restoration is not in excess of one month;
2. 80 percent when the period of restoration is in excess of one month, but not in excess of two months; or
3. 100 percent when the period of restoration is in excess of two months.

These limits of recovery are cumulative. The policy does not contain any type of coinsurance clause, as recovery is limited to a stipulated amount per month as indicated above.

The 40, 80, and 100 percent limits of recovery periods are stipulated in the newer forms of the endorsement, but the manual rules provide for writing optional percentage limits of liability and periods of restoration. When using optional percentages, it is provided that if the total amount of insurance is not exhausted at the end of the longest period of restoration provided for, such unexhausted amount may be applied to insured expenses for the remainder of the period of restoration.

Exclusions

The standard extra expense policy excludes coverage for extra expenses resulting from building laws or ordinances (e.g., demolition of a partially destroyed building and reconstruction to meet current building codes). Likewise, there is no coverage for extra expense loss caused by strikes interfering with the reconstruction process.

The policy specifically excludes coverage for loss of income to emphasize the fact that it is not a business interruption policy. The cost of repairing or replacing any kind of damaged property—buildings, equipment, records, computer tapes, and so forth—is specifically excluded except when extra expenses to repair or restore property serve to reduce the extra expense loss. "Any other consequential or remote loss" is also excluded to further underscore the policy's intent to cover only extra expense losses.

Other Insurance

If there are other insurance contracts which cover in any manner extra expense as covered by the policy, the extra expense policy applies only as *excess* insurance and only to the amount of extra expense *over and above* the amount due the insured under such forms.

As an illustration, if both business interruption insurance and extra expense were carried, the insured could recover the amount of extra expenses (or expediting expenses) necessarily incurred to reduce a business interruption loss under the expense to reduce loss clause of the business interruption policy. If expediting expenses of, say, $10,000, reduced the loss by only $7,500, then the insured could only be reimbursed $7,500 through the business interruption policy. The extra expense policy, under the other insurance clause, could respond for the $2,500 excess extra expense necessarily incurred to reduce the loss.

Amount of Insurance

There is no relationship between the cost of doing business and the extra expense necessarily incurred in order to maintain a normal volume of business after loss or damage by an insured peril. Therefore, it is difficult to determine how much insurance to purchase.

The first point to be considered is the probability of being able to continue business under emergency measures. Secondly, consideration should be given to the cost of using such emergency measures. There is no rule or principle upon which to base anticipated extra expense of maintaining a normal volume of business during an interruption, but much consideration should be given to an estimate of the probable length of time it would take to rebuild or repair the principal building and/or equipment.

By using a work sheet similar to the one illustrated in Figure 5-5 one could fairly accurately tabulate the greatest amount of expense which might reasonably be anticipated. The work sheet is designed to record only the first, second, and third months following a loss.

One way to determine the amount of extra expense insurance required would be to determine from the work sheet the probable extra expense for *two* periods of restoration: (1) a period of one month, and (2) a period covering the maximum number of months which could reasonably be anticipated for resumption of normal operations. The *minimum* amount of insurance which should be carried is determined by dividing the estimated extra expense for the one-month period by the percentage reimbursement when the period of restoration is one month

Figure 5-5
Work Sheet*

Expenses Necessary to Continue Business	First Month		Second Month		Third Month	
Rent of temporary premises						
Cleaning temporary premises						
Labor equipping temporary premises						
Rent of temporary machinery, equipment, etc.						
Net cost of equipment, etc., purchased						
Expense of moving equipment, etc.						
Light, power, and heat at temporary premises						
Labor at temporary premises						
Insurance expense at temporary premises						
Janitor and watchman at temporary premises						
Other expenses at or because of temporary premises (advertising, telephone, telegraph, legal, etc.)						
Total due to temporary premises						
Add payments to others for manufacturing or processing						
Add necessarily continuing expenses at original location after a loss						
Add bonuses for quick services, etc.						
Total expenses after a loss						
Deduct total of all expenses which would have been incurred at the original location for the corresponding period had no loss incurred						
Extra expense insurance to be carried						

*Reprinted with permission from Henry C. Klein, *Business Interruption Insurance* (Indianapolis: The Rough Notes Co., 1964), p. 253.

or less. This amount of insurance, however, might not be enough to cover the total extra expense estimated for the maximum possible interruption. In this case, the estimate for the longer period should be used.

For example, using the standard extra expense insurance form, the insured might estimate that extra expense indemnification of $8,000 for

Table 5-9

Coinsurance Building Rate Factors*

Percentage Limit Specified for the First Month	Rate Factor
40	2.0
35	1.9
30	1.8
25	1.7
20	1.6
10	1.4

*Reprinted with permission from *Pennsylvania-Delaware Rule Book* (New York: Insurance Services Office, July 1967), p. 2-14.

a one-month period of restoration would be sufficient. The minimum required insurance would be $8,000 divided by 40 percent (0.40) or $20,000. While the $20,000 total amount would assure recovery of up to $8,000 (40 percent) during the first-month period, up to $16,000 (80 percent) during a two-month period, and up to $20,000 (100 percent of the amount of insurance) for any period in excess of two months, the total amount might not be sufficient to cover estimated expenses for a longer period of time. If $30,000 of total coverage is needed, the insured could arrange the coverage for 40 percent recovery for the first month, and so on, as previously described. It is often possible to arrange for an optional combination of cumulative percentages of recovery, such as 35, 70, and 100 percent or 30, 60, 90, and 100 percent.

Rating

The rate for the standard form of extra expense insurance is two times the 80 percent coinsurance building rate. In other words, extra expense insurance is roughly twice as costly as the same dollar amount of building insurance. When an optional endorsement is used to change the standard limits of liability (40, 80, and 100 percent) or number of periods of restoration from those specified in the form, the rate is computed by multiplying the 80 percent coinsurance building rate by the appropriate rate factor determined from Table 5-9.

CONTINGENT EXTRA EXPENSE INSURANCE

As with business interruption, extra expenses can be incurred due to direct loss or damage at contributing properties.

In cases where the insured can secure the same materials or services from a third firm at still another location, it could possibly continue business without an interruption or loss of income. In such a case, the insured could replace the contingent business interruption coverage with contingent extra expense insurance. In such an event, contingent extra expense insurance would indemnify the insured for the extra expense incurred to continue business with the assistance of a substitute supplier. The contingent extra expense form would cover the cost of materials or services in excess of the price charged by the original supplier or transportation costs in excess of those normally charged.

The extra expense form may be altered to effect contingent extra expense insurance. The amount of insurance needed under the contingent extra expense form would be based only on the increase in cost of obtaining materials or services from other than regular sources. The same apportionment to periodic limits of liability (e.g., 40, 80, and 100 percent) applies to the contingent form as to the direct extra expense form. The length of time for which the contingent coverage would be needed depends on the length of time necessary for restoration of the original supplier's property. Thus, the percentages of apportionments required might change under the contingent form depending on the circumstances and conditions relating to the acquisition and transportation of substitute materials or services.

The rate for contingent extra expense insurance is computed in the same manner as that for direct extra expense insurance except, of course, that it is based upon the building fire insurance rate applicable to the contributing property.

COMBINED BUSINESS INTERRUPTION AND EXTRA EXPENSE FORM

At this point it might help to reiterate the differences between extra expense insurance and the "expense to reduce the loss" coverage of the business interruption form. The business interruption form covers extra expenses only to the extent that they serve to reduce the business interruption loss. For example, if the business interruption loss can be reduced by operating at a temporary location or by farming out operations to another supplier, business interruption coverage applies. However, business interruption coverage only applies to the extent that the actual loss sustained is reduced. If the business interruption loss is not reduced, business interruption insurance will not pay for such extra expenses.

Extra expense insurance pays for the necessary expenses of remaining in business. It does not pay for lost income as a result of the interruption. The two coverages serve different purposes. In some cases, neither coverage by itself adequately treats the loss exposure, but both coverages must be purchased in combination.

As previously illustrated, most businesses have a need for either business interruption or extra expense insurance. However, a few businesses whose major exposure is loss of earnings due to shutdown rather than extra expense, frequently discover that recovery under the expense to reduce loss portion of the business interruption policy is not enough to make up for the amount of extra expense incurred in order to get back into operation quickly. Usually, the amount of extra expense recoverable is but a small fraction of the total extra expense incurred.

An illustration will demonstrate how the businessowner can recover all of the extra expense incurred to reduce loss and get back into operation. Let us assume that the building and/or contents were damaged to such an extent that it would require a four-month period of restoration. This suspension of production would result in approximately $100,000 lost earnings. In moving some of the damaged equipment to a temporary location and by relocating some phases of the operation to a temporary location, the normal rate of production can be maintained, so there would not be the previously anticipated loss of earnings. However, the total cost of the production under temporary conditions results in an amount of $200,000 over that which would have been expended under normal conditions. The recovery under the business interruption policy's expense to reduce loss provision would be $100,000, equal to that which had been the anticipated loss of earnings. The other portion of the extra expense would not be recoverable under an unmodified business interruption policy.

By modifying the business interruption form to add some extra expense coverage in small amounts, the $100,000 of unrecoverable extra expense can be paid. If the business had $1 million in gross earnings and the policy is written with a 50 percent coinsurance clause, the limit of liability of the policy would be $500,000. By adding an apportionment of extra expense insurance equal to 8, 16, and 20 percent of the total amount of insurance for thirty, sixty, and over sixty days of recovery, there would be $40,000, $80,000, and $100,000 of extra expense insurance available for the entire period of restoration.

The business interruption form modified to include limited extra expense coverage is called the combined business interruption and extra expense form. The ordinary payroll exclusion and limited coverage modifications may not be used with this form; but otherwise, it is subject to the same rules and provisions of separate business interruption and extra expense policies.

RENT OR RENTAL VALUE INSURANCE

Rental value insurance is a type of indirect loss insurance similar to business interruption insurance. It covers an insured's exposure to the loss of income due to an insured peril and the passage of time when the insured or a tenant may not use all or a portion of the premises owned by the insured for business operations.

The owner of a building suffers a loss of rent when rent payments are discontinued because the premises are made untenantable by a fire or other covered peril. An owner-occupant suffers a loss of rental value when the premises are rendered untenantable and it is necessary to rent other quarters. Tenants may also suffer loss of rental value if the lease provides that rent payments will be continued even when premises are rendered untenantable.

There is a distinction between *rental income* and *rental value.* Rental income refers to the income actually derived from others as payment for occupancy of the landlord's premises. Rental value refers to the value of rent that could be obtained from others when the owner occupies the premises.

Usually loss of rents received by a store owner from leased departments of a store would be recoverable under a business interruption policy. The landlord could also recover the loss of rents under its business interruption policy if the tenant rents another portion of the same building owned by the landlord. However, the landlord could also cover the loss of rental income under a separate rent insurance policy, which often is written at a lower premium rate than the business interruption coverage. When the owner occupies a portion of the premises and one or more tenants rent other portions, the rental income value of the rented sections and the use value of the portion occupied by the landlord can be covered together as rental value under the rental value policy designed for that purpose. A single amount of insurance would cover the overall exposure of rental income and value. It is important to assess all income or use value for all portions of the building so that adequate insurance can be maintained.

In the analysis of rental income exposures, the method of payment of rent by tenants is important. Some leases are paid on the basis of a flat rental per month, while others are based on sales by a tenant (such as in a shopping center). In the latter case, instead of a fixed amount, the

Table 5-10
Percentage for Rates of the Contribution Form

Percent of Contribution Clause	Percent of 80% Coinsurance Clause
50	80
60	70
75	64
80	62
90	58
100	55

rental income would vary according to the sales activity of the tenant or tenants.

Rent insurance is usually written in one of two ways, using either a contribution form or a monthly limitation form.

Contribution Form

This form may be written with a contribution clause (coinsurance) percentage of 50 percent or higher. The amount of insurance to satisfy the contribution clause is based upon gross rental value of the premises for the twelve months immediately following the date of damage. If rent is paid by all tenants on a fixed basis, 50 percent of the annual rental value would cover a period of untenantability for six months, and 75 percent would cover a period of nine months. If the rents are payable on the basis of a percentage of sales, the exposure to loss for a six-month period could be 60 percent or higher if untenantability would occur during peak periods of the tenants' sales. In such a case a higher amount of insurance and coinsurance factor could be used.

Blanket rent insurance may be written over two or more separate buildings owned by the same party with either a 90 or 100 percent contribution clause. Average rates are published by the applicable rating bureau.

Rates for the contribution form are expressed as a percentage of the 80 percent coinsurance building fire rate. Table 5-10 is used to determine the applicable percentage.

Rental value insurance may be written covering a building under construction in most states. Any damage to the partially completed building will delay the date the owner can begin to collect rental income. In this case, the appropriate 80 percent coinsurance builders' risk rate is used to insure this loss exposure. Recovery would be based on the period of time required to restore the building in course of construction to the condition existing at the date of the damage.

Rental value insurance may also be modified to extend the period of indemnity beyond the time required for restoration, repair, or replacement of the damaged property by adding the endorsement extending the period of indemnity. The period of indemnity is extended until the insured's rental income is restored to that which would have existed had no loss occurred. The period of indemnity is extended from 30 to 360 days in multiples of 30 days at appropriate increases in premium.

Premium Adjustment Form The premium adjustment form is a variation of the contribution identical in concept to the premium adjustment endorsement used with business interruption insurance. This form is primarily designed to provide insurance against loss of rents which are based upon a percentage of the tenants' sales or designed for large office and apartment buildings that are subject to a fluctuating amount of vacancy. Rental income in these cases is difficult to anticipate accurately. The premium adjustment form permits the insured to carry adequate insurance and to comply with the contribution clause.

Under the premium adjustment form, the contribution clause remains in effect even though rental values may fluctuate during the policy period.

Reimbursement under the premium adjustment form will not exceed the lowest amount of the following: (1) based on the percentage of rental value specified in the declarations applying to the contribution clause, liability shall not exceed the policy's portion of that percentage of rental value that would have been earned during twelve months immediately following the loss; or (2) liability may not exceed the policy's percentage of that portion of any loss which the last statement of annual rental value received by the company prior to the date of damage or destruction bears to the actual annual rental value during the period covered by the statement.

Even though the insured, in anticipating the highest possible rental income for the next twelve months, might have to purchase more insurance, the premium adjustment clause permits the insured to get back a premium refund on that amount of insurance not needed. The insured submits a statement showing the actual annual rental value for the policy period within 120 days after cancellation. The company refunds the premium paid for the amount of insurance carried which is in excess of the policy's proportion of the specified contribution clause percentage of the actual average annual rental value.

Monthly Limitation Form

Rent insurance may also be written under a form without the contribution clause. The approach used here is similar to that in earnings insurance. The company restricts the recovery to the insured under this form in any one month to no more than that fraction specified in the declarations bears to the total amount of insurance. As in earnings insurance, the insured first should estimate the total amount of loss that would be sustained in each month due to the untenantability of the building. If the insured estimates a maximum loss of $20,000 per month and feels that it would take six months time to rebuild, the amount of insurance should be $120,000 and the policy written on a one-sixth monthly limitation. Limitations of one-ninth and one-twelfth are also available for longer periods of anticipated shutdown. This form is best adapted when flat monthly rent payments are made.

LEASEHOLD INTEREST INSURANCE

A lessee (tenant) may suffer a financial loss if the lease is canceled. One of the principal reasons for cancellation of a lease is because of substantial damage or destruction of the building or portion of a building occupied by the tenant. Most leases contain a fire clause which describes the conditions under which damage or destruction by fire or another peril would permit the owner to cancel. A typical fire clause in a lease reads as follows:

> If the building or premises is damaged by fire or other cause to the extent of 25% of the value thereof, the lease may be terminated by the lessor. If the building or premises is rendered untenantable due to damage by fire or other cause, the lessee is relieved of the payments of rents during the term that the premises are untenantable whether the lease is cancelled or not.

Some leases may have cancellation options based on 50 percent damage or upon a certain amount of time required to repair or replace damaged property.

There are a number of circumstances when a lease is so canceled that a tenant may suffer a financial loss. The following are illustrations:

1. A lessee who has a favorable lease at rent much less than the current rental value of the premises would not be able to obtain

as favorable a lease upon cancellation. (The "loss" would be the additional cost to rent equivalent premises for the duration of the current lease.)

2. A lessee who has sublet the premises to another at a profit. (The loss would be the loss of profit margin for the duration of the lease.)
3. A lessee who paid a bonus to acquire a lease. (The loss would be the unamortized value of the bonus. In some leases, however, there is a provision for the return of the pro rata unearned portion of a bonus if the lease is canceled.)
4. A lessee who installed expensive improvements and betterments. (The use of these would be lost as a result of the cancellation of the lease.)
5. A lessee who has paid advance rent which is not recoverable under the terms of the lease in the event of cancellation. (The lessee loses the value of the advance rent.)
6. A lessee who purchases an existing lease. (The lessee may lose the unamortized portion of the purchase price in the event of lease cancellation.)

In all of the above circumstances the tenant is exposed to loss if the lease is canceled. The amount of the loss depends on the unfulfilled portion of the lease, so the values exposed will continue to decline as the lease runs. There is a resemblance between this declining loss exposure and the exposures covered with decreasing term (life) insurance (e.g., mortgage life). The exposure may be treated with leasehold interest insurance, which resembles the approach taken with decreasing term (life) insurance.

The following discussion relates to leasehold interest form A designed for lessees with advantageous long-term leases or premises sublet at a profit.

Under the leasehold interest form, in the event of cancellation of the lease by the lessor after loss by fire or other insured peril (in accordance with the conditions of the lease or by statutory requirements in the absence of a fire clause), the insured may recover the actual loss sustained. Recovery will not exceed the amount of insurance remaining in force at the date of the occurrence, computed as follows: "The interest of the insured as lessee as determined by adjustment shall be paid for the first three (3) months succeeding the fire, and the net leasehold interest shall be paid for the remaining months of the unexpired lease."

The term *interest of the insured as lessee* is defined in the policy as:

> . . . the excess of the rental value of such premises over the actual rental payable (*including any maintenance or operating charges paid*

Table 5-11

Calculation of the Interest of the Insured as Lessee

Established rental value			$3,200
Less: Actual rent payable		$2,000	
Operating expense	$450		
Maintenance cost	50	500	2,500
Monthly interest of the insured as lessee			$ 700

by the insured) during the unexpired term of the insured's lease, whether the premises be occupied in whole or part by the insured or whether they be sublet to other tenants. (Italics added.)

As an illustration, assume the actual rent of $2,000 per month for a building; operating charges or expenses for elevators and janitorial service, heat, light, and power amounting to $450; and general maintenance of $50 per month. Actual rental value of the building at the time of policy inception is $3,200 per month. Then the interest of the insured as lessee is calculated as shown in Table 5-11.

The term net leasehold interest is defined as "that sum which, placed at 4% interest compounded annually will be equivalent to the interest of the insured as lessee for each separate month of the lease unexpired."

A table of leasehold interest which accompanies the policy is reproduced in Table 5-12. This table shows net leasehold interest and the amount for which a policy should be written per $1 of monthly gross leasehold interest for the number of months of unexpired lease. For example, the table shows that for 120 months of unexpired lease, the net leasehold interest is 99.1232 for each dollar of monthly gross leasehold interest. Thus, the net leasehold interest for the firm cited would be ($700 × 99.1232) or $69,386.24.

Amount of Insurance

The policy is written for the total amount of net leasehold interest of the insured for the unexpired months of the lease. It is a condition of the policy that the amount of insurance is automatically reduced from month to month as set forth in the net leasehold interest table.

For the firm cited, the policy would be written for $69,386.24. However, the amount of insurance available would decrease each month as the unexpired term of the lease becomes shorter. At the expiration of

Table 5-12
Table of Leasehold Interest Factors

Unexpired term of lease in months.	Net leasehold interest per $1 of monthly gross leasehold interest for number of months of lease unexpired.	Unexpired term of lease in months.	Net leasehold interest per $1 of monthly gross leasehold interest for number of months of lease unexpired.	Unexpired term of lease in months.	Net leasehold interest per $1 of monthly gross leasehold interest for number of months of lease unexpired.	Unexpired term of lease in months.	Net leasehold interest per $1 of monthly gross leasehold interest for number of months of lease unexpired.
1	1.00	61	55.2326	121	99.7965	181	136.4268
2	2.00	62	56.6492	122	100.4677	182	136.9785
3	3.00	63	56.8631	123	101.1367	183	137.5284
4	3.9871	64	57.6744	124	101.8035	184	138.0765
5	4.9710	65	58.4331	125	102.4682	185	138.6228
6	5.9517	66	59.2891	126	103.1307	186	139.1673
7	6.9292	67	60.0925	127	103.7911	187	139.7101
8	7.9035	68	60.8933	128	104.4493	188	140.2511
9	8.8746	69	61.5914	129	105.1053	189	140.7903
10	9.8425	70	62.4369	130	105.7592	190	141.3277
11	10.8072	71	63.2798	131	106.4109	191	141.8633
12	11.7687	72	64.0701	132	107.0605	192	142.3972
13	12.7263	73	64.8578	133	107.7079	193	142.9293
14	13.6809	74	65.6430	134	108.3533	194	143.4597
15	14.6323	75	66.4256	135	108.9966	195	143.9884
16	15.5811	76	67.2057	136	109.6378	196	144.5154
17	16.5267	77	67.9833	137	110.2769	197	145.0407
18	17.4693	78	68.7583	138	110.9139	198	145.5643
19	18.4089	79	69.5308	139	111.5489	199	146.0862
20	19.3455	80	70.3008	140	112.1818	200	146.6064
21	20.2791	81	71.0682	141	112.8126	201	147.1249
22	21.2097	82	71.8331	142	113.4413	202	147.6417
23	22.1373	83	72.5955	143	114.0679	203	148.1568
24	23.0619	84	73.3554	144	114.6925	204	148.6702
25	23.9834	85	74.1128	145	115.3151	205	149.1819
26	24.9020	86	74.8678	146	115.9357	206	149.6920
27	25.8176	87	75.6203	147	116.5543	207	150.2004
28	26.7302	88	76.3704	148	117.1709	208	150.7072
29	27.6399	89	77.1181	149	117.7855	209	151.2123
30	28.5466	90	77.8633	150	118.3981	210	151.7158
31	29.4504	91	78.6061	151	119.0087	211	152.2176
32	30.3512	92	79.3465	152	119.6173	212	152.7178
33	31.2490	93	80.0844	153	120.2239	213	153.2163
34	32.1439	94	80.8199	154	120.8285	214	153.7132
35	33.0358	95	81.5530	155	121.4311	215	154.2084
36	33.9248	96	82.2837	156	122.0317	216	154.7020
37	34.8109	97	83.0119	157	122.6303	217	155.1939
38	35.6942	98	83.7378	158	123.2270	218	155.6843
39	36.5746	99	84.4613	159	123.8217	219	156.1731
40	37.4522	100	85.1825	160	124.4145	220	156.6603
41	38.3269	101	85.9013	161	125.0054	221	157.1459
42	39.1988	102	86.6178	162	125.5944	222	157.6299
43	40.0678	103	87.3320	163	126.1815	223	158.1124
44	40.9340	104	88.0438	164	126.7666	224	158.5933
45	41.7973	105	88.7533	165	127.3498	225	159.0726
46	42.6578	106	89.4604	166	127.9311	226	159.5503
47	43.5154	107	90.1652	167	128.5105	227	160.0264
48	44.3702	108	90.8678	168	129.0880	228	160.5010
49	45.2222	109	91.5681	169	129.6636	229	160.9740
50	46.0715	110	92.2662	170	130.2374	230	161.4455
51	46.9180	111	92.9620	171	130.8093	231	161.9154
52	47.7618	112	93.6556	172	131.3794	232	162.3838
53	48.6028	113	94.3469	173	131.9476	233	162.8507
54	49.4411	114	95.0360	174	132.5140	234	163.3161
55	50.2767	115	95.7228	175	133.0785	235	163.7800
56	51.1095	116	96.4074	176	133.6412	236	164.2424
57	51.9396	117	97.0897	177	134.2020	237	164.7033
58	52.7669	118	97.7698	178	134.7610	238	165.1627
59	53.5915	119	98.4476	179	135.3181	239	165.6206
60	54.4134	120	99.1232	180	135.8734	240	166.0770

a three-year policy the loss exposure would have decreased by 36 months. The amount of insurance then can be calculated by subtracting 36 months from 120 months (84 months), checking the table to find the factor for 84 months (73.3554), and then multiplying $700 by 73.3554 to arrive at $51,348.78.

If the amount of insurance at policy inception is $69,386.24 and the amount of insurance at expiration is $51,358.78, the *average* amount of insurance is the average of these two figures, or $60,367.51. The *premium* would be based on the average amount of insurance ($60,367.51), but the *policy amount* would be the discounted value of the lease on the effective date of the policy ($69,386.24).

Premiums are based on the building fire rate but may be reduced depending on the terms of the lease.

Other Provisions

The section of the lease pertaining to cancellation of the lease due to damage of the building is incorporated into the policy. If the lease contains no conditions relative to the damage to the premises by fire, the statutory requirements of the state in which the property is situated prevail.

The policy excludes any loss to leasehold interest by reason of any act or omission of the insured; or by the insured exercising an option to cancel the lease; or by the enforcement of any local or state ordinance or law regulating or prohibiting construction or repair of buildings; or by suspension, lapse, or cancellation of any license; or for any other remote loss. The lease cancellation option may only be exercised by the lessor for the policy to provide coverage. It would be reasonable to assume that the lessor would exercise this option if, at the time of damage, there were an appreciable increase in rental value of the premises.

In some cases following a loss, the lessor may find it advantageous to permit a good tenant to remain in possession of the premises on a month-to-month basis or to negotiate another lease at less than the full actual rental value. In such cases, the reimbursement for any loss of leasehold interest for the tenant would be limited to the actual loss sustained. This amount would be the difference between the rent under the original lease and that under the new lease or on a month-to-month basis.

If the premises are rendered untenantable and the lease is *not* canceled, the lessee would lose the leasehold interest for the time it would take to restore the premises to a tenantable condition. Reimbursement under the policy would be the actual loss sustained at a rate not exceeding a specified amount per month and a pro rata proportion

Table 5-13
Leasehold Interest Policy Amounts

(1)	Amount of advance rental, bonus payment, or cost of improvements and betterments at effective date of ten-year lease (amortized $1,000 per month)		$120,000
(2)	Unamortized portion of (1) at effective date of policy, six months later		114,000
(3)	Unamortized portion at expiration of three-year policy		78,000
(4)	Amount at inception plus amount at expiration	(2) + (3)	192,000
(5)	Average amount of liability for policy term	(4) ÷ 2	96,000

thereof for less than one month, and a pro rata proportion thereof for partial untenantability for the length of time required to render the premises tenantable again. This reimbursement would not extend beyond the expiration of the lease however.

Leasehold Interest Form B

In addition to loss caused by advantageous leases or sublet premises, several other circumstances have been mentioned where the tenant has a special leasehold interest in the unexpired term of a lease. These are for *bonus payments* made at the time of the acquisition of the lease; *advance rentals* paid at the inception of the lease, which may not be returnable to the tenant in the event of building damage; and *improvements and betterments* made by the tenant during the term of the lease.

These special leasehold interests may be covered under a special leasehold interest insurance form, but the table of leasehold interest factors is not used. Instead, the policy amount is the unamortized amount of bonus paid, advance rent paid, or the unamortized value of improvements and betterments installed by the tenant.

As an example, consider the calculation in Table 5-13. As before, the amount of insurance shown in the policy would be $114,000, but the premium would be based on $96,000.

Improvements and Betterments

A tenant's use interest in improvements and betterments can be insured under a leasehold interest form B and under a property form such as form FGP-1, discussed in Chapter 3. A few observations are in order in comparing the coverage under these two forms.

FGP-1 covers loss resulting from direct damage to the improvements and betterments, whether or not the lease is canceled. Leasehold interest insurance covers loss resulting from cancellation of the lease, whether or not the improvements and betterments are directly damaged. Firms with substantial values in improvements and betterments will often find it advantageous to carry both coverages.

Improvements and betterments not replaced are valued in the same manner under the general property form as under the leasehold interest form. The general property form, however, provides coverage for the actual cash value of improvements and betterments that are repaired or replaced at the insured's expense.

TUITION FEES INSURANCE

Tuition fees insurance is a form of business interruption insurance which has been designed specifically to meet the needs of educational institutions. The private school or college which receives its income from students in the form of tuition has an exposure which differs to a degree from the mercantile or manufacturing exposure.

If a fire or other insured peril were to damage or destroy school buildings or property during the time that the school was not using these facilities and the school could not open at the beginning of the next school session, a full annual income from students not accommodated could be lost. The tuition fees form is adapted to cover this loss contingency.

The following language from the policy form illustrates how the coverage applies particularly in the case of a fire or other peril damaging buildings just prior to the beginning of a school year:

> This company shall be liable for the ACTUAL LOSS OF TUITION FEES SUSTAINED by the Insured less charges and expenses which do not necessarily continue during the period of time, not limited by the date of expiration of this policy, commencing with the date of such damage or destruction and ending (except as provided in paragraph 3) on the day preceding the beginning of the first school year following the date that the damaged or destroyed buildings, structures and contents thereof could . . . be rebuilt, repaired or replaced.

Paragraph three of the same form stipulates that if the restoration is not completed within thirty days prior to the opening day of the first school year following the damage, coverage is extended to include loss of tuition and fees sustained until the end of that school year and the beginning of the second school year.

The words, *beginning of school year*, as used in the policy, mean the opening date of school in the fall as announced in the school catalog. Therefore, if a fire destroyed a building housing an important facility of the school or college in April and reconstruction or repair could not be finished until August 15, and if the school year officially started on September 1, the policy would cover reimbursement for reduction in fees and tuition from April to September of the next school year. In such an instance, however, it is not likely that the loss would be more than a partial loss, since on a multi-building campus, temporary facilities can be used to replace others in emergency situations.

Tuition fees are defined in the policy as the sum of tuition, fees, and other income from students, less the cost of merchandise sold, and materials and supplies consumed, in services sold to students.

The form, therefore, permits coverage for income derived from the sale of supplies, books, laboratory equipment and fees, room and board in dormitories, and so on to students, in addition to tuition. The form can be modified to also include income from athletic events and from research conducted by the school for governmental bodies or private industry.

The school would have to continue its tenured professors' salaries throughout the school year as contracted. In addition, many such faculty members would be considered irreplaceable by a large school that had built up a reputation in a certain field of study. A school, primarily a boarding school, would have a considerable abatable expense in food, dormitory supplies and services, and laundry services that could be deducted as cost of materials and supplies consumed in services sold to students.

Rating

Due to the higher ratio of exposure to loss of continuing payroll for schools than for other types of commercial activities, and the possibility of a loss of income extending beyond the date of restoration of the property, a higher minimum amount of insurance would be required, and rates should be normally higher than other comparable business interruption forms. Under the tuition fees form, therefore, the contribution clause percentage is set at either 80 percent or 100 percent of the tuition fees that would have been earned for twelve months following a loss. The 80 percent loss carries a rate of 90 percent of the applicable 80 percent coinsurance building rate, and the 100 percent clause would carry a rate of 80 percent of the building rate.

Campers' Fees Insurance

In addition to schools and universities, the tuition fees form can be adapted to other exposures to loss of income due to destruction by fire or other perils. It is appropriately modified to cover the exposure of seasonal camps. Similar to schools, destruction of key facilities of a private summer camp might cause a loss of income extending beyond the beginning of the camp season if facilities are not repaired until after the season had started or just prior to its start.

Campers' fees insurance should be carried on a year-round basis, since a severe fire in the off-season could seriously curtail recruiting activity during the winter and spring months if word spread that the camp might not reopen in the summer. Parents would still be able to find alternative camps for their youngsters in such a case, resulting in almost complete loss of fees for the camp season.

A special nonstandard variation of campers' fees insurance has also been devised to cover contingencies of camp owners or operators that had to refund campers' fees because of the shutdown of a camp in mid-season or prior to the beginning of the season because of epidemic diseases, such as impetigo, polio, or encephalitis. In addition, this form would cover loss of profit if the campers had to stay beyond the normal closing date due to quarantine for such an epidemic disease. Reimbursement of campers' fees to individual campers who had to leave camp because of injury or illness could also be covered.

Usually campers' fees insurance is written only by insurers specializing in coverage for summer camps who have the facilities to insure the whole package.

Variations of Indirect Loss Insurance

A number of other variations of indirect loss insurance are available to suit the needs of particular firms. For example, there are special forms and rules to provide coverage on coal mining operations, drive-in theaters, radio and television transmitting stations and studios, and whiskey distilleries and wineries.

Indirect loss insurance for losses caused by accident involving a boiler or machinery will be discussed in Chapter 13.

Chapter Notes

1. This cost and several of the following examples normally are insured under direct damage contracts. Nevertheless, they are properly classified as consequential losses.
2. FC&S, Fire and Marine, Business Interruption B-3 (August 1970).
3. E. C. Bardwell, *New Profits—Business Interruption* (Indianapolis: The Rough Notes Company, 1973), p. 115. This is based largely on a decision of the U.S. Court of Appeals, Sixth Circuit, Shakertown Corp. v. Commissioner of Internal Revenue 277 F2d 625. If a contract is an agreement to pay a specified amount per day (or other perils) during the time use and occupancy of property is prevented, such proceeds are taxable only as capital gain if invested in replacement of the damaged or destroyed property with property similar in type and use to that which was damaged or destroyed.

CHAPTER 6

Noninsurance Treatment of Fire and Allied Lines Exposures

INTRODUCTION

Insurance enables people and organizations to manage loss exposures effectively and efficiently, but it is not the only effective and efficient method of treating loss exposures. In some situations, it is not even the most effective or efficient treatment method, and insurance should not be used to the exclusion of other techniques. Good risk management requires that the full range of risk management devices be employed in judicious mixture. Fire and allied lines insurance has been examined at some length in the past three chapters. This chapter will examine the principle facets of risk management tools other than insurance for treating property loss exposures.

When insurance has been chosen as the primary technique for treating loss exposures, supplementary risk management techniques do not diminish in importance. Only rarely does an insurance claim payment make an insured whole. Many loss effects are borne directly by the insured, including losses resulting from disruption of operations, loss of market position, and time and effort spent in accomplishing recovery (including perfecting an insurance claim). Any suffering by persons injured in connection with a loss event cannot be removed by an insurance payment. Even when insurance is carried, failure to control loss frequency or severity may lead to increased premium cost or even unavailability of coverage. Insurers pay attention to the risk management practices of insureds and vary their rates, terms, and acceptances according to the mix of risk management methods employed.

In this chapter the various noninsurance risk management devices will be grouped under two general headings: *loss control* and *loss financing*. Loss control refers to all devices aimed at reducing either the frequency or severity of losses suffered. Loss financing refers to all means of paying for losses that occur. (If a particular loss, or portion of a loss, does not occur, it has been effectively controlled. If it does occur, someone must finance it. So these two categories exhaust all the possibilities.)

Two types of loss financing techniques will be discussed in this chapter: *noninsurance transfers of loss* and *loss retention programs*. The final section of the chapter will discuss some of the factors to be considered in deciding the mix of risk management techniques to use in the treatment of fire and allied lines loss exposures.

LOSS CONTROL

"The best thing to do with a loss is not to have it." Widespread acceptance of this statement indicates the importance of loss control as a risk management device. How is it applied to the exposures subject to fire and allied lines insurance coverage?

Selection of control procedures for discussion here is based on both the overall importance of the peril (i.e., its contribution to the total number of losses in fire and allied lines insurance) and its amenability to generally available controls. Fire meets both criteria and receives considerable discussion in this chapter. Windstorm, while a rather important contributor to loss costs, is much less subject to control and so receives less attention. While explosion is less important in terms of frequency, it has considerable amenity to control and merits some discussion. Beyond these, importance drops off rapidly and, usually, so does controllability. Therefore, other perils will be discussed only briefly.

The loss control techniques to be discussed can be effective, not only in reducing direct damage losses, but also in reducing income and expense losses. Unless there is a direct loss, there will usually be no indirect loss, so a key consideration in controlling indirect losses is to limit the frequency and severity of direct losses.

Loss Control in General

Losses result from chains of events. Heinrich's domino theory was discussed in CPCU 1. The occurrence of an injury is dependent on preceding factors, like a row of dominoes standing on edge—each domino will fall only if the preceding domino knocks it over. According to Heinrich, an accident is only one of five factors in a sequence that results in an injury, as illustrated in Figure 6-1.

Figure 6-1
Heinrich's Domino Theory*

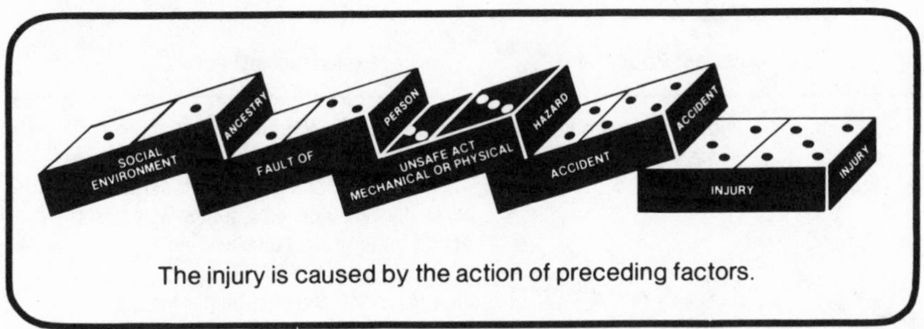

The injury is caused by the action of preceding factors.

*Reprinted with permission from H. W. Heinrich, *Industrial Accident Prevention*, 4th ed. (New York: McGraw-Hill Book Company, 1959), p. 15.

The several factors in the accident-occurrence series are explained in chronological order in Figure 6-2.

The domino theory can also be applied to property losses. The 1967 McCormick Place fire in Chicago is a good illustration of a sequence of events leading up to a major loss. It is evident that the loss might not have occurred, or would not have been as severe, were it not for a series of factors stacked up like dominoes. For example, in the McCormick Place exhibition hall, there was a failure to anticipate the needs of exhibitors for electrical outlets. The available circuits were overloaded with extension cords and an exhibitor used a defective cord. It ran among other exhibits made of light, combustible materials such as cardboard, light pressed panels, and paper. Since combustibility of contents had not been specifically considered (despite the building's intended use) and the ceiling was extremely high, the exhibition area was not sprinklered. A fire began while the guard was in another part of the building and the blaze had grown substantially before he saw it. It took three or four minutes for him to reach an alarm station. When the fire department arrived, it found that someone had left valves on the lines to the fire hydrants partially closed, seriously reducing the water pressure. The fire fighters did not know where the valves were. This series of events resulted in a $52.5 million fire and one death.[1] Many unsafe acts and physical hazards combined to produce this result, and not all of them have been mentioned. (For example, the valve problem with the hydrants [a mechanical or physical hazard] was caused by the event or chain of events that led to that condition.)

Loss control consists of insertion of devices and procedures designed to interrupt such a series of events at one or more points. Naturally, the use of specific devices depends on the nature of the particular perils and exposure conditions being attacked.

Figure 6-2

Accident Factors*

Accident Factors	Explanation of Factors
1. Ancestry and social environment.	Recklessness, stubborness, avariciousness, and other undesirable traits of character may be passed along through inheritance. Environment may develop undesirable traits of character or may interfere with education. Both inheritance and environment cause faults of person.
2. Fault of person.	Inherited or acquired faults of person; such as recklessness, violent temper, nervousness, excitability, inconsiderateness, ignorance of safe practice, etc., constitute proximate reasons for committing unsafe acts or for the existence of mechanical or physical hazards.
3. Unsafe act and/or mechanical or physical hazard.	Unsafe performance of persons, such as standing under suspended loads, starting machinery without warning, horseplay, and removal of safeguards; and mechanical or physical hazards, such as unguarded gears, unguarded point of operation, absence of rail guards, and insufficient light, result directly in accidents.
4. Accident.	Events such as falls of persons, striking of persons by flying objects, etc., are typical accidents that cause injury.
5. Injury.	Fractures, lacerations, etc., are injuries that result directly from accidents.

*Reprinted with permission from H.W. Heinrich, *Industrial Accident Prevention*, 4th ed. (New York: McGraw-Hill Book Company, 1959), p. 15.

In general, the control means available can be classified as engineering—attack by design and location of properties and equipment to reduce the number of physical hazards; and as "education, training, and enforcement"—attack by establishing appropriate behavior of people to reduce the frequency of unsafe acts. Although losses are usually caused by unsafe acts (note the several "people" failures in the exhibition hall loss chain), engineering often can be used to limit the losses resulting from unsafe acts (e.g., automatic sprinklers can successfully interrupt fire loss chains that people have started).

Fire Loss Control Principles

To break a chain of loss-causing events, it is necessary to know how the events proceed—how one thing leads to another. In simple terms, fire losses proceed by chemical processes—heat causes rapid oxidation of fuel. Thus, three things are required to have a fire: an initial source of heat; oxygen; and material that will burn, given the amount of heat and oxygen available.[2] As more fuel burns, the amount of heat present usually increases. Strong fires create their own air drafts, thus bringing more oxygen to the fuel. So fires grow, engulfing more and more fuel as the burning process literally feeds upon itself.

It follows that most fire prevention and control centers on removal or separation of one or more of the three common essentials (heat, oxygen, and fuel).

Heat Sources There are three types of energy that can create the heat sufficient to cause a fire—electrical energy, chemical energy, and mechanical (frictional) energy.

Electrical heat energy may come from natural sources (such as lightning) or artificial ones (such as power generating plants). It may be dynamic (for example, power flowing through power lines and operating motors) or static (such as the temporarily quiescent static electricity in the air or the charge in a storage battery).

Chemical heat energy is released as part of a chemical reaction. Examples include the ignition of a match, the burning of a welding torch, or spontaneous combustion of oily rags left in a closet.

Mechanical or frictional heat energy is developed when objects rub together. The brakes on a car create heat, as does the friction of a grinding wheel on a piece of metal, a belt running through a pulley, or a defective bearing. It is important to identify all the important heat sources from which fire damage might arise in order to give each proper loss control treatment. The specifics of treatment differ according to whether the source is planned or unplanned, fixed or mobile.

Planned Heat Sources. Planned sources are of two main types: those in which the heat energy is desired, and those in which it is not. Standard examples of the former include furnaces and boilers, various types of electrical apparatus, and a wide variety of heat-creating equipment, ranging from cigarette lighters to blast furnaces.

Other planned sources of heat are those in which heat is an unwanted by-product. Most common is the production of heat, including sparks, from all types of machinery or from grinding operations. Heat may also be generated by materials capable of spontaneous combustion from natural generation of internal heat. Many natural fibers generate heat while in storage, and many chemical processes necessarily produce unwanted heat.

Fixed Versus Mobile Heat Sources. Some planned sources of heat are fixed, while others move around. Furnaces and boilers for heating buildings are fixed. Welding and cutting torches are common mobile sources of heat, as are vehicles.

Fuels For a fire to start, continue, or spread, it must have fuel. Fuels vary greatly in the ease with which they can be ignited. Gasoline is thus generally more hazardous than paper, paper more hazardous than lumber, lumber more hazardous than steel, and so on. The relative combustibility or flammabililty of a fuel depends on the amount of heat required to cause it to produce burnable vapors. In a practical situation, two characteristics of a fuel are important: the temperature at which it vaporizes (a function of its chemical composition) and the extent to which it holds heat rather than spreading it (a matter strongly affected by the size and shape of the item, as well as by its chemistry).

Temperature at Which Substances Vaporize. An important characteristic of solid substances is the *ignition temperature*. The ignition temperature may be defined as the minimum temperature to which a substance in air must be heated in order to maintain combustion independently of the initial heat source.[3] A substance which has reached the ignition temperature will continue to release vapors which burn, and will continue to burn until it is extinguished or consumed.

An important characteristic of liquids is the *flash point*. The flash point is the minimum temperature at which a liquid gives off vapors that can be ignited by a spark or flame. Gasoline, for example, has a flash point of – 45°F, compared to kerosene's flash point of 100°.[4] At room temperature gasoline releases vapors that can be readily ignited. Kerosene must be heated above room temperature before it releases ignitable vapors.

Form of the Material. Wood in a toothpick and the same kind of wood in a log both have the same ignition temperature. But when the surface of a toothpick is heated, there is little place else for the heat to go and so the toothpick quickly ignites. In a log, however, some of the heat at the surface is dissipated into the interior. Hence, it takes a hotter or longer sustained supply of heat to get the log to burst into flame. And, when external heat is removed, the cool interior of the log may then absorb enough heat to bring the temperature below the ignition temperature.

Steel in most forms cannot burn because of its density and the fact that steel is a good conductor of heat. A flame applied to a steel beam is rapidly conducted away from the point of contact, which remains below the ignition temperature. Steel wool, on the other hand, can be ignited by a match because its low density reduces its ability to dissipate heat.[5]

Continuing fire represents an ongoing reaction. Thus, when one starts a wood fire in a fireplace, initial heat may be created by friction (striking of a match). It is then continued by burning of the chemicals in the match head. When the fire so generated has burned long enough, the wood of the match flames. The temperature thus created is not extremely high, but the shape and material of the match cause it to be a self-sustaining chain reaction. In the fireplace, fire is ignited in paper and light wood materials with ignition temperatures below that produced by the match. As more fuel catches fire, a higher temperature is generated. If this temperature is sustained long enough, logs can be induced to flame when heat (from other burning materials) is being applied more rapidly than it can be dissipated into the air and into the logs' interior. Eventually, if enough heat is produced rapidly enough, logs can continue to burn on their own, without any continuing outside source of heat.

The process is the same with most hostile fires. And in severe cases, the buildup of heat from the fuels that have, one by one, been heated to flaming point, increases with each additional bit of fuel consumption until the fire reaches such a point that it cannot be stopped until it has completely consumed all available fuel.

Building Contents as Fuel. The variety of building contents that may be exposed to fire is, of course, tremendous. Depending on type of operations and particular location, inventory may be paper or pig iron, alcohol or brine, sulfur or molasses. Equipment and furnishings may be combustible or noncombustible, oily or clean, light or heavy. Not only the inherent combustibility of each type, but also its spacing and arrangement determine its actual significance as fuel for fire. Each occupancy, and in some cases each part of a single occupancy, presents different exposures, so each must be evaluated on its own merits, or at least according to its own particular class. Overall, the possibilities range from such relatively light exposures as a well arranged office with metal furniture and a minimum of paper to a structure used to store dynamite.

The expected amount of combustibles available as fuel for a hostile fire in a given area is called the *fire load,* commonly expressed in terms of weight of combustibles per square foot. Heat to be expected in a fire is estimated on the basis of known calorific content of those combustibles present in a building's contents and structural components. Since physical arrangement of the material greatly affects the rate of combustion, estimation of fire load in specific cases requires expert judgment.

Most high fire loads do not result from materials recognized as especially hazardous; where possible, care is taken to limit the amount of such exposure in a building. Rather, the usual high load cases come from bulk storage of relatively low hazard materials packed together in great quantity in a minimum of space. Modern lifting equipment allows stacking to considerable height, which can create extreme fire loads. The very heaviest fire loads, however, occur in situations with large quantities of extraordinarily hazardous materials: highly flammable liquids such as light petroleum products, lacquers, or alcohols; materials that burn explosively, or nearly so, such as sulfur and some sulfides, many nitrates, some peroxides, many types of metallic or organic dusts; and so on.

Buildings as Fuel. As mentioned, fire load includes the combustible parts of a building. Frame buildings, of course, contribute more ready fuel for fire than do buildings of masonry, noncombustible, or fire resistive materials. When building materials are combustible, the result may be more damage to the building itself and faster spread of the fire to other fuel inside or outside the building.

The following discussion of construction types is based on the construction definitions used by the National Fire Protection Association (NFPA) as discussed in the 14th edition of the *Fire Protection Handbook.*

FRAME CONSTRUCTION. In pure wood frame construction, illustrated in Figure 6-3, all the materials that support the essential elements of the building—the floors, roof, and walls—are made of wood. The exterior may be clad with something else: a single thickness of bricks (brick veneer) on the walls, for example; or asphalt shingles on the roof. But everything is held up by wood in a frame structure. When that wood burns, the structure, or the involved part of it, is destroyed.

ORDINARY MASONRY CONSTRUCTION. In ordinary masonry construction, often called "ordinary construction," the walls are self-supporting masonry—they can stand without wood supports. Ordinary masonry construction is illustrated in Figure 6-4. Other supporting elements, however, are wood. Joists and beams supporting floors and roof are wood; so, usually, are the roof and floors themselves. In a fire of

Figure 6-3
Frame Construction*

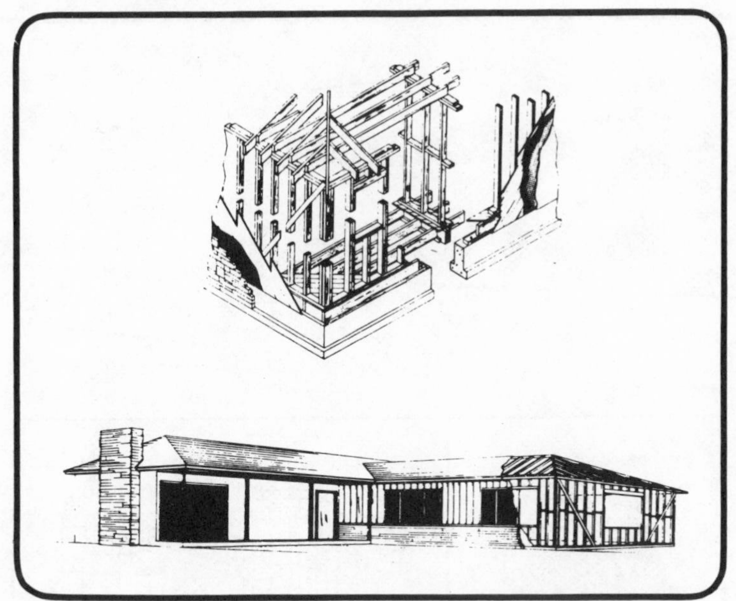

*Reprinted with permission from *Stevens Valuation Quarterly* (Los Angeles: Marshall and Swift Publication Company, July 1973), p. A-12.

considerable intensity, only a shell will be left—the bare walls. In such a fire some significant portion of the walls may even fall, knocked down by fall of the roof, or pulled or pushed down by collapsing wooden support beams. Even the bricks themselves can be damaged beyond use by heat of sufficient intensity and duration.

The principal advantage of ordinary construction appears in the much more frequent, less intense fires. To rate as ordinary, the building's exterior bearing walls must have a rated fire resistance of two hours and be arranged so as to have stability under fire conditions. (Fire resistance ratings will be discussed shortly.) Hence, the exterior bearing walls usually remain in usable, or nearly usable, condition; they continue to support the roof, and walls and roof provide some degree of protection for the interior. Obviously, ordinary construction is usually preferable to frame construction when fire occurs.

NONCOMBUSTIBLE CONSTRUCTION. "Noncombustible construction" is a specialized term in fire protection and fire insurance. Noncombustible construction is illustrated in Figure 6-5. The term is *not* applied to all buildings of noncombustible materials—many such buildings fall into the fire resistive category. A building is in the noncombustible class

Figure 6-4
Masonry Construction*

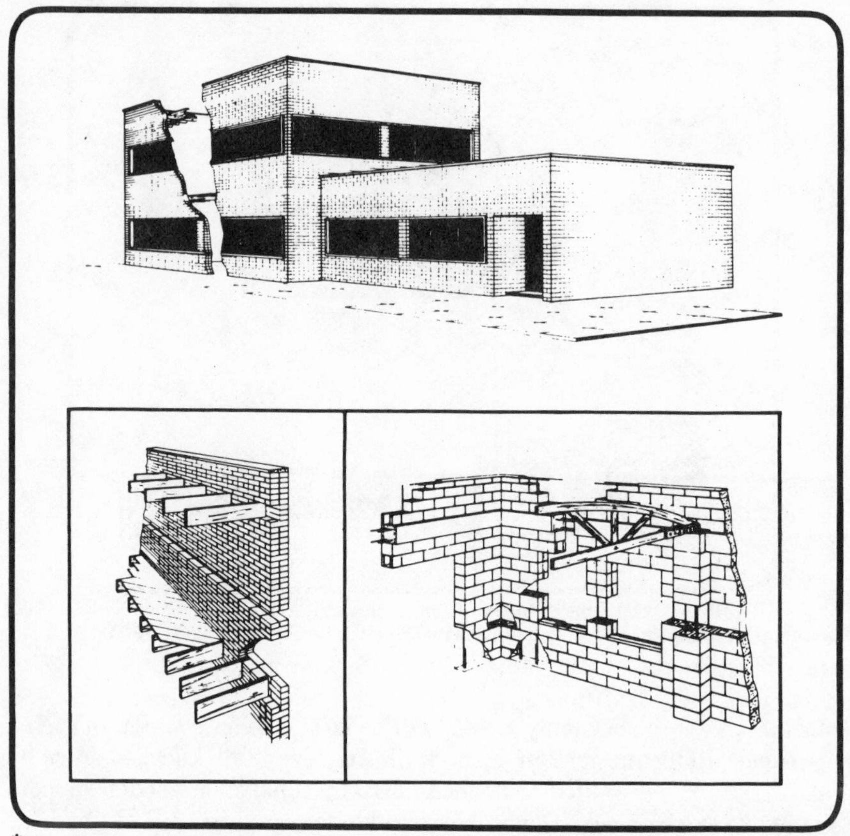

*Reprinted with permission from *Stevens Valuation Quarterly* (Los Angeles: Marshall and Swift Publication Company, July 1973), p. A-11.

when its walls, partitions, and structural members are of materials which will contribute little if any fuel to a fire. Examples of noncombustible construction include metal-framed, metal-clad buildings, or concrete block structures with a metal deck roof supported by an open web joist system. Many light noncombustible buildings do not add fuel to fires, but are readily susceptible to heat damage. They expand, twist, crack, and otherwise deteriorate in fires. Therefore, such structures often collapse in fires, meaning loss of the building, increased damage to contents, and increased threat to life safety. Although they do not contribute fuel to a fire, noncombustible buildings are not necessarily "safer" than buildings of frame or ordinary masonry construction.

Figure 6-5

Noncombustible Construction*

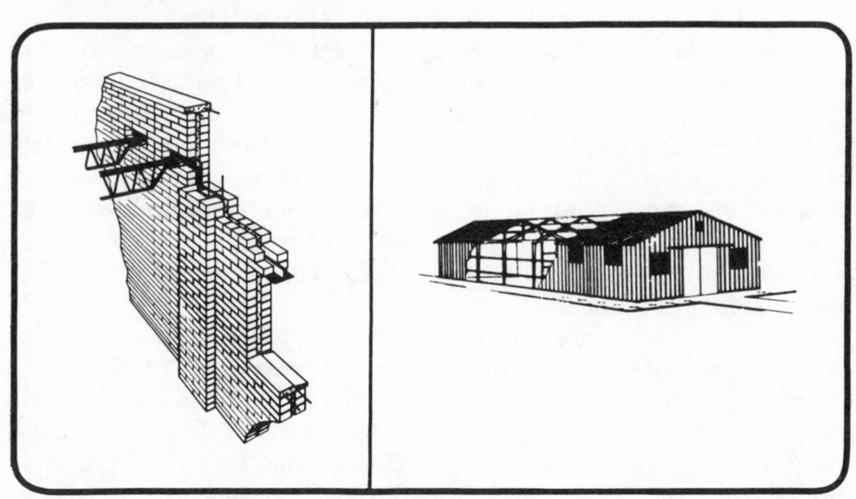

*Reprinted with permission from *Stevens Valuation Quarterly* (Los Angeles: Marshall and Swift Publication Company, July 1973), pp. A-11 and A-12.

FIRE RESISTIVE CONSTRUCTION. Fire resistive construction provides more fire protection than ordinary or noncombustible construction, but no construction is "fire proof." Materials in fire resistive construction resist heat longer than materials required for protected ordinary or noncombustible construction, but they do not resist it forever. And they do not keep fires, including large and dangerous fires, from happening. Even fire resistive buildings can be totally destroyed by fire.

Fire Resistance Ratings. Fire resistance ratings of materials are determined by standard tests in laboratories. Fire resistance of building materials as typically assembled is commonly rated by testing in furnaces specially designed for exposing the assemblies to a standard fire. An assembly rated one-hour fire resistance would meet a furnace test under load without failure for one hour.[6] Two very important practical points about the resultant ratings are the following:

1. Standard fire tests take into consideration the capacity of materials, and, in some cases, assemblies, to perform intended functions during fire exposure, and their subsequent load capacity. There is no reference to their suitability for further use (e.g., in a repaired or reconstructed building).
2. There are many reasons why performance in a standard test and performance in an actual building fire may differ.[7]

Fire Resistive Construction Defined. Fire resistive construction is defined by the National Fire Protection Association (NFPA) as that type of construction in which the structural members including walls, partitions, columns, floors, and roofs are of noncombustible or limited-combustible materials and have fire resistance ratings not less than those specified in Table 6-1. The specific materials commonly used to meet these requirements are reinforced concrete and protected structural steel for framing, reinforced concrete or masonry for bearing walls, and lighter noncombustible materials in other parts, such as curtain walls (walls which are enclosing but not load bearing). In many cases the principal differences between fire resistive and noncombustible construction are in the thickness of the concrete and masonry, the dimensions and strength of other supports, and the amount of heat shielding provided for steel supports.

In fire resistive construction, as in other types, there are no specific resistance standards for surface and trim materials. But to classify a building as fire resistive, these items "should be installed in such a manner that they do not contribute to the spread of fire. For example, the National Building Code requires that wooden trim around doors in fire resistive buildings be backed solidly with noncombustible material, thus eliminating combustible concealed spaces."[8]

Many buildings classified as "fire resistive" for insurance rating purposes are only partially fire resistive by National Fire Protection Association standards.

Heavy Timber or Mill Construction. There is a type of construction, called "heavy timber" or "mill" that is also highly fire resistive, but it is seldom used in new construction. One type of heavy timber construction is illustrated in Figure 6-6. Mill construction is a special variety of heavy timber and masonry wall construction used principally for industrial buildings. It is entirely different from ordinary construction because there are no concealed spaces. To qualify, wood timbers must meet certain minimum dimensions. For example, beams and girders must be not less than ten inches deep and six inches thick; columns must be not less than eight inches in any dimension. Loads are carried on beams resting on the outside walls and on heavy wood (sometimes steel) columns. Floors are planks providing an assembly four inches thick.[9] Large, solid pieces of wood are extremely difficult to burn. Thus, a bare wooden beam eight inches by ten inches in diameter ordinarily resists fire damage better than a bare steel beam with the same loadbearing capacity. Although the steel beam will not burn, it will warp and twist in a large fire, and lose its strength. (That is why fire resistive construction requires that structural steel be protected by a layer or layers of fire resistive materials.)

Roof Construction. A fire-spreading weakness in many fire resistive buildings has been the combustibility of the materials used to

Table 6-1

Fire Resistance Requirements for Four-Hour and Three-Hour Fire Resistive Construction*

Building Element	Fire Resistance Rating of Structural Members in Hours — Classification 4-hour	3-hour
Bearing walls or bearing portions of walls, exterior or interior	4	3
Bearing walls and bearing partitions must have adequate stability under fire conditions in addition to the specified fire resistance rating.		
Nonbearing walls or portions of walls, exterior or interior	NC or LC	NC or LC
NC—Noncombustible LC—Limited-Combustible Fire resistance may be required for such walls by conditions such as fire exposure, location with respect to lot lines, occupancy, or other pertinent conditions.		
Principal supporting members including columns, trusses, girders, and beams for one floor or roof only	3	2
Principal supporting members including columns, trusses, girders, and beams for more than one floor or roof	4	3
Secondary floors supporting members, such as the beams, slabs, and joists, not affecting the stability of the building	3	2
Secondary roof supporting members, such as beams, purlins, and slabs, not affecting the stability of the building	2	1½
Interior partitions enclosing stairways and other openings through floors	2	2
One-hour partitions of noncombustible or limited-combustible materials may be permitted under certain conditions.		

*Reprinted with permission from Gordon P. McKinnon, ed., *Fire Protection Handbook*, 14th ed. (Boston: National Fire Protection Association, 1976), p. 6-37.

Figure 6-6

Heavy Timber Construction*

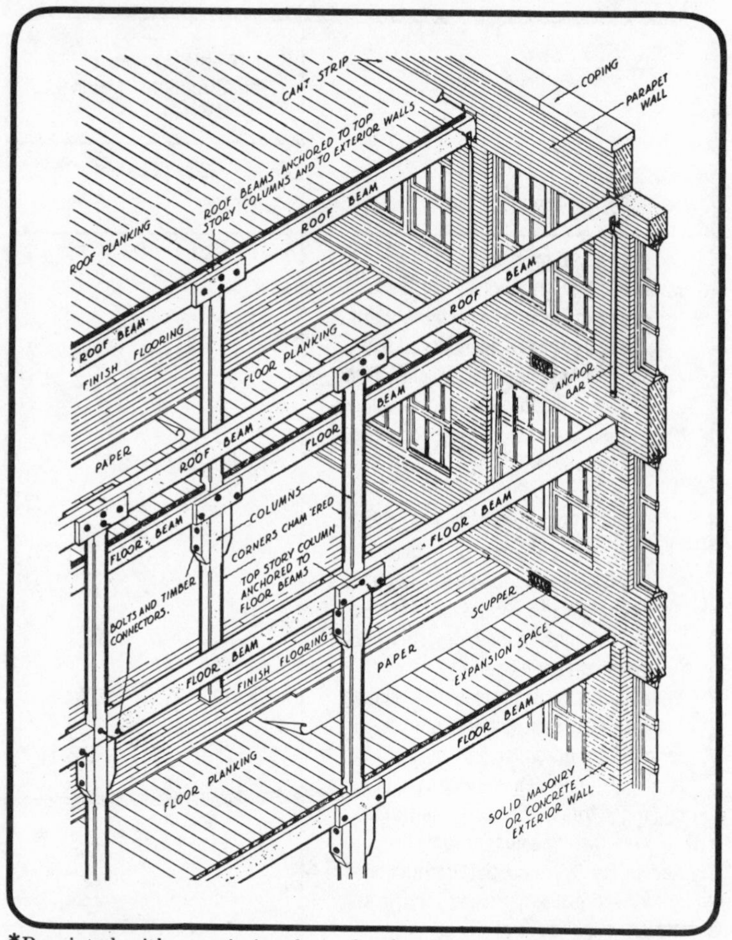

*Reprinted with permission from Gordon P. McKinnon, ed., *Fire Protection Handbook*, 14th ed. (Boston: National Fire Protection Association, 1976), p. 6-41.

coat the roof. In some major fires, such coatings have been a principal factor in fire spread. In particular, asphalt is commonly used to help provide insulation and vapor barriers in the roofs; but heat melts it, and when it oozes onto the undersurface of the roof, it furnishes very readily burning fuel for spreading a fire throughout the building. Wood shingles can also be hazardous.

ISO Definitions of Construction Types. As noted, the preceding discussion of construction types concentrated on those identified by the NFPA. The NFPA definitions are probably those most commonly used in connection with loss control, the subject of the present discussion. It should be noted that various building codes, appraisal guides, or insurance publications use definitions somewhat different from those used by the NFPA. In each case, construction types are categorized according to the needs of those using the classifications.

A different set of construction type definitions is used by the Insurance Services Office (ISO) in determining insurance rates. The ISO definitions which follow are those the ISO intends to adopt for countrywide use in property insurance rate making.

(1) FRAME: Buildings where the exterior walls are wood or other combustible materials, including construction where combustible materials are combined with other materials (such as brick veneer, stone veneer, wood-iron clad, stucco on wood).
(2) JOISTED MASONRY: Buildings where the exterior walls are constructed of masonry materials such as adobe, brick, concrete, gypsum block, hollow concrete block, stone, tile or similar materials, and where the floors and roof are combustible (disregarding floors resting directly on the ground).
(3) NON-COMBUSTIBLE: Buildings where the exterior walls and the floors and roof are constructed of, and supported by metal, asbestos, gypsum, or other non-combustible materials.
(4) MASONRY NON-COMBUSTIBLE: Buildings where the exterior walls are constructed of masonry materials as described in (2) above, with the floors and roof of metal or other non-combustible materials.
(5) MODIFIED FIRE RESISTIVE OR FIRE RESISTIVE: Buildings where the exterior walls and the floors and roof are constructed of masonry or fire resistive materials.[10]

Oxygen, Air Flow, and Related Factors Heat, fuel, and oxygen are prerequisites to a fire. Having discussed heat sources and fuels (in particular, buildings and contents as fuels for fire) the discussion proceeds to the third element of fire—oxygen.

Nearly all fires consist of extremely fast oxidation of materials. Oxidation is a process in which some of the chemical elements of the items burned are released from their original molecules and recombined into compounds containing oxygen. The normal temperature, humidity, pressure, and oxygen of the atmosphere cause some oxidation (e.g., rusting of iron, yellowing of paper). Heat hastens the process; so, often, does an increase in the oxygen supply. (There are a few substances that can burst into flame under ordinary atmospheric conditions, but these, of course, are very special cases.)

Obviously oxidation requires oxygen. The vast majority of fires, hostile and friendly, obtain their necessary supply from ordinary air (about 20 percent of which is oxygen). When they cannot get enough oxygen, they die (are "smothered"). A hot fire tends to develop its own air supply by creating a draft—air heated by the fire rises, leaving a low pressure area below into which fresh air flows.

The more favorable the arrangements for oxygen supply, the faster and better the fire burns, and when there is an abundance of oxygen, fuels flame at lower temperatures. Consequently, oxygen-rich atmospheres (used in oxygen tents in hospitals, for example, and in some industrial processes) increase the probability of a fire.

However, while an ample supply of oxygen-containing air favors flaming, too fast a flow of air can have the reverse effect, as seen in the blowing out of a match or candle. In such a case it is in part the cooling effect of the air flow that reduces the temperature below that required for a self-sustaining fire.

Flammable (Explosive) Range. Fire requires a ratio of fuel vapor to air that is neither too low ("lean") nor too high ("rich"). In an automobile engine an excess of gasoline in proportion to the amount of air can "flood" the engine—a condition brought about by too rich a mixture. On the other hand, if the choke does not operate properly, the gasoline-air mixture may be too lean for the engine to fire.

The *lower flammable limit* is the percentage of vapor below which a fire cannot occur because the mixture is too lean. The *upper flammable limit* is the range above which there is not sufficient air for a fire. The range between the lower flammable limit and the upper flammable limit is the *flammable range* or *explosive range*. For example, low octane gasoline, at room temperature in a normal atmosphere, has a flammable range from 1.4 percent to 7.6 percent.[11] Fires can be prevented if vapor concentrations can be kept below or above the flammable range, or when vapors within this range are kept free from an ignition source. Thus, it is important for firms handling flammable and combustible liquids or gases to be aware of the properties of these materials.

A few substances can burn without an outside oxygen supply. All of these are self-oxidants (e.g., nitrous oxide, nitro cellulose); their physical structure includes enough combined oxygen to support flame for awhile. And a few special chemical combinations can produce fire without any free oxygen.

Effect of Construction Characteristics on Oxygen Supply. The way a building is arranged is important in fire protection. Layout and construction have an effect on creating, stopping, or controlling air flows. In tightly enclosed spaces (e.g., a vault), a fire may be smothered for lack of oxygen, but this is not a practical solution to most building fires. More important is the control of the hot gases rising from the fire. These hot gases heat materials with which they come into contact and the heated materials give off vapors that mix with air drawn in with the fire gases. When the mixture is hot enough and sufficient air is present, flames are created, more heat and gases are generated, and the process compounds itself.

Given sufficient air supply, important factors affecting the speed of fire spread are (1) the presence of fuels above the fire, where the first and most intense heating occurs; and (2) the size of the enclosed space above the fire (in larger spaces heat is dissipated faster; in smaller spaces, heat is more concentrated and temperatures rise more rapidly). Thus, vertical shafts promote spread of flame, particularly when the shafts contain combustible materials.

Loss Control Measures. On the other hand, there are standard fire control measures that utilize concentration of heat rising from a fire. By means of baffles or curtain boards, in conjunction with roof vents, the hot gases may be prevented from spreading throughout the building, and instead be conducted to a roof vent which will remove heat from the building, thus inhibiting fire spread.

When automatic sprinkler systems are in operation, it is usually desirable to get sprinklers immediately above the fire to open quickly (by concentration of heat), and to avoid opening many sprinkler heads at once. Should a considerable number of sprinkler heads open due to the spread of rising heat, many would not be over the fire itself, and water pressure and flow may be reduced in heads over the fire. Such dilution of water concentration can inhibit extinguishing action, allowing the fire to spread.

Counteracting Fire

Once fuel, heat, and oxygen have interacted to start a hostile fire, fire fighting activities can be initiated to hold down loss severity. Usually these operate by removing one or more of the three described fire elements. In addition, it is possible to stop fires by interfering with the chain reaction mechanism in a way proven effective although not yet fully understood.

Removing the Fuel The idea of removing fuel after a fire has started is elementary and generally requires no special explanation. But its usefulness is restricted to those situations in which the fuel feeding the fire is fairly specific and subject to full control. The simplest example is turning off the supply of gas or oil in a line that has ruptured and caught on fire. Fire detection devices frequently used in restaurants shut off the supply of gas to a gas-fired stove or deep-fat fryer when a fire flares up.

A more difficult technique is the creation of a backfire to remove fuel from the path of an oncoming forest or brush fire. This technique has been successfully employed in many forest fires and in some large fires in congested cities.

The special case of dilution of fuel vapor by increasing the flow of air was noted earlier. It has occasional practical application: compressed air blasts can be effective on some fires, and explosives are sometimes used to blow out oil well fires. However, removal of fuel has limited possibilities as a means of fighting fires.

Removing the Heat Most fires are extinguished by cooling. The principal value of water in fighting fire is its strong cooling effect.

Water. When enough water can be applied to hot and burning surfaces, they are cooled below the temperature necessary to maintain combustion. Water absorbs a great deal of heat as it is converted to steam and in addition is able to cling to many substances, thus prolonging the cooling effect.

Water has some limitations as a cooling agent. It conducts electricity, so may be dangerous where there is electrical exposure. Some chemicals react violently with water, burning more actively or even exploding. Water does not wet or mix with some types of fuel. For example, many flammable liquids float on water, so application of water merely makes it easier for such fluids to spread flames over a large area, and burning gases cannot be wet by water. In addition, water does not cling well to some surfaces, and it has limited ability to reach deep inside closely packed materials, such as rolls of paper.

Sometimes, fire fighting with water is hampered by low temperatures, and problems are presented in those special cases where operations or materials are kept at temperatures below freezing. Finally, the storage of water for fire fighting purposes, in piping for automatic sprinklers, and also in tanks and standpipes is restricted to situations in which the water will not freeze while waiting to be used. However, dry-pipe automatic sprinkler systems, or systems containing antifreeze solutions, can be used in freezing temperatures. In a dry-pipe system the sprinkler piping contains only compressed air or gas until a sprinkler head is opened, allowing the air to escape and water to enter the system. Other measures can also prevent freezing, such as heating the storage tanks or using a pump to keep water in circulation.

Other Cooling Agents. There are other cooling agents. Sand, for example, when spread thoroughly over a burning surface, can act to cool it. Clearly, it is more difficult to get solid materials, such as sand, to reach and stay in contact with many burning surfaces than it is to get water (or other liquids) to do so. Nevertheless, there is one class of fires in which the cooling effect of solid particles is preferable to the use of water. Some combustible metals react violently with water; some are partially or completely self-oxidizing, so smothering does not work; some have both characteristics. For fires in many of these difficult cases, special extinguishing powders are available—different powders for different metals. Some of their effect is by cooling; some is by smothering; and some by breaking the chain reaction, depending on the powder and the type of burning metal.

Inert gases can get into small spaces better than solids or even water and can have some cooling effect. However, most of their efficacy depends on smothering (discussed below). As previously noted, ventilation is also commonly used to remove heated gases from a burning building.

Removing the Oxygen Smothering fires—interfering with their supply of oxygen—is a standard fire fighting method, especially in fires where water has an adverse reaction. Covering the fire in a pan of grease or snuffing a candle are examples of extinguishment by removal of oxygen. The use of smothering foam on major oil fires applies the same principle.

Removal of oxygen is also the principle by which carbon dioxide (CO_2) fire extinguishers work. The CO_2 or other inert gas dilutes the oxygen available to support a fire. To be completely effective, separation of fuel and oxygen must be accompanied by enough cooling of the fuel to avoid reignition when the oxygen block ceases. This point limits the usefulness of CO_2 for ordinary fires; after the flames have been extinguished, ordinary materials often retain heat longer than a blanket of CO_2 lasts. When oxygen again reaches such materials, they can reignite.

The smothering effect of foams, however, lasts longer and since foams include water, they also cool hot surfaces. Also, foam is less dense than any of the flammable liquids. Unlike water, foam can float on top of (and smother and cool) fires in liquids. Because they contain some water, however, foams are not suitable for electrical fires, or for fires in materials that react violently with water.

Breaking the Chain Reaction Experimentation uncovered the possibility of extinguishing fire with certain chemicals, such as some halogenated hydrocarbons (halogens or "Halon") and inert salts (dry chemicals). Apparently these work by interfering with the chemistry of chain reaction in a fire rather than by either cooling or smothering. Since some of these chemicals are toxic or corrosive in varying ways, care is necessary in their selection and use.

Many of the halogenated extinguishing agents, because they are either gases or liquids which rapidly vaporize in fire, leave little corrosive or abrasive residue after use. Another advantage is that they have less toxic effect than many other extinguishing agents. (Carbon dioxide, for example, would smother people when applied in sufficient concentration to smother fires.) Because halogenated agents inflict little, if any, damage to property when released and because of their low toxicity, these agents are frequently used to protect such things as computer equipment or computer rooms where evacuation of employees would be difficult. A disadvantage, however, is that Halon extinguishing agents are quite expensive.

Dry chemicals are very effective in extinguishing flames that can be reached with these chemicals and many can be used on electrical fires and flammable liquids. This effectiveness and versatility, plus ease of application, have made them popular for general use. The principal disadvantages of dry chemicals are limited penetrating power, low cooling effect, and production of a sticky residue which may damage some equipment. In order to obtain cooling, water or foam may be used. However, many foams and dry chemicals are incompatible and combinations of these must be chosen carefully.

Applying Fire Control Principles

Fires that have begun to burn can be counteracted by removal of heat, fuel, oxygen, or by breaking the chemical chain reaction. While post-loss control is important, pre-loss control is no less important. This section on applying fire control principles will discuss some of the pre-loss means available to prevent the occurrence of fires or to reduce the frequency of their occurrence.

The lines of attack to apply fire loss control principles are fairly obvious. Loss by fire is readily subject to analysis according to the energy transfer principles discussed in CPCU 1. Devices and procedures can be applied to control the buildup and release of energy, to separate released energy (hostile fire) from damageable subjects, to install less damageable subjects, and to counteract the burning process once it has gotten under way.

Controlling Heat Sources Much fire loss may be prevented by having no buildup of heat energy in heat sources not necessary to operations. For example, appropriate rules and procedures should be enforced in connection with smoking, personal cooking and heating equipment, and burning trash.

Planned Heat Sources. The necessity of planned heat sources should be questioned. Are all the sources planned for energy actually required? With sources in which heat is an unwanted by-product, can storage of the heated material or use of the heat-producing process be avoided by practical alternative arrangements?

The second question is equally important: Where there must be energy, has care been taken not to have more than is necessary? Are electrical devices overheated? Are more furnaces, forges, kilns, or whatever, in use than necessary? Are fires larger or hotter than necessary? Are there flames where something else (e.g., hot water) will do? By asking these questions, it may be possible to identify planned heat sources that can be reduced or eliminated.

Heat as a By-Product. When heat is an unwanted by-product, a variety of options is often available. In lighting, fluorescent tubes are cooler than incandescent bulbs. Machines differ in the amount of friction they create. Clearly, with self-heating materials and supplies, quantities stored should be controlled and separation of such materials into smaller amounts at segregated locations may be possible.

The release of heat energy can be controlled by dissipating heat slowly through some kind of cooling. That the atmosphere around hot processes should be kept cool seems obvious, but only methodical, step-by-step analysis gives good assurance such a move will not be overlooked.

Electrical Heat Energy. The rate and path of release of electrical energy can be controlled with proper or automatic circuit breakers and adequate grounding. Grounding can be used both to protect power circuits and to control static electricity created by moving machinery, liquids, and dust. It also applies to the mightiest "unplanned" electrical source—lightning—which can be grounded by lightning rods.

Separation of Fuel and Heat Keeping fuels and heat separated is a major means of fire loss control. Two aspects may be identified: (1) separation of friendly fires or heat sources from fuel to which they might spread, and (2) separation of additional fuel on which a hostile fire might feed from the fuel it has already reached. Separation can be accomplished by distance and by noncombustible barriers.

Separation—Friendly Fires or Heat Sources. The techniques that may be used to prevent friendly fires or heat sources from becoming a source of hostile fire vary, depending on whether the heat sources are planned or unplanned, fixed or mobile.

FIXED LOCATION PLANNED HEAT SOURCES. When fixed location planned heat sources have been identified, flammable or combustible materials must be kept away from them. The NFPA, Factory Mutuals, Industrial Risk Insurers, and others have developed standards that serve as a guide. Some involve only common sense. For example, the furnace room is not the place to keep trash, paper stocks, or janitors' materials. Other standards require more specific information. Building timbers and wood partitions should not be too close to furnaces and flues, but how close is too close? Here, recommendations are available from the above sources and should be followed.

With cooking stoves, the major fuel hazard comes from cooking oils, greases, and fats in foods. Besides the immediate exposure, there is a buildup of greasy deposits in hoods and flues—a frequent factor in restaurant fires. Regular removal of the deposits is indicated as a standard fire protection measure.

With electrical equipment, the first and most important separation device is insulation of wiring, of motor compartments, of switches, and so on. Where there is or may be arcing, common sense again dictates separation from flammable materials. Finely divided particles of any kind may provide fuel for a fire, including lints, metal dusts and shavings. Lubricating greases and oils are other obvious fuels. (It follows that finely divided particles that are oily compound the exposure.) These items may also be fuel for fires started by mechanical friction (e.g., overheated bearing), and if they do not help a fire get started, they are certain to help it spread after it has started.

MOBILE PLANNED HEAT SOURCES. Mobile planned heat sources are a significant problem in fire loss control. Welding and cutting torches are a frequent cause of fires, and portable heaters of various kinds are also significant. Even an ordinary flashlight can ignite a fire in an explosive atmosphere. "Explosion-proof" flashlights are designed for such applications.

With fixed planned sources, buildings, equipment, and operations can be designed to keep fuels away. Since the exposure does not change rapidly, the plans are relatively easy to manage effectively. But with mobile equipment, the specific exposures keep changing. The equipment has to be taken where it is needed, and those places are not restricted to areas free of fuels. Furthermore, there is a major psychological difficulty in that people are less impressed with the need to take elaborate precautions for an exposure that is going to last only a few minutes or even a few hours. If it takes, say, fifteen to thirty minutes to make an area thoroughly safe for a repair job that will last an hour and involve perhaps only several minutes of torch work, with another fifteen to thirty minutes to restore the area to operational condition, it can be difficult to get operators, and even supervisors, to take full care. Furthermore, under a variety of possible circumstances, it may be difficult to phrase rules and procedures that always define adequately what "full care" means.

UNPLANNED HEAT SOURCES. With unplanned sources of heat, the obvious approaches are prohibition and restriction, as in having "no smoking" areas and, possibly, areas specifically reserved for "smoke breaks." Employees' hot plates or coffee makers may be prohibited or restricted in number or size, and there may be a supporting practice of providing convenient alternatives in planned lunchrooms or coffee nooks. There should be a set of procedures for anticipating and handling unusual situations such as the disposal of trash during a collectors' strike or the provision of temporary heat or power to a critical operation when its regular supply has been cut off.

Separation—Hostile Fires. If friendly fires or heat sources are not adequately separated from fuel, the result may be a hostile fire. The severity of hostile fires may be reduced by effective building design.

Separation of fuel from heat may be by clear space, by barriers, or both. Within a building, how much clear space may be interposed between heat sources and possible fuels depends on the building's area relative to the space needed for storage and equipment. Inadequate space often means that materials will be crowded together and too close to heat sources. Increasing building size beyond minimum operational requirements ordinarily does not do much to separate heat from fuel effectively. When a fire does get started in some materials, its chance to reach more can be increased when there is a lot more material in the same building. Large open spaces within buildings can spawn large fires. Indeed, this is one of the most basic propositions in fire loss control.

Space is enlarged (or reduced) in two ways: in vertical height and in horizontal floor area. Since the hot air and gases generated in a fire generally rise, heating whatever they encounter, increased height is somewhat worse than increased floor area.

LIMITING VERTICAL FIRE SPREAD. Fire spread can be encouraged by vertical openings that allow heat to rise past combustible property. The most frequent examples of such vertical openings are stairwells and elevator shafts, ducts and flues, and openings used to allow pipes and wiring to get from floor to floor. Windows can also contribute to the spread of fire from one floor to another as the fire shoots out one window and in the next one above. This action is called "looping."

Another major type of exposure involves high stacking in storage. In hundreds of warehouses (and in many stores), goods in cardboard containers are stacked up, row above row, for dozens of feet. Fires that start in lower rows are thus well supplied with fuel on which to grow. Whiskey warehouses, containing alcohol in well-seasoned wood containers, present the same type of exposure but with even greater intensity, as do some drying sheds and lumber yards.

Limiting vertical rise of fire is of prime importance in designing buildings for fire loss control. Of course, it is also important to maintain the integrity of fire barriers originally designed into a building. Although this should seem obvious, it is frequently violated in practice.

Conveyor belts may be installed to deliver goods from one floor to another, piercing what was a fire resistive floor. Electrical, plumbing, or heating equipment may be installed leaving a large rough-cut opening through which fire can spread. Fire doors originally installed may be damaged or may suffer from improper maintenance.

Openings through which building service lines (pipes, wires, ducts) pass should be filled with adequate noncombustible material. Of course, air ducts are designed for movement of air through the building, and when a hostile fire occurs, its hot gases can move the same way. Therefore, insertion of movable stops (fire dampers) in all but the smallest ducts is recommended. These may be actuated by various fire-sensing devices.

Interior spaces in hollow walls and below floors (above ceilings) are other weak points. Finished walls in any type of construction may have open spaces, but wood framing provides the standard case. Open spaces between the floor of one story and the ceiling of the story below are standard features of frame and ordinary construction and are common in finished areas of other types. There are three reasons such spaces contribute significantly to spread of fire:

1. Being concealed, fire in these spaces can burn for a considerable time before it is noticed.
2. These spaces commonly contain some quantities of combustible debris, including dirt and dust.
3. With only a limited volume of air to heat, a fire in a small, contained space produces higher temperatures than it would in the open (like a fire in a stove, for example).

For these reasons, fire-stops should be inserted. These are solid pieces running from support to support of the wall or floor. In frame buildings, fire-stops inside walls often are wood two-by-fours, running horizontally from stud to stud. Although such stops are combustible, they do not burst into flame easily and they accomplish the purpose of delaying the flow of heat.

Attics are also hazardous for the same reasons. In addition, they are in the route of rising heat. In row buildings, for example, fires starting in one structure have bypassed brick walls by spreading through the common attic. Here again, while good fire resistive materials are best in the dividers, lighter materials can delay spread until fire fighters control the original fire.

Spread of heat through an attic or along the underside of any roof or ceiling can sometimes be reduced by venting, which protects by cooling (controlling the rate of release of fire energy) and by directing the flow of heat into the open, away from combustibles in the building (a form of separation of heat from fuel). Built-in venting can also prevent the problem of sudden flaming when fire fighters vent the building after a fire in it has already heated the interior.

Looping of fire from one story to the next through exterior windows is less common but can be serious. The generally recommended controls are metal framing with wired glass or other installations that will not readily burn out, soften, or fall out in high heat. Staggering the lines of windows may help. Another device is installation of parapets that extend out between in-line windows.

LIMITING HORIZONTAL FIRE SPREAD. A fire may spread horizontally almost as easily at it spreads vertically, and in the presence of readily flammable materials, there is no significant difference. (In bowling alleys, for example, the alley surfaces have sometimes supported flash spread, so that in a few minutes the whole playing area was involved.) Nearly all materials used to make walls, partitions, or doors in buildings have some value in slowing fire spread. (Unwired glass panels are a major exception.) Even a wood stud partition with a half inch of bare fir plywood on each side has a standard test rating of twenty minutes. Many plaster or wallboard partitions with wood studs test at one hour. Even twenty minutes can make a large difference in the effectiveness of prompt fire fighting; in most fires, an hour's resistance means a contained fire. The problem, however, is that fires are not always noticed right away, and then the difference between combustible and fire resistive barriers is quite significant.

As with vertical separation, adequate horizontal separation calls for barriers with no holes for heat to get through. The ideal is an unbroken wall that extends from the floor at the lowest level through and beyond the roof, with no windows near it in the exterior walls. Next in desirability is a wall with openings properly protected. In the case of doors, they should shut automatically whenever not actually in use ("self-closing doors") or be arranged to close themselves in the presence of fire heat ("automatic fire doors"). Automatic fire doors are illustrated in Figure 6-7. All materials protecting any type of opening should have adequate fire resistance rating, of course, and automatically closing equipment must not be blocked or rendered inoperable. Unfortunately, such blockage or interference is fairly common practice. A fire wall with an open door or other considerable opening is hardly more of a fire-stop than a wall of combustible materials, occasionally even less (depending on how long it takes the fire to find the opening—a process which may be speeded by the opening's providing an exhaust channel for fire gases).

When equipment (such as a conveyor line) makes solid closure impossible, special water spray protection can be used. Special sprinklers are also needed where shafts cannot be fully enclosed (as with

Figure 6-7
Automatic Door Equipment*

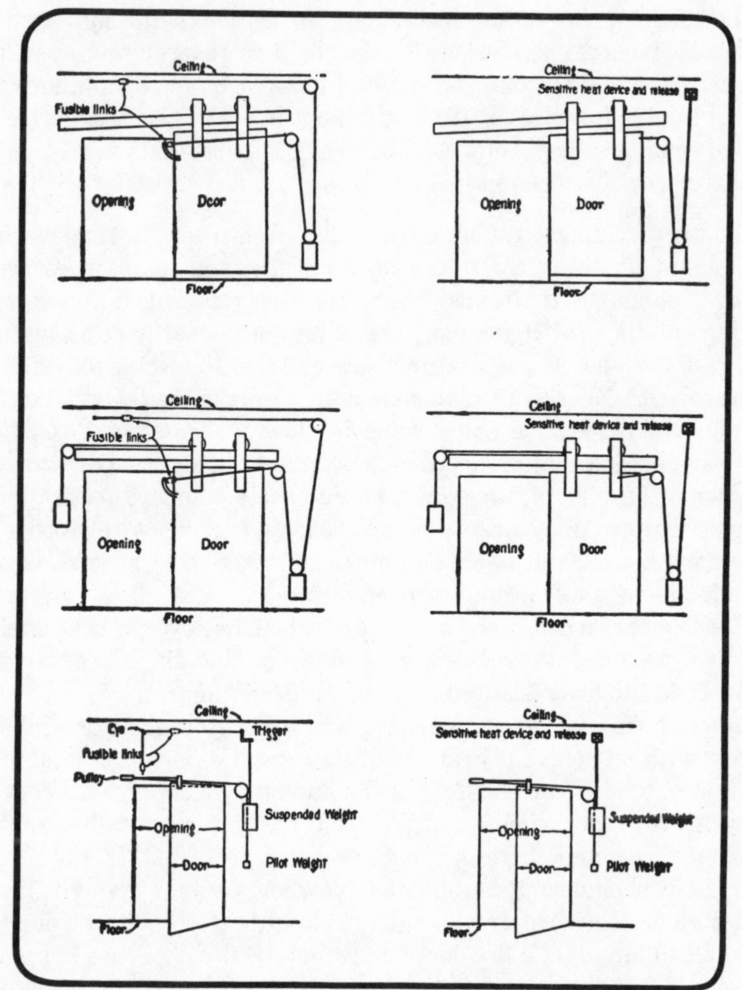

*Reprinted with permission from Charles A. Tuck, Jr., ed., *NFPA Inspection Manual,* 4th ed. (Boston: National Fire Protection Association, 1976), p. 260.

escalators, for example). Outside sprinkler heads may be used to help protect window openings in the event of a fire from outside the building.

FULL SEPARATION. When one space is sufficiently separated from another, the two are called separate "fire divisions." A self-supporting solid wall the full width and height (including lowest basement) of the building (plus adequate extensions [parapets] beyond any combustible roofs or walls), with appropriate fire resistance rating, is a "fire wall" and separates a building into fire divisions. Under most circumstances, a fire, even a very severe one, will not pass a fire wall. (There is another type of divider, less strong, and usually not extending from basement to roof, called a "fire partition." Although it can reduce the spread of fire, a fire partition does not create fire divisions.)

The other way to create a fire division or its equivalent is by outdoor open space separating two buildings. The amount of space necessary for reliable separation depends on the possible intensity of the exposing fire, the combustibility of the surfaces (walls and roofs), and the size and nature of windows and other openings in both buildings. The relative heights of two exposing buildings is also a factor. Common standards for adequacy of clear spaces regularly assume that fire fighters will arrive and be able to help protect the exposed building. When this is not the case, the amount of clear space required is much greater. (A fire in Massachusetts spread 100 feet across a river and upwind to ignite another building.)[12]

In addition, the clear space needs to be *clear*. Too frequently the value of open spaces has been compromised to the point where their effectiveness is all but destroyed by their being cluttered with combustible yard storage, small structures, etc., or by allowing grass and brush to grow between the structures.[13]

Protected openings in a fire wall significantly reduce the reliability of the wall as a fire barrier, since there is no assurance that the protection will be properly in place when needed. Therefore, the possible spread of a fire from one side of the wall to the other (i.e., no actual fire division) must be taken into account.

The protection of external openings and exposed surfaces against communication of fire or heat across a clear space increases the effectiveness of the clear area. Among the recommended devices are water spray, steel shutters, and wired glass in metal frames.

Naturally, full separation is desirable between hazardous fire sources and less hazardous operations, such as between manufacturing and office occupancies, and between operations involving materials with low ignition temperatures and other materials.

A special type of full separation is provided by the fire resistive vault. Valuable records, money, securities, jewelry, furs, or fine arts enclosed in a fire resistive vault can often survive destruction of the rest of the building. Such fire protection also provides some protection against other perils. For full protection, the vault must not only resist entry of flame; it must also insulate the contents against increase of temperature within the vault to the point where contents can ignite or be damaged. It also must withstand rupture from collapse of the containing building. (Lesser degrees of protection, as in a fire resistive file with, say, one-hour fire resistance are, of course, an improvement over ordinary cabinets or open filing with respect to fire damage.) Safes and vaults will be discussed in greater detail in Chapter 11.

Physical separation between records and duplicates of them, at totally different locations, is often the most practical method of controlling fire loss from damage to an organization's valuable papers and records.

Reducing Damageability A major method of fire control is substitution of noncombustible for combustible materials. With respect to the major components of building—as in the differences among wood frame, ordinary masonry, noncombustible, and fire resistive construction—this is obvious. It is also generally recognized in connection with special hazards, such as flammable and combustible liquids and gases. Combustibility is less frequently considered with ordinary property, such as desks and chairs. The use of steel instead of wood, or of heavy materials rather than light, can reduce damageability. Of course, the gain in resistance to fire (and other) damage, compared to the increase in cost of the safer equipment, is commonly much smaller in low hazard occupancies (such as offices) than in more hazardous ones. Combustibility of buildings and contents has not necessarily decreased in recent years with the increased use of plastic furnishings and structural components.

Reducing Fire Severity Once a hostile fire has begun, effective counteraction requires that it be detected and extinguished. Detection can be accomplished by a visual sighting and a voice alarm (employee sees the fire and yells "fire") or through simple or sophisticated automatic smoke or fire detection systems.

The two chief ways in which hostile fires are extinguished are through the use of automatic extinguishing systems and through the use of trained fire fighting personnel. Either way, rapid response is essential.

The major virtue of automatic extinguishing systems is that, when properly designed, installed, and maintained, they provide effective response with more reliability than any other device or procedure. The major drawback to trained fire fighting is the frequent delay in getting proper personnel, equipment, and supplies to the scene. The most frequent cause of this delay is in getting notification to the fire fighters that they are needed.

First Aid. Fire fighting efforts are generally divided into two classes: immediate, simple, limited efforts, sometimes called first aid fire fighting; and fully trained and fully equipped efforts. The former can be accomplished by regular personnel of the organization. Portable fire extinguishers or standpipes and hoses may effectively combat a small fire. Turning off fuel supplies and electrical power and closing fire-stops are some other possible first aid measures.

Reliance on first aid fire fighting has some serious dangers. Delay is a big problem. There is a common tendency to delay action other than first aid on the assumption that simple, limited measures will quickly extinguish the fire. As a result, there may be failure to get people out of endangered premises and delay in notification of fully trained and equipped fire fighters. Thus, when "first aid" measures are inadequate, both personal injury and property damage losses can be greatly magnified.

Users of fire extinguishers often have no training in such use. This can cause further delay while they discover how to use the equipment (or even have to discover where the equipment is) or fail to use it effectively. Untrained personnel may also use the wrong type of fire extinguisher on a fire. A fire extinguisher may be relied on to extinguish only the type of fire for which it is labeled. The various types of fire extinguisher ratings are illustrated in Figure 6-8. Fire extinguishers should also be periodically inspected and maintained to assure their operation when needed. Even trained "first aiders" are sometimes subject to another problem, having been shown only the effectiveness of the equipment, not its ineffectiveness.

Training in the use of extinguishers is important and should include instructions to all employees to see that immediate notice of any fire is given to supervisors responsible for personnel safety and to the fire brigade or fire department, regardless of first aid efforts. The training should include drills on transmitting such notice. Of course, means for prompt notice have to be available. Also, supervisors must be skilled in (not just "know") evacuation rules and procedures. Nonsupervisory employees generally should also be given practice and/or training in using fire extinguishers and in proper exit procedures.

Trained Fire Fighters. The "fully trained and equipped fire fighting personnel" may be a private fire brigade or public fire department. It is not enough for fire fighters to be fully trained—they must also be fully equipped. Inadequate water pressure and/or volume are all too frequently encountered. Other frequent problems for trained and equipped fire fighters are blank walls that impede entrance and bad weather (high winds and extremely cold or extremely hot, dry atmospheres).

A handicap that sometimes arises with large and special exposures is failure to acquaint public fire department personnel with plant layout, hazards, and fire fighting resources ahead of time. This lack of preplanning delays effective counteraction (and sometimes even leads to ineffective or dangerous courses of action) when fire does occur. For example, a public fire department may apply water to a substance that violently reacts with water. Or a fire department may fail to hook its pumper to a hidden siamese sprinkler connection to boost water pressure

Figure 6-8
Types of Fire Extinguishers*

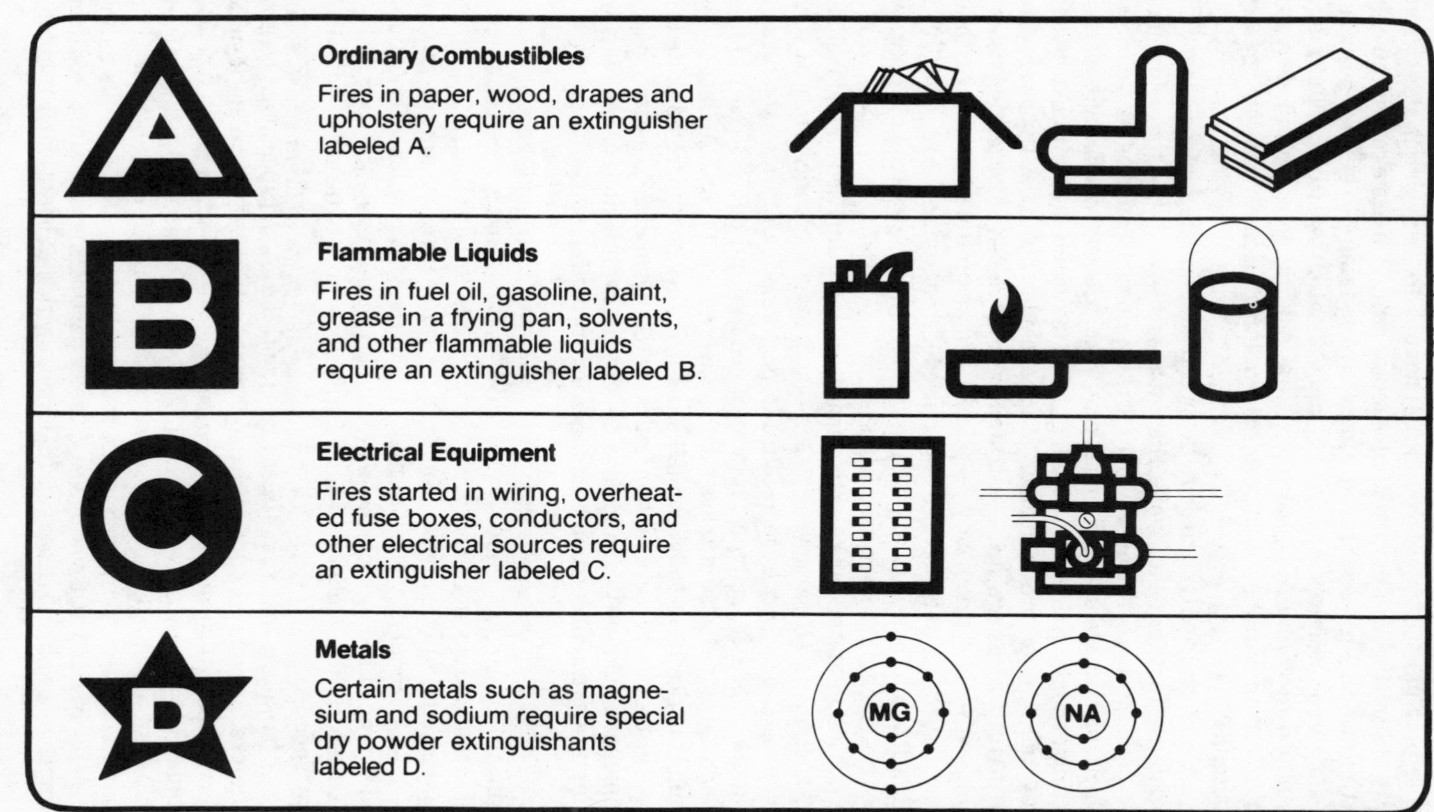

*Reprinted with permission from "This Is Your ABCD's of Portable Fire Extinguishers" (Boston: National Fire Protection Association, 1976).

at the sprinkler heads. Fire fighting personnel can get lost or trapped in an unfamiliar building.

Personnel responsible for fire safety can develop preplanning programs in cooperation with their local fire department. Fire departments are usually happy to assist in such an endeavor. Among the items which should be considered in preplanning are informing the fire department of building floor plans, locations of exits, areas where hazardous materials are stored, and which valuable files should be removed from the building if at all possible.

Delays in getting adequate equipment and personnel to a fire sometimes occur because of traffic or because resources are already tied up elsewhere. However, most delays are caused by delays in alarm. Therefore, automatic alarms are desirable for all situations in which there is special flammability or damageability of property or danger to life.

Alarms and Detection Devices. Fire detection or alarm services include (1) the manual fire alarm found in the halls of many buildings, (2) automatic smoke detection devices, (3) automatic heat detection devices, and (4) water-flow alarms that are actuated when water begins to flow through a sprinkler system because a sprinkler head has opened.

Once an automatic or manual alarm has been actuated, it signals one or more of the following types of alarm systems:

1. A *local system* sounds an alarm inside and/or outside the protected property, thus alerting the occupants to a fire.
2. A *remote station system* conducts the alarm to equipment in a remote station such as a fire or police station where someone is always on duty.
3. *Central station systems* are owned, operated, and maintained by a private concern which, on observing the alarm, will notify the fire department and may also send their own investigator to the scene of the alarm. Central station alarm companies generally provide high quality service and see to it that the transmission lines between the protected premises and the alarm company are in operation at all times.
4. *Proprietary systems* are similar to central station systems but differ in that the alarm is received at a central office on the protected property.
5. *Auxiliary systems* conduct the signal from a detection or alarm device to actuate a fire alarm box on a circuit of a municipal fire alarm system.[14]

Of these types of alarm systems, many feel the central station service is best (when available) because the system is continually monitored by the alarm company. However, there are many other circumstances which come into play in determining the type of alarm system most useful in a given situation.

For firms with low-hazard levels for both people and property, probabilities as to fire frequency and speed of spread are often considered too low to warrant the expense of automatic alarm systems. But where danger is greater—e.g., to people in schools, hospitals, hotels, theaters, night clubs, department and other large stores; or to property wherever there are readily flammable materials, concentrated property values, or large undivided areas—automatic detection and/or extinguishing systems are of prime importance in loss control. In fact, such detection and extinguishing systems are required by many building codes.

Automatic Sprinkler Systems. Automatic sprinkler systems have an impressive record in limiting fire loss severity. (Of course, they have little effect on loss frequency since sprinklers are usually activated only after a fire has begun.) According to NFPA data published in 1976, 117,770 fires in sprinklered buildings have been reported since 1897. Of these, 95 percent of the sprinklers showed satisfactory performance. Because many small fires extinguished by one or two sprinkler heads go unreported, it is possible that the actual performance record may approach 100 percent effectiveness.[15]

In cases where sprinklers have not been effective, the deficiency is almost always due to causes that could have been corrected, as illustrated in Figure 6-9.

A primary cause of automatic sprinkler ineffectiveness is failure to keep the sprinklers turned on. Some fire protection engineers suggest that sprinkler valves be chained and locked in an open position. It is further possible to attach to the sprinkler valve a sensing device that sounds an alarm when a sprinkler valve is tampered with. (This can be of particular value when an arsonist attempts to defeat a sprinkler system by closing the sprinkler valve before setting a fire.)

Another common deficiency is partial sprinkler protection. If a fire starts in or spreads to an unprotected area, a blaze may develop of such intensity that the sprinkler heads in the protected area cannot effectively extinguish the resulting blaze. However, proper design and maintenance can overcome or greatly mitigate these problems. And, as mentioned in an earlier section, sprinklers can be specially designed to reduce transmission of fire through unenclosed openings and from one building to another.

Controlling Loss from Arson For loss control, arson cases must be divided into crimes *against* the property owner and crimes *by* the property owner. While insurers need to consider the possibility of both

Figure 6-9
Reasons for Unsatisfactory
Sprinkler Performance*

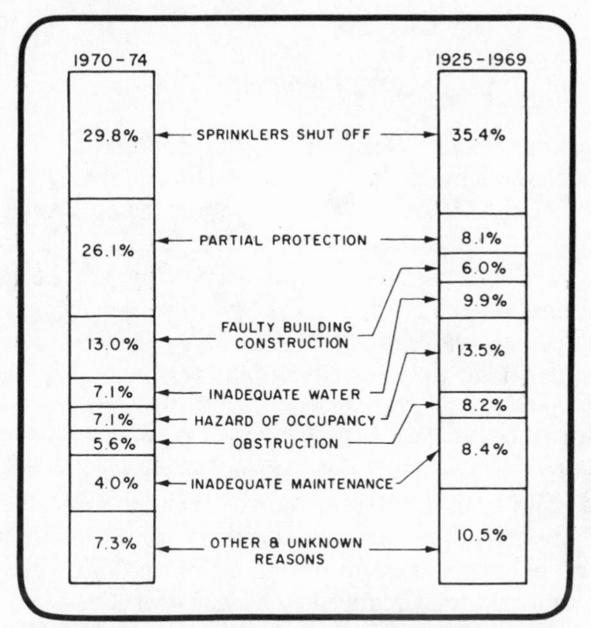

*Reprinted with permission from Gordon P. McKinnon, ed., *Fire Protection Handbook*, 14th ed. (Boston: National Fire Protection Association, 1976), p. 14-5.

types of cases, only crimes against the owner will be considered in this discussion of risk management devices other than insurance. (Arson by the owner would not be a fortuitous loss cause.)

Arson loss severity can be limited with the same types of loss control devices used to limit severity of other hostile fires—sprinklers, alarms, fire walls, and so forth. In addition to normal loss control measures, other measures are particularly useful in combating the arson hazard.

The chance of an effective arson attempt is reduced when an arsonist's opportunity to enter the premises is made difficult and when the presence of an intruder will be quickly detected. Locks, guards, alarms, and other systems effective in protecting against forcible entry of a burglar can also serve to prevent entry by an arsonist. Of course, it is necessary that areas vulnerable to an arsonist be protected, as well as those areas attractive to a thief. Loss control measures for crime losses will be discussed in greater detail in Chapter 11.

Sprinkler valves, fire alarm control devices, and similar protective devices can be protected so that any tampering by an arsonist will sound an alarm. Although such alarms may not eliminate the arsonist's opportunity to set a fire, they can reduce the amount of time during which the arsonist can work undisturbed and may send fire fighters to the scene even before the fire has been started. Any device that restricts entry or reduces the amount of time during which a would-be arsonist can work uninterrupted can reduce the chance of arson loss.

Controlling Water Damage Most fire fighting is done with water, and occasionally the water causes more property damage than the fire. (Of course, if there had been no water, the fire would have done more damage—an elementary point that is sometimes overlooked.) Also, automatic sprinklers sometimes release water when there is no fire, with some resultant damage. (Plumbing systems sometimes break or overflow, spreading water which results in the same type of damage.) Control of water damage is therefore of interest in property loss control.

Again control starts with sources. With sprinkler systems an obvious point is proper design, installation, and maintenance. There are various ways to design automatic sprinkler systems so they are less likely to respond to stimuli from sources other than hostile fires. For example, there are differing temperatures at which different sprinkler heads will open. Sprinkler heads should be chosen that will not respond to ambient temperatures produced by normal operations, and vulnerable sprinkler heads can have guards which reduce the probability of accidental damage.

Also important in reducing water damage loss severity is to provide means for water to move out of the building with minimum damage. Impermeable floors and drains and scuppers to channel the water outside are common means of control.

Most sprinkler systems have water-flow alarms which sound when water begins to flow through the system. Their primary purpose is to serve as a fire alarm. However, such alarms are also useful in providing prompt notification of an accidental discharge from a sprinkler system. In addition, sprinklers can be designed to withhold or interrupt water flow unless combinations of stimuli are received that confirm the presence of a hostile fire rather than something else. For example, there is a sprinkler head which automatically resets itself (shuts itself off) when the temperature cools. This type of head could thus automatically extinguish a small fire and then cease spraying. Due to their expense, such heads are not frequently used.

When there is a fire and valuable property is exposed to water damage from fire hoses, crews trained and equipped to put waterproof covers in place can greatly reduce loss severity. Of course, it is ordinary wisdom not to place water damageable property in basements or in lower floors below upper stories where there is serious fire hazard or other cause of water exposure.

Finally, where the possible loss from water damage is large, automatic extinguishing systems containing CO_2, dry chemicals, Halon, foam, or systems that emit water in a very fine spray ("fogging systems") may be used. (Even though foam and fogging systems contain water, it is so finely divided that it creates little or no effect on many materials that are damaged by water in its usual form.)

Experience has shown that the danger of water damage from sprinklers has often been overestimated. Electronic data processing equipment, for example, is often considered to be highly damageable by water from sprinklers. Experience with modern EDP equipment has shown otherwise.

Personnel Safety in Fires Because this is a text on property loss exposures, most of the discussion of fire loss control deals with property damage. But no discussion of the factors in origin, spread, and control of fires is adequate without special attention to personnel protection.

The key to personnel safety in hostile fires, beyond not having such fires in the first place (fire prevention), is separation; i.e., keeping the people away from fires that do occur. This in turn involves containing fires in areas away from the people and moving the people away from areas where a fire is in progress (evacuation). The first of these approaches is adequate only where fire containment is absolutely assured, a condition nearly impossible to guarantee in advance. Because of this and because a fire is always possible where people are, evacuation must always be contemplated and prearranged.

Contrary to popular belief, a majority of fire deaths are caused, not by burns, but by asphyxiation and smoke inhalation. Thus, it is important not only to protect personnel from the heat of a fire, but also from the toxic gases generated by a fire. Evacuation is often the best way to accomplish this.

Safety of evacuation depends on how much faster the people can be moved out than the fire can spread. The speed of evacuation depends on (1) speed of notice that evacuation is to commence, (2) the ability of the exit routes to speed movement, and (3) the behavior of the people in the evacuation process.

Speed of notice to the fire department has already been touched on in discussion of fire fighting responses to fire. Even more important is the necessity for prompt notice to the occupants of a burning building.

Ability of exit routes to speed movement is a function of distance to be traversed and number of people that can be handled at once. Obviously, long or narrow exit routes cause delays. Dark or unusual routes, or routes with mechanical difficulties (e.g., steep stairs, vertical ladders, slippery surfaces) also slow exit.

The behavior of people is widely known to be a critical factor in safe evacuation. In several notorious cases, panic has caused scores of injuries and deaths. A May 1977 fire at the Beverly Hills Supper Club in Southgate, Kentucky illustrates the problems that can be caused by panic. Shortly after 9:00 P.M. a busboy interrupted an act by two comedians to announce that there was a small fire in the kitchen and to ask everyone to leave the building. Many ignored the warning until smoke, billowing from behind closed doors, prompted a stampede toward the exits. The scene became pandemonium, and when it was over the huge nightclub was gutted and 164 were dead, victims of burns, trampling, and smoke inhalation.[16] In a 1974 fire in a modern skyscraper office building in Brazil, many persons were trapped in stories above the blaze. Many of the 189 deaths were caused by leaps from windows, some of them after the fire had been brought under control.

Fire protection specialists have noted that people commonly try to leave a public place by the door, elevator, or staircase through which they entered, even though that route is dangerous and others are safe. Fire gases and smoke can impair both thinking and motor control. All these factors affect efficiency of evacuation. The longer a fire and its dangerous products—heat, smoke, gases—can be kept from the people and their exit routes, the more likely a safe evacuation. Not the least of the reasons for this is reduced likelihood of panic.

Personnel safety is also, of course, a function of fire control. A fire put out in minutes by an automatic sprinkler, for example, is unlikely to cause personal injury. But an uncontrolled fire that persists and grows presents a threat, both directly (by actually causing injury) and indirectly (by inducing panic). Worst, of course, are fires that attack exit routes. This is why protection of stair openings (a natural channel of fire spread) is crucial, and fire resistive protection of stairs is among the requirements for many types of property.

Rapid spread of flame by decorative surfaces, trim, and furnishings is a serious hazard for safe exit. Many such items, particularly upholstery and plastics, produce toxic fumes, compounding the difficulty.

High-rise office buildings and apartments are nearly impossible to evacuate totally, especially if persons are at levels higher than that of the fire. The solution has to be provision of zones safely away from the fire, getting the people into them, and convincing them of their safety while there. This can be difficult. Besides building construction adequate to contain the fire against vertical spreading, it is necessary to have adequate facilities, such as standpipes, for fire fighters to put out fires which cannot be reached from the exterior of the building.

Hospitals and some other institutions have a problem when

evacuation of some patients or inmates is to be avoided. For these, a safely separated area is needed. In some cases only lateral movement is required, avoiding the problems of stairs. But there still must be a safe way to move out of the building should that need arise.

After the Fire Is Out Loss control continues to be possible after a fire is out. Property losses can be minimized by good salvage techniques, and business interruption losses can be minimized by the use of alternate resources.

Fire salvage is a specialized skill. For anyone who rarely deals with fire losses, the services of an experienced salvor are needed. The salvor may be supplied by an insurer or hired directly.

Alternate resources may be arranged in advance by having standby or underutilized equipment and facilities at another location. For some organizations, competitors' facilities may be available; occasionally there is even an informal pre-loss understanding of mutual aid in this respect. More often vacant facilities will have to be found, refurbished, and adapted to the organization's needs. Of course, temporary operation requires financing in addition to outlay for repair and reconstruction. Whether operations can be continued may depend on whether arrangements for loss financing have been adequate to cover all these expenditures.

Explosion Control

Many explosions have the chemistry of extremely rapid combustion. These explosions are, in essence, nearly instantaneous fire over the whole of a large quantity of material. Examples include explosions of flammable liquid vapors and gases, dust explosions (for example, grain elevator explosions), and the action of commercial explosives. The principles of explosion control are very similar to those for the slower combustion of fires. A major difference, of course, is the much shorter time available for explosion counteraction. There are, however, explosion suppressors that can act effectively the instant an explosion is initiated in order to suppress what would otherwise be a major explosion. Such suppression equipment detects a sudden abnormal increase in pressure and automatically floods the incipient explosion with a suppressing agent. This equipment resembles an automatic fire extinguishing system but differs in the type of detection and the extreme rapidity of response.

To prevent initial combustion that could lead to explosion, explosive materials should be properly handled. Sometimes, in addition, the material may be kept in a low-oxygen or oxygen-free atmosphere. (This is done by replacing much or all of the air in a chamber with inert gas, such as carbon dioxide or nitrogen.) Similar treatment may be provided for electrical equipment or electrical equipment may be of explosion-proof design appropriate for the explosive environment.

For explosions that are not prevented or suppressed, venting is the standard method of control—directing the force toward open air and/or a solid barrier such as an earthen bank. Thus, dynamite is stored in "igloos" with light roofs (so the explosive force is directed upwards); the "igloos" are surrounded by earth or concrete banks. The NFPA warns, however, that, "Since explosion venting is a complex subject on which much essential information is lacking, only certain generalizations can be made."[17]

Explosion of pressure and vacuum vessels is the other major type of explosion. (Technically, vacuum vessels, which rupture inwardly rather than outwardly, suffer "implosion" rather than "explosion," but the difference is not significant here.) Explosions occur in such equipment when the pressure exerted exceeds the capacity of the vessel to contain pressure. Such excess can occur from either an increase in the amount of pressure or a decrease in the strength of the vessel. Changes in strength or pressure must therefore be prevented or controlled.

Prevention and control of changes in strength of the equipment are accomplished by proper maintenance of the equipment. Periodic inspection by appropriate experts can reveal the need for repair or replacement. (Provision of inspection service is a major part of the boiler insurance contract.)

Prevention and control of pressure on such vessels depend on safe operating procedures and practices and safety release devices. Note the reference to operating procedures *and* practices. Not only must the plans and instructions for use of the equipment contain rules for safe operation; there must also be effective training in and enforcement of the procedures. There must be effective checks to verify that procedures are followed. Safety pressure release devices are only intended to overcome danger from failure in procedures and practices. But even safety devices will not work if they themselves have been improperly maintained or suffer injury that is not noticed.

Control of Windstorm Damage

Although the energy source in windstorms cannot be controlled, it is possible to locate away from areas with frequent severe storms, such as hurricanes and tornadoes. However, it is usually impractical to avoid the windstorm exposure with a choice of location. Yet, there are certain factors, such as type of building construction, that affect the probability of windstorm damage to property. Some buildings resist wind damage better than others. There is considerable correlation between ability to resist fire damage and ability to resist wind damage because it is the stronger structures which resist both types of damage.

Plate glass, attached exterior trim, and roofing are particularly susceptible to windstorm damage. Ordinary glass is readily damaged by windblown objects and, when the glass area is large, by high wind itself; light trim can be torn off by winds; and high velocity wind passing over a building creates forces that tend to lift the roof. Inadequate anchorage of the roof assembly will result in loss of the roof, followed by more loss to exposed contents. When the roof itself holds, its surface can suffer considerable stress and there may be much damage to shingles, tiles, or other attached coverings. This possibility must be considered in selection and attachment of roof surfaces. Proper maintenance is necessary, as strength of materials and their fastenings can deteriorate over time.

Flood and High Water Losses

Water damage may be caused by low ground and/or high water. In major hurricanes there is more damage from flooding than from force of wind. Natural flooding, whether from hurricanes or other storms, may be classified as three types: flooding from high tides; from rising water in rivers, streams, and lakes; and from inadequate runoff of rain water ("flash flood"). The best method of treating this exposure is to avoid areas known to have had flood experience, or at least those with a higher than average frequency of flooding. Since construction and rearrangement of the surface of the ground change runoff and flood patterns, consideration has to be given as to what these patterns may now be—preferably before construction commences.

Where property is exposed to high water, design of grounds and buildings should take this into account, as should location of particular property in the building.

The transfer of energy concept discussed in CPCU 1 can be easily applied to a discussion of flood loss exposures and their treatment.

1. *Avoid or minimize the buildup of energy.* Placement of dams and other impoundments of water can cause, modify, or reduce energy buildup.
2. *Control the injurious release of energy that has been built up.* The rate and direction of release of water energy can be controlled by creating channels and impoundments to control direction and rate of runoff and by creation of open areas over which flooded

waters can be spread out, reducing their depth and speed of flow.

3. *Separate the released energy from structures that are subject to damage.* Dikes and other barriers may be used to separate flood waters from property (and people) to be protected. Channels also effect such separation. Placing property at a high level (on high ground or in upper stories of a building) is another example of separation.
4. *Create an environment in which the injurious effects will be lessened if the released energy should reach the structure.* Property may be designed for strength against the pressure of flood waters and the effects of dampness. This can be done by making structures more solid and by giving them shapes that offer less direct impedence to water flow around and past them. Provision for runoff or pumping out water when the flood has subsided may also be necessary. (Dikes and levees sometimes increase loss by keeping water impounded longer.)
5. *Once the released energy has damaged the structure, take steps to counteract the injurious effects.* Counteraction includes such activities as emergency sandbagging, moving property to higher levels, speeding draining by pumping, and promptly drying and cleaning damaged property to minimize deleterious effects.[18]

Earthquake Losses

The transfer of energy concept also indicates some means to control loss from earthquakes. Control of buildup of energy is not possible, nor is separation of property from that energy by barriers. But separation by space (avoid high frequency earthquake areas) is common, and earthquake resistant construction is available in active earthquake zones. Some of the principles in earthquake resistant construction involve controlling and channeling the release of the earthquake's energy through the movement of components of affected structures.

LOSS FINANCING

No practical loss control program has ever eliminated all losses or loss potential. The *Titanic,* for example, was supposedly so well designed that it was immune to damage from iceberg collisions.

Because complete elimination of all exposure is virtually impossible, an important element of any risk management program is financing those losses that do occur. Loss transfers are effective arrangements for the loss to be paid by another party. Retention is financing the effects of a loss out of an organization's own resources (including its ability to obtain credit).

Loss Transfer

When loss exposures are transferred, the party exposed to loss (the transferor) transfers the loss exposure to another party (the transferee). In insurance transfers the insured is the transferor and the insurer is the transferee. In noninsurance transfers the transferee will almost always be another type of entity.

Insurance is by far the most common form of loss transference, but noninsurance loss transfers are also possible. Some of the common examples of property loss transfers will be discussed, with special attention paid to ways in which noninsurance loss transfers can serve as alternates or supplements to insurance transfers and/or retention programs.

Reimbursement and Performance Transfers Many transfer agreements call for the transferee to reimburse the transferor for some portion of the transferor's loss (or expenditure on account of loss). Most insurance transfers and many noninsurance transfers operate in this way, particularly those involving liability losses. Property loss transfers, however, may call upon the transferee to make good in kind rather than to reimburse.

Fire insurance contracts call for the transferee (the insurance company) to pay cash (reimburse) for the transferor's (insured owner's) loss of value in or cost of reconstruction of a damaged building. (The insurer generally has the option to repair or replace the damaged property.) In a lease, the transferee (tenant) is usually required to take care of the transferor's (owner's) loss by actually repairing and reconstructing the building—that is, replacement in kind.

When the transferee has accepted the obligation to restore the property, the transferor is relieved of responsibility to arrange and finance the recovery operation. This is to the transferee's advantage. On the other hand, the transferor does not now have the right to require that the new property be different from the old—more modern or better arranged—let alone for a totally different purpose. Thus, any deficiencies and obsolescences in the old property may be perpetuated.

When the tenant (transferee) occupies the entire premises under a long-term lease and the improvements are specifically adapted to the tenant's use, such transfers may effectively accomplish their intended purpose. In such a case, it is usually in the best interest of both tenant and landlord that the repaired or reconstructed property be efficient for the tenant. Two exceptional sets of conditions may change this picture. If the lease has little time to run and will not be renewed, then the tenant has more interest in economy than in efficiency of repairs. Also, if the lease has little time to run and the property would be more productive for a different use, the owner may want full control of any reconstruction. (For example, present use may be for retail stores when a restaurant would be more profitable, or vice versa.)

Transfers requiring replacement in kind sometimes occur in contracts of supply. The supplier (transferee) accepts responsibility to provide materials, goods, or services as specified. If property damage interferes with such supply, the supplier may still be required to meet specifications. Failure to fulfill any of these contracts may, of course, actually result in payment of monetary damages (for breach of the contract), but the first call under such terms is for actual performance rather than reimbursement. For example, a building contractor may be contractually obligated to produce a completed structure on the scheduled completion date despite damage during the course of construction that delayed the actual completion date. If such is the case, the contractor may be held liable for monetary damages suffered by the party which expected to have a building on that date.

Loss Control and Transfer The party controlling property has a better chance of controlling losses to that property than does an entity with no direct control. Therefore, it is important to consider the effect of a transfer of losses on the ability to control the loss exposure.

In noninsurance tranfers the transferee usually has control of the loss exposure. Thus, in the example just cited, the building contractor has active control of the property involved as opposed to the owner (transferor) who has little if any control. The situation is reversed with insurance transfers, where the insurance company (transferee) has no direct control over the property.

Combining Control and Responsibility. There is an obvious advantage in placing responsibility to pay for losses on the entity that has the opportunity to minimize loss occurrence. Splitting financial responsibility from authority to control losses invites carelessness and even fraud. (This is the essence of morale and moral hazard problems felt by insurers in insurance transfers.)

Common cases in which the principle, "Put responsibility and authority together," suggests loss transference include the following:

1. leases (of both real and personal property)—transfer losses to the lessee;
2. bailments (goods in hand of others for storage, repair, processing, or sale on commission)—transfer losses to the bailee;

3. transportation by common or contract carrier—transfer losses to the carrier;
4. property under lien or similar claim (e.g., property under mortgage or installment purchase plan)—transfer losses to the mortgagor; and
5. property being specifically worked on (e.g., property being serviced on owner's premises by contractors)—transfer losses to the contractor.

Complications. The interests of the transferor and the transferee are rarely identical. Thus, the losses the transferee wishes to control and those that affect the transferor are seldom exactly the same. A building contractor or supplier of fuel may have more interest in controlling operating costs than in spending money to assure delivery on time. (And an insurer may be more interested in having money spent on fire control equipment than on additional production machinery or inventory.)

Another moderating factor is that seldom does one have *complete* control over property belonging to another. Thus, tenants usually do not have control over basic structural qualities (including structural defects) in buildings they lease. And installers of equipment seldom have complete control over conditions and activities on the premises where the installation takes place. Therefore, complete transference usually would mean that the transferee would acquire more responsibility than control.

Mixed Arrangements. In general there are two ways for loss transference agreements to reflect mixed interests and control. One is to adjust rights of control to match financial responsibility for loss; the other is to adjust financial responsibility to reflect the facts of control. The approaches may be mixed, and both types of adjustments made at the same time.

ADJUSTMENTS IN CONTROL. There are many ways in which control can be adjusted. Construction contracts regularly give the property owner inspection privileges and the right to require constant adherence to specifications as the building progresses. Landlords commonly retain the privilege to inspect and repair their property. These two examples represent increasing a transferor's control. On the other side, building contractors commonly insist on the right to exclude occupancy of the property before completion, and tenants may have the right to make some alterations and repairs to the property without consulting the landlord. (While the primary motivations for these control rights of transferees are control of liability exposures and preservation of efficiency in the transferees' operations, they are also relevant to property loss control.)

ADJUSTMENTS IN FINANCIAL RESPONSIBILITY. There are two approaches to adjusting financial responsibility. One is to assign responsibility differently for different situations. Thus, the landlord may be responsible for damage caused by structural defects, the tenant for other damage. In construction contracts, the owner or architect may be responsible for loss from defects in design, the contractor for other damage.

The second method is to share responsibility for loss events. Many property loss transference contracts (insurance and noninsurance) transfer only direct property loss. Resulting income and other consequential losses to the parties are left with whomever they happen to hit.

It is possible to agree to share the same losses or any portions of them. Thus, some contracts provide that when a loss results from joint negligence, it is to be shared fifty-fifty. This is done more often with liability exposures than with property losses but can be applied to the latter.

Comparison of Insurance and Noninsurance Transfers. Since insurance contracts represent the extreme in separation of financial responsibility from active control of the property, they contain many examples of loss sharing devices. They are suggestive of what may be done (and needs to be done) in other cases to keep loss transference from exceeding control by too large a margin. For example, the insurance company does not accept responsibility for all aspects of the loss (e.g., may not insure income losses, loss of market share, or loss of goodwill). Some sources of loss are excluded (e.g., substantial and continuing increase of hazard on the premises and within the knowledge or control of the insured, or failure to maintain specified protective systems). And even covered losses may be transferred only in part (by use of deductibles or special limitations in the policy).

The nearest approach to the right of a property insurer to help control exposures occurs in boiler and machinery insurance. As noted in a later chapter, in these contracts the insurer has the right to inspect the covered equipment and when necessary, to cancel coverage immediately on extra hazardous cases. (But the second of these is, of course, an adjustment in responsibility necessitated by inability of the insurer actually to do anything to improve the exposure conditions.)

Efficacy in Transfer There is little point in a loss transfer when the transferee does not reimburse or replace damaged property when a loss has occurred. This may be the case when (1) there is dispute over application of the contractual transfer to the loss at hand, (2) public policy prohibits the transfer, and (3) the transferee does not have the money.

Clarity of Application. Most of the problems in contract clarity apply equally to all subject matter. The one area of special difficulty in property cases is that of the "indirect" or "consequential" losses. Which, if any, of the "intangible" losses are included under the transfer and how are those which are included to be measured? Clarity here can be difficult—so difficult that the best solution may be to include few or none of these aspects of loss in the transfer agreement (as is done with most property insurance).

Sometimes a practical alternative is to specify fixed dollar rates for such losses (called "liquidated damages"), a device similar to the use of valued per diem forms in business interruption insurance.

Public Policy. With respect to public policy, there is appreciably less aversion to private parties' agreeing to apportion their own property loss effects among themselves than there is to such allocation of public liability or bodily injury exposures. The tendency to transfer property losses is even more marked when the property loss allocation appears as part of a bargained, quid pro quo, business arrangement.

Financial Capacity. The ability of the transferee to pay deserves particular attention in property loss transfers. Two types of assurance of ability to pay are possible: (1) the transferee clearly has, and will continue to have, the necessary resources; and (2) the transferee's obligation is backed by someone else who has adequate resources—usually an insurance company.

Suppose the loss transferee is a "Fortune 100" corporation or the government of the United States. And suppose the maximum possible loss covered by the transfer is $100,000. Ability to pay without insurance protection is at least as good as ability to pay with such protection. Such cases do exist.

In situations where ability to pay is not perfectly clear, it is in order for the transferor to require the transferee to purchase insurance against the loss exposures. However, trouble is sometimes caused by trying to get coverage for uninsurable exposures. For example, consider a building on a once-in-ten-years flood plain. The tenant (transferee) is obligated by the lease "to return the premises in as good condition as received, ordinary wear and tear only excepted," at the end of a twenty-five-year lease, and the landlord wants the obligation fully covered by insurance. The limitations on the availability of flood insurance protection may make this an impossible requirement.

Suppose that a transfer includes uninsurable exposures, and the tenant (transferee) cannot be relied on to pay for the loss without insurance. Other types of guarantee may be available, such as an irrevocable letter of credit and a performance bond. Both of these, however, require that someone (the issuer of the letter of credit, or the surety on the bond) have complete faith in the ability of the loss transferee to pay when called upon. Therefore, unlike insurance, these devices are not substitutes for the ability of the transferee to finance losses. However, if the transferee cannot pay, the other party bears the loss; the original transferor is still protected. In these situations, the third party (guarantor, surety) often requires full coverage of its obligation by sound, liquid collateral.

However, if a transfer includes uninsurable exposures, the transferee cannot be relied on to pay for the loss without insurance, and other guarantees are not practical (for instance, too expensive). Some things nevertheless favor such transfer from the viewpoint of the transferor. He or she might get *part* of a major loss paid for; but more importantly, small losses are paid for by the transferee, and this may encourage some loss control. The questions then are:

1. Would the transferor be harmed by possibly bankrupting the transferee (causing loss of tenant, customer, supplier, or whatever, plus possible damage to the transferor's reputation because of that kind of business dealing)?
2. Do other terms of the contract, bargained to balance the loss transfer arrangement, make the possible post-loss gain cost more than it is worth?[19] (This second point is considered further later in this chapter.)

Economy in Transfer The final factor in determining desirable transfer of loss is economy—what is the cheapest effective way to finance losses? When all the costs and benefits of a financing method can be identified and measured, this is the only criterion. But because such complete measurement often is impossible, comparative visible net cost often has to be only one of the criteria used in a decision to transfer losses.

Factors affecting economy in loss transfer include possible savings through loss control, efficiency in loss retention, economy in insurance costs, and avoidance of litigation costs. When all facets of the loss transfer have been analyzed, it is necessary to balance the various considerations to come up with the risk management technique best adapted to the situation at hand.

Saving Through Loss Control. It has been stated that loss transfer should bring financial responsibility in line with actual control of the exposure. This statement is based on the assumption that doing so will lead the party in control to hold losses down and thus reduce overall loss costs, but such effect is not assured. Safety of buildings occupied by tenants and of property held by bailees is seldom improved by making the tenant or bailee responsible for damage by flood and earthquake. Given the tenant's or bailee's own loss in event of fire or explosion, adding financial responsibility for the building or for bailed property may produce no improvement in fire and explosion loss protection. Thus, in cases where authority to control loss costs is of little importance in a decision to transfer losses, the decision should be made according to which party can finance losses more cheaply.

Efficiency in Loss Retention. One key to efficient financing is ability of the transferee to finance the loss by *retention.* This technique is examined further in the next section, but the major factors have already been presented in Chapter 2 and in CPCU 1. Ability to retain depends on (1) the resources of the transferee (total assets, liquid assets, cash flow, earnings, and revenue) relative to the maximum possible losses under the transfer; and (2) the accuracy with which the transferee can predict its loss financing requirements. When the transferee is in significantly better shape than the transferor with respect to either financing or predictability, the transfer is likely to be economical for both. The statement assumes, of course, that the total terms of the contract are adjusted to reflect the contract's effects on the various parties' costs of treating losses.

Common applications of this statement include retention of loss by damage to leased store buildings by large retail chain store corporations where many of the buildings are owned by individuals, estates, or purely local real estate operators, or retention of damage by fire and other major perils by suppliers of leased or rented equipment to many different customers (e.g., car rental operations and leasing of computers).

Economy in Insurance Costs. Of course, the transferee may not rely just on its own ability to finance the losses. In many cases it will enlist assistance from an insurance company's financial resources and ability to predict. Then two considerations appear. One, as noted before, is the effect of transfers for which the transferee cannot get insurance. The second is the question of whether the transferor or transferee can get insurance coverage more economically. This in turn depends on such things as the cost and availability of insurance to each of the parties in the contract.

Thus, where certain types of property can be insured as either building or contents (within policy definitions), it may be desirable for the landlord to insure such items as building (because of the lower building insurance rate). Of course, a noninsurance contract between landlord and tenant should clearly spell out this division of responsibility. Where either landlord or tenant is better able to obtain insurance, perhaps because of a large volume of business with a given insurer, it may be desirable for that party to obtain insurance on the property involved.

Application to personal property must also be adapted to coverage features. Because fire and allied lines (as well as crime and most miscellaneous property) insurance makes it difficult, if not thoroughly impractical, for the owner to have insurance on property at various premises of others, the party having control of the property can insure it more efficiently. However, there are marine insurance forms, discussed in some later chapters, that are specifically adapted to covering bailed property. Some are designed for purchase by property owners, some for purchase by bailees.

Efficiency in purchase of insurance also can depend on the mix of exposures of each of the parties and each party's negotiating power with insurers. Suppose the exposure in question is either (1) small relative to total insured exposures, or (2) similar to many other exposures for just one of the parties. Then including such exposure in the total insurance program of that party will generally be cheaper than including it in the program of a party for whom the additional exposure is relatively large or unusual.

Since attorneys seldom are acquainted with these various matters about the feasibility and cost of insurance protection, risk management specialists have to work to get such matters properly taken into account when contracts are being drawn up.

Avoiding Litigation Costs. Another facet of economy of transfer is ease of enforcement. Some transfers have involved complex or conflicting conditions, and some have laid simultaneous responsibility on several parties (e.g., on several contractors and subcontractors). Then expensive litigation has been necessary to determine financial responsibility in particular cases.

Balancing The virtue of aligning financial responsibility with ability to control losses needs to be tempered with attention to simplicity and to economy of financing. Sometimes the best loss control device when one's property is to be controlled by another is just good care in the selection of who that other party is. Then the greatest economy is achieved by using loss transfer simply to make clear who is to pay in cases in which there would otherwise be (1) some doubt as to responsibility or (2) unproductive expense for insurance or administration.

Loss Retention

The guidelines for safe, economical internal financing of losses (loss retention) are presented and discussed in Chapter 2 of this text and in CPCU 1. Here attention is directed to some specific features in application of these guidelines to loss exposures for which fire and allied lines (and occasionally other types of property) insurance is available.

Frequency and Severity Characteristics In a sense, property losses are limited in severity. All one can lose in a given case of property damage are the value and income associated with that particular property. (There can be, of course, associated third-party liability losses. However, the present discussion is limited to property losses.) Thus, for an organization that has many separate properties, widely distributed and with limited interdependence in operation, property loss exposures present more limited and predictable severity than liability exposures. On the other hand, for smaller organizations, for centralized organizations, and for those with heavily interdependent operations, this relative limitation on severity has no practical significance. Maximum possible loss from property, or even probable maximum loss, is more loss than can be retained with achievement of such objectives as income maintenance or even survival.

Most property losses are small—most fires, most windstorms, most vandalism, etc., produce little damage and no interruption of operations. Such losses are readily retained. Any that have high frequency definitely should be retained. When such retention is to be combined with insurance against significant, infrequent losses, there are two regular approaches—selective insurance coverage, and deductibles.

Selective Coverage. Selective coverage involves the selection of insurance only against possible losses which are both significant and infrequent. (Insignificant, infrequent losses would thus be retained.) For example, water damage insurance may not be purchased, or small stocks of inventory at widely scattered locations may be omitted from fire insurance coverage. Plate glass insurance may not be purchased when only a few panes of glass are exposed to loss, and crime insurance may be forgone when the maximum amounts of cash on hand at any one location are within the firm's retention capabilities.

In choosing among risk management techniques, this concept becomes important in a firm's choice of insurance coverages—specifically in a choice among basic named perils forms, broad named perils forms, or "all-risks" forms of insurance. In choosing the broader coverage, it is desirable to ask whether any severe loss potential warrants the extra premium. The question is important but can be very troublesome with respect to "all-risks" protection. If no severe loss potential appears to justify expanded coverage, is the lack real or only apparent? Is the exposure truly minimal or is there only an inability to foresee all the possibilities?

Selective coverage can be carried to an extreme. Where the chance of loss is low, the insurance cost may be so slight as to make it unwise to retain the exposure. Another consideration is that selective coverage may lead to adverse selection (from the standpoint of the insurer). An insurer feeling it has been selected against may raise the premiums or decline to offer coverage, thus negating all the benefits of the selection process.

Deductibles. Deductibles gain in importance as the number of insured perils and number of exposure units increase. Broad coverage can include perils that cause small, frequent losses as well as large, infrequent ones; or a number of separate locations may generate a frequency of relatively small losses from a single peril such as fire. In either case, deductibles can be important. For example, the frequency of fire loss is greater, while the relative severity per loss is smaller, in a 500-unit chain of grocery stores than in a single store or a 5- or 10-unit chain.

Preference between an aggregate deductible and a deductible per occurrence (assuming both are available) depends on relative cost for comparable coverage. What constitutes "comparable coverage" depends on normal loss frequency and severity.

With respect to loss frequency, Table 6-2 gives some commonly accepted estimates (Poisson probabilities) that the number of losses in a given period will exceed various figures above the average rate. For example, suppose average frequency is four losses per year. Then the probability of experiencing *more than* six losses (more than two losses above average) in any twelve-month period is about 0.11 (approximately once in nine years). Probability of more than eight losses is about 0.021 (approximately one year in fifty). And probability of more than twelve losses (more than three times average) is about 0.00027 (about one out of every 3,700 years).

An example will illustrate how loss frequency probabilities can be applied in determining "comparable coverage." The figures in the example are selected for ease of illustration, but the concept may be applied when other values are involved.

Company A is a firm with a desired maximum retention of $24,000 and an average frequency of eight losses per year. An aggregate deductible of $24,000 would protect this retention goal. (This assumes that only loss under the deductible amount is relevant. Actual retention also includes losses uninsured for other reasons—uncovered perils, uncovered indirect loss, direct loss beyond the policy limits, and so forth. The stated $24,000 maximum retention must therefore be taken as $24,000 in addition to the amounts retained on all these other uncovered losses.)

If a per occurrence deductible of $2,000 were selected, more than twelve losses in a year might (depending on severity) cause the desired

Table 6-2

Poisson Probabilities of High Loss Frequency

When Average Frequency Is	Probability of Loss Frequency More Than			
	2 above average	4 above average	2 times average	3 times average
1/2	0.014	0.00017	0.090	0.090
1	0.019	0.00059	0.080	0.019
2	0.036	0.0034	0.036	0.0034
4	0.11	0.021	0.021	0.00027
8	0.18	0.064	0.0037	0.0000011
16	0.26	0.13	0.00013	†

† Less than 1/10,000,000.

retention to be exceeded. Probability of over twelve losses in a year is 0.064 (once every fifteen to sixteen years), perhaps too high to be acceptable. On this basis, a $2,000 per occurrence deductible might not be judged "comparable" to a $24,000 aggregate deductible, and lower per occurrence deductibles would be considered.

A deductible of $1,500 requires at least seventeen losses before retention under the deductible could *exceed* $24,000. Probability of more than sixteen losses is only 0.0037 (about once in 270 years). This may be low enough to judge that a $1,500 per occurrence deductible is "comparable" to a $24,000 deductible. If not, reduction of the deductible to $1,000 means twenty-five losses or more are required to have a possibility of exceeding $24,000 retention, and that probability is 0.0000011 (about once in 9 million years).

Normal loss severity enters the analysis as follows. Suppose that 80 percent of all losses comes to less than $500. Then with a $2,000 per occurrence deductible, twelve losses are very unlikely to use up the $24,000 maximum retention. (Each loss would have to equal or exceed $2,000, which is highly improbable). It will generally take at least twenty-four losses with a $2,000 per occurrence deductible before total annual retention exceeds $24,000. Thus, it is more relevant to consider the probability of having more than twenty-four losses (0.0000011).

When both frequency and severity are analyzed, it appears that the $2,000 per occurrence deductible is, in fact, "comparable" to a $24,000 aggregate deductible for Company A. However, insurance companies may offer little if any reduction in premium for a $2,000 deductible per occurrence as compared to a $1,000 deductible. So, for Company A, the practical definition of "comparable coverage" will be a $24,000 aggregate deductible and the most attractively priced per occurrence deductible of *$2,000 or less.*

Most firms attempting to compare aggregate and per occurrence deductibles for fire and allied lines insurance from the standpoint of "comparable coverage" will be large firms with average loss frequencies like those shown in Table 6-2. Small- and medium-sized firms may have much lower average frequencies. Note that the figures in Table 6-2 for probability of two or more losses above average loss frequency decrease rapidly as average frequency declines. When average frequency is very low, say one loss every twenty or fifty years, there is no practical difference between a per occurrence and an aggregate deductible because only one loss can reasonably be expected.

Note, however, that all these probabilities apply *before any loss has occurred.* The occurrence of a loss may require reassessment of the risk management technique chosen. To illustrate this point, consider Company B, a firm with an average loss frequency of 1/20, who selected a per occurrence deductible equal to its maximum retention (having given due consideration to other uninsured losses). With an average frequency of 1/20, the probability of having one loss during each twelve-month period would be 0.048 (Poisson probability). Table 6-2, if extended, would show that the probability of two losses in any one year is about 0.0012 (around one year in 800).

If Company B has a loss halfway through a given year, the probability of having two losses in that year is no longer 0.0012. It is now the probability of having one loss in half a year. This is approximately half the probability of having one loss in a whole year, or about 0.024—approximately twenty times the original probability of two losses in the year. This change may be compared with the probabilities of throwing two heads in two tosses of a coin. Before the first coin is tossed, the probability is one-fourth. But after one toss has turned up a head, the probability of the second toss turning up a head is one-half.

Having met its maximum retention in the first six months of the year, Company B may feel unwilling to chance the 0.024 probability of a second loss. Even though the initial decision in selecting a deductible was sound, Company B may now find it desirable to change its risk management strategy and revise insurance coverage to include a lower deductible or find some other technique for handling the exposure.

A final note on premium reductions for deductions is necessary. Again, suppose 80 percent of individual losses are under $500, and suppose also that 95 percent of losses are under $1,000 and 99 percent under $5,000. Then most of the premium reduction for any size deductible should be in the credit for the first $500. On the basis of claims alone, the credit for the second $500 should be only about 18 to 20 percent as large as that for the first $500. Since the relative amount allowed for reduction of underwriting expenses also tends to decline as deductibles are increased, the premium saving from additional deducted dollars commonly decreases markedly after the highest frequency losses have been cut out. (See Table 3-3 in Chapter 3.)

Because the premium credit for higher deductibles may be small and because it is more difficult to self-finance for the lower frequency, higher severity losses involved with larger deductibles, lower deductibles are often chosen even when greater retention would be possible.

Sharing Large Losses. Deductibles usually put a ceiling on the insured's participation in loss costs—the retained amount does not keep getting larger as the size of the loss increases. This is generally considered desirable, because the largest losses usually include substantial uninsurable loss effects, and increased retention of loss effects that can be insured is dangerous to achievement of risk management objectives. However, insurance can be arranged so that the larger and more important the loss, the larger the amount of retention.

RETAINING PROFIT AND EXPENSE LOSSES. Many organizations do not buy "time element" forms of insurance. Thus, they retain the income interruption and extra expense effects of otherwise insured loss events. Another common practice is to buy insurance for less than maximum possible loss. These practices mean that the insured shares in the largest losses, not just the smallest ones. How much of the omission to buy time element coverage is caused by failure to appreciate that part of the loss exposure is not known. But there are organizations that have made the decision consciously. The usual reasoning seems to be that the threat of that portion of the loss simply is not disturbing—a view that can be read as "that portion of the loss I am willing and able to retain."

RETENTION BY UNDERINSURANCE. Failure to buy insurance equal to maximum possible loss is clearly an example of retaining severe losses which are improbable.

RETENTION OF DEPRECIATION LOSSES. A related form of retention occurs when insurance is purchased on actual cash value rather than on a replacement cost basis. What is retained in any loss is the difference between present depreciated value and replacement cost of damaged property. The content and dimensions of this exposure are not easy to determine. For decades insureds had no choice but to retain it and there was no great outcry. However, rapid technological obsolescence, persistent inflation, and tax effects are increasingly important today. The importance of these factors varies greatly with respect to particular situations, so using actual cash value instead of replacement cost insurance can represent very little retention of loss effect, or a great deal. The one sure thing is that when it represents a large amount of retained loss effect, that exposure should be analyzed, and any decision to retain the depreciation exposure should be a conscious one.

Retention via Coinsurance. Retention sharing in large losses occurs when coinsurance requirements are not met. In most cases this retention is unintended and should have been avoided.

Some do propose and a few practice a deliberate deficiency in meeting coinsurance requirements as a device in loss retention. It can be demonstrated that when the maximum amount retained is set as high as the insured's ability to retain, use of a deductible is always more efficient than a coinsurance deficiency *provided* (1) the desired deductible is available, and (2) differences in insurance premiums faithfully reflect differences in expected loss costs. But of course, these provisos do not always hold in practice. Even so, great caution needs to be exercised in adopting any retention scheme that is arranged so that when the organization suffers the most from various loss effects that insurance does not ever cover, it also suffers the most from retaining loss that insurance *could* cover. This effect is compounded, of course, when there is both a coinsurance deficiency (or other underinsurance) and a lack of time element protection.

Income and Cash Flow Effects Retention and the purchase of insurance have different effects on net income and cash flow, and these can be important in determining choice between the two. Some of these effects occur after a loss, some before.

Effects After Loss. Two distinct sets of after-loss effects exist. In one set of cases loss is fully chargeable against income. Suppose, for example, there is a loss to inventory carried on the books at current cost. Or suppose that there is damage to fixed assets such that the assets are repaired (not replaced) and have essentially the same actual (not just book) value after repairs as before. In such cases the loss (loss of value in inventory or expense to repair fixed assets) can be fully charged against income for both financial reporting and income tax purposes. Assuming there is enough income that year to equal or exceed the loss charge, taxes are reduced at the regular tax rate. So the effect on reported income *and* on cash flow is less than the loss. (At a corporate tax rate of 48 percent, for example, only 52 percent of the loss is deducted from aftertax income and from cash flow. The other 48 percent is offset by the tax deduction.)

But consider what happens when the actual value lost exceeds the book and/or income tax value. This is the usual situation when a damaged fixed asset requires replacement. Book and income tax values of fixed assets are commonly below real value because (1) depreciation is taken more rapidly on the books and for tax credits than is actually suffered, and (2) inflation increases the market but not the book or tax value of the asset. (Even with inflation accounting, value of the asset for *income tax* purposes is not increased.)

When an asset is lost, the amount of deduction from earnings is the book value, not the real value of the asset. This reduces the effect of the loss on stated earnings and net worth, a feature that favors retention. But deduction from taxable income is limited, too, to the tax basis of the asset. Thus, if an asset with a real value of $5,000 has been depreciated to $2,000 for income tax purposes, only $2,000 can be deducted from taxable income after a loss. Thus, cash flow is worsened. If 48 percent of $5,000 could be retrieved by tax reduction, net cash outflow would be only $2,600 (assuming replacement with equipment of same value). But the $2,000 deduction means a net cash outflow of $4,040 for the same replacement ($5,000 less 48 percent of $2,000). When replacement consists of new or better equipment (say, an $8,000 outlay instead of $5,000), the cash flow strain is even worse.

Insurance premiums, on the other hand, are almost always fully deductible, so that type of cash outflow gets the full rate of offset from savings in taxes. This increases the value of insurance as compared to retention. Naturally this advantage is not unmixed—the world and the tax collectors do not work that way. When an insurance company pays $5,000 for loss of property that has only $2,000 value for tax purposes (as in the previous example), the insured cannot get the whole $5,000 tax free. The insured can choose to report $3,000 (excess of insurance claim over tax value of property) as taxable income in the year received. Or the insured can choose to bring the replacement equipment (purchased with the $5,000) in at the old equipment's tax value of $2,000. If the latter is chosen, the extra $3,000 provided by the insurance will eventually enter into taxable income because it can never be used to create depreciation charges that can be subtracted from taxable income. (When the insured chooses to report the extra $3,000 as income when received, there is then the opportunity to recover that same amount in later years by writing it off in depreciation charges. But to do so is to exchange *present* cash flow for a *delayed* cash flow of the same number of dollars—a trade any financial manager will avoid.)

Note that these differences in tax effects apply only to property losses. They apply particularly to fixed assets, although under some standard accounting systems they also apply to inventory. These effects do not apply to liability losses or to losses of money or securities. And, because of usual valuation practices, they seldom apply to goods in transit. That is, the limitations on tax credit as a disadvantage to retention are principally of consequence when considering retention as compared to purchase of fire and allied lines insurance; they have little or no relevance when the comparison is with liability insurance or with most crime and marine insurance.

Effects Before Loss. As noted, insurance premium payments are commonly deductible from income for both financial statement and income tax purposes. Unincurred property losses, however, are not. Therefore, funding of anticipated losses is done without the benefit of income tax deduction for the prepayments. Suppose, for example, that a firm has average annual losses of $5,000 with its actual annual experience highly variable. An insurance premium of $8,000 represents only a $4,160 reduction in net cash flow and aftertax earnings (at a 48 percent tax rate). But $5,000 placed in a contingency fund is a full $5,000 withdrawn from cash flow. It is zero reduction from earnings. Thus, retention can cause a greater reduction than insurance does in pre-loss cash flow, and retention does not allow leveling out of reported earnings between loss and nonloss years.

Captive insurance companies have been used to get tax and income deductibility for advance funding of retained losses, but accounting standards and changing income tax rules now make this more difficult.

The need for and desirability of advance funding depend heavily on the frequency of *sizable* losses. When these are infrequent, as is usually the case with the major fire and allied lines perils, protection of financial liquidity and operational efficiency in years with large losses make some form of advance funding an important adjunct of a retention program. Since such funding has the disadvantages that have been described, an extensive amount of loss retention is generally less desirable as an alternative to fire and allied lines insurance than as an alternative to many other kinds of insurance protection.

Servicing Property Loss Retention Programs Not all of an insurance premium goes to pay loss costs. A significant portion of the premium goes to the insured's overhead expenses and acquisition costs. Some of the insurer's overhead expenses are directed toward services provided to the insured—services which would otherwise have to be purchased from outsiders or provided by the insured's own personnel. It therefore behooves any risk manager considering a retention program in lieu of insurance to evaluate not only the financial impact of loss costs, but also the value of other services purchased with the insurance premium.

Notable among the associated services purchased with insurance are inspection services with boiler insurance and claims administration with liability and workers' compensation insurance. But what about fire and allied lines insurance? What services from insurers are given up with loss retention and need to be replaced so that the problem of replacing them may affect the retention decision?

One service actually provided to fire and allied lines insureds who have no claims is renewal of coverage. This service is not needed for retained losses. However, other pre-loss and post-loss services are worthy of consideration.

Pre-Loss Services. A fairly common service is to call insureds' attention to inflation in property values. Organizations using property loss retention must do this for themselves. Sometimes insurers, agents, or brokers provide some property evaluation service. The degrees of sophistication in the service vary considerably. Where this service would be provided, the uninsured property owner loses it and has to make some other provision.

Insurers offer varying degrees of loss control or engineering services to their customers. While many such services are directed at reduction of insured loss costs (for the benefit of the insurer), the benefit to the insured cannot be denied. Such services may take the form of plant inspections with recommendations for improvement made by the inspector. The fire protection engineers of some insurers can provide rather sophisticated services in the area of sprinkler system evaluation or other areas requiring specialized knowledge of fire protection techniques. The familiarity of such insurance company personnel with protective systems available or used by other businesses can be an asset.

With fully retained losses the organization forgoes such assistance as may be available from an insurer. It can, however, hire such services directly from insurers or others. Payment for such services is part of the cost of retention. When such services are provided in connection with insurance, they are paid for with part of the insurance premium.

Note that when an organization has insufficient internal resources for property exposure analysis and evaluation and cannot make efficient use of outside consultants, it is almost always too small to make full retention practical. Commonly such organizations either get evaluation and analysis services from their suppliers of insurance or forgo such services.

Post-Loss Services. Post-loss services commonly provided by insurers include loss reduction by salvage and subrogation (pursuing claims against others). These services may also be independently hired. Insurers may be able to perform them more efficiently by virtue of greater use of them, and this can have some effect in lowering premiums, but total dollar saving for the insured is small. The greatest danger in retention is that these services will simply be forgone. In general, plans for retention should include attention to salvage and subrogation and the benefits and costs thereof. But these are seldom if ever determinative of the wisdom of retention versus use of fire and allied lines insurance. (Occasionally they are important with respect to use or nonuse of some forms of crime, marine, or automobile insurance.)

A Note About Captive Insurers The formation of a captive insurance company as a risk management device has been discussed earlier in this text. (A more extensive discussion is found in CPCU 1.) As noted, there is some reason to believe that the use of a captive insurer can provide certain advantages to a firm beyond those available through a retention program. It has also been noted that the tax considerations which favored captive insurance may not persist.

Creation and management of a captive insurer is a complex matter, and users pay considerable fees for professional help in organization and management. Only large organizations can engage in captive insurer operations. Most captives are controlled by very large corporations, but some are operated by associations for the benefit of their members.

DECIDING RISK MANAGEMENT MIXES FOR PROPERTY EXPOSURES

The selected mix of loss control and loss financing devices for any set of exposures should achieve a firm's post-loss objectives (e.g., survival, profitability, growth) by means that are economical and satisfy management's pre-loss desires for legality, attention to social and political pressures, and personal peace of mind.

Meeting Post-Loss Objectives

Mixes applied to loss exposures that are subject to fire and allied lines insurance tend to be dominated by post-loss requirements for survival or profit. To meet these properly requires (1) distinguishing "large" losses from "small," and (2) determining what can be done to keep "large" losses from interfering with objectives.

Large Versus Small Losses A loss is "large" if it would interfere with achievement of objectives were not special preparation made for it. Two types of special preparation are involved—loss control and loss financing.

Analysis of which exposures present large loss potential is necessarily made based on the present condition and protection of the property. This means the resulting risk management program could be inadequate should something change the situation. Examples of such changes include filling in open space between buildings with materials or other buildings, increases in values at a location from insignificant amounts to a significant amount, loss of a water supply, and impairment of a fire resistive barrier. Possibilities of change and of failure of protective systems of many devices must be considered in determining where losses might be large. (Common cases involving failure of protective systems include sprinklers not operating, fire doors blocked, and delayed arrival of fire department or fire brigade.)

Naturally, exposures with large loss potential will be given the most attention. Those with only small potential will generally be ignored. If such treatment is to be satisfactory, the following points must be taken into account:

1. A multiplicity of small losses can add up to big money, so such loss experience should be dealt with in the interest of long-run economy, even when it constitutes no *risk* of loss that threatens organizational survival or stability of income or cash flow.
2. The separation is not between large losses and small as actually incurred, but between exposures with large loss *potential* and those with small.
3. Ability to identify large loss potential depends on knowledge, wisdom, and imagination. There is always the possibility that something important will be overlooked. An exposure identification system is necessary to minimize this danger. (Exposure identification systems were discussed in Chapter 1.)

Most loss control measures and insurance and noninsurance transfers require identification of the ways in which large losses could occur, with special attention to identification of the perils that could cause them. Specific decisions have to be made with respect to *fire* loss control, *windstorm* loss control, *flood* loss control, and so on. And the means of controlling various types of losses may be in conflict with one another. For example, bars on the windows to control crime loss may also inhibit access by fire fighters. Decisions usually must also be made with respect to which perils are and which perils are not to be insured against. Organizations for which broad difference in conditions coverage is available and useful get considerable relief from this insurance selection problem. For others, much relief may be available in primary "all-risks" coverage, but only at a cost which must be examined to determine whether it is worthwhile. This cost problem may be alleviated by use of overall or selective deductibles.

One advantage of "all-risks" coverage is that the perils that must be financed without help from insurance are better identified; they are indicated in the policy exclusions. What is not indicated, however, is their significance. For example, among the common exclusions are "mechanical breakdown" and "wet or dry rot." But to determine whether either of these presents large loss exposure and if so, what to do about it, requires more than just knowing these terms appear among an "all-risks" policy's exclusions.

Effects of Large Losses Given that a loss could interfere with achievement of objectives, the exact nature of that interference must be identified so that effective prevention or cure can be undertaken. The nature of the preventive or curative devices adopted must be related to the particular effects to be avoided. Before a problem can be properly solved, it must be properly identified. For example, if an effect could be long-term loss of market position because customers (or suppliers or key employees) would not be back after a period of interruption, the risk management program needs to prevent or at least minimize such interruption. This suggests the necessity of loss control devices, including devices to prevent or control fire damage (such as automatic sprinklers) and devices to overcome interruption (such as standby equipment, alternative premises). And it indicates, of course, that loss financing is to be geared to costs of continued operation rather than to costs of shutting down (extra expense rather than business interruption).

Alternative methods of solving the post-loss problem should be considered because economy of preparation is always a pre-loss objective. When one possibility is standby equipment, another may be arrangements for prompt borrowing, leasing, or purchasing of substitutes when loss has occurred. If both approaches will solve the post-loss problem, the one that promises lowest net cost will be chosen. One possibility is full replacement cost insurance coverage on the property with the extra expense exposure for temporary facilities after the loss financed by retention. Another possibility may be insurance covering the actual cash value of the property and extra expenses, leaving the difference between cash value and outlay for replacement to be part of the retained exposure. Again, economy will determine the choice *when both approaches will solve the post-loss problem.*

One set of loss effects that tends to be overlooked in analyses of property loss exposures is injury to persons. There is a natural tendency to think of property damage effects only in terms of property and its use. This tendency can and does lead to underprotection of people. On the basis of property values and income alone, installation of sprinklers may not seem justified, but saving of dollars on this basis can be hard to justify when the actual loss effect includes injury or death to scores of people. Unfortunately, this situation was dramatically illustrated in the previously mentioned fire at the Beverly Hills Supper Club in Southgate, Kentucky. One hundred sixty-four persons were killed in that blaze, but one expert has contended that automatic sprinkler systems "could have greatly reduced or prevented the loss of life." In addition, it was estimated that this building's annual premium would come to $22,168 if nonsprinklered and $11,000 if sprinklered. The estimated cost of a sprinkler system for this building would range from $42,000 to $68,000.

It was concluded that the premium savings alone would have paid for the sprinklers within four to seven years.[20]

The value of loss control measures is often much clearer after a loss. In this case it appears that such loss control expenditures would not only have paid for themselves but might also have saved 164 lives.

Meeting Pre-Loss Requirements

Pre-loss objectives of risk management programs, detailed in CPCU 1, can be summarized as economy, legality, and peace of mind.

Economy The approach to economy has already been discussed. From various possible plans that meet post-loss objectives, which costs least? The costs that are recognized vary from organization to organization and even from exposure to exposure within an organization. Regularly recognized are insurance premiums and capital investments in loss control. Recognition of routine or repeated expenses for control varies. (Examples of such expenses include time spent to train employees in fire response, cost of periodic recharging of extinguishers, and any reduced efficiency from safe procedures.)

To partially offset these, there may be pre-loss gains from the procedures adopted. The only one widely recognized is decrease in insurance premiums, but others can be present. Safe procedures, notably those that promote good housekeeping, actually improve operating efficiency. A variety of procedures and devices that are installed to control large losses prevent or reduce small losses as well (e.g., safer electrical equipment, proper maintenance of boilers). Employee morale may be improved by improving safety in the work environment.

Comparison between major loss control expenditures and resulting reductions in insurance premiums is a common process. This also may be done for relatively easy efforts at control. Some managers have been persuaded to improve their housekeeping, remove nonessential quantities of flammable liquids, or set up "no smoking" areas by the difference such change makes in insurance premiums (or insurance availability). Hence, how insurance rating systems reflect, or fail to reflect, various loss control measures is a significant factor in adoption or nonadoption of controls. (The ways in which insurance rating systems reflect loss control measures appear in CPCU 5.)

Insurance deductibles can be a good way to economize on recognized insurance costs. Deductibles, once rare in fire and allied lines insurance, have become more common as:

1. total loss and premium dollars have climbed to levels worth better management;

2. fire and allied lines insurance coverage has been broadened to include some perils with high frequency of loss;
3. some organizations have grown large enough to develop appreciable loss frequency with even the traditionally covered perils; and
4. knowledge and appreciation of the concepts and techniques of risk management have become more widespread.

Aggregate and per occurrence deductibles have been discussed earlier. However, aggregate forms are not always available and when they are, providing proof of an aggregation of losses can be an administrative problem.

As noted before, narrowing coverage can save premium dollars but may create a problem in meeting post-loss objectives. A common way of reducing coverage is to omit coverage that has a separate premium that seems high in view of loss frequency. A decision to forgo earthquake insurance in the eastern United States is a clear example.

Many low-frequency perils are combined in various insurance forms. The extended coverage endorsement, which includes aircraft damage, a low-frequency peril, is an example of such a coverage package. Were aircraft damage insured under a separate form with a special premium applicable to that exposure, the premium would need to be much higher because of policy writing expenses and adverse selection. But by combining the aircraft peril with the other extended coverage perils, the premium for aircraft is negligible, and there would be no point in requesting that the coverage be deleted in exchange for a premium credit (assuming such a change were possible). The extended coverage endorsement and similar packages of perils result in a total insurable loss frequency significant enough for the package of perils to develop credible loss experience on which rates can be based. But the frequency of some of the individual perils within the package may be too low to develop any credible statistical analysis.

Perils packaging is not, however, the entire solution to providing coverage for miscellaneous property exposures. If too many perils are included so that loss frequency increases substantially, the total premium for the perils package may be out of line, and it may be more desirable to retain some of the exposures. (A personal lines example emphasizes this point. The HO-5, including "all-risks" contents coverage, is much broader than the HO-3, which includes broad named perils coverage. The premium, however, is so much higher for the HO-5 that the vast majority of individuals choose to retain the additional exposures which the HO-5 might cover.)

Another possible economy measure, noted before, is care in selection of which large loss effects to insure against and which to retain. Such selection may be applied to business interruption, contingent operation of building laws (and demolition), leasehold, money, papers and records, and any other separable protection. (Note that these subjects frequently are left uninsured. However, the decision to retain the exposures is all too frequently an unconscious decision. Conscious decisions should be made regarding these items.)

A popular method of minimizing costs is to purchase insurance for less than the full amount exposed—to, say, 80 percent of "insurable value." Obviously, this may mean giving up some post-loss objective unless other means of financing the remainder are available. One means that may be available is increased borrowing following a loss. Whether this device is feasible depends on (1) the extent and nature of borrowing before the loss, and (2) whether other features of the risk management program leave the organization viable and sufficiently credit worthy after the loss. A point worth special notice is that ability to increase debt to pay for a new, more valuable building or new and more valuable fixtures, equipment, and machinery put in place after a loss, is usually greater than ability to increase debt to replace lost inventory. Any increased debt means, of course, increased interest expense plus additional drain on cash flow for debt repayment.

To determine long-run economy, many authors suggest projection of expected value of cash flow (or of earnings) that would be available during a post-loss period. A whole set of probability figures covering loss possibilities of various sizes is required. Unfortunately there are usually few clues to aid in establishing such figures, especially with respect to fire and allied lines perils. This is why many decisions are made using only clear, sure costs like readily measurable expenditure on loss control and size of insurance premiums. But reliance on these must be tempered by contemplation of the events that may give rise to consideration of the problem in the first place—occurrence of significant loss. Appraisals of the probability and significance of this event for a particular organization necessarily involve considerable error. The best one can do in most cases is to conclude that a proposed expenditure for loss control or transfer is (or is not) justified in view of the foreseen potential seriousness and guessed general likelihood of the losses that are to be prevented, reduced, or paid for. Expertise requires ability to recognize the true seriousness of the losses that can occur and not wildly misestimate their likelihood. Since underestimation of both effects and likelihood is more common than overestimation, cautious decisions are usually in order. This preference is reinforced by the extent to which errors in the direction of optimism are more expensive than those in the other direction (i.e., as the losses being dealt with have larger and larger potential effect). In practice, for example, it is usually necessary to emphasize (1) the effects a control device will have on achievement of post-loss objectives, and (2) the fact that losses do occur, in order to counterbalance the lack of reliable probability figures and the common optimism when estimating loss possibilities. Also requiring emphasis is the usual inability of insurance to substitute adequately for loss prevention and control.

Legality While much has been said about economy, legality is no less important. No proper risk management program can be developed unless it is legal in all respects. For example, various contracts of sale, leases, and debt instruments may require that property be insured. Unless this contractual requirement can be eliminated, the only legal risk management technique is the use of insurance. Therefore, as discussed earlier, insurance may be mandatory, and other risk management techniques may not be feasible, no matter how attractive they might otherwise seem.

In other cases, other elements of legality may of necessity affect the risk management decision. Building codes, for example, may require the installation of automatic sprinkler systems or other loss control devices at a certain location. Under such circumstances, the decision to utilize such loss control devices is no longer optional but mandatory.

Peace of Mind While peace of mind is an individual quality, it can be generalized as involving, in risk management, the safety and well-being of people ("these premises are safe for our employees and customers"); assurance of personal financial security ("the operations on which people rely for livelihood and vocation can survive untoward events"); and status ("the operations and finances for which I am responsible are well run, in accord with accepted good practice," or even "are much better than the general run of practice"). Occasionally another idea is influential: "If we don't do it right, the government will come up with another regulation."

The more these intangible, personal objectives can be brought out and well identified, the better chance the risk management program has to help achieve them. But, for psychological objectives to be achieved, the persons whose psyches are involved must have an accurate perception of the value of the program. A risk management program that is in fact poor—unsafe for people, unable to assure the organization's continued existence, and not up to accepted practice—may improperly be perceived as satisfactory. Or a good program may be perceived as defective. Here beauty is in the eye of the beholder, but it is easier to persuade someone that there is virtue in a thoroughly thought-out risk management program than in a haphazard program. Although highly intangible, pride is an important ingredient of any risk management program.

Chapter Notes

1. *Fire Protection Handbook*, 13th ed. (Boston, MA: National Fire Protection Association, 1969), pp. 1-69.
2. To have a fire one must also have an uninhibited chain reaction. This is of little importance in fire *prevention*. However, some chemicals used in fire extinguishers or extinguishing systems control fires by breaking the chemical chain reaction.
3. *Fire Protection Handbook*, 14th ed. (Boston, MA: National Fire Protection Association, 1976), pp. 2-4.
4. *NFPA Inspection Manual*, 4th ed. (Boston, MA: National Fire Protection Association, 1976), pp. 146-148.
5. Any attempt to verify this statement should be made with caution because the hot particles shot away from burning steel wool can cause eye injuries if protective equipment is not worn.
6. *NFPA Inspection Manual*, pp. 234.
7. *Fire Protection Handbook*, 14th ed., pp. 6-57.
8. *Fire Protection Handbook*, 13th ed., pp. 8-142.
9. *NFPA Inspection Manual*, pp. 232.
10. *Insurance Services Office Fire Class Rate Manual*, 4-75 ed. (1975), pp. 1-2.
11. *NFPA Inspection Manual*, pp. 147-148.
12. *Fire Protection Handbook*, 14th ed., pp. 6-14.
13. *Fire Protection Handbook*, 13th ed., pp. 8-212.
14. *NFPA Inspection Manual*, pp. 290-293.
15. *Fire Protection Handbook*, 14th ed., pp. 14-4—14-5.
16. *1978 Year Book Covering the Year 1977, Annual Supplement to Collier's Encyclopedia and Merit Students Encyclopedia* (New York: Macmillan Educational Corporation, 1977), p. 323.
17. Ibid., pp. 15-44.
18. Robert I. Mehr and Bob A. Hedges, *Risk Management Concepts and Applications* (Homewood, IL: Richard D. Irwin, 1974), p. 426.
19. Another possibility is to avoid the harm in such bankruptcy by not enforcing the claim if the tenant cannot pay it, which raises another whole dimension with respect to proper use of loss transfer arrangements.
20. Howard D. Tipton, administrator of the National Fire Prevention Control Administration, cited in *The National Underwriter*, Property & Casualty Insurance Edition, November 11, 1977, pp. 56-57.

CHAPTER 7

Ocean Marine Loss Exposures

INTRODUCTION

A large number of commercial enterprises have ocean marine exposures, and maritime commerce is not limited to the activities of seacoast cities. Industries and organizations all over the United States and Canada are involved in the import and export of a great variety of goods requiring transport across the oceans of the world. Many materials are also shipped on inland waterways, lakes, rivers, and canals or by oceangoing vessels between various domestic ports, such as New York and New Orleans. In addition to the vessels that carry these cargoes, there are a wide variety of other vessels engaged in transporting people, fishing for food, and building or maintaining marine facilities all over the world. Even the use of private pleasure boats has increased dramatically in recent years. All of these activities can be considered as "ocean marine" or "wet marine" exposures.

An understanding of ocean marine risks, of the physical perils that threaten ships, cargo, people, and property, and of the methods of counteracting these threats is essential to risk management. A prime characteristic of ocean marine exposures to loss are the perils unique to transportation by water. The action of the wind and waves, fog, the danger of striking rocks and shoals, and the possibility of colliding with other ships are examples of the special hazards that threaten ships and their cargoes. Even the sea itself carries with it a special threat because of its salt content. Some types of cargo regularly suffer damage from the condensation of water in ships' holds or from water that seeps or is blown into cargo holds. The motion of the ship is a hazard, as cargo that is not securely fastened will shift, possibly causing damage to itself, to other cargo, or to the ship. The shifting of cargo may even cause a ship to overturn and sink. The motion of a ship itself can cause injuries to people just as a sinking at sea presents additional risks to the lives of those at sea. As vessels move from one port to another they can pass through a variety of climates and the facilities of the ports at which they call range from modern to primitive. Each of these can present a different and changing exposure.

This chapter will first discuss the vessels and equipment, and then the cargo exposed to ocean marine perils. Because ocean marine exposures are somewhat different from other types of property exposures, the loss exposures in waterborne commerce will be discussed at length.

For centuries, various forms of insurance have been used to manage ocean marine loss exposures. This chapter concludes with a discussion of ocean marine insurance operations, tracing some of the history of ocean marine insurance from its early origins to present practices. Chapter 8 will continue the ocean marine discussion with an analysis of ocean marine insurance coverages.

VESSELS AND OTHER EQUIPMENT EXPOSED TO OCEAN MARINE PERILS

In order to evaluate ocean marine exposures, it is necessary first to examine the type of vessel or equipment exposed to loss. Different types of vessels and equipment are subject to somewhat different loss exposures. Various ship classification societies provide classifications which indicate how well a ship has been built or maintained, and these may provide an additional source of information to evaluate the loss exposure. In addition, the exposures are different for ships carrying the flags of different countries, since each ship is subject to the regulations of the country where it is registered. The liabilities of shipowners and operators differ, depending on their interest in the vessel or equipment exposed to loss, and this is yet another factor in evaluating the loss exposure.

Types of Vessels and Equipment

There are many differences among ships and the uses to which they are put. Ships that operate in ocean commerce, for instance, generally are larger and more sturdy than those designed for use on inland waters. Because the chances of loss or damage vary substantially according to the use to which a ship is put, knowledge of ship operations, design, size, age, crew, and equipment is necessary for the understanding of ocean loss exposures.

Vessels subject to ocean marine perils can be divided into five general categories: oceangoing carriers, inland and coastal cargo vessels, specialty vessels, pleasure vessels, and shore installations.

Oceangoing Carriers A distinction is usually made between oceangoing carriers that run on regular schedules (*ocean liners*) and those that do not (*tramps*). Ocean liners were the customary method of travel between various ports of the world before the airplane took over most of the passenger travel, but there are still many liners that operate on regular schedules between specified ports. A liner is defined as "a vessel sailing regularly and habitually on a publicized service and loading and unloading at specified ports." Therefore, a liner can be a ship that carries cargo alone or both cargo and passengers.

A vessel that is not engaged in a regular run between ports is generally called a tramp ship. Even a luxurious cruise ship that operates irregularly could be considered a tramp ship under this broad definition. Most tramp ships that operate in ocean commerce are cargo vessels, although some may have limited passenger accommodations.

A tramp ship's employment is constantly subject to changes in demand for shipping space. These swings in demand for ocean shipping space are sometimes extreme; and, of course, specific types of cargo have cycles—both seasonal and irregular—of their own. Wheat, for example, is subject to fluctuating conditions different from those affecting petroleum, and both are subject to weather and economic changes beyond the owners' control. Ships are not always equally suitable for all types of cargoes, nor necessarily for all routes. A vessel for which normal cargoes are not available either stands idle or is pressed into trade for which it is not well suited. This may reduce its efficiency and increase the possibility that it will suffer strain or accident.

Liners are not immune to economic cycles, but since they generally operate where trade is more stable and regularity of delivery important, they do not as a class suffer swings in demand as great as those faced by tramps.

Another category of oceangoing carrier is the *fleet* operated by the shippers themselves, the best examples being the tanker fleets operated by the major oil companies. Such shippers have the ability to coordinate carrying capacity with shipments to be made, and vice versa, to a degree appreciably beyond that available to the public carriers, including the opportunity, usually, to put maintenance on a planned schedule.

Oceangoing Cargo Ships. Based on the type of cargo they carry, ships or self-propelled cargo vessels can be divided into at least four major categories. The first is the *conventional* or *break-bulk* ship.These ships are designed with a number of large cargo compartments or holds. Entrance to these holds is through a large watertight hatch on the vessel's deck. In port this hatch is removed and individual packages of cargo are lifted into the hold and stowed away by stevedores. The cargo must be securely stowed to prevent movement during the ocean voyage and the individual packages must be strong enough to prevent damage to their contents and to support other cargo which may be stowed on top.

A second type of ship is the *container ship* or *intermodular vessel*. A container is really a large weather-tight box not unlike a truck body. These boxes are filled with cargo and then loaded on the vessel as a single unit by special cranes. The container ship has special cells designed to accept stacking of containers. Use of containers permits rapid loading and unloading and in many cases will minimize handling damage and theft.

The third type of ship is the *bulk carrier*. These ships are designed to carry large quantities of material such as ores, coal, and chemicals, particularly in their raw or partially processed states. Like most vessels the hulls of bulk carriers are divided by watertight bulkheads into a number of holds. The bulk cargo is poured or dumped in its natural state directly into the hold without any form of packing. Within the hold the cargo is frequently prevented from slipping from one side to the other as the ship rolls by dividers called shifting boards. Some bulk carriers are even designed with their own equipment for loading and unloading. Frequently the entire ship will be filled with a single cargo.

The *tanker* is a bulk cargo ship especially designed for carrying large quantities of liquids. A large portion of the world's tanker fleet is employed in the carriage of petroleum and petroleum products. The size of these vessels varies from the relatively small tanker of 20,000 deadweight tons to the very large super tankers of 300,000 or more deadweight tons. (Deadweight ton capacity is the number of long tons [2,240 pounds] of cargo and supplies that the tanker is designed to carry.) As the size of these vessels increases, their ability to maneuver decreases and the potential for a catastrophic loss increases. Where the conventional tanker of the late 1940s or early 1950s could be stopped in a few minutes, it may take twenty or thirty minutes to stop a 300,000 DWT supertanker. While tanker size has increased over the years the depth of the channels and size of the ports have not.

A relatively recent development is the transporting of liquified natural gas in specially designed vessels. The gas is refrigerated to 260 degrees below zero Fahrenheit and carried in specially insulated tanks. The controlled escape of gas helps maintain the temperature necessary to keep the gas in a liquid state.

Inland and Coastal Cargo Vessels Most commerce over rivers and canals is conducted by means of *barges*. Coal, grain, cotton, and petroleum products are typical of the bulk cargoes carried, although a considerable volume of semi-manufactured and even manufactured products are also shipped by barge. Barges are pushed or towed by *tugboats* and *towboats*. Today the largest of these barges are pushed rather than pulled, and a string of barges may extend a half-mile or more ahead of the bridge of the tug from which the captain and pilot have their view of obstacles ahead.

Great Lakes vessels are a special type, designed for the available cargoes (principally iron ore and grain) and the long narrow passageways (rivers, straits, and canals) that connect the system's open waters.

Coastal shipping refers to shipments that do not leave sheltered coastal waters for the high seas. A ship going from New York to New Orleans, although literally going along the coast, cannot stay safely within the shelter of such points as Cape Hatteras or the Florida Keys. This is, therefore, an "oceangoing" rather than "intra-coastal" voyage. The run from Seattle up the Inland Passage to Alaska, however, is a classic coastal operation, and the operations are more like those on inland waters than oceangoing.

In relatively calm ocean waters, oceangoing barges and tugs can be used. Much of the cargo between California and Hawaii is carried this way. The barges are towed by powerful oceangoing tugs. Barges also travel the intercoastal waterways stretching from Philadelphia to Florida and along the Gulf Coast.

There are, of course, vessels that operate in more than one of these categories. A tanker may, for example, travel from Houston to the St. Lawrence, up that river to Montreal—an ocean vessel route—and continue to Detroit by river, canal, and lake routes.

Specialty Vessels There are many vessels designed for purposes other than the carriage of cargo. Some vessels are for service of others, such as *tugs*. Besides towing barges, tugs are used to maneuver large oceangoing vessels while in port. There are also powerful *salvage tugs* for rescuing vessels in distress. *Service vessels* of various kinds are used to carry petroleum products to marinas, to transport pleasure vessels from summer docks to winter storage, and for a variety of other duties. The *portable dry dock* is in effect a special type of vessel that may be moved from one location to another. (A dry dock is a structure into which a ship can be floated. When the water has then been pumped out, the dock and ship are "dry" and the ship's bottom can be examined and repaired. Although designed for mobility, most dry docks are stationary.)

Some vessels are designed for operations on the water. Fishing boats are the most common example; they may be inland, coastal, or oceangoing, and used for pleasure or commercial fishing. Equipment for the clearing of channels, or for construction under or over the water (such as for laying cables or driving piling) offers a wide variety of exposures. In the form of oil rig platforms for drilling or pumping underseas petroleum, such equipment involves tens of millions of dollars, sometimes hundreds of millions. In the event of damage, there are also loss of production and possible pollution liability exposures, often amounting to tens or hundreds of millions of dollars. The exposures are often severe, as with the hurricanes of the Caribbean Sea, the extreme tempests of the North Sea, and the winter temperatures and winds of the North Atlantic.

Pleasure Vessels Pleasure vessels are the most common type of craft on inland and most coastal waters, and some are oceangoing. Larger yachts generally are operated by a crew hired for the purpose, but the owner of the yacht usually has more control over the actual operation than does a shipowner whose actual operation is in the hands of a captain and crew remote from the owner's control. This direct control by the yacht owner is an important factor increasing the probability of liability in the event of an accident. And there is, of course, a great difference in the training and experience requirements for professional masters of vessels than for many pleasure yacht owner-operators.

Shore Installations Shore installations that are closely associated with ocean marine operations are also exposed to the marine perils (e.g., damage by wind and water, or collision from vessels). The cradles and other equipment and structures used for the construction or repair of ships are examples of shore installations. The principal perils to which this property is exposed are the same as those facing most structures ashore—fire, windstorm, explosion, and so on.

Wharves, piers, marine terminals, and other waterfront installations are subject to the land perils, and in addition may be exposed to damage from collision. If a large vessel rams a dock, the dock as well as the structures on it may collapse. The size and structure of oceangoing vessels create special problems in the design of shore installations and increase the likelihood that these structures will collapse.

Classification of Vessels

A vessel may be well or poorly built, and well or poorly maintained, whatever its type. Since there is a need for a variety of interests to know details of a ship's construction (among such interests are underwriters, commercial lenders, ship charterers, and shippers), ship classification societies have been formed to classify ships according to their construction.

It is customary, when having a new ship built, to specify that it meet the requirements of a particular class (normally, the highest) of a particular society. Regular surveys are required by the various societies to verify that the vessel continues to conform to the standards of the society's original classification. The oldest classification organization is Lloyd's Register; although originated by the underwriters at Lloyd's of London, it is now an independent operation. Other commonly recognized classification societies include the American Bureau of Shipping and Bureau Veritas.

Any classification publication has to be read with considerable knowledge. The classification listed may be for operations other than those it is now going to undertake. Even lack of classification can be for different reasons: "Either the vessel is of such inferior construction that no classification society would be sponsor for the ship, or the vessel may be constructed to a standard so much in excess of the requirements of any society that the owners are not warranted in incurring the additional expense to have it classed."[1]

The "Flag" of Operation and the Hazards of Loss

Each ship is registered in a country chosen by the shipowner. The ship flies the flag of the country in which it is registered. The regulations of different countries vary greatly as to standards that must be maintained by the shipowner or operator. These regulations apply to equipment, number of crew, crew quarters, fire and life saving appliances and devices, provisions and supplies, and safety regulations in general. It is cheaper for a ship operator to operate under the flag of a country whose regulations are less stringent than those of other countries. The regulations of the United States, for example, are substantially higher than those of many other countries. Some countries are alleged to have minimal regulations in order to attract registration, as there is a financial advantage to the country in having numerous ships registered under its flag. The flags of certain countries are called "flags of convenience," because shipowners or operators are attracted to such registration in order that they may operate under minimal regulations.

The operation of a ship under the flag of a particular country may affect the use of the ship by certain shippers of cargo. A shipper may feel that the regulations of a particular country are such that cargo is subject to greater hazard than if shipped under the flag of other countries with more stringent regulations. Such a shipper may specify that cargo must be handled in ships of a certain registry or that cargo may not be handled by ships of a certain registry. There may also be political reasons why a shipper will specify the handling of cargo according to the registry of the ships.

Interests in Vessels

There is an important difference between carriers by land and carriers by water in the operation of the equipment that carries the cargo. Land carriers generally own and operate their own equipment (such as railroad locomotives, railroad cars, and trucks). There is use of rented or leased equipment in land transportation, but the lessee of such equipment generally takes full control and operates the equipment the same as if it were personally owned property.

There are many variations in the way ships are operated or leased. The liabilities of shipowners and operators differ according to the arrangements under which the ship is operated.

Shipowner The owner of a ship may personally control its operation, in which case the owner is the carrier. Passenger ships are usually operated by their owners. However, an owner may lease (or charter) the ship to some other party. A corporation may be established to own a vessel or vessels with the corporation's only assets being the vessel or vessels it owns.

Ship Operator The operator is the person or organization that has control of the ship's operation. Generally the operator is the carrier of the cargo. The position of the operator is comparable to that of the railroad or trucker in land transportation, although the liabilities differ substantially between land carriers and water carriers, as will be discussed later in this text.

Shipowner-Operator Shipowners who operate their own ships may be carriers of cargo belonging to others or they may carry their own cargo. Some of the steel companies operate fleets of ships which carry ore from the mines to the steel mills. Petroleum companies operate fleets of tankers which carry petroleum products. The business organization that must ship large quantities of cargo regularly between the same ports is likely to maintain its own fleet of ships for this purpose.

Chartering of Ships The word "charter" is used in maritime commerce to indicate the renting or leasing of a ship. The contract between the owner of the vessel and the person or organization that charters the ship is called a "charter party." The charter party spells out the responsibilities and arrangements under which the chartered ship is to operate.

A charter may apply to an entire ship or it may apply to a portion of a ship. A shipper who has a large amount of cargo destined for a foreign port may charter a portion of a ship for this purpose. This consists merely of renting a specified portion of the ship which then becomes available to the shipper for cargo. The lessee may also charter an entire ship where the needs are sufficiently large to justify this. A ship may be chartered for a specific voyage or for specified length of time.

The shipowner under some charters operates the ship. The charter then merely applies to the space in which the cargo is to be carried; the lessee has no responsibility for the operation of the ship, and may or may not be responsible for storage of cargo. Some charter parties provide that the provisions for the voyage may be supplied by the lessee. Others provide that the lessee will take over the complete operation of the ship, providing crew and provisions. These are known as "bare boat" charters. If the owner retains no degree of control at all, the arrangement is further designated as a "demise" charter. Specific conditions of charter agreements are highly individualized to meet the particular desires of the parties involved. The charter party may specify kinds of cargo, the waters in which the ship will operate, ports, speed of voyage, and any other conditions believed appropriate by the parties.

CARGOES EXPOSED TO OCEAN MARINE PERILS

The principal purpose of water transportation is to move cargo. Although there is a considerable business in the operation of cruise ships for recreational purposes and a relatively small number of passengers are carried incidentally on some oceangoing cargo ships, the majority of waterborne transportation is for the purpose of moving cargo. The risks involved in carrying passengers will be described and considered, but it should be remembered that these are a small part of waterborne commerce as a whole.

The cost of moving cargo depends upon the cargo's bulk, weight, the distance to be moved and the speed at which it is moved. Because the cost of transportation increases as its speed increases, water transportation is the cheapest method for moving a given amount of weight a given distance. The cost of moving a ton of cargo one mile by water is, for appropriate cargo, on the order of one cent. At the other extreme, for the fastest form of transportation—air transit—the cost is twenty to fifty cents per ton-mile. At one cent per ton-mile, a ton of cargo may be shipped 1,000 miles for $10. At $.20 to $.50 per ton-mile, the cost is $200 to $500.

The manufacturer of expensive items such as watches has a high monetary investment in the completed product, and therefore, it is advantageous to sell the watches as quickly as possible in order to recover the investment. Furthermore, because the weight and bulk of watches is small compared to the product's value, transportation by air saves more through reductions in financing charges than it adds to the cost of carriage. Coal, ore, and petroleum, on the other hand, are products whose bulk and weight are high compared to value per unit. There are also products whose total price is so low that even though they are not particularly bulky or heavy, cheaper forms of transportation are used to minimize the percentage markup needed to pay for carriage.

Shippers and ocean carriers who pay close attention to the actual cost of shipping by various methods may use a combination of land and ocean transport where it is more economical than an entire voyage by sea. Cargoes may go from Japan to a west coast United States port by sea, be shipped by rail across the United States, and then transshipped by sea to Europe. This arrangement, called "land bridge," is cheaper in many cases than shipment by sea through the Panama Canal. The extra distance and time required for the voyage through the canal produce a higher cost than when the cargo is sent across the United States by railroad. Similarly, although there is an all-water route from the Atlantic Ocean to Chicago or Cleveland by way of the St. Lawrence Seaway and the Great Lakes, the length of time consumed in navigating the narrow waters and locks along this route often makes shipment by railroad more economical. Cargo loss exposures are affected by the shipping methods and the terms of sale involving the cargo.

Cargo Shipping Methods

There are three basic methods of shipping cargo: bulk shipment, break bulk shipment, and container shipment.

Bulk Shipments Coal, ore, oil, and grain are common examples of cargo shipped in bulk. The characteristic of bulk shipments is that the cargo is put into the holds of the ship without any packaging. Coal, ore, and grain are poured into the holds of the ship. Petroleum and similar liquids are pumped into tanks within the ships.

Since bulk cargo is not protected by packaging or wrapping, bulk shipment presents the greatest exposure to damage from dirt, moisture, and shortage. The amount of damage that may be suffered depends in part on the nature of the cargo (e.g., wheat versus iron ore); the watertightness of the vessel—from the fit of its hatch covers to the strength and tightness of the plates covering its hull; and the quantity of the cargo that is left behind when it is transferred from shore to ship and back to shore.

Break Bulk Shipments The second method of shipping dry cargo, called break bulk, is in packages or boxes which are loaded individually into the hold of ships or on deck. This method is used for most manufactured products, such as clothing, household appliances, refined chemicals, and small or moderate sized equipment and machinery—the same kinds of goods that railroads and trucks carry in cartons and boxes. Because break bulk shipments require the individual handling of each package as it is loaded or unloaded, this method of shipment adds considerably to the cost of shipping and also increases the exposure to theft both at the port of embarkation and port of delivery. On-deck shipment of package cargo generally is considered undesirable because of the increased exposure to damage from the action of the wind and waves during transit.

Container Shipments The third type of shipment in today's commerce is by container. These containers are really large packages or boxes, many of which are as large as truck bodies. The important advantage of a container shipment over break bulk is that the entire container is moved as a unit from one mode of transportation to another—from truck or rail car to ship, and from ship to truck or rail car (also, of course, between truck and rail car). This contrasts with traditional handling, in which each ordinary package is taken in turn from the one carrier (e.g., truck), and in turn individually moved to its place on another carrier (e.g., ship).

The container can take various forms and may actually be a removable truck body that may be operated over the road as a truck trailer or on a railroad flat car to the port of embarkation where the container is lifted from the truck or railroad car and deposited on the ship. Smaller containers may be used for special types of cargo, or in situations where the cargo is transferred to another carrier that is designed to handle only smaller containers. Specially designed containers can be used for shipments of bulk liquid and refrigerated cargoes.

Another type of container operation is called LASH—lighter aboard ship. In this case the container is designed as a barge or lighter that can be picked up or dropped off by the oceangoing vessel without its having to come into port, a great saving in time and expense in some ports. LASH barges can also be towed by tugs along inland waterways to places never reached by ocean ships.

There are two principal advantages to container shipments. The first and perhaps most economically important is the reduction in the cost of handling. Once the container is loaded, there is no need to handle the contents again until they arrive at their destination. Individual package handling by longshoremen as in the loading and unloading of break bulk cargo is, therefore, eliminated, and losses due to handling are reduced. It is feasible, however, to reduce handling only if a complete container load can be put into the container at the original point of shipment, or by a freight forwarder who combines shipments of various shippers, and if the container load is then not disturbed until it arrives at its final destination.

Container shipments also reduce the exposure to loss by theft. One of the major causes of loss to marine shipments is the stealing of or opening of small packages in the loading or unloading process at the seaport. Because containers can be sealed, making it more difficult for criminals to open and steal cargo from them, theft losses are less for container shipments than for break bulk shipments. However, when an entire container is lost or damaged, the loss is much larger.

The advantages of containerization have been so great that by 1976 from 80 to 85 percent of all general cargo (i.e., not bulk cargo) movements among industrialized nations were containerized.

Terms of Sale

When cargo is transported from one destination to another, regardless of whether this transit is by truck, rail, air or water, this transportation is usually accompanied by a change in ownership of the cargo. Not only is there a change in the ownership or title to the cargo, but during the course of actual transit the cargo may be in the custody of a variety of carriers and warehousemen. It is vital that everyone clearly understand the point at which title passes, the time at which payment will be made, and the responsibilities of the buyer, the seller, and the various parties who will have actual custody of the cargo during transit.

In very general terms it might be said that there are three basic types of transactions in overseas commerce. They are: (1) sales on a cost basis (FOB or FAS), (2) sales on a cost plus freight basis (C&F), and (3) sales on a cost plus insurance and freight basis (CIF). There are many variations in the exact methods by which these three basic types are handled.

Sales on a Cost Basis A cost sale is one in which the seller's obligation ends with the shipment of the goods from the seller's place of business or with the delivery of the goods to a specified point in the same country. The seller takes no part in the overseas transaction. The cost sale agreement may specify FOB the seller's city, which means "free on board" freight cars or some other suitable transportation in that city. The seller might agree in connection with a cost sale to put the goods "free alongside" (FAS) the ship at the port from which the goods are to be shipped. With either FOB or FAS ownership of the goods passes to the buyer at the designated point. With ownership go all the owner's responsibilities and exposures to loss. However, the seller retains some interest and loss exposure until the goods have been accepted by the buyer. For various reasons, the purchaser may reject the goods. If the rejection is legally valid, the goods belong to the seller, and any damage they have suffered is the seller's loss, not the buyer's.

Sales on a Cost Plus Freight Basis The seller under a cost and freight sale (C&F) agrees to deliver the goods onto the ship and to see that space is available for the shipment. The cost of the freight (charges for overseas carriage) is included in the invoice of the seller to the buyer. However, the seller is not responsible for the safe delivery of the goods overseas. The seller's responsibility for safe delivery may end at the loading dock, on board freight cars or trucks in the seller's city, or on shipboard, depending upon the details of the sales agreement. Arrangements may be made under which the seller agrees to put the goods on shipboard. Under a C&F sale, the buyer is exposed to any loss during the overseas trip. If the goods are to be insured, it is the buyer's responsibility to obtain insurance. The important difference between a cost sale and a C&F sale is that under a C&F sale the seller agrees to see that space is available on shipboard. The seller also takes the responsibility for paying or guaranteeing payment of the freight charges. The seller then adds the amount of the freight charges to the invoice as part of the charges to be collected from the buyer.

Ocean carriers do not like to accept shipments with freight charges to be collected at the destination. A shipment under a cost sale arrangement may be refused unless the ocean carrier has some guarantee of payment or is doing business regularly with the consignee. The ocean carrier may insist upon a C&F arrangement.

Under both cost and C&F arrangements, any provision for insurance is an obligation of the consignee. Insurance is not ordinarily provided by the shipper under these arrangements, nor is any of the shipper's interest in the goods normally covered by insurance the consignee arranges.

Sales on a Cost Plus Insurance Plus Freight Basis The seller under a cost, insurance, and freight sale (CIF) is obligated not only to deliver the goods on shipboard and see that space is available but also to provide insurance to the destination in the overseas country. The contract of sale may provide for delivery at shipside in the foreign country or perhaps to an interior city. The insurance may cover continuously from the point of origin to the destination, including land transportation at both ends of the journey as well as while on shipboard.

Additional Terms and Obligations of Shippers Many variations in the contracts of sale will be found. The shipper may include the freight charges, duties, and other charges in the selling price or they may be specified separately. It is likely that the shipper will specify a sales price to which other charges will be added if the freight, duty, or insurance charges are likely to fluctuate or may be uncertain in some respect.

It should be noted that the shipper may be assuming a substantial obligation in agreeing to obtain shipping space, whether under C&F terms or under CIF; sometimes overseas shipping space is limited, in which case obtaining satisfactory carriage is difficult and expensive. The shipper usually assumes whatever obligation there may be for clearance of the shipment at port of loading.

Most countries have regulations governing imports. One of the important functions of a foreign consul in the United States is to give certification that the shipment and documents in connection with a commercial transaction are in proper form and that the regulations have been complied with. Licenses for exporting and importing may be needed for certain kinds of shipments or shipments to certain countries.

Creditors' Interests There are many situations in both domestic and foreign commerce in which cash sales or direct credit between buyer and seller are impossible or undesirable. The seller may wish payment on delivery of the goods because of a need for immediate cash or because the purchaser's credit is not acceptable. Or the problem may simply be the great difficulty in determining the credit status of a business in a foreign country. The buyer may need the goods on hand as collateral for a loan of the money needed to pay for them and therefore will not pay for them until they are received. The buyer may be reluctant to pay for goods before having a chance to examine them for defects or damage. Buyer and seller may both be reluctant to engage directly in the mechanics and risks of foreign exchange transactions. The result is that a large number of international trade transactions involve financing by banks and other professional lenders.

There are three basic methods by which payment is made for goods purchased in international commerce. If the seller and buyer have a long established relationship, and there are no problems with the obtaining of foreign exchange, an open account is utilized. As with a charge account at a department store, a bill is rendered periodically for all transactions within the foregoing month or other agreed period, and payment is made to the seller.

If "credit" has not been established between the two parties, a draft or letter of credit will be utilized. The former may be drawn to be payable on "sight" as described in paragraphs that follow or they may be payable upon the expiration of a specific time limit such as 30 or 60 days. The letter of credit is issued by the buyer's bank and is a more formal document than the draft in that it specifically prescribes the requirements for determining the value of the shipment, basis of shipment, and the placement of cargo insurance. As with the draft, the letter of credit makes it possible for the seller to be paid as soon as the shipment is underway and the necessary documents are delivered to the correspondent bank of that issuing the letter of credit.

Documentation for Overseas Shipments. The financing of overseas shipments rests on two primary points: (1) the obligation of the buyer to pay for the goods, and (2) the value of the goods as collateral. Since both of these points rest in turn on the arrival of the goods in good condition, a third base is also required—insurance protection to cover the loss in the event the goods are damaged in transit. Therefore, the group of documents—called the "commercial set"—that accompanies the transaction has three parts: (1) the bill of lading issued by the carrier, representing right to receive the goods; (2) one or more drafts, or orders to pay, addressed to the buyer; and (3) insurance certificates covering the goods en route. Also included, however, are invoices, export licenses, certificates of origin and similar papers.

The *bill of lading* is an essential document for shipment by common carriers, whether by water, land, or air. The bill of lading serves two primary functions: (1) it is an acknowledgement by the carrier that the goods have been received for shipment in good condition; (2) it also serves as a contract of carriage indicating the consignee, the destination, usually the route over which the shipment is to travel, and also who is to pay the charges for carriage.

The *straight bill of lading* instructs the carrier to deliver the goods to the consignee. The consignee is presumed in this situation to have title to the property or a right to possession of the property. This type of bill of lading is used where the goods have been paid for by the consignee, or where there is an arrangement for credit directly between the shipper and consignee, or where the shipper and the consignee represent the same interest (e.g., different offices of the same company).

The *order bill of lading* is the usual document for overseas shipments. In an "order" bill, the carrier is instructed to deliver the property to "the order of" the named consignee. This allows the order bill to be used as evidence of right to receive the goods. Typical steps in the use of the commercial set including an order bill of lading follow. An important aspect of these steps is their indication of the parties that have an interest in the property. These include the shipper, the purchaser, and the institutions financing the transaction.

1. The shipper delivers the goods into the custody of the carrier, which may be the ocean carrier or an agent of the ocean carrier.
2. The shipper receives an order bill of lading naming the shipper not only as the shipper but also as the consignee. The shipper is named consignee and may endorse the bill of lading to anyone at any time.
3. The shipper notifies the purchaser that the goods have been shipped and that the carrier will notify the purchaser when the goods arrive at the destination.
4. The shipper takes the order bill of lading and endorses it in blank. That is, the shipper's name appears in the space provided for endorsement, but the name of the party authorized to receive the goods is not filled in.This is equivalent to making out a check without putting in the name of the payee; it could be cashed by anyone in possession of it. If insurance is required the shipper also obtains the type and amount of insurance required in the sales agreement.
5. The shipper also draws a *sight draft* on the purchaser. This is a written order in which the shipper directs the purchaser to pay a specified sum of money. This sight draft usually names the shipper as the person to whom the money is paid.
6. The shipper takes the order bill of lading, evidence of insurance, and the sight draft to the bank and endorses them either to the bank or in blank, according to the procedure used by the bank.
7. The bank sends the order bill of lading, evidence of insurance, and the sight draft to a bank at the location where the goods are to be delivered. This transaction may pass through several banks and through international banking channels. The order bill of lading, evidence of insurance, and the sight draft are handled with extreme care because they are endorsed in blank and could be used by anyone who filled in a name. Such documents usually are sent by registered mail in order to reduce likelihood of loss in transit.
8. The bank in the city where delivery is to be made receives the order bill of lading, evidence of insurance, and the sight draft. The bank notifies the purchaser that it has them and that the order bill of lading will be endorsed to the purchaser on payment of the amount named in the sight draft.
9. The carrier meanwhile has carried the goods to their destination. The carrier will notify the purchaser that the goods have arrived

and will be delivered upon presentation of the order bill of lading.

10. The purchaser pays the sight draft at the bank and receives the order bill of lading. It is endorsed to the purchaser, who can now go to the carrier's office and receive the goods upon presentation of the order bill of lading.

This method of handling payment for shipments in transit is used in connection with domestic shipments as well as in connection with ocean commerce. It appears to be a complicated method of handling cash on delivery transactions but it is used so commonly that the procedure works smoothly.

An important difference between domestic and overseas shipments is the presence of the insurance documents in connection with international shipments by sea or air. This difference appears primarily because of the very limited liability of international sea and air carriers for damage to cargoes, as compared to the liability of common carriers on land in the United States.

PERILS THAT THREATEN WATERBORNE COMMERCE

Some of the perils that threaten waterborne commerce are the same as those that threaten property at fixed locations on land. Ships and cargoes are subject to fires and explosions, for example, just as is property on land. Properties in both situations are subject to damage from violent weather—windstorm, lightning, and so on—but the nature of the hazard to shipping is noticeably different. The effect of weather on a building is essentially the sheer force or energy of the wind or lightning stroke; for a ship, there is the additional complexity of interaction between the wind and the water, and the effect of the wind in driving the ship upon hazards in or around the water, such as rocks and shoals. Shipping is exposed to special perils regardless of weather—striking rocks or icebergs, or collision with other vessels; stranding on shoals; and the sheer motion of the waves puts strains on the hull and can cause dangerous shifting of cargo or equipment aboard. Finally, physical damage that would be minor ashore can be disastrous afloat; the breach in a wall that means only a partial loss to a building can mean a total loss from sinking when it happens to a ship.

Perishability of a product, and its damageability, especially by water, must also be considered in evaluating its suitability for water carriage. Modern ship design, engineering techniques, and methods of packing have reduced the likelihood of damage to cargoes, particularly routine damage under normal shipping conditions. However, the degrees of humidity and temperature met on water voyages, the corrosive effects of salt water, the mechanics of loading and unloading cargo, and the pitch and roll of ships routinely cause some damage to many kinds of products, and add to the expense of shipments by water.

For example, agricultural products shipped in bulk—such as grains, copra, and sugar—are particularly susceptible to moisture damage that either reduces their value or requires the expense of drying procedures. Some percentage of fruit shipments, as well, is regularly lost from bruising, molding, or rotting, and without special packaging, articles made of thin plastic, light wood, or ceramics are often broken.

Property in the course of transit tends to suffer more breakage, and pilferage damage, than property kept in one place. The routine events of transit—shifts, jolts and jars—cause some regular amount of breakage. Loading property onto ships and into their holds, carrying it distances during which it is subject to ships' motion, and getting it out of holds and onto shore, where it sits awaiting removal to its destination—all of these induce some damage that must be expected.

Property in transit lacks some of the physical protection and procedural controls available against theft and pilferage at fixed locations. Transshipment points in general, and wharf areas in particular, are difficult to protect and police thoroughly. Although continuous effort holds the theft rate down in some ports, the laxness of policing plus the local mores in other ports result in a high routine theft rate.

Ships and their machinery as well as cargoes suffer damage from some of these exposures. Rust, barnacles, and loosening of joints and fastenings are among the routine results of ocean exposure.

In considering the perils that can affect waterborne interests, certain perils should be examined a bit more closely since in most cases they are treated specifically in ocean marine insurance.

Violent Actions Associated with the Sea: "Perils of the Seas"

Storms and collision are not routine events, and are properly distinguished from routine contact with wind and wave. The major perils that cause damage to property on (or along) seas and that are particularly associated with seas have long been called the "perils of the seas." A United States court has noted that "perils of the seas" are identified with "marine casualties resulting from the violent action of the elements as distinguished from their natural, silent influence upon the fabric of the vessel; casualties which may, rather than consequences which must, occur."[2]

The primary examples of perils of the seas are the atmospheric perils (windstorms, including lightning) and collision (with land, reefs or shoals, icebergs, other ships, or shore installations). These are the major nonroutine causes of damage particularly associated with deep water transportation.

Other Perils

Fire and Explosion Ships and shipments are subject to the perils of fire and explosion. Again, because of the threat of sinking or stranding, these perils are even more serious afloat than ashore.

Fire aboard ship is not considered a peril of the sea; fire can occur ashore. There could be a situation where lightning was the cause of fire on shipboard. The proximate cause of the loss in such a case would be the lightning, which is a peril of the sea. Fire, like many other perils that threaten a ship, is specifically mentioned in any consideration of the hazards to marine commerce.

Loading and Unloading In ports where waters are too shallow for oceangoing ships, cargo must be carried ashore in lighters, and the chance of loss is considerably greater than where the ship can dock and unload or load directly on a pier. Goods may be dropped in the water during the transfer between the ship and the lighter. Lighters, relatively inexpensive local craft, are often overloaded, carelessly constructed and maintained, or poorly staffed. Even in the best-equipped ports, the lifting of cargo out of ships' holds, over the vessels' sides, and down onto the dock (or vice versa) present significant exposure to loss from dropping or other mishandling. During transfer, the property is at the mercy of the strength, skill, and interests of individual stevedores. Handling by crane reduces this exposure and cuts loss frequency. On the other hand, when a crane load is dropped, loss severity is greater than would occur with manual procedures.

Cargo sent by water frequently also moves overland during the same journey, creating exposure to the *perils of land transit.* (These will be discussed at length in Chapter 9.) They can be summarized as the perils that can damage or interfere with land vehicles, notably collision, upset, collapse of bridges, and derailment, plus the perils that threaten property anywhere, such as fire, explosion, violent weather, and extreme climate.

Jettison Jettison is a type of voluntary action causing loss. When an ocean venture is threatened with disaster, it may be wise to sacrifice some of the property involved to save the rest—to throw some cargo overboard to lighten a stranded ship, for example. Jettison, too, can be part of the property loss in an ocean marine voyage.

Explosion In the days of sailing vessels, the explosion hazard was generally minimal or missing; in the days of steam vessels, it was extremely important. Today, although the explosion of steam boilers used to drive the ship is much less common, there is still an explosion exposure in the ship's machinery and, of course, in some cargoes. The ship's machinery is also subject to the same hazards of sudden and accidental breakage as machinery ashore.

Machinery Damage In addition to the fortuitous perils of the seas referred to above, defects in either the ship's hull or machinery have caused loss at sea to both vessel and cargo. Damage may be caused by latent defects which could not be discovered with full diligence of owner and crew. Damage may also be caused by the crew's negligence.This exposure is particularly important because ships at sea are usually not under the direct surveillance of the owner.

Riots and Other Civil Disturbances This peril threatens shipments primarily when ashore. Just as international ports tend to be notorius for theft and pilferage, so waterfronts have historically been subject to violence in both labor and political disturbances. The intensity of this hazard varies greatly from time to time and from place to place. Again, there are times when sending cargo through such ports represents taking on a known serious hazard. On other occasions, the violence does not arise until it is too late to exercise avoidance.

Dishonesty The more important forms of dishonesty that may cause loss are barratry, assailing thieves, and theft by stealth.

Barratry includes fraudulent, dishonest, or illegal acts on the part of the master of the ship or crew which result in injury to the ship or cargo. It also includes such acts as absconding with the ship, sinking the ship, or abandoning it for some illegal or dishonest purpose. Barratry is present only if the act is committed without the knowledge of the owner.

Loss from theft by "outsiders" is another ocean marine exposure, of course. In marine exposures, just as ashore, it is common and useful to distinguish between theft by violence or threat of violence, and theft by stealth. The traditional marine terms for taking by violence are taking by "pirates and rovers" or by "thieves," which is interpreted to mean "assailing thieves." Modern hijackings of ships show that such exposure still exists, although not on the scale found in earlier centuries. Today, the major exposure to theft by force or violence is in ports and during land transportation, rather than while afloat.

Theft by stealth is primarily a port risk today. Theft loss, particularly in ports and warehouses, is such a significant hazard to marine shipping as to justify expensive packing and other protective procedures. Some shippers carefully select the ports they will or will not use on the basis of comparative theft loss rates. At one time, the port of New York suffered a significant loss in trade because the theft rate there had become so high, and the same thing has happened to other ports. (Naturally, when theft is common, it represents "normal loss," and the exposure can be managed accordingly.)

Seizure by Governmental Authority This may mean confiscation of cargo, confiscation of a ship, heavy fines, or simply significant costs from delay. Governmental seizure may be by due course of established law or by arbitrary exercise of power.

Causes for seizure under due course of established law may be for violations of regulations or to enforce or protect a civil claim. Types of regulations whose violation may lead to seizure include customs, restrictions on entry into national (or claimed national) waters, and quarantines. One example is the seizure of fishing vessels in waters claimed as territorial by the seizing nation, but as international waters by the country from which the vessel came.

Property can be seized to protect the rights of creditors or potential creditors. Lenders with a claim against the owner of a ship or cargo may obtain a court order requiring the property to be held until the claim is satisfied. Also, a vessel that has been in an accident may have been negligently operated, giving rise to a liability claim against the owner or operator. If the vessel is allowed to leave, enforcement of a later judgment against the foreign owners may be very difficult, so the local authorities may impound the ship for its value as a source of funds with which to pay off such potential judgment.

The hazard of seizure by governmental authority thus has some peculiar aspects. In some situations, such as the fishing waters controversies, the existence of the hazard becomes well known. Ship operators must be considered as taking a calculated risk when sailing into such situations. An entirely different exposure exists in sudden changes in governments, in governmental rules or processes, or in international relations. History is replete with situations in which, for one reason or another, a nation has without warning implemented a process of harassment and seizure of vessels entering its waters, and even upon the high seas. Another aspect of the hazard is inherent in the wide-ranging ocean marine exposure. It is difficult to know all the rules, regulations, and practices of all the nations affecting ocean commerce. Therefore, an established rule or procedure may be violated inadvertently. Unexpected events may bring the property within an unanticipated area for whose regulations the cargo or the vessel, and their papers, were not prepared.

War Damage The war peril was described in the early form of Lloyd's insurance policy as, "surprisals, takings at sea, arrests, restraints, and detainments of all kings, princes, and people, of what nation, condition, or quality soever." In modern usage, "war damage" generally is considered to be that resulting from acts of war between nations. This includes the capture, seizure, or detainment of a ship by a nation that is at war. Civil wars and similar actions between factions within a country are also generally considered war.

LOSS EXPOSURES IN WATERBORNE COMMERCE

Ships and their cargoes may be exposed to loss by any of the perils previously discussed. Losses in waterborne commerce, like losses on land, may have several components. There may be property and expense losses, profit and income losses, and loss arising out of liability.

Property and Expense Losses

A property loss that occurs in marine shipping is more likely to be total than a similar loss ashore. (This characteristic is peculiar to ocean marine exposures, although it is shared, today, with one other class: aviation.) Even so, the vast majority of marine losses are partial losses rather than total losses. A particular terminology and set of practices pertaining to the distinction between partial and total losses developed around marine law.

In marine practice, "total loss" means the complete loss of subject matter. If some of the property value is saved, the loss is "partial." There is a special marine term for partial losses: "average." (Although the phrase, "average loss," is sometimes used, it is technically incorrect. The word "average" itself means "partial loss.")

Total Loss Marine terminology distinguishes between three types of total loss: actual total loss, constructive total loss, and total loss of a part.

An *actual total loss* is one in which the subject property is totally lost or is so damaged physically that it has no value left. When there is no doubt that a vessel has sunk in deep water, or been blown onto land or rocks and broken up, total loss is clear. There are, however, more difficult cases.

Even today a ship can disappear at sea without a trace. A missing ship is considered to be an actual total loss after a sufficient time has expired to prove the ship has been lost. However, substantial efforts are made to determine what has happened to the ship if the value is considerable.

A *constructive total loss* occurs when the cost of salvaging the cargo or ship and of making repairs is too high relative to the resulting value saved. If a ship is ashore on rocks and the cost of recovering and repairing it exceeds what its value would be when recovered and repaired, it would be considered a constructive total loss. There may be a constructive total loss as far as a ship is concerned without there being a constructive total loss to cargo. It might be possible to save the cargo even though the ship is in such a position that it could not reasonably be saved.

Someone has to make the decision as to whether there has been a constructive total loss; that is, as to whether *salvage* efforts are likely to be worthwhile. If salvage is not worthwhile, the property will often be *abandoned*. In the first instance, responsibility for this decision rests with the property owner(s). But since much of the property in ocean commerce is insured, it is often the underwriters' rather than the owner's interest that takes precedence.

More than the value of the property may be involved. If the ship is in a position to be or to become a hazard to further navigation, the law requires that the responsible party have it removed—an undertaking that can involve large sums of money. Occasionally, removal can even cost more than the property was worth before the loss. Furthermore, operators responsible for the sinking can be held liable for damage the wreck causes to other shipping. Thus, salvage or demolition expenditures may be incurred even though there will be no salvage value.

As noted, property losses that are not total, are partial losses, or average. On its face, loss of an entire ship and all its cargo is a total loss. There is in addition, however, the concept of *total loss of a part*—total loss of one shipper's cargo, for example, without total loss to the ship or other shipments. Another example is total loss of a lighter and its cargo during unloading, other parts of the cargo from the same ocean voyage not being lost. And there may even be total loss of a part of a single shipment—total loss of one package, say, from a shipment that contains six. Hence, the phrase "total loss" sometimes requires specification of the unit or set of units that made up the total.

Partial Loss There are two types of partial loss in marine practice: particular average and general average.

Particular Average. *Average* is a loss that is not total; particular average is an average that is not general. An example of a particular average would be a case in which perils of the sea caused damage to ship or cargo. There is no voluntary sacrifice of any portion of the ship or cargo but merely direct damage from the storm. Each cargo owner and shipowner would have to stand his or her own loss. The term particular average usually applies to the loss or damage of a specific shipment or the vessel rather than damage of multiple interests.

Particular average is said sometimes to mean partial loss. This is not entirely true. A particular average is a partial loss in the sense that it does not involve the whole venture. It may involve a total loss of the property belonging to a particular interest. Loss of the entire lot of cargo belonging to one interest without loss of the ship or loss of cargo belonging to others would still be a particular average.

General Average. In some cases a ship becomes endangered so that it is necessary to lighten the load by dumping part of the cargo to prevent the entire ship from sinking. When there is voluntary sacrifice (such as jettison) of some property in order to save the rest, and certain other conditions are also met, the owners of the saved property contribute to the owners of the property that has been sacrificed. The loss, or "average," is made "general."

For example, suppose a ship and its cargo and freight charges were worth a total of $5 million. Assume further that the ship was stranded and $500,000 worth of cargo was jettisoned to lighten the load. The balance of the value, $4.5 million, was saved. Therefore, one-tenth of the total exposed value was lost and nine-tenths was saved. General average operates to distribute the loss so that *each party* or interest in the venture suffers a personal loss of one-tenth, leaving nine-tenths protected. When each owner contributes one-tenth of the saved value of his or her property, the total contribution is one-tenth of $4.5 million or $450,000. When this amount is given to the owner whose property was jettisoned, that owner has $450,000 in lieu of a $500,000 shipment. That is, one-tenth (or $50,000) is lost and nine-tenths of the original property value is protected. Thus, the loss is evenly distributed among all parties concerned.

Two important practical matters must be added:

1. Note that only loss of property is considered. Any loss the owner of the jettisoned property suffered because a customer is unhappy over lack of delivery, or because a business operation must curtail operations for lack of delivery of materials or equipment, is ignored. Those remain loss exposures inherent in ocean shipping.
2. The process of determining general average losses and contributions itself costs money. Hence, where the value of the jettisoned property was one-tenth the total value exposed, each party loses more than one-tenth of the saved value of his or her

property, as all must contribute something to the cost of having the general average adjustment made.

REQUIREMENTS FOR GENERAL AVERAGE. Modern practice in connection with general average requires that certain elements be present before a general average claim can be made by the owners of a ship or cargo. These elements are as follows:

1. There must be an imminent risk that appears to threaten all interests in the venture, including ship and cargo.
2. There must be a voluntary sacrifice or some extraordinary expense with the purpose of avoiding loss or reducing loss for the common benefit of all participants.
3. There must have been a practical effect of the effort with at least a part of the value saved.
4. There must be a freedom from any fault on the part of the interests claiming contribution from the other interests in the venture. For example, if the owners of a ship are claiming general average contribution, they must prove that they were not at fault in connection with the risk that threatened the venture.

APPLICATION OF GENERAL AVERAGE. General average originated as a method of distributing the loss in cases where there was a jettison of cargo or a portion of the ship. Modern practice has expanded this to include other expenses in addition to jettison. There have been cases where a ship was stranded and its engines were damaged in pulling the ship off a reef. Such damage to the engines in order to rescue the vessel has been recognized as a general average sacrifice. It has also come to be recognized that damage by water, steam, or other materials that are used to extinguish a fire are a general average sacrifice to prevent loss of the entire ship and cargo. Damage by the fire itself, however, would be borne only by the owner of the burned property, and would be a particular average. The problem of determining where fire damage leaves off and damage from water or steam takes up is a practical problem of loss adjustment.

A frequent form of general average today arises from the costs of putting a vessel into a port of refuge for examination and repairs necessitated by a collision or other casualty and required for the safety of the vessel, cargo, and crew. Among the expenses that could qualify for general average are cost of entering port, dock dues, cost of removing, storing, and returning cargo (as needed to allow examination and repair of the ship), and wages and maintenance of the crew in the meantime. The cost of repairing the ship would ordinarily be particular average.

There must be an actual peril that threatens all interests if a general average claim is to be recognized. A general average claim will not be recognized if the peril is imaginary and the sacrifice is made in the mistaken belief that a peril exists when in fact it does not.

Any extraordinary expenses that are incurred rest upon the interest incurring those expenses if no part of the venture is saved. This appears to be fair if the sacrifice is a jettison. It makes no difference that the jettisoned property is lost sooner than the rest of the property in cases where a portion of the cargo is jettisoned but the entire venture is subsequently lost. This practice also applies to a sacrifice or extraordinary expense of a particular interest. The other portions of the ship and cargo do not contribute to such extraordinary expense if nothing is saved. This is the practice even though this does result in placing the extraordinary expense on a particular interest in that case.

ADJUSTMENT OF GENERAL AVERAGE LOSS. The adjustment of general average losses is a specialty of marine insurance adjusters. Such an adjustment is particularly complicated where a ship contains many parcels of cargo owned by different interests. The value of the property belonging to each interest must be determined on the basis of the value before the loss, and the general average contribution must be calculated for each interest. The entire venture participates, including the ship, the cargo and the freight charges. A general average adjustment may require hundreds of pages of descriptions and figures and may take many months to complete. Each interest must guarantee that it will pay its proportion of the general average charges before its property is released. Insurance on the property is considered a sufficient guarantee if the underwriter guarantees payment of the general average charges. The owner of an uninsured cargo or ship may have to put up a bond or a cash guarantee of payment before that cargo or ship would be released.

The basic principle of general average, as presented in the example given earlier, applies everywhere, although application varies. What interests are included, and how values are determined, depend in part on which particular set of general average rules is applied. The set most widely applied is the York-Antwerp Rules, named after the cities in which they were made and modified by international agreement. Another important set is that of the Port of New York. Other variations are used elsewhere.

Voluntary Expense and Losses—Sue and Labor Efforts of the owners (or other parties at interest) to take any reasonable action or incur any reasonable expense to preserve the venture or minimize the loss are called sue and labor expenses. The possibility of total loss, plus the possiblity that there may also be loss of life, mean that considerable effort is justified to save and protect endangered ocean ventures. Emergency repairs and the costs incurred because of the delays they cause (e.g., continuing the wages of the crew while repairs are effected) can themselves be expensive. There are instances on record in which such costs have equalled the sound value of the repaired vessel. There are also cases in which rescue efforts have failed, so that the total loss included the total value of the property *plus* the expenditure on the unsuccessful rescue attempt.

Sue and labor expenses are expenses incurred for the protection or saving of particular property—a particular part of the cargo, or the vessel. General average charges arise only when the expenditure is necessary to save ship, cargo, and all.

Sue and labor expenses have been paid in cases where the property was not actually damaged. The sue and labor expenses in this case would have been expanded in order to prevent a loss. There also have been cases in which sue and labor expenses have been allowed to an insured in addition to payment for a total loss.

Salvage Marine law imposes an obligation on ship operators to try to save lives endangered at sea. No salvage award is involved solely for life-saving efforts. To encourage the saving of property, a monetary award, called "salvage award," is provided to "salvors"—persons or organizations engaging in salvage operations. It is a legally determined lien against the value of the property saved. Obviously, a salvage award cannot be worth more than the amount saved. Since salvors take the chance that considerable effort may produce little or no award, their risk taking is rewarded by generous salvage awards when they are successful. The award represents a loss to property owners in addition to the damage to property salvaged. There are three elements which are essential if a salvage award is to be made: (1) the property involved must be in peril from some hazard, (2) the salvage service must be voluntary, and (3) there must be a success, at least to some degree, to the effort.

It should be noted that the general rules applying to salvage at sea do not apply where the owner of the property has contracted with an organization to save the specific vessel in distress.

The situations that can arise involving a ship in distress can be complicated. There may be salvage charges; a voluntary sacrifice (jettison) or expenditure (e.g., for a salvage tug) may set up a general average situation; there can be sue and labor expenses if the salvage operation applies to a particular portion of the cargo or to the ship. The exact circumstances and the determination of what efforts were made, under what circumstances, and by whose orders, would all determine the contribution by the various interests involved in the maritime venture.

Profit and Income Losses

Loss of property in ocean marine ventures, as elsewhere, commonly involves losses of income as well as direct property losses and loss through expenses. There are three major categories of losses of income: profits in goods, freight and passage money, and interruption and delay.

Profits in Goods The usual reason for shipping goods is to increase their value. They are expected to be worth more where they are going than they were at their place of origin. If the goods are lost or damaged en route, not only their original cost but also the expected profit on them is lost.

Freight and Passage Money *Freight*, in marine terms, is the charge for carrying goods; *passage money* is the charge for carrying passengers. Usually, freight is prepaid by the shipper. If the voyage is not completed, it is the shipper, not the carrier, who loses that value. Of course, if there has not been prepayment, the ship operator has this loss. The same practice applies to passage money.

Interruption and Delay When completion of a voyage is delayed, the loss in profit runs beyond the effects suffered on that particular voyage. While a vessel is tied up by a delay in one voyage, it cannot be making another. Since freight charges are per voyage, not per day, any significant delay means a loss of some earning potential. Unfortunately, while earnings are lost, expenses do not drop accordingly. Even an idle vessel costs something to maintain. Many delays—such as waiting for a berth at which to unload cargo, waiting for high tide to float a vessel stranded on a bar, or in a port while waiting for a repair part to be fabricated and delivered—involve the costs of maintaining a crew and operating some machinery and equipment.

Cycles in demand for shipping will sometimes make loss from delay more serious. What income will be lost depends on the demand for shipping space the vessel could provide. Shipowners have found themselves with vessels tied up when there is a high demand for space, then available when demand has slackened. This is especially possible when a vessel is laid up for extensive repairs which can take months or longer to complete. These variations are reflected in swings in the market value of existing vessels. For example, when the Suez Canal was closed because of conflict in the Near East, the value of oil tankers capable of rounding the Cape of Good Hope increased. A vessel constructed or reconstructed during this period might have been ready for service just in time to encounter the Arab oil embargo, and sat idle piling up maintenance and interest expense until the market opened up again. These vagaries can make valuation of ships difficult. Under temporary market conditions, a usable vessel may be worth several times its replacement cost, while at other times its immediate value may be only a fraction of that same cost.

Under some circumstances, cargo losses can produce similar results. Damage to a shipment of particularly heavy equipment, or of specialized production machinery, for example, may produce serious delays in production or other operations at the location to which they were being shipped. There may be lost contracts or penalties for failure to fulfill contracts

Delay can occur without any damage to property. For example, in the mid-1970s, one African nation ordered heavy cargoes in quantities far beyond the unloading capacity of its port. Loaded vessels were tied up for weeks, waiting a chance to discharge their cargoes. Some even returned their unloaded cargoes to their original ports, without delivery, but with considerable expense of transit. In certain circumstances, delays or the impossibility of completing the venture are called *frustration of the adventure*. Strikes of longshoremen or teamsters as well as of ships' personnel have produced such losses, as have wars, revolutions, and other political upheavals. In such circumstances, not only do shipowners and operators have expensive but idle investments, but also shippers cannot collect their receivables and, typically, run up interest costs and other expenses during the wait.

Liability Interests in Ocean Marine Losses

The laws and customs apportioning financial responsibility for loss, and otherwise affecting interests in ships and cargoes, differ in many respects from the laws and customs applying to conveyance and cargoes on land.

General Nature of Ocean Marine Liability for Loss Ocean marine rules affixing financial responsibility for loss were created in response to five important characteristics of ocean marine commerce. One of these characteristics is that *ocean trade is international.* Countries differ in their laws as applied to the ships under their jurisdiction on the high seas and as applied to occurrences within their territorial waters. The discussions in this text will follow generally the laws of the United States, but particular attention will also be given to the laws of Great Britain. The development of ocean marine law (admiralty law) generally and of ocean marine insurance is closely tied to the development of British ocean trade and British maritime law. Custom and usage, which are extremely important in ocean marine law and insurance throughout the world, are to a large extent the result of British practices.

The second important factor in the rules and customs affecting interests in ocean marine commerce and property is the *considerable distance between the parties involved,* especially between buyers and sellers of goods. This means that considerable time is required to complete transactions. An important result is the considerable cost of financing a transaction while it is in progress.

A third significant factor is the *cost of oceangoing ships and the variety of conditions affecting their use.* Modern vessels may cost millions of dollars. Skill in vessel operation and ability to invest large sums do not necessarily go together. Furthermore, the shifting economics (seasonal, cyclical, and irregular) of international trade require that there be some flexibility in ships' employment. A properly maintained ship lasts decades, and during that time a wide variety of trading conditions will occur. Changes occur in demand with respect to both commodities and routes, and there are also technological changes (e.g., development of more efficient larger tankers, the cryogenic ships, and vessels specifically designed to handle containers). The combination of large long-term investments requiring considerable skill in management with the shift in demand for use has led to a sophisticated system for dividing up responsibility for ships and their operation.

The fourth conditioning factor in ocean marine laws and customs is the *significance of the physical hazards faced.* Particularly when law and customs were being developed and settled, venturing life and property at sea was a very hazardous business, and this characteristic was recognized.

A fifth conditioning factor was the *importance of ocean trade and ships to the commercial and military strength of a nation.* Hence, governments took care to encourage their nationals to engage in international trade.

These five conditioning factors together led the authorities to take great care not to impose legal liability in a way that would increase the possibility of catastrophic loss to a particular shipper, owner, or operator much beyond what was inherent in the nature of ocean trade itself.

Liability of Ship Owners and Operators

Liability for Cargo. Maritime practice and the Carriage of Goods by Sea Acts of both the United States and Britain generally provide that the ship operator is not liable for loss or damage to cargo aboard the ship if the operator has exercised due diligence and has provided a ship that is seaworthy in every respect. This principle carries forward from the practice of many hundreds of years and is based on the theory that all participants in a maritime venture take their chances on the hazards which threaten the venture. Shipowners are exposed to loss of ships and cargo owners are exposed to loss of cargo. If shipowners can prove that due diligence was exercised, they are relieved of liability. American statutes in this respect apply to commerce between the United States and other nations, including the loading and unloading of cargo. These statutes do not apply to domestic shipments by water unless the bill of lading includes reference to the statutory provisions.

The limitation of liability on the part of international carriers by sea should be contrasted to the liability of a common carrier by land. In the United States, a common carrier by land for practical purposes guarantees the safe delivery of the cargo. This extensive liability will be discussed in detail in connection with inland marine exposures and insurance in Chapter 9. The difference between carriers by land and carriers by sea is pointed out here in order to emphasize the very limited liability of the carrier by sea.

Liability for Passengers. The liability of a ship operator for passengers is limited as compared to the liability of a common carrier in the United States. Here again the theory is that the passengers aboard a ship are joint venturers with the ship operator. Due diligence on the part of the operator generally relieves the operator of liability. The ship operator, however, may be obligated to provide medical treatment for a sick passenger or crew member.

Liability for Workers. The general ocean marine rule is that a shipowner's or operator's liability for the crew is based upon the principle of exercising due diligence and providing a seaworthy ship. The operator who provides a seaworthy ship and has exercised due diligence has only a limited liability to crew members, consisting of some obligations for medical care and deviation from the normal course of the ship in order to save life. However, when a crew member is injured, courts frequently find that the circumstances of the injury themselves are evidence that the vessel was not seaworthy.

Several acts of Congress have affected the liability of ship operators and owners of vessels in United States waters or of vessels carrying the American flag. One of these was the Jones Act, passed in 1920. This provides that a crew member who is injured in the course of employment as a result of negligence, not only on the part of the ship operator or owner, but also on the part of the master or a fellow crew member, can recover damages for injuries.[3]

Liability of an employer to maritime employees other than ship officers and crew members is subject in the United States to the federal Longshoremen's and Harbor Workers' Compensation Act. This workers' compensation law applies to persons who are not crew members but are otherwise "employed in maritime employment, in whole or in part, upon the navigable waters of the United States." A major application, specified in the Act, is to longshoremen when loading or unloading cargo. This was considered "maritime" because in earlier days (and in some parts of the world today), the loading and unloading of cargo was (is) a duty of the crew. The workers' compensation laws of the various states apply to other activities of longshoremen.[4]

In many countries, including the United States, longshoremen commonly are not employees of ship operators but of stevedoring companies that contract with ship operators to do loading, unloading, and other stevedoring work. This arrangement left shipowners and operators open to tort claims from longshoremen. Many claims were based on alleged violation of the warranty of seaworthiness. In 1972, the Longshoremen's and Harbor Workers' Act was amended to provide that claims against vessels by longshoremen and by persons engaged in ship building or repair "shall not be based upon the warranty of seaworthiness or a breach thereof at the time the injury occurred."[5] This made workers' compensation the sole benefit in such cases.

Liability for Collision. The owner or operator of a ship may be held liable for resulting damage if the ship is operated negligently and property not aboard the offending vessel is damaged as a result. The liability of the shipowner or operator as a result of collision is limited in varying degrees by the size or value of the ship upon which the negligence rests. Under United States law, one limitation that can be invoked when a defendant shipowner was not personally negligent is the value of the ship after the collision, plus freight earned on that passage. However, if the claims against the shipowner include some for bodily injury, the total limitation on this class of claim cannot be less than $60 per gross ton of the vessel. British law also provides liability limits for shipowners not personally responsible. Of course, defense costs are incurred in addition to these limits, and there is always the possibility the owner will be held to have been personally negligent.

Collisions in many cases are due to fault on the part of both vessels. It was the practice for many years for the fault to be considered equal between two ships that were in collision if there was fault on the part of both ships. In 1975 the United States Supreme Court held that where American jurisdiction applies, the damages are to be apportioned according to "comparative negliglence;" that is, each party is to pay in proportion to its negligence.[6] Thus, an operator whose vessel was adjudged to have contributed 30 percent of the total negligence involved would be responsible for 30 percent of the total loss.

Liability for Pollution. The last few years have seen a rapid increase in the awareness of possible liability for damage by pollution. In general, the theory is that a vessel and its operator should be held liable for damage caused by polluting material discharged from the ship. Some states have passed laws which place almost absolute liability on the operators of ships, while other state laws and federal laws are based upon the principle of negligence.

It has been the practice for many years for ships to clean their tanks or their holds while at sea and to discharge the resultant material or debris at sea. Such polluting material may drift ashore, in which case the state, the federal government, or the owners of shore property may make claim against the operator of the ship for the damage. Present American law (The Water Quality Improvement Act) imposes a liability of $100 per gross ton or $14 million, whichever is less, for cleanup of spills of hazardous substances in the navigable waters of the United States. A civil penalty (fine) can also be assessed for spillage of hazardous substances that cannot be cleaned up.

No complete statement will be possible for several years on the degree of pollution liability to which ship operators may be subject. Law and court decisions are in a state of flux because of pressure from the people and agencies seeking to protect the environment, and because of the resistance offered by organizations that might be held liable for pollution damage. Since the law on this subject is changing rather rapidly, current publications must be consulted to determine the present status of shipowners' and operators' liability.

OCEAN MARINE INSURANCE OPERATIONS

Ocean marine insurance has a longer direct history than any other branch of insurance. Ocean marine insurance terminology and practices took much of their present shape in the late 1600s, influenced by customs and practices of the preceding 200 years. Since ocean marine was the first kind of insurance to take on modern form, other kinds of insurance operations, particularly property and liability insurance, have been strongly influenced by it.

Direct Origins of Marine Insurance

Even ancient and medieval history include references to devices similar to insurance. These consisted, in one way or another, of means whereby one person assumed a loss exposure or a portion of a loss exposure from a commercial venturer in return for the payment of what amounted to a premium. The last important step in this developmental chain was the *bottomry bond.*

The bottomry bond was a form of note which was given by the

owner of a vessel to the money lender who financed the voyage, using the ship as collateral. The shipowner paid back the amount of the loan plus an interest charge if the voyage was completed successfully. However, the owner was discharged from debt if the vessel was lost. The interest charge, to the extent that it exceeded the normal rate of interest on loans, constituted a form of insurance premium for a possible loss of the ship. It was not designated as an insurance charge but the effect was that of making an extra payment in return for discharge of the debt in case of a maritime disaster.

The term "bottomry bond" is still used today to designate a note given by the owner of a vessel in order to raise funds when all other means of securing a loan have failed. The vessel may be in distress at some port of refuge where the master has no other facilities available to obtain the funds necessary to complete the venture. The usual arrangement today for securing funds with the ship as collateral is by means of a mortgage rather than by a bottomry bond. The lender who supplies money today with a bottomry bond as security acquires an insurable interest in the ship and he has a sufficient insurable interest to justify the purchase of insurance to protect that interest.

The *respondentia bond* is similar to the bottomry bond except that the property pledged as collateral is the cargo rather than the ship. The respondentia bond survives today and is used in rare cases to secure finances where other means of getting a loan have failed. However, neither the bottomry bond nor the respondentia bond is important in today's ocean commerce. Modern mortgage and lending practices and current insurance practices are better adapted to the needs of businesses engaged in ocean commerce.

In medieval times, church officials opposed many arrangements that attempted to alleviate the results of disaster. The theory was that disaster was visited upon people by God and that it was evil to forestall such distress. Bottomry and respondentia bonds were discouraged as being contrary to the will of God. The lending of money at an interest rate was also considered to be evil. The term "usury" was applied to any interest which was charged for a loan. It was only later in America that "usury" came to mean an unjust or unreasonable rate of interest.

The discovery of America and the expanding commerce across the Atlantic Ocean brought an increased need for protection against the financial losses resulting from maritime disasters. Europe was coming into the mercantile age, and shipowners came more and more to depend upon financial support from others. It was during this period that the idea of transferring a risk to an insurer in exchange for a premium became an acceptable and desirable practice.

Development of Marine Insurance

Early insurance practices consisted of transfer of a loss exposure from one person to another person in return for the payment of a premium. There were no insurance companies in the modern sense. The insurance "policy" might consist of a piece of paper signifying that the insurer would pay an agreed amount of money to the assured if the venture were lost.

It is generally considered that the first specific statutory recognition of insurance in England was in the British law known as the Arbitration Act of Elizabeth I, passed in 1601. Its language reflected a changed attitude toward forestalling the effect of disaster, as well as a clear understanding of the basic nature of insurance. The principle of spreading the risk was expressed in the following language:

> . . . it comethe to passe that upon the losse or perishinge of any shippe there followethe not the undoinge of any man, but the losse lightethe rather easilie upon many than heavilie upon fewe. . . .

Lloyd's of London The designation "Lloyd's" comes from a man named Edward Lloyd, who in the late 1600s ran a coffee house in London. This coffee house was conveniently located near the wharves and it became a gathering place for persons interested in maritime ventures. Mr. Lloyd encouraged business by providing information regarding ships and their sailings and in 1696 he began publishing a small sheet called "Lloyd's News" which gave maritime news.

Lloyd's coffee house became a meeting place for the buying and selling of ships, and it was natural that persons who were willing to accept insurable exposures on maritime ventures would also frequent the establishment. A formal organization of underwriters was set up in 1769 and then took over the publication of the newsletter that continues today as "Lloyd's List."

Lloyd's of London today consists of several thousand underwriters who assume risks for their individual accounts. There is a corporation which is a governing body for the purpose of establishing rules of operation and that does not itself transact any business. The corporation also decides who is qualified for membership—members are not limited to British citizens, and there are several American members of Lloyd's. The financial and personal requirements for membership are high, which results in a high degree of integrity and responsibility on the part of the Lloyd's operation. Members are personally liable for all losses incurred.

The members of Lloyd's of London do their business through brokers who are familiar with the types of business that are preferred by different members. There are many groups of underwriters within the Lloyd's organization called syndicates. Several members who are interested in the same types of exposure will place responsibility for the acceptance or rejection of an exposure with one person or a small group of persons who are specialists in this area. One syndicate, for example, may be especially interested in aviation exposure; another may be interested in petroleum exposure. A member of Lloyd's of London may be a member of more than one syndicate. A member's participation may be entirely financial in that he or she will allow one or more syndicates to handle his or her business, or the member may actively participate on his or her own account or as an operating member of a syndicate.

The financial requirements for membership as an underwriter at Lloyd's are: (1) a specified amount of personal wealth fully available to pay insurance claims; (2) a deposit of funds in the Association's guaranty fund to cover the mischance that any member cannot pay claims; and (3) a deposit of each premium received, left until sufficiently long after the policy has expired to provide reasonable assurance all claims are known and can be properly reserved for (usually) three years. The amount of wealth stipulated in the first requirement has been increased from time to time. The amount of deposit in the guaranty fund depends on the types and amounts of insurance transactions in which the member will engage.

Lloyd's maintains funds on deposit in the United States to guarantee payment of claims. These assets are contractually dedicated to the protection of insureds in this country alone.

Only brokers who are approved by the Lloyd's Association may enter Lloyd's to purchase insurance for clients. American business generally reaches the floor at Lloyd's through American brokers who have arranged connections with Lloyd's brokers. This might appear to be a cumbersome channel but in practice it works smoothly and quickly. An exposure to be insured may be submitted by cable to a London broker who is familiar with the members of syndicates that would be interested in the particular submission.

The British Market Just as Lloyd's provides a source for a wide variety of insurance in addition to wet marine insurance, the British insurance market has grown over the years to include a number of stock insurance companies that also participate in writing marine business. One may find both the British companies and Lloyd's underwriters participating on the same loss exposures placed entirely in the company market. It is common in the British market to find a large number of underwriters participating on even relatively small exposures.

The American Market In the American market, there is a much stronger tendency to place an entire marine account with a single insurer. The American stock companies exercise a much stronger influence on the U.S. marine market than their counterparts do in England. The first stock insurance company in the United States was organized in the latter part of the eighteenth century and its first writings were in the marine lines. The ocean marine activities of some insurance companies are placed in the hands of marine managers who will operate for the several companies in the underwriting of marine risks. In several areas where the capacity of many companies is required for the placement of large exposures, American insurance companies have been permitted by the federal government to form underwriting syndicates. The best known of the American syndicates is the American Hull Insurance Syndicate. This group which includes a majority of the marine companies in the United States is the primary domestic market for large ocean hull exposures.

In England, much of the Protection and Indemnity (P&I) insurance for oceangoing vessels is written in mutual associations called P&I Clubs. These clubs specialize in P&I exposures and are much more like reciprocal organizations than mutual insurance companies in the U.S. On very large exposures, particularly in the area of hull coverage, it is not unusual to see part of the exposure placed in several different markets, for example, the American, British, and perhaps one or two European markets.

A large number of insurers may belong to a group for the purpose of developing policy forms and clauses. However, there is no rating bureau in the ocean marine field comparable to the insurance rating bureaus that establish rates and policy forms for insurance coverages on land.

It is characteristic of the ocean marine business that a large proportion of it is placed through brokerage offices specializing in this kind of business. The marine insurance broker is more than a sales and service representative. In many cases the broker may be involved in the application of general average and in the collection of general average charges or other assessments in connection with casualties. There is a tendency for these brokers to specialize in the handling of particular types of ships and coverages applying to different situations.

The Worldwide Market Insurance on large-valued units is spread throughout almost all of the insurers in the world. A very large crude oil carrier may be worth from $50 million to almost $100 million, including the value of the cargo. It has already been pointed out that the value of an off-shore drilling rig may run into the hundreds of millions of dollars. It takes the entire insurance capacity of the ocean marine insurers to cover such huge values.

There may be a lead group of insurance companies or of syndicates within Lloyd's of London that will arrange the coverage and suggest a rate for such a unit. There are also some "lead underwriters" outside Lloyd's. For example, most major hull insurance written in the United States is led by the American Hull Insurance Syndicate. After a lead underwriter has agreed to a set of conditions and rates, proposals for any additional coverage needed are then submitted to other underwriters, who usually then make their acceptances on the same terms and rates.

Insurance on smaller units in the United States is placed largely in American insurance companies. In cases where the value is within the capacity of a particular group (considering their automatic reinsurance capacity), the particular group can make the complete arrangements for the coverage. A large portion of the ocean marine insurance written by American companies or American branches of alien companies is handled by management offices that operate for several different insurance companies in the ocean marine field. A very large ocean marine insurance company may operate for itself, seeking the assistance of other groups when the size of the unit becomes larger than the company or group wishes to carry alone. As previously mentioned a large portion of marine insurance is written by members of Lloyd's of London.

Laws Governing Marine Insurance

The collection of laws that applies to ocean marine operations and shipping is known collectively as Admiralty Law. Within this section, both United States and British Admiralty law will be discussed.

United States Law Federal law and state laws in the United States relating to ocean marine insurance tend to be general in nature. This is a reflection of the international character of the market and the necessity for flexibility in the writing of ocean marine coverages.

For many years, property and liability insurance operations in the United States were divided by law into separate classes, such as fire, windstorm, automobile physical damage, automobile liability, and burglary and robbery. These individual classes were grouped into four major divisions: fire, marine, liability, and surety. In most states, an insurer that wrote fire and marine could not write liability and surety business, and vice versa. This was known as, "separation of underwriting powers." Regulations were, and in many states still are, different for different classes and groups, especially the marine group. In particular, all states exempt ocean marine insurance from any rate or form filing requirements.

It has therefore been necessary to identify what is, and what is not, "marine" and "ocean marine" insurance. In the early 1930s most states adopted a generally standard "Nation-Wide Marine Definition and Interpretation of the Insuring Powers of Marine and Transportation Underwriters." (The title "Nation-Wide Marine Definition" was adopted in 1933.) In addition, companies writing most of the marine insurance premium volume agreed among themselves to use the Definition even in those states in which it did not have the force of law. The development and acceptance of multiple-line underwriting in the early 1950s considerably reduced the significance of the Definition. Its present effect will be considered more fully in the discussion of inland marine insurance in Chapter 9. Its effect on ocean marine insurance was principally in classifying imports and exports as subjects of ocean marine insurance. Imports could be covered by ocean marine insurance until such time as they became mixed with the general property in the United States; exports could be covered by ocean marine insurance as soon as they are designated for export. Thus, marine insurance could cover imports and exports from the point of origin to destination, even though origin and destination were many miles from a seaport. This is known as warehouse to warehouse coverage.

British Law British law forms the basis for much of the world law and practices affecting ocean marine insurance. This is largely due to the importance of England as a trading nation during the past several hundred years and also to the fact that the British Parliament passed several acts which define important principles in connection with marine insurance. The British principles tend to be followed everywhere unless there is specific local law to the contrary.

The definition of Marine insurance which is contained in the Marine Insurance Act, 1906, of the British Parliament is thus widely accepted as the definition of such insurance:

> A contract of marine insurance is a contract whereby the insurer undertakes to indemnify the assured, in manner and to the extent thereby agreed, against marine losses, that is to say, the losses incident to marine adventure.

It is obvious that further definitions are required in order to state what constitutes a marine adventure and what are maritime perils. The act further provides that there is a marine adventure where:

(a) Any ship, goods or other movables are exposed to maritime perils. Such property is in this Act referred to as "insurable property."
(b) The earning or acquisition of any freight, passage money, commission, profit, or other pecuniary benefit, or the security for

any advances, loan, or dispersements, is endangered by the exposure of insurable property to maritime perils.

(c) Any liability to a third party may be incurred by the owner of, or other person interested in, or responsible for, insurable property, by reason of maritime perils.

Note that marine insurance by these definitions includes not only insurance against loss of insurable property but also loss of income and loss because of liability to a third party. This recognizes the practice in ocean marine insurance of providing coverage on freight, money, and third party liability coverage under the running down, collision and protection and indemnity coverages. These will be discussed in detail in Chapter 8.

The law's reference to "maritime perils" means the perils consequent on, or incidental to, the navigation of the sea, as previously discussed. The law also allows the addition of perils "either of the like kind or which may be designated by the policy." This makes it permissible to cover other perils such as theft or fresh water damage as well as those which traditionally have been covered by marine insurance.

The British Marine Insurance Act of 1906 recognized the warehouse to warehouse coverage as a marine risk. Its provisions relating to "mixed sea and land risks" also recognized that certain situations that are analogous to marine risks may also be covered by marine insurance, including ships in course of construction and shipyard facilities.

Efforts by fire insurers to prevent marine insurers from invading the fire field resulted in an interesting rule that was effective during the days when insurance in the United States was divided into categories. The Nation-Wide Marine Definition adopted in 1933 specified that bridges and tunnels could be insured under marine policies only if the coverage were of an "all-risks" nature. A marine policy could not be written merely for fire and certain other perils of the extended coverage nature. Marine coverage on piers and wharves had to exclude fire and wind coverage. The British Marine Insurance Act of 1906 does not contain any such limitation.

Modern Ocean Marine Insurance Practices

From its ancient origins, ocean marine insurance has developed into a sophisticated business. In order to evaluate ocean marine exposures and select the proper insurance and noninsurance techniques for treating those exposures, it is helpful to consider some of the factors which affect modern ocean marine insurance practices. Many of the factors considered by marine insurers must also be considered by the risk managers of firms with ocean marine exposures. (Ocean marine insurance coverages will be discussed in Chaper 8.)

Exposure Factors World trade conditions, weather, and other natural and human phenomena make it necessary for ocean marine insurers continuously to adapt rates and coverages to changing conditions. A ship that takes a cargo to Europe in mid-winter meets entirely different conditions than a ship making the same voyage during the summer. And one extra stop in a hurricane-prone area during the late summer can add an additional hazard that must be recognized in providing coverage.

Political conditions can change exposures rapidly. The closing of the Suez Canal for example, forces ships to take the much more hazardous route around Africa. Labor trouble or political unrest in a port or nation exposes cargoes to additional hazards from delays, lack of adequate care, and sabotage; ships are delayed, the number of vessels in the area increases as unloading is slowed, increasing chance of collision; ships and cargoes are diverted to other destinations, changing exposures. Changes in shipping trade demand cause changes in usage of ships; ships and crews are used for unaccustomed cargoes and on unaccustomed routes. New types of vessels and new shipping methods are developed, all needing insurance coverage before there has been enough experience with them to see their actual propensities for loss. Finally, international competition among both insureds and insurers puts much pressure on each side to match the best terms obtainable anywhere.

To cope successfully with these conditions, marine insurers use a considerable amount of judgment based on long experience and certain basic elements that apply to ocean exposures generally. The following factors are some of those which insurers might consider in determining whether to insure a particular exposure, the rate or premium which would be charged, and what conditions would be imposed on the insured:

1. The ship or the ships in the fleet and the general record of the shipowner in maintaining seaworthiness.
2. The route over which the ship or ships will operate, and the weather conditions at the time of the year if coverage is for a specific voyage.
3. The condition of the harbors into which calls will be made, and the world political situation in those areas.
4. The type of cargo to be carried and any inherent hazards in the cargo.
5. The coverage granted in the policy, including participations and deductibles.

6. The experience of the shipowner, operator, or cargo shipper, and whether this experience includes operations similar to the one projected for the trip or the term of the policy.
7. The competitive situation in the world insurance market.
8. The age and registry of ships.
9. The methods of packing cargo.

Marine insurers maintain their own records of their policyholders or prospective policyholders. The loss experience of a fleet operator or shipper is an important factor in determining the rates to be charged and the breadth of coverage to be provided. Ocean marine underwriters are truly dependent upon personal knowledge and expertise in achieving success in this field.

Ocean Marine Insurance Rates Ocean marine insurers are their own actuaries and rate makers. As each exposure is proposed, the insurer must determine the rate and conditions for it. This requires great flexibility and makes regulated rates generally impractical. In addition, as previously noted, direct international competition for marine insurance requires that ocean marine insurers have freedom to meet changing international competitive conditions.

Sources of Rate-Making Information Experienced insurers maintain a large volume of information regarding ships, shipping and cargoes. The nature of each ship and its apparent ability to operate safely are important factors. The ship that is designed for operation in the Great Lakes, for example, would not be considered for operation in the North Atlantic Ocean during the winter season. One of the important factors that is considered is the design of the ship and whether it will be operating in waters and carrying cargo for which it is considered to be suitable.

Information concerning many factors relevant to the setting of ocean marine insurance rates must come from the applicant, which explains the insistence upon utmost good faith. In practice, the information comes through marine insurance brokers.

Special Situations The coverage of war risks is one example of a special situation. The war risk exposure is covered under special conditions or policies and at rates that are adjusted frequently and quickly in accordance with conditions in different parts of the world.

Another special situation that must be considered involves new types of ships, such as very large crude petroleum tanker ships. Several of these ships have been lost due to conditions that are inherent in such vessels and their operation. Some of the losses occurred during the cleaning of the tanks within the vessel. It appeared that the cleaning operation produced flammable vapors that perhaps were not anticipated in the design or building of ships. Thus, experience must be followed carefully in connection with any newly designed ships. Insurers maintain careful records of the experience not only of their own policyholders but also that of other underwriters or ship operators.

As noted earlier, one of the important developments in connection with ocean marine insurance during the past few years has been the extensive use of containers. Containers have generally reduced the amount of pilferage and theft at ports, but since containers may be carried on deck, some instances have occurred where such containers were washed overboard.

Insurers try to anticipate the results of such new developments and then adjust promptly to experience as it develops. Thus, they have learned what to require in the way of the securing of on-deck containers and to recognize the differences in hazards between ships specifically designed for on-deck carriage of containers and ordinary ships where some containers are put on deck as a matter of adding cargo capacity. Similarly, provision must be made for other developments such as super tankers, cryogenic tankers, LNG carriers, and oil drilling rigs of new design and in new locations (such as the stormy North Sea), and the hundreds of new materials and designs in products shipped as cargoes.

Insurable Interest The application of the principle of insurable interest is basically the same in relation to all property and situations, but there are particular aspects that apply to hull, cargo, freight, and liability. The simplest insurable interest in a ship is that of owner. However, the interest also may be as mortgagee, as a lessee under a charter party, as the lender of money under a bottomry bond, or the operator of a ship under any circumstances where the loss of the ship or damage to it would cause a financial loss.

The simplest form of insurable interest on cargo is that of ownership. A bailee also has an insurable interest because that person has a responsibility for the property. Insurable interest in cargo may also exist in a person to whom the property is shipped on consignment. A person who is to receive a consignment of goods would be precluded from earning a commission if the goods were lost. In addition, the person whose interest in the freight charges would be lost due to the destruction of the goods also has an insurable interest. That person may secure insurance against the loss of the freight that would have been earned had the goods been safely delivered.

The operator of a ship also acquires an insurable interest in the safe operation of the ship by reason of possible liabilities to others whose person or property might be damaged by an occurrence. In particular, the lessee under a charter has an exposure of possible liability for damage to the chartered vessel. Under a demise charter, this exposure essentially represents liability for all damage other than normal wear and tear. The charter party may specify the responsibility. A lessee has an exposure of possible loss of use of the vessel for the unexpired portion of the charter term.

Mere possession of an insurance policy on the property, or possession of the package of documents in connection with shipment of cargo, does not convey an insurable interest. There must be an actual possibility of financial loss before the person acquires an insurable interest in the property.

General rules of insurable interest apply. Thus, insurable interest must exist at the time of loss. It is permissible to buy the coverage before the interest exists when there is a reasonable expectation that an interest will develop. Thus, it is common practice for shipowners to buy insurance on new vessels while they are still under construction with the condition that the insurance is to take effect at time of delivery of the ship. It would be at such a time that the actual insurable interest would occur. Another situation might be where goods are purchased "free on board." The buyer in that case has no insurable interest until the goods are actually shipped, but can buy insurance to take effect at the time when the property is delivered on board and becomes at the buyer's risk.

A partial interest in property is insurable. The exact extent of a partial interest does not need to be known at the time insurance is purchased for there to be a proper insurable interest.

Utmost Good Faith Marine insurance contracts are based upon *uberrimae fidei*, the principle of utmost good faith. If utmost good faith is not observed by either party, the contract may be voided by the other party. The owner of property which may be subject to marine insurance is very likely to have important information regarding the subject of the insurance and is obligated to disclose to the insurer every detail of information available. Concealment of any kind, regardless of whether it arises because of accident, negligence, inadvertence, or mistake, will be fatal to the insurance contract if it is material to the contract. Such concealment, even though unintentional, would be given the same effect as if it were intentional or fraudulent.

This requirement for utmost good faith between the parties is much more stringent in connection with ocean marine insurance than it is in connection with insurance on land. In the United States, unintentional concealment in connection with insurance other than ocean marine is held not to avoid the contract. There have been many cases with insurance on land where a court has held that withholding of information by an insured is not fatal to the insurance contract if the insurer had the information available from other sources or even if the insurer could have obtained the information by diligent inquiry into the situation. The remoteness of time and distance in connection with ocean marine insurance has led to the absolute requirement for utmost good faith between the parties.

The obligation of the insured to reveal facts to the insurer is limited to *material* facts. Generally, it may be said that every circumstance is material which would influence the judgment of a prudent underwriter in fixing the premium or in accepting the exposure. A greater exposure would justify a larger premium, or might influence an insurer to accept a smaller commitment than would be acceptable for a smaller risk. Such facts are material to the underwriter's consideration and must be revealed by the insured to the insurer.

Subrogation The right of an insurer to subrogation appears in marine insurance on the same basis as in other types of insurance. Ocean marine insurers may depend upon the existence of this right under the law, or they may insert a specific provision in the policy under which the insured is obligated to assign its rights against other parties who may be responsible for the loss. Such a clause usually obligates the insured to cooperate in the recovery effort, and the insured is entitled to the amount of any recovery in excess of the amount paid by its insurers less recovery costs.

Warranties The application of warranties to contracts of insurance applying to exposures ashore has been largely removed, particularly in the United States, by court decisions and statutes. But warranties are still important in marine insurance, particularly wet marine—a situation that accords with the continuing emphasis in marine insurance on utmost good faith.

Significance. A warranty is a condition of coverage which must be strictly complied with whether or not it is material to the risk. It is a promise that a particular thing shall be done, that a condition will be fulfilled, or something that the insured affirms or negatives as to its existence. A breach generally voids the coverage from the time of the breach, and the coverage is not reinstated when the breach is corrected. Among subjects that warranties have dealt with have been size and nature of a ship's crew, the areas in which the ship will sail, and the types of cargo it will carry.

Warranties are not treated as seriously in connection with insurance on land as they are with ocean marine insurance. Court decisions relating to insurance on land exposures tend to treat warranties as representations. Some states have passed laws providing that warranties are to be considered as merely representations. A representation must be materially false and made with intent to deceive before it voids the contract.

Affirmative and Promissory. A warranty as it affects an insurance contract may be affirmative or promissory. An affirmative warranty assures that certain facts are true when the contract is effective. A promissory warranty assures that certain conditions will be carried out during the term of the contract.

Implied Warranties. There are certain conditions that are understood to exist in connection with a maritime venture. These are implied warranties. They are just as binding upon the insured and the insurer as if they were expressed in the policy.

The implied warranties generally affecting a maritime venture are: (1) that the ship is seaworthy, (2) that the venture is lawful, (3) that there will be no delay beyond the normal time for starting the venture, and (4) that there will be no deviation from the customary route. All of these implied warranties are subject to interpretations that have developed over a period of several hundreds of years.

SEAWORTHINESS. The insured under an ocean marine insurance policy warrants by implication that the ship is seaworthy at the beginning of the voyage. Seaworthiness requires the following:

1. a competent crew,
2. adequate stores, and
3. machinery and hull in condition to make the voyage.

A ship may leave port under apparent seaworthy conditions but later developments may indicate that the ship was not seaworthy. It then becomes a question of fact, which may eventually have to be determined by a court, whether the ship actually was seaworthy when it left port. A definition of seaworthines, as stated in the British Marine Insurance Act of 1906, is, "A ship is deemed to be seaworthy when she is reasonably fit in all respects to encounter the ordinary perils of the seas of the adventure insured."

It is important to note the requirement that the ship be reasonably fit to encounter the "ordinary perils of the sea of the adventure insured." The mere fact that a ship is lost does not constitute *prima facie* evidence of unseaworthiness. There may be some unusual action of the wind or the waves, or loss due to some other peril. Facts that could be considered as indicating an unseaworthy condition might be the overloading of a ship so that it settled below the load line mark which is painted on the side of the vessel, or starting a voyage with inadequate fuel or provisions or with engines known to be in questionable condition.

In a case which was decided by a British court, it was discovered after a vessel left port that the ship's boilers were defective. The ship returned to port to have the boilers repaired, and was then lost after going to sea the second time. The court decided that the warranty of seaworthiness had been broken by the fact that the ship originally started its voyage with defective boilers and was not seaworthy at that time. The warranty being broken, the underwriters were relieved of liability even though the ship appeared to have been seaworthy when the voyage was started the second time. This is an illustration of the principle that warranties are applied literally, and that once a warranty has been breached the insurance coverage is voided and is not reinstated by correction of the breach.

Changing conditions in maritime commerce bring about modifications from time to time in the application of this implied warranty of seaworthiness. A large part of ocean commerce now is carried on fleets of ships, and it is the obligation of the fleet operator to see that a ship starts each voyage in a seaworthy condition. Time policies on ships are written to cover from one date to another date, and many ships of the fleet may be at sea when the insurance takes effect. It would be impossible for the operator of a large fleet to determine whether each vessel in the fleet is actually seaworthy at the moment that the insurance takes effect. Therefore, the implied warranty of seaworthiness under these circumstances is interpreted to mean that each vessel will be seaworthy at the time it starts each voyage.

Modern conditions relating to cargo have brought about a relaxation of the seaworthiness warranty as it applies to loss of cargo. Insurance policies covering loss to cargo usually agree that seaworthiness is admitted between the shipper and the underwriters. This recognizes the fact that many commercial shippers of cargo have no idea on what particular ship the cargo may be carried. Even where the cargo owner may arrange for carriage on a particular ship, there may be no opportunity to determine that the ship is seaworthy at the time the venture is started.

The admission of seaworthiness of cargo may not be effective if the cargo is being shipped on a vessel which is owned by the shipper or which is chartered to the shipper. A cargo of petroleum, for example, may be carried on a ship that is under the same ownership as the cargo. Such a shipowner or operator under those circumstances would have an opportunity to determine seaworthiness, so that the warranty generally would apply to cargo as well as to the ship.

LEGALITY. There is an implied warranty that the venture is legal. It is not considered proper nor in the public interest for insurers to protect a person against loss in some illegal enterprise. It is important to note that this is the only one of the implied warranties that cannot be modified or negated by a provision in the marine insurance policy.

The implied warranty of legality of the venture does not require that the venture comply with every law of every country in the world.

The laws and regulations of the various countries are so numerous and so complicated that it is impractical to require strict compliance with every law. The American courts, for example, would apply the laws of the United States, and British courts would apply the laws of that country. The breach of some foreign law ordinarily would not be considered a breach of the warranty of legality, especially if the breach were without the privity of the insured.

An example of an illegal venture that would not be covered by a marine insurance policy would be a smuggling venture. There is an enormous traffic in the smuggling of cocaine and marijuana into the United States through the southeastern states along the Gulf of Mexico and the Atlantic Ocean. One of the methods used is to buy an old freighter (usually obtainable for its break-up value) and bring the drugs from South America into international waters off the coast of the United States. The drugs are then off-loaded to high speed motor boats for delivery into one of the hundreds of coves along the shore. The freighter cannot be touched by the United States Coast Guard because it never enters United States waters, and the speedboats are so small and so fast that it is very difficult to catch them. Such an operation is an illegal venture. No underwriter would knowingly insure such vessels. However, should insurance be secured, it would be void because of the implied warranty that the venture is legal.

Consider, however, a liner that unknowingly carries a smuggler among its passengers, or a freight ship operator who unknowingly has contraband cargo aboard. The operation of the liner and freighter themselves is legal, and insurance carried by the owner, operator, and others whose goods are legal is not affected by the illegal actions of persons beyond their knowledge or control. However, the insurance of an owner whose ship is used for illegal means by a charterer of the entire vessel is jeopardized by such use. Also, when ship or goods are damaged by governmental actions taken against illegal activities aboard, that peril is generally not one covered by insurance.

NO DELAY. Underwriters base their premiums for a venture and the acceptance of the risk on expected conditions. If there is a delay in starting a voyage there may be a change in the weather, or a change in international conditions that would make the voyage subject to increased hazards. Some ports become congested at certain times of the year and this may increase the danger of casualty or it may require that a ship stand off from a port to await a berth and thus be exposed to sea perils at a time when it should have been sheltered in port. Therefore, the underwriters covering a specific voyage or venture are entitled to assume that the voyage will start within a reasonable time.

A determination of what is reasonable or unreasonable in the start of a venture would be affected to some extent by custom. For example, a custom that ships making a certain voyage usually wait at some port for a time would be considered in determining whether that delay actually was unreasonable within the implication that the voyage would be started without delay.

The implied warranty of no delay may be modified in time policies or in policies covering cargo. Time policies generally are issued to cover all operations of an insured within the term of the policy, and the insured is assumed to continue normal operations. Premium and acceptance of the exposure by underwriters are based upon the normal operations of the insured so that the insurance is not tied as completely to specific voyages as is the case where the insurance specifically applies to a venture. The shipper of cargo in many cases has no knowledge or control of the time at which the venture starts, so that the warranty of no delay customarily is eliminated under the terms of the policies covering cargo.

NO DEVIATION. Deviation from the customary route may have an effect on the chances of loss. It is emphasized here that an ocean marine policy is based upon an assumption by the underwriters that there will be no deviation from the most direct or customary route for the voyage insured. Here again, the implied warranty of no deviation is not effective under a time policy in which all operations of the insured during any term of the insurance policy are covered. Cargo insurance policies also customarily contain a deviation waiver clause. The shipper or cargo owner normally has no control over the vessel's course, and may be required by the terms of the policy to notify the underwriters if a deviation is discovered. There may be also a requirement that additional premium be paid because of any additional risk that the underwriters cover because of the deviation.

It should again be pointed out that certain deviations are permitted without jeopardizing the insurance coverage. For example, a deviation for the purpose of saving life or to rescue persons involved in the disaster of another ship would be excused. A deviation would also be permissible if it were required for the safety and preservation of the venture covered.

Express Warranties. Sometimes particular conditions on the handling of the property or on the voyage are inserted as express warranties in ocean marine policies. In the early days, the armament carried by the ship was a frequent subject of such warranty; others were the size and nature of the crew, and identity of the ship's captain. The custom grew of calling these and other limitations as "warranties," even those beyond the control of the insured or any ship operator.

Thus, instead of stating that loss by capture or seizure is

"excluded," the common wording is that the property is "*warranted* free from capture and seizure." Thus, ocean marine express warranties are really of two kinds: those of the usual type, relating to *hazards* which may affect the probability of loss of the kinds insured against; and those that exclude certain *perils* and *losses* from coverage. In one important way, the effect of the two types is the same—if either is violated, the insurer does not pay. But when a warranty relating to *hazards* is violated, the contract is voidable; it may be completely unenforceable.

When a "warranty" excluding certain perils or losses is violated, the effect is really not on the whole contract, but merely on the insurer's obligation to pay for the particular loss excluded. For example, if the policy contains a warranty that the vessel will not sail in certain areas, violation could be the end of all coverage on that voyage; even though a loss occurred independently and later, it would not be paid. But when the policy contains the common provision that the property is "warranted" free from partial damage amounting to less than 5 percent of its value, the fact that such damage was in fact suffered does not prevent recovery for a later total loss caused by a peril insured against.

With respect to any warranty that is applicable, and whose violation would void the contract, an insured who learns that compliance will be difficult or impossible should give immediate notice to the underwriters and ask for permission to breach the warranty. The underwriters may be willing to give permission for the breach, particularly if an additional premium commensurate with the additional risk can be secured. This discussion of warranties will become more meaningful when ocean marine insurance coverage is discussed in Chapter 8.

Chapter Notes

1. William D. Winter, *Marine Insurance*, 3rd ed. (New York: McGraw-Hill, 1952), p. 100.
2. Pillsbury Flour Mills Co. v. Becker S. S. Co., D.C., N.Y., 49 F. 2d 648, 650.
3. The Jones Act is discussed further in CPCU 4, Chapter 6.
4. The Longshoremen's and Harbor Workers' Act is discussed further in CPCU 4, Chapter 6.
5. 33 U.S.C. Sec. 905(b) (1972). For a resume of the effect of this amendment, see Paul N. Daigle, "Third Party Liability under 1972 LSHWCA Amendments," 17 *For the Defense* (July, 1976), pp. 89-94.
6. United States v. Reliable Transfer Co., Inc., 95 S.Ct. 1708 (1975).

CHAPTER 8

Ocean Marine Insurance

INTRODUCTION

The parties to an ocean marine insurance contract are not bound by law or regulation to use any standard form. This is in contrast to the situation in fire insurance, for example, where standard fire policy forms are required by law or regulation.

However, standardization has benefits for both underwriters and insureds. In order to gain these benefits, the members of Lloyd's of London agreed in 1779 that all would use a standard insurance policy that they had developed. This contract was submitted to the British Parliament, as was customary with business developments at that time, was approved, and as a result, has been the basis for ocean marine insurance contract wording ever since. The British Marine Insurance Act of 1906, still in force, contains wording for marine insurance very similar to the 1779 Lloyd's form. Legislators, underwriters, and insureds have been reluctant to change the wording because court interpretations have established its meanings during the past two hundred years. However, there have been efforts by marine underwriters to modernize the language wherever that could be done without disturbing the world marine insurance market.

The American Institute of Marine Underwriters, organized in 1898, has played an important role in formulating and clarifying ocean marine insurance policy clauses.

POLICY FORMS

The basic ocean marine policy still essentially resembles the Lloyd's policy that has been in use for about two hundred years. It was officially recognized (but not required to be used) in the British Marine Insurance Act of 1906. This policy is a skeleton of what a complete insurance contract should be. The practice today is to use this language in the makeup of "combination" policies. The policy is amended or modified by one or more of the following means:

1. Clauses that are not to apply to the particular contract may be overprinted.
2. Printed clauses (such as the "forms" which are attached to property and casualty policies in the United States) may be attached to provide additional or necessary conditions.
3. Additional provisions and clauses may be written or typed onto the policy itself.

The provisions of the basic policy itself are such that they may apply to both hull and cargo, but the actual property covered would be specified.

Lloyd's General Form

Groups of insurers throughout the world have developed combination policies and clauses that are used to provide the exact coverage needed for a specific case, but all are based in part at least on the old Lloyd's form. Therefore, an examination of the Lloyd's policy is necessary to understand the further discussion of the coverage and the effect of this document. Following is the S.G. form of the Marine Insurance Policy that was adopted in 1779, and printed in the Marine Insurance Act of 1906. The designation "S.G." originally appears to have meant "ship" and "goods." It will be noted that the conditions are such that they can apply to both ship and goods (or cargo). The exact application is made by additional terms that are added to this skeleton policy.

S.G. Form of Marine Insurance Policy

Be it known that ______________ as well in ________________own name, as for and in the Name and Names of all and every other Person or Persons to whom the same doth may, or shall appertain, in part or in all, doth make Assurance and cause ______________ and them, and every one of them, to be insured, lost or not lost, at and from ______________. Upon any kinds of goods and Merchandise and also the Body, Tackle, Apparel, Ordnance, Munition, Artillery, Boat and other Furniture, of and in the good Ship or Vessel called the ______________ whereof is Master under God, for this present voyage, ______________ or whosoever else shall go for Master in the said Ship, or by whatsoever other names or names the same Ship, or the Master thereof, is or shall be named or called; beginning the Adventure upon the said Goods and Merchandise from the loading thereof ______________ aboard the said Ship ______________ upon the said Ship, etc., ______________ and shall so continue and endure during her Abode there, upon the said Ship, etc.; and further, until the said Ship, with all her Ordnance, Tackle, Apparel, etc., and Goods and Merchandise whatsoever, shall be arrived at ______________ upon the said Ship, etc., until she hath moored at Anchor Twenty-four Hours in good Safety; and upon the Goods and Merchandises until the same be there discharged and safely landed; and it shall be lawful for the said Ship, etc., in this Voyage to proceed and sail to and touch and stay at any Ports or Places whatsoever ______________ without Prejudice to the Insurance. The said Ship, etc., Goods and Merchandises, etc., for so much as concerns the Assured by Agreement between the Assured and Assurers in this policy, are and shall be valued at ______________.

Touching the Adventures and Perils which we the Assurers are contented to bear and do take upon us in this Voyage, they are, of the Seas, Men-of-War, Fire, Enemies, Pirates, Rovers, Thieves, Jettisons, Letters of Mart and Countermart, Surprisals, Takings at Sea, Arrests, Restraints and Detainments of all Kings, Princes and People, of what Nation, Conditions or Quality soever, Barratry of the Master and Mariners, and of all other Perils, Losses and Misfortunes that have or shall come to the Hurt, Detriment or Damage of the said Goods and Merchandise and Ship, etc., or any Part thereof; and in case of any Loss or Misfortune, it shall be lawful to the Assured, their Factors, Servants, and Assigns, to sue, labour, and travel for, in and about the Defence, Safeguard and Recovery of the said Goods and Merchandises and Ship, etc., or any Part thereof, without Prejudice to this Insurance; to the Charges whereof we, the Assurers, will contribute, each according to the Rate and Quantity of the Sum herein assured. And it is especially declared and agreed that no Acts of the Insurer or Insured in recovering, saving, or preserving the property insured, shall be considered as a waiver or acceptance of abandonment. And it is agreed by us, the Insurers, that this Writing or Policy of Assurance shall be of as much Force and Effect as the surest Writing or Policy of Assurance heretofore made in Lombard Street, or in the Royal Exchange, or elsewhere in London.

And so we, the Assurers, are contented, and do hereby promise and bind ourselves, each one for his own Part, our heirs, Executors, and Goods, to the Assured, their Executors, Administrators, and Assigns, for the true Performance of the Premises, confessing ourselves paid the Consideration due unto us for this Assurance by the Assured, at and after the Rate of ______________

IN WITNESS whereof we, the Assurers, have subscribed our Names and Sums assured in LONDON.

The following note, called a Memorandum Clause, was also a part of the policy as generally written. It was introduced into the Lloyd's policy about 1748.

N.B.—Corn, Fish, Salt, Fruit, Flour and Seed are warranted free from Average, unless General, or the ship be stranded—Sugar, Tobacco, Hemp, Flax, Hides, and Skins are warranted free from Average under Five Pounds per cent; and all other Goods, also the Ship and Freight, are warranted free from Average under Three Pounds per cent, unless general, or the Ship be stranded.

Language of Ocean Marine Insurance Policies

As noted there has been great reluctance to change the basic clauses of ocean marine policies. Court interpretations in the United States and Great Britain, as well as other countries, have established the meanings during the past two hundred years. Marine underwriters through their associations, such as the American Institute of Marine Underwriters and the London institutes of marine underwriters, have attempted to clarify and modify the language wherever this could be done without disturbing the court-determined meanings.

Perils

While practically every term in the policy quoted above has been interpreted by the courts, the most important interpretations involve the perils insured. These perils and their interpretation are summarized here, in the order in which they appear in the contract. (Refer to the sentence of the policy that begins, "Touching the Adventure and Perils which we the Assurers are contented to bear. . . .")

Perils of the Seas The perils of the seas include the effects of heavy weather, stranding, foundering, collision, and other effects of the wind and waves. This is not intended to provide an "all-risks" type of coverage, but to cover the unexpected and fortuitous damage to a ship or cargo that might result *from unusual action of the oceans.* It has been held that perils of the seas does not include bad stowage, being exposed to theft or embezzlement by the master or mariners, nor to seawater damage to cargo which entered through a leak in the hull which was not the result of actual damage to the ship in a storm. Damage by rainwater is not generally considered a peril of the sea inasmuch as this would be a normal occurrence during ocean transit.

Men of War Damage resulting from the acts of men of war generally would be war damage. Today, most ocean marine policies contain an exclusion (which is usually worded as a warranty) that the coverage is "free of capture and seizure." War risk may be covered but this would be done specifically under a separate policy or endorsement and subject to special conditions and rates.

There could be a situation where damage resulting from action of a warship might be unrelated to a true act of war. The coverage in such a case would depend on whether the damage would be considered war damage.

Fire Fire is a serious peril at sea but is not considered to be a peril *of* the seas. However, the peril is specifically mentioned in the policy in order to make clear that it is covered. Damage done by steam or water used to extinguish fire is considered damage by fire. However, use of steam or water in the mistaken belief that there is a fire in a hold when in fact none exists would not be considered fire damage.

There have been some interesting cases in connection with the spontaneous heating or spontaneous ignition of cargo. Cargo insurers may deny liability for such loss if the shipper knowingly put a cargo into a hold in a condition that would make spontaneous ignition probable. The denial might be based on the principle that the insured did not disclose a material fact to the insurer when placing such material in the hold, or the inherent vice of the cargo itself.

Enemies, Pirates, and Rovers Damage resulting from the action of enemies at sea, pirates, and rovers is not as likely under today's conditions as it was a few hundred years ago. However, questions have arisen recently as a result of hijackings or threatened hijackings of vessels. Actual piracy probably would be considered a war risk.

Piracy was defined in a case involving an incident in the Far East in 1873 as forcible robbery at sea whether committed by marauders from outside the ship or by mariners or passengers within it. Marine insurers usually exclude from marine policy loss which results from a warlike operation and to cover the exposure specifically under a war risk policy. The exact circumstances of any occurrence would determine under which policy coverage applied.

Thieves The intent of the policy is to cover loss from "assailing thieves"; that is, loss from theft by violence. It is not intended to cover theft by stealth nor theft committed by anyone of the ship's company regardless of whether the thief is a member of the crew or a passenger. Some of the modern ocean marine policies have changed the wording to cover loss by "assailing thieves."

Some ocean marine policies today do cover pilferage and other theft by steath, as well as theft from piers and wharves, without a requirement that violence be involved. This is a special coverage which is subject to rates commensurate with the risk, and also probably subject to deductibles or participation by the insured in the loss.

Jettisons As explained in Chapter 7, jettison is a voluntary sacrifice of some property to save the rest. The policy is intended to cover loss resulting from a jettison made to save the venture. Of course, an insurer that pays a jettison loss becomes subrogated to the insured's claim for *general average*. Voluntary sacrifice of cargo which is carried on deck would be recognized as a jettison loss. However, cargo accidentally washed overboard would not be considered a jettison.

Letters of Mart and Countermart, Surprisals, Restraints, and Detainments These perils are of little importance in modern marine insurance. Because they relate to war perils, coverage under these perils is virtually eliminated by means of a "free of capture and seizure" (FC &S) clause. Damages from these perils would be covered under war risk insurance, which can be written separately.

There have been several cases during recent years where vessels have been seized by national governments for violations of territorial waters. One of the more frequent occurrences of this kind has been the seizure of fishing vessels within waters that are claimed to be the territorial waters of the nation. This is not a war risk. The question of whether such a seizure would be excluded by the free of capture and seizure clause would depend upon the exact circumstances of the seizure.

A frequently used free of capture and seizure clause excludes, among other things, seizure and confiscation whether in time of peace or war and whether lawful or otherwise. It appears that such an exclusion would exclude coverage for the seizure of a fishing boat under the circumstances described. It would probably also exclude the confiscation of cargo because of some violation of national law.

Barratry of the Master and Mariners Barratry includes illegal acts committed by master or crew, but not negligence or carelessness. To constitute barratry, an act must be intended to injure the goods or the ship, such as the deliberate sinking of a ship by the master or crew, the embezzlement of the cargo, or the committing of some act such as smuggling which would make the ship or cargo subject to confiscation. Insurance coverage against barratry, a fraudulent act, may be compared roughly to fidelity coverage which is issued in connection with land exposures to protect against loss by dishonesty of employees. It should be noted that deliberate destruction of a ship by its owners would not be an act of barratry. The act must be committed against the owners and without their knowledge or connivance.

***All Other Perils*—Ejusdem Generis** The concluding portion of the policy relating to the covered perils specifies, "all other perils losses and misfortunes, that have come or shall come to the hurt, detriment or damage of the subject matter insured or any part thereof." This may appear at first glance to be comparable to the "all-risks" type of insurance that is commonly written to cover property on land, but it is not so intended. The term "all other perils" under an ocean marine policy covers only perils that are similar in kind to the perils specifically mentioned in the policy. This is an example of the legal principle of *ejusdem generis* (and other things of the same kind). Originally there was uncertainty as to whether the principle applied, and, if so, which other perils were and which were not sufficiently similar to be covered. Court decisions over the years have established that the principle does apply, and have settled the classification of most perils.

In modern practice, marine insurers tend to specify whether other specific perils are covered by the policy in order to eliminate any question. Modern policies may specify that the policy applies to, "all other *like* perils, losses and misfortunes."

Two important perils that fall into this "all other *like* perils" category are machinery damage and explosion.

Machinery Damage. The introduction of steam power for the operation of ships brought about new chances of damage to ships and cargo. A question arose whether damage from breakage of machinery was a peril of the sea or another "like peril" to those covered in the hull insurance policy. The question was decided by the British House of Lords (acting as a supreme court) in connection with a steamer named the Inchmaree. Damage had occurred to the ship's machinery, apparently as a result of negligence on the part of the crew. The Lords decided that the loss was not the result of "another like peril" to those covered by the policy, and coverage did not apply.

Shipowners, realizing that breakage or other damage to machinery could be very costly, asked underwriters to extend the hull policy to cover loss from breakage of machinery. Underwriters developed a clause which specifically extends the coverage of the ocean marine insurance policy to this type of loss. The clause became known as the "Inchmaree clause" and it is commonly found in marine insurance hull policies today.

INCHMAREE CLAUSE. The Inchmaree (or negligence) clause extends the coverage of the hull policy to loss resulting from the bursting of boilers, from breakage of shafts, from latent defects in the machinery, hull or appurtenances, or from faults or errors in the navigation of the ship or its management by the master, mariners, mates, engineers, or pilots. The Inchmaree clause excludes, "the cost and expense of replacing or repairing the defective parts." This is intended to make it clear that the coverage extension applies to damage resulting from the breakage of a part or machine, but it does not cover the replacement of the part which actually broke. Underwriters occasionally are willing to extend the coverage further to include repair or replacement of such a part by means of a "liner" clause, so called because underwriters were more willing to extend the coverage to ocean liners than to tramp ships. They felt that the operation and maintenance of liners were more often of sufficient quality to justify this extension of coverage.

Explosion. Current practice is to cover explosion specifically in addition to the other perils. Sometimes this is accomplished by addition of a specific separate provision; at other times, it is done by rewriting the Inchmaree clause so it refers to explosions in general rather than only to boiler explosion.

Cancellation

Cancellation practices differ materially between ocean marine insurance and property insurance on land. Marine underwriters do not consider it important to have the right of immediate or nearly immediate cancellation except for the perils of war, strikes, riots, and civil commotion, where the danger may increase greatly within a matter of days or hours. The perils of the seas, however, do not change materially from year to year, and the integrity of the insured is determined before the policy is written. Therefore, underwriters generally are willing to continue coverage to the normal expiration of the policy with the exception of coverage against war and riot.

There are some exceptions to this practice, however. While voyage policies commonly are written without provision for cancellation by either party, term policies frequently provide for cancellation with thirty days' notice. Open cargo policies that have no specified expiration date have cancellation provisions, of course; again, thirty days' notice is usually required. Cancellation clauses usually provide that the cancellation does not affect any exposure on which the insurance has attached prior to the effective date of notice. This means that property already at sea or otherwise under the policy's protection is covered until it is delivered to the point where the insurance would otherwise terminate.

Cancellation of war, strikes, riots, and civil commotion may be made with as little as forty-eight hours notice, but again this cancellation would not apply to voyages already in progress.

"Other Insurance" Practices and Provisions

Cases where different policies insure different interests in the same event are not subject to "other insurance" provisions in any kind of insurance. When more than one policy applies to the same interest in the same loss, special provisions are needed. In ocean marine insurance, three types of these latter situations must be distinguished:

1. Large exposures are often shared, each insurer taking its specified share of the whole amount and of each loss.
2. Cases in which one of the policies is limited to coverage of total loss only, while the other is not. This situation occurs with hull insurance, which is discussed later.
3. Other multiple cases.

With respect to "other multiple cases," United States practice is for the policy with the earliest effective date to be considered the primary insurance. The policy with the next earliest effective date is excess over the first, and so on. Policies with the same effective date share losses on a pro rata basis. Sometimes American policies contain provisions that spell out this succession of coverage.

Under British policies, however, each underwriter or group of underwriters is liable for the full amount of its policy. The insured may collect from any one of its insurers, but it cannot collect more than the loss. The other insurers are then liable to the insurer that paid the loss for their pro rata share of the loss. This sharing of the loss may be entirely among the insurers after the insured has collected the amount of its loss from the chosen insurer.

Multiple insurance without a share arrangement is rare because insured and insurer usually agree on the value of the property and the placing of the insurance on that value, as a part of the total insurance transaction.

Assignment of Coverage

Assignment of Cargo Coverage Assignment provisions in ocean marine policies are different from those used in most other lines of insurance. Assignment of cargo coverage is handled differently from assignment of hull coverage. Insurance on cargo usually is written so that the benefit of the ocean marine insurance policy will follow changes in title or interest. These policies can be assigned or indorsed to other parties having an interest in the cargo or as their interest develops. This is necessary in order to carry out the functions of ocean marine insurance on carge in relation to commercial transactions.

Assignment of Hull Coverage The transfer of a ship to a new owner may result in a different and less desirable exposure. Underwriters usually are not willing to allow the insurance coverage automatically to follow the ownership of the vessel. The ship may be insured, "for the account of whom it may concern," but this provision usually is limited so that change of ownership or management cancels the coverage unless the underwriters agree to the change in writing.

There may, however, be a provision that in the case of an involuntary and temporary transfer, by requisition or otherwise, without the prior execution of a written agreement by the insured, the cancellation will take place fifteen days after such a transfer. This is considered necessary to permit an insured to handle temporary and unexpected situations. A possible further provision is that if the vessel has cargo on board and has already sailed from its loading port, or is at sea in ballast, the cancellation shall be suspended until arrival at final port of discharge (if with cargo) or at port of destination (if in ballast). Other provisions may limit coverage as far as any charter or transferee is concerned. There may be a further provision that any loss payable under a delayed cancellation provides the underwriters with a right of subrogation to all rights of the insured against the transferee.

Interests of Insurer and Insured

Insurers' interests in ocean marine losses generally follow the interests of their insureds, subject to policy exclusions and conditions. But there are occasions when the interests of an insured and the insurer are not identical, such as those involving: (1) possible abandonment, or (2) voluntary expenditures to save or protect the property (sue and labor).

Abandonment Ocean marine insurance is one of the relatively few kinds of property loss insurance under which the insured has the right to offer abandonment of property to the insurer. This right ties in with the principles applying to constructive total loss. It is usual for marine policies to provide that the property will not be deemed subject to constructive total loss unless cost of recovery will exceed the value of the saved property (e.g., in American Institute of Marine Underwriters Cargo clauses) or the agreed value of the property as stated in the policy (e.g., in American Institute of Marine Underwriting Hull clauses).

It is customary in connection with total loss payments for marine insurers to take an assignment of the property where there is hope that some salvage can be secured. The owner of the ship or cargo can tender abandonment to the insurers and ask for payment of total loss where the owner determines that the ship or cargo are damaged to an extent that salvage would cost more than could be saved. The insurers may accept abandonment, in which case they would pay the insured for a total loss.

When the insurers accept abandonment, they may or may not

accept ownership. The advantage of accepting ownership is that it includes the owner's rights to whatever can be salvaged. The disadvantage is that it also includes the owner's liability for damage to vessels or other property that might come in contact with the wreck. The owner may also be obligated to remove the wreck, or render it harmless to navigation—sometimes an expensive undertaking.

The insurers may refuse to accept abandonment, in which case the insured is obligated to use all reasonable means to salvage the property until it can be demonstrated conclusively that a constructive total loss has occurred. Abandonment is optional with the insured and cannot be forced by the insurers. However, the insured is obligated to tender abandonment promptly if the situation is such that abandonment is desirable. The acceptance of abandonment by the insurers cannot be changed once the tender has been made and acceptance has been made. This follows the principles applying to any contract in which an offer and acceptance have been completed.

Charges and Expenses for Saving and Protecting Property Ocean marine practice recognizes three categories of expenses and charges incurred to save or protect threatened property. When such expenses or charges—sue and labor, general average, or salvage award—arise from threat by a peril covered in the policy, and are obilgations of the insured, they are covered by standard ocean marine insurance forms. This coverage is, however, subject to adjustment procedure that treats the coverage as though it had a 100 percent coinsurance clause. Thus, if the amount of general average charge against the insured is based on, say, a value of $100,000 for property, while the insured has only $80,000 of insurance, the insurer will pay only 80 percent of that general average obligation.

Payment is in addition to the property damage coverage. Should sue and labor expenditures be unsuccessful (the property is lost anyway), the insurer would pay for the expenses in addition to the total loss of the property. Sue and labor expenses *may* be paid even though the property was only threatened, not actually damaged, by an insured peril.

Insurance coverage of general average and salvage charges provides an important benefit in addition to payment of the costs themselves. The process of determining each party's share of such charges is complicated and can be time-consuming. While it is going on, the authorities in charge require guarantees that each party's share will be paid promptly upon determination. The property involved (ship and cargo) therefore is impounded and not released until a satisfactory bond or other assurance of payment has been provided. The guarantee of a reputable insurer usually is accepted as such assurance, and the insured can then reclaim its property. The next section of this chapter discusses insurance coverage that applies to vessels, called *hull insurance*.

HULL INSURANCE

Types of Hull Policies: Navigation, Port Risk, and Special Hazard Covers

In general, navigation policies cover the operation of ships. Port risk policies cover ships laid up in port and not subject to navigation hazards. A variety of ocean marine insurance forms apply to other specialized exposures, most of which involve at least some exposure ashore.

Perils Insured Against

While current hull forms follow the original British form in many respects, the coverage provided in the forms is more complex. Of current hull forms, one of the best known and broadest is the American Institute of Marine Underwriters Time Hull Form of June 2, 1977. This form in addition to insuring the perils previously discussed in the basic perils clause includes the risk assumed in the Inchmaree clause, explosion, lightning, accidents in loading, discharging or handling of cargo, and other additional named perils.

Riot and Civil Commotion

In general, there is not any great concern about damage to hulls from strikes, riots, and civil commotion. The chances of loss from such perils are mostly from fire while the ship is in port. Actual damage by strikes, riots, and civil commotion is not covered by the ocean marine hull policy which has been described. However, coverage for damage as a consequence of strike, riot, or civil commotion action is important protection which marine insurers have regularly provided by endorsement for extra premium charge.

The exposure from these perils is considerably greater to ships under construction, in dry dock, or otherwise in port for an extended period. A marine port risk policy or a policy on ships under construction or repair usually would exclude damage by strikes, riot, or civil commotion unless it is specifically covered and an additional premium paid.

Identification of Insured Property

When a ship is insured, the insured property includes the hull, materials and equipment, stores and provisions for the officers and crew, and in the case of vessels engaged in a special trade, the ordinary fittings requisite for the trade. Also included are the machinery, boilers, and the fuel supplies owned by the insured. Usually, equipment installed for use on board the vessel but not owned by the insured is also covered if the insured has assumed responsibility for its safety.

The term "ship" is seldom used in describing the property covered by an insurance policy. Insurance coverage may apply specifically to the hull, to the machinery, or to other supplies and equipment. It is necessary, therefore, to understand the actual property that is included within the various terms as they are used in the insurance policies.

Hull The term "hull" includes the basic structure of the ship and certain equipment such as electrical equipment that is not a part of the propulsion machinery. For example, refrigerating machinery that is required for the protection of cargo may be considered as part of the hull if it is not specifically covered and also if it is not connected to the propulsion machinery. Generally, donkey engines, winches, cranes, and windlasses are considered part of the hull for insurance purposes.

Machinery The term "machinery" refers primarily to propulsion machinery (for the propelling of the ship). However, this may be further extended by the description of the insured machinery as "boilers, machinery, refrigerating machinery and insulation, motor generators and other electrical machinery, and everything connected therewith." The distinction between machinery which is considered part of the hull and that which is covered under the separate item of "machinery" is not precisely delineated. However, most policies state clearly what property is covered under these different items.

The amount of insurance on the hull and on the machinery may be specified separately, or the hull and machinery may be covered by a single amount of insurance over both types of property. It is more satisfactory from the standpoint of the insured to have a single item of insurance over both hull and machinery. A separation of the insurance between hull and machinery could result in an inadequate amount of insurance on one item or the other under some special circumstances.

Other Property The cargo is not part of the hull even when the ownership of the hull and the cargo are the same. The insurance policy definitions of hull and machinery are such that cargo would not be included. In addition, there is an established maritime custom that cargo is not hull.

Provisions and stores for the operation of the ship may be covered under the hull insurance if the definitions are so worded, but personal effects of passengers and crew are not. Provisions for the passengers would not be covered under the hull insurance.

Running Down Clause

Ocean marine hull insurance contracts contain some important liability insurance coverage called collision liability, or the running down clause. It covers liability for damage *to other ships and their cargoes* from collision involving the insured vessel. Note there is no coverage for damage to other types of property—not for damage to cargo on board the insured vessel, and not for damage to any types of property (e.g., wharves, piers, bridges) except other ships and their cargoes. There is no coverage for liability for bodily injury to anyone. All these other liability exposures require other insurance, notably protection and indemnity insurance, discussed later in this chapter.

Fleet Policies

A hull policy may be written to cover only a single vessel or to cover an entire fleet. Fleet coverage may be applied not only to vessels directly owned, but also to vessels indirectly owned, and to others chartered to the same management. The policy may cover additional vessels from the time they are delivered or acquired, with payment of a pro rata premium for the period covered. The covered vessels may be scheduled, or the coverage may be blanket in form, called "floating" coverage.

A fleet policy may provide that each vessel is deemed to be covered by separate insurance. This provision means that a breach of warranty with respect to one vessel does not affect coverage on the others.

A large fleet may be covered by several different insurers. All the policies should be identical. Each will state the total amount of insurance provided, and the share or percentage of that total provided by that particular policy. Each insurer receives a share of the total premium and pays a share of each claim accordingly. By this device, each insurer gets a spread of exposure over many vessels, and between the older and less desirable ships and the newer and better ships. Sometimes this is the only way older vessels are acceptable to the underwriters. Even on individually acceptable vessels, the insurance rate may be lower under fleet coverage, because of the spread of exposure provided by this method of writing.

Values Insured and Amount of Insurance

Hull insurance contains special provisions about valuation of the insured property. There are also related provisions about the amount of insurance on the property.

Valuation of Vessels Marine insurance is commonly on a valued basis. Hull policies generally contain a specific statement that the insured ship is valued at a specified amount.

Several factors have to be taken into account in determining the insurable value of a ship. The replacement cost of the vessel, its age and condition, and the current market value if the ship could be sold are all important physical facts to be determined. Two other factors to be considered are the amount of net freight that could be earned by the vessel during its probable remaining lifetime, and the break-up value when it would be broken up for scrap at the end of its useful life. The value of a relatively new vessel may be close to its replacement cost. Older vessels for which there is little demand may be valued at the market value for which the vessel could be sold.

Sometimes two valuations are given, one applying to total losses (actual and constructive) and one applying to partial losses. This is advisable when repair costs are high in relation to the market value of the ship. For example, the replacement cost of a particular ship may be $500,000, but the market value may be only half that amount. Insurers would be willing to pay only the market value ($250,000) in the case of a total loss. However, the cost of repairing a partial loss would be related to the $500,000 replacement cost of the vessel. Therefore, the valuation for total loss purposes may be set at $250,000, whereas the valuation for distribution of partial losses would be set at a figure close to the $500,000 replacement cost. Insurers would take a percentage of the $250,000 in case of a total loss and a percentage of the $500,000 value for any partial losses. For example, if a particular group of insurers took 25 percent of the insurance, they would issue an insurance policy for 25 percent of $250,000, or $62,500 for total loss purposes, and $125,000 for partial loss purposes. The balance of either or both valuations may be entirely insured or partially retained by the shipowners. Either way, the insurers with 25 percent of established value pay 25 percent of partial losses (particular and general average), sue and labor charges, and of total losses. Naturally, if the cost to repair the ship exceeds its actual value, a constructive total loss has occurred, and the total loss insurance will be paid, rather than the partial loss coverage.

The amount of hull insurance taken is often less than the agreed value of the ship, as insurers may not be available to cover the full value, or the premium for the ship at its full value may be more than the insured is willing to pay. When insurance is less than agreed value, the insured pays its proportion of any loss in relation to the proportion of underinsurance. This operates the same as a 100 percent coinsurance clause in fire insurance.

Disbursements Warranty—Increased Value Insurance The valuation provisions of the hull insurance policy are intended to limit the amount of insurance on the ship to the amount specified. A shipowner might be tempted to insure a ship for a low value in order to establish a small premium, and then try to buy insurance on collateral exposures in order to build up the total recovery in case of loss. The hull policy usually contains a warranty which limits the amount of insurance that may be purchased to cover collateral and intangible risks in addition to the insurance on the hull. This is called a *disbursements warranty* because one of the principal additional expenses that may be covered are the disbursements that a shipowner has made in connection with the venture (such as outlays for crew's wages and provisions and for ship's fuel and supplies).

A customary disbursements warranty limits to 25 percent of the value stated in the hull policy the amount that may be insured to cover disbursements, manager's commissions, profits, freight or increased value of hull and machinery.

There are occasions when a ship is insured for total loss only. This may happen with an older ship that is chartered for a single voyage or with a ship that is engaged in a hazardous undertaking. Underwriters may be willing to insure against the chances of a total loss but may be unwilling to provide coverage for any partial losses that might occur. The shipowner is responsible for the repair of any partial losses to the ship regardless of extent, and can collect from the insurers only if there is a total loss or a constructive total loss. Such a policy usually would specify whether sue and labor and salvage charges are covered by the insurers in addition to the coverage on the ship itself. The standard American form of disbursements cover is a total loss form; it pays only in the event of actual or constructive total loss, and also provides coverage on general average, salvage, and sue and labor charges, and collision liability for loss in excess of the amount paid by the insured's full-form cover.

Deductibles

Hull insurance policies sometimes contain deductibles, and both straight deductibles and franchise clauses are used. Sometimes the straight deductible does not apply to total losses. (Of course, since all losses over a certain amount are covered in full under a franchise clause, no franchise clause deductible would apply to a total loss).

For years, standard terms contained a 3 percent franchise, or $4,850, whichever was smaller. The dollar figure was set in 1920 and eventually became too small. In 1970, when a figure of about $45,000 represented about the same relative amount of damage, change was made from franchise to straight deductibles. And where the franchise had applied on a per voyage basis, the deductible became applied per accident. (However, the policy provides that all damage suffered from heavy weather between two consecutive ports of call will be considered caused by a single accident.)

New for Old Materials in Repairs

Wooden ships were considered to deteriorate materially during their lifetimes, and the replacement of new wood for old in a sailing vessel was supposed to improve its condition. It was customary at one time for insurers to deduct one-third of any loss where repairs were made to a vessel. This principle of "thirds-off" was a means of applying a depreciation charge.

The replacing of damaged portions of a metal hull with new metal in most cases does not actually improve the condition of the ship. Therefore, the principle of "thirds-off" has largely been abandoned in the writing of ocean marine insurance and the settlement of losses, and it is customary to pay for new material to be used in making repairs without any deduction for possible improvement.

Trading Warranties

Trading warranties are important in hull insurance. A trading warranty specifies the geographical area within which a ship may operate. Breach of a warranty such as these generally voids coverage.

The expected routes and conditions of a particular voyage may be expressed in the policy. However, it is not possible to express all of these conditions in policies that cover a fleet of vessels or a multitude of shipments on a time basis. Time policies may provide for geographical limits within which trading is permitted (coverage applies). For hulls, these limits customarily are shown as warranties regarding certain geographical areas. For example, it may he warranted that ships will not operate in the Great Lakes or the St. Lawrence Seaway, or that they will not operate in the Baltic Sea, or any other area which the insurers do not contemplate in their premiums and conditions of coverage.

Seasonal restrictions may also be imposed in the trading warranties. Winter conditions in the northern part of the Atlantic Ocean, for example, are more hazardous than summer conditions. Vessels may be prohibited from operating north of certain specified latitudes during winter months.

In the absence of provision to the contrary, these are full-fledged warranties and violation of them voids the contract. However, the policy may provide that departure from the specified limits is held covered by the policy, in which case the insurers must be notified of such exposure, and appropriate premium paid. The additional premium may be fixed in the policy or it may be "to be agreed," which in effect means that the additional premium will be determined by the underwriters in accordance with the additional hazard involved.

Warranties relating to entering especially hazardous areas may apply to war risks or to other known hazards. Such a warranty is similar in form to trading warranties, but in spirit is akin to war risk warranties previously discussed (the free of capture and seizure and neutrality warranties).

Voyage Policies and Time Policies

The variations in the nature of ocean marine policies are as numerous as the needs of shipowners and cargo shippers.

A voyage policy may be written to cover a specified voyage from one port to another. Time policies usually are written on fleets. These cover for a specified period of time in much the same way that policies cover property on land. A time policy may be written to cover voyages anywhere in the world, or anywhere within certain geographical limits, such as points within the Western Hemisphere, or within the range of specified degrees of latitude.

A time policy can expire when one of the covered ships is at sea, of course. If the vessel is then in distress, a problem of coverage arises. Hull policies customarily provide for continuation of coverage for vessels in mid-voyage (in distress or not) at expiration date, provided previous notice has been given the insurer. Of course, a pro rata premium is charged for any extension in time covered.

Coverage "At and From" An ocean marine hull policy covering a specified voyage applies "at and from" the port named. The words "at and from" indicate that the insurance policy is intended to cover while the ship is in port. Use of the word "from" by itself would indicate that coverage would be effective only from the time the ship sailed.

Coverage on the ship continues, "until she hath moored at anchor twenty-four hours in good safety." An insurance policy covering during calls at several ports would be written to cover continously during such calls and until the ship has been moored safely for twenty-four hours at the destination named in the policy. British law provides that, "where a ship is insured at and from a particular place, and she is at that place in good safety when the contract is concluded (i.e., is agreed to) the risk attaches immediately. If she be not at that place when the contract is concluded the risk attaches as soon as she arrives there in good safety." In addition, the policy may contain an express warranty that the ship is in "good safety" at a designated place or time. Insurance containing such a warranty does not attach unless the ship is actually in good safety at the time or place specified.

Insurance for Expense, Profit, and Income Losses

As noted in Chapter 7, shipowners are exposed to substantial collateral losses in addition to the value of property lost as a result of a sinking or other casualty. The insurance of these collateral losses is handled differently from business interruption practices applying to property on land.

Freight As noted in Chapter 7, freight charges are commonly prepaid and, if the voyage is interrupted, the shipper may be exposed to the loss of freight charges. This exposure is commonly covered by including it in the valuation of the property.

When the exposure is that of the ship operator, and the hull insurance is on a voyage basis, freight value is ordinarily included in valuation of the hull. However, freight coverage is also available separately when desired—by an operator who does not own and insure the ship, for example. The "freight" to be insured is the total amount of such charges for all of the bills of lading applying to the goods on board.

Future freight earnings are sometimes insured where there is a contract or other assurance that the ship will be in use for some future time so the anticipated freight is reasonably expected. Such insurance can be written on a total loss or constructive total loss basis only.

Passage Money The money that is paid by passengers for passage aboard the ship is not "freight" and, therefore, is not insurable as "freight." The passenger who has paid on amount of money for passage on a trip could insure that against the loss that might result from a casualty to the ship.

The shipowner has an insurable interest even though there is no legal obligation to provide any refund or to provide the cost of forwarding a passenger to an agreed location. It is customary, when a ship is lost but passengers are saved, for a shipowner to arrange for passengers to continue on to their destination, to return to their port of embarkation, or to receive a refund of their passage money. Because shipowners are thus exposed to loss, insurance has been made available to cover the exposure to loss of passage money. A tour operator can likewise insure against the loss of passage money that has been paid.

Tugboat Insurance

The function of a tugboat is to assist other vessels—it does not carry cargo. Tugboats in port areas assist bigger ships which need extra power or towage assistance in docking and in negotiating difficult waterways. Another important function of the tugboat is the towing or pushing of barges. There is an extensive traffic on the navigable waterways of the United States of cargo carried in barges. These barges have no power of their own and must depend upon tugboats, many of which are specially designed for operation on rivers and canals. The "tow" moved by a single tug may contain many barges in two or more rows making quick maneuvering impossible, especially against the current.

Hull insurance for the tugboat owner follows the general practices of ocean marine hull insurance with two important differences. The running down clause is ordinarily written to protect the tugboat operator when negligence results in damage to the property being towed.

The liability exposure of a tugboat operator may be more extensive than the usual liability exposure of a ship operator at sea. The tugboat with its accompanying barges or other vessels may be operated in narrow channels and through locks where expert handling is necessary. An error in judgment that might be held to be negligence could produce damage to the object being towed, or to locks, bridges, or other property along the waterway—a large property damage liability loss exposure.

It is important for the tugboat operator to secure *towers liability protection and indemnity* insurance because the usual running down clause would not apply to structures along the waterway nor would it normally apply to the property being towed. The tugboat operator may also have a need for *excess protection and indemnity* coverage. (Protection and indemnity coverage is discussed in greater detail later in this chapter.)

The fact that tugboats operate largely on inland waters is likely to subject such an operator to the thinking of land courts as contrasted to maritime courts; therefore, liability might be imposed according to the general principles applying to liability on land. (Liability rules on land in the United States are discussed extensively in CPCU 4.)

Insurance for Drilling Rigs

Offshore drilling rigs constitute a relatively new type of equipment that is insured under ocean marine policies. It is customary for the offshore drilling rig to be constructed or partially constructed on land, and then be transported to the drilling site. Transportation to the drilling site involves not only the ordinary maritime hazards, but also the fact that ordinarily the rig is bulky and unwieldy compared to a seaworthy ship. The rig may be transported to the drilling site on its side. Upon arrival at the drilling site, it is then sunk in its upright position to the ocean floor.

The hazards to which the rig is exposed do not end when it is in place. The ocean floor is constantly being changed by erosion from ocean currents, and undermining of the foundations to the rig may cause it to tilt or capsize. There are also substantial weather hazards to the rig, both from wind and from action of the waves. Rigs are subject to collision damage from ships used to service the operations and other ships using the area.

Drilling rigs are also exposed to damage by fire, lightning, explosion, blowout, and cratering. The blowout and cratering hazards are similar to those which also occur at drilling operations on land. An unexpected pressure of gas, oil or water may force to the surface an opening outside the drilling holes. A crater may form around the drill hole and may cause the entire rig to become unstable.

The equivalent of business interruption insurance sometimes is requested by the operator of a drilling rig. This coverage tends to follow more the practices of business interruption insurance on land than any of the normal ocean marine practices. The drilling operation may be interrupted for a period of months by some accident, and the loss to the operator, and consequently to the underwriters, can be extensive under these circumstances.

The insuring of offshore drilling rigs is a highly specialized insurance operation. Conditions and premiums are subject to negotiation between the operator and the underwriters. Many underwriters are reluctant to insure an off-shore drilling operation unless they also have all or a substantial portion of the insured's other coverage.

Possible liability for pollution from offshore oil rigs can be very expensive, and most marine insurers are reluctant to take on such exposures at prices operators can afford.

Miscellaneous Vessels

There are many types of vessels built for special purposes. Barges, dredges, fishing boats, shrimp boats, car floats, and ferry boats are built specifically for carrying out certain functions. All of these may be insured under ocean marine policies following the general practices. Vessels that operate in inland waters may be subject to the extra liability hazards that have been described for tugboats.

Port Risk Policies

A ship may be insured under a port risk policy when it is laid up and is not subject to navigation hazards. A warranty is required that the vessel is out of commission and laid up, and that it will be confined during the period of coverage under the policy. Privilege may be granted in the policy for the vessel to change docks or to go into dry dock, or otherwise to make some change necessary for coverage of the intended situation. The collision clause and the machinery damage clause probably will be included in the coverage in order to protect the owner from loss because of situations to which these clauses apply. There may also be a relaxation of limitations on partial loss, or particular average. There may be a greater exposure to loss if the ship is laid up in or adjacent to navigable waters as compared to being laid up at a dock. The rate for port risk normally is low, unless the ship is anchored in or near a seaway where it is exposed to collision from other ships under navigation.

Ship Construction, Servicing, and Repair

Servicing and repair of ships and ship construction involve shore exposures. A ship ashore is not subject to navigation and even some port risks, but ships' structures are designed to be supported by the pressure of water all along the hull, and removal of such support presents engineering problems in designing mechanical substitutes on land. In addition, ship building, servicing, and repair operations involve special hazards for fire and accidents (e.g., the use of welding and cutting torches and cranes for removal of parts).

Dry Docks and Marine Railways The principal device for major servicing and repair of ships is the dry dock. Water is pumped into the dry dock, permitting a ship to be floated in. When the water has been pumped out, the ship's bottom is exposed for examination and necessary work.

Small vessels can be handled by marine railways. The railway is equipped with a cradle which is lowered far enough into the water to allow the ship to slip into it. Then the cradle and ship are pulled up an incline onto the shore.

Because these structures are closely associated with marine exposures, and marine underwriters traditionally willing to consider any risk associated with marine operations, insurance on these structures developed as ocean marine insurance. In the case of portable dry docks, which can be moved by water from one location to another, the exposure while undergoing such movement is essentially a hull exposure, and is so written. "At location" covers are adapted to particular needs, and bear some similarity to the "inland" marine covers provided for "instrumentalities of transportation and communication," discussed in Chapter 10.

Builders' Risks It has become customary to use a marine policy in connection with shipyard operations. This is reasonable because the risks of a shipbuilder extend to both land and water operations. The use of a marine policy permits continuous coverage from the time the keel is laid until the ship has passed its acceptance tests for the owner. The builders' risk policy covers marine perils similar to other ocean marine policies and in addition covers:

> All risks, including fire, while under construction or fitting out, including materials in buildings, workshops, yards and docks of the insured, or on quays, pontoons, craft, etc., and all risks while in transit to and from the works or the vessel wherever she may be lying, also all risks of loss or damage through collapse of supports or ways from any cause whatsoever, and all risks of launching and breakage of the ways.

Insurance usually is written to cover the ship from the time work is started on the laying of the keel until after launching, during test runs, and until the ship is accepted by its owners. Considerable additional expense may be incurred if a ship fails to launch. This additional expense is a part of the cost covered by the "all-risks" shipbuilder's policy.

Furthermore, the ocean marine builders' risk policy does more than insure against loss from accidental occurence. It is in the nature of a guarantee of the materials used in the construction. Damage from latent defects in materials that appear during trial runs are covered, including the replacing of the defective parts unless the loss results from lack of due diligence on the part of the builder or the owner.

Insurance coverage applies to marine perils similar to the ocean marine policies already described. Additional coverage is on an "all-risks" basis, including fire. Coverage also applies to materials in buildings, workshops, yards, and docks of the insured, and while in transit to or from the workshops and the vessel. This coverage on materials can be effective from the time the particular material is designated for use in the construction of that ship. This means that it is possible to cover the material from the time it is designated for use in constructing that ship even though the material at the time may be many miles away.

There are some exclusions in a builders' risk insurance policy. For example, it is customary to include an FC&S clause in order to exclude war damage. There may be an exclusion of damage by strikers and locked-out workers unless additional premium is paid for this coverage. There may also be exclusions of damage due to earthquake, an exclusion of consequential loss, and an exclusion of loss from delay in the construction.

It is important for the protection of the insured that the policy contain a negligence clause and also that protection and indemnity insurance be included in the coverage.

Marine builders' risk policies do not ordinarily cover workers' compensation or employers' liability during the construction period on land. The builder normally would buy a workers' compensation and employers' liability policy for the construction work in the shipyard as a land-based insurance. However, the protection and indemnity insurance would provide coverage of the maritime risks during the trial run and after launching of the vessel.

Ships under construction customarily are insured for completed value. This is comparable to completed value builders' risk coverage under a fire policy form. Policies may contain provisions that allow for additional insurance during construction if it develops that the completed cost will be more than originally estimated. The values involved in the construction of a ship may be so large that a very broad market is necessary in order to cover the entire value. For example, a very large crude oil carrier might be valued at $50 million or more upon completion. A cost overrun might require additional amounts of insurance. It is customary in marine insurance for the amount of coverage to be specified and to be agreed to by the underwriters. Therefore, there has to be provision to permit additional amounts of insurance if it becomes necessary during the construction period. Usually there is a time limit in the policy during which the insurance is effective. There may be provision for a refund of a portion of the premium if the vessel is completed in a shorter time than is specified in the policy.

Bailee's Exposure During Repairs The repair of ships is related to builder's risk policies. Shipbuilders who engage in the repair of vessels will buy a coverage that is comparable to builders' risk insurance, and their liability for the vessel may be compared to bailee liability. The exposure to loss and the insurance coverage written to cover this situation are comparable to those which affect builders' risks.

CARGO INSURANCE

The exposure of cargo to loss is different in many respects from the exposure of the ship to loss. There is, of course, a threat to cargo from perils of the seas, from fire, and the possibility of total loss of a cargo shipment from the same perils which also threaten the ship. Some additional perils that threaten cargo are loss by theft, water damage, handling damage, and contamination from other cargo.

It has become customary for insurance on cargo to be written separately from insurance on hulls. The situation today is very different from that of several hundred years ago, when a ship operator in many cases was carrying personally owned cargo. Today the owners and operators of ships are mostly carriers who transport the goods of other people. Some companies such as petroleum companies operate their own fleets of ships, but even in such cases hull and cargo insurance are written separately. This permits the insurance on the hull and the insurance on the cargo to cover more particularly the perils that threaten each type of property.

As noted before, the liability of a ship operator for loss of cargo is limited in comparison to the liability of a carrier of goods by land. In general, cargo owners retain their own exposure to loss unless they purchase insurance.

Property Covered

"Cargo" in ocean commerce means only the property that is accepted by the carrier for transportation and for which a freight charge is paid. It does not include the personal effects of passengers or crew or other miscellaneous property that is not being carried as cargo. (It is possible for passengers and crew members to obtain insurance to cover their personal effects, but this is not considered cargo insurance.)

Cargo may be insured for a particular voyage or under *open cargo policies*, which are in the nature of reporting form policies. Which type of policy is chosen by the shipper depends on the volume and frequency of ocean shipments. Either form can be arranged to meet the coverage needs of an insured.

Voyage Policies A voyage policy is issued to cover a single trip described in the policy.

Open Cargo Policies Under an open cargo policy, voyages and the nature of goods covered may be specified. The insured is required to report all shipments of such goods and pay premiums as provided in the policy. The underwriter is required to insure them (as long as the open policy is in force). Other types of goods are not covered unless the contract so indicates specifically. When these other goods are covered, shipments of them must also be reported, and conditions and premiums for their coverage negotiated.

The open cargo policy might also be called a master policy. It is basically designed for the shipper who has a volume of overseas shipments. It is most often written without a specific expiration date, although some policies are written for a specific term, usually one year. The holder of an open policy is obligated to report all shipments covered by the policy in accordance with the valuation clause. Premiums are based on the rates established in the policy for various shipments and paid to the insurer as shipments are made.

Many insureds will submit monthly reports of shipments. However, in addition to the open policy, there is another policy or certificate frequently used for ocean cargo shipments. This special marine policy or certificate describes the details of a given shipment and may be used as evidence of cargo insurance as part of the documentation for export shipments. In addition to supplying details of the specific shipment such as a description of the cargo, its point of origin, its destination, the means of shipment and a specific value for the shipment, it provides the consignee with instructions on what to do in the event of a loss. It also provides the means for having a loss settled at the destination without having to return all claims papers to the shipper for presentation to the insurer. The special marine policy can be issued either for the assured who has only one shipment or for the shipper making many shipments each month. In the case of the latter the insurance companies often authorize individual insureds to issue special marine policies themselves in accordance with the terms of their open policy.

Duration of Cargo Coverage

Ocean marine insurance originally covered property such as cargo only from the time it was loaded on shipboard until it was discharged at the port of destination. This was adequate coverage when most transportation was by water, but the development of railroads during the last century permitted the delivery of cargo to inland cities by means other than over water. This created a need for continuous coverage from point of origin to declared destination even though there might be many miles of land transit involved. Such coverage is commonly provided under ocean marine policies by including the warehouse to warehouse clause.

Warehouse to Warehouse Clause Current wording of the American Institute of Marine Underwriters warehouse to warehouse clause is as follows:

> This insurance attaches from the time the goods leave the Warehouse and/or Store at the place named in the Policy for the commencement of the transit and continues *during the ordinary course of transit*, including customary transhipment if any, until the goods are discharged overside from the overseas vessel at the final port. Thereafter the insurance continues whilst the goods are in transit and/or awaiting transit until delivered to final warehouse at the destination named in the Policy or until the expiry of 15 days (or 30 days if the destination to which the goods are insured is outside the limits of the port) whichever shall first occur. The time limits referred to above to be reckoned from midnight of the day on which the discharge overside of the goods hereby insured from the overseas vessel is completed. Held covered at a premium to be arranged in the event of transshipment, if any, other than as above and/or in the event of delay in excess of the above time limits arising from circumstances beyond the control of the Assured.

The fifteen/thirty-day limitation on coverage after discharge at final port is a recognition that ocean marine insurance is generally intended to cover transit and is not ordinarily supposed to provide continuous coverage at an insured's permanent location. However, insurers recognize that circumstances beyond the control of the insured may delay the delivery of the goods for more than fifteen/thirty days.

Extension of coverage is provided but this extension is dependent upon notification to the insurer and the payment of additional premium that may be required. Note should also be made of the underlined phrase during ordinary course of transit. The insurer's intent is to provide coverage during those normal delays over which the owner of the goods has no control; but, should the owner direct that transit be interrupted and the goods placed in storage prior to arrival at destination, the goods would no longer be considered in due course of transit.

Marine Extensions Clauses Because of the uncertainties of long ocean transit, even the coverage provided by the warehouse to warehouse clause was found to be inadequate in many cases to fully protect cargo during transit. A ship may break down before reaching the intended port of discharge and be forced to terminate its voyage, or the intended port of discharge may be closed by natural disaster, civil authorities or even strikes of port workers. Under such circumstances cargo cannot be discharged. The marine extensions clauses (MEC) were developed to cover contingencies such as these. When these clauses are incorporated in a cargo policy they supersede the terms of the warehouse to warehouse clause. One version of the marine extension clauses includes the following provisions:

1. This insurance attached from the time the goods leave the warehouse at the place named in the Policy, certificate or declaration for the commencement of the transit and continues until the goods are delivered to the consignees' or other final warehouse at the destination named in the Policy, certificate or declaration. In the course of this transit the goods are covered during
   (i) Deviation, delay beyond the control of the Assured, forced discharge, re-shipment and transshipment.
   (ii) Any other variation of the adventure arising from the exercise of a liberty granted to the shipowner or charterer under the contract of affreightment.

The provisions of this clause shall be subject to those of clauses 2 and 3 hereunder.

2. If owing to circumstances beyond the control of the Assured either the contract of affreightment is terminated at a port or place other than the destination named therein or the adventure is otherwise terminated before delivery of the goods into consignees' or other final warehouse at the destination named in the Policy, certificate of declaration, then, provided notice is give immediately after receipt of advices and subject to an additional premium if required, this insurance shall remain in force until the goods are sold and delivered at such port or place or, if the goods are forwarded to the destination named in the Policy, certificate or declaration or to any other destination, until the goods have arrived at consignees' or other final warehouse at such destination.
3. If the goods are sold (the sale not being one within the provisions of clause 2) while this insurance is still in force but before the expiry of 15 days from midnight of the day on which the goods are discharged overside from the overseas vessel at the final port of discharge and following the sale the goods are to be forwarded to a destination other than that to which they are insured by this Policy, this insurance shall remain in force only until the expiry of the said period of 15 days at the final port of discharge or until the goods commence transit at that port at the risk of the buyer, whichever first occurs. If such sale takes place after expiry of the aforementioned period of 15 days but while this insurance is still in force the insurance shall cease as from the time of the sale.
4. Held covered at a premium to be arranged in case of change of voyage or of any omission or error in the description of the interest vessel or voyage.

5. This insurance shall in no case be deemed to extend to cover loss damage or expense proximately caused by delay or inherent vice or nature of the subject-matter insured.
6. It is a condition of this insurance that the Assured shall act with reasonable dispatch in all circumstances within their control.
7. It is necessary for the Assured when they become aware of an event which is "held covered" under this Policy to give prompt notice to underwriters and the right to such cover is dependent upon compliance with this obligation.

All other terms and conditions of the Policy remain unchanged, it being particularly understood and agreed that the F.C.&S. clause remains in full force and effect, and that nothing in the foregoing shall be construed as extending this insurance to cover any risks of war or consequences of hostilities.

Several basic points can be recognized from a careful reading of these clauses. A voyage may have to be changed or terminated without any fault of the cargo owner, and the cargo owner may have to sell the goods at an unintended port or to arrange for transshipment to the original destination. Coverage is continued during such unusual or unexpected time, but the insured is expected and obligated to pay any extra premium justified by extra hazards resulting from the unexpected situation. The insured is obligated to do everything in his or her power to preserve the goods from harm because of the delay or termination.

These provisions merely extend the time and place of coverage. No additional perils are covered under these clauses, and there is no coverage for any damage or other loss due to the delay. When a cargo is sold at a port where the voyage is prematurely terminated, there may be a loss to the shipper because this sale is for less than the intended value at the destination. The difference between the intended value at destination and the amount recovered by sale at the port where the voyage is terminated would be a loss due to the change in the voyage. Such loss is not covered by the insurance policy as ordinarily written. The effect of the marine extension clauses in such a case is merely to continue the insurance on the cargo until such time as the cargo is sold at such a port.

Lost or Not Lost Ocean marine insurance policies may be written covering the property "lost or not lost." This means that coverage applies even if the property has already been lost at the time the policy is negotiated, *provided* that the insured did not know of a loss and had no reason to suspect there actually had been a casualty. This practice is particularly advantageous to those who are continuously engaged in overseas commerce. Open policies on cargo are written so that they cover all of the goods described while they are in transit. It is possible for a cargo to be lost before the insured knows that it has been shipped.

The clause is also needed when coverage is being transferred from one insurer to another while a ship is at sea.

Other Important Clauses

Bailee Clause A limitation, found in ocean and inland marine as well as in other types of property insurance, is that the shipper's insurance "shall not inure, directly or indirectly, to the benefit of any carrier or bailee." Cargo insurance is for the benefit of cargo interests only, not for the benefit of ship operators, warehousemen, and others hired to carry, store, and process the goods.

"Both to Blame" Clause When two ships collide, and both are negligent, all the loss is shared. Thus, the owner or operator of Ship A will have to contribute toward the damage to cargo aboard Ship B. But bills of lading often require that the shipper reimburse the operator of Ship A to the extent Ship A has to pay Ship B for damage to the shipper's goods. Under the "Both to Blame" clause in cargo policies, the shipper's insurance claims for damage to goods includes any such reimbursement that must be made to Ship A. The result is that the shipper's insurer gets the benefit of damage claims against other ships only to the extent another ship, not the one carrying the cargo, was at fault.

Perils Insured

The traditional perils clause of the ocean marine contract has already been discussed in some detail. This clause enumerated the perils against which marine insurers were willing to provide insurance. In the modern marine market, coverage is based on either these traditional named perils (and modifications) or on the more popular "all-risks" approach. Both have to be examined in a bit more detail.

Although the marine perils clause enumerates the perils which marine underwriters were willing to insure, it does not define the extent of coverage which is provided by any given policy. This is usually found in a second clause called *average terms*. There are many variations of average terms and only three will be mentioned here.

Average Terms The first is *total loss only*. When wording to this effect is included in the average terms it limits recovery under the insurance to only those cases where the cargo is a total loss as a result of the perils named in the basic perils clause.

The second variation is *free of particular average* (FPA). The

American version of this clause (free of particular average American conditions FPAAC) includes the following:

> Warranted free from Particular Average unless caused by the vessel or craft being stranded, sunk, or burnt, but... Assurers are to pay any loss... which may reasonably be attributed to fire, collision or contact of the vessel... with any external substance (ice included) other than water, or to discharge of the cargo at port of distress.

This clause still represents a considerable restriction of the coverage. It leaves only general average, salvage charges and total loss of the property fully subject to coverage against the original list of perils.

The FPAAC cover may be broadened by providing that 100 percent loss to an individual shipping package qualifies even though other parts of the same shipment were not totally lost. It is customary in any event to provide coverage for individual packages totally damaged or lost during loading, transshipment, or discharge. There is a second version of the FPA clause, FPAEC. The EC refers to English Conditions. Under English Conditions stranding, sinking, or burning do not have to cause the loss, but only have to occur during the course of the voyage.

The third basic variation in the average terms is frequently referred to as *with average* terms. This calls for payment of any loss caused by the named perils. The wording itself says that the insurance "will pay average irrespective of percentage."

Institute Clauses Even the broad "with average" coverage leaves a cargo shipment exposed to a variety of fortuitous losses. This gap has been closed over the years from two directions. The first direction has been the addition to cargo forms of certain standard or Institute clauses. These clauses are now found on most cargo policies and are not subject to the limitations of the average terms. They include shore perils, explosion, Inchmaree, and pilferage.

Shore Perils. Initially, the warehouse to warehouse clause, extending coverage to property ashore, was not accompanied by any specific reference to perils. A claim was made inferring that this omission implied "all-risks" coverage ashore, but the court disagreed. Since the standard ocean marine perils are inadequate ashore, specific perils applicable ashore were inserted. The standard list now contains fire, lightning, windstorm, rising navigable waters, sprinkler leakage, accident to a conveyance (specified in various ways), and collapse of docks or wharves.

Explosion. This clause covers damage to cargo resulting from explosion unless the cause of the explosion is one excluded by either the strikes warranty or the war risk exclusion.

Inchmaree. This clause extends coverage to include damage from bursting boilers, latent defect in the vessel or its machinery, and errors in handling of the vessel by the master or crew.

Pilferage—Theft by Stealth. It has already been pointed out that the coverage against loss from "thieves" under the ocean marine insurance policy was intended to cover only theft by violence or by "assailing thieves." Conditions in many ocean ports result in substantial loss of cargo from ordinary theft or pilferage and many ask their insurers for coverage against such loss. This coverage may be provided, usually at an additional premium that is sometimes substantial. Coverage may also be extended to loss from nondelivery or shortage of cargo upon reaching its destination. One of the restrictions sometimes placed upon the coverage against theft, pilferage, or nondelivery is a provision that there is "no risk after discharge," or "no risk after landing." The underwriters may be willing to cover the risk of theft, pilferage, or nondelivery of cargo while the cargo is on shipboard, but they may be unwilling to cover the risk in those ports for which the cargo is destined. These are all factors which are negotiated between the insured and the insurer when arranging coverage.

Other perils that may be added include damage by oil, fresh water, sweat, cargo handling hooks, and by other cargo.

"All-Risks" Coverage Naturally restricted coverage is written at lower rates than the broader forms of coverage. In actual practice the more limited coverage is usually applied to bulk commodities or raw materials, or is used in cases where the shipper wishes to retain normal losses and buy insurance only for major losses or disasters.

The alternative to named perils coverage is "all-risks" coverage. Today this coverage is provided for a wide variety of finished and semi-finished products. This approach is intended to cover losses not expected to happen, something fortuitous—an accident or casualty. Sometimes additional wording is included to clarify the designation. Thus, specific exclusion of loss, "proximately caused by delay or inherent vice or nature of the subject matter insured" frequently appears. Or, the insuring provision may read, "all risks of loss or damage from any external cause." "All-risks" coverage is subject to the exclusions in the free of capture and seizure (FC&S) clause, and loss by strikes, riots, and civil commotions is often specifically excluded.

Franchise and Deductible Clauses

Straight deductible clauses like those used in other types of insurance do appear in ocean cargo insurance contracts. However, *franchise* deductibles are also used, and formerly were standard in ocean marine coverage. With a franchise clause, the insurer pays nothing when the loss is no more than the specified amount. When the franchise amount (often called just "the franchise") is exceeded, the loss is paid in full when other policy conditions are also met. The franchise amount is usually stated as a percentage (e.g., 3 or 5 percent) of the value of the insured property.

The percentage specified in a franchise type of clause varies with the type of cargo. The figure varies according to the amount of routine damage that type of cargo can be expected to suffer. Over the years, a standard franchise provision was developed and included in the memorandum clause, stating percentages generally applicable. This clause appears at the end of the standard Lloyd's policy. Under it, a franchise of 3 percent is applied to goods in general, with some particular commodities subject to 5 percent and others subject to FPA. (Note that the FPA and the 3 percent franchise provisions do not apply if the vessel has experienced stranding.) The memorandum percentages apply only if other franchise figures are not inserted, and insertions of other figures are frequent.

Loss that exceeds the franchise amount is paid only if other conditions of the contract are also met, such as the requirement the loss be caused by a covered peril. This seems obvious, but the ways in which various clauses are inserted into ocean marine contracts are such that, while reading one part, it is sometimes difficult to keep all their interactions in mind. Hence this reminder that franchise provisions do not of themselves provide that particular average exceeding the franchise amount will be paid.

Franchise clauses apply only to particular, not general, average and do not apply to sue and labor or salvage charges. The franchise amount may apply per event or be cumulative over the entire voyage. When the per event basis is not specified, the per voyage basis applies.

Franchise and deductible clauses are used to a lesser extent in connection with package or containerized cargo because such property is better protected from the miscellaneous losses, such as leakage or errors in weighing or measuring. In general, franchise and deductible clauses are more common on policies issued to importers than on policies covering exports.

Special Conditions

On-Deck Shipments Traditionally, all cargo was presumed to be shipped under deck. Ships generally were not built to withstand the extra stress of cargo loading above deck, and on-deck cargo was exposed to additional hazards, such as damage by sea water and the possibility of being washed overboard. If ship operators loaded cargo on deck, they were responsible for the safe carriage of that cargo, and the cargo insurance did not apply.

There were some exceptions to this rule. Certain hazardous types of cargo were required to be shipped on deck so as not to expose general cargo under deck to the extra hazards. Insurers accepting insurance on such cargo were presumed to know the regulations.

The situation has been changed substantially by the development of containerized shipping. Many of the new specially built container ships have provision for carrying large numbers of containers above deck. This is less hazardous because the ships are so constructed that the containers are not likely to be washed overboard, and the cargo has the extra protection of being in presumably weather tight containers.

Cargo should still be loaded under deck on conventional ships that are built to carry cargo in their holds and not on deck. The newer rules apply to containerships that are built specifically to handle the on-deck container situation.

The shipper of cargo may not know whether the cargo is stowed beneath deck or whether it is on deck. It is customary in open cargo insurance policies to provide that particular average will not be paid on cargo above deck unless the loss is caused by the ship being stranded, sunk, on fire, or in collision with another vessel, or by fire, jettison, or washing overboard. The policy may further provide, however, that if the cargo is shipped on deck without the knowledge and consent of the shipper, it will then be treated as under-deck cargo as far as the insured is concerned. There can be a question of additional liability on the part of the ship operator if the cargo is loaded on deck contrary to general requirements or custom and without consent of the shipper. The objectives of these changes is to protect the shipper of the cargo when a loss occurs because of some circumstance over which he has no control.

Loss of Special Parts Sometimes the consequences of loss of one part of an item are considerable. Two types of cases receive special attention in cargo insurance policies: (1) loss or damage to parts of machinery, and (2) loss of labels.

Parts of Machinery. The regular provision appears in one form as, "these Assurers shall be liable only for the proportion of the insured value of the part lost or damaged, or at the Assured's option, for the cost and expense... of replacing or repairing the lost or damaged part...; but in no event shall these Assurers be liable for more than the insured value of the complete machine." The intent of the first statement is to exclude payment for consequential loss in the value of the total machine beyond the value of the lost or damaged part itself. The second statement allows the insured to make up for this by replacing the part at the insurer's expense unless that exceeds the total insured value of the machine.

Labels Clause. Loss of labels, capsules, or wrappers is treated as follows: the insurance covers the cost of relabeling, encapsulating, or wrapping unless that cost exceeds the original insured value. (The cost of reidentifying sealed goods, or of reconditioning unwrapped goods or contents lost from capsules, can easily exceed the cost of original manufacture and packaging.)

Variations and Extensions of Coverage Ocean cargo policies are an unfiled form of insurance. As such, there are many variations and extensions of basic coverage which can be provided in the ocean cargo coverage. The extensions relating to air shipments and import duties are summarized below.

Air Shipments. Many of the same characteristics also apply to international air shipments. It is quite common now to extend the terms of a cargo policy to include air shipments made by the insured. Most terms of the policy remain unchanged although the average terms applicable to air shipments are usually "all-risks." Of course, air voyages are of shorter duration than water voyages. Rates for air shipments will frequently be lower than rates for waterborne shipments even though damageability and theft hazards may be as great or greater.

Import Duties. Some countries require payment of an export duty on goods leaving the country. This becomes a part of the expense of getting the cargo to its destination, and is therefore a part of the value of the goods.

Import duties ordinarily are not assessed against cargo until the cargo has reached its destination, or the port of entry. However, there are circumstances where, even if the cargo is damaged, the tariff laws require payment of the full duty. The duty forms an important part of the cost with certain types of property, so that it could result in a substantial additional loss if the full duty has to be paid on property that has been damaged.

When insurance coverage includes transit to an inland site, the value of any property lost during land transit normally would include the import duty which has been paid on the property as it entered the country. This could be taken into account in determining the value of the property for cargo insurance. However, when loss occurs before the duty has been paid, duty cost ordinarily is not incurred. The premium for separate insurance on duty charges recognizing this fact, so to save premium money, some shippers buy separate insurance. (Remember that the method used in adjusting ocean marine losses means that if duty cost *is* included in the insured value of the cargo, that increased value increases the size of claims payment even when the loss occurs before the duty becomes payable.)

Strikes, Riots, Civil Commotion, and War. Two common exclusions are found in almost all American cargo policies. The first of these warrants the insurance shall be free of claim from strikes, riots, and civil commotions. The second warrants that the insurance shall be free of claim from a variety of perils associated with hostile action or war.

Cargo insurance policies may be extended to cover damage from strike, riot, or civil commotion. An additional premium is usually charged because of the additional exposure. The coverage ordinarily applies to physical damage to the cargo but does not cover loss from delay or loss of market.

Insurers sometimes find it difficult to distinguish between a riot situation and a war risk situation. Rebellion is considered "war," but the distinction between rebellion and riot often is not clear. Whether a given incident is one or the other depends on such factors as the objectives of the uprising (e.g., to overthrow the government or just to protest a particular law or procedure) and the numbers and organization of the persons involved (e.g., a well-drilled armed body from a large segment of the population or just a mob of disgruntled individuals armed with clubs and stones). To illustrate these semantic problems, recent situations in Northern Ireland, Jordan, and the Watts district of Los Angeles have been termed variously, "rebellion," "civil war," "riot," and "civil commotion."

Another problem in connection with strike and riot coverage is the probable loss from theft or pilferage during a riot. Strike and riot coverage is written in such a way as to cover theft when the theft, pilferage, or destruction is caused by vandalism attendant upon a riot.

STRIKE, RIOT AND CIVIL COMMOTION COVERAGE. Strike, riot, and civil commotion coverage is accomplished by means of a special policy or special clauses added to the ocean marine policy. The endorsement or policy spells out the coverage in considerable detail. Cancellation provisions in connection with strike, riot, and civil commotion coverage are similar to the coverage on war risk. The insurer as well as the insured usually has the privilege of canceling strike and riot coverage. Underwriters consider this a necessary right because a strike and riot situation can develop into an intolerable exposure within a short period of time.

WAR RISKS COVERAGE. Cargo policies can also, at the option of the insured, be extended to cover war risks in the same manner that coverage is provided for strikes, riots, and civil commotions. In fact both coverages are usually included at the same time. There are special clauses which are used for this purpose. The war risk coverage does not attach until cargo is loaded on the vessel and will normally terminate with the arrival of that vessel at the port of discharge.

Like strikes, riots, and civil commotion coverage, war risk coverage responds only for actual physical loss or damage to the insured property and does not cover any form of consequential loss. War risk coverage is normally subject to cancellation with forty-eight hours notice although this cancellation applies only to new exposures and does not affect shipments already at sea.

While both strikes, riots, and civil commotion coverage and war risk coverage can normally be obtained for cargo shipments as additional coverage for which premium is charged, the delay warranty excluding claims for loss of market or for loss arising from delay is usually not one which insurers are willing to provide coverage.

SPECIAL CLAUSES. It should be mentioned that special clauses have been developed to meet the requirements for special groups of commodities. The bulk oil clause, for example, contains terms and conditions particularly applicable to shipments of liquids in bulk. Similar clauses exist for grain, lumber, coffee, refrigerated cargoes, and similar items.

Valuation of Cargo

With single shipments of specific cargo, such as machinery or other individual items, a specific agreed value may be set. However, it is seldom practical for an open cargo insurance policy to list an individual valuation for every shipment that is made, particularly for a shipper sending hundreds of shipments a year. The alternative is to provide a method by which the value of the cargo can be determined for insurance purposes. Usual practice is valuation at the amount of invoice, including all charges such as prepaid or guaranteed freight, *plus a stated percentage*. This added amount above the invoice cost is intended to take care of the additional value of the cargo to the consignee at the destination. The percentage to be inserted in the valuation clause depends upon the circumstances, the type of merchandise, and the anticipated value at the destination. Ten percent is commonly used.

It is necessary in connection with valuation clauses to determine the intent of the parties. A customary wording specifies that property "shall be valued at," followed by a space in which a valuation may be inserted. It is important to note that a valuation must be inserted in the blank space in order that a valuation might be agreed upon. The use of the words "shall be valued at" do not in themselves convert the policy to a valued policy. An open policy sometimes uses the expression "to be subsequently declared and valued." Such a policy remains an unvalued policy in respect to any shipments which may arrive or be the subject of loss before a value has been declared or established. The policy may specify a valuation procedure for cases in which a declaration of value has not yet been made.

Cargo cover, like that on hulls, includes coverage for the insured's obligations to pay general average or salvage awards, and for sue and labor expenses incurred. Again, if the cargo value in the policy is less than the value on which the general average assessment is based, the insured will bear a part of the assessment proportionately.

Exposure Limits Under an open cargo policy, the insurer does not know in advance the value of any given shipment which may be declared by the insured under the terms of the open policy. The valuation clause which establishes in advance the manner in which shipments are to be valued eliminates the possibility of disagreement about the value of a shipment if loss happens to occur before it is declared to the insurer. Open policies will, however, contain a limit of insurance showing the maximum liability the insurer is willing to accept on any one vessel. Since the exposure of cargo shipped on deck is much greater than under deck it is not unusual to also find a separate limit in open cargo policies for "on-deck" shipments. A distinction is usually made between "on-deck" shipments and those in regular containers which are stowed by container lines either under or on deck. Where coverage is provided for air shipments a limit may also be found for air shipments.

Percentage of Value Lost Coverage of loss from direct damage to the described insured property is the principal part of ocean marine insurance. A significant characteristic of this property coverage is the custom of evaluating the damage in terms of "percentage of value lost." Thus, if the damage is estimated to be 40 percent of what the value of the property would have been without damage, 40 percent of the *insured amount* is paid for the loss. This practice gives ocean marine insurance policies the effect of "valued policies"—in the event of total loss, the face of the policy is always paid. It also gives the effect of a 100 percent coinsurance clause *when the amount insured does not exceed the value of the property*. For example, assume a property's actual value is $500, with insurance of $400; further assume a loss of $100 or one-fifth of actual value. Under 100 percent coinsurance, payment would be calculated at 400/500 times the $100 loss, producing payment of $80. Under marine practice, payment would be 100/500 times the insured value of $400, also producing $80. The student can determine these two results will always be the same in case of underinsurance.

When the amount of insurance exceeds the value of the property, the marine computation proceeds the same way. With $600 of insurance on the $500 of property, payment for a $100 loss (one-fifth of actual property value) would *still* be one-fifth of the insured amount; that is, one-fifth of $600, or $120. This practice has arisen from a combination of need and opportunity. Part of the need comes from the fact that ocean cargo losses often must be settled in distant places, under complex market conditions, and with speed. Suppose a cargo of cotton bound for Liverpool from Madras were lost in the Indian Ocean. If "actual cash value" were to be used as the basis of settlement, then value in what place at what time? Value in Madras, in Liverpool, or at some point in between? Value as of the day the voyage began, as of the day it should have reached Liverpool, or as of the day of the loss when that is known?

Under marine insurance practice, none of these questions has to be asked when loss is total. For partial losses, only the immediate market—the present price in the market to which the goods are delivered—needs to be known. The percentage loss in that market and the amount of insurance together determine the amount of the insured claim. The adjuster does not have to know about prices in other markets or at other times. In the early days of ocean marine insurance, this arrangement was essential.

Another part of the need comes from the general property insurance problem of equitable rates for both total and partial losses. Ocean marine valuation and settlement practice gives the same effect as 100 percent coinsurance, and exists for the same reason as coinsurance; that is, to make premiums equitable as between policies that cover only the more frequent partial losses and those that are large enough to cover total losses as well.

Marine insurers can use a method that pays some insureds more than their loss because of the special conditions of ocean marine trade. This is feasible because the insured usually has a limited ability to deliberately create a loss, especially as a reaction to changing conditions. When the market for cotton collapses, the merchant with cotton enroute from Madras to Marseilles may wish it at the bottom of the sea, but has little opportunity to bring about that wish. Even the owner of the vessel has only limited control under those circumstances. (Of course, in the earlier days, when ship and cargo owners might be on board their vessels and directly in charge, the exposure of their own lives was a deterrent to destroying the venture.)

Another significant condition created by the relations among participants in the ocean marine market is that they are a somewhat limited group. Insurers protect themselves by being careful about the brokers through whom they accept business. (For example, as previously noted, only selected brokers are allowed into Lloyd's to deal with the underwriters at Lloyd's.) Brokers, to protect their access to markets, try to avoid dishonest insureds.

There is also the support of legal enforcement of *uberrimae fidei* (the utmost good faith). Thus, those who attempt to deceive the insurers seldom get a second chance to do it.

Finally, insurers are careful about the agreed amount of value set in the policy. Much of the cargo valuation is by sales invoice, of course, particularly under open cargo policies. When invoice value is not available, an agreed formula or method of valuation has to be substituted in open cargo forms.

Loss of Profit, Expense, or Income

Shippers of cargo face some unique and extensive exposures to loss of expense, profit, or income which were identified in Chapter 7. Insurance is available to cover some of these loss expense exposures.

Loss of Profit Margin in Goods The profit margin in goods insured under ocean marine forms is covered in a manner similar to that provided by a selling price or market value clause in fire and allied lines insurance. That is, insurance covers for the sales price rather than the cost price. However, there is a difference in that in fire and allied lines, a special selling price clause is usually required before loss is adjusted by sales price or market price. In ocean marine insurance, on the other hand, policies are treated as valued policies. The amount of insurance is set at the invoice price of the goods plus a margin for expenses not included in the invoice, and the profit margin in the invoice price is thus covered.

Interruption and Delay Profit losses caused by interruption and delay—termed "frustration losses"—are not commonly insured in ocean marine practice. However, the flexibility of the ocean marine insurance market is such that, where a demonstrable need for insurance exists, interruption and delay covers may be negotiated (although not always, of course, on terms the prospective insured considers acceptable).

Freight The freight cost is commonly prepaid, and hence the shipper is exposed to loss of "freight." This exposure can be covered by making the insured amount large enough to include it—a common practice. When the ship operator bears the exposure, it may be specifically insured.

Prepaid Expenses The coverage of shipper's expense for prepaid freight was noted above. Other shipping expenses (such as prepaid premium for insurance) are similarly included in the valuation of the insured property. The same holds for valuation of ships. The "insurable value" of a ship normally is its value at the commencement of the exposure, including value of provisions and stores for the voyage, money that has been advanced for sailors' wages, and other disbursements that may have been incurred to make the ship fit for the voyage. Note the difference from treatment ashore. Suppose, near the end of a voyage, a ship is lost, with little fuel left in its bunkers. In marine insurance, the insured value lost includes the cost of the oil the ship had in its bunkers at the *beginning* of the voyage. This is because the real value of that oil was in its contribution to the voyage, and that value has been lost.

LIABILITY COVERAGE

From early times, ocean marine insurance responded to the needs of ship and cargo owners for insurance regardless of whether the exposure was from loss of property or from liability to the person and property of others. Ocean marine policies cover both collision liability and general liability (protection and indemnity).

Collision Liability

As ocean marine insurance developed, a distinction was made between: (1) liability in connection with collision between ships, and (2) other liability cases.

Running Down Clause Standard hull insurance policies include a collision liability or running down clause that applies to damage to another ship and its cargo. As in liability insurance ashore, "damage" includes loss of use, and costs of investigation and defense. The running down clause does not cover liability for damage to piers, wharves, or other structures, loss to the insured ship or its cargo, loss of life, or bodily injury. Also, the only cause of loss covered is collision; liability arising from negligence in causing or allowing other perils to occur is not covered. Thus, if a fire on board ship is negligently allowed to spread to another ship, liability for such loss is not covered under collision liability. (A fire loss to another ship as a result of collision with that ship is covered, of course.)

Coverage is excluded for any obligation under statutes or other governmental regulations to remove wreckage, even when the wreckage resulted from a collision. (Note that liability to another private party for costs to *salvage* ship or cargo *is* covered. What is excluded are costs incurred because of governmental requirements that channels be kept clear, without regard to the salvage value of the material removed.) In addition, hull policies provide that coverage ceases when the insurer pays for a total loss. This prevents the collision liability coverage from continuing to apply to the wreck. (Coverage for incidents that occurred before payment is, of course, unaffected.)

The insurance which is provided by the running down clause is a separate amount of insurance in addition to the insurance on the value of the ship itself. The amount of coverage under the clause customarily is the same as the amount of insurance on the vessel itself. A rationale of this limit is the previously mentioned rule that the liability attaching to the offending vessel would not be higher than the remaining value of such vessel *if* the owner was not personally negligent. It can be seen that, in case of a total loss of the insured ship plus a liability on the part of that ship for damage to another vessel, the loss to the underwriters could be twice the amount of coverage on the insured ship. And of course the insured has the extra exposure if the claims are not limited to the remaining value of the ship. This applies not only to presence of personal negligence, but also when there are bodily injury claims. Excess collision liability cover may be purchased for claims falling under collision liability cover; protection and indemnity insurance is necessary for other claims.

It is important to note that laws imposing liability vary among jurisdictions, as do insurance contracts. For example, British insurance practice is to limit recovery under the running down clause to three-fourths of the insured's liability. American insurers usually cover the full liability of the insured (up to the policy limit, of course). Thus, examination of the actual policies is required.

Sister Ship Clause A so-called "sister ship" clause usually is included in the running down coverage on a fleet of ships. This provides that if two ships of the same fleet or belonging to the same owner are involved in a collision, the damages shall be assessed as if the two vessels were separately owned and separately insured. This differs from liability insurance coverage on land vehicles. The owner of two land vehicles which collide cannot collect under liability insurance because such an owner cannot be legally liable to himself or herself. It would be necessary for an automobile owner to buy collision insurance to cover under such circumstances.

General Liability—Protection and Indemnity

Liability coverage in addition to that provided by the running down clause is provided by protection and indemnity (P&I) insurance. This is a third-party personal injury and property damage liability insurance. It has been pointed out that the collision or running down clause forms a part of many ocean marine hull policies. The protection and indemnity coverage, in contrast, usually is provided under a separate insurance policy. The most common exception to this separation is in yacht policies. Forms for covering charterers also regularly combine collision liability and P&I protection. Sometimes P&I coverage is included in a builder's risk policy or port risk policy. These last are exposures in which the third-party liability may be nominal, so that the property underwriters can accept this additional liability exposure without serious hazard to themselves.

Exposures Covered The P&I coverage protects against many possible liabilities. An important exposure is the possibility of damage to bridges, piers, wharves, and other structures along waterways. There have been several cases where ships have caused extensive damage to bridges. Another covered loss that could be very expensive is the cost of raising, destroying, or removing the wreck if the ship is sunk and constitutes a hazard to navigation.

The coverage of liability to persons includes passengers, ship visitors, the crew, and stevedores working on or about the ship. Included is liability for expenses in getting sick or injured crew to shore plus wages to the end of the voyage for crew disabled by sickness or injury. Crew members who must be left at foreign ports must be brought home at the expense of the P&I insurance. Injury or death of a member of a ship's crew is one of the most important factors in P&I coverage but not all P&I forms automatically include crew.

The liability of a ship operator for damage to cargo aboard ship is substantially less than the liability of a common carrier on land in the United States. However, there are circumstances under which a ship operator is liable to cargo owners for damage. One source of carriers' liability for cargo carried is the doctrine of comparative negligence. When Ships A and B collide, with negligence on both sides, Ship A is liable for damage to cargo on board Ship B, and vice versa. Suppose total property damage is $2 million, of which $400,000 is to cargo aboard Ship A. If Ship A's comparative negligence is assessed as 60 percent, Ship A's operator or owner is liable for 60 percent of $2 million, including 60 percent of the $400,000 of damage to cargo aboard Ship A.

Another cause of carriers' liability to cargo is, as previously noted, failure to provide a seaworthy ship (including a competent captain and crew). In such a case, P&I insurance covers liability for damage to cargo aboard the insured ship.

The P&I policy also covers the insured shipowner's or operator's liability for fines of a state or country that may be imposed for violation of laws. However, this particular liability coverage may be subject to a deductible in order that a ship operator is not encouraged to violate laws knowingly.

Amount of Insurance The P&I coverage usually is issued in the same amount as the insurance on the ship. This is adequate where the shipowner is permitted to limit personal liability to the value of the ship. However, the limitation of liability to the value of the ship ordinarily is dependent upon a lack of privity, or knowledge, on the part of the owner with respect to the particular conditions or events that caused the loss. In the case of a yacht owner who may be on board or may actually be operating the yacht personally, an absence of privity could not be claimed in case of accident. There can be other circumstances where either a commercial operator or a yacht owner is privy to a particular situation that results in a liability claim against the ship. It is desirable in such circumstances for the ship operator to have an excess P&I insurance for amounts above the value of the ship.

The exposure of the shipowner or operator to liability for loss of life, personal injury, or property damage is generally limited to cases of negligence. The most important form of operator negligence is lack of seaworthiness in the vessel.

Workers' Compensation As noted in Chapter 7, in the United States the Longshoremen's and Harbor Workers' Compensation Act makes an employer liable for injury to employees in "maritime employment" on the navigable waters of the United States. This includes employees on dry docks but it does not include the master or crew of a vessel. Coverage for the liabilities imposed by this act normally is written with a standard workers' compensation policy. (The Longshoremen's and Harbor Workers' Act, and the use of workers' compensation insurance to provide coverage under that act are discussed in more detail in CPCU 4, Chapters 6 and 7.) While coverage can be provided as part of the ocean marine policy, this is only customary in yacht coverage. The owner of a yacht may be an individual who does not have any other reason to buy workers' compensation coverage, and it is convenient for it to be provided in the yacht policy.

There are several miscellaneous activities that come within the coverage of the act. The owner of a vessel, and particularly a yacht owner, may not realize that coverage should be provided for such activities as a machinist repairing a launch, a rigger making ready a vessel for a voyage, or the scraping and painting of a ship that is tied up at a wharf. The hiring of someone to work on a vessel that is subject to the act may create an unexpected and unknown exposure. Therefore, it is desirable for any owner or operator of a vessel that could be subject to the act to have this coverage.

Pollution Liability To provide protection required under American law for liability for discharge of hazardous substances into navigable waters of the United States, a group of U.S. underwriters have formed the Water Quality Insurance Syndicate. This syndicate issues separate pollution liability policies. The large oil companies that operate tankers have their own pool for sharing liability for pollution losses worldwide. This coverage is entirely separate from liability provided by P&I forms.

YACHT INSURANCE

The yacht is a pleasure vessel—it does not carry cargo. Ordinarily it is not for hire, although a yacht may be used in a commercial operation for carrying passengers. The insurance coverage for commercial operation is different from the insurance coverage for a pleasure yacht. Commercial operation of such a pleasure boat creates exposures similar in most respects to the passenger-carrying ships, although on a smaller scale.

The yacht owner needs full ocean marine coverage even though the exposure from some features of the yacht operation are relatively minor compared to a commercial operation. Often, there are some important exposures not commonly faced by most commercial operators, notably the hazards of hauling and launching of pleasure vessels not kept regularly in the water, and exposures during long mooring periods and seasonal lay-ups.

In contrast to the normal treatment of commercial vessels where separate forms will usually apply to hull coverage and P&I (liability) coverage, yacht insurance is commonly sold as a package policy containing both physical damage and liability coverages even though separate charges may be included for the liability exposures.

Perils Covered

Yacht insurance coverage on the hull is comparable to that under other ocean marine hull policies. The perils covered usually are those that have already been discussed, and war damage is almost always excluded by a free of capture and seizure (FC&S) clause. The yacht owner ordinarily does not need war damage coverage, and is not under any compulsion to buy a policy covering such hazards. Coverage of loss from strikes, riots, and civil commotion may be subject to negotiation between the insured and the insurer, although some may offer this coverage to all yacht owners. Some policies include damage to hull or machinery from accidents in loading, discharging, or handling stores and fittings; or in taking on fuel, or in hauling or launching, or moving in shipyards. The coverage relating to hauling, launching, or moving the yacht is important where yachts are laid up during a part of the year.

Some other type of coverage may be valuable to the yacht owner. Windstorm, flood, and collapse of a building or shoring may be important in cases where the yacht is laid up in an area exposed to windstorms and weather. Protection against the bursting of boilers, the breakage of shafts, and damage from latent defects, similar to machinery breakage coverage on commercial vessels, can be important.

Many insurance companies today provide a broad "all-risks" form of hull coverage for the better yachts. This form will normally contain additional exclusions to eliminate claims for normal wear and tear or depreciation. Another common exclusion is for loss or damage to masts, spars, and sails during races.

Property Covered

One standard representative policy provides coverage: "upon the hull, spars, sails, tackle, apparel, provisions, stores, machinery, boats, and other furniture of and in the yacht." Also, it is customary to provide coverage for equipment of the yacht that is separated from the yacht and laid up on shore. This may be limited to 20 percent of the amount of insurance on the yacht.

A yacht policy may be extended to cover a boat trailer. This provision normally would be associated with coverage on the yacht itself during land transportation. However, ordinarily only the property, not the liability, parts of the policy are so extended.

Insurance on small boats, and particularly outboard motorboats, is likely to be provided under inland marine types of policies rather than ocean marine types. Coverage for outboard motor boats and similar vessels will be discussed in connection with inland marine insurance.

Warranties of Conditions

A private pleasure warranty is customary in order to avoid the extra exposure that would result from commercial operations, such as renting out the vessel. It is also customary for yacht policies to show the period of navigation and the period of lay-up, if any. Navigation limits are usual—yachts operated in the ocean are charged higher premiums than those operated in more sheltered waters.

Yacht policies issued on power boats may contain a provision prohibiting or restricting water skiing operations. When water skiing is covered, contracts commonly require at least two crew members in the boat (one to operate it, the other to watch for any accident involving the skier).

Sailboats are frequently used for racing, so that racing of sailboats is generally considered a normal hazard. However, policies often exclude or "warrant free of loss" spars and sails during the racing of sailing vessels.

Liability Coverage

Yacht policies issued by most insurance companies in the United States include running down (collision liability) coverage as well as P&I provisions. These coverages are important for the yacht owner, partly because there may have been no occasion to buy comparable workers' compensation type of coverage for any other reason.

Liability coverage under the P&I provisions may differ from general ocean marine concepts in its provisions for high limits of liability. The yacht policy of many companies tends to follow practices comparable to liability insurance on land in this respect. Coverage may be on the customary land insurance basis, with one limit applying to any one person and another limit applying to any one accident. A separate limit usually applies to property damage.

An interesting addition in many yacht policies as compared to usual ocean marine practices is a provision for medical payments coverage. This follows generally the medical payments provisions that are written in connection with automobile policies in the United States.

NONINSURANCE TECHNIQUES FOR TREATING OCEAN MARINE EXPOSURES

From its earliest days, ocean marine exposures have been almost inextricably tied to insurance. It should be obvious that marine law, in many cases, exists because of the availability of insurance, and vice versa. Because of the values and numerous interests involved, it is almost unthinkable that the owner of a large commercial ship would choose to retain the loss exposure.

Exposures to cargo loss are more frequently retained by shippers. In some cases, the retention may be unconscious because the shipper is unaware that most losses will be borne by the shipper. To determine whether or not the shipper is exposed, it is necessary to examine the terms of any sales agreement. In some cases, the exposure may be consciously retained, if the potential severity of any one loss would not severely damage the shipper's financial condition.

The terms of sale determine who bears the exposure of loss to cargo in transit. Transference of the exposure, by use of an appropriate sales agreement, is a noninsurance technique frequently used.

Loss control techniques are important as adjuncts to ocean marine insurance. Many such techniques have been discussed in passing in previous portions of the two chapters on ocean marine exposures and their treatment. A few of these points will be summarized in the following section.

Loss Control

Ocean marine underwriters, despite their physical distance from the subject of insurance, exert an important influence on losses. One factor which encourages loss control efforts by the insured is that ocean marine insurance rates are based largely upon the experience of the insured. Shipowners are encouraged to install loss prevention devices and procedures because a bad loss record will bring about higher rates.

Prevention and reduction of cargo losses are encouraged by associations of shippers, who investigate the best methods of packaging and recommend proper methods to their members. A series of losses involving a particular kind of cargo would be investigated by them to determine the cause.

Theft and pilferage in certain ports has been one of the principal causes of marine losses in recent years. Theft by dock workers, hijacking of trucks in the terminals or after leaving the port, failure of consignees to claim merchandise on time, port congestion which causes misshipment of goods, and delays in getting goods cleared through customs have all contributed to losses. Associations of shippers can exert pressure on local and federal authorities to arrest and prosecute thieves, and security measures can be instituted by authorities when pressure is sufficiently strong. Individual shippers will control loss exposures by routing their goods through ports that are known to be reasonably safe for cargo. As the safety factor of a certain port may change from time to time, the alert shipper may be able to use mainly ports that currently have good security systems.

Surveys of vessels, packing and loading inspections, and careful scrutiny of loss patterns often assist both insurers and insureds in the elimination of potential loss factors.

Index

A

B

C

D

E

F

G

H

I

J

L

M

N

O

P

Q

R

S

T

Y